F.B.

Bases Abroad

sipri

Stockholm International Peace Research Institute

SIPRI is an independent international institute for research into problems of peace and conflict, especially those of arms control and disarmament. It was established in 1966 to commemorate Sweden's 150 years of unbroken peace.

The Institute is financed mainly by the Swedish Parliament. The staff, the Governing Board and the Scientific Council are international.

The Governing Board and Scientific Council are not responsible for the views expressed in the publications of the Institute.

sipri

Stockholm International Peace Research Institute
Pipers väg 28, S-171 73 Solna, Sweden
Cable: PEACERESEARCH STOCKHOLM
Telefax: 46 8/55 97 33
Telephone: 46 8/55 97 00

Bases Abroad
The Global Foreign Military Presence

Robert E. Harkavy

sipri

Stockholm International Peace Research Institute

OXFORD UNIVERSITY PRESS
1989

Oxford University Press, Walton Street, Oxford OX2 6DP

Oxford New York Toronto
Delhi Bombay Calcutta Madras Karachi
Petaling Jaya Singapore Hong Kong Tokyo
Melbourne Auckland
and associated companies in
Berlin Ibadan

Oxford is a trade mark of Oxford University Press

Published in the United States
by Oxford University Press, New York

British Library Cataloguing in Publication Data
Harkavy, Robert E.
Bases abroad: the global foreign military presence.
—(SIPRI monographs).
1. Overseas military bases
I. Title   II. Series
355.7
ISBN 0–19–829131–0

Library of Congress Cataloging in Publication Data
(data available)

Set by Oxford Text System

Printed and bound in
Great Britain by Biddles Ltd,
Guildford and King's Lynn

Acknowledgements

I wish to thank a number of persons and organizations who have aided in the preparation of this book. Needless to say, none are to blame for its inevitable shortcomings.

Billie Bielckus, my editor at SIPRI, did a truly excellent job of helping me with sources, maintaining current research files, repairing my sometimes errant syntax, negotiating with cartographers and, overall, of organizing the whole project. She was a joy to work with, and helped maintain my sanity during some rocky periods. Connie Wall, SIPRI's sage editor-in-chief, likewise provided badly needed encouragement and assistance of various sorts.

Joanne Ostergaard, my former secretary at Penn State, did a very fine job of typing the manuscript and of managing the entire enterprise at the Pennsylvania end. One could not find a better secretary. When Joanne moved to Oregon, Michelle Sherman did an excellent job of picking up and carrying on. Additional secretarial assistance was provided by Melanie Romig and Jill Larue.

Laura Stanonis ably organized some of the SIPRI data for me, in the capacity of research assistant. Additional assistance was provided by Preston Keat.

Richard Fieldhouse and Simon Duke, both of whom know more than I about some areas of this subject, reviewed the draft ·manuscript and each offered numerous helpful criticisms and suggestions, for which I am deeply grateful. Thanks are also due both to the SIPRI and the Penn State library staffs.

Tami Mistrick, cartographer at Penn State's Deasy GeoGraphics Laboratory, Department of Geography, did a fine job of constructing the maps for figures 2, 3, 4, 7, 9, 10 and 11, ably aided by David Hayward.

So many other persons provided valuable assistance and encouragement to me during this project that it would be impossible to list them all. But I would like to offer special thanks to Frank Blackaby, Eva Rosdahl, Staffan Tillander, Anna Helleday and Robert Butterworth. I apologize if I have inadvertently left someone off the list.

Several organizations outside of SIPRI provided me financial assistance in connection with this project. The Liberal Arts College research office at Pennsylvania State University granted some research funds, as did the University's Political Science Department, headed by Trond Gilberg. Administrative assistance of all sorts was provided by Penn State's Institute for Policy Research and Evaluation (IPRE), directed by Irwin Feller. In 1984, I worked on the beginnings of this project while I was an Alexander von Humboldt fellow at the University of Kiel, FR Germany. I received a Fulbright research grant to work in Stockholm at SIPRI during the summer of 1985, and my university granted me a half-year sabbatical leave to work on this project. Finally, I would like to thank Dr Walther Stützle, Director of SIPRI, for offering all the facilities of the Institute, which enabled me to write this book.

This book is dedicated to my wife Jane, my son Mike, and to my parents, Samuel and Helen Harkavy. Jointly, they sustained me through a long and difficult job.

Robert E. Harkavy

Contents

Acronyms, abbreviations and conventions

ABM	Anti-ballistic missile
ACDA	(US) Arms Control and Disarmament Agency
ACE HIGH	Allied Command Europe Communications Network (NATO)
ADM	Atomic demolition munition
AEW	Advanced electronic warfare system/airborne early-warning system
AFB	Air Force Base
AFSATCOM	Air Force Satellite Communications System
AFTAC	Air Force Technical Applications Center
AGI	Soviet intelligence collection vessel
ALCM	Air-launched cruise missile
ANZUS Treaty	Australia, New Zealand and United States Treaty
ARC	Acoustic Research Center
ARM	Anti-radiation missile
ASAT	Anti-satellite warfare
ASEAN	Association of South East Asian Nations
ASROC	Anti-Submarine Rocket
ASW	Anti-submarine warfare
ATGW	Anti-tank guided weapon
AUTEC	Atlantic Underseas Test and Evaluation Center
AUTODIN	Automatic Digital Network
AUTOSEVOCOM	Automatic Secure Voice Communications System
AUTOVON	Automatic Voice Switching Network
AWACS	Airborne Warning and Control System
BAOR	British Army of the Rhine
BMEWS	Ballistic Missile Early Warning System
BMP	Soviet amphibious personnel carrier
BW	Biological warfare
C^3I	Command, control, communications and intelligence
CADIN	Continental air defense integration north
CAP	Combat air patrol
CDAA	Circularly Disposed Antenna Array
CEP	Circular error probable
CENTAG	Central Army Group
CENTO	Central Treaty Organization
COB	Collocated operating base
COD	Carrier-on-board delivery (aircraft)

COMINT	Communications intelligence
CONUS	Continental United States
CRAF	Civilian Reserve Air Force
CVN	Nuclear-powered aircraft carrier
CW	Chemical warfare
DCS	Defence Communications System
DEBS	Digital European Backbone System
DEW	Distant Early Warning
DF	Direction-finding
DMSP	Defense Meteorological Satellite Program
DSCS	Defense Satellite Communications System
DSP	Defense Satellite Program
ECCM	Electronic counter-countermeasure
ECM	Electronic countermeasure
EEZ	Exclusive economic zone
ELDO	European Launcher Development Organization
ELF	Extremely low frequency
ELINT	Electronic intelligence
EMP	Electromagnetic pulse
EORSAT	Electronic Intelligence Ocean Reconnaissance Satellite
EPARCS	Enhanced Perimeter Acquisition Radar Attack Characterization System
ESA	European Space Agency
ESC	Electronic Security Command (USAF)
ESF	Economic Support Fund
ESMC	Eastern Space and Missile Center
EUCOM	European Command
FBIS	Foreign Broadcast Information Centre
FBS	Forward based systems
FEBA	Forward edge of the battle area
FISINT	Foreign instrumentation signals intelligence
FLIR	Forward-looking infra-red
FLO-FLO	Float-on/float-off
FLOT	Forward line of troops
FLTSATCOM	Fleet Satellite Communications
FMP	Foreign military presence
FMS	Foreign Military Sales
FOBS	Fractional orbital bombardment system
FROG	Free-rocket-over-ground
GCHG	Government Communications Headquarters

GEODSS	Ground-based Electro-Optical Deep Space Surveillance system
GIUK	Greenland–Iceland–United Kingdom gap
GLCM	Ground-launched cruise missile
GLONASS	Soviet global navigation system
GPS	Global Positioning System
GWEN	Ground Wave Emergency Network
HF	High frequency
HF/DF	High-frequency direction finders
HILAT	High-altitude research satellite
HUMINT	Human intelligence
ICBM	Intercontinental ballistic missile
IDCSP	Initial Defense Communication Satellite Program
IISS	International Institute for Strategic Studies (London)
IMET	International Military Education and Training Program
INF	Intermediate-range nuclear forces
INS	Inertial navigation system
INSCOM	Intelligence and Security Command (US Army)
IONDS	Integrated Operational NUDETS Detection System
IRBM	Intermediate-range ballistic missile
KGB	Committee of State Security (USSR)
LANDSOUTH	Allied Land Forces Southern Europe
LF	Low frequency
LORAN-C	Long-range aid to navigation, modification C
LOW	Launch-on-warning
LPD	Amphibious transport dock
LSM	Landing ship medium
LST	Landing ship tank
LUA	Launch-under-attack
MAAG	Military Advisory Assistance Group (US)
MAB	Marine Amphibious Brigade (USMC)
MAD	Mutual assured destruction
MADM	Medium Atomic Demolition Munition
MAJRELSTA	Major Relay Station
MAP	Military Assistance Program
MAU	Marine Amphibious Unit
MBFR	Mutual and balanced force reductions
MBT	Main battle tank
MCMV	Mine counter-measure vessel
MILS	Missile Impact Location System

MILSTAR	(Communications satellite system)
MIRV	Multiple independently targetable re-entry vehicle
MORFLOT	Soviet merchant marine
MPS	Maritime Prepositioning Ships
MRBM	Medium-range ballistic missile
MVD	Ministry of Internal Affairs (USSR)
NADGE	NATO Air Defense Ground Environment system
NAMFI	NATO Missile Firing Installation
NARS	North Atlantic Relay System
NASA	National Aeronautics and Space Administration
NATO	North Atlantic Treaty Organization
NAVSPASUR	Naval Space Surveillance
NAVSTAR	US navigation satellite system
NORAD	North American Air Defense Command
NORSAR	Norwegian Seismic Array
NORTHAG	Northern Army Group
NPT	Non-Proliferation Treaty
NTPF	Near-Term Prepositioning Force
NSA	National Security Agency (USA)
NSG	Naval Security Group (USA)
NUDET	Nuclear detection or nuclear detonation
NWFZ	Nuclear weapon-free zone
OECD	Organization for Economic Co-operation and Development
OKEAN-75	Soviet naval exercise, 1975
OMAR	Organization Mondiale Inter-Armee de Transmissions
OMIT	Organization Maritime de Transmissions
OPEC	Organization of Petroleum Exporting Countries
OTH	Over-the-horizon radar
PACBAR	Pacific Radar Barrier
PAVE PAWS	Phased Array Warning System
PHOTINT	Photographic intelligence
POL	Petroleum, oil and lubricants
POMCUS	The European Prepositioning of Materiel Configured to Unit Sets (USA)
PRC	People's Republic of China
PTBT	Partial Test Ban Treaty
PVO	Soviet air defence organization (PVO)
R&D	Research and development
R&R	Rest and recuperation
RADINT	Radar intelligence

RAF	Royal Air Force (UK)
RENAMO	Resistência Nacional Moçambicana
RDF	Rapid Deployment Force
RDJTF	Rapid Deployment Joint Task Force
RDSS	Rapidly Deployable Surveillance System
RO-RO	Roll-on/roll-off
RORSAT	Radar ocean-reconnaissance satellite
RSS	Regional Security System
RSTN	Regional Seismic Test Network
RV	Re-entry vehicle
RW	Radiological warfare
SAC	Strategic Air Command
SACLANT	Supreme Allied Commander Atlantic, NATO Command
SALT	Strategic arms limitation talks
SADM	Special Atomic Demolition Munition
SAM	Surface-to-air missile
SATRAN	Satellite Reconnaissance Advance Notice system (USA)
SCF	Satellite control facility
SCOT	British shipborne satellite communication system
SCUD	SS-1 Army level mid-range battlefield missile
SDI	Strategic Defense Initiative
SDS	Satellite Data System
SEAL	Sea–Air–Land force
SEATO	Southeast Asia Treaty Organization
SHAPE	Supreme Headquarters Allied Powers Europe, NATO headquarters at Casteau-Mons, Belgium
SHF	Super-high frequency
SIGINT	Signals intelligence
SLBM	Submarine-launched ballistic missile
SLCM	Submarine-launched cruise missile
SLOC	Sea lane of communication
SNF	Short-range nuclear forces
SOFNET	Solar Flare Network
SOON	Solar Optical Observing Network
SOSUS	Sound surveillance under sea
SPADATS	Space Detection and Tracking System
SRAM	Short-range attack missile
SRBM	Short-range ballistic missile
SSB	Non-nuclear-powered ballistic missile submarine
SSBN	Nuclear-powered ballistic missile submarine
SSGN	Guided missile submarine (nuclear powered)
SSN	Nuclear-powered submarine
STADAN	Satellite Tracking and Data Acquisition Network

SUBROC	Underwater-to-air-underwater missile
SURTAS	Surveillance towed array system
SWAPO	South West Africa People's Organization
TACAMO	Take charge and move out—US communications aircraft
TARE	Telegraph Automatic Relay Equipment (NATO)
TELINT	Telemetry intelligence
TELS	Transporter-erector-launchers
TERCOM	Terrain-contour matching
TLAM	Tomahawk land attack cruise missile
TOW	Tube-launched, optically tracked, wire-guided missile
TRANET	Tracking network
TUSLOG	Turkish–US Logistics Group
TTBT	Threshold Test Ban Treaty
TVD	Theatre of military operations (Soviet)
UHF	Ultra-high frequency
UKADGE	(British component of NADGE)
UKUSA	UK–USA security agreement
UNFICYP	UN Force in Cyprus
USAF	US Air Force
USMC	US Marine Corps
VHF	Very-high frequency
VLF	Very-low frequency
VOA	Voice of America
V/STOL	Vertical/short take-off and landing
VTOL	Vertical take-off and landing
WTO	Warsaw Treaty Organization

Conventions

..	Data not available or not applicable
—	Nil or a negligible figure
m.	Million
b.	Billion (thousand million)
$	US $ unless otherwise indicated

1. Introduction

In recent years, various aspects of the major powers' rivalry over foreign basing access—or, more broadly, 'foreign military presence' (FMP)—have persistently drawn attention as prominent, front-page news. Indeed, this vital aspect of the competition between the rival power blocs has cut across virtually the entire swath of contemporary power diplomacy involving, among other things, rival alliances, the strategic nuclear race, the arms trade and wars between Third World states.

The US invasion of Grenada in 1983 was, presumably, largely impelled by fear of the imminence of a new Soviet/Cuban base in the Caribbean; similarly, the USA has been very concerned with possible later Soviet acquisition of basing facilities in Central America, specifically in Nicaragua. Britain's successful retaking of the Falklands/Malvinas Islands hinged critically on the use of staging facilities on Ascension and at Gibraltar.[1] The 1979 Soviet invasion of Afghanistan provided the USSR with access to air bases within closer striking range of the Persian Gulf; that invasion on top of the Iranian revolution the same year impelled the USA to seek new or enhanced air and naval access in Oman, Egypt, Kenya, Somalia, Turkey and Morocco. More recently, the USA has laboured, largely without success, to acquire additional access to facilities in Saudi Arabia, Kuwait and other Gulf states amid the ongoing crisis surrounding the 'reflagging' of oil tankers.

The US loss of vital intelligence facilities in Iran—useful for monitoring Soviet missile tests in connection with verification of SALT I—led to compensatory efforts at acquiring or keeping access in Turkey, China, Pakistan and Norway (there were clear links here with the US impasse over the Greece-Turkey imbroglio, with its balancing act between India and Pakistan, and with the USA's playing of the 'China card' at the expense of Taiwan). Growing Soviet access to air and naval facilities in Viet Nam, Ethiopia, South Yemen, Mozambique and Angola caused Western anxieties about potential interdiction of sea lanes of communication (SLOCs) for oil in certain circumstances. The USA also worried about maintaining presences in Iceland and Greenland vital to anti-submarine activities and strategic bomber refuelling; the USSR worried about keeping a presence in Cuba for similar and additional reasons. And for 40 years both superpowers have retained massive presences in Central Europe on the soil of allies. While both have also fielded military advisory groups in numerous places, the Soviet Union has also financed and armed large-unit Cuban 'surrogate' or 'proxy' forces in Ethiopia and Angola.[2]

Pakistan, meanwhile, was reported to have stationed some 10 000 troops in Saudi Arabia, a reminder that the politics of FMP might become more than a two-power or two-bloc game as new aspirants to the status of regional power arise in the Third World.[3] (North Korea, for instance, was in 1987 rumoured to

be considering sending troops to Angola.[4]) On the perhaps less obtrusive end
of what is subsumed under foreign military presence, there are the important
phenomena of aircraft overflight rights, naval port visits, access for commercial
airliners, oceanographic research vessels and fishing boats—some with less
benign purposes than advertised—and human intelligence (HUMINT) activities. And, in an area of somewhat convergent superpower interests, both the
USA and the USSR maintain a variety of overseas installations devoted to
surveillance of other nations' nascent and often covert nuclear activities, as
well as well-publicized nuclear tests by already established second-tier nuclear
powers. This in turn is an example of one area in which ongoing technological
developments (such as satellites and more accurate stand-off seismic devices)
may reduce the number of overseas facilities required by the major powers.
These examples illustrate the scope and complexity of some current FMP activities and requirements. It is a large, diverse and complex subject, in both its
technical and political aspects.

I. The historical context

There is, needless to say, nothing altogether new about the use by one military
power of access to another's soil. There is, indeed, a long history to basing
access and its associated diplomacy: Thucydides wrote of basing issues which
arose during the Peloponnesian wars.[5] Closer to the present, the successive
maritime empires—regional to global—of Venice, Portugal, Spain, Holland
and Britain were all reliant on external naval bases which were objects of
military rivalries (they were both reflective of, and determinants of, maritime
supremacy).[6] Admiral Mahan looked upon the combination of undivided sea
control and pre-eminent basing access as crucial to the rise and fall of imperial
naval power;[7] ironically, the supersession of sailing vessels by those powered
by steam increased the dependence of major powers on bases, that is, coaling
stations.[8] The British exploited the openings of both the Napoleonic wars and
World War I by picking off rivals' overseas assets—such were the easy fruits
of maritime dominance.[9] Admiral Gorschkov's writings reflect a very bitter
and traditional Great Russian dismay at earlier naval weakness; specifically,
the absence of a global basing network which might have circumvented reliance
on British bases and hence altered the embarrassing outcome against Japan
in 1905.[10] The USA emerged from World War II determined not to repeat its
earlier, almost cavalier, disregard for the importance of external bases—it
learned the importance of the facilities acquired from the UK under the Lend-
Lease agreement in 1940 as well as the effective use put to mid-Pacific bases
by Japan at the outset of World War II, both for offensive and defensive
purposes.[11]

    The modern period—here somewhat arbitrarily defined as that since the close
of World War I—has seen three more or less identifiable phases of global access
diplomacy, albeit somewhat telescoped and hence not altogether discrete:[12]

1. The colonial period, from 1919 up to and beyond World War II.
2. The early post-war period, characterized by a tight, bipolar, ideologically based alliance structure.
3. The most recent period, characterized by greater multipolarity, ideological diffusion, proliferation of independent sovereignties, and changing North–South relations.

The inter-war period—as an extension of the pre-World War I global system—saw most of what is now referred to as the Third World remain under colonial control. Thus, basing networks, in a relative sense, were mostly a function of the scope of rival empires. Britain had by far the largest global basing and military deployment structure, followed in turn by France, Spain, Portugal, the Netherlands, Italy, Japan and the USA. The USSR had virtually none; neither had defeated Germany. Hence, in contrast to the present day, there was little congruence between the overall facts of relative military power and the extent of basing access.[13] In other words, the vaunted 'rise of the peripheral powers' around declining Europe was not at first accompanied by large-scale overseas presence.[14] In addition, the latter was an important object of revisionist diplomatic aims, that is, a contributing cause of war.

Further, the inter-war period was characterized by shifting, relatively impermanent alliances (less clearly ideologically based than would later be the case), and there was no pre-World War II equivalent to the later highly structured and durable North Atlantic Treaty Organization (NATO) and Warsaw Treaty Organization (WTO).[15] Hence, there was little if any stationing of forces by major powers on their allies' soil—that applied to naval and air bases as well as to ground force deployments.[16] Some German utilization of Italian and Spanish bases in the late 1930s and contemporaneous Japanese access to Siamese (Thai) facilities were among the few exceptions.[17] These patterns constituted an extension of what had been normal practice for centuries, so that it is the recent period which constitutes an anomaly, an important point not readily discerned by the casual observer. Also lacking by comparison with the present period was a nexus of arms sales to granting of basing access—the arms trade of that period was still conducted on a 'free-market' basis, that is, it was removed from governmental licensing restrictions.[18] In other words, arms sales were not a major instrument for acquiring basing access. Nowadays, that relationship has become a hallmark of contemporary diplomacy.

The early post-war period saw the retention of most pre-war colonial holdings by the Western powers, which holdings gradually were reduced and eliminated over the next 30 years. But of greater importance, the West—underwritten by massive US military and economic aid—was able to fashion an elaborate system of formal alliances around the Eurasian rimland, as primarily embodied in the NATO, Central Treaty Organization (CENTO) and Southeast Asian Treaty Organization (SEATO) alliances, and supplemented by Washington's bilateral or otherwise multilateral security ties to Japan, South Korea, Taiwan and the Australia, New Zealand and United States (ANZUS) Treaty powers.[19] These alliances provided the West with an elaborate basing structure, usable for the whole range of conventional and strategic-nuclear purposes.

During this period, which preceded the partial unravelling of *Pax Americana* beginning in the 1960s, there was assumed a convergence of security interests between the USA and most of its allies and clients, so that access was usually freely granted and was not normally the subject of grudging negotiations over quid pro quo, nor of 'status of forces', that is, contingent restriction of access.[20]

The Soviet Union, meanwhile, with a few early exceptions (China, Finland and Albania) was constrained within its contiguous heartland empire and had little in the way of external access.[21] Such developments were to await not only political upheavals in the Third World, but also the building of a Soviet blue-water navy and long-range air transport capability, which would not only produce new basing requirements but also provide the power projection capability to sustain and (if necessary) defend a basing structure.

The more recent period has seen gradual but cumulatively profound changes, resulting in a qualitatively different pattern of access and associated diplomacy. The Soviet Union's leapfrogging of the old containment ring has eventuated in the acquisition of facilities, with varying degrees of access, in numerous Third World locales: Algeria, Angola, Cuba, Ethiopia, India, Kampuchea, Libya, Mozambique, Peru, South Yemen, Syria and Viet Nam, among others.[22] Basing is now almost entirely a two-bloc game and is fully enmeshed in the big-power competition for global influence. The old colonial empires have almost completely vanished, and as many ex-colonial nations have not allowed a continued Western presence (some, indeed, now host a Soviet presence) numerous former points of access have been lost to the West.

Increasingly, indeed, the USA has found it difficult to persuade many of its erstwhile clients that their security interests are convergent with its own. The result in many cases has been a move towards decoupling, resulting variously in full denial of access, the imposition of more restrictive terms of access or, in combination, the imposition of higher costs in the form of rent, increased security assistance and economic aid, political quid pro quo, and so on.[23]

The above-mentioned decoupling and growing perceptions of a decline in convergence of security interests (access in exchange for protection and/or extended deterrence) have resulted in a somewhat altered diplomacy of access. Access is no longer so automatically granted to hegemonic alliance leaders on the basis of past friendship, nor gratitude for liberation in World War II, nor mere ideological congruence on one side or the other of the great power divide. Access must now be bargained for, and the reciprocal balance of leverage involved appears in many cases more symmetrical than in the past. Primarily, the instrument of arms supplies (or more broadly, security assistance) has become the foremost item of exchange. Many US clients—Greece, Morocco, the Philippines, Portugal, Somalia, Spain and Turkey, among others—have sought and obtained large annual assistance packages (in actual fact a form of rent) ranging close to US $1 billion per year.[24] Sometimes too, the qualitative aspects of arms supplies (the sophistication of aircraft, missiles, etc., and their lethal accessories) form the basis for bargaining. The same has been true regarding Soviet overseas military presence, as witness the (disparate) course of developments in Algeria, Egypt, Libya and Viet Nam, among others.

By the late 1980s, these trends had been extended to the point at which one might speculate as to whether a distinct, fourth phase of basing diplomacy could be discerned. Difficult to label, it might be characterized as one in which basing diplomacy had, to a degree, become depoliticized (in an ideological sense) and placed, increasingly, on an almost crass commercial basis. Burma, a neutral nation in dire economic straits, was rumoured to be offering the USA a base on its Coco Islands.[25] Greece abjured expelling the US presence—for a big price—seemingly only because it needed the rent.[26]

Within the Soviet orbit, there were increasing signs of a Soviet retreat from the long-escalating effort at enhancing overseas power projection, just because the economic quid pro quo for bases was becoming too burdensome for the strained Soviet economy.[27] Curiously, these trends appeared to presage a return to the practices of the seventeenth or eighteenth centuries, during the 'Golden Age of Diplomacy' and the heyday of mercenary forces. The Soviet and US uses of 'surrogate forces', linked to basing diplomacy, seemed to reinforce this point.[28]

Generally, as is elaborated upon below, basing access correlates with a close arms supplier–client relationship, featuring a sole or predominant major power role. On the contrary, the now fairly large number of Third World countries which acquire arms from both sides of the cold war bloc divide tend, in most cases, to be free of a superpower presence, at least as pertains to major facilities.[29] And, shifts in arms transfer client relationships across the ideological divide usually result in concomitant shifts in access patterns—witness the recent volte faces in China, Egypt, Ethiopia, Somalia, Sudan, and so on.

The modern era has seen technological as well as political changes which, in some cases, have profoundly altered patterns of foreign basing access, if only gradually. Several major changes stand out. First, missiles, particularly intercontinental ballistic missiles (ICBMs), have largely superseded strategic bombers. Then, the longer ranges of aircraft (in particular) and ships—and the development of aerial refuelling—have greatly reduced the earlier requirements for extensive chains of access needed, for instance, in aerial resupply of arms or troops during war. This trend has been reinforced by the now far smaller numbers of ships and aircraft of all types in all countries (more combat capability is packed into fewer systems)—in the 1930s, even some medium-range powers such as Argentina or Romania fielded 1000 or more combat aircraft and far more surface vessels than at the present time.[30] The result: fewer bases, all round, both at home and abroad, with one source reporting that the number of US bases has been reduced to about 700 from almost 7000 during World War II's peak.[31] Concomitantly, this meant enhanced vulnerability to preemptive strikes, occasioning a newer emphasis on dispersion and mobility.

The contrast can be seen rather starkly using a comparison of large-scale US airlifts to the Middle East, in 1941–42 and 1973 respectively. In the former, the

USA, in mounting an airlift (also in ferrying fighter aircraft) to beleaguered British forces in the Middle East, had to make use of an elaborate chain of air-staging bases stretching from Florida via Cuba, Puerto Rico, Barbados, Trinidad, British Guiana, north-east Brazil (Recife, Natal), Fernando de Noronha, Takoradi (now in Ghana), Lagos, Kano (now in Nigeria), Khartoum and on to Egypt.[32] A shorter though still elaborate staging network was utilized to ferry aircraft to the UK via Newfoundland, Labrador, Greenland, Iceland and Northern Ireland. In 1973, by contrast, the USA needed only Portugal's Lajes Air Force Base in the Azores islands (abetted by US aircraft carriers) to mount a massive arms airlift to Israel; afterwards still newer technological advances (the C-141 aircraft 'stretch' programme, enhanced refuelling capability) would enable the USA, if required, to mount a similar airlift from Dover, Delaware to Tel Aviv without the use of any intermediate stops.[33] As the example of the Azores illustrates, however, the dwindling number of bases has made the superpowers more vulnerable to host nations demanding extravagant concessions.

Similar trends have been evidenced regarding naval bases necessary to support a global maritime presence. In the 1930s, the British Royal Navy utilized numerous main operating bases to establish a presence across the whole of the Indian Ocean and western Pacific littorals; today, with smaller fleets (but some nuclear-powered ships, better at-sea refuelling and other provisioning) the same approximate mission (albeit minus that of colonial control) is performed with a small number of US bases: Yokosuka, Guam, Subic Bay and Diego Garcia support an extensive US naval deployment all the way from the Central Pacific to the South-West Asia/Persian Gulf area; Cam Ranh Bay in Viet Nam performs a roughly analogous function for the USSR.

But that is not the whole story. Whereas the sheer quantitative requirements for traditional air and naval bases has declined, there has been an enormous increase in requirements for numerous new 'technical' basing facilities, many of which are neither very visible nor widely publicized, but which are crucial to a modern, global military establishment. That trend has been gradual but ineluctable. Before World War II, there were some such 'technical' requirements: radio receivers, transmitters, relays, and so on; terminals and relays for underwater cables; and some rudimentary radar and communications intercept facilities.[34] But in combination these functions were of limited importance *vis-à-vis* those of naval and aircraft main bases.

Now, the number and functions of such new basing requirements have expanded dramatically: signals intelligence (SIGINT), space tracking (telescopes, radars, laser sources), satellite control and data relay, ground terminals and data-processing facilities for underwater sonar cables (anti-submarine warfare), early-warning radars (for missiles, bombers), seismological detection, navigation and positioning aids for aircraft and submarines, downwind detection of air samples (nuclear explosion monitoring), communications all along a spectrum from extra-low frequency (ELF) to ultra-high frequency (UHF), and a vast array of research and environmental testing activities involving everything from weapon tests to the weather.[35] As implied here, these new requirements have coincided with the expansion of modern military activity fully to three dimensions: surface (land and sea), underwater and outer space. Indeed, these newer technical facilities—alone or in combinations—often deal with the inter-relationships of military activities extending across all of these domains. Anti-submarine detection can involve satellites; navigation satellites assist mid-flight corrections for missiles launched from underwater, and so on. Communications traverse all these media as part of integrated networks.

These trends and relationships will become still more important if, as now seems highly possible, the militarization of space and rival strategic missile defensive systems are to move ahead. Extensive strategic defence deployments on either or both sides will, presumably, produce a host of new external basing requirements even as, paradoxically, satellites gradually supersede some basing functions previously conducted on land or at sea.[36] Generally speaking, the real-time surveillance, communications and targeting capabilities of modern weapons appear to increase the vulnerability of military forces to pre-emptive strikes, occasioning a newer overall emphasis on dispersion, mobility and hiding. This would in turn appear to presage enhanced requirements for global access, even as the political climate for such access appears to be becoming more constrained.

II. Definitions

There is a certain amount of semantic confusion involving a number of terms and concepts now used to envelope the subject which, by common convention, long fell under the heading of 'basing' or 'overseas bases'. Indeed, book titles earlier sported these terms without any self-consciousness about definitional ambiguity. As is so often the case, what is involved is not merely a matter of alternative or optional scholarly usage, but some subtle political and ideological issues as well.

At issue are such matters as degrees and types of foreign access, the political or economic terms of such access, and the extent to which it (access) is temporary or permanent.

On the narrowest basis, one frequently (and interchangeably) sees the terms 'base', 'facility' and 'installation'.[37] The last-named usually takes on the character of a strictly technical term, devoid of political/ideological content—it refers usually to one finite physical operation with one function. The terms base and/or facility appear to be a bit broader in scope; although they are often used interchangeably they have come to connote very separate sets of circumstances. 'Base'—a much more frequently used term for centuries up to the recent past—has come to define a situation in which the user nation (i.e., the foreign presence) has unrestricted access and freedom to operate. 'Facility', meanwhile, has come to be the preferred term where the host nation exerts ultimate sovereignty and where the user nation's access is contingent, restricted and subject to *ad hoc* decisions about use in given situations. By these definitions, European access to installations in former colonial holdings would have defined a base; so too those situations of highly unequal power and leverage involving sovereign states where 'status of forces agreements' had given more or less open-ended access and use to the foreign presence, as was so often the case for US basing access earlier on in the post-war period. But then, as most of what used to be called basing now really refers to the above definition of facility, it is now often claimed that in an era of lapsed colonialism and diffused global sovereignty there are virtually no more bases, only facilities. That is formally or nominally true, but most writers continue to use the former term, if only after a formal demurrer regarding definitions.

One might prefer the use of a still broader term, 'foreign military presence'.[38] Everything that falls under the headings of bases and facilities would thereby be included. So too would large military formations (combat units, etc.) and military advisory groups, and headquarters operations which may be spread around office buildings in the centre of a host city.

Still broader, however, is the notion of military access (sometimes co-terminously referred to as 'strategic access' but intended to connote a broader purview than would apply merely to strategic nuclear forces).[39] This concept subsumes not only permanent or durable basing facilities, but also such disparate activities as naval ship port visits, regular or occasional access for fishing fleets or oceanographic vessels (some with 'grey area' military purposes), overhead use of airspace (aircraft overflights), *ad hoc* military aircraft staging (sometimes involving use of commercial airports), HUMINT activities, whether fully clandestine or not, smaller military advisory groups, and so on. Clearly, the dividing line between this concept and those previously discussed is often indistinct, involving blurred, grey areas. For instance, more than occasional use of a port for warship visits can come, at some point, to define a facility, though a formal definition of the latter might require permanent stationing on land of shore personnel engaged in maintenance, repair, reprovisioning, and so on. Similarly, frequent and more or less regular use of access to airports becomes, at some point, a 'staging base', or rather, a commercial 'staging facility'.

III. Emerging macro-political trends and bases

The above review of historical developments leads to a discussion of emerging macro-political trends which may now and in the near future have a fundamental effect on basing access. Such an analysis—admittedly speculative and probably also subject to the danger of over-reliance on mere extrapolation from current trends—merges the somewhat distinct but overlapping endeavours of futurology (hence the terminology of macro-political trends) and of international systems analysis (identification of basic variables useful for describing *any* historical epoch).[40] Systems analysis, considered by many scholars the most promising road to a general theory of international relations, might be used to 'explain' why the USA has experienced a long-term, seemingly ineluctable reduction in its access to bases over the past several decades, or cautiously to 'predict' whether those trends are likely to be extrapolated or reversed.[41]

Ranging from the relatively abstract to the relatively mundane, some of the areas which appear most relevant to an analysis of emerging macro-political trends, as they would in turn affect basing politics, are listed below.

1. Broad changes in the global political 'climate' for big-power basing, involving a complex web of essentially subjective, psychological factors revolving around issues of sovereignty, national dignity/humiliation, etc.

2. Shifting conditions of international economics, involving North–South, East–West, intra-OECD dimensions: trade, investment, raw materials.

3. Changing global political structure, involving such factors as polarity (bipolarity versus trends towards multipolarity), the continued role of ideology in determining alignments, propensities towards or against neutralism on the part not only of Third World countries but also of nations now firmly within the Western or Eastern military blocs.

4. The future of arms control, centrally involving SALT/START, test bans, and outer space but, as it applies to basing, also potentially involving arms transfers, nuclear weapon-free zones, nuclear non-proliferation, and perhaps conventional arms control in Central Europe (MBFR—mutual and balanced force reductions).

5. The remnant 'decolonialization' of the Third World, i.e., how many and what additional new nations might be created from still non-independent island groups.

6. Trends in intra-Third World warfare: how many wars, what types (conventional or unconventional), extent of big-power involvement, etc.

7. Trends in conventional weapon developments, and the relationship to arms transfers and warfare in the Third World.

8. Changes in the extent of nuclear proliferation, i.e., a possible large-scale expansion of the number of nuclear-armed states.

A comprehensive analysis of the myriad interrelationships among the above areas is beyond the scope of this chapter. Some illustrative points, however, are offered below.

Generally, regarding the 'climate' for big-power access, it is clear that recent years have seen an increasingly less permissive environment for foreign access. A foreign presence is, for obvious reasons, almost nowhere welcome, except where it can be construed as contributing directly and visibly to protection. But, indeed, almost everywhere, both in the Third World and within the US orbit of Western democracies, governments are subject to pressures regarding a foreign presence. Bruised dignities and compromised sovereignties are here involved, often at the level of rivalry over local women in areas adjacent to bases or (as witnessed by US problems in Greece and the Philippines in recent years) over wages paid to local personnel.[42] In Western countries, and in US clients in the Third World, the USSR conducts a daily onslaught of propaganda designed to unhinge US basing access—the USA in turn is engaged in various base denial activities directed at Soviet access.[43] Bases are very visible political targets.

Further, there is now a lot of 'lateral' pressure among Third World countries involving superpower basing presences, echoed in UN resolutions and, for instance, such manifestations as the Iraqi Charter floated several years ago, which called on all Third World countries to eliminate foreign bases.[44] Some of these pressures are global; some regional (e.g., discussions among Indian Ocean littoral countries about demilitarization of that region—in reality, specifically directed against Diego Garcia; and intra-Arab pressures linking US bases in Oman, Morocco, etc., to the Israeli issue). And, of course, the USA seems to be targeted—asymmetrically relative to the USSR—by these pressures, for all of the usually cited reasons, that is, the legacy of Western colonialism, the failures of US public diplomacy, the seeming irrationalities of anti-Americanism.[45] The moves towards 'closure' of the seas and overland airspace as evidenced by the 1982 Law of the Sea regime is, of course, illustrative of this pattern.[46]

Additionally, recent years have witnessed the spread of anti-nuclear and environmental movements throughout the Western world and elsewhere, generally associated with the radical left. The recent US problems in New Zealand well illustrate how such factors can constrain US basing access even in connection with an old US ally, and one rather remote from the cold-war front lines.[47] Pressures have been felt in the UK and Canada as well.

It is likely that the psychological environment, generally, for foreign military access—particularly that involving nuclear weapons or even nuclear-powered vessels—will become even less permissive. That trend could, presumably, be reversed—in some circumstances—by increased global tensions which at least in some places made a US protective presence more desirable. That in turn could depend upon perceptions of US strength and resolve though, paradoxically, that same strength can induce resentment. Otherwise, it is also possible that in the future Soviet basing access will suffer from the same pressures as now apply more seriously to the USA. Soviet problems in Egypt—there clearly related to issues of national pride and independence—could be the forerunners of a more general phenomenon.

It might be said that the present seeming trend towards 'decoupling' of the major powers' basing access could be disaggregated into largely distinct nuclear and conventional components. On the one hand, numerous clients and basing hosts of the major powers have come to fear the consequences of hosting nuclear-related facilities if war should erupt. Hence, scenarios such as that in Tom Clancy's *Red Storm Rising* (reflective of reported war games and other projections in Washington) have US allies making secret deals with the USSR, or simply closing down US access, when push comes to shove—fear and intimidation come to outweigh paper alliance commitments when the balloon really does go up.[48]

On a distinct plane, however, are such phenomena as France's refusal to allow US aircraft overflights *en route* to the Libya bombing raid, or Kuwait's refusal to allow access for US helicopters operating over the tense Persian Gulf.[49] These actions represent not so much the duress of imminent destruction, or involvement in an unwanted war, as they do narrow, pragmatic political calculations which carefully weigh the economic and political trade-offs where competing interests and political cross-pressures are involved. The Arabs fear a US embrace because of the Israeli problem; France contemplates loss of economic advantage in the Middle East if it supports a US military action against any Arab state, and so on.

It is, of course, also difficult to predict just what macro-economic trends, possible economic crises or cataclysms, or shifts in the global economic power balance, will unfold in the near to distant future, much less what impact they will have on basing access. The uncertainties are no more obvious in the light of various recent surprises and reversals: oil glut replaces oil shortage, the resurgence and then fall of the US dollar *vis-à-vis* other major currencies, debt problems in Latin America and elsewhere among countries earlier thought to be on the verge of 'take-off', and so on. But one can speculate on some issues, some possibilities. For instance, there is the question, particularly for the USA, as to whether Third World debts or, more generally, worsening economic circumstances, can be used to acquire leverage for basing access in a period seeing the supersession of political by economic factors as a basis for acquiring access. The rumoured example of Burma, cited above, may be a straw in the wind. But as is discussed below, by the late 1980s, both the USA and the USSR appeared more and more affected by budgetary constraints and by the cost of their military presences—on both sides there was greatly increased concern about the 'burdens of empire'. Indeed, by 1988, the improved climate for a variety of arms control arrangements seemed driven, on both sides, more than ever before, by mounting economic pressures.

Any of a number of possible broad structural changes in the international system could affect basing structure, involving dramatic shifts in political alignments. Though it is unlikely, Western Europe and the USA could split, perhaps dramatically (this could, of course, involve partial split-offs). FR Germany's *Ostpolitik* could be pushed much further, perhaps even to a 'second Rapallo'. The People's Republic of China (PRC) could become more closely aligned with the USA; contrariwise one might envision a revival of the Sino-Soviet alliance. Historically, long-term, stable, ideologically based alliances have been more conducive to basing access; multipolar global systems with more rapidly shifting alignments less so. There seems now an overall trend towards alliance de-coupling—if so, access will presumably become more precarious and tenuous, or at least more costly, all round. Alliances based on 'pragmatic' (hence, also probably more unstable) rather than ideological grounds are probably less conducive to access.

It is important to emphasize in this above regard that not merely the structure of alignments, but also the very basis of superpower foreign policies—ideological versus pragmatic, aggressive or expansionist versus cautious or neo-isolationist—may have a major impact on basing diplomacy. The USA, for instance, which once had a near-maximizing policy on base acquisitions, became far less ambitious in this regard after the Viet Nam War, tending to seek to retain a bare minimum of necessary overseas facilities.[50]

Analyses of Soviet basing and alignment policies began to take on a different character in 1986–87, both before and after the emerging outlines of Gorbachev's *Glasnost* policy came to be staples of public discussion. Some earlier analyses in this period saw a waning of the Soviet drive for power projection capability and associated basing access—this was attributed primarily to shifting military priorities in the direction of focusing naval power on protection of the SSBN (nuclear-powered ballistic missile submarine) bastions, and on the capability for interdicting sea lanes of communication in the Atlantic and Pacific oceans in the event of a major war.[51]

In 1987, however, new indications of what might become a more fundamental shift in Soviet foreign policy emerged. A major effort was underway to open new lines of communication and political and economic relationships with moderate or even pro-Western Third World states—Argentina, Brazil, Egypt, Indonesia, Kuwait, Mexico, Saudi Arabia, Thailand. This was said to be at the expense of—or in lieu of—relations with long-time Soviet clients such as Angola, Cuba, Libya, Mozambique, Nicaragua, Syria, Viet Nam, and so on, most if not all of which were said to have become economic, if not political, burdens to the USSR at a time when it badly needed to reform its economy and enhance its role in the international economy (most of the latter group had also failed heretofore to become showpieces of socialist political economy).[52]

The Soviet Union has its major overseas bases in the latter group, however, and with regard to the former group of states, it is not likely that such access could be obtained no matter what the level of enhanced economic and cultural ties. Whether this was consonant with a reduced Soviet interest in power projection—or simply a recognition that the cost had become too high—was not entirely clear. Neither was the nature of the debate thereon within the Soviet hierarchy clear, between conservatives and 'progressives' linked to Gorbachev.

The overall future of arms control is, at the time of writing, very unclear, both generally and with respect to specific arms control domains. It is also presumably subject to volatile short-term as well as long-term political shifts within the USA and the USSR—the effects of the 1988 US election remain to be seen. Whether the (until recently) frozen 'SALT structure' will survive or be transformed by a new START treaty is unclear, as are the futures of test ban treaties and those possibly pertaining to anti-satellite (ASAT) weapons. The outcomes could affect basing requirements in response to changing (that is, allowed) weapon deployments; for instance, ground and/or space-based laser weapons, cruise-missile deployments, missile launching facilities, command, control, communications and intelligence (C^3I) installations connected to ballistic missile defence, numbers of externally based nuclear-powered ballistic-missile submarines, seismological stations, and so on. And certain arms control arrangements which might be envisioned, however dimly, for Central Europe—

mutual and balanced force reductions, nuclear weapon-free zones—might also critically affect basing issues, for instance by re-opening the question of US forward based-systems (FBS) in Central Europe and/or the Mediterranean in the wake of the 1987 Treaty between the USA and the USSR on the Elimination of Their Intermediate-Range and Shorter-Range Missiles (the INF Treaty).

As of 1987, there were few seeming adumbrations of new arms control regimes directly related to basing issues. Ten years earlier, of course, Indian Ocean demilitarization—then effectively involving a prospective trade-off between US access to Diego Garcia and Soviet access to Somalia—had at least made its way on to the agenda. More recently, a nuclear weapon-free zone in the south-west Pacific has at least been broached. But as yet, there is nothing concrete to match the (temporarily successful) basing aspects of the inter-war Washington Naval Agreement, which respectively limited inter-war British and Japanese basing efforts in the Pacific and East Asia, albeit only temporarily.[53]

The post-war decolonialization process is, so it would appear, nearly complete, but for a few remnant, nagging issues such as Namibia, and apart from essentially non-issues occasionally pressed within the UN as, for instance, that of Puerto Rico. But there may be further pressures in international forums which could involve Ascension, Bermuda, Diego Garcia, the Falklands, Greenland, the various quasi-independent states now emerging from US trusteeships in the Central Pacific, the Canary Islands, Gibraltar, Mayotte, and so on, to cite a few salient situations. Some of these do involve important Western basing assets (note Ascension's crucial importance in the Falklands War as well as for space tracking and tanker refuelling). The central Pacific islands could well become an important focus of superpower contention at some point, given their strategic location. The overall climate of North–South relations could have an ultimate bearing on the disposition or use of some of these small strategic prizes.

Regarding Third World warfare, it is important to note that some of these wars, particularly because of the diplomacy of big-power arms resupply, have had a large impact on basing access. Enhanced Soviet access to Viet Nam was almost explicitly bargained for in the context of Soviet aid to Viet Nam during its war with the PRC in 1979.[54] Soviet access to Syria has been widened as a result of the crisis in Lebanon, as has French access to Chad amid the latter's conflict with Libya. US access to Argentina has now been curtailed because of Washington's tilt towards the UK in the Falklands crisis.[55] And, of course, there is the matter of Soviet bases in Afghanistan; and, perhaps later, in Central America. Soviet and US bases were reversed after the Horn War of 1977–78. Generally speaking, it is worth noting that some analysts are predicting an increase in the frequency of 'traditional' conventional warfare in the Third World which, if it eventuates, could strongly affect basing diplomacy.[56]

The future of arms transfer diplomacy—related to the above—will be important, both generally and with reference to specific cases, to the future of basing diplomacy. As indicated, arms transfers—modified by the ideological component of alignments—have become, overwhelmingly, the major coin of basing diplomacy. There are few cases indeed where significant basing access has been granted either superpower without a significant arms transfer relationship, though the reverse of this proposition does not necessarily hold, that is, arms transfers do not always or automatically translate into access, as witness the recent US experience in and around the Persian Gulf. Overall leverage here is critical. Current analyses of the currently evolving trends in arms transfers tend to coalesce around some of the following points, all germane to the future of basing access diplomacy.[57]

1. The overall volume of transfers to the Third World may now be declining, mainly as a result of the decline of the Organization of Petroleum Exporting Countries (OPEC)—a huge proportion of recent arms transfers has been accounted for by oil states—and also to the debt problems of other states. Otherwise, the near 'saturation' of some arms markets, and the vastly increased unit costs of modern weapons such as high-performance aircraft and main battle tanks have been important factors.

2. The USA seems to be overtaking the USSR as an arms supplier, as measured by new orders, reversing the trend of recent years. This has resulted in part from the relaxation of self-imposed US restraints as embodied in a Presidential Directive issued by President Carter in 1977 (PD-13). It may also have resulted from the successes of US arms in Lebanon and the corresponding Soviet débâcle, that is, a perception in the Third World that US arms technology is ascendant.

3. Superpowers may increasingly be able to tilt some local arms balances with infusions of qualitatively more advanced systems, i.e., electronic countermeasures (ECMs), electronic counter-countermeasures (ECCMs), precision bombing technology, forward-looking infra-red (FLIR), and so on. If so (if that is one lesson of Lebanon) it may result in greater big-power leverage in bargaining for bases via arms sales, i.e., the quality and sophistication of those sales may be paramount. Contrariwise, the Iraq–Iran War points to the problem of 'absorption' as often overriding that of technology.

4. More and more Third World countries—also some developed ones—are demanding technology transfer, i.e., assistance to indigenous arms production programmes. As the case of the recent US–Turkish agreement may indicate, this too may become part of the arsenal of leverage available to a major power seeking basing access.

The future impact of nuclear proliferation on basing diplomacy appears somewhat indeterminate; indeed, there is wide disagreement even among experts about how many additions to the nuclear club there may be by the year 2000 or 2005. What, for instance, would be the impact—on basing—of the addition of some or all of the following: Argentina, Brazil, India, Iraq, Pakistan, South Africa, South Korea and Taiwan? Many 'theoretical' studies of nuclear proliferation project an overall 'decoupling' of alliance systems, a kind of disaggregation in which superpowers attempt to distance themselves from nuclear clients who, in a variety of circumstances, might trigger escalation towards a superpower nuclear exchange. But one could equally argue that access might be enhanced in some cases, were big-power defensive or deterrent assistance offered to clients threatened by newly 'nuclearized' neighbours.[58] In addition, some would-be nuclear powers might utilize the lure or carrot of basing access so as to reduce pressures against their nuclear programmes—Pakistan's recent bargaining with the USA might thus be characterized.

IV. The scope and boundaries of the subject

The above discussion of definitions—revolving mainly around the terms foreign military presence, access, strategic access, base, facility, installation, and so on—serves to initiate a discussion of the boundaries of this study. Those boundaries are cast rather wide to encompass virtually anything that might satisfy the virtually self-explanatory criterion of fitting all three of the words which constitute FMP—'foreign', 'military' and 'presence'. That would incorporate not only the obvious—large air and naval bases, satellite tracking facilities, etc.—but also port visits, overflights and perhaps cadres of military advisers beyond the usual handful normal to an arms transfer relationship. But there are some other issues: those of historical location in time and of geographical scope or emphasis.

For the most part, this study is intended to provide a relatively current analysis of the global state of FMP—something of a snap-shot. Even with that intention, however, one must inevitably recognize the dynamics of an ever-evolving situation and the need to explain how the present structure of basing facilities is rooted in past political relationships and past military-technological requirements.

Some basing presences have remained relatively static or unchanging over a long period of time, for instance, US ground-troop deployments in FR Germany, or air defence radar installations in Canada. But even in these cases, and more so in others, there is gradual change wrought by the onward march of technological development and associated upgrading of facilities and weapon systems.[59] At air bases in Japan, F-16s replace F-4s; and SR-71s replace U-2s as the US spy planes flown out of bases in the UK. The number of Soviet ships and aircraft deployed in Viet Nam has gradually increased since 1979 though the number of discrete facilities has remained the same.

Geographically speaking, there are no boundaries to the study, which is intended to be global and hence, in this sense, comprehensive. One minor caveat intrudes, however. In sheer quantitative terms, the massive FMP of the two superpowers in their respective East and West European alliance domains can almost overwhelm a comprehensive data base on this subject. A mere cataloguing, for instance, of the Soviet and US ground force presences in the two Germanies fills a small volume—hundreds, if not thousands, of barracks areas, hospitals, depots, and so on. Hence, at the risk of introducing a new asymmetry or distortion, these details—and partly because they are intrinsically less interesting in a study of this sort than the quantitatively smaller but far more obtrusive and prominent FMP in some Third World states—are here collapsed or summarized to a greater degree than their counterparts in the politically more contentious cases in the Third World.

At least three other methodological or boundary issues bear mention at the outset, as they relate to a clear, full definition of FMP: ship port visits, aircraft overflights and small military advisory groups. Each involves daunting problems of data collection as well as difficult grey area boundary problems in relation to more obvious (for inclusion) aspects of FMP.

Regarding naval facilities, at one end of the spectrum are the main naval bases replete with dry-docking facilities and the like. At the other end are occasional port visits for essentially diplomatic or symbolic 'showing the flag' purposes. In between, however, are more routine and maybe (in a deterrence sense) more militarily relevant ship visits for provisions, refuelling, rest and recreation (R & R), and so on, involving numerous grey area cases in which it is arguable whether or not a 'facility' or 'base' can be discerned; such visits are perhaps also subject to fairly frequent fluctuations.[60]

If all port visits were considered indicative of FMP, the data management problem would, obviously, be formidable as it would also be for aircraft overflights. Yet, this is a terribly important matter at times, the circumstances surrounding the 1973 airlifts to the Middle Eastern combatants, those in 1977–78 to Ethiopia and Somalia, and US problems in connection with its recent raid on Libya being illustrative. About all we can do with this subject is to discuss its parameters, highlight its importance and illustrate the latter with some salient cases.[61]

Finally, there is the grey area regarding ground-force FMP between actual units (combat or otherwise) deployed in other nations, and the routine small training missions which accompany almost any arms sales transaction, of which obviously there are many. The celebrated issue of the Soviet 'brigade' in Cuba, which helped torpedo SALT II in 1979, is illustrative of the issue as are also, for instance, periodic rumours about Israeli 'advisers' in Guatemala or Ethiopia, Taiwanese pilots in North Yemen, and so on. For the sake of economy, the present analysis is relegated to significant, operating field units clearly beyond the level of handfuls of seconded advisers, while still highlighting the close relationship between security assistance and basing access.

One additional prefatory note involves data sources and the completeness or inclusiveness of the data presented here. For obvious reasons, information on US, British and French FMP is easier to come by than that involving Soviet access to facilities. This is particularly the case where detailed information on 'technical' facilities is involved, that is, those involving intelligence, communications and other space-related functions. And, as is noted below, the Soviet practice of utilizing ships in lieu of land-based facilities—relative to the US case—may exacerbate the problem to the extent that the amount of data available on US facilities will greatly outweigh that for the USSR, perhaps serving to provide a somewhat false impression of asymmetries in capabilities, if not the impression that Soviet facilities simply go unreported. This is dealt with in chapter 6.

V. A typology of FMP

This work is basically organized around 10 types of FMP, which constitute the chapters at the core of the book.

Needless to say, the dividing lines between these categories are occasionally somewhat fuzzy, unavoidably so. The contemporary tendency in the literature to classify some discrete facilities as dealing principally with C^3I bespeaks of a grey area between two of the categories, in actuality perhaps more a semantic than a real problem. Naval aircraft, including helicopters, located at or adjacent to naval bases might be classified in either of the first two categories. Some space and intelligence functions, as defined here, may be difficult in some cases to separate; as may some environmental and research functions. Aircraft utilized for ocean surveillance and/or anti-submarine warfare may be discussed either under the rubric of naval forces or that of intelligence-related facilities. By and large, however, the typology below appears apt and useful, as well as near-exhaustive across the whole range of activities subsumed under FMP.

1. Airfield—or any other site concerned with the operation of aircraft for military purposes;

2. Naval—port or any other site concerned with the operation of ships for military purposes, such as repair dockyards, mid-ocean mooring buoys;

3. Ground force—any site concerned with the conduct of land warfare, such as army bases, exercise areas, fortifications, fixed artillery;

4. Missile—sites concerned primarily with the maintenance and launching of missiles, fixed artillery sites, etc.

5. Space—sites concerned with the operation or monitoring of military satellites other than communications satellites;

6. Communications and control—sites concerned with military communications or the control of military systems;

7. Intelligence and command—sites concerned with intelligence gathering by non-satellite means, and sites exercising command over military systems.

8. Environmental monitoring—sites carrying out monitoring of environmental factors of military importance, such as military meteorological stations;

9. Research and testing—sites associated with military research and with developmental testing of military systems;

10. Logistic—sites not obviously assignable to airfield, naval or ground force, and concerned with production, storage and transport of military *matériel*, administration of military forces, and the housing, medical treatment, etc., of military personnel.

At the risk of some (hopefully minimal) redundancy, the somewhat static data categories listed above—once defined and presented in tandem—are reorganized along more 'functional' lines. They can be grouped in any number of ways to illustrate their combined uses for various types of military or logistical oper- ation. Perhaps the most obviously appropriate dividing line, however, is that between conventional and nuclear military operations; or short of actual combat, deployment for the eventuality of such contingencies. In the con- ventional realm, one can discuss US and/or Soviet basing structures as they are configured to support global power projection capabilities: (hypothetical) major power wars, larger and smaller interventions in various Third World areas, support for client states and/or surrogate forces; also arms resupply operations on behalf of arms clients at war. Both sides also have elaborate basing structures for supporting their nuclear force postures, designed primarily for 'normal' peacetime deterrence, but also for various levels of alert (involving dispersion, higher levels of readiness) during crises or even during hypothetical protracted conventional phases of superpower conventional war. Some overseas facilities will, of course, be configured for both conventional and nuclear purposes, for instance, satellite-surveillance systems' ground down-links, various com- munications facilities, air tanker bases, and so on. And, a protracted 'con- ventional phase' which saw both sides on high nuclear alert status while attempting to improve, relatively, their nuclear postures, would blur these categories.

In the above analysis, in leading into the overarching format of this book, data on bases or facilities are organized according to two dimensions: (*a*) domains of military endeavour and classes of military technology (ground forces, air forces, naval forces, intelligence, space, communications, etc.); and (*b*) the by now 'functional' breakdown between facilities for nuclear forces and those used for conventional force projection. There is, however, a third dimension; indeed, that by which the data *are* most basically organized: by country (host or user) and by region. That is, there is a geographical dimension. One might, indeed, have assayed a chapter breakdown by region but, instead, that dimension has been subsumed under the others.[62] But there is more involved than the formality of the structure of a book.

A number of years ago, Saul Cohen, in writing what was to become known as a classic study of geopolitical theory, defined geopolitics in terms of 'the world that matters', that is, what is important in the geography of power relations between the major powers of a period.[63] Otherwise stated, this pertains to the 'strategic high ground' between competing major powers, or to crucial 'zones of decision'. Hence, the 'heartland' and 'rimland' so dear to theorists such as Mackinder and Mahan, can be seen to fit such a definition—they speak of the crucial importance of rivalry between continental land power and surrounding sea power on the Eurasian rimlands, which, even today, largely defines the geopolitical competition between the USA and the USSR. In the 1950s, similarly, there was considerable talk about control of the airspaces over the Arctic as constituting a crucial zone of decision during the era of dominance by strategic bombers.

As applied to current FMP matters it may be said that a long-term review of basing problems will reveal rather clear periodic shifts in attention between nations and regions, as the major power focus on ever-new points of crucial contention shifts with changing technology, global resource economics and political rivalries. One can trace this back a half-century or more, almost in the form of a 'content analysis' of press and journal offerings.

In the late 1930s, a study of basing access problems (as revealed in the press and in new declassified intelligence documents) would have revealed enormous interest and accompanying tensions over, in particular: access to nations in proximity to the Panama Canal (Colombia, Panama, Costa Rica, the Galapagos Islands), the Gibraltar Straits (Spain, Portugal, Tangiers, Libya, the Canary Islands), the Central Pacific (the Marianas, the Marshall and Caroline Islands), South-East Asia (Hainan, the Spratly Islands, Indo-China, the Philippines, Formosa) and, particularly for the USA, the Atlantic littoral from Labrador all the way to north-east Brazil. The reasons for these foci are presumably altogether apparent in the light of defence planning for the initial stages of what would become World War II.

In the 1950s, the literature on bases (and the day-to-day drumbeat of front-pages news) focused on the forward-based rim of the US-led containment alliance around Eurasia. Basing in connection with nuclear deterrence (bombers, tankers, intelligence functions, etc.) was foremost. In the 1960s, there appeared an altered focus on the gathering Soviet maritime expansion, particularly as regards the Mediterranean and the Indian Ocean. Later, in the 1970s, the focus shifted again, particularly to the Persian Gulf in the wake of OPEC's success. The most prominent basing issues were the US quest for access (Oman, Kenya, Somalia, Morocco, Egypt) in connection with the Rapid Deployment Force (RDF) and the basing implications of a new Soviet foothold in Afghanistan. Africa, generally, in relation to resource access and SLOCs became another focus, amid new tentative geopolitical formulations, that is, the newly found importance of the 'southern seas'.[64]

In the mid-1980s, in updating a SIPRI data base for this book (and, hence, perusing newspapers and journals on a continuous basis) the author became aware of several dominant foci, geographically related to a number of recent political events or points of superpower competition. The US effort at acquiring new access in Central America in relation to the aftermath of the Nicaraguan revolution was one. So too the several new island republics of the south-west Pacific (and some remnant colonial possessions there), as the USSR began to 'fish' (via fisheries agreements) for new points of access. Generally, the effects of the growing superpower naval competition in the western Pacific could be seen, even as talk grew about the coming global economic dominance of the Pacific Basin. Viet Nam, the Philippines, Japan and the US trusteeship island groups were constantly in the news in relation to military facilities. And, there appeared a major focus on access related to anti-submarine warfare—sound surveillance under sea (SOSUS), bases for anti-submarine warfare (ASW) air-craft, the geography of access in proximity to the Soviet submarine 'bastions' in the Norwegian and Barents seas and the Sea of Okhotsk, etc.—no doubt reflecting the growing importance of SSBNs as the primary deterrent force and strategic reserve as doubts about ICBM vulnerability on both sides grew. Generally speaking, the Norwegian and Barents seas, the Norwegian coast, Iceland, Greenland and the Greenland–Iceland–United Kingdom (GIUK) gap chokepoints can be seen as a contemporary 'strategic high ground,' as reflected in almost all scenarios for a major US–Soviet conflict in Europe.[65]

These historical developments signal caution in attempting to extrapolate to the strategic basing concerns of the 1990s. The history is one of surprises. That point notwithstanding, there were the beginnings of interest in the possible geographical access implications of SDI on both sides of the superpower divide. Control of space began to loom as the crucial zone of decision for the future— the 'high frontier'. This is expected to ramify importantly into the basing diplomacy of the 1990s and beyond.

VI. The politics and economics of FMP

While the bulk of this work is devoted essentially to description and explanation of the various forms of FMP (what and where), the final chapter is devoted to analysis of their associated politics and economics, that is, who has FMP where, at what cost and on what political terms. The basis for such an analysis is hinted at in the historical coverage above, which outlines the progression of FMP politics from an essentially colonial/imperial phenomenon to one based on a far more symmetrical (between user and host) quid pro quo relationship.

Several related areas of inquiry are involved here, some of which involve problems of available data or of a required complexity beyond the scope of this work, hence dictating a somewhat sketchy, cursory or indicative treatment. There is that of the legal or administrative status of facilities, that is, the relative degree of host nation or user nation control. In some cases these considerations are spelled out in overt treaties or status of forces agreements; in others, the arrangements are secret or hidden, and one can merely infer from ongoing activities, which may or may not predict what will happen in a crisis. The mix of personnel at given facilities can take any number of forms along a spectrum: all foreign nation personnel, all host nation personnel, joint foreign and host nation personnel; various mixes of military, non-military and contractor-operated representation—some facilities too are unmanned. The various possibilities for the administrative status of facilities are:

1. Sites located in colonies, possessions, territories, etc., where the foreign nation has sovereignty.

2. Sites located in enclaves in which the foreign nation has sovereign rights.

3. Sites administered by the foreign nation, and located within the host nation according to a treaty or similar agreement.

4. Sites at which the foreign nation has its own facilities within the host nation facilities, and joint foreign/host nation use of host nation facilities.

5. Sites financed/constructed/operated/used by forces of multilateral alliance.

6. Sites with facilities operated by the host nation mainly on behalf of the foreign nation, and generally planned/constructed/financed by the foreign nation.

7. Host nation facilities which contribute significantly to the functioning of a foreign nation military system.

8. Host nation sites to which the foreign nation has access and of which it makes permanent or repeated use.

9. Foreign presence at the invitation of, and administered by the host nation, e.g., for the training of host nation forces.

The financing of a facility—or the financial terms of a basing presence—is important but often difficult to determine. On the poles of a spectrum, there can be sole, full financing by either the host or user; that in turn may say something about the overall political relationship, that is, whether the host is a reluctant one (perhaps because of alliance commitments) or whether, on the other hand, it eagerly desires the security or protection associated with the FMP.

But indeed, the quid pro quo involved in a basing relationship is usually far more complicated than is revealed in line-item budgets or balance sheets. In recent years, the USA has had to bargain for retention of its facilities in countries such as Greece, the Philippines, Portugal, Spain, Turkey, and so on, with extensive economic and military aid, which actually is a form of rent, but rarely admitted or characterized as such in those same words. Otherwise, US, Soviet and other basing presences have been facilitated by a variety of political and/or economic 'quid': qualitative upgrading of arms transfers, intelligence co-operation, trade concessions and commodity arrangements, airline landing rights, nuclear 'sweeteners' (peaceful nuclear technology transfer), tacit political deals of all sorts involving security commitments, other trade-offs, and so on. Generally, the balance of leverage, overall, appears to have shifted in recent years towards the hosts whose demands for 'quid' tend to escalate constantly, all the more so when a geographical or technological substitute for a given FMP/facility is not readily available.

Because arms transfer relationships have in the modern era become arguably the single most telling indicator of the state of alignments between industrialized and Third World countries (particularly as systemic trends have dictated a much lessened propensity on the part of all nations to formal alliances), arms transfer data are here juxtaposed to those for FMP in an effort to illuminate the core of modern basing diplomacy. Essentially, this involves juxtaposing information on facilities to one or another variant of the by now standard classification of donor–recipient arms transfer patterns. That classification involves a spectrum from sole or predominant client relationships, to mixed or multiple source relationships, with the latter further, crucially subdivided according to within- or across-bloc patterns. That, in essence, allows us to gauge the correlation or congruence of political alignments—perhaps best reflected by arms transfer patterns—with those of basing access. Whether these patterns have been altered over time is an interesting question, which returns us to systems analysis.

VII. Summary

As the above suggests, what is assayed here is a fairly comprehensive coverage of the modern status of basing access and its associated diplomacy. The data are largely available, albeit of mixed specific detail and perhaps more comprehensive for the West than for the USSR and its clients. It is very easy to be overwhelmed by a blizzard of detail—there are thousands of installations which fall under the heading of FMP. Hence, those data must be collapsed, re-ordered and analysed so as to provide some sense of their vital meaning. Not to be obscured in this process, however, is the fact that basing access is a key consideration of modern diplomacy; indeed, one of the primary ends of that diplomacy as well often as a means to other ends.

Notes and references

[1] See Zakheim, D., 'The South Atlantic conflict: Strategic, military and technological lessons', eds A. Coll and A. C. Arend, *The Falklands War: Lessons for Strategy, Diplomacy and International Law* (Allen and Unwin: Boston, Mass., 1985), chapter 11, especially p. 167; and The Sunday Times of London Insight Team, *War in the Falklands* (Harper and Row: New York, 1982), especially pp. 103–104. Herein it is said that Britain alternatively considered staging points in Chile, Uruguay, Sierra Leone and South Africa (Simonstown), but ruled them out as politically impossible.

[2] The concept of 'surrogate' or 'proxy' forces, subsequently to be enlarged upon, is developed in David, S. R., 'The use of proxy forces by major powers in the Third World', eds S. Neuman and R. Harkavy, *The Lessons of Recent Wars in the Third World: Comparative Dimensions*, Vol. 2 (D. C. Heath: Lexington, Mass., 1987), pp. 199–226.

[3] The International Institute for Strategic Studies, *The Military Balance: 1986–1987* (IISS: London, 1986), p. 165.

[4] 'The selling of terrorism: profit from a lucrative export', *The Washington Times' Insight*, 20 July 1987, pp. 30–31; and 'Cuba pays for Soviet aid by policing worldwide Marxism', *The Washington Times*, 28 Nov. 1986, p. 5E.

[5] Thucydides, *The Peleponnesian War*, translated by R. Warner (Penguin Books: Baltimore, Md., 1954), especially p. 447.

[6] See Boxer, C. R., *The Portuguese Seaborne Empire* (Knopf: New York, 1969); Boxer, C. R., *The Dutch Seaborne Empire, 1600–1800* (Knopf: New York, 1965); Kennedy, P. M., *The Rise and Fall of British Naval Mastery* (Scribner's: New York, 1976); Graham, G., *The Politics of Naval Supremacy* (Cambridge University Press: Cambridge, 1965); and Cole, Brig. D. H., *Imperial Military Geography*, 12th edn (Sifton Praed: London, 1956).

[7] See Graham (note 6), p. 12; and Rosinski, H., *The Development of Naval Thought* (Naval War College Press: Newport, R.I., 1977).

[8] See Brodie, B., *Sea Power in the Machine Age* (Princeton University Press: Princeton, N.J., 1941), chapter 7, under 'War at sea under steam: Strategic geography and the fuel problem'.

[9] See Kennedy (note 6), pp. 86–87 and 154–57.

[10] Gorschkov, Admiral S. G., *Sea Power of the State* (US Naval Institute Press: Annapolis, Md., 1979).

[11] This is discussed in Weller, G. A., *Bases Overseas: An American Trusteeship in Power* (Harcourt, Brace: New York, 1944); and Weigert, H., 'Strategic bases', eds H. Weigert, V. Stefansson and R. Harrison, *New Compass of the World* (Macmillan: New York, 1949), pp. 219–37. See also Blaker, J. R. and Walter, K. T., *U.S. Global Basing: Historical Overview of the U.S. Overseas Basing System*, report by the Hudson Institute, HI 3793–RR, for the US Department of Defense, Aug. 1987, pp. 5–47, under 'An historical overview'. The legislation embodied in the Lend–Lease Act of

1940 is discussed in Stettinius, E., *Lend–Lease, Weapons for Victory* (Macmillan: New York, 1944).

[12] This analysis of phases is developed in Harkavy, R. E., *Great Power Competition for Overseas Bases: The Geopolitics of Access Diplomacy* (Pergamon: New York, 1982).

[13] Harkavy (note 12), chapter 3.

[14] The rise of the peripheral powers around declining Europe is a central focus of Holborn, H., *The Political Collapse of Europe* (Knopf: New York, 1959).

[15] International systems analysis, as applicable to the historical analysis of FMP, is developed in Kaplan, M., *System and Process in International Politics* (Wiley: New York, 1957).

[16] Detailed information on inter-war FMP can be gleaned from the files of the Navy and Old Army Branch, the US National Archives, Record Group 165 (Records of the War Department, General and Special Staffs), Military Intelligence Division (MID), Washington, DC.

[17] German access to Italy's Libyan bases at the outset of World War II was crucial to the attack on British forces in Egypt; those provided by Spain in the Canary Islands were apparently important for refuelling German U-boats.

[18] Harkavy, R. E., *The Arms Trade and International Systems* (Ballinger: Cambridge, Mass., 1975), especially chapters 1 and 2.

[19] The development of the US-led alliance structure from 1950 to 1970 is detailed in Paul, R., *American Military Commitments Abroad* (Rutgers University Press: New Brunswick, N.J., 1973); and *United States Security Agreements and Commitments Abroad*, US Senate, Committee on Foreign Relations, Hearings Before the Subcommittee on US Security Agreements and Commitments Abroad, 91st Congress, vols I and II (US Government Printing Office: Washington, DC, 1971).

[20] This is discussed in Hagerty, H. G., *Forward Deployment in the 1970s and 1980s* (National Defense University: Washington, DC, 1977), National Security Affairs Monograph 77-2.

[21] See Remnek, R., 'The politics of Soviet access to naval support facilities in the Mediterranean', eds B. Dismukes and J. McConnell, *Soviet Naval Diplomacy* (Pergamon: New York, 1979), appendix D. See also 'Soviet military withdrawals', *Gist*, May 1987, Bureau of Public Affairs, US Department of State.

[22] A good introduction is in US Department of Defense, *Soviet Military Power* (US Government Printing Office: Washington, DC), published annually since September 1981.

[23] See, among others, 'When the stepping stones of world power are rocky bases', *US News and World Report*, 23 Nov. 1987, pp. 30–31; and 'Shrinking power: Network of U.S. bases overseas is unraveling as need for it grows', *Wall Street Journal*, 29 Dec. 1987, p. 1.

[24] See *Congressional Presentation for Security Assistance Programs: Fiscal Year 1988* (US Government Printing Office: Washington, DC, 1987), especially 'Introduction'.

[25] 'Burma said to offer U.S. waterfront real estate', *The Washington Times' Insight*, 20 July 1987, p. 37.

[26] 'Greece, U.S. reach accord maintaining bases for 5 years', *International Herald Tribune*, 16–17 July 1983, p. 1.

[27] See Fukuyama, F., 'Soviet military power in the Middle East; or, Whatever became of power projection?', eds S. Spiegel, M. Heller and J. Goldberg, *The Soviet–American Competition in the Middle East* (D. C. Heath: Lexington, Mass., 1988), pp. 159–82.

[28] David (note 2).

[29] This typology was originally developed in Leiss, A. C., *et al.*, *Arms Transfers to Less Developed Countries*, c/70-1 (MIT Center for International Studies: Cambridge, Mass., 1970) and Harkavy (note 18).

[30] Harkavy (note 18), p. 22.

[31] *Wall Street Journal* (note 23), p. 5.

[32] Harkavy (note 18), chapters 3 and 4.

[33] The Sunday Times of London Insight Team, *The Yom Kippur War* (Doubleday: Garden City, N.Y., 1974), p. 284; or Luttwak, E. and Laqueur, W., 'Kissinger and the Yom Kippur war', *Commentary*, vol. 58, no. 3 (Sept. 1974), pp. 33–40, especially p. 37.

[34] Kennedy, P. M., 'Imperial cable communications and strategy, 1870-1914', *English Historical Review*, vol. 86, no. 141 (1971), pp. 728–52; and Kemp, G. and Maurer, J., 'The logistics of Pax Britannica: lessons for America', paper presented at Fletcher School Conference on 'Projection of power', 23–25 Apr. 1980, Boston. On a narrower, case-study level, see Hart-Davis, D., *Ascension: The Story of a South Atlantic Island* (Doubleday: Garden City, N.Y., 1973), especially pp. 150–71 under 'Communications center: 1860-1927'.

[35] These various categories are covered in, among others, Richelson, J. T. and Ball, D., *The Ties that Bind* (Allen and Unwin: Boston, Mass., 1985).

[36] ' "Space Wars" bases likely in Europe', *Daily Telegraph*, 10 July 1984. The long-range implications are further implied in 'New clues on a Soviet laser complex', *New York Times*, 23 Oct. 1987, p. A14.

[37] This distinction is discussed in Hagerty (note 20).

[38] This term or concept has long been standard in SIPRI publications. See SIPRI, *World Armaments and Disarmament: SIPRI Yearbook 1972* (Taylor and Francis: London, 1972), under 'Foreign military presence, 1971: armed forces and major bases', chapter 7.

[39] A still broader construction of the notion of 'strategic access', also encompassing access to raw materials, is in Critchley, H., 'Defining strategic value: Problems of conceptual clarity and valid threat assessments', eds R. Harkavy and E. Kolodziej, *American Security Policy and Policy-Making* (D. C. Heath: Lexington, Mass., 1980), pp. 45–65.

[40] A standard point of departure is that of Kahn, H., *The Year 2000* (Macmillan: New York, 1967). On a less ambitious scale, but illustrative of the US Government's systemic futurology, see *Discriminate Deterrence*, Report of the Commission on Integrated Long-Term Strategy (Co-Chairmen: F. C. Iklé and A. Wohlstetter) (US Government Printing Office: Washington, DC, Jan. 1988), pp. 5–11; and in more detail, 'Sources of Change in the Future Security Environment, Summary Report of the Future Security Environment Working Group', Commission on Integrated Long-Term Strategy, Washington, DC, Apr. 1988. See also Blaker, J. R., Tsagronis S. J. and Walter, K. T., *US Global Basing: US Basing Options*, Hudson Institute, Report for the US Department of Defense, HI-3916-RR, Oct. 1987, pp. 4–21, under 'Trends in the U.S. overseas basing system'.

[41] Regarding international systems analysis, see, among others, Kaplan (note 15); Rosecrance, R., *Action and Reaction in World Politics: International Systems in Perspective* (Little, Brown: Boston, Mass., 1963); Gilpin, R., *War and Change in World Politics* (Cambridge University Press: Cambridge, Mass., 1981); and Waltz, K., *Theory of International Politics* (Addison-Wesley: Reading, Mass., 1979), especially chapters 3 and 4.

[42] See 'U.S. base in Athens is besieged', *New York Times*, 24 July 1984, p. A5; and 'Accord reached in Philippines strike', *New York Times*, 2 Apr. 1986, p. A3.

[43] See, among others, Cottrell, A., 'Soviet views of U.S. overseas bases', *Orbis*, vol. 7, no. 1 (spring 1963), pp. 77–95.

[44] This is discussed in Weinland, R. G., 'Superpower access to support facilities in the Third World: Effects and their causes', paper delivered at the meeting of the International Studies Association, Philadelphia, 18–21 Mar. 1981; and in 'Iraq: Frustration in the Gulf', *Middle-East Intelligence Survey*, vol. 8, no. 8 (16–31 July 1980), pp. 60–61.

[45] Regarding anti-Americanism, see Rubinstein, A. Z. and Smith, D. E. (eds), *Anti-Americanism in the Third World* (Praeger: New York, 1986), especially a chapter by Evin, A., 'Anti-Americanism in Turkey', pp. 121–36, which discusses the impact of FMP on national pride. See also Haseler, S. *Anti-Americanism: Steps on a Dangerous Path* (Alliance Publishers: London, 1986), for the Institute for European Defense and Strategic Studies, especially chapter III.

[46] See, among numerous sources, Pontecorvo, G., *The New Order of the Oceans* (Columbia University Press: New York, 1986); Exman, B. H., Caron, D. D. and Buderi, C. L., *Law of the Sea, U.S. Policy Dilemma* (Institute for Contemporary Studies: San Francisco, Calif., 1983); Gamble, J. K., *Law of the Sea*, Proceedings of the Law of the Sea Tenth Annual Conference, 22–25 June 1976, University of Rhode Island, Kingston, R.I. (Ballinger: Cambridge, Mass., 1977).

[47] See Alves, D., *Anti-Nuclear Attitudes in New Zealand and Australia* (National Defense University Press: Washington, DC, 1985), A National Security Affairs Monograph.

[48] Clancy, T., *Red Storm Rising* (G. P. Putnam's Sons: New York), 1986.

[49] See Oakes, J. B., 'More than Libya was ground zero', *New York Times*, 8 May 1986, p. A27.

[50] See US Senate, Committee on Foreign Relations, *United States Foreign Policy Objectives and Overseas Military Installations*, prepared by Congressional Research Service, Library of Congress, Washington, DC, 1979.

[51] Fukuyama (note 27), pp. 159–82. For a less assertive or more tentative view, see Papp, D., *Soviet Policies Toward the Developing World During the 1980s* (Air University Press: Maxwell AFB, Ala., 1986), especially chapter 12. See also Hosmer, S. and Wolfe, T. W., *Soviet Policy and Practice Toward Third World Conflicts* (D. C. Heath: Lexington, Mass., 1983).

[52] See, for instance, 'Soviet courts South America with an eye for trade', *New York Times*, 4 Oct. 1987, p. E3, which discusses Soviet Foreign Minister Shevardnadze's visit to Argentina, Brazil and Uruguay.

[53] See Collier, B., *The Lion and the Eagle* (Putnam: New York, 1972), p. 248; and Benns, F. L. and Seldon, M. E., *Europe: 1914–1939* (Appleton-Century-Crofts: New York, 1965), pp. 155–57, 438–39.

[54] See Jencks, H., 'Lessons of a "Lesson": China–Vietnam, 1979', eds R. Harkavy and S. Neuman, *The Lessons of Recent Wars in the Third World: Approaches and Case Studies* (D. C. Heath: Lexington, Mass., 1985), pp. 139–60.

[55] This is detailed in 'Argentina, U.S. to conduct first naval exercises since '82', *Washington Times*, 9 Apr. 1986, p. 9A. It reports that public demonstrations blocked an attempt by US ships to take on provisions—in 1984—at Puerto Madryn and that subsequently the Argentine Government refused to participate in joint ship exercises.

[56] This is predicted in Cohen, E. A., 'Distant battles', in Neuman and Harkavy (note 2), chapter 2.

[57] See US Arms Control and Disarmament Agency, *World Military Expenditures and Arms Transfers 1986* (ACDA: Washington, DC, 1987), especially pp. 6–10.

[58] This prospect is broached, in the context of US contingency defence planning, by Jones, R., *Small Nuclear Forces and U.S. Security Policy* (D. C. Heath: Lexington, Mass., 1984).

[59] The relationship between basing and ongoing technological development is covered in Blaker, Tsagronis and Walter (note 40), pp. 37–47, under 'Technological solutions to base site decline'.

[60] For a good outline of the various purposes served by naval access, see Blechman, B. and Weinland, R., 'Why coaling stations are necessary in the nuclear age', *International Security*, no. 2 (1977), pp. 88–89. Regarding quantification of ship port visits, see Watson, B. (ed.), *The Soviet Navy* (Westview Press: Boulder, Colo., 1986), especially appendix tables 13–25.

[61] The sole extant general coverage of this subject is Dadant, P. M., 'Shrinking international airspace as a problem for future air movements—A briefing', Report R-2178-AF, RAND, Santa Monica, Calif., 1978.

[62] There is a partial breakdown by region and individual country in Arkin, W. M. and Fieldhouse, R. W., *Nuclear Battlefields: Global Links in the Arms Race* (Ballinger: Cambridge, Mass., 1985), especially chapters 6 and 7.

[63] Cohen, S., *Geography and Politics in a World Divided* (Random House: New York, 1963), chapter 1.

[64] Kemp, G., 'The new strategic map', *Survival*, vol. 19, no. 2 (Mar./Apr. 1977), pp. 50–59.

[65] Other analyses, however, focus on chokepoints in relation to Third World resources. Hence, under 'Soviet Third World involvement related to maritime choke points', John Collins' map highlights the Indonesian Straits, Strait of Hormuz, Suez Canal, Bab El Mandeb, Madagascar Channel and the Panama Canal. See Collins, J., *U.S.–Soviet Military Balance 1980–1985* (Pergamon-Brassey's: Washington, DC, 1985), p. 14. Otherwise, under 'Militarily important naval choke points', p. 151, he cites the Kuriles, Japanese, East Indies and Caribbean Straits, the GIN gaps, Danish and Turkish Straits, and Gibraltar. Similarly, see also 'Reagan's "choke points" stretch from sea to sea', *New York Times*, 13 Feb. 1986, p. A12.

2. Naval facilities

I. Introduction and historical background

Almost any discussion of bases, or basing systems or networks, conjures up the historical image of the serial, successive reigns of the Portuguese, Spanish, Dutch and British global maritime empires, all crucially hinged upon global maritime dominance. Indeed, a central thesis of Admiral Mahan's theory of seapower was that of the requirement for, and virtual inevitability of, indivisible global sea control, which of necessity requires, but paradoxically also provides, a global basing system.[1] And, indeed, the history of major powers' rival global basing systems has long been bound up in the imagery of heartland and rimland, of continental land power versus extra-continental (Eurasian) sea power.[2]

Land and sea power have not always, however, been perceived necessarily as mutually exclusive—Mackinder, aware of Napoleon's ambitions and fearful of future German or Russian capabilities, postulated the global dominance of a heartland land power which might also become a pre-eminent global naval power.[3] Admiral Tirpitz's 'risk fleet' before 1914 envisaged the neutralization of pre-eminent British seapower as Germany was also in the process of becoming a naval power.[4] These themes, familiar to students of traditional geopolitical theory are, of course, very reflective of recent events in the US–Soviet competition for global naval power: the rise of Admiral Gorschkov's navy, the development of the recent US maritime strategy, and so on.[5]

The succession of maritime pre-eminence reflected in near-exclusive unipolar global basing systems—Portuguese, Netherlands, British, US—is one historical trend worth noting. There are others, particularly as concerns the relationship of evolving naval technology to the quantitative requirements for global basing points. Generally, as indicated in chapter 1, there has been a reduction in the quantitative requirements for surface naval bases because of (a) the greater ranges of modern ships, (b) advances in refuelling at sea and in the more effective use of a variety of support ships, and (c) the long-term trend towards smaller navies, as measured solely by numbers of ships.[6] The replacement of sailing ships by coal-driven vessels in the nineteenth century temporarily reversed the first-named of these trends, as measured at least by refuelling, though not by other criteria dealing with replenishment of consumables, that is, food, water, and so on. But, generally, the trend has been ineluctable; nuclear power has been one more development furthering it. Indeed, the Portuguese and Dutch basing systems of the sixteenth, seventeenth and eighteenth centuries were, actually, as measured by numbers of main bases, considerably more elaborate than those utilized today by the USA and the USSR.[7]

Britain, at the peak of its naval power in the late nineteenth and early twentieth centuries, had a truly elaborate, massive naval base structure to go with a navy which at times deployed thousands of surface combatants. It had main bases (homeported ships; major repair facilities) at Shanghai, Singapore, Hong Kong, Mauritius, Bombay, Karachi, Trincomalee, Aden, Alexandria, Basra, Port Sudan, Simonstown, Freetown, Mombasa, Malta, Haifa, Gibraltar, Halifax, Trinidad, Kingston, and many other places.[8] And, indeed, the far larger— relative to today—US naval deployments of the late 1940s and 1950s also saw a far more elaborate basing structure. That structure has since become much tauter. In part, this has involved the politics of base divestiture because of decolonialization, the radicalization of numerous Third World states, and the decoupling or fraying of many US alliances; hence, the US Navy (sometimes via its NATO allies) has lost important access to major facilities in Iran, Jamaica, Libya, Madagascar, Morocco, Mozambique, Pakistan, the Seychelles, South Africa, Taiwan and Viet Nam.[9] In other locales, use is now more restricted and (according to the specific situation) contingent—Australia, Bahrain, Greece, Japan, New Zealand, the Philippines, Portugal, Singapore, Spain and Turkey; maybe also Canada, Italy and the UK.

Otherwise, however, the now more restricted US naval basing system has resulted from reduced requirements—the USA can now support a global naval presence by a mere handful of main operating bases overseas. The expansion of the US Navy undertaken by the Reagan Administration under the leadership of its former Secretary of the Navy, John Lehman—intended to produce a 600-ship surface fleet—has altered these requirements only slightly, if at all (on the other hand, the room for error regarding future loss of access may have been narrowed).[10] The Soviet Union, meanwhile, in line with the recent expansion of its navy to a truly global presence and deployment, has increased the number of associated main basing points, which in sheer numbers now about equals those available to the USA.[11]

The above comments are rendered with the recognition that changing technology has also produced new needs for naval access, even as that for surface ship main bases has declined. Some of these: air bases for naval aircraft involved in anti-submarine warfare, ground terminals for ASW hydrophone arrays, facilities related to down-links for ocean surveillance satellites, and others, are discussed in chapter 6.

In relation to traditional geopolitics, US–Soviet competition for access has followed a somewhat curious, perhaps historically unique pattern. For the first decade or more, the US forward containment policy—hinged on the linked NATO, CENTO and SEATO alliances—made a near-perfect fit to the classic Mahanian rimland thesis. Emphasis was on rapidity of movement around the rim, control of chokepoints controlling egress from the heartland, and total control over the nether hinterlands of the rimland and its waters.[12] US military and economic aid policies joined to the remnants of colonialism ensured that. The USSR, without a serious blue-water navy, remained pinned within the contiguous heartland empire defined by what was accepted up to the early 1960s as the 'Sino–Soviet bloc'.

In the 1960s, a series of major changes became evident, which dramatically changed the spatial configuration of the superpower struggle and, with it, the nature of the rivals' competition for FMP. They were, in brief:

1. Decolonialization of the European overseas empires, and the resultant shift of numerous new states to either a form of neutralism or to more radical Soviet-leaning client status.

2. Unravelling of some of the US alliance structure.

3. The Sino–Soviet split.

4. Soviet development of a blue-water navy and long-range air transport capability.

5. Soviet rise to co-leadership with the USA, as a global arms trader, as arms transfers became the primary quid pro quo for basing access.

6. Decline in the US relative economic position and concomitant lessened US capacity for economic and military aid.

7. The Cuban Revolution and resulting Soviet access there.

8. Soviet access to the Middle East and South Asia, as related to the superpowers' roles in the Arab–Israel and India–Pakistan disputes.

9. The US Viet Nam débâcle and subsequent withdrawal of US power under the banner of the 'Nixon Doctrine'.

10. Massive constriction of British and, to a lesser degree, French basing assets overseas.

11. The oil crisis and rise to primacy of the Persian Gulf as a perceived strategic prize, in turn inspiring the 'Carter Doctrine'.

In the wake of these profound changes, the spatial configuration of the superpowers' global naval competition was gradually altered. The USSR, in numerous places, leap-frogged the old containment ring—the rimland was no longer indivisible after a Soviet presence had been established, at one time or another, in Guinea, Angola, Equatorial Guinea, Mozambique, Somalia, South Yemen, Libya, Egypt, Syria, Iraq, India, Viet Nam, Kampuchea and Peru, among others.[13] Rather, the global competition took on the character of a more fluid, rapidly shifting game; perhaps too, previously rigid ideological foundations for alignment gave way in some cases to more traditional balance of power considerations.

The US effort at maintaining FMP to block Soviet egress from homeland naval bases—particularly with regard to submarines—was a reminder that the old rimland containment strategy remained operative and valid. Other strategic interests also came to appear at stake, however, in connection with the naval competition. The Persian Gulf came to be perceived as an all-important strategic prize; with that came a central focus on sea lanes of communication (SLOCs) leading from there to Western Europe and Japan and, hence, on *en route* basing points astride crucial straits and chokepoints such as those in Indonesia, the Mozambique Channel, Bab El Mandeb, and so on.[14] One writer at least was to herald a newer geopolitical focus on the 'southern seas'.[15]

In a curious way, the long and heretofore durable 'cold peace' between the USA and the USSR also gave rise to paradoxical questions about the very meaning, in practical terms, of the struggle over FMP. Assumptions that a superpower war would quickly escalate to a devastating all-out nuclear exchange caused some analysts to downgrade the traditional concerns about a struggle for overseas sea control at the beginning of a conflict. Similarly, the seeming improbability of Soviet attempts at interdicting SLOCs short of major war led some to question the importance of *en route* basing access to protect these SLOCs. Some critics were sceptical about the geopolitical imagery evoked by fears about blocked chokepoints, 'outflanked' positions, and press and magazine news briefs which displayed the coloured dots and flags charting the progress of FMP naval competition. Others, however, insisted on the importance of the *perceptions* of global power shifts (momentum); of 'presence', coercive diplomacy, crisis management, day-to-day deterrence, and so on. They also pointed to the importance of naval bases as 'trip-wires', that is, deterrents to attack upon clients and friends. And, finally, the interminable small wars of the Third World, many pitting respective US and Soviet clients against each other, provided a continuing rationale for various forms of basing—naval bases in particular, along with air staging facilities—as crucial to resupply of arms, movement of 'advisors' and surrogate forces, and so on.

All in all, however, the very meaning of global naval base competition seems to have been altered, from something thought crucial to and/or reflective of maritime primacy (and hence of advantage in access to resources and security of their transport) to a far more subjective, arguable and multifaceted matter, seemingly more essentially psychological in nature than before. That is one view. Military planners who thought in terms of possible protracted superpower conflict (maybe initially on a conventional level, then escalating to a limited nuclear exchange; perhaps restricted altogether to 'conventional' naval exchange) have retained a more traditional view of naval access as crucial to potential war-fighting scenarios.

By the mid-1980s, there were a number of extant, prominent issues or 'debates' regarding naval warfare, which in turn ramified into questions about basing requirements. There was the 'big carrier versus small carrier' debate, further fanned by the 'lessons learned' literature emerging from the Falklands War—crucial to this was the question of whether new satellite technology (radar and ELINT ocean-reconnaissance satellites—RORSATs and EORSATs) had fundamentally altered the basis of naval warfare, among other things, towards a more marked pre-emptive character.[16] There was the question of whether either side would have a strong incentive to pre-empt with nuclear weapons against the other's fleets in the event of a general, escalating conventional war in Europe or elsewhere.[17] And there were nagging unknowns about the future of ASW versus the hiding of submarines, an arcane but deadly serious technological race at the very core of the modern military competition.[18] All of these issues ramified into basing access.

Superimposed on these narrower issues was, at least in the USA, the wider debate on the new 'maritime strategy' associated with Secretary to the Navy John Lehman and a coterie of defence intellectuals associated with the Reagan

Administration. As it happens, exactly what was involved with this new strategy was a source of dispute, not least because its essentials seemed to shift or at least evolve between 1981 and 1987. One critic, John Mearsheimer, saw its major elements as general maritime superiority, horizontal escalation, offensive sea control, counterforce coercion (nuclear), and direct military impact (on Central European land operations), with different emphases in different phases of the administration.[19] A supporter, Colin Gray, listed the following, some overlapping those above, under the heading of 'the value of the fleet'.[20]

1. To keep NATO in the war, whether the war is short or long.
2. To assist NATO ground forces by flank distraction.
3. To provide leverage to help offset NATO loss elsewhere.
4. To apply pressure in a global protracted conflict.
5. To contest a Soviet siege of the Americas.
6. To protect the US SSBN fleet.

All of these various desiderata involve bases and basing diplomacy, often conjoining air and naval forces (air bases in Norway and Iceland are critical to offensive sea control in the Norwegian Sea). Most critically, however, the newer emphasis on horizontal escalation (note the historical analogy to Britain's strategy *vis-à-vis* Napoleonic France and, later, Germany) spotlighted the role of naval facilities as compensatory strategic pawns as well as their strategic importance in relation to potential naval combat all around the Eurasian periphery.[21] The geopolitical arguments of the turn of the century were revisited—the indivisibility of sea control, 'risk fleets', maritime versus land-power/continental strategies, and so on.

II. Forms and functions of naval FMP

The maritime component of FMP—mostly naval bases and/or facilities—can assume any number of forms across a spectrum describing the types or mix of ships provided access; levels, extent, frequency of permitted access, permanence, use for various contingencies, and so on. One summary article divided the functions served by naval shore facilities into four categories: replenishment of consumables, repairs, direct combat support, and intelligence and communications (the last-named is dealt with in chapter 6).[22] More broadly construed, naval FMP may be interpreted to subsume port visits, use of offshore anchorages (within or outside territorial limits); access for fishing vessels, merchant ships, and oceanographic research vessels (to the extent used for military purposes), and so forth.[23] And, for strictly analytical purposes, because of the standard methods of breaking down naval forces' orders of battles, functions, and so on, a division between bases respectively utilized for surface and submarine craft is used here, the partial overlap in some cases between the two categories notwithstanding.

The consumable-replenishment category involves a wide variety of items, such as water, food, supplies, fuels and lubricants, spare parts, disposable equipment (such as sonabuoys and wing tanks for aircraft), and ordnance, as well as the replenishment of the morale of sailors needing periodic shore leave ('R&R'). The need for *matériel* replenishment is paced by the finite storage space on ships (often subject to trade-offs between combat capability and personnel comforts), though the requirements for shore storage facilities can be mitigated by the extensive use of supply ships accompanying fleets.[24] That is normally considered a fall-back expedient where shore bases are not available, as was the case for Soviet operations in many areas prior to the new acquisition of shore access, and is still the case in some areas. On the contrary, more extensive use of supply ships in lieu of land bases lessens political vulnerability, particularly in crises.

Some of the needed items—such as food and water—are available commercially in all ports, but political contingencies may dictate the availability of more permanent and assured access, as port clearances are subject to denial during crises or even on a more or less permanent basis.

Use of shore facilities for R&R is not merely a trivial or superfluous matter. It may be important for the morale, hence the combat effectiveness, of a fleet. Indeed, one recent article reported that the (US) 'Navy plans to cut the time aircraft carriers, the most visible sign of American naval power, sail in foreign waters in an effort to reduce the strain on the large crews and to save money . . .'.[25] The article went on to state that one of the major rationales for limiting deployments at sea was that of improving crew morale and hence re-enlistments. Traditionally, the Soviet Union has seemed to worry less about that problem, though it is hard to assess the practical effects.

The arrival of a fleet, even if only for replenishment, can have sensitive political overtones, particularly given the colonial history of gunboat diplomacy, the awesome symbolic display of military might involved, and the always explosive potential for violence when large numbers of sailors are disgorged *en masse* to roam the local bars. The latter problem earlier led US access to Turkey to be curtailed, and there have been untoward incidents in the Philippines, Kenya, Argentina and elsewhere.[26] Even the close restrictions placed on Soviet sailors in port has not prevented some instances of local resentment, for instance, earlier in Egypt.[27]

Shore facilities provide convenient and secure places to store often bulky and expensive equipment (missiles, large parts) which could be shipped from home bases—but only at great expense and with a time penalty. Such facilities are therefore important for the major powers' prepositioning of *matériel* for conflict contingencies, and it is for that reason that the USA expressed concern when the Soviet Union apparently acquired shore-based missile storage facilities in Somalia, in proximity to potential combat zones in the Indian Ocean-Red Sea-Persian Gulf area.[28] Similarly, the United States has been accorded an advantage in the nuclear strategic context by its forward Polaris submarine bases in Scotland, Spain and Guam (only the first-named is still used), for crew rotation as well as for replenishment and resupply of *matériel*. Some current strategic analyses point to the looming importance of overseas submarine and ship ordnance reloads in the event of protracted war.[29]

Ship repair facilities abroad—both for minor and preventive maintenance or for major overhauls—are highly sought after by all major naval powers, given the enormous costs and time involved in having to bring ships all the way home, and the resulting loss of ship-days on station and readiness for war contingencies. Though some repairs may be done at sea by accompanying tenders (which carry tools and spare parts), and others by tenders in ports, some will still require large dry-docks and heavy cranes, necessitating a permanent shore facility. Some commercial yards may be used (as at present in Singapore and perhaps Greece), but their continued use may be subject to diplomatic vicissitudes in an era, unlike earlier periods, in which all commercial harbour facilities operate under restrictive political controls.[30]

The need for forward repair facilities has long presented a potential disadvantage for the United States in maintaining transatlantic and transpacific fleets far from home. Also, few overseas shipyards can carry out the sophisticated maintenance and repairs required for large warships; building new large repair facilities from scratch is an expensive proposition, and that is not to mention the problem of availability of a necessary skilled labour force. Hence, the United States relies precariously, for its Pacific fleet, on facilities in Japan and the Philippines. To replace these with new repair facilities, say in Guam, would be very expensive. The Soviet Union, on the other hand, has long relied on floating dry-docks and in-port tenders in lieu of more permanent land-based repair facilities.

Direct combat support facilities involve permanent overseas basing of ships, ranging from individual vessels to small flotillas to large fleets, or smaller units where extensive administrative support is often involved. For the United States nowadays, large fleets are homeported in Japan and Italy, and smaller flotillas, such as that based in Bahrain on the Persian Gulf, may be intended primarily as a 'presence' and as a potential nucleus for a buildup in time of crisis. Otherwise, shore facilities may also provide land-based aircraft for defending fleets—and for attacking rival fleets—as well as for maritime patrol, ASW, reconnaissance and electronic warfare.[31] Bases deploying aircraft for the defence of fleets may be more highly sought after where aircraft carriers are not available; hence, this has long been a primary Soviet consideration, as reflected in its land-based naval air deployments in several places.[32]

The time required to deploy ships to combat in an arc around any forward base is a prime item of calculation in locating bases and in dispersing fleet elements to different bases.[33] Such calculations may also involve the possible use of naval marines in amphibious or helicopter-borne operations.

As noted, many ship support functions can be located either on shore or aboard support ships, involving trade-offs between the greater sophistication and variety afforded by shore facilities (also the absence of adverse weather factors where heavy seas can impede operations) and the freedom from political interference provided by portable shipborne support facilities. Generally, however, shore-based repair shops, warehouses, fuel tanks, magazines, radios, radars or dry-docks can be substituted for on ships, if only at the cost of reallocating naval budgets towards 'more tail and less tooth,' in the form of tenders, repair ships, fuel-tankers or barges, ammunition, storage, communications and electronic ships, hospital vessels and floating dry-docks. Many overseas deployments actually make use of both types of facility. The Soviet Union has long had to make more extensive use of support ships and offshore mooring points than has the United States (and, similarly, more use of seaborne intelligence gathering ships in lieu of shore-based facilities), because of the relative lack of overseas bases, a situation which may recently, however, have changed somewhat.

The Soviet Union, in particular, has also made extensive use of offshore anchorages in international waters for refuelling, maintenance, and idling and rendezvousing of ships, usually where onshore facilities are not available or where political conditions dictate a low profile. These anchorages, replete with permanent mooring buoys, have been dispersed all over the Mediterranean, the Indian Ocean and offshore Asia, often barely beyond the traditional three-mile limits demarcating national sovereignty from international waters.[34] Though perfectly 'legal,' however, the willingness to use anchorages in near proximity to other nations' coastlines may to some extent depend upon the state of political relations—or also asymmetries in coercive power—given the still sensitive symbolic issues involved. These problems were highlighted a few years ago by Soviet naval activities just off the Egyptian coast.[35] And seemingly impending routine global extensions of national control over greater distances from coastlines (most nations now assert 200-mile economic zones on top of 12-mile naval maritime limits) may in the future restrict the use of such anchorages, perhaps creating some serious points of friction. Use of anchorages where port visits are not made available does, of course, carry the disadvantage of precluding shore leave for ship personnel, which, again, may be important both for morale and effectiveness.

Some 'traditional' naval and air facilities, or rather modes of access, may fall into a grey area between civilian and military use. The Soviet Union, for instance, has developed an extensive network of access for its very large fleets of fishing and oceanographic vessels, many of which may have less benign than advertised purposes—such as electronic warfare, military communications relays, shadowing of others' ships, anti-submarine detection, disruption of and interference with communications cables and underwater sonar arrays, SIGINT, space tracking, and so on.[36] Cuba has made similar use of its extensive fishing fleets. The Soviet merchant marine has also operated as a wing of the Soviet Navy, involved in, among other things, the transport of arms and the smuggling of intelligence agents into friendly and neutral ports.[37] Often, the USSR has attempted to use the acquisition of seemingly benign access for its fishing fleets as an opening wedge for broader access,[38] as witness recent bargaining with the Maldives, Mauritius, Tonga, Vanuatu, Papua New Guinea and others.[39] (Newly independent island groupings in the south-west Pacific seem to have become salient recent targets.) Indeed, the pattern of efforts to establish new access for fishing or oceanographic research vessels may be one (tentative) indicator of emerging strategic requirements for naval basing access.

III. Preferred locales of naval facilities

It is noted above that the number of major naval basing points now utilized by the major powers has been reduced to a mere handful on either side. That, in turn, raises the question of why access is sought in particular places, beyond the (geographically) somewhat random facts of political alignment. Basically, this comes down to three distinct criteria: location, characteristics of a port and the political disposition of the host nation.

Regarding location, it is worth noting that extant analyses of US and other fleet deployments and overseas basing access devote considerable space to measurements of sailing time from bases to potential trouble spots or sites of confrontation. Perceptions of the likelihood of location of conflict will, of course, vary; similarly, the perceptions of the strategic value of certain nations and locales will vary. Earlier, in the inter-war period, British and US analysts devoted considerable attention to steaming times in connection with the key Panama and Suez Canal chokepoints. In recent years, the Persian Gulf area and adjacent chokepoints and SLOCs have become all-important foci; hence, the frequent analyses of sailing times from Diego Garcia, Subic Bay, Cockburn Sound, Mombasa, and so on (and equivalent measures of Soviet sailing times

Table 1. Approximate ship transit times between present Pacific bases. The average speed is 18 knots

Base to base	Approximate distance (nm)	Time Hours	Days
A. US West Coast (San Diego)			
1. Pearl Harbor	2 150	119.4	5.0
2. Guam	5 380	298.9	12.5
3. Yokosuka	5 000	277.8	11.6
4. Subic Bay	6 700	372.2	15.5
B. Pearl Harbor			
1. Guam	3 320	184.4	7.7
2. Yokosuka	3 400	188.9	7.9
3. Subic Bay	4 820	267.8	11.2
C. Yokosuka			
1. Guam	1 350	75.0	3.1
2. Subic Bay	1 760	97.8	4.0
D. Subic Bay			
1. Guam	1 500	83.3	3.5

Source: Feeney, W. R., 'The Pacific basing system and U.S. security', eds W. T. Tow and W. R. Feeney, *US Foreign Policy and Asian-Pacific Security: A Transregional Approach* (Westview Press: Boulder, Colo., 1982), table 7.4, p. 197.

from Aden, Port Blair, Cam Ranh Bay, etc.), all converging upon the Straits of Hormuz.[40] US anxieties about the possible loss of naval bases in the Philippines should a collapse of, or political reorientation of, the present government lead to a withdrawal of the US presence has spawned considerable analysis of possible 'fall-back positions'—Cockburn Sound, Djakarta, Guam, Kaohsiung, Sattahip,

Singapore, Yokosuka, etc.—mostly couched in the simple mathematics of sailing days and/or operating radii of fleets located far afield.[41] The location of Diego Garcia's prepositioned *matériel* in relation to a variety of conflict scenarios in South-West Asia has received similar attention.

Tables 1 and 2 and figure 1 illustrate some typical analyses seen frequently in the USA in recent years amid anxieties about projecting naval force to the Far East and to the Indian Ocean and Arabian Sea and illustrate the simple mathematics of ship sailing days and combat radii involving crucial strategic areas. Excerpts from one analysis of these problems, as applied to US force projection problems involving the Pacific and Indian Ocean/Arabian Sea areas respectively, illustrate this:

[Table 1] outlines the distances and steaming times between existing Pacific bases. These factors become important when forces from one sector are deployed to reinforce units in another sector on a north–south axis (Yokosuka–Subic Bay). In this case the requisite transit time is four full days. However, the distance-time problem is greatly magnified

Table 2. Approximate ship transit times from present major Pacific bases to operating stations.
The average speed is 18 knots.

Operating station from base	Approximate distance (nm)	Time	
		Hours	Days
A. Kurile Islands (A)			
1. Yokosuka	650	36.1	1.5
2. Subic Bay	2 300	127.8	5.3
3. Pearl Harbor	2 850	158.3	6.6
4. US West Coast	5 000	277.8	11.5
B. Okinawa (B)			
1. Yokosuka	730	40.6	1.7
2. Subic Bay	850	47.2	2.0
3. Pearl Harbor	3 710	206.1	8.6
4. US West Coast	5 860	325.6	13.6
C. Northern South China Sea (C)			
1. Subic Bay	400	22.2	0.9
2. Yokosuka	1 710	95.0	4.0
3. Pearl Harbor	4 830	268.3	11.2
4. West Coast	6 980	388.8	16.2
D. Malacca Straits (D)			
1. Subic Bay	1 180	65.6	2.7
2. Yokosuka	2 700	150.0	6.3
3. Pearl Harbor	5 880	326.7	13.6
4. US West Coast	8 030	446.1	18.6
E. Arabian Sea (E)			
1. Subic Bay	4 900	272.2	11.3
2. Yokosuka	5 860	325.6	13.6
3. Pearl Harbor	9 170	509.4	21.2
4. US West Coast	11 320	629.9	26.2

Source: Feeney, W. R., 'The Pacific basing system and U.S. security', eds W. T. Tow and W. R. Feeney, *US Foreign Policy and Asian-Pacific Security: A Transregional Approach* (Westview Press: Boulder, Colo., 1982), table 7.5, p. 200.

by east–west movement from support bases on Guam, Pearl Harbor and the U.S. West Coast to forward installations. Indeed, for ships to travel from the West Coast to Yokosuka or to Subic Bay requires the better part of eleven days and fifteen days, respectively, while from Pearl Harbor it is nearly eight days and over eleven days, respectively. During the northern passage to Japan, however, naval units become susceptible to interception by Soviet submarines and naval aircraft operating from Petropavlovsk-Kamchatskiy which lies only 500 to 750 nautical miles north of the usual transit routes (at most, one to two days underwater travel time for submarines, one to two hours for turboprop aircraft, and one-half hour for the Backfire B bomber).

Similar problems confront U.S. forward-based and reinforcement naval units. In time of alert, every effort would be made to move ships already underway and those in port on ready status to pre-determined operating stations to meet a variety of contingency situations (see [table 2] for a breakdown of distances and transit times to operating stations). Units based in Japan would be within two days sailing time to combat stations near Okinawa or northeast of Japan off the Kurile Islands. Reinforcements from Subic Bay to the Okinawa area would take two days, but from Hawaii or the West Coast from seven to fourteen days would be needed. Again, these units might be forced to run a dangerous gauntlet unless U.S. aircraft and attack submarines could provide continuous combat patrols . . .

The worst contingency in terms of necessary positioning time is naval movement to the Persian Gulf area. Current logistical limitations of the joint U.S.-U.K. forward base at Diego Garcia which is still being expanded and specific access arrangements for potential bases in Oman, Kenya, and Somalia continue to rule out any extensive American force multiplier effect for the time being. Subic Bay units would require no less than thirteen days to reach station in the Arabian Sea, and Yokosuka units would take a full two weeks. As noted, efforts are underway to construct an enlarged air base and naval facilities on Diego Garcia which is 1000 miles south of the Indian subcontinent and 2500 miles southeast of the Strait of Hormuz. But this forward Indian Ocean base which is a part of the British Indian Ocean Territories cannot be used as a main operations staging area for ground forces because of its small size and the distance from the Persian Gulf. On the other hand, the island will be highly useful as a transit point for large cargo planes and as a support base for U.S. naval forces operating in the Indian Ocean. [See figure 1.]

At no time were geographical problems more pressing than during the 1980 crisis in Iran and Afghanistan. U.S. force requirements were shifted dramatically from the western Pacific to the Indian Ocean and the Persian Gulf. For several months Northeast Asia was left temporarily without an operational carrier task force for the first time since the end of World War II, when the Midway and several support ships were redeployed into the Indian Ocean. Not only did this transfer seriously impair U.S. Pacific defense capabilities, but it also forced a time-consuming movement of replacement units from Pearl Harbor and Third Fleet bases on the U.S. West coast.[42]

Again, the focus of such attention will shift in response to the changing tide of events. The rise in tensions in Central America has spotlighted respective US and Soviet capabilities for projecting force into the Caribbean and Pacific littorals of that region; the Falklands War shifted attention to the South Atlantic.[43] Areas around Southern Africa are perceived potentially important because of the spectre of war there as well as the relationship of SLOCs leading from the Persian Gulf to Western Europe. Some recent reports assert a Soviet interest in

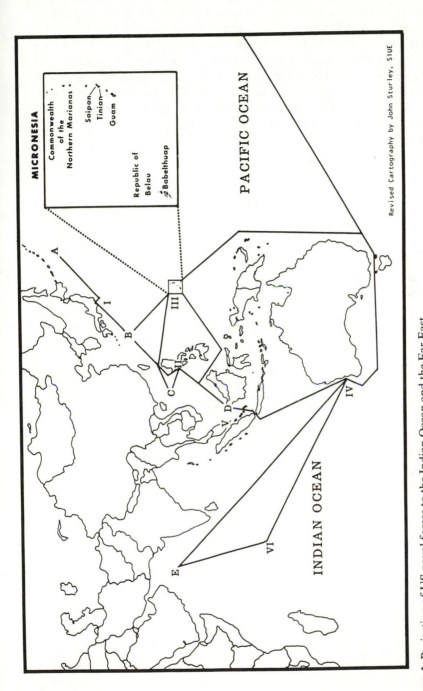

Figure 1. Projection of US naval forces to the Indian Ocean and the Far East
Letters refer to operating stations listed in table 2. Roman numerals refer to present/alternative US basing facilities: I = Yokosuka; II = Subic Bay; III = Guam/Saipan/Tinian; IV = Cockburn Sound; V = Singapore; VI = Diego Garcia.

Source: Tow, W. T. and Feeney, W. R., *US Foreign Policy and Asian–Pacific Security: A Transregional Approach* (Westview Press: Boulder, Colo., 1982), p. 199.

projecting naval power to the South Pacific, which in turn directs attention to possible basing diplomacy involving new island nations in that area; perhaps too the western coast of South America.[44] On an illustrative historical note, it is often forgotten that there was a major debate in the UK in the 1920s over retention of major British naval bases in British Columbia and in Jamaica, the arguments then revolving about the reality of continuing possible US–British naval rivalry and its relation to the Panama Canal.[45] In the 1950s, meanwhile, US naval deployments in the Western Pacific took seriously the possibility of naval confrontation with China, among other things then highlighting the importance of US bases in Taiwan.

Table 3. Comparison of several ports considered as back-ups to US use of Subic Bay

Port		Facilities			
	Size[a]	Shelter afforded	Repairs	Dry-dock	Supplies and services[b]
(a) Western Pacific					
Australia					
Hobart	M	Excellent	Limited	Medium	f,w,p,c,m,e
Melbourne	L	Excellent	Major	Medium	f,w,p,c,m,e
Sydney	L	Excellent	Major	Large	f,w,p,c,m,e
Newcastle	L	Excellent	Major	Large	f,w,p,c,m,e
Brisbane	L	Excellent	Major	Medium	f,w,p,c,m,e
Darwin	M	Excellent	Limited		
New Zealand					
Wellington	L	Good	Major	Medium	f,w,p,c,m,e
Auckland	L	Excellent	Major	Large	f,w,p,c,m,e
Port Lyttleton	M	Good	Major	Medium	f,w,p,c,m,e
Singapore	L	Good	Major	Large	f,w,p,c,m
Philippines					
Manila	L	Excellent	Major	Medium	f,w,p,c,m,e
Cebu	M	Excellent	Moderate	Medium	f,w,p,c,m,e
Hong Kong	L	Excellent	Major	Large	f,w,p,c,m,e
Taiwan					
Kaohsiung	M	Fair	Limited	Small	f,w,p,c,m,e
Keelung	M	Fair	Major	Medium	f,w,p,c,m,e
South Korea					
Pusan	L	Good	Moderate	Medium	f,w,p,c,m
(b) Indian Ocean					
South Africa					
Simonstown	V	Good	Major	Large	f,w,p,c,m,e
Port Elizabeth	M	Fair	Moderate		f,w,p,c,m,e
East London	M	Good	Major	Large	f,w,p,c,m,e
Durban	L	Good	Moderate	Large	f,w,p,c,m,e
Mozambique					
Maputo	M	Good	Moderate	Small	f,w,p,c,m,e
Beira	M	Good	Moderate	Small	f,w,p,c,m,e
Mocambique	S	Good	Limited	..	c,m,e
Tanzania					
Dar es Salaam	M	Good	Limited	..	f,w,p,c,m,e
Kenya					
Mombasa	V	Fair	Limited	..	f,w,p,c,m,e

Port	Facilities Size[a]	Shelter afforded	Repairs	Dry-dock	Supplies and services[b]
Somalia					
Mogadiscio	S	Fair	Limited	..	f,w,p,c,m,e
Berbera	S	Good	Limited	..	w,p,c,m,e
Afars & Issas					
Djibouti	S	Good	Limited	..	f,w,p,c,m,e
People's Dem. Republic of Yemen					
Aden	M	Good	Limited	Small	f,w,p,c,e
Oman					
Muscat	V	Fair	..	..	p,m
Pakistan					
Karachi	M	Good	Limited	Large	f,w,p,c,m
India					
Bombay	L	Good	Major	Large	f,w,p,c,m
Cochin	M	Good	Moderate	Small	f,w,p,c,m
Vishakhapatnam	M	Poor	Moderate	Medium	f,w,p,c,m
Calcutta	L	Good	Major	Small	f,w,p,c,m

[a] L: large; M: medium; S: small; V: very small.
[b] c: crane service; f: fuel oil; w: water; p: provisions; m: medical facilities; e: electrical repairs.

Source: US Defense Mapping Agency, *World Port Index*, Publication 50, 5th edn (Defense Mapping Agency: Washington, DC, 1976).

Location momentarily aside, the very finite number of truly suitable ports for naval bases directs attention to the mix of variables which determine their worth. These variables can be read out of the *World Port Index*, and are often used to discuss the suitability of ports as fleet anchorages, locales for major repairs, and so on (regarding the latter, of course, building of new repair facilities, dredging of channels, etc., can alter these capabilities over time).[46] Generally, the variables taken into account include: size, type of harbour (natural or breakwater), shelter afforded, anchorage depth, turn area, repair capabilities, dry-docking, supplies and services (crane service, fuel oil, water, provisions, medical facilities, electrical repairs), and labour force (including wage levels). For purposes of illustration, table 3 provides a comparison of several ports considered as back-ups to US use of Subic Bay, should that be necessary; and table 4 shows the characteristics of ports around the Mediterranean where US access has been increasingly in jeopardy and where (until recently) Soviet access was expanding.

The political conditions attendant upon a major power's use of a given facility can, of course, be important. It is noted that, generally speaking, user or status of forces agreements have become less permissive or more constrained, in the light of the increased leverage acquired by hosts jealous of their sovereignty. Several nations now apply restrictions on visits by US ships carrying nuclear weapons, as was made vivid in the recent US confrontation with New Zealand.[47] Most host nations require *ad hoc* permission for use of ports in cases of conflict or crisis, for instance, US use of Subic Bay or Diego Garcia or Souda Bay might become highly doubtful in another Middle Eastern crisis involving US security support for Israel. Some such questions are both highly interesting and con-jectural—would, for instance, the US Navy have access to Taiwanese naval facilities in the case of a hypothetical major war between China and the USSR? Generally, the USA and the USSR must now, increasingly, judge the three major criteria discussed here in planning permanent naval access applicable to a variety of contingencies, crises and long-term political changes.

Table 4. Comparison of port facilities in the Mediterranean

Port	Size[a]	Shelter afforded	Repairs	Dry-dock	Longshore	Electrical	Steam	Navig. equipment	Electrical repairs	Provisions	Water	Fuel oil	Diesel oil	Deck	Engine
France															
Marseille	L	Excellent	Major	Large	X	X	X	X	X	X	X	X	X	X	X
Toulon	M	Good	Major	Large	X	—	—	—	—	X	X	X	X	X	X
Spain															
Rota/Cadiz	M	Good	Major	Large	X	X	X	X	X	X	X	X	X	X	X
Barcelona	L	Good	Limited	Medium	X	X	X	X	X	X	X	X	X	X	X
Cartagena	M	Fair	Major	Medium	X	—	—	X	X	X	X	X	X	X	X
Italy															
Naples	L	Excellent	Major	Large	X	X	X	X	X	X	X	X	X	X	X
Taranto	M	Good	Major	Small	X	—	—	X	X	X	X	X	X	X	X
Livorno	M	Good	Major	Large	X	X	X	X	X	X	X	X	X	X	X
La Spezia	M	Good	Major	Large	X	—	—	X	X	X	X	X	X	X	X
Greece															
Piraeus	L	Excellent	Major	Medium	X	X	X	X	X	X	X	X	X	X	X
Souda Bay	V	Fair	Limited	Small	—	—	—	—	—	—	—	—	—	X	X
Turkey															
Istanbul	M	Fair	Moderate	Small	X	X	X	X	X	X	X	X	X	X	X
Izmir	M	Good	Limited	..	X	X	—	—	—	X	X	X	X	X	X
Antalya	S	Poor	..	..	—	—	—	—	—	X	X	X	X	—	—
Iskenderun	S	Fair	Limited	..	X	X	—	—	—	X	X	—	—	—	—
Israel															
Haifa	S	Fair	Major	Medium	X	X	—	—	—	X	—	—	—	X	X
Ashdod	S	Fair	Limited	..	—	—	—	—	—	X	X	X	—	—	—
Egypt															
Alexandria	L	Fair	Major	Medium	X	X	X	X	X	X	X	X	X	X	X
Port Said	L	Good	Major	Large	X	X	—	—	—	X	X	X	X	X	X
Libya															
Tobruk	S	Good	..	Small	X	X	—	—	—	X	X	X	—	—	—
Tripoli	M	Fair	Limited	Medium	X	X	—	—	—	X	X	X	X	—	—
Tunisia															
Tunis	M	Good	Moderate	..	X	X	—	—	—	X	X	—	X	—	—

Port	Size[a]	Shelter afforded	Repairs	Dry-dock	Longshore	Electrical	Steam	Navig. equipment	Electrical repairs	Provisions	Water	Fuel oil	Diesel oil	Deck	Engine
		Facilities					**Services**					**Supplies**			
Bizerte	..	..	Moderate	Large	X	X	—	—	—	X	X	X	X	—	—
Algeria															
Mers El Kebir	S	Good	Major	Large	—	—	—	—	—	—	—	—	—	—	—
Algiers	L	Good	Major	Small	X	X	—	—	—	X	X	X	X	X	X
Yugoslavia															
Tivat	V	Fair	Major	Medium	—	—	—	—	—	X	X	X	—	—	—
Split	M	Fair	Major	Medium	—	—	—	—	—	X	X	X	X	—	—
Sibenik	M	Good	Limited	Small	—	—	—	—	—	X	X	—	—	—	—

[a] L: Large; M: medium; S: small; V: very small

Source: US Defense Mapping Agency, *World Port Index*, Publication 50, 5th edn (Defense Mapping Agency: Washington, DC, 1976).

IV. The superpowers' global naval deployments and FMP

A brief review of the current US and Soviet overseas naval deployments and associated basing points and requirements is given below, and figure 2 shows the location of the main and secondary naval operating bases of the USA and the Soviet Union. As noted above, there is a modest level of disagreement about definitions of levels of access, that is, about whether port X or Y deserves to be called a US or Soviet base or facility. Sometimes these arguments are over the sheer facts of access and presence; otherwise, they may serve as covers for highly polemical, political arguments intended to 'expose' or 'reveal' the other side's access so as to encourage political pressures for their removal.

The levels of access are divided into three categories, again, in reality involving a spectrum with no clear, discrete demarcations. First, we cite and discuss the powers' main operating bases, that is, those of most vital importance, usually entailing homeporting of fleets, flotillas or squadrons, and the performing of the entire range of maintenance, provisioning and repair; most crucially, dry-docking facilities for the largest warships. These are the *bases* (the term here used to denote size and significance aside from the matter of sovereign control over disposition) which usually merit a star or an anchor on global maps describing rival basing networks.

At a slightly lesser level of prominence—sometimes denoted on maps by anchors rather than the stars reserved for main operating bases—are the more numerous 'facilities' where the naval units of major powers are normally availed of access for replenishment, R&R, minor repairs, and so on—many shade into

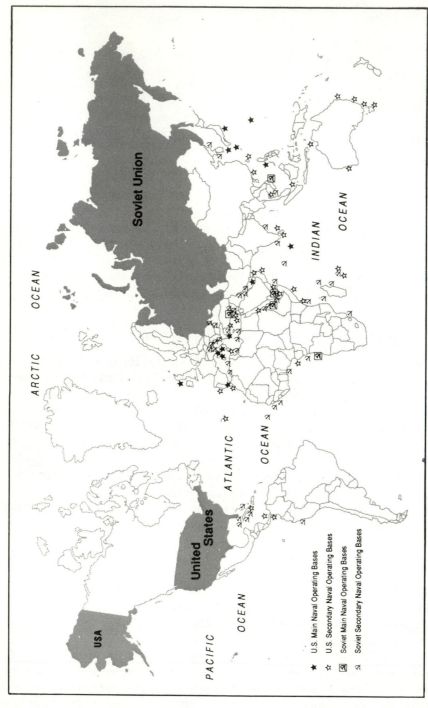

Figure 2. US and Soviet naval operating bases world-wide

Source: SIPRI data

the above-discussed 'base' category. These facilities do not routinely carry out major repairs, are not designated as homeports, and relative to the first category are of contingent, doubtful use to a major power in a crisis or intervention unless the user's and host's political interests should happen to converge in that given instance. Bahrain might, for instance, be available to the USA for naval operations against Khomeini's Iran; use on behalf of Israel would obviously be another story.

Finally, at the other end of a spectrum, are the occasional port visits—courtesy calls, 'shows of the flag'—which are a diplomatic tradition. These, like those in the previous category, can involve provisioning, R&R, minor repairs, and so on. But they are usually sporadic and *ad hoc*, often involving pairs of hosts and users whose political ties are weak, even relatively hostile. By no means can such access be expected in a real crisis or in connection with the conduct of war. However, there is often a significant political component to such visits—they can act as a barometer of shifting political winds. Such an interpretation might be given, for instance, to recent proposed visits by US Navy ships to China, planned explicitly to signal, symbolize, or ratify an increasingly close security tie.[48]

Summing up, there appear to be three basic relative criteria determining whether a naval FMP 'deserves' to be designated a 'main operating base', merely a base, a facility, or whatever: (*a*) size and scope of functions performed; (*b*) permanence (i.e., whether personnel or ships are permanently stationed or homeported); and (*c*) the political problem of the latitude or discretion allowed by the host for the users' operations, in turn divisible into routine and crisis situations. To some extent or in some instances, there will be congruence across these three criteria—but not always. The large US bases in Spain and the Philippines may operate under strict constraints, particularly regarding Middle Eastern contingencies. The much smaller US facility at Diego Garcia probably is, on balance, less politically constrained, because of the nature of the US–British relationship as well as the role of the USA in building the base on a once obscure and near-empty island, one from which demonstrations against US presence are not likely to be launched.

US Naval FMP

According to the *The Military Balance* (IISS), the US Navy of late has fielded some 92 000 personnel abroad (of a total of 564 800 US personnel abroad), of whom some 56 000 are afloat.[49] Its surface fleet is now organized around 14 aircraft carrier battle groups (with one additional carrier in long-term overhaul) and three battleship groups based on the World War II Iowa-class behemoths now being re-configured as cruise-missile carriers. Four of the aircraft carriers are nuclear (CVNs), the others conventionally powered. There are some 205 other principal surface combatants (cruisers, destroyers, gun/ASW destroyers, frigates, gun frigates, etc.); some 89 minor surface combatants (patrol boats, minesweepers); 60 amphibious warfare ships and 54 amphibious landing craft;

some 84 principal auxiliary ships (ammunition, stores, fast sea lift, oilers, destroyer tenders, subtenders, repair, salvage/rescue, etc.); a variety of Military
Sealift Command ships (36); 356 strategic sea lift ships, mobility enhancement
and maritime prepositioning ships, and an active and ready reserve force. Each
carrier group usually contains 8-10 escorts, which include cruisers, destroyers
and submarines, as well as supply ships that sail with each carrier in a battle
group. Each also comprises an air wing averaging 86 planes—fighter and attack
aircraft, ASW, ECM and airborne early-warning system (AEW) craft.

Outside the USA, these naval forces are geographically organized as follows
(personnel numbers as of 1986–87):

1. Atlantic (2nd Fleet): 31 SSBNs, 50 attack submarines, 93 principal surface
combatants, 24 amphibious craft. Main bases: Cuba (Guantanamo Bay) 2100;
Bermuda 1500, Iceland (Keflavik) 1900; UK (Holy Loch and other) 2200;
NATO-assigned personnel 14 800.

2. Mediterranean (27 200), 6th Fleet: up to 4 SSNs, 2 carriers, 12 surface
combatants, 11 support ships, 1 amphibious ready group (3–5 ships), 1 maritime
pre-positioning squadron (MPS), 5 depot ships. Main bases: Italy (Gaeta,
Naples, Sigonella, La Maddalena) 5200; Spain (Rota) 3600.

3. Eastern Pacific, 3rd Fleet: 5 SSBNs, some 25 SSNs, 4 carriers, 72 principal
surface combatants, 26 amphibious craft, 32 support ships. Main bases: Pearl
Harbour and CONUS.

4. Western Pacific (41 400), 7th Fleet: some 15 SSNs and SS, 2 carriers (1
helicopter carrier), 6 amphibious and 8 support ships, 1 MPS. Main bases:
Japan (Yokosuka) 7400; Philippines (Subic Bay) 5300; Guam, Midway 4900
including Marine detachments; Australia, some 600.

5. Indian Ocean (11 000), 7th/2nd Fleet detachments: 1 carrier battle group
(6 surface combatants), 5 MPSs. Base: Diego Garcia 1300.

6. Middle East (Persian Gulf/Bahrain): 1 command ship, 4 destroyers/
frigates.[50]

Basically, the Indian Ocean force acts as a hinge, with reinforcements or
surges ('swing' forces) of forces being provided during crises or potential conflicts from the Western Pacific or Mediterranean,[51] transit from the latter now
normally being possible via the Suez Canal, in line with improved US–Egyptian
relations.[52] Hence, the US Indian Ocean naval presence will often constitute a
mix of the permanently stationed Middle East force based in Bahrain, and the
usually much larger seconded elements of the 6th and 7th Fleets.

In the recent past, when the US Navy had 12 carrier battle groups, six were
usually based on each coast, with two in port, two in training, and two on
six-month cruises abroad. The recent expansion of the carrier groups to 14 in
conjunction with reduced foreign sailing time, will apparently leave the overseas
carrier deployments approximately steady, with perhaps even some decrease
allowed for by the occasional substitute by battleship groups to maintain a
'presence'.[53]

The above outline of US fleet deployments leads easily to a description of their overseas supporting base structure. As noted, this is hinged on a very small number of main operating bases, abetted by others available for port calls, replenishment and perhaps minor repairs. Table 5 provides more detailed information on the scope of basing activities at each.

Table 5. Main and secondary surface-ship and submarine operating bases of the US Navy

Host nation and base	Description
For surface ships	
Japan	
Yokosuka	Major naval base, HQ for US Naval Forces Japan and homeport for aircraft carrier *Midway* and about 10 other 7th Fleet ships; available for contingencies in West Pacific; also used by nuclear attack submarines; extensive dock facilities, naval munitions maintenance and storage, naval hospital, ship repairs including largest USN dry-dock west of CONUS; supply depot
Sasebo	Base used jointly with Japan; naval ordnance facility, docking storage facilities for 7th Fleet; homeport for a nuclear attack submarine, dry-docks capacity for aircraft carriers, large-scale naval fuel storage, munitions storage for USMC
White Beach (Okinawa)	Berthing and storage for 7th Fleet ships; occasional use by SSNs
Taiwan	
Kaohsiung	Occasional port use by US ships
Guam (US overseas possession)	
Apra	Major naval base; ship repairs, logistics wharf, explosives and fuel storage; formerly Polaris homeport for 8 SSBNs; patrol boats and mine flotilla based here
Philippines	
Subic Bay	Major USN base, HQ for US Naval Forces, Philippines; major ship repair facility with 4 floating dry-docks which can accommodate all but largest aircraft carriers; piers and other support facilities—support 7th Fleet operations throughout West Pacific and Indian Ocean; 60 per cent of all 7th Fleet repairs performed here
Australia	
Cockburn Sound	Australian base, can accommodate 4 submarines and 4 destroyers; possible expansion to accommodate carriers; US considered homeporting a destroyer here; mostly potential US base, offered earlier as such by hosts; port calls at Hobart, Melbourne, Sydney, Brisbane, Darwin
Thailand	
Sattahip	Military port constructed by USA; major port of entry for military supplies to US bases in Thailand; peaked at end of Viet Nam War
Hong Kong	Periodic port calls
Singapore	
Sembawang	Some overhauls, reprovisioning for USN ships, potential for expanded use
Sri Lanka	
Colombo	Alleged use by USA for R&R

Host nation and base	Description
Trincomalee	Port calls
Djibouti	Port calls by US Indian Ocean task force; refuelling and reprovisioning, no shore leave; US leases fuel storage for own use
Réunion	Port calls
Somalia	
Berbera	Some use by US Indian Ocean task force; possible storage of *matériel* for rapid deployment force
Mogadiscio	US improving facilities; port visits; possible storage of equipment and supplies for Central Command
Oman	
Muscat (Mina Qaboos)	Restricted USN use by Indian Ocean task force; contingent use for Central Command in Persian Gulf crisis
Mina Raysutt	Restricted US use
Masirah	Port calls
Bahrain	
Al Jufair	USA took over British facilities in 1949; now homeport for 'Mideast Force' of 4 destroyers; communications, storage, barracks, berth, hangars, co-use of adjacent airfield; resupply of Indian Ocean task force; low-key use because of political problems; quiet access for greatly expanded US presence in 1987
Kenya	
Mombasa	US port visits, possible pre-positioning of *matériel* for use in South-West Asia
Diego Garcia	US naval support facilities; berths Central Command's *matériel* storage ships; lagoon being dredged to create sufficient anchorage for a carrier battle group
Mauritius	Rumoured USN port visits; R&R and reprovisioning
Azores (Portugal)	
Ponta Delgada	Fuel storage; breakwaters; frequent visits by NATO warships
Spain	
Rota	Major naval base; also airfield and communications station; major repair capabilities; can berth aircraft carriers; former Polaris SSBN base; fuel depot; weather station; naval hospital
Italy	
Naples	Major support complex for US 6th Fleet; HQ for attack submarines; homeport for destroyer tender, communications centre
Gaeta	Main base; homeport for flagship of US 6th Fleet; refuelling facilities
Greece	
Souda Bay	NATO naval base; anchorage large enough for entire 6th Fleet; extensive underground fuel and munitions storage
Athens/Piraeus	US use of commercial port facilities increasingly in jeopardy during Papandreou regime
Turkey	
Istanbul	USN port visit
Izmir	USN port visit
Antalya	USN port visit

Host nation and base	Description
Portugal	
Lisbon	USN port visits
Israel	
Haifa	Periodic USN port visits
Tunisia	
Tunis	USN port visits
Egypt	
Alexandria	USN port visits, periodically
Sudan	
Port Sudan	USN port visits
Cuba	
Guantanamo Bay	USN port visits, training and exercises; naval air station, dry-dock, sheltered anchorage, naval hospital; in reality mostly a political bargaining chip
Panama	
Rodman Naval Station	Fleet support, logistics, small craft training facility
Balboa	Naval ship repair facility
For submarines	
United Kingdom	
Holy Loch	SSBN forward base, homeport for 10 Poseidons; submarine tender permanently berthed; large floating dry dock
Japan	
Yokosuka, Sasebo	(See previous mention)
Italy	
La Maddalena	Homeport for submarine tender; base for patrols by SSNs in Mediterranean

Source: Compiled from SIPRI data and the many references cited for this chapter.

In the crucial Western Pacific—now witnessing a major Soviet buildup of naval forces and expansion of the Soviet presence in Viet Nam—the primary US naval bases are at Yokosuka in Japan and Subic Bay in the Philippines, backed up further east by the US bases in Pearl Harbor, Guam and Adak. The presence in Japan—also involving a smaller facility at Sasebo and also access to Okinawa—is, of course, directed at the Soviet Far Eastern main bases at Vladivostok and Petropavlovsk; the adjacent, enclosed Soviet naval bastion in the Sea of Okhotsk; and the associated crucial chokepoints represented by the Soya, Tsugaru and Korean Straits. They are vital, of course, for underpinning the security of Japan and South Korea.

Subic Bay further south, while obviously in proximity to South-East Asia, the South China Sea, and the critical Indonesian Straits, derives further importance because of its relation to contingencies in the Indian Ocean/South-West Asia/ Horn of Africa region, that is, the so-called 'arc of crisis'. For that reason, that is, its location, it is considered a vital link in the US naval presence hinging the Pacific and Indian Ocean theatres.[54]

The US Navy is availed of other less permanent facilities in the Far East, on a regular or contingency basis. Sasebo has been mentioned as a secondary base in Japan. Pusan in South Korea and Okinawa have frequently been utilized; further south so have Singapore, Djakarta and the US-constructed port of Sattahip near Bangkok in Thailand.[55] Taiwan's naval bases of Kaohsiung and Keelung, sometimes mentioned as potential fall-backs if Subic Bay should be lost to US access, are now infrequently used so as not to perturb Chinese sensibilities in the now lengthy aftermath of the Shanghai communiqué.[56] Saipan and Tinian in the Marianas are available as fall-back positions; so too is probably the large Koror anchorage area in the Belau Islands, which would require extensive construction if it were to serve as more than an anchorage. In Western Australia, Cockburn Sound adjacent to the Perth/Fremantle area is available for US Navy use; indeed, it has periodically been mentioned as a possibility for homeporting a small permanent naval presence, though none has as yet eventuated.

In the 2nd Fleet area (Western Atlantic–Caribbean), proximity to the US mainland allows for most basing functions to be carried out in US ports: Norfolk, Charleston, Kings Island, Mayport, Newport, New York, Boston and others. The USA otherwise maintains a large installation, utilized primarily for training purposes, at Guantanamo in Cuba, an anomalous remnant from pre-Castro Cuba—there is also a fairly important main operating base at Roosevelt Roads in Puerto Rico astride the main Atlantic–Caribbean SLOCs.[57] The USA retains access in Panama and, as the Central American imbroglio has deepened in recent years, has sought and acquired additional limited access to facilities in Honduras and Colombia. Bermuda and the Azores provide basing access in the Atlantic; for refuelling and provisioning, and so on, and more importantly for ASW and other technical functions to be discussed later. And, a variety of NATO ports in Western Europe are available—the UK, Iceland and Norway are important—in an area, however, where the British Navy maintains primary responsibility for NATO maritime security.

The Mediterranean 6th Fleet utilizes Naples as its homeport and main base; Spain's Rota is perhaps the second most important facility in that area.[58] In the past, the USA has made extensive use of Antalya, Istanbul and Izmir in Turkey, and Piraeus and Souda Bay (Crete) in Greece; all of which are nominally available and still used for port calls, but (particularly in the case of Greece) in a worsening political climate (for the USA).[59] In recent years, the 6th Fleet has increased port calls both at Alexandria and Haifa, reflective of the post-Camp David realignment in that area and of the extensive US military and economic aid funnelled to Egypt and Israel.[60] US ships have also frequently visited Morocco (Rabat, Casablanca), Tunisia (Bizerte), southern France, Gibraltar and Portugal—the latter has figured in some recent press accounts as a target for a US quest for enhanced naval access in an obviously crucial area.

In the Middle East/Indian Ocean region, the USA has, since the Soviet invasion of Afghanistan in 1979, the fall of the Shah of Iran and the initiation of the Iraq–Iran War, made a major effort towards beefed-up naval access directed at the contingency of combat (or deterrence thereof) in or around the

Persian Gulf. Building of a greatly enhanced facility at British-owned Diego Garcia—some 3000 miles, however, from the Shatt-Al-Arab—has been one key element of this buildup—it provides a transit point between Subic Bay and South-West Asia.[61] Otherwise, US diplomacy, underpinned by significant arms and economic aid, has achieved ship access (lacking formal agreements, contingent upon *ad hoc* permission for use) in Kenya (Mombasa), Somalia (Berbera, a former Soviet base, and Mogadishu) and Oman (Muscat, Masirah).[62] At the time of the crisis in 1987 featuring the Iraqi sinking of the *USS Stark*, it was reported that this force, operating out of Bahrain, had expanded to a consistent level of seven frigates and destroyers, intended as a 'presence'.[63] Afterwards, it was expanded much further to some 25 vessels.[64]

A small, permanently homeported presence also remains in Bahrain, long-known as the US Middle East Force, though the overall size of the US presence in the Gulf was greatly expanded in connection with protection of tankers during the Iraq–Iran War.[65] Although Saudi Arabia and Egypt have been cautious about allowing US use of facilities (a planned US base at Egypt's Ras Banas on the Red Sea has now been aborted), there are some ship visits allowed. US ships also make some use of Djibouti (a French base), Port Sudan, Karachi, Trincomalee (Sri Lanka) and Mauritius in an area increasingly subject to the rival powers' shows of force, 'presence' and potentially, more serious forms of coercive diplomacy.

Given the difficulties the US Navy has had of late regarding bases and visits by nuclear-armed ships, it is worth noting here those facilities still available for such purposes.[66] For nuclear-armed surface ships the USA relies heavily on Crete in the Mediterranean area and on Subic Bay in the Pacific. Guam and Holy Loch have allowed for overseas SSBN deployments even as the need for that has declined with the phasing-in of the Ohio-class (Trident-missile) fleet. Attack submarines, vital among other things for hunting SSBNs, now deploy overseas in Guam's Apra Harbor (a US possession), Pearl Harbor and at La Maddalena on Sardinia.

Navy élite units

The US Navy utilizes not only facilities for large warships and submarines, but in an area closer to the activities of the Army, also utilizes some overseas access for its élite Sea–Air–Land (SEAL) force. That force features frogmen who specialize in underwater demolition, beach clearing, infiltration and reconnoitre, comparable to some functions performed on the Soviet side by *Spetsnaz* units. It is also deployed for anti-terrorism activities.

Now being enlarged to an overall size of some 3000 personnel, units of SEAL forces have been reported permanently stationed overseas in Scotland (Machrihanish), the Philippines (Subic Bay) and Antigua; as well as in Hawaii and Puerto Rico (Roosevelt Roads).[67] Not to be ignored—both for US and Soviet élite special forces units—are the possibilities for their use at the outset of major general wars as each side moves to degrade the other's strategic postures through sabotage and the sowing of confusion. The Navy is not alone in its overseas role here—US Army Special Forces units are stationed in FR Germany (Bad Tolz, Berlin) and South Korea.

Soviet Naval FMP

Regarding the interplay between geographical location and naval strategy, the Soviet Navy's position and deployments in some ways provide almost a mirror image of those of the US Navy. Long considered primarily a continental land power (in Mackinder's imagery, also a near-invulnerable fortress protected on its coast by impenetrable ice and rivers draining to the Arctic), the Soviet (earlier Russian) naval strategy had long been assumed essentially defensive, and the Soviet Navy virtually a coastal defence force.[68] Indeed, in the late nineteenth century, the Russian navy compensated for its maritime weakness by emphasizing the construction of numerous small patrol boats, again perceived as a largely defensive measure usable close to home.[69] True, there was the centuries-long quest for warm-water ports; also a fairly sizeable naval buildup in the late nineteenth century leading to the 1905 disaster at Japanese hands in the Straits of Tsushima. But even as recently as the late 1950s, the Soviet Navy had little in the way of 'blue water', long-range power projection capability, nor overseas basing access. The early post-war exceptions were use of a Chinese base at Port Arthur, Porkalla in Finland and a three-year interregnum (1958–61) when Soviet submarines were granted access to Albanian bases in the Mediterranean.[70]

What has occurred since, subsequent to the Cuban missile crisis débâcle, is familiar history: the major naval buildup under the aegis of Admiral Gorschkov; the vastly increased on-station deployments in first the Mediterranean, then the Indian Ocean, Caribbean, and South Atlantic; the vast buildup of naval forces in the Far East in recent years, and so on.[71] The Soviet fleet is now quantitatively larger than its US counterpart as measured by major surface combatants, both SSBNs and nuclear-powered attack submarines (SSNs), and patrol craft; still far weaker in the crucial domain of large aircraft carriers, but with their initial deployment impending. And, of course, the Soviet Union has acquired access to numerous overseas basing points, so that, as indicated, the superpowers' maritime competition has assumed a more global and fluid or inter-mixed character, somewhat altered away from the traditional heartland versus rimland pattern. The ambitious US maritime strategy notwithstanding, few assume the USA to be capable of indivisible sea control.

The Soviet Navy now fields some 269 principal surface combatants (including 3 Kiev carriers with one more imminent), 2 ASW helicopter carriers, some 36 cruisers of which 2 (Kirov-class) are nuclear, 61 destroyers (of which 33 are specialized for ASW), and 167 escorts including 100 corvettes.[72] In addition, there are some 762 minor surface combatants: vast numbers of missile patrol boats, fast attack craft, minesweepers, minelayers, radar picket ships, 197 amphibious ships and smaller craft, 372 principal auxiliary ships (replenishment, tankers, missile support, supply, cargo, submarine tenders, repair, hospital, submarine rescue, salvage/rescue, training ships, etc.). There are some 62 intelligence collection vessels (AGI), 456 naval research vessels, 74 tankers, 298 support ships, 1900 merchant ships, and numerous civilian oceanographic, fishery, space-associated and hydrographic research vessels.[73]

The Soviet submarine fleet is equally formidable, comprising some 360 vessels. It fields 63 SSBNs and 14 non nuclear-powered ballistic-missile submarines (SSBs), with a total of 983 submarine-launched ballistic missiles (SLBMs)—39 SLBMs and 15 submarines are outside the SALT limits—some 214 attack submarines (of which 70 are nuclear-powered); and 63 cruise missile submarines, 48 of which are nuclear (SSGNs).[74]

Amid this blizzard of detail, several key general points stand out, as they specifically relate to Soviet external basing requirements and utilization, particularly by comparison with the US case. First, of course, the Soviet Navy is, numerically speaking, huge, with respect to both surface and submarine forces, even if also subject to the historical trend towards numerically smaller but more potent navies. Second, the very outsized force of auxiliary ships reminds us that many functions performed on shore by the US Navy are of necessity carried out at sea by the Soviet Navy; the cost to crew morale or other efficiencies is hard to gauge. Similarly, third, the large force of AGIs, plus fishing and oceanographic vessels, is used extensively to perform many functions, for which the USA utilizes land facilities: SIGINT, communications relay, space-tracking, and so on (of course, this also directs attention to the use by these ships of foreign ports for repair, replenishment, etc.).[75] Fourth, the absence of large aircraft carriers should not allow us to ignore the very large Soviet naval aircraft force, which, utilizing stand-off missiles, performs many combat functions in lieu of carriers, geographical limitations kept in mind.[76] That force comprises some 915 combat aircraft: 120 Tu-22M Backfire B bombers; 275 medium bombers (240 Tu-16 Badger C and 35 Tu-22 Blinder B); and others, including some 205 Bear F, IL-38 May and Be-12 ASW aircraft.[77]

The deployment of the Soviet Navy is characteristically divided as follows: an Arctic Command comprising the Northern Fleet; an Atlantic Command comprising the Baltic and Black Sea Fleets, and a Mediterranean squadron; and the Pacific Fleet. The Arctic Command, with headquarters at Severomorsk and main bases at Motovskij Gulf, Kola Inlet, Gremikha, and Polyarny, deploys 42 SSB/BNs, 117 other submarines, 75 major and 45 minor surface combatants, 65 mine countermeasure vessels (MCMVs), 14 amphibious ships, and 119 auxiliaries.[78] The Baltic Fleet has 34 submarines, 45 principal and 105 minor surface combatants, 120 MCMVs, 50 amphibious ships, and 58 auxiliaries; its main bases are at Baltiysk, Kronstadt, Paldiski, Liepaja, Klaipeda and Riga, with its headquarters at Kaliningrad.[79] The Black Sea Fleet, headquartered at Sebastopol and its major bases there and at Balaclava, Poti and Odessa, fields 34 submarines, 69 principal and 105 minor surface combatants, 90 MCMVs, 75 amphibious ships and 67 auxiliaries.[80] The Mediterranean squadron is composed of ships drawn from the other fleets. The Pacific Fleet, headquartered at Vladivostok and with its main bases there and at Petropavlovsk and Sovjetskaya

Gavan, deploys 31 SSB/BNs, 77 other submarines, 82 principal and 136 minor surface combatants, 96 MCMVs, 59 amphibious ships and 128 auxiliaries.[81]

As noted, the Soviet Navy still labours under its age-old geographical problem of chokepoints and blocked egress; its forward basing strategy is largely directed at achieving extended access to overcome that problem. The Northern Fleet must deal with the US/NATO blocking position across the Greenland-Iceland-UK (GIUK) gap—or, alternatively, the Greenland-Iceland-Norway (GIN) gap; the Baltic Fleet with the Danish Straits; the Black Sea Fleet with the Turkish Straits; the Mediterranean Eskadra with the Gibraltar Straits; and the Pacific Fleet with the several chokepoints leading out of the Sea of Okhotsk and the Sea of Japan. And, while information on Soviet SSBN deployments (as well as similar US deployments) is limited, it is known that this largely entails utilization of two 'bastion' areas; one in the Barents Sea/Norwegian Sea area; the other within the Sea of Okhotsk. Unlike the USA, at least until recently, the USSR has not forward-based its SSBNs; rather, it has rotated them back and forth from firing stations to their homeports in the Kola Peninsula and Siberia/Far East areas. However, Soviet attack submarines—both nuclear and diesel-powered—make extensive use of external bases: in Cam Ranh Bay (Viet Nam), Cienfuegos (Cuba) and Aden (South Yemen), among others.[82]

Table 6 details the Soviet overseas naval basing structure which, it is important to note, has experienced some major changes in recent years as reflective of the vicissitudes of external political alignments. Several external main operating bases are crucial to Soviet naval deployments: Cam Ranh Bay (Viet Nam) in the Far East/Pacific area; Aden and Socotra (South Yemen) and the Dahlak Archipelago (Ethiopia) in the western Indian Ocean/Horn of Africa area; Luanda (Angola) in the South Atlantic; Latakia and Tartus (Syria) in the Mediterranean; and Havana, Cienfuegos and Mariel (Cuba) in the western North Atlantic. Beyond that, the Soviet Navy has required degrees of access—secondary bases, minor facilities, port visits, etc.—in numerous other locales (often the subject of debate over facts and interpretations).[83] These include Cambodia, India, Iraq, Mauritius, the Seychelles, Madagascar, Mozambique, Angola, Congo, São Tomé and Príncipe, Cape Verde, Guinea Bissau, Benin, Guinea, Algeria, Libya, Yugoslavia, Spain (Canary Islands), Nicaragua and Peru.[84] That may not yet be a truly global basing structure, but it is something well beyond what would accord with a strictly defensive, coastal defence navy, or with the assumptions and expectations of a generation ago.

Some of these Soviet facilities are particularly important. Cam Ranh Bay has become the largest Soviet naval forward deployment base outside the WTO. Aside from the basing of reconnaissance and strike aircraft (discussed below), this involves support for deployment of some 20–25 ships to the South China Sea, including surface combatants, attack and cruise-missile submarines and naval auxiliary and amphibious ships. The vertical/short take-off and landing (V/STOL) aircraft carrier *Minsk* has called at Cam Ranh as part of its distant-water operations.[85]

Table 6. Main and secondary surface-ship operating bases of the Soviet Navy

Host nation/base	Description
Viet Nam	
Cam Ranh Bay	Main external Soviet naval base in Far East—guided-missile cruisers, frigates and minesweepers based here; also, attack submarines; on average, deployment is 4 submarines, 2–4 combat vessels, 10 auxiliaries
Cambodia	
Kompong Som (Sihanoukville)	Reported access for Soviet warships, i.e., replenishment, refuelling, etc.
North Korea	
Najin	Some port access, earlier reports of submarine base
India	
Vishakhapatnam	Indian naval base built with Soviet assistance; some Soviet port calls, refuelling, etc.
Cochin	Port calls, refuelling, etc., reported
Iraq	
Umm Quasr	Soviet assistance in improving facility here, earlier reported accessible to Soviet warships; access limited during Iraq–Iran War since 1980
Az Zubayr	Earlier reported used by Soviet submarines and SIGINT vessels
Al Fao	Iraqi port, reported availed to Soviet Union after 1974 agreement
South Yemen	
Aden	Soviet main base for Indian Ocean operations: fuel tanks, replenishment, reports of submarine pens alongside berthing for major surface ships
Socotra Island	Anchorage used by Soviet ships, possible shore facilities
Ethiopia	
Dahlak Archipelago	Large anchorage for Soviet Indian Ocean naval squadron
Assab	Important Soviet naval facility; floating dry dock formerly moored at Berbera now apparently here
Massawa	Port access, routine
Perim Island	Former British facility, reportedly being improved by Soviet Union
Mauritius	Reported port calls (note concurrently reported US access)
Mozambique	
Nacala	Periodic port calls
Maputo	Periodic port calls
Tanzania	
Zanzibar	Available, port calls
Angola	
Luanda	Now main Soviet naval base on West African coast, having replaced Conakry; guided-missile destroyer and several accompanying craft stationed here
Madagascar	
Diego Suarez	Available, port calls
Tanative	Available, port calls
Benin	
Cotonou	Periodic port calls

Host nation/base	Description
Guinea	
Conakry	Formerly hosted small West African flotilla; use now apparently curtailed, if not eliminated
Congo	
Ponte Noir	Reported occasional port calls
Guinea Bissau	
Geba Estuary	Port calls
Algeria	
Mers El Kebir	Port calls
Annaba	Soviet repair ships deployed, submarine repair capabilities reported
Libya	
Tripoli	Regular access, Soviet Mediterranean squadron
Benghazi	Regular access, Soviet Mediterranean squadron
Bardia	Soviet Union reported constructing naval base here
Syria	
Latakia	Main base for Soviet Mediterranean squadron: fuel, replenishment, etc.
Tartus	Regular access, maintenance facility for attack submarines, oiler, tender
Ras Shamra	Soviet submarine base alleged under construction
Yugoslavia	
Tivat	Repair of Soviet ships and submarines
Rijeka	Port calls
Pula	Port calls
Sibenik	Port calls
Split	Port calls
Greece	
Siros Island	Ship repairs, commercial, at Neorian shipyard
Cuba	
Cienfuegos	Replenishment base for Soviet attack submarines, mooring of submarine tender occasionally rumoured
Mariel	Port calls
Nipe Bay	Port calls, Golf-class submarines, intelligence collectors
Havana	Access for Soviet surface ships
Santiago de Cuba	Access for Soviet surface ships
Peru	
Calleo	Occasional ship visits since Soviet–Peruvian arms deal
Romania	
Mangalia	Reported Soviet submarine base on Black Sea
Sulina	Forward supply base for Soviet Danube flotilla

Source: Compiled from SIPRI data and the many references cited for this chapter.

In the western Indian Ocean, the main base is at Aden, where the Soviet Navy enjoys nearly unlimited access; there is additional access to an anchorage at Socotra Island.[86] In addition to basing of naval reconnaissance aircraft, that includes facilities for delivery of military and economic aid; trans-shipment of petroleum products; trans-shipment of cargo to Ethiopia and other parts of Africa; crew rest and recreation; refuelling and provisioning; and alongside berthing and anchoring space for naval combatants, cargo ships and units of the Soviet fishing fleet. In addition, the Soviet communications and intelligence collection facilities in South Yemen could greatly assist the Soviet Indian Ocean Squadron's capabilities during a crisis or conflict. In 1987, as tensions in the Persian Gulf area mounted and simultaneous with the Iraqi attack on the *USS Stark*, it was announced that Soviet naval forces would accompany and protect oil tankers *en route* to and from Kuwait. The Soviet naval units involved were based on South Yemen—by contrast, the US Navy was availed of access within the Gulf at Bahrain[87]—and have utilized periodic access to ports in Mozambique, at Beira, Nacala and Maputo.[88]

In the Mediterranean, the important Soviet presence in Syria includes naval access to the port of Tartus, which is the primary maintenance facility for Soviet submarines operating in the area. A Soviet submarine tender, a yard oiler and a water tender are stationed there. And the base appears recently to have been upgraded, perhaps to become the home port for the Soviet Fifth Fleet.[89]

Over the years, there has also been varied degrees of naval access to Algeria, Libya and Yugoslavia. Soviet submarines have been reported serviced at Annaba in Algeria, and its ships refuelled and maintained at several Yugoslav ports in the Adriatic, at Tivat and Sibenik.[90]

In Guinea, despite some curtailment of long-maintained access for Soviet Bear reconnaissance aircraft, the USSR routinely uses Conakry harbour as a facility for its West African patrol.[91] But Luanda in Angola has now become the most important port for Moscow's West African naval units—since 1982 that has involved an 8500-ton floating dry-dock capable of handling most major Soviet naval combatants.[92] In Ethiopia, the installation at Dahlak Archipelago is a maintenance facility and supply depot for Soviet naval combatants operating in the Indian Ocean and Red Sea, normally ranging from 20 to 25 units, including surface ships, attack and cruise-missile submarines and auxiliaries. This facility includes an 8500-ton floating dry-dock, floating piers, helipads, fuel and water storage, a submarine tender and other repair ships. Guided-missile cruisers and nuclear-powered submarines regularly call at Dahlak for repair and supplies.[93]

In the Caribbean, Nicaragua may now become another site for Soviet naval activities. Heretofore, this has involved intermediate stops by Soviet ships. According to some sources, the direct passage of the Soviet ship *Bakuriani* from the port of Nikolayev on the Black Sea to Corinto on the west coast of Nicaragua in November 1984 marked a new, more assertive turn in Soviet efforts.[94]

In Cuba, in addition to enjoying access for port visits, maintenance, and so on, Moscow permanently bases a submarine tender at Cienfuegos, used primarily, if not solely, for servicing attack submarines—access for SSBNs might be construed as a violation of the agreements emerging out of the Cuban missile crisis.[95]

At another level, Soviet access to Peruvian ports has provided logistics support and maintenance for some 200 fishing vessels that operate off the coast of South America. This involves, among other things, extensive rotation of merchant seamen and fishermen.[96]

Future strategic basing of submarines

Heretofore and by contrast to the US experience, the Soviet Union has not utilized overseas maintenance and refuelling bases for its strategic submarines—SSBNs. These have been home-based in the Kola Peninsula area and in Vladivostok and Petropavlovsk in the Far East, transiting to nearby firing positions in the associated 'bastions' in the Norwegian and Barents seas and in the Sea of Okhotsk. But the advent of a US space-based defence—particularly if it should involve a boost-phase intercept capability—could force a change. Moscow might then choose to disperse its SSBNs to areas of lesser vulnerability to interdiction by space-based defences. Though it is still purely hypothetical, this could direct attention to a variety of possible new overseas submarine bases, perhaps along the western littoral of South America, in the south-west Pacific, West Africa or the Caribbean. Such bases would have to be within targeting distance of the continental USA, yet also relatively distant from the US ASW bases, not an easily achieved combination.

Use of off-shore anchorages in lieu of shore facilities

During the long segment of the post-war period in which Soviet naval access was limited by the paucity of (politically aligned) hosts, a strategy of self-sufficiency dictated extensive use of offshore anchorages. Also, far more than the USA, the Soviet Union has made use of mooring buoys in places relatively sheltered from inclement weather. These sites usually act as points of more or less continuous deployment for ships conducting specific missions; minesweeping, intelligence, submarine support, and the like. Relative to use of shore facilities, there are, of course, costs: crew morale in connection with limited shore leave; the need for more extensive use of auxiliary ships; the need for rotation back to home ports for more than minor repairs. On the reverse side, there is the routinized development of the capacity and habit of operating free of the political constraints which can be applied—perhaps only amid crisis—by reluctant base hosts.[97]

Among the major Soviet Mediterranean anchorages and mooring buoys are those at Kithira (south of Greek Peloponnisos), Hammamet (off the Tunisian coast), Crete East, and in the Alboran Basin some 100 miles east of Gibraltar, off the Chella Bank. Kithira, nearby major US Sixth Fleet bases, often has several warships at anchor, and is used for refuelling, replenishment and some repairs. Hammamet is used by submarines and surface combat ships, while anchorages at Alboran allow for support of ships deployed near the strategic

Gibraltar exit. That off Crete is used by combat ships during crises in the Middle East.[98]

Numerous other secondary anchorages have been developed by the Soviet Navy throughout the Mediterranean: off Cape Andreas near Cyprus; off Limnos Island in the Aegean on the route to and from the Black Sea; at Hurd Bank and Lampedusa Island south of Sicily; off Cape Passero near Sicily, near Gavdos Island south of Crete; and at the Bank le Sec north-east of the Tunisian–Algerian border adjacent to the Tyrrhenian Sea.[99]

In the Indian Ocean, the main anchorages have been at Socotra (warship and support ships), Cape Guardafui off Somalia, and another south-west of Aden, all concentrated near the crucial Cape Bab El Mandeb. Others used, more widely dispersed around the Indian Ocean, have been off the Chagos Archipelago near Diego Garcia, at Coetivy Island near the Fortune Bank; and also near the Seychelles, at Cargados Carajos in the Persian Gulf, and off the Nicobar and Laccadive Islands.[100]

In the Pacific, there are frequently used anchorages off Pagan Island in the Philippines, not far from Subic Bay, and another south of Singapore.

In a purely definitional sense, offshore anchorages in international waters do not constitute FMP as such. But it is important to note that there may be a grey area here, that is, use of such anchorages may be eased by at least mildly friendly relations with nearby states and vice-versa. After Sadat's expulsion of the Soviet Navy in the early 1970s, there was considerable Egypto–Soviet tension over use of an anchorage in the Gulf of Sollum, just outside the 12-mile territorial limit. The Egyptians attempted, apparently with eventual success, to move the Soviet ships away, among other things by conducting live firing exercises in the vicinity.[101]

Grey area access: fishing and maritime fleets

It is at least arguable that any discussion of Soviet naval FMP ought not omit the matter of access for fishing and commercial transport fleets, generally deemed an important adjunct arm of the Soviet military, and in which civilian and military functions appear somewhat blurred. Space, communications and intelligence functions are performed in large measure by a variety of Soviet seaborne vessels, in contrast with the far more extensive US use of land facilities. Discussion of fishing fleets is therefore confined to the sections on these functions in chapter 6.

The by now huge Soviet merchant marine fleet is often used to support the Soviet Navy; according to one source it was 'under central naval control ultimately directed by Admiral Gorschkov' (the British use of commandeered merchant vessels for supplying the Falklands operation and current US plans to develop similar capacity indicate that the Soviet practice here need not be perceived as wholly unique).[102] Soviet merchant ships have participated in exercises such as OKEAN-75 and have been used to monitor Western naval operations.[103] The Soviet Navy, in particular, has made extensive use of merchant tankers, which may provide as much as one half of the fleet's fuel requirements.[104] Soviet merchant ships have greatly increased their calls to Third World ports in recent years, not only in client states, but significantly in countries such as Brazil, Tunisia, Malaysia, Spain, Greece, Singapore and India. Otherwise, joint maritime firms have been established with India, Sri Lanka, Egypt, Spain, the Philippines, Iraq and Somalia—creating another aspect of naval FMP.[105]

Other nations' naval FMP

Somewhat in the face of historical nostrums associated with Mahan and others, it is apparent that the competition—if that is what it is—for overseas naval access has become largely a two-nation game. In that sense at least, bipolarity unquestionably reigns. There are, none the less, a few not altogether insignificant instances of naval FMP retained by—or recently acquired by—some other nations: France, Britain, Australia, the Netherlands and maybe others. Of course, almost all navies conduct periodic port visits abroad, variously involving 'presence', solidification of political friendships, broadening of horizons for naval personnel, and so on.

France has the most significant naval FMP besides the superpowers, most notably represented by its Indian Ocean Flotilla (Alindien) of five frigates, three minor combatants, two amphibious and four support ships (also a small naval marine detachment). That force is deployed out of Djibouti (hence is within combat range of the Persian Gulf), also making extensive use of bases at Réunion and Mayotte (Mozambique Channel), both French overseas possessions (earlier, up to 1973, France had extensive access to Diego Suarez in Madagascar).[106] There is also a significant (and recently beefed-up) naval presence in the Pacific: five frigates, five minor combatants, seven amphibious and twelve support ships. That force operates out of Nouméa, New Caledonia; also patrolling via Tahiti (Papeete), Muroroa and other French dependencies in the south-west Pacific.[107] Two small ships are also normally rotated about between the Antilles (Port Louis, Guadeloupe) and Guyana.[108] The French Navy also makes extensive use of a number of other ports, mostly in closely aligned African nations: most notably Dakar (Senegal), Abidjan (Ivory Coast) and Libreville (Gabon). During the events of 1987, France's access to Djibouti allowed for a significant naval presence in the Gulf of Oman, outside the Straits of Hormuz. That presence was reported as consisting of three minesweepers, three escorts, one anti-submarine ship, the aircraft carrier *Clemenceau* and two frigates.

Great Britain's once near astonishing network of overseas naval bases and access has by now dwindled to a very small remnant, aside from still extensive routine port calls by the Royal Navy. Small naval forces are still permanently deployed in Belize, Gibraltar and Hong Kong.[109] A relatively large force including an ASW carrier, an SSN and several escorts and auxiliaries remains in the Falklands in the wake of that (not wholly resolved) dispute. A small naval detachment (one or two destroyers or frigates and a couple of support ships) moves about the Indian Ocean, making use of Diego Garcia, Singapore, Perth, and so on, and has quietly been used to escort ships in the Persian Gulf. That presence, which apparently utilizes access to Bahrain, was reported in 1987 to consist of two warships, one fleet tanker, four minesweepers and a supply ship.[110] Otherwise, within NATO, only the Netherlands permanently deploys a tiny naval presence outside Europe—the Dutch retain a small presence at Curacao in the Caribbean.[111] (Spain is reported to have established a small 'fishing' presence in Equatorial Guinea after the expulsion of the Soviet Navy from Luba.)[112]

Regarding more extensive or 'routine' naval access than periodic port calls, only a scattered handful of disparate additional examples could be cited, subject to rapid change. Saudi Arabia, bent on hegemony over the Red Sea, apparently moves some naval units back and forth across to Sudan. Earlier, Israel reportedly had a somewhat covert naval presence on some Ethiopian islands in the Red Sea—that ended with the demise of Haile Selassie's reign.[113] Australia's contribution to the West's presence in the Indian Ocean (a destroyer and a couple of patrol boats) makes regular visits to Singapore and other facilities within the ASEAN grouping. China was much earlier claimed to be seeking access to Sri Lanka's port at Trincomalee.[114]

V. 'Presence'

Further along a spectrum encompassing naval FMP, broadly construed, are the activities falling under 'port calls' and 'ship-days' in various bodies of water. Together, in writings which precede our inauguration of the concept of FMP in lieu of bases, these matters usually fall under the heading of 'presence', or of 'showing the flag'.

Traditionally, such efforts to 'show the flag' have represented one measure of naval powers' capability to sustain forces 'out of area'. And, even in the absence of actual or threatened combat, data in these areas do convey something about deterrence, latent coercive power and regional influence. In a way they may be said to measure levels of confidence, status, or even boldness, particularly as such deployments may become routinized over time.

Data of this sort are not easily come by. Almost ironically, there is no general, comprehensive source for US or other Western navies' port calls or ship-days in various oceans. On the other hand, at least for the period up to 1980, such data for the Soviet Navy have been compiled by Bruce Watson and by a team at the US Center for Naval Analyses.[115] The subject is, therefore, merely touched upon here, using the data for the Soviet Navy, which will at least illustrate what is involved.

Both of the above sources show a growing Soviet maritime presence from the 1960s to the 1980s, in all three major oceans and the Mediterranean. This was, of course, the period of the major Soviet naval buildup under Admiral Gorschkov's aegis—the data for 'presence' largely mirror those regarding access to facilities.

Watson provides data for 'out of area' ship-days by geographical area from 1956 to 1980, beginning near the time of the Suez war and shortly after the Soviet arms deals with Egypt and Syria which kicked off the major burst of Soviet expansion in the Third World. (See table 7.)[116]

Table 7. Soviet out-of-area ship-days—distribution by geographical area, 1956–80[a]

Year	Mediterranean Sea	Atlantic Ocean	Indian Ocean	Pacific Ocean	Caribbean Sea	Total
1956	100	500	0	200	0	800
1957	600	1 500	0	200	0	2 300
1958	1 000	1 300	0	900	0	3 200
1959	4 100	2 100	0	900	0	7 100
1960	5 600	1 600	200	400	0	7 800
1961	2 300	2 200	0	700	0	5 200
1962	800	4 300	100	1 400	0	6 600
1963	600	3 600	100	1 800	0	6 100
1964	1 800	5 300	0	2 000	0	9 100
1965	3 700	5 400	0	2 500	0	11 600
1966	5 400	5 500	0	2 800	0	13 700
1967	8 800	5 800	200	3 600	0	18 400
1968	11 700	5 900	1 200	4 200	0	23 000
1969	15 400	9 600	4 100	5 900	300	35 300
1970	17 400	13 600	4 900	7 100	700	43 700
1971	18 700	14 800	4 000	6 200	700	44 400
1972	17 700	14 500	8 900	5 900	1 900	48 900
1973	20 600	13 000	8 900	6 300	1 400	50 200
1974	20 200	13 900	10 500	7 400	1 200	53 200
1975	20 000	13 200	7 100	6 800	1 100	48 200
1976	18 600	14 000	7 300	6 500	1 000	47 400
1977	16 300	15 800	6 700	7 500	1 200	47 500
1978	16 600	16 100	8 500	6 900	1 300	49 400
1979	16 600	16 900	7 600	10 400	1 100	52 600
1980	16 600	16 900	11 800	11 800	700	57 800

[a] Data for the years prior to 1969 have been extrapolated from approximate information and are not considered as valid as those for the years 1969–80. Ship-days in the Indian Ocean prior to 1967 reflect ship transits through the ocean and are not ships deployed specifically for Indian Ocean operations.

Source: Watson, B. W., *Red Navy at Sea: Soviet Naval Operations on the High Seas, 1956–80* (Westview: Boulder, Colo., 1982), table 2, p. 183.

Several points may be imputed, cautiously, from these data. First, although there was an enormous expansion of the Soviet global naval presence over the 25-odd years surveyed, most of that expansion came in the period before 1973. After that year, there was a levelling off and the Soviet presence in the Mediterranean actually declined somewhat, a result no doubt of the severing of security ties with Egypt. Not surprisingly, the one area with some post-1973 expansion has been the Pacific Ocean, related undoubtedly to the growing Soviet presence in Viet Nam as well as to the growth of the Soviet Pacific Fleet.

Noteworthy, too, is the relatively even division of presence in the four major regions represented: the Mediterranean Sea and the Atlantic, Pacific and Indian oceans.

Watson also presents extensive data on Soviet port visits, by regions and by individual nations and their ports. Some of these data are aggregated in table 8, utilizing the top 10 countries—as measured by total ship-days—in each of the relevant regions. Any number of salient, albeit in some cases speculative, points may be imputed from this information, which in Watson's work is supplemented by data for individual ports and by appended explanations of what, centrally, was at issue in each case.

Table 8. Cumulative totals of Soviet naval port visits, 1953–80

Atlantic Ocean Country/ total ship-days		Mediterranean Sea Country/ total ship-days		Indian Ocean Country/ total ship-days		Pacific Ocean Country/ total ship-days	
Guinea	8 488	Egypt	38 966	Somalia	6 199	Singapore	5 078
Cuba	7 781	Syria	13 739	Ethiopia	4 812	Viet Nam	2 866
Angola	3 394	Albania	11 283	S. Yemen	4 625	Japan	330
Canary Is	1 011	Yugoslavia	8 062	Bangladesh	3 920	Canada	100
Morocco	666	Algeria	2 252	Egypt[a]	1 599	N. Korea	82
Sweden	540	Tunisia	1 695	Iraq	1 386	Fiji Is	55
Benin	462	Greece	742	Mauritius	965	Peru	48
Senegal	446	Italy	603	Sri Lanka	548	Mexico	42
Canada	317	Gibraltar	425	India	374	Kampuchea	34
Uruguay	300	Spain	171	Mozambique	261	Ecuador	29

[a] Red Sea Coast.

Source: Watson, B. W., *Red Navy at Sea: Soviet Naval Operations on the High Seas* (Westview: Boulder, Colo., 1982), tables in appendix.

Clearly, there are not many surprises in the biggest cases. The Soviet presence, measured in this manner, has largely been concentrated where it has had its most extensive basing access underpinned by major security assistance relationships: Cuba, Guinea, Angola, Syria, Viet Nam, South Yemen, Ethiopia, and (earlier) Somalia and Egypt. The seemingly outsized numbers for Albania reflect the Soviet use there of submarine bases from 1958 to 1961.[117] There are, however, a few surprises. Singapore did extensive overhaul and yard work on Soviet ships at least up until 1980, when further access was denied in the wake of the Afghanistan invasion.[118] Yards at Chiba and Yokahama in Japan have carried out extensive overhaul work on Soviet auxiliary ships. And there has been the surprising level of Soviet access to Las Palmas in Spain's Canary Islands since 1969, used by auxiliary ships to support naval operations in Guinea and elsewhere in the Atlantic.[119] The inclusion of Morocco, Sweden, Senegal, Canada, Tunisia, Greece, Italy, Gibraltar, Fiji, Mexico and Ecuador in these lists is interesting and gives rise to various political, if not merely commercial, interpretations. Indeed, Watson's longer lists include a plethora of NATO nations and others closely aligned with the United States. But regarding these nations, nothing much more than traditional courtesy visits among nations not at war may be inferred.

Overall, the combination of data for ship-days and port calls would appear to portray a significant and expanding Soviet global naval presence, one now made routine at a fairly high level. Though difficult to gauge and interpret, these facts do seem to underscore the extent to which the Soviet Navy had by 1980 leap-frogged the old Eurasian containment ring. But more recently, since the 1980 compilation of Watson's data, some analysts have produced newer and altered analyses.

In a recent contribution by Francis Fukuyama of the RAND Corporation entitled, indicatively, *Soviet Military Power in the Middle East: or, Whatever Became of Power Projection?*, the thesis is cogently propounded that the USSR had by 1985 curtailed its apparent previous emphasis on building a blue-water navy and associated basing structure, so as to pursue ever-increased interventionism in the Third World, a thesis long accepted as unarguable in the West.[120] In part, this shift is attributed to internal Soviet politics involving inter-service rivalries and personality clashes; specifically, the demise of Admiral Gorschkov and Marshall Grechko, the two men deemed most responsible in the 1970s for the Soviet push towards global power projection capability. The evidence is compelling: more modest overseas intervention activities including no new ventures, lagging levels of economic assistance, defections of states like Mozambique from the Soviet camp, and most of all the de-emphasis of the navy, as reflected both by shipbuilding programmes and deployment patterns. In the absence of comprehensive data equivalent to Watson's, the point is nevertheless made that Soviet ship-days in major oceans and seas, and port calls, have been curtailed.

Fukuyama does actually provide another reason for these trends—beyond the obvious possibility of Soviet disillusionment with the record of its Third World engagements and the performance of some of the Marxist clients it has supported, including Viet Nam, Ethiopia, South Yemen, Cuba and Angola, which collectively had become a drain on the Soviet economy.[121] That reason has to do with technological change—specifically, longer-range SLBMs on SSBNs (US Ohio-class and Soviet Typhoon-class)—which has allowed both superpowers to deploy these submarines closer to home and/or Arctic waters. According to Fukuyama, the primary reason for the earlier expansion of Soviet fleet deployments in the Mediterranean and, to a lesser degree, the Indian Ocean was ASW and protection of countering attack submarines. Now that the Soviet Navy no longer has to track Polaris submarines in these two areas, its emphasis has shifted to the protection of SSBNs in the bastions of the Norwegian and Barents Seas and the Sea of Okhotsk. Naval deployments and basing requirements are deemed to have changed accordingly.

Fukuyama does note that although Soviet naval expansionism does appear to have levelled off and then declined, the USSR has retained a strong interest in protecting existing points of influence and access—in Viet Nam, South Yemen,

Ethiopia, Angola, Cuba, Syria and other countries. This raises interesting questions about Soviet perceptions regarding a minimal level of naval access required for presence, coercive diplomacy, intervention scenarios requiring power projection, deterrence of US activities, and so on. It also raises questions about a possible minimal-sized system of access required to perform various global technical functions—even as supplemented by ships and satellites—that is, communications, SIGINT, satellite tracking, and so on. The juxtaposition of these (evolving) requirements to those of altered Soviet naval requirements is not altogether clear.

VI. Coercive diplomacy

Though it is not really a form of FMP as such, it is important to note that various forms of FMP provide the basis for coercive diplomacy, otherwise referred to—as reflected in the most well-known work on the subject—as 'politics without force'. This subject has been comprehensively canvassed in the works of Barry Blechman and Stephen Kaplan, who have produced two volumes—one for the USA and the other for the USSR—in an attempt to conceptualize, measure and assess this difficult subject.[122] Needless to say, in line with the vivid meaning attached to 'gunboat diplomacy', naval forces have played a large role in coercive diplomacy, even if not as routinized or formalized as in the days when, for instance, the USA had 'station fleets' routinely patrolling the Caribbean as a latently coercive force.

Thus, according to Blechman and Kaplan:

Throughout the postwar period the United States has turned most often to its Navy when it desired to employ components of the armed forces in support of political objectives. Naval units participated in 177 of the 215 incidents, or more than four out of every five . . .

This reliance on naval forces has been the case in all parts of the world throughout the postwar period. It has been sensitive neither to Soviet or Chinese participation in the incidents nor to the political context which led to the U.S. use of force. Navy participation ranged from a 'low' of 77 percent of the incidents in Sub-Saharan Africa and South Asia to a 'high' of 85 percent of the incidents in East Asia. Navy participation in other regions fell within this relatively narrow range. Although Navy participation sometimes varied sharply from one year to the next, it has been consistently high over time. Indeed, in only five years (1949, 1953, 1955, 1960, and 1966) did the Navy participate in less than 70 percent of all incidents. For nine of the years the Navy was involved in every political use of the armed forces. Since 1955 the Navy has been involved, on the average, in more than nine out of every ten incidents . . .

In short, the Navy clearly has been the foremost instrument for the United States' political uses of the armed forces: at all times, in all places, and regardless of the specifics of the situation. The reasons for this dominance are not difficult to discern. First, ships are easier to move about than are Army or land-based aircraft units, and can be moved at less incremental cost and more rapidly than can any land-based unit of comparable size. Because a larger portion of the Navy's support is organic to the combat unit (that

is, a ship as compared to a battalion or a squadron), the establishment of communications and logistics flows can be accomplished with less difficulty.

Second, warships on the scene of a disturbance are less disruptive psychologically
than are land-based forces and thus are likely to be less offensive diplomatically; if
desirable, naval forces can remain nearby but out of sight.[123]

These authors provide numerous illustrations of the utility of foreign bases
in connection with coercive diplomacy. US support for Thailand in the early
1960s was enabled by use of nearby bases in the Far East, for instance, in the
Philippines and Okinawa. US naval threats against India in the 1971 Indo-
Pakistani war were mounted by naval forces based at Subic Bay and in Viet
Nam, but assembled off Singapore.[124] Threats against Syria in 1970 when the
latter menaced Jordan were underpinned by naval forces with access to various
ports around the Mediterranean. Kenya and North Yemen were supported in
crises by naval forces moved from the Far East.

The USSR has also made use of naval facilities in connection with coercive
diplomacy. Hence, according to Kaplan:

The navy was the pre-eminent instrument of Soviet coercive military diplomacy when
the Kremlin looked beyond nations contiguous to the USSR and Central Europe. Naval
vessels participated in two-thirds of these incidents. The navy was also the principal tool
of Soviet cooperative military diplomacy. Communist and third world nations with
which the Kremlin was attempting to improve relations were the targets on a number
of occasions, but the most frequent focus of cooperative actions—usually a port call by
one to three warships—were Western European nations when Moscow sought to improve relations at important crossroads or to otherwise cultivate special relationships.
Discernible in each of these instances was a Soviet interest in weakening NATO unity
or relations between a neutral nation and NATO.

Surface combatants provided the usual expression of coercive naval diplomacy.
Cruisers, frigates, destroyers, or other escorts were involved in four-fifths of these
incidents. The typical operation took one of two forms: a visit or offshore presence by
one or two such vessels, often accompanied by a submarine, minesweeper, amphibious
craft, oiler, or other type of ship in a situation where violence was not immediately
present; or an offshore presence or naval demonstration by many surface combatants
supported by other vessels. No coercive operations involving more than three surface
warships took place before 1967.[125]

In particular, Kaplan's work points to the use of Soviet naval forces in
connection with several crises in West Africa, specifically, in support of Guinea
and Sierra Leone. More recently, Soviet naval forces based in South Yemen
were crucial to coercive activities on behalf of a radical new government in the
Seychelles.

But apropos some of the above comments regarding an alleged declined
Soviet interest in maritime power projection capability, it is also claimed by
some that the Soviet inclination to use coercive diplomacy may recently have
waned. Thus according to D. K. Hall:

During the Lebanon War when the United States had concentrated four aircraft carriers within striking distance of the Soviet Union, Moscow failed to augment the Fifth Eskadra to anything approaching the level of October 1973. The Soviets had surged their fleet during crises in 1967, 1970, 1971, and 1973; the contrast to Lebanon is striking and indicates a reduced interest in using the navy as an instrument of crisis diplomacy.[126]

VII. Summary

Overall, the picture presented is that of what remains a predominantly two-power or bipolar competition for overseas naval access, mirroring the overall facts of naval power. What earlier, however, was an overwhelming US advantage in access has somewhat dissipated, though the *rate* of change as concerns a shifting balance of assets has appeared to level off since about the mid-1970s.

What once was a huge and redundant US network of naval bases rimming the Eurasian 'heartland' has now been reduced to a far more taut and precarious structure, but one still easily adequate to the projection of sea power in virtually all areas of the globe (that situation could substantially change if Subic Bay were removed from the list of US facilities, or if access to several nations around the Mediterranean—Greece, Turkey, Egypt, Spain, Italy—were simultaneously to be jeopardized in response to changing political conditions).

The Soviet Union, meanwhile, has now acquired access to important naval facilities in all of the major ocean areas, hinged principally on Cuba, Ángola, Ethiopia, South Yemen and Viet Nam. At a minimum, that represents an overcoming of the old US-enforced containment rim even if, in a broader sense, US naval superiority—measured by overall ship-days, presumed power projection capabilities, etc.—appears substantially intact.

The thesis of the indivisibility of global sea power has long been an established canon of naval doctrine, as it has been propounded by Mahan and others. That doctrinal assumption, perhaps largely inferred from the history of British naval dominance, pertained largely to the outcome of naval warfare at the outset of major wars, as those outcomes then further translated into dominance measured by global basing networks. (This pattern, evidenced during the Napoleonic Wars, was also illustrated when Holland superseded Portugal as a naval power.)

It remains to be seen whether in the current era, the traditional linkage between sea-power dominance and basing dominance will be maintained. With major wars rendered more unlikely by the spectre of nuclear destruction, the current situation of bipolar competition for bases, without actual warfare, seems likely to continue. That in turn directs attention, aside from matters of prestige and the symbols of power, to coercive diplomacy, shows of force, and support for clients in Third World conflicts. Naval bases are crucial to such purposes; they in turn often determine the progress of the competition for access.

Notes and references

[1] This is discussed in the collection of essays written by Rosinski, H. and edited by Simpson, B. M., III, *The Development of Naval Thought* (Naval War College Press: Newport, R.I., 1977), pp. 23–25.

[2] See Cohen, S., *Geography and Politics in a World Divided* (Random House: New York, 1963); Gray, C., *The Geopolitics of the Nuclear Era* (Crane Russak: New York, 1977); Weigert, H., Stefansson, V. and Harrison, R. (eds), *New Compass of the World* (Macmillan: New York, 1949).

[3] This is noted in Weigert, H., *Generals and Geographers* (Oxford University: London, 1942), p. 136.

[4] See Wainstein, L., 'The Dreadnought Gap', eds Art, R. J. and Waltz, K., *The Use of Force* (Little, Brown: Boston, Mass., 1971), pp. 153-69; and Woodward, E. L., *Great Britain and the German Navy* (Oxford University: London, 1935).

[5] Regarding the by now fairly extensive analytical literature on the new US maritime strategy, see, among others, Watkins, Admiral J. D. (ed.), *The Maritime Strategy* (US Naval Institute: Annapolis, Md., 1986); Kaufmann, W. W., *A Thoroughly Efficient Navy* (The Brookings Institution: Washington, DC, 1987), especially chapter 2; Mearsheimer, J. J., 'A strategic misstep', *International Security*, vol. 2, no. 2. (Fall 1986), pp. 3-55; and Gray, C., 'Maritime strategy', *Proceedings of the U.S. Naval Institute*, Feb. 1986, pp. 34-42.

[6] Brodie, B., *Sea Power in the Machine Age* (Princeton University Press: Princeton, N.J., 1941), p. 437.

[7] Boxer, C. R., *The Portuguese Seaborne Empire, 1415-1825* (Knopf: New York, 1969); and Boxer, C. R., *The Dutch Seaborne Empire: 1600-1800* (Knopf: New York, 1965).

[8] See, among others, Cole, D. H., *Imperial Military Geography*, 12th edn (Sifton Praed: London, 1956); and Kennedy, P. M., *The Rise and Fall of British Naval Mastery* (Scribner: New York, 1976).

[9] Earlier, the decline of the US basing system was detailed in Cottrell, A. and Moorer, T. H., 'U.S. overseas bases: Problems of projecting American military power abroad' (Georgetown CSIS: Washington, DC, 1977), paper no. 47.

[10] See 'Rust to riches: The navy is back', *U.S. News and World Report*, 4 Aug. 1986, pp. 28-33; and 'Maritime superiority goal keyed to 600-ship fleet', *Aviation Week & Space Technology*, 31 Aug. 1981, pp. 38-63.

[11] The best recent summary is in US Department of Defense, *Soviet Military Power 1987*, 6th edn (US Government Printing Office: Washington, DC, 1987), chapter 7, under 'Political-military and regional policies'. An earlier but more detailed coverage is in *Soviet Military Power: 1985*, 4th edn, chapter 7 under 'Global ambitions'.

[12] See Weigert, H., *et al.*, *Principles of Political Geography* (Appleton-Century-Crofts: New York, 1957), especially chapter 8 under 'The impact of location on strategy and power politics'. See also Spykman, N., *The Geography of the Peace* (Harcourt, Brace: New York, 1944), especially chapter 7. For a different view (imputed to the USSR) on chokepoints, see Hanks, R. J., *The Unnoticed Challenge: Soviet Maritime Strategy and the Global Choke Points* (Institute for Foreign Policy Analysis: Cambridge, Mass.), Special Report, Aug. 1980.

[13] *Soviet Military Power 1985* (note 11).

[14] See, among numerous sources, McNaugher, T. L., *Arms and Oil: U.S. Military Strategy and the Persian Gulf* (Brookings Institution: Washington, DC, 1985); Cordesman, A., *The Gulf and the Search for Strategic Stability* (Westview Press: Boulder, Colo., 1984).

[15] Kemp, G., 'The new strategic map', *Survival*, vol. 19, no. 2 (Mar./Apr. 1977), pp. 50-59.

[16] See Burrows, W., *Deep Black* (Random House: New York, 1986), pp. 269-72; Richelson, J., *Sword and Shield* (Ballinger: Cambridge, Mass., 1986), pp. 103-105; and 'Soviets launch ocean surveillance satellite', *Aviation Week & Space Technology*, 7 June 1982, p. 16; 'Soviet COSMOS spacecraft providing land, sea imagery', *Aviation Week & Space Technology*, 12 Nov. 1984, p. 212.

[17] Daniel, D. C. F., 'The Soviet navy and tactical nuclear war at sea', *Survival*, vol. 29, no. 4 (July/Aug. 1987), pp. 318-35; MccGwire, M., *Soviet Military Objectives* (Brookings Institution: Washington, DC, 1987); Ball, D., 'Nuclear war at sea', eds S. Miller and S. Van Evera, *National Strategy and National Security* (Princeton University Press: Princeton, N.J., 1988), pp. 303-31; and Posen, B., 'Inadvertent nuclear war? Escalation and NATO's northern flank', in Miller and Van Evera, pp. 332-58.

[18] 'In battle of wits, submarines evade advanced efforts at detection', *New York Times*, 1 Apr. 1986, p. C1; 'Navy warns of crisis in anti-submarine warfare', *New York Times*, 19 Mar. 1987, p. A19; 'Can submarines be hidden?', *New York Times*, 11 Dec. 1984, p. C1; 'Defense Department says Soviet subs may have hit a U.S. sonar device', *New York Times*, 5 Nov. 1983, p. 10; and 'Quiet Soviet subs can evade U.S. defenses', *Defense Week*, vol. 5, no. 33 (16 July 1984), p. 17; and Tierney, J., 'The invisible force', *Science 83*, vol. 4, no. 9 (1983), pp. 68-78.

[19] Mearsheimer (note 5).

[20] Gray (note 5).

[21] Epstein, J. M., 'Horizontal escalation: Sour notes of a recurrent theme' in Miller and Van Evera (note 17), pp. 102–14.

[22] Blechman, B. and Weinland, R., 'Why coaling stations are necessary in the nuclear age', *International Security*, no. 2 (1977), pp. 88–99.

[23] These various domains are covered, on the Soviet side at least, in Dismukes, B. and McConnell, J. (eds), *Soviet Naval Diplomacy* (Pergamon: New York, 1979).

[24] Blechman and Weinland (note 22).

[25] 'Navy plans to pare time aircraft carriers are deployed overseas', *New York Times*, 30 Apr. 1985, p. A7.

[26] Regarding Turkey, see Evin, A., 'Anti-Americanism in Turkey', eds A. Z. Rubinstein and D. E. Smith, *Anti-Americanism in the Third World* (Praeger: New York, 1985), pp. 121–36; and 'U.S. reports harassment in Turkey', *International Herald Tribune*, 9 Aug. 1975. Regarding demonstrations in Argentina after the Falklands War—which resulted in blocking of the replenishment of US ships at Puerto Madryn, see 'Argentina, U.S. to conduct first naval exercises since '82', *Washington Times*, 9 Apr. 1986, p. 9A. See also 'U.S. worries about security of 2 big bases in Philippines', *New York Times*, 28 Oct. 1985, p. A1.

[27] See Remnek, R., 'The politics of Soviet access to naval support facilities in the Mediterranean', in Dismukes and McConnell (note 23), p. 373, who notes Soviet refusal to allow President Sadat access to the naval base at Mersa Matruh. See also Rubinstein, A. Z., *Red Star on the Nile* (Princeton University Press: Princeton, N.J., 1977), especially chapters 6 and 9; Sella, A., *Soviet Political and Military Conduct in the Middle East* (St. Martin's: New York, 1981), pp. 76–77; 'U.S. presence in Egypt: Uneasiness comes easy', *International Herald Tribune*, 31 July 1980.

[28] Petersen, C. C., 'Trends in Soviet naval operations', in Dismukes and McConnell (note 23), p. 71; Remnek, R., 'Soviet policy in the Horn of Africa: The decision to intervene', Center for Naval Analyses, Alexandria, Va., Professional Paper 270, Jan. 1980; and 'Somalia–USSR: Major naval complex nearly ready', *Defense and Foreign Affairs Daily*, vol. 6, no. 5 (7 Jan. 1977), p. 1.

[29] On protracted war, generally, see Gray, C. S., 'Global protracted war: Conduct and termination', National Institute for Public Policy, Fairfax, Va., Sept. 1985.

[30] 'Aid to Russia: Greek refit deal', *Daily Telegraph*, 8 Sept. 1979; 'Greece will stop servicing ships from Soviet fleet', *New York Times*, 9 Apr. 1981, p. A6; and 'Greece will stop fixing Soviet ships', *New York Times*, 24 Feb. 1981, p. A2; and 'Singapore: New contract for Soviet ship repair', *Defense and Foreign Affairs Daily*, 3 Mar. 1977, p. 2.

[31] See Blechman and Weinland (note 22), p. 90, who also point to the use of overseas land facilities for carrier on-board delivery (COD) aircraft for transshipping people and cargo to fleets.

[32] See Vernoski, K., 'Soviet naval aircraft', eds B. Watson and S. Watson, *The Soviet Navy: Strengths and Liabilities* (Westview Press: Boulder, Colo., 1986), chapter 9; and *Soviet Military Power: 1985* (note 11), pp. 101–102, 114.

[33] Blechman and Weinland (note 22); and Feeney, W. R., 'The Pacific basing system and U.S. security', eds W. T. Tow and W. R. Feeney, *U.S. Foreign Policy and Asian-Pacific Security: A Transregional Approach* (Westview Press: Boulder, Colo., 1982), pp. 163–225.

[34] Petersen (note 28), chapter 2, especially p. 66; and Harkavy, R., *Great Power Competition for Overseas Bases* (Pergamon Press: New York, 1982), pp. 189–95.

[35] Cooley, J. K., 'Soviet ships prowl for new havens', *Christian Science Monitor*, 7 Apr. 1976, pp. 18–19.

[36] Davidchik, M. D. and Mahoney, R. B., 'Soviet civil fleets and the Third World', in Dismukes and McConnell (note 23), appendix A, pp. 317–35; Stuart, G. and Taylor, L., 'The Soviet naval auxiliary force', in Watson and Watson (note 32), chapter 8; Rees, D., 'Soviet sea power: The covert support fleet', *Conflict Studies*, no. 84 (June 1977), p. 5; and *Soviet Military Power 1985* (note 11), pp. 105–106.

[37] Smalley, C., 'The Soviet merchant fleet's role in USSR global strategy', *Conflict*, vol. 6, no. 3 (1985), pp. 229–38. Regarding Papua New Guinea see 'South Pacific island calls for Moscow talks', *International Herald Tribune*, 30–31 Aug. 1986, p. 2.

[38] Cable, J., 'As the Soviet Union casts its net wide', *Daily Telegraph*, 20 June 1983.

[39] 'Fishing yields Soviet a South Pacific toehold', *New York Times*, 17 May 1987, p. A22; 'Pacific isle anti-communists chase off Soviet cruise ship', *New York Times*, 3 Feb. 1987, p. A3; 'South Pacific island calls for Moscow talks', *International Herald Tribune*, 30–31 Aug. 1986, p. 2; Warner, D., 'South Pacific: America may have missed the boat', *International Herald Tribune*, 1 Aug. 1986, p. 4; 'Soviet seeks a larger role in Southeast Asia', *New York Times*, 8 Apr. 1986, p. A17; 'Vanuatu may open port to Soviet Pacific trawlers', *International Herald Tribune*, 31 July 1986, p. 6.

[40] One excellent analysis is Feeney (note 33).

[41] Feeney (note 33); and 'Environments for U.S. naval strategy in the Pacific–Indian Ocean area, 1985–1995', Proceedings of a Conference Coordinated for the Center for Advanced Research, US Naval War College, by the Institute for Foreign Policy Analysis (Cambridge, Mass., 1977); and Feeney (note 33), pp. 209–13.

[42] Feeney (note 33), pp. 196, 198.

[43] Pittman, H. T., 'Geopolitics and foreign policy in Argentina, Brazil, and Chile', eds E. G. Ferris and J. K. Lincoln, Latin American Foreign Policies: Global and Regional Dimensions (Westview Press: Boulder, Colo., 1981); and Hayes, M. D., Latin America and the U.S. National Interest (Westview Press: Boulder, Colo., 1984).

[44] 'Soviet seeks a larger role in Southeast Asia', New York Times, 8 Apr. 1986, p. 4.

[45] The U.S. National Archives, Military Intelligence Division (MID) file number 2667–14. This discusses British Conservative Party resistance to Labour Party proposals for closing British bases in the Western Hemisphere amid the euphoria of the Kellogg-Briand Pact. As a goodwill gesture to the USA, Britain considered dismantling the naval base at Kingston, Jamaica.

[46] Along with the annual World Port Index, 10th edn (US Defense Mapping Agency: Washington, DC, 1986), published by the Defense Mapping Agency, see 'Environments for U.S. naval strategy in the Pacific–Indian Ocean Area, 1985–1995' (note 41). The matter of labour supply and costs is noted on p. 266 amid a discussion of Guam as a possible US fall-back position.

[47] See 'New Zealand rebuff: A baffling furor', New York Times, 7 Feb. 1986, p. A10; 'New Zealand rejects visit by U.S. ship, citing anti-nuclear policy', New York Times, 5 Feb. 1985, p. A13; 'New Zealand's Premier-elect will try to ban nuclear ships', New York Times, 16 July 1984; 'U.S. formally suspends defense of New Zealand', International Herald Tribune, 13 Aug. 1986, p. 1; and more generally, McMillan, S., Neither Confirm nor Deny: The Nuclear Ships Dispute Between New Zealand and the United States (Greenwood Press: New York, 1987).

[48] 'China said to bar visits by A-weapon ships', Washington Post, 29 Mar. 1986; and 'Vessey starts talks', New York Times, 13 Jan. 1985, p. 12.

[49] International Institute for Strategic Studies, The Military Balance: 1986–1987 (IISS: London, 1986), p. 21. Data in the subsequent two paragraphs are drawn from the same source, pp. 22–24.

[50] IISS (note 49), pp. 28–29.

[51] Dunn, K. A. and Staudenmaier, W. O., Strategic Implications of the Continental-Maritime Debate, The Center for Strategic and International Studies, The Washington Papers 107 (Praeger: New York, 1984), p. 9; and 'Reagan selling naval budget as heart of military mission', New York Times, 11 Apr. 1982, p. A24.

[52] US transiting of nuclear-powered carriers through the Suez Canal with Egyptian permission and the policy of keeping two carriers in the Mediterranean indefinitely after the Libyan crisis of 1986 are noted in 'Ships to stay in the Mediterranean', Centre Daily Times, 12 June 1986, p. A2.

[53] This is discussed, in the context of by then increasing constraints on the US naval budget, in 'Navy Secretary visits ships to describe cutbacks', New York Times, 13 Nov. 1985, p. A23, wherein it is reported that there was a new policy whereby each ship was to be in its home port 50 per cent of the time.

[54] 'Is "Yankee go home" the writing on the Philippine wall?', The Economist, 9 Apr. 1988, p. 37.

[55] See 'U.S. ships leave Singapore', Daily Telegraph, 30 Jan. 1980.

[56] But continued use after Washington's normalization of relations with Peking is noted in 'U.S., Taiwan remain close despite split', International Herald Tribune, 18 May 1979. Generally, regarding fall-back positions should Subic Bay be lost, see Gregor, A. J. and Aganon, V., The Philippines Bases: U.S. Security at Risk (Ethics and Public Policy Center: Washington, DC, 1987), especially chapter 5 under 'Alternative basing arrangements'.

[57] 'Gitmo: 7,500 Americans on a hostile shore', New York Times, 27 Feb. 1971.

[58] Plans for relocation or enlargement of the major naval headquarters at Naples are discussed in 'Navy fights for space in Italy', Centre Daily Times, 9 Mar. 1987, p. A5.

[59] The strategic importance of Souda Bay is noted in Sulzberger, C. L., 'Some strategic islands and the U.S. Sixth Fleet', International Herald Tribune, 3 Aug. 1974; and 'U.S. forces keep low profile in Greek areas', International Herald Tribune, 20 Feb. 1976. Earlier, for three years up to 1975, the USN had homeported a squadron of six destroyers at Elefsis in Greece; this ended with the change of government in Athens. See 'Strong fleet without friends', Time, 12 May 1975, pp. 27–28; and 'Greece and America conclude new bases agreement which cuts down privileges of U.S. troops', The Times, 14 Feb. 1976.

[60] 'Egypt portrays itself as major U.S. asset', New York Times, 16 Jan. 1985, p. A4. The contingent use of Haifa was previewed in 'Israel port seen for U.S. fleet', International Herald Tribune, 20 Aug. 1974. The broader problem of US access to Israel in the context of the Carter Doctrine and the

formation of the Rapid Deployment Force is discussed in Kupchan, C., *The Persian Gulf and the West* (Allen and Unwin: Boston, Mass., 1987), pp. 134–37, 152–55.

[61] See, among numerous sources, 'Digging in at Diego Garcia', *Time*, 14 July 1980, p. 29; 'Diego Garcia', *New Republic*, 9 Mar. 1974; 'U.S. naval base in Indian Ocean nearing completion', *Los Angeles Times*, 3 Oct. 1979, part VI, p. 7; and 'U.S. studying $1 billion expansion of Indian Ocean base', *New York Times*, 6 Apr. 1980, p. 16.

[62] 'In Mideast turmoil, Kenya stands up to be counted', *U.S. News and World Report*, 31 Mar. 1980, p. 51; 'U.S. can use Kenya's ports to get forces to Persian Gulf, *Washington Post*, 22 Feb. 1980, p. 23; 'U.S. would link aid to access to bases', *Washington Post*, 28 Feb. 1980, p. 24; 'U.S., Kenya in accord on allowing greater use of port facilities', *Washington Star*, 28 June 1980, p. 12; 'Kenya allows U.S. facilities at Mombasa', *Daily Telegraph*, 25 Feb. 1980. Regarding Muscat, see 'U.S. is seeking port expansion in Indian Ocean', *Washington Star*, 19 Dec. 1979, p. 1; and 'Oman emerges as firm U.S. ally in Gulf', *New York Times*, 26 Mar. 1985; and 'The Iran-Iraq War', *Christian Science Monitor*, 12 Feb. 1985, p. 21. Regarding Bahrain, see 'U.S. Navy keeps wraps on its only Persian Gulf port', *Baltimore Sun*, 28 Nov. 1979, p. 2; 'Iran crisis, U.S. in Gulf area', *New York Times*, 8 Feb. 1979, p. 3; 'Bahrain shift seen', *International Herald Tribune*, 7 Oct. 1974; and Kupchan (note 60), pp. 55–56, 72. Kupchan (note 60), pp. 129–30, also discusses US access to Oman, Somalia and Kenya—and Saudi Arabia—in the context of the Carter Doctrine. Regarding Djibouti, where US ships apparently can take on fuel and provisions but not disgorge sailors, see 'Djibouti off limits to U.S.', *Washington Post*, 10 June 1980, p. 17. Regarding Mauritius, see 'U.S. influence over strategic island states in Indian Ocean dwindling', *Washington Star*, 27 Apr. 1980, p. 5. There have also been reports of resumed US access to Seychelles ports to match Soviet access—see 'Navy docking agreement near in Seychelles', *The Times*, 27 July 1983.

But the USA has denied seeking expanded access to the Makran coast of Pakistan, Trincomalee in Sri Lanka and Chittagong or St. Martin's Island in Bangladesh. See 'State Department official says U.S. seeks no bases in South Asia', *New York Times*, 4 Mar. 1984, p. 3. Further on renewed access to Pakistani ports, see 'A new round of American installations in Pakistan', *Asian Defense Journal*, May 1982, pp. 29–35, specifically regarding the basing potential of Gwadar and Jiwani on the Arabian Sea coast.

[63] 'Why did this happen?', *Time*, 1 June 1987, pp. 17–23; 'U.S. readies a battleship for Gulf', *International Herald Tribune*, 25 June 1987, p. 2.

[64] 'Attack on the Stark: Answers to key questions are beginning to emerge', *New York Times*, 21 May 1987, p. A18.

[65] By August 1987, the US naval presence in the Persian Gulf had been expanded to some 30 vessels—the 9-ship Middle East Force (based at Bahrain), the *USS Guadalcanal*, *USS Raleigh* with 3 minesweepers in the Gulf, *USS Constellation*, plus 6-ship battle group in the Arabian Sea. See *Newsweek*, 24 Aug. 1987, p. 23, under 'The mines of August'.

[66] '3 nuclear storage depots to close as B-52 missions change', *New York Times*, 16 May 1988, p. A18 which notes that ships with nuclear weapons on board may stop off in Japan and the Philippines. But by 1988 there were signs that nuclear access in the Philippines might be cancelled— 'Antinuclear move in the Philippines', *New York Times*, 7 June 1988, p. A6.

[67] See 'U.S. navy hunting for seals', *USA Today*, 27 Feb. 1987, p. 3A.

[68] Mackinder, H., *Democratic Ideals and Reality* (Norton: New York, 1962).

[69] See Newbold, J. T. W., *The War Trust Exposed* (Blackfriars: London, 1916), p. 28, which describes the British Navy in a near-panic in 1884, worried about a 'torpedo boat gap', after Russia had acquired 112 such vessels while Britain had none.

[70] Remnek, R., 'The politics of Soviet access to naval support facilities in the Mediterranean', in Dismukes and McConnell (note 23), p. 359.

[71] This is perhaps best gauged by a review of Watson, B., *Red Navy at Sea: Soviet Naval Operations on the High Seas, 1956–1980* (Westview Press: Boulder, Colo., 1982); and in the various recent editions of *Soviet Military Power*.

[72] IISS (note 49), p. 39.

[73] IISS (note 49), p. 40.

[74] IISS (note 49), p. 36.

[75] Stuart, G. and Taylor, L., 'The Soviet naval auxiliary force', in Watson and Watson (note 32), chapter 8.

[76] Pierce, P. L., 'Aircraft carriers and large surface combatants', in Watson and Watson (note 32), chapter 6. Regarding the future possibility of large-deck Soviet carriers, see Anderson, J., 'Soviets want to control the oceans', *Centre Daily Times*, 21 June 1984, p. A4.

[77] IISS (note 49), p. 35; and Blechman and Weinland (note 22), p. 99, which refers to fleet air defence as the 'Soviet Navy's Achilles' heel'.

[78] IISS (note 49), p. 42. See also Allen, K., 'The northern fleet and North Atlantic naval operations', in Watson and Watson (note 32), chapter 18.

[79] IISS (note 49), p. 43. See also Wyman, R. D., 'The Baltic fleet', in Watson and Watson (note 32), chapter 19.

[80] IISS (note 49), p. 44. See also Allen, K., 'The Black Sea fleet and Mediterranean naval operations', in Watson and Watson (note 32), chapter 22.

[81] IISS (note 49), p. 45. See also Thomas, G. S., 'The Pacific fleet', in Watson and Watson (note 32), chapter 23.

[82] Soviet Military Power: 1985 (note 11), chapter 7; SIPRI data; see also 'U.S. asserts a Soviet submarine has entered South Yemen port', New York Times, 6 Aug. 1979, p. A4; and 'Soviet activity found growing in Aden Region', New York Times, 10 June 1980, p. A13.

[83] Watson (note 71), appendix.

[84] The seemingly anomalous case of Soviet fishing boats allegedly conducting intelligence operations out of the Canary Islands is discussed in 'Spain charges Soviet monitoring hot spots', Washington Post, 31 Jan. 1976; and 'Spanish leader hoping for entry to NATO in '81', New York Times, 14 Apr. 1981, p. A8; and 'Canaries counting on Soviet shipping', The Times, 14 June 1983. Soviet access to Yugoslav shipyards, specifically at Tivat, is discussed in Remnek (note 70), pp. 382–83. Mauritius is discussed in 'Indian Ocean: The U.S. and the Soviet Presence', New York Times, 19 Apr. 1981, p. 3. Mozambique is discussed in 'South Africa: A bet on U.S.?', New York Times, 16 Mar. 1981, p. 1. Peru is discussed in 'Peru: More reports of a Soviet deal', Defense and Foreign Affairs Daily, Weekly Report on Strategic Latin American Affairs, vol. 3, no. 3 (20 Jan. 1977), and in Soviet Military Power 1985 (note 11), p. 123. The latter, pp. 121–23, also discusses growing Soviet naval access to Nicaragua. The possibility of a new Soviet naval base on São Tomé and Principe is raised in 'New West African base for Russian forces', Daily Telegraph, 12 Oct. 1984.

[85] 'U.S. reports Cam Ranh Bay now major Soviet naval base', International Herald Tribune, 3 Apr. 1984; 'Soviet bases in Vietnam worry U.S.', International Herald Tribune, 31 Jan. 1984; 'The Soviets test the waters', Newsweek, 20 May 1985, pp. 32–33; and 'Japan warns of a Soviet military buildup in Asia', New York Times, 15 Sep. 1984, p. 4; 'Soviet naval challenge to U.S. grows in Pacific', International Herald Tribune, 30 July 1985, p. 1; and 'Soviet fleet conducting huge exercises', International Herald Tribune, 18 Aug. 1986, p. 2.

[86] Regarding Socotra, see 'Soviets deepen military role in Red Sea Region', Washington Star, 30 Sept. 1979, p. 1. See also 'Russia is said to seek a base for its navy in Indian Ocean', International Herald Tribune, 15 June 1974, which reports Moscow's efforts towards increased access to Mauritius beyond that for fishing vessels; also 'Seychelles: New outpost for Russians?', U.S. News and World Report, 24 Mar. 1980, p. 36; and 'René denies Seychelles is a Soviet base', The Times, 1 Dec. 1984.

[87] 'Persian Gulf', Centre Daily Times, 1 June 1987, p. A-8. Earlier, before the Iraq–Iran War, the Soviet Union had naval access to Iraq's Um Quasr on the Persian Gulf. See 'Iraq to let Soviets use bases', Philadelphia Inquirer, 5 Nov. 1976, p. 3.

[88] 'Soviet ships sent to Maputo after South African raid', International Herald Tribune, 23 Feb. 1981; and generally regarding access to Mozambique ports, see also O'Ballance, E., Tracks of the Bear (Presidio Press: Novato, Calif., 1982), p. 185. The USSR has also sought access to Madagascar's deep-water port at Diego Suarez. See 'Madagascar: East, West still maneuver for influence', International Herald Tribune, 3 Aug. 1983, p. 6.

[89] 'New Soviet base', Near East Report, vol. 32, no. 5 (1 Feb. 1988); and Soviet Military Power 1985 (note 11), p. 124. Moscow has also had access to ship repair facilities in Tunisia—see 'Explosion on ship', Daily Telegraph, 12 June 1981.

[90] Remnek (note 70), pp. 382–83 (regarding Yugoslavia), and pp. 386–88 (regarding Algeria).

[91] See 'New West African base for Russian forces', Daily Telegraph, 12 Sep. 1984; Shulsky, A., 'Coercive diplomacy', in Dismukes and McConnell (note 23), pp. 130–31.

[92] Soviet Military Power 1985 (note 11), p. 123; and Hritsik, M., 'The West African naval contingent', in Watson and Watson (note 32), pp. 203–207.

[93] Anderson, J., 'Israel aiding Mengistu in Ethiopia', Washington Post, 2 Jan. 1985, p. E19; 'Soviet navy using "base" off Ethiopia', AEN, 11 Jan. 1980; 'Soviets deepen military role in Red Sea region', Washington Star, 30 Sept. 1979, p. 1; Carolla, M. A., 'The Indian Ocean squadron', in Watson and Watson (note 32); Watson and Watson (note 32), pp. 241–46; and Soviet Military Power: 1985 (note 11), p. 123.

[94] *Soviet Military Power 1985* (note 11), p. 121; and Norton, F. W., 'Caribbean naval activity', in Watson and Watson (note 32), pp. 208–13.

[95] 'Disabled Soviet sub surfaces off South Carolina', *New York Times*, 4 Nov. 1983, p. A1 reports on a Soviet submarine tender based at Cienfuegos. Regarding access for Soviet submarines to Cuban ports subsequent to the 1962 missile crisis, see Blechman, B. and Levinson, S., 'Soviet submarine visits to Cuba', eds M. MccGwire and J. McDonnell, *Soviet Naval Influence* (Praeger: New York, 1977), pp. 436–41. See also 'Soviets still use Cuba as submarine base', *Washington Star*, 16 Feb. 1978, p. 8; Abel, C. A., 'A breach in the ramparts', *U.S. Naval Institute Proceedings*, July 1980, pp. 47–50; and 'Soviet Union building sub base in Cuba', *Baltimore Sun*, 30 Mar. 1979, p. 4.

[96] *Soviet Military Power 1985* (note 11), p. 123.

[97] Petersen, C., 'Trends in Soviet naval operations', in Dismukes and McConnell (note 23), chapter 2.

[98] Note 97, p. 65.

[99] Note 97, p. 65.

[100] Note 97, p. 66.

[101] Cooley, J. K., 'Soviet ships prowl for new havens', *Christian Science Monitor*, 7 Apr. 1976, pp. 18–19.

[102] Rees, D., 'Soviet sea power: The covert support fleet', *Conflict studies*, no. 84, June 1977, p. 5; and Davidchik, M. and Mahoney, R., 'Soviet civil fleets and the Third World', in Dismukes and McConnell (note 23), p. 323. See also Ackley, R., 'The merchant fleet', in MccGwire and McDonnell (note 95), pp. 291–310.

[103] Davidchik and Mahoney (note 102), p. 323.

[104] Davidchik and Mahoney (note 102), p. 323.

[105] Davidchik and Mahoney (note 102), p. 321.

[106] 'Malagasy port faces decline as French end 90-year stay', *International Herald Tribune*, 3 June 1975. Earlier, the USA too had had some access to Diego Suarez, before the 1973 Middle East War—see 'Madagascar bars visit by 4 U.S. destroyers', *New York Times*, 27 Dec. 1973.

[107] IISS (note 49), p. 66; 'France bolstering New Caledonia Base', *New York Times*, 21 Jan. 1985, p. A3; and 'France sends forces to New Caledonia', *Washington Post*, 13 Jan. 1985, p. A1.

[108] IISS (note 49), p. 66 and SIPRI data.

[109] IISS (note 49), p. 60. Gibraltar's naval base was maintained after ship repair services were terminated—see 'Britain to shut Gibraltar naval yard and reduce "Rock's" air operations', *International Herald Tribune*, 26 Nov. 1981.

[110] 'The mines of August', *Newsweek*, 24 Aug. 1987, p. 23. For a longer and broader view, see Kupchan (note 60), chapter 8, under 'The out-of-area problem for NATO'.

[111] IISS (note 49), p. 73.

[112] 'Spain rushes to aid new regime in Equatorial Guinea', *New York Times*, 12 Sep. 1979, p. A5; and 'Equatorial Guinea warms up to Spain', *New York Times*, 26 Dec. 1979, p. A5; 'Russia to quit post in Equatorial Guinea', *International Herald Tribune*, 21 Dec. 1979; 'Russia out', *Sunday Times*, 23 Dec. 1979.

[113] This is discussed in 'Soviet influence diminishing at approaches to Red Sea', *Washington Post*, 24 Mar. 1977, p. A21.

[114] See 'China to build base in Lanka', *Hindustan Times*, 10 July 1972.

[115] Watson (note 71); and Petersen, C. C., 'Showing the flag', in Dismukes and McConnell (note 23), chapter 3. See also Tsouras, P., 'Port visits', in Watson and Watson (note 32), chapter 27.

[116] Watson (note 71), appendix, pp. 183–228.

[117] Dismukes, B. and Shulsky, A., 'Non-Third World cases of Soviet naval diplomacy', appendix C, in Dismukes and McConnell (note 23), pp. 362–64.

[118] Petersen (note 28), p. 72. 'The Soviets have also used to Keppel shipyard in Singapore quite extensively, but only for repairs on naval auxiliaries because no combatants are permitted.' See also Watson (note 71), p. 137, who states that Moscow lost its access there in 1980.

[119] See 'Spain charges Soviets monitoring hot spots', *Washington Post*, 31 Jan. 1976, which reports that 'Soviet fishing trawlers based at Spain's Canary Islands are ranging as far south as Angola for electronic monitoring of U.S.-backed forces fighting in the former Portuguese colony.' Years later, with Spain trying to gain entry to NATO, it appeared prepared to reduce such access. See 'Spanish leader hoping for entry to NATO in '81', *New York Times*, 14 Apr. 1981, p. A8, which refers to 'the strategic Canary Islands, where Soviet "fishing" vessels, laden with sophisticated radar, are known to be engaged in extensive electronic espionage'.

[120] Fukuyama, F., 'Soviet military power in the Middle East; or, Whatever became of power

projection?', eds S. Spiegel, M. Heller and J. Goldberg, *The Soviet–American Competition in the Middle East* (D. C. Heath: Lexington, Mass., 1988), pp. 159–82.

[121] Fukuyama (note 120). See also Wolfe, C., Jr., Crane, K., Yeh, K. C., Anderson, S. and Brunner, E., *The Costs and Benefits of the Soviet Empire*, R-3419-NA (RAND: Santa Monica, Calif., Aug. 1986).

[122] Blechman, B. M. and Kaplan, S. S., *Force Without War: U.S. Armed Forces as a Political Instrument* (The Brookings Institution: Washington, DC, 1978); and Kaplan, S. (ed.), *Diplomacy of Power: Soviet Armed Forces as a Political Instrument* (The Brookings Institution: Washington, DC, 1981). See also Cable, J., *Gunboat Diplomacy 1919–1979: Political Applications of Limited Naval Force*, 2nd edn (St. Martin's: New York, 1981); Luttwak, E., *The Political Uses of Sea Power* (Johns Hopkins University Press: Baltimore, Md., 1974); Shulsky, A., 'Coercive diplomacy', in Dismukes and McConnell (note 23), chapter 4; and Mandel, R., 'The effectiveness of gunboat diplomacy', *International Studies Quarterly*, vol. 30, no. 1 (Mar. 1986), pp. 59–76.

[123] Blechman and Kaplan (note 122), pp. 38–41.

[124] Blechman and Kaplan (note 122), p. 88.

[125] Kaplan (note 122), pp. 49–50.

[126] Hall, D. K., 'Naval diplomacy in West African waters', in Kaplan (note 122), chapter 12; Soviet use of Dakar, Senegal in connection with a demonstration on behalf of Guinea is mentioned on p. 553.

3. Air force facilities

I. Introduction

With the arrival of air power to a position of dominance in contemporary warfare—a position fully entrenched after 1945 in connection with nuclear weapons—the rival powers' access to external bases acquired a concomitant importance. Air bases came to rival their naval counterparts as the 'coaling stations' of contemporary geopolitics, and control of the air came to be seen as vital in the winning of wars.[1] By the 1980s, access to foreign air bases had become vital across a whole range of military activities spanning defence (war-fighting), deterrence and coercive diplomacy. These activities included, crucially: forward basing of strategic (bomber) and tactical (fighter) aircraft; tanker refuelling bases for both of the aforementioned; staging bases for long-range transport logistics, ferrying of tactical aircraft, arms resupply and interventions; bomber recovery and dispersal basing; anti-submarine warfare, anti-ship missions and ocean-surface surveillance; airborne communications and signals intelligence; airborne recovery of space capsules; airborne launch of anti-satellite weapons; back-up communications from the air to underwater submarines; ferrying of supplies to aircraft carriers; fighter interception, primarily for 'continental',that is, anti-strategic bomber defence; airborne collection of downwind nuclear debris; high-altitude photographic intelligence; and still others.

Needless to say, the USA and the USSR compete across the board for global networks encompassing most if not all of these activities; medium powers such as the UK and France are restricted to a narrower range of them, and on a much more limited geographical basis; some still lesser military powers may utilize external bases for one or two purposes or in one or two places.

In chapter 1 a number of long-range, secular historical trends are suggested to have had a cumulative effect on the mix and quantity of required bases. Some of these trends, which encompass both technological and political or 'systemic' factors, are worth restating here, as they apply specifically to the basing of aircraft.

First, as alluded to above, modern air forces deploy far fewer discrete aircraft now than was the case a generation ago, a point made obvious by, for instance, the numerous contextual discussions of the staggering rise in unit costs of US tactical fighter bombers and the associated gradual shrinkage of the number of aircraft acquired.[2] This means, in effect, that far more combat power is being packed into a much smaller number of aircraft—fewer pilots are required, but the unit investments involved are huge; hence too, there are severe vulnerabilities even to a few losses. In 1938, even modest powers such as Argentina, Romania and Poland fielded over a thousand combat aircraft, then costing about $20 000 apiece. Today, countries at that level of relative power are financially stretched to deploy 200–300 combat aircraft, at unit costs ranging well above $10 million—the difference is obviously only partly accounted for by the accumulated inflation of nearly half a century.

Meanwhile, the ranges of aircraft—even without refuelling—have greatly increased. This is far more the case for transport and reconnaissance aircraft with intercontinental or transoceanic ranges; less so for tactical fighters which, while of longer range than their predecessors, are often still restricted to combat radii of several hundred miles, greatly depending upon flight profiles (ferry ranges are much longer), but again, on refuelling either by tanker or by 'buddy' aircraft of similar type. The US C-5B, for instance, even without refuelling, can now carry a sizeable cargo load from Dover, Delaware to Cairo or Tel Aviv; Soviet Antonovs can do almost as much over similar distances.[3] Some other powers, now including the UK, Israel, Australia, Saudi Arabia and Iraq, also utilize tankers—the list is somewhat reflective of the obvious facts of geography and long-range military requirements.[4]

The combined impact of fewer aircraft, longer ranges and tanker refuelling has, of course, resulted in quantitatively lesser needs for overseas bases, particularly for long-range bombing, long-range transport logistics and for the ferrying of fighter aircraft. Whereas prior to and during World War II, the USA, the UK, Japan and other powers utilized large numbers of overseas bases—hundreds of them (Japan had a score on Hainan Island alone)—nowadays requirements can be met by a far more limited, albeit strategically placed, number of air bases.[5] That trend parallels a similar one with respect to naval facilities. But now, the growing vulnerability of relatively scarce and vital air bases appears to be driving a new emphasis on redundancy and contingency or dispersal bases.[6] Indeed, there is the overall question of the future of manned aircraft. The increasing vulnerability of air bases and their pilots by modern surface-to-air missiles impels speculation about wholesale replacement by missiles and drone technology.[7]

However, while developing technology appears gradually to have decreased the quantitative requirements for air bases, political factors have, of course, rendered them far more difficult to acquire either on a permanent, *ad hoc*, or contingency basis. Decolonialization, sensitivities about sovereignty, Third World peer pressures brought to bear on foreign military presences, and perhaps a shift of overall political leverage away from the major powers—all have made base acquisitions more difficult for the latter. Therefore, even the lessened requirements have become difficult to sustain, and a given nation or locale can assume overwhelming importance, as witness US relations—in connection with air bases—with Turkey and the Philippines, or Soviet relations with Viet Nam. Also associated with these difficulties has been a growing trend towards closure of overhead airspaces, in many cases forcing rival air forces to fly much more circuitous and longer routes, either for routine peacetime patrols or for actual combat missions—this factor too has tended to counterbalance the above-mentioned technological ones militating towards longer aircraft reaches.[8]

In relating the joint impact of political and technological trends, it should further be noted that the massive proliferation of new sovereignties in the Third World has also been associated with a vastly increased number of conflicts.[9] Many of these have been revolutionary or civil wars, of varying levels of intensity. But whereas colonial control tended to mute levels of Third World conflict, decolonialization has multiplied them. That in turn has greatly heightened the importance of arms resupply to combatants and, hence, requirements for air staging points around the globe, particularly where resupply is 'time urgent'.[10] This factor has tended to modify the impact of other political and technological trends which have decreased the need for bases.

There have been other trends, some with counteracting implications with regard to numerical requirements for air base facilities. Satellites have reduced some needs for aircraft in the areas of signals and photographic intelligence— but aircraft still fulfil vital needs, for instance, that of rapid close-in photographic surveillance of trouble spots, as has been performed by the US SR-71 and Soviet MiG-25.[11] And SIGINT aircraft flying along a nation's periphery can still be used to great advantage as ferrets, forcing defensive radars to switch on and hence to reveal capabilities. But overall, there is an ineluctable trend towards increased use of satellites for these purposes. Aircraft do remain vital, however, despite rival technologies (SOSUS, ship-towed sonars, satellites) for anti-submarine warfare and ocean surveillance—in recent years, bases from which to deploy aircraft over key, potentially contestable, ocean areas has become a vital requirement for both superpowers. The USA also uses its TACAMO (take charge and move out) aircraft for communicating with submarines beneath the sea, supplementing other, ground-based modes of communications.[12]

For long-range strategic deterrence, both the USA and the USSR, in maintaining their traditional triad postures, have retained significant strategic bomber forces. Generally, this has resulted from a desire for a 'recallable' leg of the triad, to complicate defences, to enable more flexible, omnidirectional targeting (for instance, involving the intra-war location of mobile ICBMs), and so forth.[13] But with ballistic missile defences now contemplated on both sides, the bomber (along with cruise missiles, some of which are launched by bombers) may now acquire a greater importance, if only because it will complicate defences or compel more elaborate and costly ones. Development of effective stealth technology may enhance this tendency, if itself not soon countered by effective defences, for instance, those involving look-down radars.[14]

II. A typology of air FMP

The above discussion of long-term trends determining air-base requirements provides a list of functions served by such bases. Most fundamentally, this involves the categories of long-range bombardment, forward placement of tactical aircraft to provide air cover for ground troops collocated in the vicinity, air transport staging, reconnaissance and ASW. Some general comments are in order regarding the superpowers' rival uses of these forms of access.

The United States has also long fielded nuclear attack bombers in forward positions; from the 1950s in Spain, Morocco and the UK, and continuing to the present in the latter.[15] Other facilities, for instance in Spain, have been designated as recovery bases for Strategic Air Command (SAC) bombers in case of all-out war (in such an event, numerous *ad hoc* arrangements might be anticipated). Cuban bases may be intended by the Soviet Union for similar purposes with the arrival of the Backfire bomber (this was much argued over during the SALT II debate), and they also host shorter-range aircraft (such as the MiG-23) which could possibly be used by Soviet pilots for nuclear strikes against the United States.[16] Also at the strategic level, there are crucial air-base facilities (for the United States, mostly in Arctic regions) for tanker refuelling aircraft, which enable great extension of ranges for bombing missions.[17] In the nuclear strategic context, recovery and refuelling bases are now of perhaps declining but still residual importance in an era dominated by long-range land- and sea-based missiles.

Of course, if a broader definition of 'strategic' is utilized—as is often suggested by Soviet arms control spokesmen—then still other air facilities come into play. US F-111s deployed in the UK and numerous forward-based systems (FBS) such as F-16s in FR Germany, also can deliver nuclear weapons to Soviet territory, as can carrier-based aircraft in the Mediterranean.[18] (If these earlier were marginal considerations, they may become of increased importance to Western deterrence as theatre and perhaps tactical missiles are removed or reduced by arms control.[19]) Soviet-manned MiG-23s in Cuba could arguably be placed in the same category.

Forward-based tactical aircraft on the part of either superpower normally are—in a broad sense—collocated with major ground force deployments. Thus, US tactical air bases in FR Germany, the Netherlands, Turkey, the UK and Italy (abetted by tactical reconnaissance craft, aircraft shelters, munitions storage, barracks, fuel storage, communications, etc.), and also British and Canadian aircraft in FR Germany, exist primarily in relation to contingencies for providing air cover, close ground support and deep interdiction missions (conventional or nuclear) in case of large-scale conflict in Europe. Those in Japan, Okinawa and Korea—and Soviet tactical aircraft in the German Democratic Republic, Poland, Hungary and Mongolia—are deployed for similar contingencies. Forward-based US aircraft in the Philippines or in Turkey, on the other hand, are not collocated with major ground force units. They are for local defence of an ally—or for deterrence in that connection—or for contingencies elsewhere in the respective regions; in the case of Turkey, the relationship to the Persian Gulf is obvious.[20]

Actually, the tactical air forces of the major powers, which are concentrated in the main European and Asian areas of potential conflict, comprise a number of different and specialized aircraft. Indeed, there seems now a reversal of a long-term historical trend which had seen a reduction in functionally specialized aircraft types—during World War II, the US, German, and other air forces had utilized fighter/interceptors, torpedo bombers, dive bombers, light/

medium/heavy bombers, and so on. Nowadays, there is a breakdown involving air defence fighters (used to fly combat air patrols—CAP), ground-attack fighters (often just differently configured models common to air defence fighters), light bombers, reconnaissance aircraft (usually specially configured models of fighter or other aircraft), airborne early-warning or command and control/battle management aircraft, electronic warfare aircraft (used for radar surveillance, jamming, other countermeasures, etc.), forward air control craft (to call in strikes on targets by other aircraft), specially configured aircraft carrying anti-radiation missiles (ARMs) for interdiction of surface-to-air missiles (SAMs), such as the US 'wild weasels', and some special operations aircraft, in addition to a variety of types of helicopter. Generally speaking, recent years have seen greatly increased attention, as reflected in numerical deployments, particularly on airborne warning and control and electronic warfare aircraft. The importance of these (previously considered auxiliary systems) was well demonstrated by Israel in the 1982 Lebanon War.[21]

In some cases, particularly regarding Soviet tactical aircraft overseas, there may be definitional problems regarding FMP, that is, regarding the line between it and simple arms transfers. Soviet fighter aircraft based in Libya, Syria, Angola and South Yemen (earlier also in Egypt) may be flown by Soviet pilots; perhaps also by Cubans, North Koreans, North Vietnamese or other 'surrogates'.[22] These are grey area cases where (Angola excepted) collocated major-power combat units are not involved.

Forward-based aircraft are valuable but also concentrated and vulnerable assets, so that on all sides, there has been considerable attention to hardening (underground shelters or revetments) and placing of fuel and munitions underground. Aircraft so located can, of course, be moved temporarily to crisis areas elsewhere—the Lebanon hostage crisis reportedly saw some US F-16s moved to Turkey from elsewhere within NATO.

Staging of transport aircraft for arms supplies, personnel and other *matériel* accounts for numerous overseas facilities (sometimes collocated with combat functions), sometimes involving large installations with permanently stationed user personnel, but also often involving joint control or use of client states' facilities on a more or less *ad hoc* basis.

Some facilities of this type are used on a more or less normal basis during peacetime for routine arms and personnel shipments, while at other times they must be bargained for just before and during crises. During crises, particularly in the case of out-of-area operations, access may be denied. Hence, the United States gained the use of Portuguese staging facilities in the Azores during the 1973 war, but not those of other European allies[23] (Britain, for example, denied the USA access to her bases in Cyprus), while in recent crises in Iran and Nicaragua, the use of nearby bases in Turkey and Costa Rica, respectively, had to be bargained over.[24] The complexity of the operation against Libya in 1987 was increased when France, FR Germany and Spain refused overflights or use of bases. This was violated when a US F-111 made a forced landing in Spain. Whether or not British permission for staging supplies through Diego Garcia would be granted in the case of another Middle Eastern crisis involving Israel is an open question.[25] Use of staging facilities in Spain, Portugal and Italy for arms supplied to Middle Eastern countries other than Israel has also apparently been subject to bargaining.[26] Meanwhile, both the USA and the USSR also have made periodic use of commercial airports throughout the world for various air staging operations, where *ad hoc* permission during crises may also be at issue. France, Britain and other middle-range powers will also require staging bases for long-range logistics operations. Thus, in moving troops and supplies to Chad in 1983 and 1985, Paris utilized staging bases in Cameroons, the Central African Republic and Niger. Britain has reportedly used Brazilian bases for resupplying its garrison in the Falklands in the wake of the 1982 war.[27]

Many staging bases are also used for ferrying short-range tactical aircraft over long distances, often where time constraints preclude or render less desirable alternative movement by ship. The now longer ranges of such aircraft, and in some cases, their mid-air refuelling capabilities, now render this function somewhat less vital than was the case before and during World War II, when the United States had to utilize numerous short-hop ferrying routes to Europe, Africa and the Near East.[28] Generally, for both staging and ferrying operations, the importance of a given base may be gauged only in the light of regional chains or networks providing routes of access and forward deployment, in conjunction with the availability of overflight corridors.

Recent vast increases in aircraft ranges and in the development of sophisticated in-flight refuelling techniques have somewhat lessened the requirements for numerous overseas bases to support a global air staging network. With the inter-war period used as a baseline, the change is seen to have been dramatic. Using large numbers of tankers, new cargo aircraft such as the US C-5A may now transport large numbers of troops and massive cargo tonnages throughout the world with the use of only a small number of well-placed staging and tanker deployment points.[29] Hence, one recent analysis indicated that the USA's continued use of British-owned Ascension and Diego Garcia islands could alone, in conjunction with tanker refuelling, provide the United States with the capability for extensive aerial supply to much of Africa and the Middle East.[30]

But the trends are still of mixed import. Even with the longer transport ranges, the use of intermediate refuelling stops can improve the ratio of cargo to fuel carried, and hence improve the economics of airlift. And the (political) availability of tanker facilities may themselves be in doubt during crises, as were those in Spain in 1973.[31] Further, in the event of a general war, it is anticipated that there will be serious competition for use of tankers between strategic bombers and long-range air transports. The USSR, meanwhile, is just beginning to make extensive use of tanker refuelling, as it deploys its new fleet of IL-76 Midas aircraft. None of its previous transports have had refuelling capability, and this will apparently not change with the huge incoming AN-124 Condor. Addition of refuelling capability for the Backfire bombers could double their ranges and transform them into long-range strategic systems.[32]

The now longer ranges of fighter aircraft and their configuration for aerial refuelling have somewhat mitigated the need for short-run ferry routes, but not entirely.[33] And the lessened need for strategic air bases may now be balanced somewhat by the increased need for fleet air cover from ground bases (for the Soviet Union as well as the United States) in a period witnessing the increased vulnerability of surface ship concentrations to interdiction by air- and sea-launched missiles. (One notes here the central focus on Norway and Iceland, and on Soviet control of Viet Nam.) And, finally, crisis contingencies may require the quick dispatch of aircraft from nearby countries, where movement from the homeland may be prohibitively slow.

As noted, facilities for ASW and (related) long-range ocean surveillance have become major basing requirements for both superpowers; to a lesser degree in some areas, for France as well. Both sides fly regular patrols over ocean areas known to be inhabited by rivals' nuclear-powered ballistic-missile submarines (SSBNs) and nuclear-powered attack submarines (SSNs), practising or simulating actual combat missions by hunting the latters' submarines. This is done, variously, by the dropping of sonabuoys and use of various airborne detection instruments (including analysis of ocean wake movements, magnetic anomaly detectors, etc.).[34] The USA flies its P-3C ASW aircraft all over the North Atlantic, North Pacific and Indian oceans. Long-range Soviet Bear-D ocean-surveillance aircraft traverse the North Atlantic in a triangle between the Kola Peninsula, West Africa and Cuba, and also the Indian and Pacific oceans.[35] Some US ASW aircraft bases are thought to store nuclear depth charges for all-out war contingencies; alternatively, they serve as potential locales for quick forward deployment of such weapons in a crisis.[36] Soviet forward bases presumably may serve similar functions, even if less well publicized.

The US TACAMO communications aircraft and smaller naval aircraft called carrier-on-board delivery (COD) demonstrate two other modern functions for land-based aircraft. In the former case, low-flying aircraft trailing communications gear in the water are used to communicate with submerged SSBNs, as a back-up to the extremely low frequency (ELF) and very low frequency (VLF) land-based communications systems.[37] The COD aircraft—usually based in proximity to major areas of fleet concentrations such as in the Mediterranean or the Indian Ocean—help replenish ships at sea, by landing on aircraft carriers. As such, they may reduce the need for support ships and/or for port calls (though they obviously cannot be used for refuelling or provisioning of water).[38]

A final general category of air FMP is that covering a broad area of intelligence (SIGINT, photographic intelligence—PHOTINT, etc.) and surveillance. It includes such varied activities as the flying of electronic intelligence (ELINT) and communications intelligence (COMINT) ferret aircraft along the rim of a rival's borders, and high-altitude reconnaissance overflights. Some of these activities have, as noted, gradually been taken over by satellites, but by no means all—witness the US response to the loss of its Iranian bases in seeking further access for its U-2s in Cyprus along with use of Turkish airspace.[39] Retention of redundancy in these areas might, at any rate, be considered prudent because of the now looming ASAT threat in the event of war. For a long time, indeed, there was an asymmetry of requirements in these areas between the USA and the USSR. With the latter a more 'closed' society, the USA was impelled in the early post-war period to undertake a massive effort at sur- veillance of the USSR from its Eurasian rimland peripheries and also from overhead. The advent of satellites partly resolved that. The USSR, on the other hand, has long laboured under the disadvantage of relatively more restricted basing access in proximity to the USA—the Cuban revolution in 1960 went far to rectify that disadvantage but has involved putting a lot of assets in one place, there being at present no fall-backs such as those availed the USA after the fall of the Shah of Iran.

Photo-reconnaissance bases, meanwhile, are important not only for mon- itoring the activities of a rival superpower, but also for closely monitoring Third World conflicts, in some instances with an eye to providing battlefield information to a favoured client state.[40] As in other ways, this highlights the connection between base location and the locales of Third World flashpoints.

For the future, there is the promise of overseas basing access for Stealth aircraft, now often characterized because of their projected cost as well as combat value, as 'silver bullets'. The USA is clearly well advanced in the de- velopment both of Stealth bombers and fighter attack aircraft. The future will no doubt see some of these aircraft deployed in Europe, presumably at existing bases in FR Germany and elsewhere. These are seen as particularly useful for covert deep penetration and interdiction of high-value targets—bridges, communications nodes, oil and weapon depots, Soviet second-echelon forces/ operational manoeuvre groups, and so on, that is, Soviet conventional strategic reserve or 'follow-on' forces deemed vital to effecting and exploiting a break- through on the ground. The Soviet Union will no doubt also later deploy similar systems.

Outside the European theatre, it might be speculated that Stealth aircraft will be of particular use in Third World areas for reconnaissance missions, or for quick strikes equivalent to the US raid on Libya in 1986, where circumventing overflight restrictions may be both important and possible. This may later involve important basing implications.

III. US air bases abroad

The USA utilizes virtually the whole spectrum of aircraft types discussed above, along with related types of facility, in addition to the overhead airspace of numerous nations. Some of these facilities, of course, involve 'permanent' or continuous stationing of aircraft and associated personnel and ancillary systems; variously, for tactical fighter aircraft, bombers, tankers, airborne warning and control, ASW or reconnaissance craft, and so on. Others are, by degrees, more *ad hoc*, for instance involving the staging of men or *matériel* in connection with arms transfers—either under normal peacetime conditions or amid war or crisis—or for periodic, *ad hoc*, or sporadically routine ocean reconnaissance.

There is great variety. Overall, there are some 135 000 USAF personnel located overseas.[41]

Fighter aircraft bases

The primary locales for the basing of tactical fighter aircraft are, as one would expect, those nations (FR Germany, South Korea) which also host large-scale US ground forces in regular combat units; and a few countries such as Japan, the UK and the Philippines, where there are no such ground formations but where there are major naval bases and an elaborate infrastructure of technical facilities.

The US Air Force has a number of main fighter air bases in FR Germany: Zweibrücken, Bitburg, Hahn, Spangdahlen, Ramstein and Sembach. These deploy some six combat air wings with 328 combat aircraft. At its core this involves some 72 F-16 A/Bs, 96 F-4Es (half soon to be replaced by F-16s), 24 F-4Gs, 72 F-15 C/Ds, plus 18 RF-4C reconnaissance aircraft.[42] There is the additional related deployment of two squadrons of 42 OV-10A tactical air control planes plus another deploying seven CH-53C helicopters. Some additional bases—at Leipheim, Ahlhorn and Norvenich—are apparently designated as forward operating locations for A-10 attack craft main-based in the UK; as 'host nation' air bases with US maintenance detachments and munitions storage igloos.[43] Several others are designated as collocated operating bases (COBs) at which the USAF has its own refuelling, munitions storage and maintenance facilities on West German 'host nation' air bases. Considering what is at stake and the magnitude of the overall US military presence in FR Germany, this is still a somewhat taut and concentrated group of main tactical air bases, with an overall presence of some 40 000 personnel. As of 1988, it appeared that some of these aircraft deployments—particularly where dual-capable systems are involved—might become subjects of arms control negotiations, in connection with possible reductions of conventional force levels in Central Europe.

The US Air Force also deploys a large combat force in the UK: over 290 combat aircraft organized in four combat air wings, and 16 squadrons, overall involving 27 500 personnel. There some 150 F-111 E/Fs (actually deployed as a nuclear strike force with strategic or tactical implications), 12 EF-111 Raven electronic warfare aircraft, 108 A-10s, and 18 RF-4C reconnaissance craft—the A-10s, as noted, are home-based in the UK but can rapidly be deployed forward in FR Germany.[44] These aircraft are based at several sites: Lakenheath, Alconbury, Upper Heyford, Woodbridge and Bentwaters.[45] Alconbury also hosts 18 F-5E 'aggressor' aircraft.[46] Elsewhere within NATO, the USAF bases a squadron of (24) F-15 C/Ds at Soesterberg in the Netherlands and an air defence squadron of 18 F-15s at Keflavik in Iceland. As a result of the 1988 decision of the Spanish Government 72 F-16 A/Bs are being removed from Torrejon and will be redeployed to Italy (Sicily).[47] Some nuclear-capable F-4s are forward-located at Incirlik in Turkey. Other tactical aircraft are regularly 'rotated' forward elsewhere in Turkey and at Aviano in Italy—a plethora of bases within NATO are designated as collocated host bases available for crises, situations demanding coercive diplomacy or outright major war. In the Netherlands, Spain, Italy, Greece, Turkey and Iceland, there are respectively 2000, 5300, 5800, 2700, 3800 and 1700 US Air Force personnel.[48]

The USAF also bases fighter aircraft forward in Japan, the Philippines and South Korea. In Japan, with 16 200 USAF personnel, are based three squadrons of 72 F-15 C/Ds, 18 RF-4Cs, and 48 F-16s at Yokota and Misawa; also some US Marine Corps V/STOL Harriers at Iwakuni, and some T-39 craft.[49] Two squadrons of F-4 E/Gs are permanently stationed at the Clark Air Force Base in the Philippines; additionally, a dozen F-5E 'aggressor' aircraft.[50] In Korea there are 36 F-4Es and RF-4Es, 48 F-16s, and 24 A-10s and a tactical control group with 24 OA-37 Dragonflies located at main operating bases at Osan, Kunsan and Taegu; the newer F-16s are based at Kunsan.[51] In South Korea and the Philippines, there are 11 200 and 9300 USAF personnel, respectively.[52]

Bomber forces and tankers

As indicated above, the USA does not directly rely on overseas facilities for main basing of strategic bombers, as it earlier did in the eras of B-29s and B-47s. But there are some roles for overseas bases in this connection. F-111s (which would be augmented in a crisis) are based in the UK, and nuclear-configured tactical aircraft capable of reaching targets in the USSR are based in Turkey and FR Germany. In addition, some overseas facilities—their identities are kept secret but one can assume they are those US facilities located in proximity to the USSR—are apparently designated as dispersal bases for SAC's B-52 force, as indeed are numerous secondary bases within the USA. Similarly, some overseas facilities could be used for recovery purposes or as emergency landing sites for bombers returning from nuclear bombing missions in the event of a major war. In earlier years Spain and Morocco were mentioned in this connection.

Collocated operating bases (COBs), standby operating bases, forward operating bases

In recent years, as detailed by Campbell, the USA (or NATO) has erected an elaborate structure of COBs, standby operating bases and forward operating bases (FOBs). The FOBs provide advance facilities and right of use to SAC bombers (B-52s and FB-111s) normally based in the USA. Bases at Upper Heyford, Fairford, Brize Norton and Marham are designated for this purpose. Three other British bases—Sculthorpe, Wethersfield and Greenham Common— are designated as 'stand-by operating bases'.

Recent attention to USAF reinforcement or augmentation in Europe has focused mainly on the plan for COBs, originally said to have been developed in response to the removal of US Air Force bases from France after 1967 and also to the 'flexible response' doctrine of developing greater conventional warfare capability.[53]

According to Campbell, USAF originally selected 73 air bases belonging to its European allies from which US forces might operate during a war, and rights for such use have since been obtained for 53 bases in 10 countries.[54] These rights involve a priori technical agreements with 'sponsors' on sharing of the facilities and construction of 'minimum essential facilities' for Americans (communications, fuel storage, munitions sites, intelligence centres, 'starter kits' of spare parts, ammunition, etc.). Several of the COBs allocated to the USA in the UK are current or former RAF V-bomber or tactical nuclear bases (Finningley, Wittering, Coltishall, Waddington) and have Special Storage Areas for nuclear weapons. The US-based aircraft which would be brought to the British COBs include F-4 Phantoms, A-7 Corsairs, F-16s and F-111s, all nuclear-capable. Other COBs in the UK are located at Bedford, Benson, Boscombe Down, Cranwell, Leeming and Odiham. NATO nations other than the UK have air bases designated as COBs or Standby Deployment Bases—the latter can involve old bases not presently used, but where the tarmacs are usable. Some examples should suffice. Norway apparently can host five squadrons of aircraft on its COBs during crises, including provision for handling A-6s from US aircraft carriers.[55] Denmark has designated COBs for five USAF squadrons and two RAF squadrons. The US squadrons would go to COBs at Ålborg, Karup, Vandel, and Skrydstrup; the British squadrons to another at Tirstrup.[56] Others in Turkey are mentioned above.[57]

Numerous US overseas facilities are regularly used to base tanker refuelling aircraft. Many of these aircraft can be used for multiple purposes, that is, to refuel strategic bombers in crises or wars, cargo aircraft in connection with long-range logistics (including large-scale arms resupply operations) and fighter aircraft being ferried overseas. But they are most commonly counted as part of the US strategic forces.

The USAF now has some (613) KC-135 A/Q and (48) KC-10A tankers, with a greatly expanded number of the latter now being phased in (another (103) KC-135 A/Qs are attached to reserve forces).[58] Like the B-52 bombers they are intended primarily to service, these tankers may, in a crisis or war (or for Third World arms resupply or intervention contingencies) be redeployed to dispersal bases (note for example the British dispersal of tankers to Ascension to assist in the logistics for the Falklands War). On a more regular basis, tankers are kept on station in a number of places: in the UK (Mildenhall, Fairford), Spain (Zaragoza), the Philippines (Clark AFB), Okinawa (Kadena), Diego Garcia, Iceland (Keflavik) and also Guam (Anderson AFB)—Thule in Greenland and Goose Bay and Harmon in Canada were earlier used for similar purposes.[59] Still earlier, up to 1963, SAC's KC-97s were based in Canada at Namao, Churchill, Cold Lake and Frobisher—some of these are still designated for dispersal and refuelling operations for currently deployed KC-135s.[60]

Transport aircraft

The USA also utilizes some overseas facilities for regular or permanent basing of transport aircraft—this is distinct from and in addition to the more *ad hoc* use of a global system for staging or transiting transport aircraft.

The primary US aircraft for long-range lift operations—some 269 C-141Bs and 70 C-5As—are all home-based in the USA, though again, they may be dispersed abroad for a variety of contingencies.[61] But the USAF also has some 218 C-130s organized into 14 squadrons which are designated for tactical purposes (i.e., with shorter ranges and able to utilize shorter runways).[62] Some of these C-130s are home-based in foreign facilities, among them, Rhein Main (FRG), Howard AFB (Panama), Mildenhall (UK), Clark AFB (Philippines), Yokota (Japan) and Kadena (Okinawa)—there are groups of 16 C-130s organized as tactical transport wings in the UK, Japan, the Philippines and FR Germany (in the latter are based an additional 18 C-23A Sherpas).[63]

It must once more be pointed out that use of numerous other facilities for tactical airlift operations may be envisaged or have occurred; for instance, the USA reportedly staged the C-130s used in the abortive Iran hostage raid out of either Qena or Cairo West in Egypt.[64] It is noted below that otherwise-configured C-130s—for instance, for satellite film recovery and communications with submerged submarines—also make extensive use of overseas facilities.

For the future, the USAF plans, budgetary authorizations permitting, to acquire some 220 new C-17 aircraft, which it prefers to the C-5A.[65] According to one source, 'The C-17, while carrying fewer troops or lighter loads, would be designed to fly farther and directly into rough airfields in combat zones, and it would cost less to operate.'[66] The basing implications, including those involving tankers, are not yet clear.

ASW

Aside from tactical and strategic combat aircraft, and long and short (tactical) airlift or cargo craft, the perhaps next most important element of external basing of US aircraft has to do with anti-submarine warfare. This involves, of course, continuous efforts—in peace as well as in war—to track or monitor the movements of rival powers' SSBNs and SSNs, which strive to hide within the ocean depths and not to reveal paths of egress and ingress from and to homeports. Of course, aircraft are but one of several systems used in ASW activities—the roles of attack submarines, of SOSUS grids linked to on-shore computer analysis terminals, of surface ships with active sonars on their hulls and of helicopters—land or ship-based—dragging active sonars through the waters are noted in chapter 6. In an area shrouded in secrecy, these various methods are presumed complementary and often redundant—all involve external basing.

The primary current US aircraft used for ASW surveillance—and surface ocean surveillance as well—is the P-3C Orion, in reality a roomy old propeller-driven aircraft loaded down with various instruments devoted to ASW. According to one description:

There was radar for spotting a periscope sticking a few inches out of the water. Heat from an engine near the surface could be picked out by equipment that measured infrared radiation. A thin fiberglass tube protruding straight back from the tail encased a device for measuring disturbances in the Earth's magnetic field caused by the iron in a submarine's hull. Bathythermograph buoys dropped from the plane could radio back the changing water temperatures below the surface. This information was crucial to the most important means of sub detection: sonar . . . another crew member picked up a three-foot long yellow cylinder called a sonabuoy. It was shoved into a tube and dropped into the water 5,000 feet below.

The U.S. navy has compiled a catalog of the signatures of Soviet subs enabling listeners to match a sound with a type of submarine, sometimes even with a particular vessel.[67]

The P-3Cs are armed primarily with conventional torpedoes for killing submarines they can locate. But, numerous recent reports have detailed that the US Navy can configure the P-3Cs with 'atomic depth charges' which, if not regularly stored overseas, can be deployed during crises or war, insofar as allowed for by alliance diplomacy.[68] Given the utter centrality of submarine warfare to all major war scenarios, the basing aspects of this activity are clearly crucial.

The US P-3Cs, of which there are some 375 in various configurations, are based along both coasts of the USA, for instance, at Brunswick, Maine. They are also forward-based so as to provide surveillance over those ocean areas most likely to involve stationing or transiting of Soviet SSBNs or SSNs (including areas with potential for 'out of area' conventional conflict which could engage superpower navies).[69] Particular attention is paid to the North Atlantic (particularly waters near the GIUK gap), the western Indian Ocean, the western Pacific Ocean (including the South China Sea and the Indonesian Straits); also more specifically to obvious egress points such as Gibraltar and the Kurile Islands area.[70] All around these areas, the USA has acquired access for regular basing and for staging of P-3C flights, and those of the older, usually carrier-based S-3A Viking, 110 of which are used for ASW work.[71]

Around the Indian Ocean littoral, among the air facilities often cited as basing or allowing refuelling of US P-3Cs are Mogadiscio (Somalia), Emba/Zasi/Nairobi (Kenya), Masirah (Oman),[72] Diego Garcia, Tahkli (Thailand), Singapore and Djibouti; earlier, under different political conditions, Mahe (Seychelles) and Bandar Abbas (Iran) were also part of this network.[73] In the western and central Pacific, along with Pearl Harbor, Midway and Adak (Alaska), P-3Cs may utilize Misawa and Iwakuni (Japan), Cubi Point (Philippines) and, again, Singapore. Dakar in Senegal apparently is utilized in the equatorial

Atlantic area; further north in the Atlantic submarine grounds, Keflavik (Iceland), Bermuda, the Azores and Rota (Spain) are engaged. In the Mediterranean, in addition to Spain's Rota, Sigonella on Sicily is a main base for US P-3C operations.[74]

AWACS

More recently, in response to changing technology which has brought battle management aircraft to the fore, the USA has begun use of several overseas bases for its Airborne Warning and Control Systems (AWACS). This form of access may, of course, be assumed critical for future conventional aerial combat. It is noteworthy that the US AWACS designated for the primary potential areas of conflict—particularly in Western Europe—are home-based well back of the lines of confrontation, so as to mitigate the chances of pre-emptive strike.[75] Between one and three AWACS are now reportedly being deployed at Keflavik in Iceland (note the relationship to air control over the key GIUK-gap area), a number in FR Germany (Geilenkirchen) and three in Japan.[76] Future deployments are scheduled to forward operating bases at Trapani, Italy; Konya, Turkey; and Oerland, Norway.[77] The NATO Airborne Early Warning Command (NAEW) at Maisières, Belgium controls NATO's AWACS and British Nimrod early-warning aircraft. Other AWACS, manned by US crews, are based in Saudi Arabia, nominally under control of the Saudi Government, to provide battle management for potential air combat in and around the Persian Gulf.[78] The issue of similar basing of AWACS in Pakistan has recently arisen at Islamabad's request.[79]

As it is, the AWACS were not the first of a new contemporary breed of special-purpose technical or electronic warfare craft to be deployed alongside the traditional combat types. Others—to be taken up in connection with intelligence facilities—were in evidence as far back as the 1950s, when the USA deployed overseas its ferret aircraft for SIGINT flights around the periphery of the Soviet bloc. Nowadays, as was so graphically demonstrated by the Israeli air force in Lebanon, other combat auxiliary aircraft are specifically configured not only for battle management *per se*, but also for electronic countermeasures (ECMs) and electronic counter-countermeasures (ECCMs), for jamming or blinding of ground radars and various other activities under the heading of electronic warfare. For instance, in the UK, the USAF fields 15 EF-111 Raven aircraft (reconfigured F-111s) for such purposes; in Spain and Turkey (Diyarbakir) it deploys some EA-3B 'Sentry' SIGINT aircraft. Several other aircraft systems have been used as SIGINT platforms: the EC-135, EC-121 and RC-135.[80]

The EC-121, now phased out, was a version of the old C-121 Super Constellation transport with a crew of 30 and ability to stay in the air for 20 hours. It was used from the 1950s to 1970s as a radar picket and COMINT aircraft, utilizing a variety of bases. It has been superseded by the RC-135, a modified Boeing 707 which can remain in the air for 18 hours, and is used for a variety of COMINT/ELINT purposes, that is, monitoring of radars and telemetry.[81]

Some are based in the USA; others overseas at RAF Mildenhall, Hellenikon (Greece) and Kadena on Okinawa.[82] The EC-135, a modified KC-135 Strato-tanker, is also used as a radio and telemetry intercept aircraft, as well as a flying command post for SAC. Four of these 'Silk Purse' US European Command (USEUCOM) centres are based at RAF Mildenhall.[83]

Reconnaissance and communications

At least two other functions requiring overseas basing or continuous routing of aircraft bear mention: high-altitude photo-reconnaissance and communications with underwater SSBNs; functions performed respectively by the US Air Force and Navy. The initial U-2 deployments in the 1950s noted above were brought to public prominence by the furore surrounding the shooting down of Gary Powers' flight over Sverdlovsk by Soviet SAM-2s. In that era, the U-2s utilized Wiesbaden (FRG), Bodø (Norway), Atsugi (Japan) and Peshawar (Pakistan), among other basing points.[84]

Although satellites have now largely superseded the earlier crucial importance of these photo-reconnaissance missions, the USA has continued the development of ever more-sophisticated aircraft of this type. The U-2 was superseded by the SR-71 Blackbird; the latter is now being replaced by the very new TR-1. Although the basing and staging of these aircraft receive little mention in open sources, there have been, for instance, frequent reports of U-2s operating out of the British base at Akrotiri on Cyprus. This became an issue during the debate over SALT II verification around 1979, concurrent with the US loss of Iranian SIGINT facilities which might have been compensated for, to a degree, by U-2s operating out of Cyprus and along the Turkish–Soviet frontier.[85] Both U-2s and SR-71s have been mentioned in connection with US monitoring of Middle East crises and for verifying compliance with the Camp David accords—they too presumably fly out of Akrotiri.[86] Otherwise, SR-71s have visited bases in the UK (Mildenhall) and on Okinawa (Kadena).[87] Two of the newer TR-1s are now also permanently deployed in the UK, at Alconbury.[88]

As a supplement to land-based communications (ELF and VLF) with US SSBNs, the USA also relies upon so-called TACAMO aircraft—retrofitted C-130 transports loaded with communications gear. More specifically, these are radio-relay planes equipped with VLF antennas 'that are supposed to convey orders from the President to the US submarines on patrol'. Further, according to one writer: '. . . the large land-based VLF antennas that normally broadcast orders to the submarine fleet are soft targets that could be destroyed at the outset of a nuclear attack. An airborne system was therefore established to provide "post-attack" communications.'[89]

According to the same source, the USA attempts to keep one TACAMO aircraft aloft at any given time over both the Atlantic and Pacific areas where its SSBNs move about among firing stations.[90] Over the Atlantic, this has apparently involved use of bases at Bermuda and in the UK (Alconbury); in the Pacific, on Guam, Wake Island and Hawaii.[91]

The future may see some altered patterns of external basing for US aircraft. In the past few years, the USA has gained extensive access to air bases in Honduras—at Palmerola, La Cieba, San Lorenzo and others—in connection with the ongoing effort at overturning the Sandinista Government in Nicaragua.[92] It has also acquired much access to El Salvador.[93] And, as an example of emerging new forms of access requirements, one could point to reports that the USA has negotiated with Chile over access to remote Easter Island, where F-15 fighters configured for ASAT missions might be based.[94]

IV. Soviet aircraft bases

Numerically speaking the Soviet Air Force is huge, comprising—in varying degrees of readiness—some 5000 combat aircraft.[95] More than half of these are primarily configured as interceptors, that is, they are for strategic and/or tactical defence; the remainder are configured mostly as ground-attack craft. Still others have as their primary functions reconnaissance and electronic countermeasures; 540 and 30 craft, respectively.[96] In its strategic forces, the USSR has some 165 long-range, 567 medium-range, and 450 short-range bombers, 68 long-range reconnaissance craft, some 100 ECM machines and (here deficient relative to the USA) a growing force of some 50 Bison and Badger tankers.[97]

As indicated above—and in line with the fact of Soviet ground and naval deployments—most permanent external deployments of aircraft are in the immediately contiguous areas of Eastern Europe within the WTO, Mongolia and Afghanistan. Otherwise, however, recent years have seen the Soviet Air Force break out of the confines of Eurasia to establish more or less permanent bases in Viet Nam, South Yemen, Angola and Cuba.

The USSR has some 2000 tactical aircraft deployed in Eastern Europe. The MiG-23 Flogger is by far the most numerous fighter-interceptor; followed by late-model MiG-21 Fishbeds and older Su-15 Flagons. Other less numerous fighter-interceptors include the Foxbat, Firebar, Fiddler and the new MiG-31 Foxhound and MiG-29 Fulcrum.[98] The Fulcrums are being phased in to replace the Fishbed, Flagon and some Floggers. The Foxhound and the Su-27 Flanker will probably replace Fishbed, Flogger, Flagon and older Foxbat aircraft.

Among the ground-attack aircraft, the most common are the Su-17 Fitter and MiG-27 Flogger, though reportedly the best interdiction aircraft in the Soviet inventory is the Su-24 Fencer.[99] Other units are comprised of MiG-23 Floggers, the new Su-25 Frogfoot and older MiG-21 Fishbed and Su-7 Fitter As. Reconnaissance aircraft deployed in Eastern Europe include MiG-21 Fishbeds, Su-17 Fitters, MiG-25 Foxbats and Yak-28 Brewers.

In the GDR, there are large numbers of attack and interceptor fighters, a total of 685 combat aircraft, comprising 315 attack aircraft (Su-17s, Su-24s, Su-25s, MiG-27s); 300 fighter interceptors (MiG-21/25/27s); 50 reconnaissance craft (Su-17s, MiG-25s); plus 20 ECM and 40 light transport aircraft.[100] These are forward-based at some 17 bases; quantitatively speaking, there are both more aircraft and bases than are fielded by the US and British counterparts in FR Germany. These are at: Zossen-Wiensdorf, Stralsund, Peenemunde, Parchim (Hind-24 helicopters and long-range transports for troop exchanges), Finow, Werneuchen, Oranienburg, Wittstock, Neuruppin, Zerbst (MiG-25 reconnaissance aircraft), Juterborg, Kothen, Welzow, Finsterwalde (Su-20 'Fitter B' fighter regiment), Merseburg, Grossenhein and Alternburg.[101]

In Czechoslovakia, the USSR regularly deploys some 105 combat aircraft, located mostly in the Bohemian region along the German border and in the area north-west of Prague. There are some 45 MiG-27 Flogger D/Js, 45 Flogger Bs and 15 Su-17 reconnaissance craft.[102] Among the some 30 military airfields in Czechoslovakia, Soviet combat aircraft are reported stationed at Prague's Ruzyne airport, Milovice, Cheb/Horni Dvory, Dobrany, Karlovy Vary, Zatec, Mimon, Tchorovice and Panensky Tynec.[103]

In Hungary, the Soviet Air Force has six major air bases in addition to joint use of some Hungarian bases and also some dispersal strips. There are about 240 combat aircraft deployed, including Su-17 Fitter and Su-24 Fencer attack craft, MiG-23 interceptors, and Su-17 reconnaissance aircraft.[104] Tokól in Budapest, a major Soviet base used jointly with Hungary, deploys fighters, bombers, transports and helicopters and is also the headquarters for the Soviet Air Force in Hungary. Other important bases are at Kaposvar, Pápa, Veszprem, Debrecen, Mezokovesd, Pecs and Szombathely. There is joint use of other installations at Kalocsa, Szolnok, Kecskemet, Sarmellek and Szeged.[105]

In strategically located (relative to the main potential theatre of operations along the West German frontier) Poland, the USSR earlier based combat aircraft at Legnica, Gniezno, Puscza Bolimowska, Gdansk (naval air Backfires), Zagan, Brzeg, Opole, Szczecin, Kolobrzeg, Szczecinek and Koszalin,[106] but according to the International Institute for Strategic Studies (IISS) in London, there are now no regularly based combat aircraft there, only 10 transport aircraft. Arkin and Fieldhouse, however, cite bases at Zagan and Szprotawa as hosting Su-24 Fencer aircraft.[107]

In Bulgaria, the closest Soviet ally, there are no Soviet garrison forces as such, nor any extensive Soviet air deployments. However, the Bulgarian Air Force, utilizing Soviet aircraft, is presumed fully integrated into that of its major alliance partner. Romania, which once hosted a major Soviet Air Force headquarters and aircraft deployment (up to 1958) now also lacks such deployments.

In the Far East, again associated with a major ground force deployment, there are in Mongolia about six squadrons of Soviet combat aircraft, including MiG-21/23/25/27s. They are at Choybalsan north-east, Ulan Bator south-west, Nalayh, Bayan Suma and two facilities around Sayn Shand which field MiG-23s.[108] These are large deployments comparable to those in Eastern Europe, reflecting the size of the Soviet presence *vis-à-vis* China. In addition some 30 MiG-23s are based on Eterofu Island in the Kuriles (disputed with Japan), along with 8000–10 000 troops.[109]

One other site of external Soviet aircraft basing contiguous to the USSR is, of course, Afghanistan, where war raged from 1979 until 1988. Recent Soviet air deployments there were, of course, primarily intended for prosecution of the ongoing war itself, which saw extensive use of helicopters and attack aircraft, most recently including the MiG-29, for counter-insurgency, and basing of helicopters and transports for tactical movement of troops and *matériel*. Of course, one of the several reasons often cited for the Soviet invasion of Afghanistan (along with elimination of a potentially subversive presence immediately next door to Soviet Muslim Central Asia) is that of acquisition of air bases in closer proximity to the Persian Gulf and adjacent Indian Ocean waters.[110] In that connection numerous Western strategic analyses dwell on the range and other capabilities of Backfire bomber, the MiG-23 and other attack fighters in relation to potential conflict scenarios in and around the Gulf, the future of Pakistan's Baluchistan, future internal developments in Iran, and so forth.[111]

Amid the ongoing war, the Soviet Air Force has established a major presence in at least five air bases, some of which are being expanded and upgraded. These are at Kabul, Kandahar (important for airlift and for naval reconnaissance over the Indian Ocean), Bagram (MiG-23 base and reported Tu-95 Bear bomber deployment), Shindand (a squadron each of MiG-21s and MiG-23s, two squadrons of Su-20 fighters, and 60 Mi-6 helicopters), and Jalalabad near Pakistan and the Khyber Pass, where 100-plus Soviet helicopters are reported stationed.[112] It remains to be seen whether this presence will be reduced or eliminated in line with the recent accords signed in Geneva.

Outside of the old (Western-imposed) Eurasian containment rim (or 'out of area' relative to the USSR), the Soviet Air Force has by now established bases, *ad hoc* facilities and staging rights in virtually all of the world's major regions. Concerning the 'permanent' or continuous deployment of aircraft (or sporadic deployments approaching that status), this involves, most importantly, both combat and naval reconnaissance aircraft. The major deployments are, as one might expect, collocated with the major naval facilities in some of the Soviet Union's closest allies in the Third World, such as, Viet Nam, South Yemen, Cuba, Syria, Libya and Angola. Still, relative to USAF access overseas, the paucity of permanent deployment of combat aircraft stands out. Perhaps of greater significance is the growing access for Soviet naval reconnaissance aircraft—developments between 1965 and 1985 are depicted in figure 3.

In Viet Nam, alongside the major naval deployments at Cam Ranh Bay, the Soviet Union now deploys some 24 reconnaissance or combat aircraft, 8 Tu-95 Bears and 16 Tu-16 Badgers D/K, 10 of the latter having strike capabilities.[113] The Badgers' ranges extend the Soviet strike capability over the entire South-East Asian region, notably including the US bases in the Philippines, but also over Guam and the other US facilities in the islands of the Central Pacific.[114] Support facilities have also been upgraded to provide for additional permanently deployed aircraft, notably including a squadron of MiG-23/Flogger fighters.[115] The Soviet Air Force presumably has contingent access to some of the earlier US main air bases in Saigon (Ton Son Nhut), Bien Hoa, Pleiku, and so on.

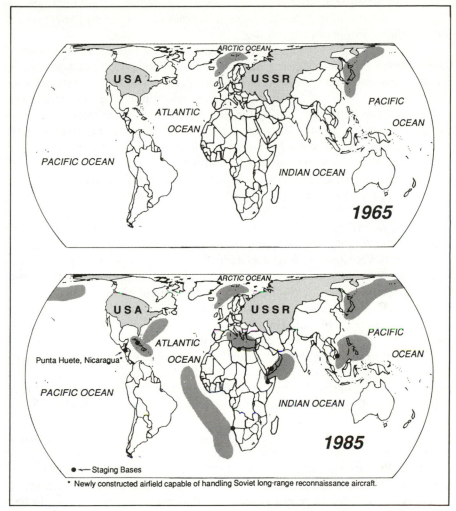

Figure 3. Soviet naval reconnaissance aircraft operating areas in 1965 and 1985

Source: Based on US Department of Defense, *Soviet Military Power 1985* (US Government Printing Office: Washington, DC, 1985), p. 114.

In the South-West Asia/Indian Ocean area, the Soviet Union, since 1978, has been provided access to Aden International Airport and to a military airfield at Al-Anad, for IL-38/May naval reconnaissance aircraft, the Soviet equivalent to the US P-3C.[116] (These are transited further south to Ethiopia and Mozambique.) In the Mediterranean, there has been similar access for IL-38s in Libya since 1981, at Okba ben Nafi, the former US Wheelus Air Force Base. Additionally, there are a large number of Soviet Air Force advisers and maintenance personnel in Libya, whose air force comprises MiG-25s, MiG-23s, MiG-21s, Su-22s and Mi-24 Hind helicopters—as well as Tu-22 Blinder bombers and IL-76 Candid and AN-26 Curl transports.[117] These significant deployments might well be available to Soviet pilots in a crisis or war, given their outsized nature relative to Libyan capabilities.

The case of South Yemen provides perhaps a rare example of an 'out-of-area' locale (which excludes Afghanistan) where Soviet combat aircraft piloted by Soviet pilots have been involved in combat. (There was also some brief such involvement on behalf of Egypt versus Israeli pilots in 1970 during that area's 'war of attrition.') In 1985, during the South Yemen civil war pitting two rival pro-Soviet factions against one another, Soviet pilots were reported to have flown sorties on behalf of the faction headed by Abd al-Fattah Ismail.[118]

In Syria there is a somewhat parallel situation. There, Soviet naval reconnaissance aircraft which monitor the Mediterranean Sea have access to airfields at Tiyas and Umm Aitigah, where pairs of intermediate-range IL-38s are periodically deployed.[119]

In sub-Saharan Africa, Tu-95 Bear D reconnaissance aircraft, which often traversed the Atlantic to Cuba, earlier enjoyed access to Conakry, Guinea.[120] Those flights were apparently cancelled in 1977, though Conakry appears to be still available for staging of transport aircraft.[121] But further south, the Soviet Union now has access for the Bear Ds and Fs at Luanda in Angola; they are reported to deploy in pairs about 3–4 times a year.[122] Mozambique has provided access to airfields at Maputo and Beira. In Ethiopia, which provides extensive naval access, the USSR deployed two IL-38 ASW aircraft to Asmara airfield until they were destroyed by Eritrean rebels in May 1984[123] and has had access to the Johannes IV airfield. Earlier, up to 1977, it had utilized access to several airfields in Somalia: at Birihao, Hargeisa, Gallaci, Amin, Uanle and Belet Uen.[124] It was also earlier reported to be building two airfields in Mali for Soviet use.

Cuba, of course, provides extensive air access to the USSR, in addition to itself deploying large numbers of combat aircraft such as the MiG-23 which could, under some circumstances, be married to Soviet pilots. Both Tu-95 Bear D and Tu-142 Bear F naval reconnaissance and ASW craft have made numerous deployments to Cuba in recent years, often flying in pairs from the Kola Peninsula, along the US east coast, to Cuban bases at Jose San Marti Airport in Havana or San Antonio de los Banos.[125] And although there have been as yet no similar deployments to Nicaragua, the USSR has been reported to have constructed a new airfield there at Hueté capable of handling long-range reconnaissance aircraft.[126]

The maps in figure 3 depict clearly the primary Soviet interests in coverage for ocean surveillance and ASW. The focus on waters adjacent to the two main Soviet SSBN bastions—Barents/Norwegian Sea and Sea of Okhotsk—is clear; similarly, the Mediterranean, the western Indian Ocean/Bab El Mandeb/Strait of Hormuz area, the sea lanes of communication between Africa and South America, the US east coast and the Caribbean. Regarding combat aircraft, the Soviet Union appears still to rely on the air forces of close allies flying late-model Soviet aircraft.

V. Other nations' use of foreign air bases

As in so many other areas of FMP, the matter of external basing of aircraft remains primarily a two-nation game, reflective of the tenacious hold of bi-polarity which has characterized global basing networks in the post-colonial era. Earlier, of course, the primary colonial powers—Britain, France, Italy, the Netherlands, Portugal, Spain—all had extensive networks of air bases closely associated with colonial garrisons and with colonial rivalries among the Euro-pean powers themselves. In the 15–20 years after 1945, these assets gradually dwindled and in the process the number of bases available to the USA and, more generally, to the Atlantic Alliance contracted. But there are still some remnants and in the case of France, at least, even the hint of a slight recent expansion of an overseas air power presence.

Of course, there is some intra-NATO alliance forward basing of aircraft in FR Germany; again, associated for obvious reasons with land-force deploy-ments and, indeed, located immediately to the rear, westward of those forces. The British Army of the Rhine is backed up by significant forward Royal Air Force (RAF) deployments, involving 12 aircraft and two helicopter squadrons, six deploying nuclear-capable Tornado strike aircraft (co-developed in a con-sortium with the FRG and Italy), one of Jaguar reconnaissance aircraft, and two of Phantom fighters; also among these are two squadrons of Harrier jump jets (to be made nuclear-capable) and one of Pembroke communications aircraft.[127] These aircraft are stationed at several main air bases in northern Germany: Laarbruch, Bruggen, Wildenrath and Gutersloh. Canada's con-tribution, further south in Baden Wurtemberg, consists of forward deployment of three squadrons of 36 CF-18s at a base at Baden Sollingen, supported by liaison aircraft and 2700 personnel.[128] In addition, the West German Luftwaffe has training and some support facilities in Portugal, the USA, the UK and Canada, and has permanently based 18 Alpha jets at Beja in Portugal, mostly in connection with training activities.[129]

Elsewhere, overseas, some remnants of what obviously once was a much larger RAF presence remain. There are some aircraft or helicopters permanently stationed at the Falkland Islands, Ascension, Belize, Brunei, Cyprus, Gibraltar and Hong Kong.[130] Of these, the RAF maintains only helicopters and/or utility aircraft in Brunei, Cyprus (Akrotiri), and Hong Kong, though Phantoms and Lightning fighters are sometimes deployed to Cyprus.[131] There are apparently Victor bomber and Hercules C-18 tanker detachments on Ascension, no doubt to provide the wherewithal for another logistics operation to the Falklands, if that should be necessary. (More recently, a larger airfield which can take larger transports has been built in the Falklands.[132]) There is a helicopter squadron at Hong Kong, as the latter's reversion to China looms. In Belize, a lingering point of tension in connection with Guatemalan irredentist aims, the supporting British force includes four Harriers and also four Puma and four Gazelle heli-copters. Gibraltar, seemingly *en route* to political change which will involve some degree of loss of British sovereignty, still sees occasional deployments of

Jaguar fighter aircraft.[133] In the Falklands themselves, the UK—to deter another invasion which could see an enhanced Argentinian air assault—maintains on station a full squadron of nine Phantoms and Harrier vertical take-off and landing (VTOL) aircraft, Hercules tactical transports, and several Sea King and Chinook helicopter detachments.[134] This is, almost quixotically, the largest RAF presence outside of Europe. Overall, the RAF has some 17 000 personnel stationed abroad.[135]

The UK also deploys some ASW aircraft at overseas bases, supplementing the near-global presence of the large US force of P-3C Orions. The British equivalent is the nuclear-capable Nimrod MR2 aircraft. These are periodically deployed at Wideawake Airfield on Ascension; Kindley Naval Air Station, Bermuda; Akrotiri, Cyprus; Stanley Airfield in the Falklands; Gibraltar; Keflavik, Iceland; Sigonella, Sicily and perhaps also Konya Air Base, Turkey.[136]

Some additional external installations are used for training purposes because of the limited air and ground space in the UK. Training exercises with Buccaneers, Harriers and Tornados are conducted at Cold Lake, Alberta and Goose Bay, Newfoundland, Canada;[137] a bombing range at Vlieland in the Netherlands is used by RAF units stationed in FR Germany.[138]

The French Air Force, again in direct association with army detachments, maintains a fairly significant presence in several African states. These forces have been directly engaged in some local wars where, even in small numbers, they can be decisive or at least telling because of an absence of counterweights, at least so long as Soviet or Cuban pilots are not directly engaged. At minimum, they can act as tripwire deterrents—for several Francophone regimes—against local aggression or external involvement.

The main points of present or recent deployment have been in Djibouti, the Central African Republic, Chad, Gabon, the Ivory Coast and Senegal. Jaguar fighter-bombers (co-developed with the UK) are deployed in the Central African Republic, Chad and Gabon; Mirage F-1C aircraft have also been deployed to Chad.[139] Djibouti has a squadron of 10 Mirage IIIs. Alouette and Puma helicopters are stationed in all of these countries; in the Ivory Coast they constitute the only French Air Force presence. There are C-160 Noratlas transport aircraft deployed to the Central African Republic, Chad, Djibouti, Gabon and Senegal;[140] in the latter case, France has based at Dakar and also at Djibouti Breguet Atlantique maritime-surveillance aircraft in areas not far from frequent Soviet naval deployments in West Africa and the Indian Ocean.[141] The Noratlases provide for speedy movement of French or other surrogate forces in case of crisis or conflict.

Aircraft based in Chad were earlier militarily engaged, as were those based in Senegal, which flew missions on behalf of Mauritania and Morocco earlier on during the (still ongoing) Western Sahara War.[142] Outside of Africa, France has no permanently stationed combat aircraft, though helicopters and utility aircraft are deployed in Martinique, Guadeloupe, French Polynesia, Réunion and the Mozambique Channel Islands.

Otherwise, one can point merely to a few, scattered external deployments of aircraft represented by still other members of the Western alliance. The Netherlands has deployed some Neptune ASW aircraft at Curacao in the Caribbean, and rotates some P-3Cs through Keflavik, Iceland and through British air bases at St Mawgan and Machrihanish. Australia has kept two squadrons of Mirages in Malaysia as its contribution to the defence of South-East Asia;[143] New Zealand up to 1982 had also had a small air presence in Singapore. Outside the Western orbit, Libya earlier forward-based some aircraft in Chad prior to its débâcle in 1987. The disparate, scattered nature of these relatively small activities indicates just how little remains of old colonial-based presences and the extent to which superpower rivalry now dominates the game of basing access diplomacy.

Running somewhat contrary to the above point, several Third World states have donated pilots to other countries' air forces, sometimes obviously in close connection to transfers of aircraft from a superpower. Cuban, North Korean and other nations' pilots have flown Soviet aircraft in Syria, Ethiopia and Angola; Taiwanese and Pakistani air force personnel have similarly served in Saudi Arabia and perhaps in other Persian Gulf states.[144] This underscores again the increasing trend towards use of mercenaries or 'surrogates' even as basing diplomacy itself seems increasingly characterized by commercial considerations.

VI. Aircraft overflights

One of the less visible forms of FMP, also one which involves movable and transitory presences, is that of aircraft overflight privileges. It is a form of FMP which under 'normal' circumstances, that is, outside of wars and crises, receives scant attention and is the subject of little political controversy. But that often changes during major crises, as witness the attention given to overflights amid the rival airlifts during the 1973 war, or the more recent fuss over French and Spanish refusals to allow overflights by US F-111 bombers *en route* from bases in the UK to targets in Libya.[145]

This occasionally crucial matter of aircraft overflight privileges involves a complex range of practices and traditions, some of which have, in an overall sense, been altered by time in an era of increasingly 'total' warfare, diplomacy and ideological rivalries. In parallel with—and closely bound up with—what has been wrought by nations' increasing insistence upon extension of sovereign control further outward from coastlines (now more or less institutionalized by 200-mile Exclusive Economic Zones—EEZs), the trend here has been towards tightened restrictions on overflights.

In the past—and in some cases continuing to the present—some nations have allowed others more or less full, unhindered, and continuous overflight rights (perhaps involving only *pro forma* short-term notices, i.e., filing of flight plans).[146] In other cases, however, where political relations are weaker or not based on alliances, *ad hoc* formal applications for permission to overfly must be made well ahead of time, which may or may not be granted depending upon the purpose and situation, be it routine or crisis. It is also to be noted that this does not only involve military overflights—the tragic events surrounding the shooting down of Korean Air Lines 007 over Sakhalin Island illustrate that commercial flights are similarly affected.

It is to be stressed that the day-to-day diplomacy of overflight rights is a very closed and obscure matter, albeit of often crucial importance. We have little data—the subject periodically emerges to prominence during crises such as the 1986 US raid on Libya. Of course, it is precisely when urgent military operations are involved that the subject acquires the most importance.

Nowadays, of course, well past the introduction of radar and its widespread global distribution, few overflights can be made on a covert basis, as was common before World War II, when detection depended primarily on visual observation from the ground. Not only 'host nation' radar, but now also the superpowers' satellite reconnaissance makes such 'covert' activities almost impossible, particularly if a small nation has access to information from one of the superpowers, be it on a regular or *ad hoc* basis. This in turn may have important ramifications for intra-Third World rivalries, specifically, regarding the balance of diplomatic leverage involved. Nations inclined, for instance, to provide overflight rights in connection with a US airlift to Israel will know that Soviet satellite reconnaissance will provide information about that to Arab governments. That is a powerful deterrent.

Now, however, the impending advent of Stealth aircraft technology may bring still another cycle of change. It may negate many small powers' radar capabilities for detecting overflights, though the superpowers' satellites may still be able to detect most of the stealth overflights from above, because of the much larger radar cross-sections provided.

Some overflights are made without permission (as with the respective use by the United States and the USSR of U-2 and MiG-25 reconnaissance flights), overtly or covertly or with a tacit or resigned wink by the overflown nation. Often a nation whose airspace is violated will not openly complain for fear of international or domestic embarrassment over its impotence, or untoward diplomatic repercussions by a strong power.[147] Hence, the USSR is thought to have overflown Egypt and Sudan, among others, without permission in supplying arms to Ethiopia during the 1977–78 Horn War;[148] earlier, its MiG-25 and Tu-95 reconnaissance aircraft apparently flew with impunity over Iran's airspace. The United States is thought to have threatened overflights in some places for future arms resupply of Israel, if it should be utterly necessary.

All in all, the rather sharp division of the world into hostile ideological camps—and the proliferation of jealous and politically volatile sovereignties produced in the wake of decolonialization—has rendered the granting of overflight privileges a perhaps increasingly important and sensitive matter. That has been borne out in numerous recent wars and crises, some of which are cited above. There have been many others.

In the 1973 war, Turkey and Yugoslavia granted the USSR overflight rights, while some of the USA's NATO Allies did not grant similar access to the USA on behalf of Israel.[149] During the Ethiopia–Somalia War of 1977–78, the USSR was apparently embroiled in complicated problems with several South-West Asian and African nations over overflights—in addition to Egypt and Sudan, also Pakistan and Iraq (the latter backed Somalia despite its hitherto close Soviet ties). The Soviet airlift to Angola in 1975 involved utilization of the airspace (and staging bases) of a number of West African states along the route south from Algeria or Libya:[150] Benin, Mali, Guinea, Equatorial Guinea, Congo. Belgium subsequently had problems with its support of Zaïre during the Shaba II conflict in 1978.[151] India was apparently overflown by Soviet aircraft *en route* to arms resupply of Viet Nam in 1979 during the latter's war with China.[152] The USA, meanwhile, apparently had to conduct some quiet or covert overflights *en route* to the Iran hostage raid in 1981 from bases in Egypt— Saudi Arabia and Oman were mentioned, speculatively, in press reports.[153] Israel's raid on Entebbe clearly required Kenyan permission for overflights, but may as well have involved covert use of the airspace of other nations, perhaps Sudan or Ethiopia. As is more generally the case for basing access, overflight privileges may be required as a quid pro quo for arms transfers. It is reported that a recent Soviet agreement to supply advanced MiG-23 attack aircraft to North Korea was related to the latter's now allowing Soviet military overflights *en route* to the East China Sea and to Viet Nam.[154]

Generally, gauging the possibilities and problems for overflights in particular circumstances requires close attention to the political alignments of nations along various corridors or axes—north–south and east–west across Africa, south from the USSR across various parts of the rimland, across South America, across portions of South-East Asia, and so on. But, in recent years, the telescoping of several developments—large-scale use of tanker refuelling, the closure of straits less than 24 nautical miles wide (twice the 12-mile territorial limit per country), and the possibility of 200-mile EEZs being used to exclude overflights—has focused attention on long-range flights overseas by what earlier would have been considered circuitous routes. This has applied to long-range airlift (for instance, for arms resupply operations or support of military interventions) and to long-range deployment of, or ferrying of, fighter bombers by major powers.

Figure 4, showing maps from a recent US government-sponsored report, indicates the long-range trends regarding US and Soviet access to airspace. An earlier RAND study, meanwhile, had underlined the critical need for US retention of access to the two British island bases, Diego Garcia and Ascension, particularly if tankers could be based at each. If so, the USA could then mount airlift operations almost anywhere in the world, even in the face of overflight restrictions, including those associated with narrow straits and EEZs.

There is, of course, a close connection between air-staging networks and overflight rights, even aside from the tendency to congruence between the two, such that major powers will be provided with both by some host nations. Blocked overflight corridors, however, place a premium on staging points which can compensate, if only with great penalties in required ranges. As Kemp and

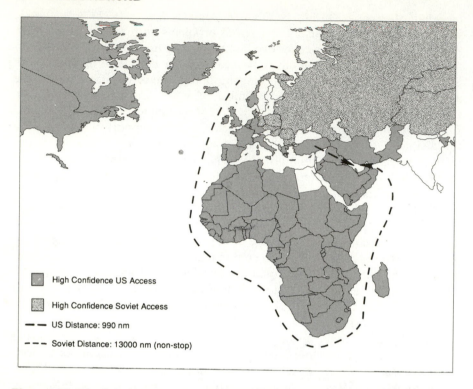

Figure 4 (a). Trends in US and Soviet access to airfields or airspace in the mid-1950s
In the mid-1950s the USA had base access and overflight rights that allowed it to send forces quickly from Europe to the Persian Gulf or other nearby areas, while Soviet airlift to the Near East or South Asia was not feasible.

others have noted, this has, in some circumstances, led to the disproportionate strategic importance of islands such as Ascension, the Cocos Islands, Diego Garcia, the Maldives, the Seychelles, and others, which line major air routes around large continents; note too the extensive Soviet effort to gain a foothold in the south-west Pacific. It may also lead to the disproportionate importance of small nations located at vital points, as witness Oman's role on behalf of the West.

Though the varied possibilities for utilizing staging routes—again, either for long-range transport or for ferrying of fighter aircraft—during or out of crises or wars are almost limitless, a few points can be made. Mostly, this has to do with a number of routes or corridors frequently utilized or often required by the respective superpowers.

The USA has, of course, required staging points for arms resupply of Israel—that has directed attention in the past particularly to Portugal's Azores air base at Lajes.[155] Contingency plans for staging *matériel* to the Persian Gulf area have focused attention on air facilities in Morocco, Italy's Sicily (Sigonella), Egypt and Turkey—or, coming from the other direction, Guam, the Philippines and

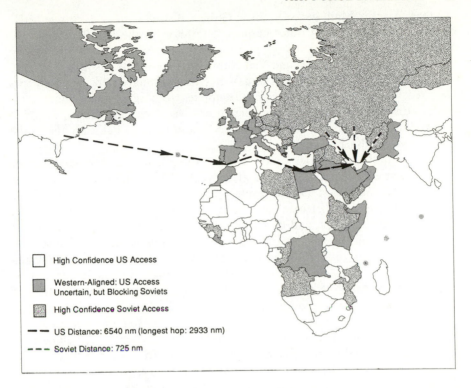

Figure 4 (b). Trends in US and Soviet access to airfields or airspace in 1987
By 1987, access to airfields and airspace had changed dramatically. The USA must use intercontinental airlift to send ground forces to the Gulf, but *en route* staging is uncertain. The USSR can airlift forces quickly from nearby, without staging or refuelling. Even US Allies such as Turkey have on occasion allowed the USSR to transit their airspace when resupplying client states in a crisis.

Source: Based on the Commission on Integrated Long-Term Strategy, *Discriminate Deterrence* (US Government Printing Office: Washington, D.C., 1988), pp. 24–25.

Diego Garcia,[156] and Oman, as well as Somalia and Kenya.[157] The USA, along with its European allies, earlier used the Ivory Coast, Senegal and Liberia for the rescue effort mounted on behalf of Zaïre's Shaba Province and, more recently, has used airfields in Zaïre to stage *matériel* to UNITA forces in Angola.[158] Because of its control over Hawaii and Guam, the USA need not worry about staging transports or fighter aircraft to the entirety of the Western Pacific littoral. It is worth noting, however, that long-maintained US access to facilities in New Zealand for staging C-130 flights to Antarctica (as part of 'Operation Deep Freeze') has been called into question, if only over a technicality over inspections for nuclear weapons.[159] It remains to be seen whether this presages difficulties elsewhere as part of a growing global trend.

The Soviet Union, in particular, is concerned about a north–south staging route reaching down into southern Africa—that focuses attention on facilities in Libya, Algeria, Mali, Benin, Guinea, Guinea-Bissau, Congo, Tanzania, Ethiopia and Angola, among other nations.[160] Otherwise, the USSR is also concerned about a west-east staging route running from North Africa through the Middle East and on to India and Viet Nam—that spotlights Libya, Syria, Iraq, South Yemen, India, Cambodia and Viet Nam, among others. Such an axis was used, for instance, in ferrying arms resupplies from Egypt—then a long-term Soviet arms client—to India during the latter's war with Pakistan in 1971.[161] It was also used to resupply Viet Nam via India and perhaps Pakistan during the former's war with China in 1979.[162]

For the future, the Soviet Union is likely to seek some other points where obvious barriers now exist to a global network. The seeming Soviet drive for access in the south-west Pacific would appear related to the possibility of a staging link between Viet Nam and Peru, both Soviet arms clients. Grenada would have provided an additional link *en route* to Central America or one between Cuba and West Africa;[163] bases in Nicaragua would provide staging assistance *en route* to the western coast of South America. Now that Guinea has somewhat restricted access to the Soviet Air Force, a replacement may be sought in West Africa. Noteworthy too have been Soviet pressures on some of the new Indian Ocean island nations—Seychelles, Maldives, Mauritius, all located along vital air logistics routes.[164] It remains further to be seen whether—or to what extent—the USSR will be able to match US tanker refuelling capabilities, so as to reduce requirements for staging facilities and overflight rights, allowing for critical reliance on a smaller number of basing points.

Some middle-range powers as well may have to concern themselves with long-range staging routes, either during crises or under more normal conditions. France's requirements for staging *matériel* south into Africa are noted above. Britain, in the wake of the Falklands War, is reported to have utilized Brazilian bases for refuelling aircraft used to reprovision its forces in the Falklands.[165]

VII. Summary

The discussion in this chapter indicates that when it comes to forward stationing of combat aircraft, both for potential conventional and nuclear purposes, most of the two superpowers' deployments are in Europe, within the confines of the rival NATO and WTO alliances. There are a few exceptions, for instance, the rival deployments of attack aircraft in Viet Nam and the Philippines. Indeed, perhaps the most vital external bases in the Third World, used by the superpowers to deploy aircraft in peacetime, are those devoted to ASW and ocean surveillance, including in some cases the prepositioning of nuclear depth charges.

Otherwise, the most important aircraft-related FMP has to do with the superpowers' competition for influence in the Third World and their competitive roles as suppliers of arms (including resupply during conflict), as interveners in conflict, and as constant participants in the ongoing game of coercive diplomacy.

These purposes, as we have noted, direct attention to permanent or *ad hoc* use of staging facilities and of overhead airspace, and (at least for the USA) to global networks of tanker refuelling facilities. That in turn directs attention to the bases for Third World alignments with superpowers, be they ideology, formal security pacts, and so on, or rather military and/or economic aid as quid pro quo, whether or not cemented by ideological ties.

Notes and references

[1] The 'airman's view' as a phase of geopolitical theory can be seen in Jones, S., 'Global strategic views', *The Geographical Review*, vol. 45, no. 4 (July 1955), pp. 492–508; and Warner, E., 'Douhet, Mitchell, Seversky: Theories of air warfare', ed. E. Earle, *Makers of Modern Strategy* (Princeton University Press: Princeton, N.J., 1941), chapter 20.

[2] See Harkavy, R. E., *Great Power Competition for Overseas Bases: The Geopolitics of Access Diplomacy* (Pergamon: New York, 1982), p. 21.

[3] See 'In-flight refueling to aid C-5 wing life', *Aviation Week & Space Technology*, 12 July 1976, pp. 32–34; and 'Importance of U.S. munitions to Israel assayed', *New York Times*, 2 Dec. 1974, p. 3. According to US Department of Defense, *Soviet Military Power 1987*, 6th edn (US Government Printing Office: Washington, DC, 1987), p. 98, both the C-5B Galaxy and An-22 Cock have ranges of 4200 km with maximum payloads.

[4] These are itemized in International Institute for Strategic Studies, *The Military Balance: 1987–1988* (IISS: London, 1987), in country-by-country orders of battle. In the Iraqi case, regarding refuelling of fighter aircraft over the Persian Gulf during the Iraq-Iran War, see 'On crucial Strait of Hormuz, Omani "traffic cops" ', *New York Times*, 22 Dec. 1986, p. A18.

[5] Harkavy (note 2), pp. 82–83 and p. 104, note 177, wherein it is reported that the RAF had some 20 air bases in Tanganyika alone in the 1930s, the Italians 11 main bases and 69 additional airstrips in Ethiopia to support over 200 combat aircraft. These data were originally drawn from the US National Archives, Navy and Old Army Branch, Record Group 165, Military Intelligence Division (MID).

[6] This is best illustrated, with particular attention to contingency and dispersal bases in the UK, in Campbell, D., *The Unsinkable Aircraft Carrier: American Military Power in Britain* (Paladin: London, 1986), especially pp. 255–71, which discusses the distinctions between main operating bases, stand-by operating bases, collocated operating bases, and forward operating bases.

[7] This issue was raised by the Israeli use of RPVs during the Lebanon war of 1982. See Gabriel, R. A., *Operation Peace for Galilee* (Hill and Wang: New York, 1984), pp. 98–99; and Bellamy, C., *The Future of Land Warfare* (St. Martin's: New York, 1987), pp. 27 and 259. More generally, see 'RPVs under scrutiny', *Aerospace*, vol. 9 (Dec. 1982), p. 28; and 'Cost factor key to unmanned vehicles', *Aviation Week & Space Technology*, 9 Aug. 1982, pp. 65–67.

[8] On overflights, generally, see Dadant, P. M., *Shrinking International Airspace as a Problem for Future Air Movements—A Briefing*, Report R-2178-AF (RAND: Santa Monica, Calif., 1978); and *Discriminate Deterrence*, Report of the Commission on Integrated Long-Term Strategy, US Government Printing Office, Jan. 1988, especially pp. 24–25.

[9] See Starr, H. and Most, B., 'Patterns of conflict: Quantitative analysis and the comparative lessons of Third World wars', eds R. E. Harkavy and S. G. Neuman, *The Lessons of Recent Wars in the Third World: Approaches and Case Studies* (D. C. Heath: Lexington, Mass., 1985), pp. 33–52; and 'The world's wars: Turn south for the killing fields', *The Economist*, 12 Mar. 1988, pp. 18–22; and Keegan, J. and Wheatcroft, A., *Zones of Conflict: An Atlas of Future Wars* (Simon and Schuster: New York, 1986).

[10] See Harkavy, R., 'Arms resupply during conflict: A framework for analysis', *The Jerusalem Journal of International Relations*, vol. 7, no. 3 (1985), pp. 5–40.

[11] Arkin, W. M. and Fieldhouse, R. F., *Nuclear Battlefields: Global Links in the Arms Race* (Ballinger: Cambridge, Mass., 1985), p. 73, notes the additional role for the SR-71 (and the U-2) of telemetry intercepts from Soviet missile tests. Soviet use of MiG-25s operating out of Libya for reconnaissance missions over the Mediterranean is noted in 'Libya: The mysterious weapons store', *Middle-East Intelligence Survey*, vol. 7, no. 15 (1–15 Nov. 1979), p. 119.

[12] Arkin and Fieldhouse (note 11), pp. 80–81.

[13] Arkin and Fieldhouse (note 11), pp. 80 and 127. See also 'Britain agrees to Diego Garcia plan

for loaded B-52s', *Daily Telegraph*, 14 Aug. 1981. But, many analyses of B-52 basing in Diego Garcia see the primary purpose as that of conventional interdiction of Soviet forces advancing through Iran—see Kupchan, C., *The Persian Gulf and the West* (Allen and Unwin: Boston, Mass., 1987), p. 110; McNaugher, 'T. L., *Arms and Oil: U.S. Military Strategy and the Persian Gulf* (Brookings Institution: Washington, DC, 1985), chapter 3; and '3 nuclear storage depots to close as B-52 missions change', *New York Times*, 16 May 1988, p. A18, which reports that 'removing nuclear weapons from the base on Guam means the Air Force will no longer have long-range nuclear weapons in the Pacific region'.

[14] 'Plan to re-equip B-52s is proposed', *New York Times*, 18 Sep. 1987, p. A7. Regarding the attack routes, missions, and basing requirements for the B-2 Stealth bomber expected to be deployed around 1992, see 'Stealth bomber takes shape: A flying wing and crew of 2', *New York Times*, 16 May 1988. Herein it is stated that the bombers will be based at Whiteman AFB, Missouri and other inland bases, will be armed with SRAMs and iron bombs, and will require tanker refuelling *en route* to and on return from (hypothesized) missions in the USSR.

[15] Goodie, C. B., *Strategic Air Command* (Simon and Schuster: New York, 1965); Holst, J. J., 'Comparative U.S. and Soviet deployments, doctrines, and arms limitation', University of Chicago, Chicago, 1971, Occasional Paper of the Center for Policy Study; and Campbell (note 6), chapter 1.

[16] 'Cuba's secrets probed', *Centre Daily Times*, 18 Mar. 1980, p. 4 discusses whether the length of runways at Cienfuegos and at other airfields could accommodate Backfire bombers. See also 'Allies foresee wartime peril in Cuban base', *New York Times*, 3 Dec. 1979; 'Russia's backfire bomber; red threat or a red herring?', *New York Times*, 7 May 1978, part IV, p. 4; and 'Senate panel calls hearings on Soviet troops in Cuba', *New York Times*, 7 Sep. 1979.

[17] SIPRI data on Canada, Iceland, Greenland, etc., regarding stationing of tankers; and Arkin and Fieldhouse (note 11), p. 78.

[18] But the USA has in recent years striven for additional access for its B-52 bombers in Australia and Diego Garcia, claimed by many to involve 'strategic' purposes, i.e., the possibility of launching ALCMs at the USSR from the south. See, for instance 'Bombers wait for Reagan', *Financial Review*, 1 May 1981.

[19] 'U.S. officials divided on approach to INF', *Washington Post*, 19 Oct. 1986, p. A1; 'Commander of NATO is opposed to ridding Europe of all missiles', *New York Times*, 21 Apr. 1987, p. A6.

[20] 'U.S. woos Ozal for military foothold', *The Times*, 3 Apr. 1986; 'U.S. improves Turkish bases', *Financial Times*, 15 Nov. 1984; and 'Young Turks maneuvre to invade Iraq', which cites recent construction of bases usable by the USAF in eastern Turkey at Diyarbakir, Bitlis, Van, Erzerum and Kars, some possibly for B-52s, others in connection with the Rapid Deployment Force. See also McNaugher (note 13), chapter 3, especially pp. 55-63; and 'U.S. to pay for upgrading Turkish military airfields', *New York Times*, 16 Oct. 1982.

[21] See Gabriel (note 7), p. 7.

[22] See Rubinstein, A., *Red Star on the Nile* (Princeton University Press: Princeton, N.J., 1977), chapter 4; and Sella, A., *Soviet Political and Military Conduct in the Middle East* (St. Martin's Press: New York, 1981), p. 26.

[23] Some sources have claimed that the USA used KC-135 tankers based on Torrejon for refuelling US planes flying supplies to Israel during the 1973 Middle East War even though Spain refused to permit US use of Spanish bases to help Israel. See 'Spain reportedly urges U.S. to quit air base near Madrid', *International Herald Tribune*, 25 Feb. 1975. An opposite view is forwarded in 'Portugal cool to idea of U.S. sending spare parts to Iran via Azores base', *Christian Science Monitor*, 4 Nov. 1980, p. 11, which also discusses Lisbon's reluctance to allow US use of Lajes for logistics in connection with crises around the Persian Gulf.

[24] See, for instance, 'Costa Ricans expel U.S. Air Force unit', *New York Times*, 11 July 1979.

[25] Britain in 1973 refused for several days to allow US U-2 spy planes to use the British base in Akrotiri, Cyprus, for flights over the Middle East battlefields. See 'British–U.S. intelligence links are expected to become even closer', *New York Times*, 12 Mar. 1979, p. A4. Regarding Diego Garcia and possible future resupply of Israel, see Siegel, L., 'Diego Garcia', *Pacific Research*, vol. 8, no. 3 (Mar.–Apr. 1977), p. 5.

[26] See 'Use of bases may become thorny issue for U.S., Spain', *Washington Post*, 30 Jan. 1979, which discusses 'Spain's reluctance to allow U.S. F-15s bound for Saudi Arabia to land at Torrejon air base outside Madrid', in turn impelling alternative use of Portugal's Lajes base in the Azores. See also 'Spain tosses a wrench into U.S. F-15 plans', *Baltimore Sun*, 12 Jan. 1979, p. 2; and 'Spain bars refueling of U.S. planes', *Baltimore Sun*, 8 Aug. 1980, p. 2, wherein 'In the past two months, the sources said, Spain has twice denied this authorization to U.S. combat and transport aircraft

en route to the Middle East.' Then see 'U.S. eyes updating of airbase in Azores', *Washington Star*, 25 July 1980, p. 5, wherein: 'Spain recently refused permission for a squadron of U.S. Air Force F-4 Phantom jet fighter-bombers to refuel at American-built air bases there on the way to a three-month training exercise in Egypt.'

[27] See 'Rebels set to take Chad town', *Daily Telegraph*, 11 Aug. 1983; and 'Niger's president is dead of a brain tumor in Paris', 11 Nov. 1987, p. A6. See, regarding the UK, 'Hercules refuel in Brazil', *The Guardian*, 6 Mar. 1983.

[28] Harkavy (note 2), pp. 67–71.

[29] See 'Importance of U.S. munitions to Israel assayed', *New York Times*, 2 Dec. 1974. Herein, referring to the C-5A's performance in 1973: 'Refueling in the Azores, one of the giant transports carried 148,000 pounds of supplies to Israel. On a non-stop, unrefueled flight the freight weight was 67,000 pounds.' See also, for discussion of cargo loads and fuel requirements for the various US airlift transports, 'The U.S. airlift has growing strategic role', *New York Times*, 15 Nov. 1975.

[30] Dadant (note 8).

[31] Again, see 'Spain reportedly urges U.S. to quit air base near Madrid', *International Herald Tribune*, 25 Feb. 1975.

[32] US Department of Defense, *Soviet Military Power 1988*, 7th edn. US Government Printing Office: Washington, DC, 1988), pp. 51, 107, 110 and 150 discusses the MIDAS tanker, and on pp. 39, 93, 131 and 136 the AN-24 transport. MIDAS apparently will be used to refuel air defence fighters for longer loiter time, and also long-range bombers carrying ALCMs.

[33] See 'Demand for aerial refueling increasing', *Aviation Week & Space Technology*, 7 Feb. 1983, p. 76; and 'Upgrade aerial refueling capabilities', *Aviation Week & Space Technology*, 11 Aug. 1980, pp. 57–60.

[34] See, for instance, 'ASW: A deadly underseas game', *US News and World Report*, 15 June 1987, pp. 40–41.

[35] Richelson, J., *Sword and Shield* (Ballinger: Cambridge, Mass., 1986), pp. 105–106; and 'Soviets increase close-in flights along E. coast', *Washington Star*, 20 Mar. 1981, p. 7.

[36] 'Shultz, in Iceland, is said to discuss arms dispute', *New York Times*, 15 Mar. 1985, which says sites earmarked for these nuclear devices are Canada, Spain, the Azores (Portugal), Bermuda, Puerto Rico, the Philippines and Diego Garcia. See also 'U.S. tries to reduce allied resistance to American arms', *New York Times*, 14 Feb. 1985, p. A13, which cites reports on crisis contingency plans earmarking nuclear weapons for Puerto Rico, the Azores, Philippines, Spain and Diego Garcia.

[37] Regarding TACAMO, see Arkin and Fieldhouse (note 11), pp. 80–81; and Ford, D., *The Button* (Simon and Schuster: New York, 1985), pp. 95–97.

[38] On COD aircraft, see Blechman, B. M. and Weinland, R. G., 'Why coaling stations are necessary in the nuclear age', *International Security*, no. 2 (1977), pp. 88–89 and p. 90.

[39] 'Cyprus vital for spy planes to monitor Salt-2', *Daily Telegraph*, 23 May 1979.

[40] For instance, US photoreconnaissance aircraft are reported closely to have monitored the 1967 and 1973 wars as well as the subsequent truces and peace arrangements in Sinai. See, for instance, Richelson, J. T., *The U.S. Intelligence Community* (Ballinger: Cambridge, Mass., 1985), p. 116, wherein it is stated that during the 1973 war, 'an SR-71 was sent to overfly the Negev desert on the basis of information that Israel was preparing to arm its Jericho missiles with nuclear warheads.' See also 'U.S. plans to use new U-2s to monitor Soviet missiles', *International Herald Tribune*, 6 Apr. 1979, which discusses reconnaissance missions in the Middle East.

[41] International Institute for Strategic Studies, *The Military Balance: 1986–1987* (IISS: London, 1986), p. 30.

[42] Note 41, p. 29 and SIPRI data.

[43] SIPRI data.

[44] SIPRI data and Campbell (note 6), chapters 9 and 10.

[45] See also 'Airstrip one,' *Sanity*, Oct./Nov. 1980, p. 14.

[46] See 'Aggressor F-5E aircraft', *Air Force Magazine*, vol. 65, no. 4 (Apr. 1982), p. 39.

[47] Regarding the removal of F-16s from Torrejon, see 'Spain rejects U.S. deal on bases, foreshadowing the treaty's end', *New York Times*, 5 Nov. 1987, p. A1; 'Weinberger, opposed in Spain, backs U.S. bases', *New York Times*, 18 Mar. 1987, p. A12; 'Spain to press U.S. for a timetable on removal of F-16 jets near Madrid', *International Herald Tribune*, 26 June 1987, p. 2; 'When the stepping stones of world power are rocky bases', *U.S. News and World Report*, 23 Nov. 1987, pp. 30–31; 'U.S. asks Italy to take F-16 jets that Spain has ordered removed', *New York Times*, 4 Feb. 1988, p. A6; and 'Global view: Europe: Italy', *Journal of Defense and Diplomacy*, vol. 6,

no. 5 (May 1988), pp. 56–57. Herein it is reported that three Italian bases were being considered for the F-16s: Comiso, Aviano, and Gioia del Colla.

[48] IISS (note 41), p. 29.

[49] IISS (note 41) and 'U.S. begins F-16 deployment in Japan in bid to rival Soviet buildup in Asia', *International Herald Tribune*, 4 Apr. 1985.

[50] See 'Aggressor F-5E aircraft', *Air Force Magazine*, vol. 65, no. 4 (Apr. 1982), p. 8.

[51] See 'U.S. aide vows steps to offset new Soviet jets to North Korea', *International Herald Tribune*, 15 Aug. 1985, p. 4.

[52] IISS (note 41), p. 30.

[53] Campbell (note 6), pp. 78–82.

[54] Campbell (note 6), pp. 261–62.

[55] See, regarding 8 COBs in Norway and the 'Invictus' programme involving US carriers, Lodgaard, S., 'Threats to European security: The main elements', eds S. Lodgaard and K. Birnbaum, *Overcoming Threats to Europe: A New Deal for Confidence and Security*, SIPRI (Oxford University Press: London, 1987), p. 24.

[56] See 'Denmarks's defence', special issue of *Defence Today*, published by The Information and Welfare Services of the Danish Defence, Copenhagen, Aug. 1986, p. 27.

[57] See, additionally, 'Bulgaria upset by air base NATO is building in Turkey', *New York Times*, 6 Jan. 1984, p. 4, which discusses a base at Corlu which might be adapted to take radar warning planes.

[58] IISS (note 41), p. 20.

[59] SIPRI data.

[60] SIPRI data and Arkin and Fieldhouse (note 11), p. 78.

[61] IISS (note 41), p. 27.

[62] IISS (note 41), p. 27.

[63] IISS (note 41), pp. 29–30, and SIPRI data. Earlier, up to 1973, a squadron of C-130s had been based on Taiwan, and Ching Chuan Kang air base. See 'U.S. air squadron leaves Taiwan', *New York Times*, 2 Sep. 1973.

[64] 'U.S. military is no secret in Egypt', *Washington Post*, 20 June 1980, p. 1.

[65] 'Air force wants new cargo plane', *New York Times*, 5 Mar. 1984, p. A1.

[66] Note 65, p. A15, continued.

[67] Tierney, J., 'The invisible force', *Science 83*, vol. 4, no. 9 (1983), pp. 68–78.

[68] For a description of the P-3's capabilities see 'Iceland: Military intelligence crossroad', *The Christian Science Monitor*, 26 Nov. 1975, p. 10.

[69] Tierney (note 67), p. 70.

[70] This is discussed in Arkin and Fieldhouse (note 11), p. 62.

[71] Arkin and Fieldhouse (note 11), p. 62, which also notes the similar role of over 100 SH-3 ASW helicopters. See also IISS (note 41), p. 25.

[72] Regarding Oman-based P-3s, see 'U.S. wants more flights by AWACS over the Gulf', *International Herald Tribune*, 12 June 1987, p. 4.

[73] Regarding use of Singapore, see 'U.S. stepping up Indian Ocean activity', *Los Angeles Times*, 23 June 1978, p. 1B, which notes this followed loss of US access to Thailand. In 'Thais won't allow U.S. Indian Ocean flights', *Japan Times*, 14 July 1974, it is said US access—for reconnaissance flights—to Utapao Air Base had been halted. But continued use of Tahkli is noted in 'U.S. military still using Thai base for refueling', *New York Times*, 21 Oct. 1976; and 'U.S. air crews at war base in Thailand again', *Chicago Tribune*, 21 Oct. 1976.

[74] SIPRI data.

[75] AWACS can also be temporarily based or 'rotated through,' for training purposes or those of a political demonstration. See 'U.S. planes test Egypt's air bases', *Washington Post*, 9 Jan. 1980, p. 1; and Kupchan (note 13), p. 132, which reports on the sending of four AWACS to Riyadh in 1980 to deter Iranian attacks on Saudi oilfields at the outset of the Iraq–Iran War. See also 'U.S. calls back AWACs planes from Chad war', *International Herald Tribune*, 24 Aug. 1983, describing US dispatch of these aircraft to Sudan during hostilities between France and Libya in Chad.

[76] IISS (note 4), p. 25; SIPRI data.

[77] See 'AWACs base open in Turkey', *New York Times*, 26 Oct. 1983. See also 'Greece will be AWACs base by end of 1985', *Financial Times*, 10 Oct. 1984, which further reports on a plan to rotate AWACS through a Greek base at Preveza.

[78] 'Fig leaf hunting', *Near East Report*, vol. 31, no. 24 (15 June 1987), p. 95; 'U.S. expects Saudis to extend protection for AWACs', *Internationl Herald Tribune*, 20–21 June 1987, p. 2; 'U.S. wants more flights by AWACs over the Gulf', *International Herald Tribune*, 12 June 1987, p. 4.

[79] 'Flying into a tight corner', *Time*, 22 June 1987, p. 41, which notes Pakistan's request for control aircraft to direct F-16s against intruders along the border with Afghanistan; and 'White house seeks increase in sales of arms overseas', *New York Times*, 2 May 1988, p. A1.

[80] Arkin and Fieldhouse (note 11), p. 73, note the RC-135 Cobra Ball planes fly from Shemya Island to cover Soviet Pacific tests. See also Richelson, J. T. and Ball, D., *The Ties That Bind* (Allen and Unwin: Boston, Mass., 1985), pp. 182–83; and Hersh, S., *The Target is Destroyed* (Random House: New York, 1986), pp. 37–43. Arkin and Fieldhouse (note 11), p. 73, also report the EC-135N Advanced Range Instrumentation Aircraft (ARIA) is based at Wright-Patterson AFB in Ohio and can fly out of 40 airfields around the world to monitor tests.

[81] One RC-135 based on Shemya Island, Aleutians, was involved in the shooting down of Korean Air Lines flight 007 in 1983. See 'Why the Russians did it', *Newsweek*, 19 Sep. 1983, pp. 23–24.

[82] Regarding the use of Hellenikon for monitoring Libyan communications, see 'U.S. Planes in Greece, instead of heading north, veer south to listen in on Libya', *International Herald Tribune*, 29 Oct. 1981. See also 'U.S. doubt over Greek bases', *Financial Times*, 5 Apr. 1984, which also reports on the role for reconnaissance flights of the base at Iraklion on Crete.

[83] Campbell (note 6), p. 241.

[84] U.S. loss of access to Peshawar long after the Powers incident is discussed in 'U.S. base in Pakistan phasing out after 10 years', *Christian Science Monitor*, 27 June 1969.

[85] 'U.S. plans to use new U-2s to monitor Soviet missiles', *International Herald Tribune*, 6 Apr. 1979; 'Cyprus vital for spy planes to monitor Salt-2', *Daily Telegraph*, 23 May 1979; 'Turkey still considering U-2 overflights by U.S.', *International Herald Tribune*, 14 Sep. 1979; 'Turkey refuses to consult Russians about spy flights', *The Times*, 5 July 1980; 'U.S. panel says Turkey to allow flights by U-2s', *International Herald Tribune*, 5–6 July 1980.

[86] Britain in 1973 refused for several days to allow US U-2 spy planes to use the British base in Akrotiri, Cyprus, for flights over the Middle East battlefields. See 'British–U.S. intelligence links are expected to become even closer', *New York Times*, 12 Mar. 1979, p. A4. Regarding Diego Garcia and possible future resupply of Israel, see Siegel, L., 'Diego Garcia', *Pacific Research*, vol. 8, no. 3 (Mar.–Apr. 1977), p. 5.

[87] 'Second SR-171 deployed to England', *Aviation Week & Space Technology*, 31 Jan. 1983, p. 59.

[88] Arkin and Fieldhouse (note 11), p. 234.

[89] Ford (note 37), p. 95.

[90] Ford (note 37), p. 96.

[91] Ford (note 37), p. 96, and SIPRI data. See also Arkin and Fieldhouse (note 11), appendix A.

[92] 'U.S. to spend millions on Latin bases', *New York Times*, 16 May 1984, p. A3; 'Work in Honduras prompts criticism', *New York Times*, 19 Apr. 1984, p. A7 (which discusses another base at Aguacate); 'Honduras targeted for U.S. air base', *Centre Daily Times*, 15 May 1984, p. A2 (which focuses on Palmerola and San Lorenzo); 'At Honduran base, mystery over role', *New York Times*, 14 Dec. 1983, p. A20 (focuses on Aguacate); and 'U.S. Latin force in place if needed, officials report', *New York Times*, 23 Apr. 1984, p. A1, which notes (p. A8) that 11 OV-10 Mohawk reconnaissance planes are based at La Palmerola; and 'U.S. army units to build 6th airfield in Honduras', *New York Times*, 3 Mar. 1986, which discusses a new base at Mocoron which can handle C-130 aircraft. See also 'Operations: Nicaragua', *Journal of Defense Diplomacy*, vol. 6, no. 3 (1988), p. 6, which reports on still another Honduras base at El Cisne used by the USA and the contras; and Goldman, F., 'Lost in another Honduras', *Harper's*, vol. 273, no. 1637 (Oct. 1986), pp. 49–57, which also identifies a USAF radar post outside Tegucigalpa at Cerro de Mole.

[93] 'Salvadoran air base is called center for CIA operations', *New York Times*, 15 Oct. 1986, which concerns the air base at Ilopango.

[94] 'Easter Island's runway fracas', *Newsweek*, 8 July 1985, pp. 22–23; and 'NASA seeks right from Chile for Easter Island abort site', *Aviation Week & Space Technology*, 17 June 1985, p. 127.

[95] IISS (note 4), pp. 36–38.

[96] IISS (note 4), p. 34.

[97] IISS (note 4), p. 34.

[98] *Soviet Military Power 1987* (note 3), p. 78.

[99] *Soviet Military Power 1987* (note 3), p. 78.

[100] IISS (note 4), p. 41.

[101] SIPRI data for the GDR.

[102] IISS (note 4), p. 41.

[103] SIPRI data on Czechoslovakia.

[104] IISS (note 4), p. 42.

[105] SIPRI data on Hungary.

[106] SIPRI data on Poland.

[107] Arkin and Fieldhouse (note 11), appendix B, p. 267.

[108] IISS (note 4), p. 44, and SIPRI data on Mongolia.

[109] 'MIGs spotted', *The Times*, 31 Aug. 1983; 'Russia puts MIGs on isle off Japan', *International Herald Tribune*, 31 Aug. 1983.

[110] Furlong, R. D. M. and Winkler, T., 'The Soviet invasion of Afghanistan', *International Defense Review*, no. 2 (1980), pp. 168–70; 'Russians build Afghan bases', *The Guardian*, 21 Nov. 1984; 'Soviet units in Afghanistan dig in as if for a long stay', *New York Times*, 9 Oct. 1980, p. A20; SIPRI data on Afghanistan; regarding the relative weight of basing and resources as motives for the Soviet invasion see Bradsher, H., *Afghanistan and the Soviet Union* (Duke University Press: Durham, N.C., 1983), pp. 159, 192.

[111] 'Moscow's spring offensive: Two Afghan options?', *New York Times*, 10 Mar. 1980, p. A12 discusses the earlier perceived possibility of deployment of Backfires in Afghanistan, with 5500 mile ranges.

[112] SIPRI data on Afghanistan; *New York Times* (note 111); 'In Afghanistan, 2 Soviet trends now emerging', *New York Times*, 30 Oct. 1979, p. A6; and 'Soviet units in Afghanistan dig in as if for a long stay', *New York Times*, 9 Oct. 1980, p. A20.

[113] 'Russians expand Vietnam base to aid military clout in Pacific', *International Herald Tribune*, 22 Dec. 1983. Regarding the role of TU-95s, see 'Soviet "air spies" over S.E. Asia', *Daily Telegraph*, 4 Nov. 1983.

[114] Some sources have hinted at Backfire bombers rotated to Viet Nam from Kamchatka. See 'Backfire bombers "a threat in the Pacific" ', *Daily Telegraph*, 30 Oct. 1982.

[115] 'Russians expand Vietnam base to aid military clout in Pacific', *International Herald Tribune*, 22 Dec. 1983—which also discusses the possibility of Soviet stationing of advanced Su-24s in Viet Nam. See also 'Russian MiG's in Vietnam', *Daily Telegraph*, 2 Jan. 1985.

[116] US Department of Defense, *Soviet Military Power 1985*, 4th edn (US Government Printing Office: Washington, DC, 1985), p. 118.

[117] Note 116, p. 125.

[118] See 'South Yemen loyalists reported holding on', *New York Times*, 22 Jan. 1986, p. A8.

[119] Note 116, p. 124.

[120] Note 116, p. 123.

[121] See also 'New west African base for Russian forces', *Daily Telegraph*, 12 Oct. 1984, which depicts Moscow trying to acquire access to São Tomé and Principe to replace that being lost in Guinea.

[122] Richelson (note 34), p. 106; and *Soviet Military Power 1985* (note 116), p. 123.

[123] Richelson (note 34), p. 106; and *Soviet Military Power 1985* (note 116), p. 120.

[124] Regarding the airfields in Mali, see 'From Moscow to Timbuktu', *Christian Science Monitor*, 28 June 1977, p. 27. Regarding those in Ethiopia and Somalia see SIPRI data; and Petersen, C., 'Trends in Soviet naval operations', eds B. Dismukes and J. McConnell, *Soviet Naval Diplomacy* (Pergamon: New York, 1979), p. 75.

[125] Petersen (note 124), p. 120. See also, 'Spy planes a threat to U.S.', *Washington Post*, 14 Sep. 1979, p. D15; 'Soviets increase close-in flights along East coast', *Washington Star*, 20 Mar. 1981, p. 7; see also Richelson (note 34), p. 106.

[126] *Soviet Military Power 1985* (note 116), p. 121. There were also reports of a Soviet AN-30 photo-reconnaissance aircraft in Nicaragua. See 'Soviet spy plane seen over Nicaragua', *Centre Daily Times*, 12 June 1986, p. A9; and 'U.S. says Soviet survey plane is aiding Nicaragua', *New York Times*, 12 June 1986, p. A19.

[127] IISS (note 4), p. 82.

[128] IISS (note 4), p. 59 and SIPRI data on Canada.

[129] IISS (note 4), p. 66. See also *Journal of Defense and Diplomacy*, vol. 5, no. 10 (1987), p. 50, under 'Global view: Europe: Portugal'.

[130] IISS (note 4), p. 82, and SIPRI data.

[131] It is worth recalling that Britain, up to 1975, based nuclear-armed V-Bombers at Akrotiri on Cyprus—see 'End of era at air base', *Daily Telegraph*, 24 Sep. 1977.

[132] Nine F-4M Phantoms have also deployed in the Falklands. See 'British deploying F-4Ms in Falklands', *Aviation Week & Space Technology*, 6 Dec. 1982, p. 127; and IISS (note 4), p. 82.

[133] As late as 1985, London still deployed a squadron of Jaguars on Gibraltar. See 'The cloudy outlook for Gibraltar's commanding view', *New York Times*, 10 Feb. 1986, p. E5.

[134] IISS (note 4), p. 82. An additional detachment of Hercules transports is now stationed on Ascension Island.

[135] IISS (note 4), p. 82.

[136] Arkin and Fieldhouse (note 11), appendix C, p. 278.

[137] Arkin and Fieldhouse (note 11), appendix C, p. 278.

[138] Arkin and Fieldhouse (note 11), appendix C, p. 278.

[139] 'France reluctant to return to gendarme role in Chad', *Financial Times*, 12 Aug. 1983; 'Gunships sent to back French troops in Chad', *International Herald Tribune*, 5 Sep. 1983. One report also cites a French base at Bouar in the Central African Republic 'developed both as a supply post and an electronic listening base linked to Breguet Atlantic high level airborne listening posts'. See 'Chad to be test ground for new weapons', *Guardian*, 19 Aug. 1983.

[140] IISS (note 4), p. 64.

[141] Arkin and Fieldhouse (note 11), p. 288.

[142] Regarding French use of Jaguars against the Polisario, said based on Dakar and Nouakchott, see *Arab Report*, 6 June 1979; and 'Polisario claims aircraft hit in new French attack', *Financial Times*, 22 Dec. 1977.

[143] 'Australia faces dilemma on future of Malaysia air base', *Guardian*, 16 Feb. 1984.

[144] Regarding Cuban and East German pilots in Ethiopia, see 'Ethiopia held trying to drive out Somalis', *International Herald Tribune*, 14 Feb. 1980. Regarding Pakistani pilots in the Arabian Peninsula, see 'Pakistan said to offer to base troops on Saudi soil', *New York Times*, 20 Aug. 1980, p. A5.

[145] See 'U.S. says raid hurt Libya's ability to "direct and control" terror', 16 Apr. 1986, p. A20; 'French beef up air defenses on southern coast', 25 Apr. 1986, p. A33.

[146] See Harkavy (note 2), pp. 21–22.

[147] Sometimes they do complain, with other allies for an audience, see: 'Saudis allege trespass by Israeli planes', *Baltimore Sun*, 10 Nov. 1981, p. 2; 'Soviets deny planes flew over Philippines', *Washington Post*, 9 May 1980, p. A13; and 'Pakistanis accuse Russians of border overflights', *New York Times*, 17 June 1980, p. A5. France's former President Valery Giscard d'Estaing reported that his air force overflew some countries without permission when flying troops to Chad to protect the latter from Libya. See Oakes, J., 'More than Libya was ground zero', *New York Times*, 8 May 1986, p. A27.

[148] See 'U.S. charges Soviet mounts big airlift to Ethiopian army', *New York Times*, 14 Dec. 1977, p. A1, which also cites Yugoslavia, Libya and Pakistan as nations overflown, the last-named perhaps without permission. Egypt in turn overflew Kenya *en route* to Somalia during this war and had one plane seized in the process—see 'Shootout on Cyprus overshadows Mideast peace efforts', *Washington Post*, 24 Feb. 1978, p. A19. And, according to Petersen (note 124), p. 57, beginning in 1968, Soviet Tu-95Ds overflew Iran, Afghanistan and India from the USSR at the time of the Luna spacecraft recovery operations in the Indian Ocean.

[149] But Yugoslavia apparently refused to give Moscow permanent overflight rights after 1973— see 'Yugoslavs report that Tito rebuffed Brezhnev on air and naval rights and a role in Warsaw Pact', *New York Times*, 9 Jan. 1977, p. 10.

[150] According to one article, the USA protested to Yugoslavia over alleged stopovers there by Soviet aircraft carrying supplies to the popular movement. See 'Africa tension mounts on Angola meeting', *Washington Post*, 10 Jan. 1976.

[151] Mangold, P., 'Shaba I and Shaba II', *Survival*, vol. 21, no. 3 (May/June 1979), pp. 107–115.

[152] 'Soviet arms airlift to Vietnam hinted as combat goes on', *New York Times*, 23 Feb. 1979, p. A1, which also indicates some nation along a route via South Asia must also have been utilized for refuelling.

[153] Some reports also hinted at actual use of Omani air bases for the raid—see 'U.S. cargo planes use Oman but link with raid denied', *The Times*, 28 Apr. 1980; and 'The 'plan: How it failed', *Newsweek*, 5 May 1980, pp. 27–28. Regarding reported use of the Egyptian air base at Qena to launch C-130s for the hostage raid, see 'U.S. military is no secret in Egypt', *Washington Post*, 20 June 1980, p. 1.

[154] Jong-Chul Choi, 'United States security policy in Asia and the U.S.–Japan–South Korea Collective Security Cooperation System', M.A. thesis, Pennsylvania State University, 1988, p. 29.

[155] But more recently, Lajes had been discussed in terms of the Rapid Deployment Force's logistics *en route* to Egypt. See 'Portugal bargains for U.S. military aid with strategic mid-Atlantic base', *Christian Science Monitor*, 24 Mar. 1981, p. 9. See also 'Deadlock reported at Azores talks', *Guardian*, 26 July 1983; 'Portugal, U.S. sign base pact', *International Herald Tribune*, 14 Dec. 1983; and 'Accord reached on Portugal's Azores air base', *Financial Times*, 14 Dec. 1983.

[156] See 'Preparing for future crises: U.S. is talking with Saudis on bases', *International Herald Tribune*, 19 Dec. 1979; 'Offer by the U.S. to guard tankers in gulf reported', *New York Times*, 17 May 1984, p. A1; 'House panel cuts money for bases', *New York Times*, 17 May 1984, p. A7; 'The Iran–Iraq war', *Christian Science Monitor*, 12 Feb. 1985, p. 21. Earlier US aspirations for access to Egyptian bases, particularly regarding construction of a major new base at Ras Banas, have been shelved. See 'Egypt portrays itself as major U.S. asset', *New York Times*, 16 Jan. 1985, p. A4; 'U.S.–Egyptian base scrapped', *Near East Report*, vol. 29, no. 4 (28 Jan. 1985), p. 13; 'Secret U.S. air base is revealed in Egypt amid broader buildup', *International Herald Tribune*, 24 June 1983; and McNaugher (note 13), p. 55. The latter article also discusses Morocco, where the Reagan Administration is reported to have spent $25 million on runway improvements to accommodate C-5s and C-141s going to and coming back from Egypt.

[157] Regarding Oman, particularly Masirah Island, see 'U.S. may use desert island airfield as base for defense of Persian Gulf', *Washington Post*, 11 Oct. 1980, p. A21; and 'Bright star: Omanis play balancing act', *New York Times*, 7 Dec. 1981, p. A9. Regarding Somalia and Kenya, see 'Qaddafi is new chip in Horn of Africa poker game', *New York Times*, 21 Sep. 1981, p. A2; 'U.S. is reported to study offer of a Somali base', *New York Times*, 23 Dec. 1979, p. A1; 'Kenya agrees to expand U.S. use of military bases', *New York Times*, 28 June 1980, p. 5; 'U.S. and Somalia expected to conclude pact on bases', *New York Times*, 19 Aug. 1980, p. A8; and 'House panel skeptical on U.S. pact with Somalia', *New York Times*, 17 Sep. 1980, p. A14. See also McNaugher (note 13), p. 55.

[158] 'U.S. arms airlift to Angola rebels is said to go on', *New York Times*, 27 July 1987.

[159] Blaker, J. R., Tsagronis, S. J. and Walter, K. T., *U.S. Global Basing: U.S. Basing Options*, Hudson Institute, Alexandria, Va., report for the US Department of Defense, HI-3916-RR, Oct. 1987, p. A3, note that Christchurch in New Zealand hosts a facility providing logistics support for Antarctic operations.

[160] Soviet testing of its logistical lines with a massive airlift to the Middle East and Africa is reported in 'Russia's secret airlift', *Newsweek*, 26 Nov. 1980, p. 33.

[161] See Haselkorn, A., 'The Soviet collective security system', *Orbis* (spring 1975), p. 240.

[162] 'Soviets pouring aid into Viet', *Pittsburgh Press*, 3 Sep. 1978, p. B4, reports that both India and Pakistan allowed Soviet planes to refuel in resupplying Viet Nam during its invasion of Cambodia.

[163] Regarding Grenada as an additional link to Central America see '1,900 U.S. troops, with Caribbean allies, invade Grenada and battle leftists', *New York Times*, 26 Oct. 1983, p. A1, which notes the construction of a 10 000 foot runway at Port Salines on Grenada. See also 'Grenada's leader is reported shot', *New York Times*, 20 Oct. 1983, p. A3; and 'Cuba says workers fought for 3 hours against Americans', *New York Times*, 26 Oct. 1983, p. A17.

[164] Regarding reports about Soviet efforts to gain a foothold at the Gan air base in the Maldives, see 'Gan airbase offered for rent', *Daily Telegraph*, 31 Dec. 1976; 'Russia fails in bid for ex-RAF base', *Daily Telegraph*, 28 Oct. 1977; and 'Maldives: New regime, old problems', *International Herald Tribune*, 13 July 1979. Similarly, regarding the Seychelles, see 'Seychelles "ruthlessly wooed" by Russia', *Daily Telegraph*, 29 June 1980.

[165] See 'Hercules refuel in Brazil', *The Guardian*, 6 Mar. 1983, which also reports on London's diplomatic efforts to obtain staging rights in Uruguay.

4. Ground-force FMP

I. Introduction

The ground-force aspect of FMP—foreign ground-force deployments and in-stallations—is perhaps the most visible, traditional and quantitatively imposing one. It is perhaps also the most politically intrusive, that is, most threatening to a host's sovereignty and dignity, just because it often includes a large-scale and permanent presence and, no matter what the actual purpose, is suggestive of an 'occupation' of sorts.

The historical context of current ground-force FMP or, rather, the sig-nificance of current foreign ground-force deployments in relation to the recent development of the international system is stressed here. A generation ago, most such FMP, virtually all, would have been accounted for by colonial presences in what is now designated the Third World; that is, by imperial garrisons and related deployments for interventions against anti-colonial insurrections. Nowadays, with the Western colonial era all but spent, such garrisons constitute only a small corner of the subject. Far more important are the large-scale land-army presences in Western and Eastern Europe associated with the rival NATO/WTO alliances in Central Europe. Whereas a lengthy swath of in-ternational relations preceding World War II saw an absence of such durable alliances underpinned by security pacts and associated military deployments, the history of the post-war era has been one of relatively fixed and stable bipolarity. Forward deployments of ground forces associated with the central, hegemonic, military alliances have been the most salient fact of contemporary ground-force FMP; periodic predictions about a systemic shift towards a more multipolar structure, or short of that, the neutralization of Central Europe, have remained speculation.

Just because of the collapse of Western colonialism, however, the overall requirements for FMP on land may have been reduced. During the first 20-odd years of the post-war period, the ex-colonial powers—particularly Britain and France—maintained extensive overseas troop garrisons so as to combat or, at least, control the pace and direction of decolonialization. But there was the long and ineluctable history of British redeployments of forces as the empire dwindled, so well chronicled by Gregory Blaxland, many of which still engaged in (ultimately futile) rearguard actions in Kenya, Oman, Egypt and other coun-tries.[1] The French, Dutch and Portuguese experiences were similar, though on a smaller scale. The primary dimensions of ground-force FMP are:

(*a*) forces deployed in or stationed in other nations as a result of war, inva-sion, etc., either ongoing or in an (often unsettled) aftermath;

(*b*) remnant colonial or other garrisons involving highly dependent or asym-metric security relationships;

(c) 'advisers', surrogate forces, trip-wires, or praetorian guards, all including FMP at or near the size of combat units, often collocated with naval and/or air bases;

(d) small military training missions or arms purchasing teams;

(e) pre-positioned *matériel* and associated personnel;

(f) training areas for a variety of functions, climates, and terrains;

(g) pre-emptive occupations of contested territories, particularly small islands;

(h) use of cross-border sanctuaries and staging grounds by unconventional/ revolutionary forces;

(i) peacekeeping forces, either UN contingents or other; and

(j) temporary troop deployments in the form of training exercises or manoeuvres.

II. Large-scale, alliance-related, ground-force deployments

Both NATO and the WTO have engaged in large-scale deployment of the forces of alliance partners in the crucial areas of the central military confrontation line in Central Europe. This involves, centrally, US, Canadian, Dutch, Belgian, French and British forces in FR Germany (also US forces in Italy); and their counterparts, Soviet forces in the GDR, Poland, Czechoslovakia and Hungary. In this general category of ground-force FMP—primarily defined by the sheer magnitude of deployments—we may also include the US forces in South Korea (abetted by a small number of other, token, UN forces) and the large-scale Soviet ground forces in Mongolia which are one component of the Soviet deployments in Asia *vis-à-vis* China.

To a certain extent some of these forces can be considered multi-purpose; their mix of functions over time can also be said to have (gradually) changed from among: defence of the host country and its hinterland from invasion; garrisoning or occupation of a country so as to forestall a possible revolution, irredentism or revisionism in relation to a past war; or the provision of a forward base for regional or even extra-regional military operations.[2] The US, British and French armies in FR Germany, for instance, while primarily deployed in-line and in-depth to defend against an attack from the East, also earlier had a post-war garrisoning function—there may be some in Western Europe who still perceive the continuing need for that function, however limited and conjectural.[3] Soviet forces in Eastern Europe have long had a clearer dual purpose along such lines with their deployment both against NATO and against potential internal insurgencies such as those in Hungary, Czechoslovakia and Poland in 1956, 1968 and 1981, respectively, and in particular the spectre of East German revolt. And, the US forces in Europe—or at least units of them—are normally thought available for contingencies in the Middle East or North Africa; similarly, weapons pre-positioned in Europe may in some circumstances—as demonstrated during the 1973 Middle Eastern War—be used to resupply client states engaged in combat outside of Europe.

Both the non-German NATO forces in FR Germany and the Soviet forces in the four relevant East European countries (the GDR, Poland, Hungary and Czechoslovakia) contain the entire panoply of installations, functions, personnel, types of combat and support units, and so on, that one would normally expect to find in a military structure of such magnitude. A cursory review of the deployments on both sides reveals, among other things: hundreds of barracks or *kasernen*; maintenance and storage depots for armoured vehicles, trucks and so on; hospitals, recreation facilities; depots for prepositioned *matériel* (such as the so-called US POMCUS—Prepositioning of Material Configured to Unit Sets— stocks); airfields for light fixed-wing aircraft and helicopters; air defence (missiles and guns) installations and associated radars; fuel storage depots; training areas for a variety of purposes (tank and artillery firing ranges, simulated urban-warfare environments, bivouac areas); nuclear weapon storage sites; and a variety of major and lesser command headquarters.[4] From top to bottom— field armies through corps, divisions, regiments, battalions, companies and platoons—there is the characteristic mix of combat functions: infantry, armour, field artillery, air defence artillery, quartermaster, ordnance, transportation, signals, engineering, intelligence, medical, special forces, and so on. In categories covered in other chapters, there are the various facilities (some under command of air forces) collocated with the ground forces, often at the same bases: SIGINT, surface-to-surface and surface-to-air missiles; air defence radars; a variety of communications transmitters, relays, receivers, and so on.

III. US and other NATO foreign-based ground forces

Europe

The various non-German NATO ground forces are, as is familiarly known, interspersed with German forces along the whole West German border with the GDR and Czechoslovakia; in line from Lübeck in the north to Passau in the south, and in depth back to the borders of the Netherlands, Belgium, Luxembourg and France. Basically, for command purposes, that includes a three-way regional division: (*a*) north—Northern Army Group (NORTHAG); (*b*) central—Central Army Group (CENTAG); and (*c*) south—directed from the US European Command HQ (EUCOM). The US forces are primarily concentrated in the south and central portions of the front.[5]

There are some 204 000 US Army forces in FR Germany (out of an overall total of about 217 000 based in Europe). Those are controlled by one Army and two corps-level headquarters.[6] They are organized in combat units as follows: two armoured and two mechanized divisions; one armoured and one mechanized brigade; two armoured cavalry regiments; seven field artillery brigades; and four independent artillery groups. The armoured and mechanized brigades are from the divisions in the USA earmarked to reinforce the 7th Army in a crisis, and which would be 'married' to the prepositioned *matériel* (POMCUS stocks) in place in FR Germany.[7] Crucially, these forces deploy some 5000 main battle tanks (MBTs); additionally there are attached some 30 air defence batteries with HAWK-SAMs; and two battalions with Patriot SAMs (each with six batteries).

The remaining (and relatively limited in numbers) US Army personnel in NATO Europe, none of which are organized in actual combat units except for an infantry brigade in West Berlin, are as follows: Belgium (1160), Greece (470), Italy (3450), the Netherlands (930), Turkey (1200), West Berlin (4300) and other (1840).[8] Those in Italy under Allied Land Forces Southern Europe (LAND-SOUTH) headquartered in Verona, mostly service and technical forces, are basically intended to stiffen the Italian forces deployed south of the Alps in relation to possible contingencies emanating from or through Austria and/or Yugoslavia.

Britain's ground-force FMP in FR Germany is represented by the British Army of the Rhine (BAOR) with some 56 000 personnel.[9] Under one corps headquarters, it consists of three armoured divisions, which comprise eight armoured and one air-mobile brigade, one artillery brigade, three army-air regiments, two air-defence regiments and seven engineering regiments.[10] In addition, there is a 3000-man Berlin Infantry Brigade.[11] Located in the north German plains, these forces are heavily weighted towards armour, and field large numbers of Chieftain and Challenger main battle tanks. Earmarked reinforcements in the UK constitute an additional brigade.

France, the third of the original occupying powers, also has a significant land-army presence within FR Germany, located contiguously (to France) in Pfalz, Baden and Saarland. Some 50 000 forces are organized into three armoured divisions with 400 AMX-30 main battle tanks, and an additional 2700 men in Berlin comprise an armoured and an infantry regiment.[12]

The other NATO ground forces in FR Germany are much smaller. Canada has some 4200 men deployed, most of them in a mechanized brigade group, fielding some 60 Leopard tanks, with 1415 reinforcements earmarked from Canada.[13] Belgium has around 25 000 forces: a corps and division headquarters; one armoured and one mechanized infantry brigade plus a variety of support units located in the Rhineland east of Belgium.[14] These forces deploy some 240 main battle tanks. The Netherlands deploys about 5500 men in FR Germany: an armoured brigade plus reconnaissance and engineering battalions.[15]

With a few minor exceptions, there are no other ground force deployments intra-NATO; that is, most of what is involved are the various deployments forward on West German territory. The minor exceptions have to do with small support or headquarters units, whose functions can vary. There is a small such US Army presence in the UK. FR Germany has small support units in the Netherlands and Portugal; in the former case, dictated by the obvious realities of geography, that is, the limited depth of German defence deployments in northern Germany relative to the projected forward edge of the battle area (FEBA).

The Western ground-force deployments in Europe have been surprisingly stable for a long time. Whether that stability will be retained or whether there are hints of fundamental change, is hard to say. There is a lot of talk about US troop withdrawals from Europe within the US Congress. There are the (long-stalemated) Mutual and Balanced Force Reductions (MBFR) negotiations, now perhaps to be superseded by more promising negotiations within another format.[16] There is also much discussion of the need for an enhanced West European conventional force posture in the wake of the INF Treaty and the possibility of still more ambitious reductions of nuclear weapons in Central Europe. There are increasing signs of tightened Franco-German military relations, which could later affect ground-force FMP, perhaps to the extent of larger French troop deployments within FR Germany.[17] NATO's asymmetric concentration of force in NORTHAG could change in response to perceived changes in Soviet offensive strategies. Some analyses point to greater utilization of 'high-tech' weaponry, particularly for targeting well behind the FEBA;[18] others to a newer strategy (such as the Dutch 'rim' defence) featuring quickly mobilizable, light reserve forces.[19]

Rest of the world

The US Army has only one major ground-force deployment outside of Central Europe, that in South Korea. That force has been in place since the close of the Korean War in 1954, though it is now smaller. In 1977 the Carter Administration considered near-full withdrawal or large-scale reduction of the US Army in Korea, but ultimately bowed to countervailing Korean and domestic US pressures.[20] That force now consists of some 30 000 men, with one infantry division of 13 900 men constituting the major combat unit. (An additional 2100 US Army personnel in Japan act largely as a support force for the units in Korea, and include a corps headquarters.) Not coincidentally, arms control discussions in recent years about no-first-use of nuclear weapons have centred on FR Germany and Korea, the two areas of large—but still outnumbered— US Army forces often characterized at least in part as trip-wires whose overrunning might trigger escalation to the nuclear level.[21]

Aside from the usual, perfunctory small military advisory missions, there are only a few other US ground-force deployments abroad, none major. The USA has some 6730 Army forces in Latin America and the Caribbean: in the Panama Canal Zone with its Southern Headquarters and jungle training school; and a small trip-wire and guard force at Guantanamo in Cuba.[22] There is now also the somewhat politically controversial 500-man or so advisory group in Honduras which deploys *vis-à-vis* Nicaragua and supports the 'Contra' forces inside Nicaragua.[23] There are a handful of US troops in such disparate locales as Greenland, Taiwan, the Philippines, and so on; and some in the buffer force in Sinai which helps separate Israeli and Egyptian forces and monitor the Camp David Accords.[24] The US Marine Corps has some 42 500 forces abroad, some on land, some afloat.[25] The bulk, some 38 100, are in Okinawa, including a 23 000-man Marine Amphibious Force. Others are in Panama, Cuba

(Guantanamo), with the 7th Fleet in the Philippines, and afloat in the Indian Ocean and the Mediterranean.

IV. Soviet foreign-based ground forces

Europe

The counterpart to NATO's large-scale land-army presence in FR Germany is the massive forward Red Army deployment in Eastern Europe: in the GDR, Czechoslovakia, Poland and Hungary, only the first two of which border upon FR Germany. Soviet ground forces in the latter two provide depth and reserves for potential combat as well as serving a continuing garrison function.

Soviet deployments in Central and Eastern Europe comprise some 565 000 ground-forces, organized for combat into 30 divisions (16 tank and 14 motorized rifle), plus attached artillery units.[26] All these divisions are considered, by Soviet terminology, in a 'Category 1' state of readiness, that is, at 75–100 per cent of full strength.[27] Altogether they deploy some 10 500 main battle tanks, exclusive of still others in reserve. These forces are divided as follows among the WTO allies:[28]

1. GDR: 380 000 troops; one Group and 5 Army headquarters; 10 tank and 9 motorized rifle divisions; 1 artillery division; 1 air assault division; 5 attack helicopter regiments with some 600 Mi-8 Hip and 420 Hind attack helicopters.
2. Czechoslovakia: 80 000 troops; 1 Group and 1 Army HQ; 2 tank and 3 motorized rifle divisions; 1 air assault battalion; 1 artillery brigade, 2 attack helicopter regiments with 100 Mi-8 Hip and Mi-24 Hind helicopters.
3. Poland: 40 000 troops; 1 Group and 1 Army headquarters; 2 tank divisions, 1 attack helicopter regiment with 120 Mi-8 and Mi-24 helicopters.
4. Hungary: 65 000 troops; 1 Group and 1 Army HQ; 2 tank and 2 motorized rifle divisions, 1 air assault brigade with 65 Mi-8 and Mi-24 helicopters.[29]

In a related context, it is important to note that those forces are immediately backed up by those stationed in all of the European Soviet Military Districts, comprising some 65 divisions (23 tank, 37 motorized rifle and 5 airborne).

In recent years there has been considerable analysis and speculation as to whether the USSR has forward-positioned sufficient combat forces near the inter-German border, so as to allow for a sudden, surprise pre-emptive attack in which NATO would be denied early warning. Particular attention has been paid to the deployment of the 3rd Shock Army and the 8th Guard Army, both positioned across from NATO's CENTAG.[30] The former is headquartered at Magdeburg and comprises the 47th Guard's Tank Division at Hillersleden, the 207th Guards Motor Rifle Division at Stendahl, the 10th Guard's Tank Division at Kranznitz and the 12th Guard's Tank Division at Neuruppin. The latter, headquartered at Weimar-Nohra, comprises the 39th Motorized Rifle Division at Ohrduf, and the rest of the Army is stationed at bases around Jena. To the north, opposite Lower Saxony, the Soviet 2nd Guards Army has its two motor rifle divisions, the 21st and 94th, at Perleberg and Schwerin, facing NATO's NORTHAG.[31]

Rest of the world

Outside Europe, the only permanent major (peacetime) Soviet ground-force deployment in an allied country is in Mongolia. There, the Red Army deploys two tank and three motorized rifle divisions, 65 000 troops in all (earlier there were 75 000) *vis-à-vis* China.[32] These forces fill a gap in the Sino-Soviet confrontation line amid a much larger overall Soviet deployment in the Far Eastern theatre of some 53 regular divisions (7 tank, 45 motorized rifle, 1 airborne) abetted by four artillery divisions and two air assault brigades.[33] There is a smaller proportion of tank units here relative to the European theatre, no doubt a mixed function of the expected nature of combat, the terrain and the constraints of long-range logistics.

In mid-1986, amid a flurry of arms control proposals and other new diplomatic initiatives by the new Soviet leader Mikhail Gorbachev, the USSR broached the withdrawal of some or all of its forces in Mongolia as part of an effort to improve long-frayed relations with China (there was also then the gesture of a token withdrawal of forces from Afghanistan).[34] Some offered concessions with regard to boundary disputes along the Ussuri River were part of the context of this new initiative.

The Soviet Union's other main external ground force has, of course, been the large army of some 118 000 troops engaged in combat in Afghanistan, which included 10 000 Ministry of Internal Affairs (MVD) and Committee of State Security (KGB) troops. That force remained, numerically speaking, at a fairly constant level from the initiation of hostilities in 1979, with some gradual increases;[35] though in 1988 full withdrawal appears a serious possibility now that the Geneva negotiations on conflict termination are concluded.[36] This is by far the most significant combat deployment of Soviet troops during the post-war period. In 1970, however, some 20 000 Soviet troops were engaged in air-defence activities along the Suez Canal during Egypt's war of attrition with Israel.[37] There are also 8–10 000 Soviet troops forward-located in the Kuriles, still disputed with Japan.

There are several other locales where clusters of Soviet-bloc advisers and military technicians are significant beyond the 'norm' for standard military missions. These are in Algeria (1000), Cuba (8000), Ethiopia (1500), Libya (2000), North Yemen (500), South Yemen (2500), Syria (4000) and Viet Nam (2500), with smaller numbers in India, Iraq, Kampuchea, Laos, Mali, Mozambique, Nicaragua and Peru.[38] Each is a major recipient of Soviet arms. The much-argued 'Cuban brigade'—whether defined as a combat formation or as a collection of support troops—achieved some notoriety in 1979 when publicity over its presence (and arguments about whether it represented a violation of agreements made at the close of the 1962 Cuban missile crisis) was important to the aborting of the SALT II Treaty by opposition in the US Senate.[39] Soviet forces in Syria have become important in the wake of the latter's débâcle in the 1982 war with Israel—they man the some 48 long-range SA-5s which could contest Israeli air control even over the Mediterranean in the event of new hostilities. Earlier, prior to 1972, there was a large force of Soviet troops— some 20 000—deployed in Egypt's Suez Canal area, mostly to man air defence installations. In 1977–78, some Soviet forces aided Ethiopia in its war against Somalia.

V. Second-tier powers' foreign-based ground forces

Among the second-tier powers, France has probably the most significant—if still rather modest—overseas ground-force deployments outside the NATO area (as in the case of naval bases, the UK has withdrawn relatively further from its earlier imperial presence). Some of these French ground forces are collocated with the small naval squadrons mentioned in chapter 2: Antilles-Guyana (a marine infantry regiment and battalion, one Foreign Legion regiment); Mayotte and Réunion (one marine infantry regiment, two infantry companies); New Caledonia (one marine infantry regiment, four infantry companies); and Polynesia (one marine regiment, one Foreign Legion regiment).[40] These may in some instances be perceived as garrisons for the remnants of colonial empire (New Caledonia and Mayotte have seen recent political turmoil, raising some doubts about ultimate political control).[41] Réunion, however, is a fully fledged French *département*, politically linked to the metropole. All of these outposts can, of course, act as bases for regional power projection or interlocking defence: forces in Tahiti can be moved expeditiously to New Caledonia in the event of trouble; those in Martinique can similarly be moved to Guyana, or vice-versa.

The remainder of the French overseas land presence is in Africa. In all cases former colonies are involved, now fully independent nations which have retained strong economic and political ties to the former colonial power—the contrast with the former British possessions in Africa is in this regard striking. Again, the ground-force deployments coincide with naval and air access available not only to France but, in some cases or for some contingencies, also to the USA. (Djibouti and Dakar, Senegal, most notably.) The forces deployed are as follows:

(*a*) Central African Republic: one battalion group including two motor companies; AML and L-19 armoured cars, Milan anti-tank guided weapons (ATGWs), 120-mm mortars;
   (*b*) Chad: 1300 men in three infantry companies, with Puma helicopters;
   (*c*) Djibouti: 4000 men, two regiments, including light tank units;
   (*d*) Gabon: a marine infantry battalion, 350 men;
   (*e*) Ivory Coast: a marine infantry battalion of 480 men; and
   (*f*) Senegal: 1250 men, including a marine infantry regiment.[42]

Altogether, this is a significant presence in Africa (earlier there were additional deployments in Niger and Cameroon[43]) available for a variety of contingencies, and one implicitly acting on behalf of pro-Western interests on the continent, if only to serve as a deterrent. Implicitly too, these forces may be viewed as praetorian guards, if only in a deterrent sense, in a region of endemic political instability. These countries are, of course, all primarily recipients of French arms.

In the case of Chad, although the government received considerable US security assistance during the conduct of its offensive against Libya in 1987, during the heavy fighting of that year French forces remained south of the 15° parallel, in place to protect the incumbent government and its capital but not used for offensive operations against Libya.[44] (In a curious parallel, Cuban forces in Angola have remained north of a line some 200 miles north of Namibia.[45])

Britain's remnant overseas ground forces, roughly of the same overall magnitude, are distributed among fewer, but more globally dispersed countries:

(a) Belize: 1200 troops; infantry battalion; armed reconnaissance unit; field-artillery battery; air-defence, engineering and helicopter units;

(b) Brunei: Ghurka infantry battalion; Royal Marine company—900 men;

(c) Cyprus: 3250-man force; infantry, engineering, reconnaissance units, etc.;

(d) Falkland Islands: 2000 troops; infantry battalion group plus supporting units;

(e) Gibraltar: 770 men; infantry and engineering units; and

(f) Hong Kong: 8000 British and Ghurka troops; infantry plus supporting units.[46]

Politically speaking these deployments include a variety of situations and associated functions. The units in Hong Kong and Gibraltar are trip-wires or 'presences' in remnant imperial holdings—Hong Kong will soon revert to China and Gibraltar appears to be en route to some sort of arrangement involving enhanced Spanish sovereignty (but its vital geographical importance dictates NATO's continued interest). Belize, now independent, uses a small British force to deter further Guatemalan designs on that new nation, a responsibility reluctantly but openly conceded by the UK. The force in the Falkland Islands is now larger than that before the war of 1982 (though it is being reduced) and is clearly intended to help deter a repetition; though that deterrence function falls mostly to the Royal Navy and Air Force. The force in Cyprus, some of which is formally attached to UNFICYP (UN Force in Cyprus) as a peace-keeping presence,[47] provides a potential interposition between contending Turkish and Greek forces; also, it provides a ground complement and deterrent in relation to the important air base at Akrotiri, which is used by the USA as well as the UK mainly for reconnaissance aircraft, such as the U-2 and SR-71. The British force in Brunei can be viewed as serving to stiffen a pro-Western regime which is also a relatively important oil producer.

Outside the major and second-tier powers, there is merely a handful of other, minor territorial FMP. Australia, for instance, has long fielded small numbers

of ground forces in Papua/New Guinea and Malaysia/Singapore as its con-
tributions to the Association of South East Asian Nations (ASEAN) and nearby
south-west Pacific security.[48] New Zealand long maintained a battalion in
Singapore, which is now being withdrawn and perhaps designated for other
purposes in the increasingly tense south-west Pacific area.[49]

VI. Invasion forces, surrogates, advisers, defence planning, manoeuvres, training, and so on

The remaining categories of ground-force FMP are beset with questions of
definitions, designations, labels, and so on, which run across the divides of
ideology (North versus South, East versus West), rival superpower perspectives
on the 'legitimacy' of certain political arrangements, short- and long-term perspectives, the left–right political spectrum, and so forth.

For instance, there is the matter of large-scale invasions and wars which have
resulted in highly intrusive 'foreign presences' in some places, however those
situations might be defined (what are invasions for some people are seen as
'invited presences' by others). The USSR has, for some six years, had an army
of more than 110 000 men in Afghanistan. Libya had deployed sizeable forces
within northern Chad, until they were driven out in 1987, in a situation whose
ultimate outcome remains uncertain. (At its peak, some 5000 troops organized
in two mechanized and two tank battalions, with T-55 tanks and BMP armoured
personnel carriers were involved.[50]) Viet Nam, in pursuing hegemony over the
remainder of Indo-China and in supporting its friends in neighbouring countries, has some 170 000 forces in Cambodia to bolster the Heng Samrin Government (2 front headquarters, 12 army divisions plus support troops)[51] and
another 40 000 (three infantry divisions and support troops) in Laos.[52] South
Africa has some 14 000 troops in Namibia and, sporadically, some within
Angola.[53] Iraq and Iran, at war since 1980 and now stalemated fairly close to the
status quo ante in a conflict increasingly relegated to air and missile exchanges
interspersed with sporadic ground fighting, still have some forces ensconced
within each other's territories along the border. Syria maintains force deployments in Lebanon,[54] and there have been other examples.[55]

There are, of course, some politically debatable presences involving the super-
powers' 'acquisitions' at the end of World War II. The USSR maintains some
ground forces in the Kurile Islands, islands which are still forcefully claimed by
Japan. The USA deploys some forces on the Northern Marianas Islands of
Saipan and Tinian; the Marianas are now emerging into US Commonwealth
status, but their eventual permanent political status remains undefined. In the
South China Sea, Viet Nam and China respectively occupy portions of the
Paracel Islands; Taiwan, Viet Nam and the Philippines are similarly installed in
the Spratly Islands.[56] The Arabs consider Israel's annexation of the Golan
Heights to constitute a foreign presence. These may be characterized as
pre-emptive occupations pending final resolution of territorial claims—the

occupations could, of course, themselves eventually define 'permanent' solutions, as the accrual of time confers gradual legitimacy.

In some cases, FMP may take the form of guerrilla or revolutionary forces which use the territories of contiguous or nearby countries as sanctuaries. The Polisario, contesting Morocco for Western Sahara, utilizes such sanctuary in Algeria. The Nicaraguan 'Contras' do the same in Honduras; the Afghan rebels in Pakistan. The Khmer Serieu operates out of Thailand, the South West Africa People's Organization (SWAPO) out of Angola. There are no doubt numerous other such examples in a world riddled with little publicized, but nasty, low-intensity conflicts.[57]

Table 9. Cuban expeditionary forces overseas, 1986

Location	Numbers
Afghanistan	100
Algeria	200–300
Angola	37 000
Benin	30–50
Congo	400–3 000
Ethiopia	2 000–8 000
Ghana	50
Guinea	240
Guinea-Bissau	125
Iraq	400
Libya	3 000
Madagascar	150
Mozambique	750–2 500
Nicaragua	3 000–9 000
São Tomé and Príncipe	300–600
South Yemen	800–1 000
Syria	300
Viet Nam	Unknown
Western Sahara	75

Source: Katz, S., 'Cuba pays for Soviet aid by policing worldwide Marxism', *Washington Times*, 28 Nov. 1986, p. 5E.

There has been considerable debate over the use of the term 'surrogate' forces. Often 'surrogates' are defined in the context of the superpowers' client forces being used in a manner reminiscent of old-fashioned mercenaries—to pursue the larger powers' military interests.[58] Cuban forces, for example, have been used in recent years to provide the crucial margin of victory for Ethiopia over Somalia in the Horn War (1977–78), and in the larger and earlier civil war in Angola which peaked in 1975.[59] There are now some 2000–8000 Cubans in Ethiopia; 37 000 in Angola. Numbers of Cuban expeditionary forces overseas, according to Katz, are shown in table 9. Those in Angola have become embroiled in the bargaining over possible South African withdrawal from Namibia even as civil war in Angola rages on between the incumbent regime and rival forces under the leadership of Jonas Savimbi. Earlier, during the 'Shaba I' and 'Shaba II' invasions of Zaïre's Katanga province (in 1977 and 1979), Moroccan troops which successfully bolstered Mobutu's Zaïre were commonly characterized as surrogates (for the USA, France and Belgium)—they were with-drawn after the conflicts.[60] Some Moroccans have also been reported acting as French 'surrogates' in Gabon.

Table 10. Other intra-Third World forces abroad, 1987

Foreign nation	Host nation	Numbers (approx.)	Comments
Egypt	Oman, Sudan, Iraq, Somalia, Zaïre	. .	
Iran	Lebanon	1 000	Revolutionary guards
Israel	Lebanon	1 500	Border patrol, buffer
Libya	Chad	2 000	Occupation, northern strip
	Sudan	700–1 000	
Morocco	South West Sahara	100 000	Occupation, counter-insurgency
	Equatorial Guinea	300	
Syria	Lebanon	20 000	Occupation, interposition
Malawi	Mozambique	400	Counter-insurgency
South Africa	Angola	3 000	Fighting vs. Cubans
Tanzania	Mozambique	650	Counter-insurgency
Zimbabwe	Mozambique	6 000–12 000	Counter-insurgency
North Korea	Angola	1 000	Counter-insurgency
	Iran	300	
Pakistan	Saudi Arabia	10 000	Praetorian guard, deterrent
	Oman, UAE, Kuwait, Libya	10 000	
Viet Nam	Laos	50 000	Being reduced by half
	Kampuchea	140 000	Being reduced
India	Sri Lanka	80 000	Occupation, peace-keeping

Source: International Institute for Strategic Studies, *The Military Balance: 1987–1988* (IISS: London, 1987) and press reports cited elsewhere in this chapter.

Other intra-Third World forces abroad are listed in table 10. At least one case may be identified as exemplifying a significant intra-Third World ground-force deployment, in the mixed form of forward combat deployment and praetorian guard. Pakistan now reportedly has some combined 30 000 forces in Saudi Arabia, Jordan, Libya, Oman and the United Arab Republic, more than 10 000 (including armoured units) of which are in the first-named. Those forces have bolstered the Saudi National Guard in the capital at Riyadh, but are also claimed to have been deployed in relation to possible combat contingencies which might pit Saudi Arabia against Israel in the area east of Israel's port of Eilat. As of late 1987, however, these forces were apparently being withdrawn at Saudi request because of complications produced by the Iraq–Iran War.[61]

There are, of course, numerous cases in which 'foreign military advisers' are actually deployed as combat forces, if not in large-scale units then in connection with the manning of particular weapon systems. In 1970, for instance, the Soviet Union deployed more than 10 000 air defence personnel to Egypt to expand and control that country's air defence system.[62]

A good current example is in Syria, where there are now more Soviet military advisers—approximately 4000—than in any other Third World country with the exception of Afghanistan. These include 1100 ground-force advisers, and 2000 air-defence advisers—the remainder are assigned to the Syrian Air Force and Navy. After Syria's defeat by Israel in 1982, the Soviet presence was augmented by 600 air-defence personnel. These have manned two operational SA-5 Gammon missile complexes located at Dumayr and Homs, which were the first operational SA-5s outside the USSR.[63] Since then, SA-5s involving Soviet personnel have also been installed in Libya, with ranges of 180 miles out into the Mediterranean.[64]

Additional Soviet advisers have their headquarters in Damascus. Directly subordinate to the Soviet General Staff in Moscow, they are assigned to the Syrian Ministry of Defence, the headquarters of all three services, operational units, repair and maintenance facilities, and various schools and military academies.

In the past, pilots of Pakistan, North Korea, Cuba, North Vietnam, the USSR and perhaps other countries have been reported in combat against Israel. Taiwanese pilots have been reported flying aircraft of US-origin for North Yemen and perhaps other Arab countries;[65] Taiwanese advisers and also Israelis and Argentinians have been claimed to be involved in Central America on behalf of US friends—here one returns to the terminology of 'surrogates' if only in a more numerically limited way.[66] In the insurgency war in Mozambique, incumbent government forces have been assisted by contingents from Zimbabwe (12 000 troops), Tanzania and Malawi as well as by Soviet and Cuban advisors in battling insurgent RENAMO forces.[67]

These advisory forces will at some point on the spectrum shade into the historically 'normal' use of advisers for training purposes, usually closely correlated to the facts of arms-client relationships, that is, to the main sources of arms. Both the USA and USSR have scores of such advisory groups, usually in small numbers; in the USA and other Western nations' cases, this often also includes corporate contract personnel assigned to train weapon users and assist in installation and maintenance of systems. The USA has in recent years had large numbers of such contract personnel in Saudi Arabia, Kuwait, other Gulf States, Iran (before 1979), and so forth.[68]

In some instances, the major powers may use overseas training areas (not just areas such as those in FR Germany, which are amid large force deployments) to take advantage of terrain, climate, relatively uninhabited space, and so on, not easily found or acquired within the home countries. The USA has long trained troops for jungle warfare in tropical Panama, and on Pacific islands such as Palau.[69] The Soviet Union, largely bereft of suitable places for practising amphibious island landings, has apparently used South Yemen's Socotra Island for that purpose.[70] The USA has used Okinawa for similar purposes. US cold weather forces' training in Norway can probably be defined in the context of trip-wires and 'presence' (showing the flag) as an additional rationale; in this case, the training takes place at an obviously contingent point of possible actual future combat, one that would be crucial in a major NATO–WTO war.

One other form of ground-force FMP worth noting is that of periodic large-scale military manoeuvres on the soil of the superpowers' client states. This involves not only the familiarization of major power forces with climate and terrain where they may one day be called upon to fight, but also an exercise in related long-range logistics. These are sometimes referred to as 'command post exercises'. Then too, such manoeuvres may be used to signal strong support for client states, to threaten or intimidate the clients' rivals, or to establish a warning to would-be foes of the client. Hence, the USA has now institutionalized its annual 'Bright Star' manoeuvres in Egypt, Oman and Jordan;[71] also, it has periodically conducted fairly large-scale manoeuvres in Honduras next door to neighbouring Nicaragua, some of which apparently have involved National Guard forces.[72] There are also the 'Team Spirit' exercises with Japan and South Korea involving forward rotation of forces from Hawaii and elsewhere,[73] perhaps to be interpreted as signalling continued resolve to deter attacks upon South Korea. Earlier, the Central Command had held a large-scale air defence exercise called Jade Tiger, involving Oman, Sudan and Somalia along with US forces. The USA has also been involved in numerous 'command post exercises' with Moroccan forces on the latter's home soil.

Sometimes, such manoeuvres are used as a very thinly disguised form of coercive diplomacy.[74] A recent example in 1987 was the US manoeuvres in Honduras called 'Solid Shield', used to:

> . . . serve notice that the USA is prepared to deploy an attacking force within hours of trouble in Central America. That maneuver initially involved 1,800 Marines, 1,500 paratroopers, and supporting air and naval forces; ultimately some 40,000 personnel were involved. According to one former Reagan Administration official, those manoeuvres and similar ones in the Middle East were more than exercises. . . . They're the modern equivalent of gunboat diplomacy.[75]

The USSR has also used manoeuvres as a form of coercive diplomacy; for example, exercises in neighbouring East European states were clearly a signal of brute force to Poland's opposition Solidarity movement.

Some manoeuvres are held jointly with host country personnel; hence, they may serve the several purposes of training, coercive diplomacy, and shoring up often shaky political regimes. Honduran troops, in small numbers, have participated in US manoeuvres; Egyptian forces have done so on a much larger scale.

The matter of forward pre-positioned ground-force *matériel* (weapons, ordnance, petrol, etc.) might also fit within a discussion of ground-force FMP; note the important role of the US POMCUS stocks in Western Europe, prepositioned US *matériel* in proximity to the Persian Gulf, in Diego Garcia, Kenya, and so on.[76] The Soviet Union is similarly reported to have prepositioned massive war stocks in Syria, Libya and perhaps Ethiopia, howsoever disguised as regular arms transfers for the specific use of the recipients, some of which could not easily absorb the quantities involved.[77] These matters are more extensively discussed in the section on logistics in chapter 9.

Under normal circumstances, one of the military advisors' primary roles is that of marketing their nation's arms. That is done not only by the 'on-the-ground' advisors, but also by more *ad hoc* survey teams sent abroad to analyse the weapon needs of host nations. That is, military advisors are often heavily involved in the defence planning process of host (and arms recipient) nations, an obvious and necessary adjunct to the associated training function.[78] In the early part of the US Carter Administration, when that administration's policy of arms sales restraints—embodied in the famous PD-13 (Presidential Directive)—dictated restrictions on such sales (by volume and number of recipients), the number of US Military Advisory Assistance (MAAG) groups overseas was reduced. That was done in connection with the associated so-called 'leprosy clause' which restricted the marketing activities of the salesmen of arms-producing corporations.

Generally, there is a high correlation between FMP and arms transfers. Almost all nations hosting FMP will receive arms predominantly from that source. The converse, however, is not always the case—many nations do not grant significant FMP to their primary or significant arms sources, particularly where the political relationship is short of a formal alliance and/or where there are multiple significant sources of arms, or where the political leverage of a recipient state *vis-à-vis* an arms supplier is high, as in the case of Saudi Arabia relative to the USA. This subject is discussed in chapter 10.

Table 11. Soviet and Cuban military personnel in the Third World, 1985

Region	Soviet personnel	Cuban personnel
Latin America (including Cuba)	7 900	2 500–3 500
Sub-Saharan Africa	3 600–4 000	35 000–37 000
Middle East and North Africa	9 000	500
Asia (including Viet Nam)	3 500	
Afghanistan	115 000	

Source: US Department of Defense, *Soviet Military Power 1985*, 4th edn (US Government Printing Office: Washington, DC, 1985), p. 116.

In Libya, Soviet (and East European) advisors assist in training Libyan personnel and in maintaining the large amounts of Soviet-supplied armour and other equipment that Libya has in storage, often characterized, as noted, virtually as a Soviet forward, prepositioned depot. In Algeria, advisors work in various schools and academies and are assigned to equipment repair installations and individual combat units—these include T-62 and T-72 tank units; and air-defence units with SA-2, SA-3 and SA-6 SAMs.[79] Soviet advisors in Nicaragua help maintain the some 200 Soviet armoured vehicles and the

Mi-8/HiP and Mi-24/Hind D attack helicopters already delivered there. In Peru, 150 Soviet advisors and technicians provide maintenance and instruction on Soviet equipment, including the SA-3 60A air defence missiles. Table 11 details the regional distribution of Soviet and Cuban advisory personnel.

On a somewhat more disaggregated basis, their US counterparts may be identified in table 12 provided by the Pentagon. These data are all-inclusive including military training, purchasing missions and embassy personnel, in addition to personnel associated with definable military units.

Table 12. Active duty US military personnel strengths by regional area and by country, 31 December 1985

Regional area/country	Total	Army	Navy	Marine Corps	Air Force
US territory and special locations					
Continental United States (CONUS)	1 318 110	467 736	274 307	145 022	431 045
Alaska	20 765	7 786	1 943	198	10 838
Hawaii	46 375	18 004	12 261	9 428	6 682
American Samoa	1	1	0	0	0
Guam	9 015	30	4 571	386	4 028
Johnston Atoll	150	144	0	0	6
Midway Islands	10	0	10	0	0
Puerto Rico	3 699	465	3 033	161	40
Trust Territory of the Pacific Islands*a*	63	48	2	0	13
Virgin Islands of the US	10	9	0	0	1
Wake Island	7	0	0	0	7
Transients	79 001	29 424	19 214	10 454	19 909
Afloat	188 259	0	187 209	1 050	0
Total US Territory and special locations	**1 665 465**	**523 647**	**502 550**	**166 699**	**472 569**
Foreign countries					
(1) Western and Southern Europe					
Austria	30	6	0	22	2
Belgium*	3 117	1 326	120	34	1 637
Cyprus	13	3	0	10	0
Denmark*	61	8	20	10	23
Finland	20	5	2	11	2
France*	72	18	10	34	10
FR Germany (incl. West Berlin)*	247 349	205 985	346	90	40 928
Gibraltar	3	0	3	0	0
Greece*	3 541	517	495	14	2 515
Greenland*	313	0	0	0	313
Iceland*	3 127	2	1 758	94	1 273
Ireland	10	2	0	8	0
Italy*	14 926	4 133	4 846	253	5 694
Luxembourg*	11	5	0	6	0
Malta	6	0	0	6	0
Netherlands*	2 882	918	17	10	1 937
Norway*	219	37	38	21	123
Portugal*	1 702	71	383	13	1 235
Spain*	9 310	24	3 879	202	5 205
Sweden	14	1	2	6	5
Switzerland	32	3	0	26	3
Turkey*	5 024	1 222	97	19	3 686
United Kingdom*	28 952	210	2 346	358	26 038

Regional area/country	Total	Army	Navy	Marine Corps	Air Force
Vatican City	6	0	0	6	0
Afloat	14 639	0	12 123	2 516	0
Total Western and Southern Europe	**335 379**	**214 496**	**26 485**	**3 769**	**90 629**
(*European NATO)	**(320 606)**	**(214 476)**	**(14 355)**	**(1 158)**	**(90 617)**
(*European NATO permanently assigned)	**(321 145)**	**(214 498)**	**(14 306)**	**(1 158)**	**(91 183)**
(2) *East Asia and Pacific*					
Australia	714	10	413	10	281
Burma	11	3	0	6	2
China	23	5	3	12	3
Fiji	1	0	1	0	0
Hong Kong	44	14	14	11	5
Indonesia	45	10	12	12	11
Japan (including Okinawa)	47 632	2 204	7 323	21 922	16 183
Malaysia	22	9	1	9	3
New Zealand	69	1	52	6	10
Philippines	15 611	62	4 959	1 306	9 284
Republic of Korea	43 252	30 445	391	1 227	11 189
Singapore	23	3	12	6	2
Thailand	110	57	10	13	30
Afloat	12 000	0	11 587	413	0
Total East Asia and Pacific	**119 557**	**32 823**	**24 778**	**24 953**	**37 003**
(3) *Africa, Near East and South Asia*					
Afghanistan	4	0	0	4	0
Algeria	9	3	0	6	0
Bahrain	89	1	87	0	1
Bangladesh	9	2	0	7	0
Burkina Faso	6	0	0	6	0
British Indian Ocean Territory (includes Diego Garcia)	1 244	0	1 237	0	7
Cameroon	8	2	0	6	0
Chad	15	3	0	12	0
Congo	8	0	2	6	0
Djibouti	6	0	0	6	0
Egypt	1 404	1 288	30	27	59
Ethiopia	7	0	0	7	0
Gabon	6	0	0	6	0
Ghana	11	3	0	8	0
India	40	6	5	24	5
Israel	73	25	9	22	17
Ivory Coast	14	4	0	9	1
Iraq	6	0	0	6	0
Jordan	32	20	0	8	4
Kenya	46	10	12	21	3
Kuwait	27	14	2	8	3
Lebanon	20	5	0	15	0
Liberia	19	8	2	7	2
Madagascar	8	0	2	6	0
Malawi	3	3	0	0	0
Mali	5	0	0	5	0
Mauritius	6	0	0	6	0
Morocco	52	14	3	22	13
Nepal	7	3	0	4	0
Niger	7	1	0	6	0
Nigeria	16	3	0	10	3

Regional area/country	Total	Army	Navy	Marine Corps	Air Force
Oman	21	3	1	9	8
Pakistan	42	14	3	17	8
St Helena (includes Ascension Island)	2	0	0	0	2
Saudi Arabia	460	190	43	22	205
Senegal	13	1	2	10	0
Sierra Leone	6	0	0	6	0
Seychelles	4	0	0	0	4
Somalia	35	22	4	6	3
South Africa	22	2	3	13	4
Sri Lanka	12	0	3	9	0
Sudan	31	7	0	11	13
Syria	11	3	0	8	0
Tanzania, United Republic of	8	0	0	8	0
Tunisia	27	10	2	11	4
United Arab Emirates	12	5	1	5	1
Yemen (Sanaa)	13	6	0	4	3
Zaïre	26	10	0	10	6
Zambia	6	0	0	6	0
Zimbabwe	8	2	0	6	0
Afloat	9 500	0	9 302	198	0
Total Africa, Near East and South Asia	**13 466**	**1 693**	**10 755**	**639**	**379**
(4) Western Hemisphere					
Antigua	75	0	73	0	2
Argentina	22	4	2	11	5
Bahamas, The	47	0	22	7	18
Barbados	19	10	2	7	0
Belize	4	3	1	0	0
Bermuda	1 500	0	1 416	84	0
Bolivia	14	4	0	7	3
Brazil	52	11	9	27	5
Canada	521	9	389	12	111
Chile	19	3	1	13	2
Colombia	29	8	4	13	4
Costa Rica	16	6	0	10	0
Cuba (Guantanamo)	2 274	0	1 839	433	2
Dominican Republic	18	4	2	10	2
Ecuador	25	5	3	10	7
El Salvador	69	37	0	28	4
Grenada	7	1	0	6	0
Guatemala	21	6	0	14	1
Guyana	6	0	0	6	0
Haiti	14	5	0	8	1
Honduras[b]	883	848	3	24	8
Jamaica	14	1	3	10	0
Mexico	33	10	3	14	6
Nicaragua	13	2	0	10	1
Panama	8 865	5 868	445	191	2 361
Paraguay	13	3	1	7	2
Peru	35	4	11	13	7
Suriname	3	3	0	0	0
Trinidad and Tobago	6	0	0	6	0
Uruguay	15	4	2	7	2
Venezuela	31	3	4	8	16
Afloat	818	0	818	0	0
Total Western Hemisphere	**15 481**	**6 862**	**5 053**	**996**	**2 570**

Regional area/country	Total	Army	Navy	Marine Corps	Air Force
(5) *Antarctica*	133	34	99	0	0
(6) *Eastern Europe*					
Bulgaria	12	2	0	8	2
Czechoslovakia	13	1	0	9	3
German Democratic Republic	52	45	0	7	0
Hungary	16	4	0	11	1
Poland	14	3	0	10	1
Romania	12	3	0	8	1
USSR	61	7	5	42	7
Yugoslavia	29	4	1	20	4
Total Eastern Europe	**209**	**69**	**6**	**115**	**19**
(7) *Undistributed*					
Ashore[c]	689	11	194	0	484
Total undistributed	**689**	**11**	**194**	**0**	**484**
Total foreign countries	**484 914**	**255 988**	**67 370**	**30 472**	**131 084**
Ashore	447 957	255 988	33 540	27 345	131 084
Afloat	36 957	0	33 830	3 127	0
Total world-wide	**2 150 379**	**779 635**	**569 920**	**197 171**	**603 653**
Ashore	1 925 163	779 635	348 881	192 994	603 653
Afloat	225 216	0	221 039	4 177	0

[a] Includes five civic action teams of approximately 13 persons each (1 in Palau and 4 in the Federated States of Micronesia).

[b] Number includes military personnel on temporary duty for planning and conduct of exercises.

[c] Ashore includes temporarily shore-based.

Source: US Department of Defense, table P309A, 1985, unpublished.

Several points stand out in observing these data. First, the proportion of US active duty personnel outside the USA and its territories, including those afloat, is in the range of 20–25 per cent, comprising nearly half a million persons. Of those, more than half are Army forces, but with a strong representation from the Air Force. As expected, the Army presence in particular, but also that of the Air Force, in FR Germany dominates the picture, comprising about half the overall US foreign presence. The Army presence in Korea and the Air Force data for Japan (mostly Okinawa) also stand out. In Third World areas where US personnel representation is scattered and thin, the dominance of the Panama presence in Latin America and the at least significant numbers for Egypt and Saudi Arabia in the Middle East stand out. The data could, overall, be dramatically altered by any significant US force withdrawal from Western Europe, Japan and Korea.

British advisors are in Ghana, Nigeria, Saudi Arabia, Swaziland, Uganda and Zimbabwe; and as well as those locales noted previously as hosts to French combat units, there are French advisors/technicians in Algeria, Bahrain, Côte d'Ivoire, Madagascar, Mauritania, Morocco, Niger, Rwanda, Saudi Arabia and Zaïre. In these cases the numbers involved are much smaller than for the USA or the USSR.

VII. Multilateral peacekeeping forces

The United Nations has long maintained multilateral peacekeeping forces in various hot spots, usually positioned between contending sides of still unresolved conflicts, such as those between the Arabs and Israel, Greece and Turkey on Cyprus, India and Pakistan in Kashmir, and so on. This too constitutes a form of FMP.

For instance in the Golan Heights, the UN deploys the 1410-man Disengagement Observer-Force (UNDEF) with contingents from Austria (532), Canada (226), Finland (495) and Poland (157). The UN Interim Force in Lebanon (UNFIL) consists of some 5827 men, from France (1391), Fiji (627), Finland (514), Ghana (690), Ireland (746), Italy (51), Nepal (800), Norway (864) and Sweden (144).

The Egyptian–Israeli border is patrolled by the 2665-man Multinational Force and Observers (MFO) set up under the Israeli–Egyptian Peace Treaty; contingents come from the USA (1186), Canada (136), Britain (38), Colombia (500), Fiji (500), France (40), Italy (90), the Netherlands (105) and Uruguay (70).[80]

VIII. Summary

This chapter stresses that as measured in quantitative terms, the bulk of the current ground-force FMP phenomenon consists of forward deployments of large NATO and Soviet armies in Central Europe; and to a lesser degree deployment in Korea and Mongolia. These deployments may be viewed as a (somewhat historically unique) function of the durable, long-term alliances which have been the hallmark of the post-war international system. Otherwise stated, these deployments are a correlate of what is often characterized in the literature of international relations theory as a tight bipolar system, only perhaps now gradually evolving towards a degree of relative multipolarity.

Although numerically speaking a less prominent feature of contemporary politics, most other ground-force FMP involves one degree or another of major-power involvement in Third World wars, conflicts and confrontations. Variously, this involves the related aspects of surrogate forces, trainers and advisors, attached small-unit combat forces; these are often involved in wars of nerves, coercive diplomacy, deterrence functions, maintenance of local balances of power, and so on. Such presences are also often adjuncts to major power air and naval forces, in turn acquired as quid pro quo for security assistance and/or the protection provided by small-scale ground-force FMP.

Notes and references

[1] Blaxland, G., *The Regiments Depart* (William Kimber: London, 1971); and Barnet, C., *Britain and Her Army: 1509–1970* (William Morrow: New York, 1970).
[2] The preferred current terminology is: 'out of area' missions, as usually applied to NATO

activities outside Europe. See Kupchan, C., *The Persian Gulf and the West* (Allen and Unwin: Boston, Mass., 1987), chapter 8, under 'The out-of-area problem for NATO'.

[3] These functions are reviewed in Hagerty, H. G., *Forward Deployment in the 1970s and 1980s*, National Security Affairs Monograph 77-2 (National Defense University: Washington, DC, 1977); and Foster, R. B., *et al.*, 'Implications of the Nixon Doctrine for the defense planning process', Stanford Research Institute, Menlo Park, Calif., 1972, pp. 114–25.

[4] SIPRI data, particularly those for the US Army presence in the FRG and the corresponding Red Army presence in the GDR.

[5] For a basic outline of the relevant force deployments, see Karber, P. A. and Whitley, A. G., 'Operational continuity and change within the Central European conventional arms control competition', notes prepared for the West Point Conference on 'NATO at Forty', New York, 4–7 June 1987; and Collins, J. M., *U.S.–Soviet Military Balance 1980–1984* (Pergamon-Brassey's: Washington, DC, 1985), especially Annex A, part E, pp. 254–66.

[6] International Institute for Strategic Studies, *The Military Balance 1986–1987* (IISS: London, 1986), p. 28.

[7] Weinberger, C. W., Secretary of Defense, *Annual Report to the Congress, Fiscal Year 1984* (U.S. Government Printing Office: Washington, DC), pp. 215–16.

[8] IISS (note 6), p. 28. See also, for roughly comparable data, Department of Defense, *List of Military Installations*, including FY 1987 *Authorized Full Time Assigned Personnel*, provided to the author by the Office of the Secretary of Defense.

[9] IISS (note 6), p. 60.

[10] IISS (note 6), p. 60.

[11] IISS (note 6), p. 60.

[12] IISS (note 6), p. 66.

[13] IISS (note 6), p. 62.

[14] IISS (note 6), p. 57.

[15] IISS (note 6), p. 73.

[16] On MBFR, see US Arms Control and Disarmament Agency, *Annual Report to Congress, 1986* (US Government Printing Office: Washington, DC, 1986), pp. 52–55; Prendergast, W. B., *Mutual and Balanced Force Reduction: Issues and Prospects* (American Enterprise Institute: Washington, DC, 1978); Feld, W., *Arms Control and the Atlantic Community* (Praeger: New York, 1987), pp. 18–19; and Dean, J., 'Arms control in Europe: Prospects and problems', ed. W. F. Hanrieder, *Arms Control, the FRG, and the Future of East–West Relations* (Westview: Boulder, Colo., 1987), pp. 49–60. Regarding the current prospects for conventional arms reductions in Europe, see 'Issue of conventional forces is a priority at NATO summit', *International Herald Tribune*, 1 Mar. 1988, p. 2; and 'Soviet offers to adjust imbalance of conventional forces in Europe', *New York Times*, 24 June 1988, p. A1.

[17] See Yost, D., 'Franco–German defense cooperation', *The Washington Quarterly*, vol. 11, no. 2 (spring 1988), pp. 173–95, which argues the still limited import of new developments in this area.

[18] An earlier general framework for analysis is Deitchman, S. J., *New Technology and Military Power: General Purpose Military Forces for the 1980s and Beyond* (Westview: Boulder, Colo., 1979). The 'Air-Land Battle' concept is discussed in, among others, Corcoran, E. A., 'Improving Europe's conventional defenses', eds R. Kennedy and J. Weinstein, *The Defense of the West* (Westview: Boulder, Colo., 1984), pp. 349–74; Schemmer, B., 'NATO's new strategy: Defend forward but strike deep', *Armed Forces Journal International*, Nov. 1982, p. 65; Huntington, S., 'The renewal of strategy', ed. S. Huntington, *The Strategic Imperative: New policies for American Security* (Ballinger: Cambridge, Mass., 1982), pp. 1–52; Makins, C., 'U.S. strategy and the world of the 1980s, some Western European perspectives', eds K. Dunn and W. Staudenmaier, *Alternative Military Strategies for the Future* (Westview: Boulder, Colo., 1985), chapter 2; and Collins (note 5), pp. 129–30. This concept emphasizes deep-strike weapons and related intelligence capabilities, as note US Department of the Army, *Operations*, FM 100-5, 20 Aug. 1982, chapter 7.

[19] See Canby, S., 'NATO defense: The problem is not more money', eds R. Harkavy and E. Kolodziej, *American Security Policy and Policy-Making* (D. C. Heath: Lexington, Mass., 1980), chapter 5.

[20] 'Carter delays most cuts in forces in South Korea', *International Herald Tribune*, 21–22 July 1979, reviews the history of this matter, 1977–79. See also 'When the stepping stones of world power are rocky bases', *U.S. News and World Report*, 23 Nov. 1987, p. 31.

[21] Blackaby, F., Goldblat, J. and Lodgaard, S. (eds), SIPRI, *No-First-Use* (Taylor and Francis: London, 1985).

[22] IISS (note 6), p. 30.

[23] The numbers and roles of US advisory personnel in Honduras is discussed in 'U.S. Latin force in place if needed, officials report', *New York Times*, 23 Apr. 1984, p. A1.

[24] See also, for details, Department of Defense (note 8).

[25] IISS (note 6), p. 29.

[26] IISS (note 6), pp. 31–46; and pp. 223–27 under 'The East–West conventional balance in Europe'.

[27] IISS (note 6), p. 37.

[28] IISS (note 6), pp. 42, 43.

[29] The USSR has not, in recent years, been able to station troops in Romania, though it has made demands to that end with contingencies involving Yugoslavia in mind. See 'Pressure on Ceausescu by Russia', *Daily Telegraph*, 15 Jan. 1980.

[30] Karber and Whitley (note 5).

[31] Earlier Soviet gestures at unilateral draw-downs of its forces in Eastern Europe, valid or not, are discussed in 'Fresh troops expected to nullify Soviet reduction', *The Times*, 5 Aug. 1980; 'Moscow begins second stage of troop reduction in E. Germany', *Financial Times*, 10 June 1980; and 'Soviet military withdrawals', *Gist*, May 1987, US Department of State, Bureau of Public Affairs.

[32] IISS (note 6), p. 46.

[33] IISS (note 6), p. 45.

[34] 'China, Mongolia sign agreement to upgrade ties', *International Herald Tribune*, 11 Aug. 1986, p. 1; and in 'Soviet military withdrawals', *Gist*, May 1987, U.S. Department of State, Bureau of Public Affairs.

[35] IISS (note 6), p. 46.

[36] Actually, as Soviet forces were being withdrawn in 1988, the official Soviet figure was somewhat lower. See 'Moscow says its force in war was 100,300', *New York Times*, 27 May 1988, p. A11, quoting Soviet armed forces' Chief of Staff Marshal Sergei F. Akhromeyev.

[37] Rubinstein, A., *Red Star on the Nile* (Princeton University Press: Princeton, N.J., 1977), p. 190; and Sella, A., *Soviet Political and Military Conduct in the Middle East* (St. Martin's Press: New York, 1981), p. 77, which estimates the Soviet presence between 15 000 and 21 000 men.

[38] IISS (note 6), p. 46.

[39] 'Soviet brigade: How the U.S. traced it', *New York Times*, 13 Sep. 1979, p. 16; 'Russians in Cuba: How the pieces began falling into a pattern', *Asahi*, 17 Sep. 1979; 'U.S. says Soviet brigade resumes Cuba maneuvers', *International Herald Tribune*, 3 Mar. 1980.

[40] IISS (note 6), p. 66.

[41] The stationing of 3000 French peacekeeping forces in New Caledonia during the crisis of 1985 is discussed in 'New Caledonia: A divided paradise', *New York Times*, 17 Jan. 1985, p. A1; and 'Some New Caledonians fear clash over vote', *New York Times*, 21 May 1987, p. A7; and 'France bolstering New Caledonia base', *New York Times*, 21 Jan. 1985, p. A3.

[42] IISS (note 6), p. 67.

[43] France's earlier detachment of troops in Niger is noted in 'Niger tells France to withdraw troops', *International Herald Tribune*, 17 May 1974.

[44] The earlier role of French combat troops in Chad *vis-à-vis* Libya is discussed in 'France reluctant to return to gendarme role in Chad', *Financial Times*, 12 Aug. 1983; 'France is said to send troops to Chad capital', *International Herald Tribune*, 10 Aug. 1983; 'Chad to be test ground for new weapons', *The Guardian*, 19 Aug. 1983; 'Gunships sent to back French troops in Chad', *International Herald Tribune*, 5 Sep. 1983.

[45] More recently, Cuban forces have been deployed further south. See 'Cuba's wider role cheers Angolan', *New York Times*, 17 May 1988, p. A3.

[46] IISS (note 6), p. 60.

[47] IISS (note 6), p. 60.

[48] IISS (note 6), p. 151.

[49] IISS (note 6), p. 164.

[50] 'Heavy fighting rocks town in Northern Chad', *International Herald Tribune*, 11 Aug. 1983; 'Chad claims Libyan tanks roll south to attack French', *Guardian*, 24 Aug. 1983.

[51] But this was reduced in 1988, after rising from a level of 120 000 at the time of the 1978 invasion. See 'Hanoi plans 50,000-man pullout from Cambodia', *New York Times*, 26 May 1988, p. A18; and 'Ending an entanglement', *Time*, 6 June 1988, p. 51.

[52] 'Vietnam said to withdraw some troops from Laos', *Washington Post*, 24 May 1988, p. A18; and 'Hanoi cuts force in Laos by half', *New York Times*, 27 May 1988, p. A7, reporting on withdrawal of 20 000 to 25 000 troops.

[53] The magnitude of the South African military involvement in Angola is discussed in 'South Africa gives details of Angola military role', *New York Times*, 20 Apr. 1988, p. A11; and 'Angola war: South Africa presses role', *New York Times*, 21 Dec. 1987, p. A8.

[54] 'The battle for South Beirut', *Time*, 30 May 1988, p. 39. After the 1982 war, Syria had some 50 000 troops in Lebanon, and Israel 15–20 000. See 'Israel, Lebanon set to sign pact', *International Herald Tribune*, 16 May 1983, p. 2; 'Russians tell Syria to cool Beka'a tension', *Guardian*, 30 May 1983; and 'Lebanon urges Soviet pressure on Syria to join pullout talks', *International Herald Tribune*, 21–22 May 1983.

[55] For instance, some 21 000 Tanzanian troops were in Uganda in 1979–1980. See 'Tanzania force to quit Uganda', *Daily Telegraph*, 3 Mar. 1980.

[56] 'China and Vietnam say ships exchanged fire', *International Herald Tribune*, 15 Mar. 1988, p. 1, reports that Viet Nam has troops on 10 of the Spratly Islands.

[57] Sometimes counter-insurgency forces as well may constitute an FMP, by agreement. See 'Hassan orders his troops out of Mauritania', *International Herald Tribune*, 10 Aug. 1979, which details the end of Morocco's stationing of 6000 troops in Mauritania, 1977–79, to combat Polisario guerrillas. At about the same time, South Africa had forces in Rhodesia for counterinsurgency purposes. See 'South Africa has under 1,000 troops in Rhodesia', *Daily Telegraph*, 15 Dec. 1979.

[58] David, S. R., 'The use of proxy forces by major powers in the Third World', eds S. Neuman and R. Harkavy, *The Lessons of Recent Wars in the Third World: Comparative Dimensions* (D. C. Heath: Lexington, Mass., 1987), pp. 199–226.

[59] 'Outsiders stoke Angola civil war with men, weapons, and bases', *New York Times*, 31 May 1988, p. A9; '4 nations to discuss withdrawal of outside forces from Angola', *New York Times*, 30 Apr. 1988, p. 3; 'Cubans on patrol in South Angola', *New York Times*, 16 Dec. 1987, p. A11; and 'Cuba is mired in Angola', *New York Times*, 1 July 1987, p. A7.

[60] David (note 58), pp. 207–208 and 210; and 'Morocco to send troops to fight Zaire invaders', *Washington Post*, 8 Apr. 1977, p. A16. 'U.S. role in Zaire grows with Gabon, Senegal airlift', *Washington Post*, 7 June 1978, p. A21.

[61] 'Pakistan said to offer to base troops on Saudi soil', *New York Times*, 20 Aug. 1980, p. 5; and IISS (note 6), p. 165. According to the State Department's Saudi desk only a portion of these troops, mostly those utilized for training purposes, was being withdrawn in early 1988.

[62] Rubinstein (note 37), pp. 190–91; and Sella (note 37), pp. 76–77.

[63] Regarding SA-5s in Syria, see 'Syrian armed forces: Playing waiting game?', *New York Times*, 7 Jan. 1984, p. 4; 'Soviet is said to deploy new missiles in Syria', *New York Times*, 18 Jan. 1983, p. A4; and US Department of Defense, *Soviet Military Power 1985* (US Government Printing Office: Washington, DC, 1985), p. 124.

[64] 'A Soviet connection to carnage?', *Washington Times*, 30 Dec. 1985, which sites the SA-5 batteries in Libya near Derna and Tobruk along the Mediterranean coast; and 'U.S. fleet that struck Libya starts to scatter', *New York Times*, 3 Apr. 1986, p. A13.

[65] Safire, W., 'Saleh in our alley', *New York Times*, 3 Dec. 1979, p. A25.

[66] 'Nicaragua rebels reported to raise millions in gifts', *New York Times*, 9 Sep. 1984, p. 1.

[67] 'Guerrillas force war deeper into Mozambique provinces', *Guardian*, 29 June 1983.

[68] Regarding Saudi Arabia and the contract role of the Vinnell Corporation, see McNaugher, T. L., *Arms and Oil: U.S. Military Strategy and the Persian Gulf* (Brookings Institution: Washington, DC, 1985), pp. 162 and 209.

[69] 'U.S. is likely to maintain key role at military training base in Panama', *International Herald Tribune*, 30 Aug. 1983, which notes the role of the US training facilities in Panama for training personnel from all over Latin America.

[70] 'Soviets show flag in Aden', *Washington Post*, 1 June 1979, p. A11.

[71] See 'U.S. ends secretive exercise in Egypt', *Guardian*, 6 Sep. 1983; and 'Sudan quits U.S. military exercise: Some officials fear Libyan influence', *International Herald Tribune*, 2 Aug. 1985, discussing the Bright Star exercise involving 9000 US personnel and troops from Egypt, Jordan and Somalia.

[72] Regarding President Reagan's exercising of 3200 paratroopers in Honduras in Mar. 1988, see 'Troop moves stir war of words', *USA Today*, 19–21 Mar. 1988, p. 1. Earlier exercises involving some 7000 troops are discussed in 'Army games due with Hondurans', *New York Times*, 27 Mar. 1985, p. A6; in 'U.S. flexes muscles with war games', *USA Today*, 12 May 1987, p. 1; 'New U.S. exercise seen in Honduras', *New York Times*, 17 Nov. 1984, p. 6; and 'GI's will train in Honduras again', *New York Times*, 24 Feb. 1984.

[73] *People's Korea*, 28 Mar. 1987, cited by Jong-Chul Choi, 'United States security policy in

Asia and the U.S.–Japan–South Korea Collective Security Cooperation System', M.A. thesis, Pennsylvania State University, 1988, p. 156.

[74] In 1988, the USA held joint manoeuvres with Zaïre, reportedly intended to put pressure on Angola and to support the forces of Jonas Savimbi. See 'Angola says U.S. uses Zaire bases to train rebels', *New York Times*, 26 May 1988, p. A10. Regarding a US exercise named 'Exotic Palm' with the several Caribbean members of the 'Regional Security System' see 'Caribbean war games: Not everyone is delighted', *New York Times*, 16 Sep. 1985, p. A2.

[75] 'U.S. flexes muscles with war games', *USA Today*, 12 May 1987, p. 1.

[76] Weinberger (note 7), pp. 215–16.

[77] Sella (note 37), p. 137, wherein: 'Libya was of course an additional bonus for the USSR—it was paying for stockpiles of equipment which Libya had no use for, and which was being kept there for use either in the Middle East or in Africa.'

[78] The issue of the US use of military advisers in Honduras and El Salvador—their limits in the context of executive-legislative relations—is discussed in 'Honduras approves U.S. proposal for training base, more advisers', *International Herald Tribune*, 28–29 May 1983.

[79] *Soviet Military Power 1985* (note 63), p. 126.

[80] IISS (note 6), pp. 89–90, under 'The Middle East and North Africa: Peace-keeping forces'.

5. Missiles

The post-war period has seen the advent of missiles—in a by now bewildering mix of types, ranges and functions—as a key weapon type in the hands of all significant military powers. Indeed, in an era increasingly characterized by one-shot 'smart weapons', and as so well demonstrated in the recent wars of the Middle East and the south Atlantic, missiles have become the primary conventional battlefield killers of aircraft, ships, tanks and other missiles. At the strategic nuclear level, missilry accounts for two of the three legs of the familiar triad, plus most of the countering defensive systems.

Beyond the cold numbers—particularly those describing ranges—which form the context for the geopolitics of missile basing one may note political and doctrinal elements to the FMP aspects of missilry. Some missile emplacements may be desired by either superpower in close proximity to the other's homeland so as to reduce warning time, thereby also raising the spectre of, or providing the possibilities for, first-strike capability. But, forward basing (as practised by the USA in Europe and, earlier, the Soviet Union in Cuba) may also be intended to serve a deterrent trip-wire function, that is, to underscore the major powers' political/military commitment to clients' security, the matter of actual credibility aside. The sometimes confusing, complex and subjective arguments surrounding this subject were highlighted and well-publicized during the negotiations over mutual withdrawal of US and Soviet intermediate- and short-range missiles in Europe, which led to the 1987 INF Treaty.

Finally, there is an aspect of missile FMP which is somewhat analogous to the important FMP domain of aircraft overflights. The question of missile overflights is only really significant, hypothetically, in the event of actual war. Recent US–Canadian diplomacy, and some incidents involving Soviet missiles in Scandinavia, have brought this subject to public prominence, in parallel with increasing attention to forward basing of nuclear weapons and transiting of nuclear-armed ships.[1] Mostly this involves matters of intra-alliance war contingency planning and related deterrence postures; much less, a continuous issue of FMP. But it is an aspect of the current trend towards 'decoupling' of alliances.

I. Problems of classification

To a degree, however, the above developments complicate the categorization of systems or combat functions for the purposes of this analysis. Earlier, the three-way division corresponding to the three traditional services—land, naval and air—provided for a neat, if not perfect, categorization. Nowadays, in the mixed nomenclature of modern missilry, these clear distinctions are blurred. In the US forces, for instance, the Air Force handles strategic nuclear missiles, while the Army controls theatre and tactical surface-to-surface systems. The Air Force and Army, meanwhile, both deal with air defence astride the dividing line between aircraft and surface-to-air missiles; the Navy has both for fleet defence. Each of the three US services fields cruise missiles targeted at land targets—ground-launched cruise missiles (GLCMs), submarine-launched cruise missiles (SLCMs) and air-launched cruise missiles (ALCMs), corresponding with their traditional media, that is, land, sea and air, respectively. The Soviet forces, meanwhile, are organized more along the lines of combat functions cutting across traditional service lines.

There are a number of ways of categorizing missiles, specifically, as that categorization applies to an analysis of FMP. Those categories include such criteria as: origin and destination according to the realms of land, sea and air; range; payload; nuclear versus conventional, sometimes involving dual configuration; ballistic versus guided; fixed versus mobile missiles; single versus multiple warheads; exo- and endo-atmospheric; and so on. However, most of what is relevant in connection with FMP involves surface-to-surface and surface-to-air missiles associated with the rival NATO and WTO forces in Europe. But, that is not the whole story, and it is one which may well be in the process of change.

As indicated, there is a basic breakdown of missile types according to the realms from which they are fired and the targets to which they are directed. There are air-to-air, air-to-surface, air-to-ship, surface-to-surface, surface-to-air, ship-to-ship, shore-to-ship, and ATGW missiles. Some specific models of missiles can be used for more than one of these roles; for instance, the French Exocet and US Harpoon missiles can both be configured for use on either aircraft or ships (or on land) or for missions against ships; several of the ATGWs such as the US TOW (tube-launched, optically tracked, wire-guided) missile can be fired either by ground crews or from helicopters. The Chinese Silkworm shore-to-ship missiles in Iran, which figured prominently in the news in 1987, are variants of older Soviet model ship-to-ship missiles.[2]

Some of these categories of missiles obviously involve organic relations with service-related forces, and are, therefore, difficult to discuss in isolation. Ship-to-ship and ship-to-air missiles clearly require discussion—in relation to FMP—in the context of overseas naval facilities. Similarly, air-to-surface and air-to-air missiles are inextricably bound up with aircraft and hence air bases. Those cases are clear. That of surface-to-air (air-defence) missiles is less clear. Regarding the US Army, for instance, whereas Chaparral/Vulcan air-defence systems are organic to virtually all large combat formations (and involve a dual-mounted missile and gun combination), the longer-range Improved Hawk (and now Patriot) missiles and the nuclear-armed Nike-Hercules are deployed in separate units and may perhaps be more appropriately discussed as a distinct form of FMP, even if virtually always collocated with Army units. In some cases on the Soviet side, however, such air-defence installations are less closely tied to Soviet Army force units.

Surface-to-surface missiles, the primary category warranting inclusion under

FMP, have traditionally been categorized in the strategic literature by range. This has involved some variation in common usage, but the following list is close to standard:[3]

1. *Intercontinental ballistic missile* (ICBM): as implied, intercontinental ranges, i.e., over 5500 km.
2. *Intermediate-range ballistic missile* (IRBM): ranges *c*.2400–5500 km.
3. *Medium-range ballistic missile* (MRBM): ranges *c*.800–2400 km.
4. *Short-range ballistic missile* (SRBM): ranges of up to about 800 km.
5. *Battlefield or tactical missiles*: ranges of less than 400 km.

The Pentagon's annual 'posture statements' have recently leaned towards a less formal and precise set of definitions, involving the adjustment of terminology to geopolitical specifics and to actual force structures. Missiles of intercontinental ranges are defined as strategic. Intermediate-range nuclear forces (INF) are those capable of striking targets beyond the general area of the battlefield, but still not capable of intercontinental range. Within that rubric there is reference to 'Longer-Range INF forces', which include missiles with ranges of 1800 km to 5500 km (roughly similar to the old IRBM category), and 'Shorter-Range INF forces', with missiles of ranges from beyond the immediate battlefield to 1800 km (spanning the older MRBM and SRBM categories).[4] Short-range nuclear forces include missiles capable of striking targets only in the battlefield area. These latter categories are utilized to group missiles, rockets, artillery and aircraft into discrete categories according to potential combat functions. They form the basis, or provide a baseline, more or less, for contemporary arms control discussions, as fully evidenced by the INF accords.

As noted, there are other ways to categorize missiles which constitute FMP. Some are nuclear-armed, others conventional. Some, such as the US Lance (SRBM), or Soviet Scud B (MRBM) are dual-purpose and can be armed either for nuclear or conventional strikes or, additionally, for CW (chemical warfare), BW (biological warfare) or even RW (radiological warfare) missions.

Some, actually most, are strictly ballistic missiles; others, such as most modern cruise missiles (often referred to in US military jargon as 'air breathers'), can be provided mid-course guidance or corrections; variously, by on-board inertial guidance systems, terrain-matching technology, radio guidance, infra-red, and so on—as a result, they can be brought to pinpoint accuracy. Some missiles are in fixed positions, either hardened in silos or exposed on the surface, and the time taken to fuel them or otherwise prepare them for firing can vary greatly. Others are very mobile; some are more movable than actually mobile, relying upon cumbersome transporter-erector-launchers (TELS). Some fly entirely within the earth's atmosphere at relatively flat trajectories (endo-atmospheric); others go out of the atmosphere (exo-atmospheric), a distinction of possibly considerable importance in connection with emerging space-based missile defence systems. (The earlier Soviet-bruited fractional orbit bombardment system (FOBS) was an—hypothetical—extension towards a space-based nuclear weapon.[5]) Some are solid-fuelled, others liquid-fuelled—launch-time after warning is much slower in the latter case. Some are single-shot, others can be reloaded, which directs attention to associated storage areas (perhaps hidden or covert) for weapon reload as an aspect of FMP.

There is also the traditional breakdown, familiar in analyses of the strategic nuclear balance, utilized for comparing the strengths of rival forces: launchers, throw-weight, megatonnage, warheads, equivalent megatonnage, and so on.[6] The larger the throw-weight, of course, the greater the scope and possibilities for megatonnage and, hence, for multiple independently targetable re-entry vehicle (MIRV) systems, a reality which has been highlighted in debates over the measurement of the theatre balance in Europe, as well as of the overarching superpower strategic balance.

II. Surface-to-surface missiles

The post-war history of the external basing of surface-to-surface missiles—particularly those mounting nuclear warheads—has evidenced some very visible and prominent political issues and crises. This underscores the seriousness of the hosting of such weapons.

Beginning in the mid-1950s, the USA began deployment of what was to become a series of SRBMs (the Honest Johns, Corporals, Sergeants, etc.) in Western Europe, mostly under the 'dual-key' system. (Nuclear-armed Honest Johns were deployed with the Greek and Turkish armies as well as in Central Europe.[7]) This reflected an implicit concession on NATO's part that its conventional forces were not a match for rival Soviet ground forces, and that there was therefore a requirement for a threat to move up the ladder of escalation in response to overwhelming conventional attack. It also reflected a realization in the USA, beginning in the mid-1950s, of the coming inevitability of mutual second-strike deterrent capability at the strategic nuclear level—'mutual assured destruction (MAD)' or a 'balance of terror'—that was recognized as negating the credibility of the massive retaliation doctrine enunciated at the close of the Korean War which, essentially, hinged upon the assumption of some approximation to a US first-strike capability. The fading of that assumption led to doctrines of flexible response, and to possibilities for limited, controlled nuclear war, crucially involving the stationing of tactical nuclear weapons in Western Europe and in Korea.

In the late 1950s, the vaunted US 'missile-gap scare' resulting from the Soviet *Sputnik* launch and reports of precocious Soviet ICBM developments led Washington, fearing a 'technological Pearl Harbor', to the forward emplacement of intermediate-range missiles in Europe (as an interim measure)—in Turkey, Italy and the UK.[8] This involved, specifically, two Jupiter missile squadrons in Italy, another in Turkey, and additional Jupiter and Thor missiles in the UK (105 missiles in total) to bolster the still very formidable nuclear deterrence threat posed by the Strategic Air Command's B-52 and B-47 bomber force.[9]

By the early 1960s, a large-scale US nuclear buildup under the Kennedy Administration—featuring deployment of Atlas, Titan and Minuteman ICBMs, and then Polaris SLBMs—erased the feared US missile gap (satellite reconnaissance following the famed Gary Powers U-2 incident had led to a lower estimate of Soviet ICBM developments).[10] In turn, the Soviet Union came to question its own second-strike capability. The growing US advantage impelled Soviet leader Nikita Khrushchev to gamble with the introduction of medium-range ballistic missiles (MRBMs) into Cuba—only some two years after the Cuban revolution had provided the Soviet Union with a forward base in near proximity to the USA. That precipitated the Cuban missile crisis, eventuating in the withdrawal of those Soviet missiles, but also the removal of US Jupiters in Turkey as a (somewhat indirect) quid pro quo.[11]

Less publicized but also important were the emplacements of shorter-range US nuclear missiles in the Far East, targeted upon Soviet military installations in the latter's eastern provinces and also against the PRC during the long period of Sino-American hostility coincident to the Sino-Soviet alliance. This involved the stationing of some Matador missiles (from the 1950s) in Taiwan and of 2500-mile range Mace missiles (beginning in the early 1960s) on Okinawa—the former were intended primarily as a deterrent vis-à-vis the PRC and as a trip-wire protection for Taiwan in the wake of the Korean War.[12] The earlier developments can be seen—as measured by political sensitivity—as precursors of the more recent events surrounding planned US deployment of Pershing IIs and GLCMs in Europe in response to the Soviet buildup of SS-20 theatre weapons.

By the mid-1980s, of course, both the USA/NATO and the USSR deployed large numbers of externally based, nuclear-armed missiles in Europe, constituting a massive and critical FMP. Centrally, this involved Soviet deployment of short-range theatre weapons and tactical weapons in Eastern Europe (SS-12/22s, SS-23s and SS-7 'Frogs') and countervailing US deployment of Pershings, cruise missiles and Lance battlefield weapons.

The Soviet SS-20 theatre missiles which were at the centre of the INF negotiations were first deployed in 1977. These missiles, carrying three nuclear warheads with ranges of 3400 miles (5000 km) were phased in to replace the older SS-4s.[13] The latter were first deployed in 1959, with a single warhead platform and a range of 1120 miles.[14]

By 1987, it was typically reported that over 300 SS-20s were deployed against NATO west of the Ural Mountains, with another 100 or so in Soviet Asia, for a total of 441.[15] None of these were based outside the USSR (nor were any of the 112 reported remnant SS-4s which were still deployed in the western USSR), as indicated in figure 5 showing pre-INF Treaty missile deployments in 1987.[16] They were based in several fields in the western Soviet Union and near the Caspian Sea. The SS-20s threatened the entirety of NATO-Europe with their 5000-km ranges, as well as many other important targets—the Azores, Greenland, Shemya Island, Philippines, Guam, Okinawa, and so on.[17]

As it happens, the figures formally published in the INF Treaty itself were somewhat at variance with those cited above, or at least presented in a more

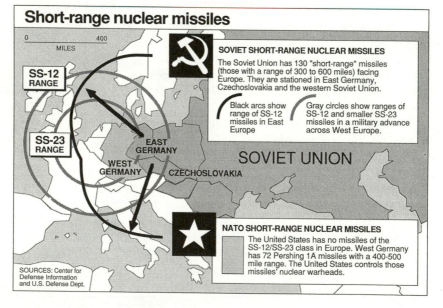

Figure 5. Pre-INF Treaty missile deployments in Europe
Source: *Centre Daily Times*, 19 April 1987, p. B5.

complex way. The USSR was gauged as having 484 deployed and 124 non-deployed intermediate-range launchers (SS-20s and SS-4s); and with those, 470 deployed and 356 non-deployed missiles.[18] Again, none were deployed outside the USSR.

Table 13. US and Soviet foreign-based systems to be removed under the INF Treaty

Party	System	Location	No. of missiles	No. of launchers
USSR	SS-20	. .	. .	. .
	SS-4	. .	. .	. .
	SS-12 (Scaleboard)	Koenigsbruck (DDR)	19	11
		Bischofswerda (DDR)	8	5
		Waren (DDR)	22	12
		Wokuhl (DDR)	5	6
		Hranice (Czech)	39	24
	Sub-total		**93**	**58**
	SS-23	Weissenfels (DDR)	6	4
		Jena-Forst (DDR)	47	12
	Sub-total		**53**	**16**
USA[a]	Pershing II	Schwäbish-Gmünd (FRG)	40 incl. 4 spares	36
		Neu Ulm (FRG)	40 incl. 4 spares	43 incl. 7 spares
		Waldheide-Neckarsulm (FRG)	40 incl. 4 spares	36
	Sub-total		**120 incl. 12 spares**	**115 incl. 7 spares**
	BGM-1096	Greenham Common (UK)	101 incl. 5 spares	29 incl. 5 spares
		Molesworth (UK)	18	6
		Comiso (Italy)	108 incl. 12 spares	31 incl. 7 spares
		Florennes (Belg)	20 incl. 4 spares	12 incl. 8 spares
		Wüschheim (FRG)	62 incl. 14 spares	31 incl. 9 spares
	Sub-total		**309 incl. 35 spares**	**109 incl. 29 spares**

[a] On the US side, the Treaty also covers another missile operating base at Woensdrecht, Netherlands (zero deployments); a launcher repair site at E.M.C. Hausen, Frankfurt, FRG; a missile repair site at SABCA Gosselies, Belgium; and a missile storage site at Weilerback, FRG.

Source: Treaty Between the United States of America and the Union of Soviet Socialist Republics on the Elimination of Their Intermediate-Range and Shorter-Range Missiles, US Department of State Publication 9555 (Bureau of Public Affairs: Washington, DC, Dec. 1987).

As shown in table 13, however, the USSR did have a number of shorter-range INF missiles and launchers, deployed in the GDR and Czechoslovakia, all of which were subject to dismantling as the Treaty came into force. This included the 900-km range SS-12 Scaleboard, first deployed in 1979, and by 1987 involved some 58 launchers and 93 missiles at four sites in the GDR and another in Czechoslovakia.[19] It also involved the 500-km range SS-23 (first deployed in 1979–80 as a follow on to the 300-km range SS-1c Scud B), for which there were two sites in the GDR involving 16 launchers and 53 missiles.[20] The Scaleboard, which is actually an MRBM, came to be forward-based in Eastern Europe only in 1984 and is also deployed within the USSR proper along the Chinese border.

At the division level, widely deployed in Eastern Europe, is the unguided free-rocket-over-ground (FROG) missile, deployed in battalions of four launchers with ranges of 70 km. These in turn are being replaced by the longer-range

(100 km) and more accurate SS-21s.[21] About 500 FROG and SS-21 launchers are facing NATO, another 215 are targeted on the PRC and the Far East, and some (all within the USSR) are targeted on South-West Asia and Turkey. Locations of FROG and SS-21 battalions in Eastern Europe and Mongolia are shown in table 14. There are more than 20 FROG and SS-21 battalions in the GDR.[22] These would, of course, be the subjects of any follow-on to the INF Treaty which pursued the so-called 'triple-zero option' involving the elimination of tactical or battlefield nuclear-armed missiles.

On the NATO side too there have been significant deployments of longer-range INF missiles and of tactical/battlefield missiles. In the former category, prior to the INF Treaty, this involved the Pershing IIs and BGM-109G cruise missiles; in the latter category, primarily Lance missiles. In 1979, the USA and its NATO allies embarked upon the so-called 'dual-track' process, whereby the USA committed itself to negotiating with the Soviet Union over arms control in this connection in exchange for commitments by the Europeans to move ahead with deployment if no accords on limitation were arrived at.[23] That ultimately involved plans by NATO for deployment of 108 Pershing IIs and 464 ground-launched cruise missiles in several NATO countries: FR Germany, Italy, the UK, Belgium and the Netherlands.

The Pershing II, feared by the Soviet Union as a first-strike capable weapon, is a highly accurate mobile missile (with terminal guidance), with a range of up to 1800 km, capable of being mounted on trucks. As noted in table 13, those missiles were deployed at three sites in FR Germany prior to the INF Treaty, sites at which US-manned Pershing 1as had previously been located.

Originally, the USA planned to deploy 464 GLCMs—a version of the US Navy's Tomahawk. They have ranges of about 2500 km, are mobile, and have one variable-yield warhead apiece, in the 10-50 kt range. They are highly accurate, with terrain-contour matching (TERCOM) guidance, but are too slow to constitute an effective first-strike threat. As shown in table 13, at the time of the INF Treaty's consummation, the USA had deployed only 109 launchers and 309 missiles en route to the planned 464.[24] Those planned for deployment in the Netherlands had not yet been installed.

Some reports in early 1988 indicated that withdrawal of US land-based missiles from Europe under the INF Treaty might result in other, countervailing deployments with FMP implications, also dependent upon possible follow-on arms control agreements. One report indicated a possible US plan for increased reliance on B-52s carrying highly accurate, stand-off conventional weapons in lieu of GLCMs.[25] Still other options were a new ground-based Lance missile with a range of up to 300 miles, dispatching more F-111 bombers to Europe, increasing the number of planned F-15 and F-16 aircraft that can fire nuclear-armed air-to-surface missiles, allocating more missile-firing submarines to the NATO military commander, and building up the number of sea-launched cruise missiles on ships and perhaps on submarines.[26]

The Lance is a short-range, highly mobile missile, with a range of 115 km, and with a variety of yields up to 100 kt; it can also be utilized in a non-nuclear

Table 14. FROG and SS-21 battalions in Eastern Europe and Mongolia, 1985

Country	Location
Bulgaria	Plotchik
	Markovo
	Plovdiv
	Shabla
	Petritch (near Karnobat)
	Kavarna/Kyutstendil
	Haskovo
	Harmanli
	Vidin
Czechoslovakia	Bruntal
	Ceske-Budejovice
	Havlickuv Brod
	Milovice, Prague
	Pilsen
	Susice
	Tabor
	Topolcany
	Vysoke, Myto
	Zvolen
German Democratic Republic	Bernau
	Dallgow-Doberitz
	Dessau-Rosslau
	Dresden
	Dresden-Klotzsche
	Eggesin
	Erfurt
	Grimma
	Halle
	Hillersleben
	Jena
	Jüterbog
	Krampnitz
	Naumburg-Saale
	Neuruppin
	Neustrelitz
	Ohrdruf
	Perleberg-Prignitz
	Riesa (Sachsen Zeithain)
	Schwerin
	Stendal-Altmark
	Vogelsang-Templin
	Wittenberg-Lutherstadt
Hungary	Esztergom
	Kecskemet
	Szekesfehervar
	Szombathely
	Tatabanya
	Veszprem
Poland	Borne
	Swiebodzin
Mongolia	Barun Urt
	Choybalsan (Urf Durfal)
	Sayn-Shand

Source: Arkin, W. A. and Fieldhouse, R. W., *Nuclear Battlefields: Global Links in the Arms Race* (Ballinger: Cambridge, Mass., 1985), appendix B.

mode.[27] Lance missiles were initially deployed in 1976, and there are now six US-manned Lance battalions with six launchers each in FR Germany with a total of 108 warheads.[28] Additional Lances are deployed with the British, Belgian, Netherlands, Italian and West German armies—technically those in Italy with the Italian forces do not fall under the rubric of FMP.[29] The British Army deploys 14 Lance launchers at Rheindahlen and Belgium also forward-bases a small number of Lance missiles based on five launchers.[30] NATO deploys a total of 88 Lance launchers, with about three missiles apiece.

The Pershing 1a was the longest-range and highest-yield Army nuclear weapon missile deployed until its (one-to-one) replacement by the Pershing IIa.[31] There were earlier some 180 launchers in FR Germany, 108 of which were operated by the US Army, the other 72 by the West German Air Force, but with US control of their nuclear warheads.[32] This mobile missile with a range of up to 740 km—which replaced the Sergeant missile in 1962—had only one warhead—of 60, 200, or 400 kt—and there was about one reload for each missile in FR Germany.[33] The German-manned systems were based at Landsberg and Tevren, and they too will be eliminated under the INF Treaty.[34]

Otherwise, there are hardly any additional overseas deployments of surface-to-surface missiles worth mentioning in connection with FMP. In the 1973 Middle Eastern War, there were rumours of Soviet nuclear warheads deployed in Egypt, and even of the 'test-firing' of a non-nuclear Scud missile near the Gaza Strip as a warning to Israel.[35] If those Scuds were, as it may be assumed, under Soviet control, it then illustrated the possibilities of external basing of sophisticated surface-to-surface missiles during crises. Other Scud and FROG missiles in Syria, Iraq and Libya are not necessarily assumed to be under Soviet operational control and as they are not nuclear-armed, constitute merely a long-range but relatively inaccurate conventional terror bombing threat.[36] The extent of Soviet control over Scud and SS-21 missiles in Syria, believed armed with chemical warheads, is not clear.[37]

By 1988, however, there were confirmed reports of the installation of 1600-mile range Chinese CSS2 ('East Wind') missiles in Saudi Arabia and corresponding discussions about whether they might ultimately be armed with either chemical or nuclear warheads. It may be surmised that Saudi Arabia could not, by itself, operate such missiles, and that they would require a large, accompanying Chinese military presence, perhaps as large as 1500 personnel.[38]

III. Surface-to-air missiles

The USSR deploys a far more diverse mix of surface-to-air (SAM) missiles than does the USA, across the whole spectrum of effective altitudes and ranges. This reflects the traditional, asymmetrically stronger Soviet emphasis on air defence, further underscored by the relatively far more numerous Soviet air-defence fighter aircraft. Quantitatively speaking, the Soviet Union deploys altogether some 10 000 SAM launchers at over 1200 sites for strategic defence—these are virtually all within the USSR. They have more than 5000 launch vehicles for tactical SAMs, subordinated to nearly 445 launch units, many of which are outside the USSR proper, particularly in Eastern Europe.[39] Five missiles—SAMs 1, 2, 3, 5 and 10—are utilized primarily for strategic defence.

Regarding tactical SAMs, the Pentagon describes current Soviet developments as follows:

Because of their continuing concern about the threat of NATO aerodynamic systems to their ground forces, the Soviets have put increasingly heavy emphasis on their traditionally strong commitment to ground force air defense. This structure consists of a dense array of mobile SAMs, antiaircraft guns, and handheld SAMs. The SA-11 and SA-12A systems are replacing the SA-4 in non-divisional air defense units. The 57-mm gun, still deployed at division level in many low-priority Soviet and NSWP units, is gradually being replaced by the SA-6 and -8 SAMs. At regimental level, a newer gun system, the ZSU-X, is beginning to supplant the ZSU-23/4. The SA-14 and new, highly accurate SA-16 handheld SAMs are replacing the SA-7 in tactical units.[40]

There are approximately 180 Soviet tactical SAM-missile batteries in Poland, comprised mostly of SA-2/3s, SA-6/8s, SA-9/13s, and SA-11s.[41] These are concentrated in a zone behind the East German border and around Warsaw; also around key Vistula River bridges. There are some 30 such batteries in Hungary, 60 in Czechoslovakia—many operated by Czech forces but integrated with and under the control of the Soviet Air Defence Organization (PVO)—and a truly massive number of such batteries in the GDR.[42] It is a formidable force—there are over 8100 SAM launchers and anti-aircraft pieces (mostly the ZSU-23/4 self-propelled model), not including the far more numerous shoulder-fired SAMs located with all Soviet units.[43]

Outside the WTO, there are but a few acknowledged deployments of Soviet SAMs under actual Soviet military control. The SA-5 deployments in Syria replete with Soviet operators have been noted.[44] There have been reports of a Soviet SAM-missile battery at Amrat in South Yemen near to other important facilities.[45] It is expected, yet publicly not confirmed, that other key overseas hosts of Soviet facilities—Cuba, Viet Nam, Ethiopia, Angola, etc.—have Soviet SAM installations manned wholly or partly by Soviet or other East-bloc personnel.[46] Earlier in the 1970s, of course, there was the elaborate belt of SAM-2s and SAM-3s set up and manned by some 20 000 Soviet personnel during Egypt's 'war of attrition' with Israel.[47]

US forces also extensively deploy SAM installations overseas. All US combat units in FR Germany and Korea have organically attached Chaparral/Vulcan units, with low-altitude missiles married to rapid-firing cannons to defend against enemy low-level air strikes. In FR Germany, the USA has some 30 separate I-Hawk batteries; additionally, there are now two battalions of Patriot missiles, each with six batteries deploying eight quad missiles.[48] The latter will become the principal theatre-level SAM against high- and medium-level aircraft. The US I-Hawks are also deployed in South Korea (the South Korean forces also use them); earlier, up to 1973, others were stationed in the Panama Canal Zone.[49]

Until recently, the USA also deployed a considerable number of Nike-Hercules nuclear-capable air-defence missiles overseas—these actually had once been ringed around some US cities and military installations but were phased out in the mid-1970s. US Nike-Hercules missiles—to be replaced by the Patriot—have until recently been stationed in Greece, Italy and FR Germany in Europe; Belgian, Dutch and German-operated missiles of the same type have been located in FR Germany.[50] (The Belgian missiles have now been dismantled.) These had relatively modest 1-kt warheads, but with long slant ranges of up to 160 km. Earlier they were sited at important US overseas facilities, for instance, at Thule in Greenland. Some 100 Nike-Hercules SAMs are apparently still active with the South Korean forces, albeit in a non-nuclear mode, and apparently are also dual-capable for surface-to-surface firing.[51]

The British Army of the Rhine deploys some British-produced SAMs in FR Germany. Some 108 Rapier SAMs, 16 of which are on self-propelled carriers, are there fielded in lieu of the US-origin I-Hawks utilized by much of the remainder of the NATO forces.[52] Otherwise, within NATO, the all-NATO missile-firing installation (NAMFI) on Crete is noteworthy. This facility is used for the test-firing of missiles rather than for actual combat-contingency purposes.[53]

An analysis of the basing aspects of the strategic nuclear balance, an area in which missilry is a focal issue, is given in chapter 8.

IV. The future

At the time of writing, the future of numerous US and Soviet surface-to-surface missiles based on the soil of NATO and WTO allies is unclear amid the ongoing negotiations in 1988 over arms control, which might result in a significant reduction of nuclear forces in Central Europe, and perhaps conventional forces as well.

The INF Treaty requires removal of all Soviet and US intermediate-range and shorter-range missiles with ranges of over 300 miles. With regard to FMP, that means removal of US Pershing IIs from FR Germany and GLCMs from Italy, the UK, Belgium and FR Germany; and removal of Soviet SS-12/22s and SS-23s from the soil of WTO allies in Eastern Europe.

At the time of writing in 1988, the implications of further possible arms control arrangements for FMP remain unclear. One possibility is that of the so-called 'triple-zero' option, regarding the elimination or reduction of tactical or battlefield missiles, that is, those of under 300-mile range. For the most part this would involve the Lance missiles on NATO's side, and the more numerous FROG and SS-21 missiles on the Soviet side.[54] Nuclear artillery (see chapter 8) could also be involved in negotiations.[55] Some reports hint that differences between the USA and FR Germany over both the 'triple-zero' option and the issue of nuclear force modernization (Lance follow-on missiles, new aircraft, stand-off weapons, etc.) ought to be resolved by compromise, involving trade-offs between these issues. That is, the triple-zero option ought to be pursued along with modernization of aircraft and delivery systems. But then, some reports about informal superpower negotiations over conventional force reductions in Europe speak of Soviet demands for reduction in US dual-capable aircraft (such as the F-16) in connection with (asymmetric) reductions of Soviet tank forces in Eastern Europe. There is much on the table.[56]

Further, some emerging reports about the state of US–Soviet START negotiations in 1988 reveal that Moscow is pushing for associated limits on sea-based cruise missiles. The USA had, apparently, planned to deploy some 2643 conventionally armed and 758 nuclear-armed TLAMs (Tomahawk land-attack cruise missiles), a total of 3401.[57] According to some reports, the USSR is suggesting much lower limits on conventional and nuclear-armed SLCMs, perhaps 600 conventional and 400 nuclear-armed systems—a total of 1000.[58] This could in turn affect other FMP issues in Europe, for instance, the progress of negotiations on tactical, battlefield weapons.

There are still other extended, albeit indirect, possible FMP implications of these various arms control negotiations. The reduction of nuclear weapons in Central Europe has, in the eyes of many Western defence experts, attached more importance to the facts of Soviet advantage in conventional forces and also to chemical weapons. This has impelled more urgent discussions of the enhancement of NATO conventional capabilities, including both force levels and new weapon developments. Some who fear the inevitability of US troop withdrawals and the weakening of the nuclear deterrent to Soviet conventional attack, have pinned their hopes on the compensatory possibilities of enhanced Franco-German military co-operation. Though not seen as imminent, that could later involve increased forward deployment of French forces in FR Germany, perhaps even to include nuclear-armed missiles.

Notes and references

[1] 'Cruise missile lands in Canada', *Centre Daily Times*, 23 Jan. 1986, p. A2; 'U.S. cruise missile tested', *New York Times*, 2 Mar. 1987, p. A6; and Arkin, W. M. and Fieldhouse, R. W., *Nuclear Battlefields: Global Links in the Arms Race* (Ballinger: Cambridge, Mass., 1985), p. 79, where the role of Canadian terrain for simulating similar terrain in the northern USSR is noted. Regarding a Soviet cruise missile which flew over Norway and Finland, see 'Soviet cruise missile said to stray across Norway and into Finland', *New York Times*, 3 Jan. 1985, p. 1, and 'Norway and Finland report Moscow apology on missile', 5 Jan. 1985, p. A4.

[2] 'Iran's fast missile: what it can do', *New York Times*, 28 May 1987, p. A13.

[3] International Institute for Strategic Studies, *The Military Balance: 1985–1986* (IISS: London, 1985), p. 165. See also, Polmar, N., *Strategic Weapons: An Introduction* (Crane Russak: New York, 1982), under 'Glossary of terms'; and Cochran, T. B., Arkin, W. M. and Hoenig, M. M., *Nuclear Weapons Databook, Vol. 1: U.S. Nuclear Forces and Capabilities* (Ballinger: Cambridge, Mass., 1984), Glossary.

[4] The Joint Staff, *United States Military Posture, 1988* (Department of Defense: Washington, DC, 1987), especially pp. 44–49.

[5] Polmar (note 3), p. 84, which says that the Soviet Union tested FOBS up to 1971, employing the SS-9 missile. As noted in Danielsson, S., 'The ABM Treaty: to be or not to be', ed B. Jasani, *Space Weapons and International Security*, SIPRI (Oxford University Press: Oxford, 1987), p. 174, FOBS was banned by SALT II.

[6] See various editions of IISS, *The Military Balance*; Cochran, Arkin and Hoenig (note 3),

Glossary; and Grieco, J., *A Military Assessment of SALT II* (Cornell Peace Studies Program: Ithaca, N.Y., 1979), Occasional Paper No. 12.

[7] SIPRI data; and Cochran, Arkin and Hoenig (note 3), pp. 280–83. See also Arkin and Fieldhouse (note 1), p. 60, who note the initial deployments of Honest Johns in 1954. Campbell, D., *The Unsinkable Aircraft Carrier: American Military Power in Britain* (Paladin: London, 1986), p. 105, notes that the Honest John was replaced by the Lance missile in 1973.

[8] Among numerous sources, see Klass, P., *Secret Sentries in Space* (Random House: New York, 1971), especially p. 42.

[9] SIPRI data; Campbell (note 7), pp. 72, 260 and 324; and Klass (note 8). For background, see also Schwartz, D., *NATO's Nuclear Dilemmas* (Brookings Institution: Washington, DC, 1983), chapter 4.

[10] See, among others, Holst, J. J., 'Comparative U.S. and Soviet deployments, doctrines, and arms limitation', Occasional Paper of the Center for Policy Study, University of Chicago, Chicago, Ill., 1971; and Klass (note 8), especially p. 107.

[11] See, among others, Steel, R., 'Lessons of the missile crisis', ed. R. Divine, *The Cuban Missile Crisis* (Quadrangle Books: Chicago, Ill., 1971), pp. 219–22; and Dinerstein, H., *The Making of a Missile Crisis: October 1962* (Johns Hopkins University Press: Baltimore, Md., 1976), pp. 228–29.

[12] SIPRI data. Regarding the Matadors in Taiwan, see also Hsieh, A. L., *Communist China's Strategy in the Nuclear Age* (Prentice Hall: Englewood Cliffs, N.J., 1962), pp. 62, 66 and 166. The Mace-D missiles deployed in the 1960s (4 batteries) had a range of 2500 km.

[13] International Institute for Strategic Studies, *The Military Balance: 1986–1987* (IISS, London, 1986), p. 204.

[14] IISS (note 13).

[15] The earlier widely assumed figures of 441 SS-20s and 112 SS-4s are shown in 'What's on the table?' *Washington Post*, 10 Oct. 1986, p. A30. Actually, the official figures associated with the INF Treaty were 405 deployed missiles and 245 more not deployed, as seen in 'New data reduce Russian missile force', *New York Times*, 10 Dec. 1987, p. A18.

[16] *New York Times* (note 15) which, at the signing of the INF Treaty, cited 65 deployed SS-4s and 105 undeployed.

[17] See the excellent 'Missile coverage maps' carried by IISS (note 13) as a large insert sheet.

[18] 'Treaty Between the United States of America and the Union of Soviet Socialist Republics on the Elimination of Their Intermediate-Range and Shorter-Range Missiles' (the INF Treaty), US Department of State Publication 9555, Bureau of Public Affairs, Washington, DC, Dec. 1987, p. 10.

[19] INF Treaty (note 18), p. 32.

[20] INF Treaty (note 18), p. 33.

[21] US Department of Defense, *Soviet Military Power 1985*, 4th edn (US Government Printing Office: Washington, DC, 1985), p. 38; and *Soviet Military Power 1987*, 6th edn, p. 41.

[22] *Soviet Military Power 1987* (note 21); IISS (note 13), p. 42; and Arkin and Fieldhouse (note 1), appendix B.

[23] For general background see, among others, Record, J., *NATO's Theater Nuclear Force Modernization Program* (Institute for Foreign Policy Analysis: Cambridge, Mass., 1981); Reed, J. D., *NATO's Theater Nuclear Forces*, National Security Affairs Monograph Series 83-8, National Defense University: Washington, DC, 1983; and Schwartz (note 9), especially chapter 7.

[24] For background on the history of the INF Treaty, see Talbott, S., 'The road to zero', *Time*, 14 Dec. 1987, pp. 18–30; and also Talbott, S., *Deadly Gambits* (Alfred Knopf: New York, 1984), for a more detailed history of the earlier phases of negotiations.

[25] 'Air Force would arm B-52 with nonnuclear missiles', *New York Times*, 16 Dec. 1987, p. A20.

[26] 'Plan to re-equip B-52's is proposed', *New York Times*, 18 Sep. 1987, p. A7. Regarding the proposed 300-mile range Lance follow-on, see 'Top Pentagon officials back plan keeping arms balance in Europe', *New York Times*, 23 Jan. 1988, p. A1. The options of dispatching more F-111 bombers to Europe and increasing the number of planned F-15 and F-16 aircraft that can fire nuclear-tipped air-to-surface weapons are discussed in 'Missile pact prompts talks on West's nuclear defense', *New York Times*, 4 Nov. 1987, p. D31. The earlier bruited but aborted idea of converting the US Pershing IIs to a shorter-range version was discussed in 'Hard choice over missiles', 27 Mar. 1987, p. A9.

[27] IISS (note 13), p. 200.

[28] IISS (note 13), p. 28. Arkin and Fieldhouse (note 1), p. 236, claim that there are 600 Lance missile warheads in FR Germany, overall.

[29] SIPRI data and IISS (note 13), which gives the following numbers of Lance missiles in

W. Europe: Belgium 5, Britain 12, FR Germany 26, Italy 6, Netherlands 6, for a total of 55 in addition to 36 US launchers. See also, Cochran, Arkin and Hoenig (note 3), pp. 285-86.

[30] SIPRI data.

[31] Cochran, Arkin and Hoenig (note 3), p. 88.

[32] Arkin and Fieldhouse (note 1), p. 236, report a total of 340 Pershing IA warheads.

[33] Cochran, Arkin and Hoenig (note 3), p. 280; and regarding the range, see IISS (note 13), p. 202.

[34] SIPRI data. The removal of the Pershing Is as part of the INF Treaty is noted in Talbott, 'The road to zero' (note 24), p. 18. The initial controversy over whether FR Germany's Pershing Is would have to be included in the INF reductions is discussed in 'Pershing missiles are Soviet focus', *New York Times*, 7 Aug. 1987, p. A1. See also, 'Now the hard part', *New York Times*, 17 Apr. 1987, p. A8; and 'Soviet draft accord would cover U.S. warheads for Bonn missiles', *New York Times*, 28 Apr. 1987, p. A10.

[35] Herzog, C., *The War of Atonement* (Weidenfield & Nicolson: London, 1975), p. 245; and Insight Team of the London Sunday Times, *The Yom Kippur War* (Doubleday: Garden City, N.Y., 1974), pp. 411-12.

[36] IISS (note 13), pp. 97, 102 and 109, reports 48 FROG-7s and 70 SCUD-Bs in Libya; 18 FROG-7s, 12 SS-21s and 18 SCUD-Bs in Syria; and 30 FROG-7s and 20 SCUD-Bs in Iraq. Karp, A., 'Ballistic missile development', *Journal of Defense and Diplomacy*, vol. 5, no. 12 (1987), p. 17, also notes FROG and SCUD missile deployments in Iran, Kuwait, North Korea and Southern Yemen.

[37] 'Countering a missile threat', *Near East Report*, vol. 31, no. 19 (11 May 1987), p. 75; 'Bio-chemical warfare must be examined, controlled', *Journal of Defense and Diplomacy*, vol. 6, no. 1 (1988), pp. 56-57, and 'The danger grows', *Near East Report*, vol. 32, no. 2 (27 June 1988), p. 105.

[38] Private conversation with Washington defense consultant. Generally, regarding the CSS2, see 'Israelis aided China on missiles', *Washington Post*, 23 May 1988.

[39] IISS (note 13), p. 38; and *Soviet Military Power 1987* (note 21), p. 59.

[40] *Soviet Military Power 1987* (note 21), p. 75.

[41] SIPRI data.

[42] SIPRI data.

[43] IISS (note 13), p. 59.

[44] *Soviet Military Power 1985* (note 21), p. 124, regarding two SA-5 Gammon missile complexes at Dumayr and Homs.

[45] SIPRI data on S. Yemen.

[46] See 'U.S. fleet that struck Libya starts to scatter', *New York Times*, 3 Apr. 1986, p. A13, regarding SAM-5s in Libya; and also 'A Soviet connection to carnage?' *The Washington Times*, 30 Dec. 1985, discussing a SAM-5 belt in Libya from Derna to Tobruk with a 180-mile radius.

[47] Sella, A., *Soviet Political and Military Conduct in the Middle East* (St. Martin's Press: New York, 1981), chapter 2; and Rubinstein, A., *Red Star on the Nile* (Princeton University Press: Princeton, N.J., 1977), chapter 4. Freedman, L., *Soviet Policy Toward the Middle East Since 1970* (Praeger: New York, 1982), p. 32, gives a lower estimate of 10 000-15 000 troops.

[48] IISS (note 13), p. 28.

[49] SIPRI data list the following South Korean sites for Nike or HAWK missile batteries: Tong-duchon, Seoul, Nijongbu (2), Suwon, Pyong Taek, Anyang-up, Kimpo (Seoul International Air-port), Sochon, Kunsan, Ansong-up, Tangjin-up, Seoul, Hongson. The earlier Panamanian HAWK sites are also listed in the SIPRI data.

[50] SIPRI data and Arkin and Fieldhouse (note 1), appendix A. For a graphic picture of earlier Nike-Hercules sites in FR Germany, see the map accompanying 'Nuclear arms become neigh-borhood issue', *Washington Post*, 15 Nov. 1981, p. A24.

[51] IISS (note 13), p. 161.

[52] IISS (note 13), p. 60.

[53] SIPRI data; and Arkin and Fieldhouse (note 1), p. 220, which sites the NAMFI facility at Canea, Souda Bay.

[54] 'U.S. and Bonn agree on need for arms control', *New York Times*, 20 Feb. 1988, p. 6; 'At NATO parley, Reagan reassures', *New York Times*, 2 Mar. 1988, p. A10; 'NATO shifts stand on arms in Europe', *New York Times*, 3 Mar. 1988, p. A3; and 'For NATO, reassurance', *New York Times*, 4 Mar. 1988, p. A6.

[55] 'W. German would scrap NATO nuclear artillary', *Washington Post*, 6 May 1988, p. A28.

[56] Dunn, L. A., 'NATO after global "double zero" ', *Survival*, vol. 30, no. 3 (May/June 1988), pp. 195-209.

[57] 'Soviet said to harden stance on missiles', *New York Times*, 14 Feb. 1988, p. 3. See also, Arkin and Fieldhouse (note 1), p. 125, who earlier saw US planning for a total of 3994 Tomahawks: 758 for nuclear attack missions, 593 for conventional anti-ship missions and 2643 for conventional land attack missions.

[58] *New York Times* (note 57), and private discussions with US government officials.

6. Overseas 'technical' facilities: intelligence, space and communications

I. Introduction

In a relative sense, and increasingly, the US–Soviet global competition for basing access has come to be centred on a variety of what, for want of a better term, might be characterized as 'technical' facilities, that is, those outside the 'traditional' categories of air and naval bases, and land-army garrisons and encampments. Most of these facilities may be subsumed under the broad headings of communications, intelligence and space-related activities. They include such disparate functions as satellite tracking, command and control; signals interception of rivals' communications, radar signals, missile telemetry, and so on; underwater detection of submarines, accurate positioning of missile-firing submarines; space-based ocean surveillance; nuclear-explosion detection; and a bewildering variety of functionally specific communications systems running along the entire spectrum from extra-low to ultra-high frequencies. The increasing importance of all these systems has paralleled the extension of contemporary military activity to an increasingly integrated, three-dimensional game involving outer space, land and sea surfaces and the global underseas realms—submarines communicate via satellite with land-based headquarters; satellites and land-based SIGINT stations locate surface fleets by intercepting their radar emissions; satellite early warning is transmitted, variously, by ground terminals, underwater cables, via other satellites, and so on.

C^3I

Until recently the terminology of 'technical systems' implied something peripheral, merely supplementary, and certainly subordinate to the more visible 'big ticket' platforms and launchers; this is no longer the case. In recent years, the critical nature of C^3I systems has been recognized and there has been significant discussion of these matters in the open literature.[1] Even more to the point, C^3I has become a central focus of the Reagan Administration's strategic modernization programme, in good measure in response to a growing wave of concern in the USA about the efficacy, indeed, survivability, of the nation's strategic communications in response to a major attack.

These questions may be examined at any of several levels, or from any of several angles. First, they may be discussed, in general terms, in the context of several of the familiar, prominent concepts central to the strategic literature: first- and second-strike capabilities; structural and crisis stability; centralized versus more disaggregated control of strategic forces, and the relation thereof to survivability and accidental war; war fighting and intra-war deterrence; massive retaliation and flexible-response doctrines, and so on.

A large proportion of the recent literature, certainly that published in the USA and thus dealing with the US strategic perspective, has dwelt on issues of survivability, assured second-strike capability and, hence, the effectiveness of US deterrence of a Soviet first strike, be it premeditated (a 'bolt from the blue') or a pre-emptive response amid an escalating crisis. For the most part, as exemplified in the works of Ford, Blair, and others, but also echoed in various US military publications, this has involved a pessimistic evaluation of the system's capabilities. It is perceived as highly vulnerable to a pre-emptive strike, one involving targeting of key C^3I basing nodes abroad and in the USA, and to the varied and combined effects of communications jamming, ASAT and electromagnetic pulse (EMP) effects created by atmospheric nuclear explosions.[2] Hence, correspondingly, there are the elaborate corrective and prescriptive analyses, mostly directed at the need for wholesale dispersion, mobility and redundancy for C^3I systems; variously, involving proliferation of communications cables and nodes, satellites, satellite launchers, command aircraft, and so on.[3] The importance of these considerations in the event of protracted nuclear war are obvious, as an extension of the problems inherent in maintaining retaliatory capability in the face of an all-out first strike. Hence too, there is the common suggestion that vulnerability of C^3I systems—to the extent it brings retaliatory capability into question—militates automatically in the direction of (at least implicit) launch-on-warning (LOW) or launch-under-attack (LUA) doctrines.[4]

If survivability of C^3I assets in the face of a first strike—and hence the efficacy and credibility of second-strike deterrence—is one general issue, another involves the trade-offs between centralized control on the one hand, and dispersion of authority and, hence, retaliatory capability, on the other. The exact nature of the command chains involved—for both the USA and the USSR— has long been a matter of considerable secrecy. It has also been a staple of the literature on accidental war, it being assumed that dispersion and devolvement of launch authority increases the chances of unauthorized launch.[5]

To a great extent, much of the importance attributed to C^3I at the nuclear level is embodied in the concept of 'flexible response'. A survivable C^3I system allows for a deliberate, rational, thought-out response by command authorities to attacks anywhere along a spectrum of magnitude. It lessens the chances for accidental war, and allows national command authorities to act without the pressure embodied in the phrase 'use 'em or lose 'em'. To the extent that the possibility of limited nuclear war is allowed for, it is based on the near-imperative of an effective C^3I system which can allow not only for measured responses but also for negotiations, and tacit signalling to foes, in a manner which signals the control and authority of recognized leadership.

Indeed, much of the recent literature is devoted to the question of whether, from the perspective of a Soviet leadership assumed by many Western intellectuals to be determined to acquire something approaching a first-strike capability, targeting C^3I is the overarching priority, above that of targeting each or all of the familiar legs of the triad.[6] Some are convinced that it is. And, almost as a mirror image, there is a growing belief that new US strategic systems—Trident, air-launched cruise missiles (ALCMs), more accurate Minuteman warheads, MX-missiles—confer enhanced US capability for a disarming strike. There have been public debates over the efficacy of a 'decapitating' targeting posture aimed at Soviet political and military élites, a strategy usually proposed as one not so much aimed at 'winning', as one geared to providing deterrence (asymmetric regional targeting could also threaten to alter the nature of the Soviet regime or alter that nation's ethnic composition to the disadvantage of Slavic groups).[7] As with the reverse Soviet strategy, it has produced debates about intra-war bargaining and/or war termination in a situation in which C^{3}I is decentralized and leadership fragmented and perhaps difficult to identify. On both sides, countering vulnerability of C^{3}I assets has led to an emphasis on mobility, dispersion and concealment, and to redundancy of C^{3}I as well as of launching systems.

As it happens, there is more than one side to the growing tide of literature (particularly American) on C^{3}I vulnerability. One recent article by Daniel Shuckman offers an alternative view, stressing the role of command devolution and the spectre of chaos amid an uncontrolled war in continuing to provide adequate deterrence, the vulnerability of command and control facilities notwithstanding.[8] As such, Shuckman has further countered what is implicit in the writings of Blair, Steinbruner, and others, namely, that US C^{3}I vulnerability lends itself to a pre-emptive first-strike posture, declaratory policies notwithstanding. To some degree these largely technical arguments (revolving crucially around highly classified aspects of command devolution) serve as covers for political debate clearly demarcated along recognizable ideological lines.

So necessary would these various systems be to the conduct of nuclear war between the superpowers, or a protracted conventional war between them which involved the danger of nuclear escalation, that considerable attention is now being paid to the possibility of mutual destruction of related basing facilities during a 'protracted conventional phase', as each side might, in such a circumstance, attempt to improve its position in the nuclear equation at various levels of escalation. In other words, tit-for-tat destruction of such facilities might form one kind of action point on a ladder of escalation, a form of vertical escalation, but also one providing possibilities for horizontal, that is, essentially geographic, escalation.[9] Soviet destruction of US C^{3}I facilities in Hawaii or Alaska could, for example, be envisaged as answered by a US attack on similar facilities in Viet Nam or Cuba.

The importance of global C^{3}I systems, including or even emphasizing their space components, is by no means restricted to the realm of strategic nuclear warfare or day-to-day maintenance of an adequate nuclear deterrent posture. There is an increasing trend towards the centralized control of conventional warfare, mainly involving real-time targeting and use of precision-guided munitions, that is, all that is included in the concept of 'air–land battle'.[10] Whether or not this trend has been overstated or prematurely accepted, it is clear that in the future satellite reconnaissance, communications and targeting will be much more important. That, in turn, directs attention to the related basing implications, for instance, those involving data down-links and long-range communications.

Even without the involvement of satellites, the outlines of future conventional warfare were made apparent in 1982 in Lebanon, where the war fought by Israel was heralded by some military analysts as providing a glimpse of a new era of battle, much as the Spanish Civil War had done a generation ago. That war featured, *de novo*, extensive use of battle management and electronic warfare aircraft, remotely-piloted vehicles, and centralized control of the entire battle-field from command posts well removed from the battle front.

The future of conventional warfare (or preparations for it), particularly as applied to the NATO–WTO stand-off, will certainly see an extension of these trends, linking the various domains of land, air, space, ocean surface and the underseas with high technology. Critical importance will adhere to space-based communications and sensors, to proliferated air and land-based sensors and communications nodes, and to related seaborne and underwater technologies. It follows that the foreign bases of the major powers utilized for these purposes will be critical.

The increasing importance of such facilities—the eyes, ears and mouths of contemporary warfare and its a priori deterrence—has led to greatly altered perceptions of the strategic value of various locales throughout the globe, amounting virtually to a 'new geopolitics' of contemporary military rivalries. The crucial importance of monitoring the movements of strategic nuclear sub-marines through various 'chokepoints' or routes of egress from home bases has, for instance, centred attention on the Greenland–Iceland–United Kingdom (GIUK) gap, the Indonesian straits, the Gibraltar exit from the Mediterranean and the several straits in and around Japan, Korea and Soviet Siberia.[11] The US need for satellite-based SIGINT from geosynchronous orbit above the Horn of Africa earlier put a premium on data down-links in that region so as to afford rapid transmission of data back to the USA. The earlier need for ground-based extremely low frequency (ELF) communications to SSBNs directed attention to apt locations in relation to those submarines' normal firing stations; similarly, the USA has needed air bases from which to fly its TACAMO ('take charge and move out') communications aircraft in proximity to those submarine cruis-ing areas. To monitor Soviet signals, the USA has required listening stations along the Soviet periphery, particularly in South-West Asia; the Soviet Union, similarly, has found Cuba a particularly well-located vantage point. The ex-amples could be multiplied, and it must be kept in mind that very little space is needed for most of these facilities, so that access by a superpower to a favourably located but small state may be deemed a vital matter. That point has been highlighted by recent events in Grenada, Vanuatu and elsewhere.

Politics and technical facilities

The increasing importance of technical facilities has also altered the politics of their access, in a perhaps paradoxical way. Whereas traditional naval and air bases involve large and intrusive presences, more often than not in proximity to areas of large local populations, most C³I bases are small, unobtrusive, and often located in remote areas. Their personnel do not cause major problems with local women or with violence in big-city restaurants, nor do they dominate the local economy and employment as do US facilities in the Philippines and Greece, for example. Instead, because many of these facilities are not only remote but also involve very esoteric, classified, mysterious, often indiscernible functions, they provide a different type of problem for public diplomacy. Local politicians and intellectuals want to know what is going on and whether the foreign presence is dangerous in inviting a pre-emptive attack from a rival superpower.

Because many such activities involve intelligence matters or other highly classified activities, their existence often gives rise to wild rumours about their functions, sometimes verging upon paranoia. In this context, both superpowers, have been engaged in determined 'base denial' activity, involving propaganda, disinformation, covert actions, and so on, to 'expose' their rivals' technical facilities and to incite public opinion against their presence (see chapter 10). As part of that equation many host states have increasingly demanded 'participation' in the use of technical facilities on their soil, involving some sharing of intelligence information, access to satellite capabilities, dual use of communications facilities, and so on.[12] That sharing may enhance the security of the host state by increasing its own intelligence capabilities, but it also ensures that its government is privy to the nature of the activities involved. This issue has arisen even in relations between 'developed' allies, namely, the USA and Australia.[13]

Such presence has also given rise to much speculation about superpower access to facilities during crises or wars. They would be important targets and, hence, the objects of threats and blackmail. Ironically, while the use of such facilities is usually assumed assured under normal conditions where allies, friends and clients are concerned, there are real questions about alliance decoupling in crisis or war, under the shadow of threats. That spectre has, in turn, encouraged both superpowers to acquire redundant, proliferated C³I facilities, involving not only many client states, but also the (increasing) use of satellites and sea-borne platforms as contingent surrogates.[14] Indeed, a major conceptual question involves the relative vulnerabilities of satellites and land-based facilities in a crisis or at the onset of war.

Contrariwise, in some cases, targeting of technical facilities may be rendered less likely just because their destruction might engender escalation of a still conventional conflict to the nuclear level. This is particularly true of early-warning satellites and their associated communications down-links—destruction of ocean-surveillance satellites and other sensors might also be similarly destabilizing. Stated another way, 'keeping the hostages alive' in the form of sensors, during a conventional conflict, could be perceived as a form of intra-war confidence-building measure, or as a self-imposed measure of limitation or restraint.

II. A historical note

As noted, the importance of the non-traditional forms of access has increased gradually, beginning near the turn of the century. Aside from its being an interesting historical datum, there is an additional interesting point of historical analogy with contemporary security problems. That has to do with stability and pre-emptive imperatives during crises and/or escalation of early stages of conflict.

Before World War I Britain developed an elaborate and unrivalled global network of underseas telegraph cables—by far the most important early precursor to modern 'tech' facilities. At that time all of the key British overseas possessions were linked together by that network, providing advantages in early warning and command and control of naval forces, and in the ability to control and influence news broadcasting, an earlier form of 'public diplomacy' used as an instrument of competition.

British strategists worried endlessly before 1914 about the possible wartime vulnerability of their cable communications system, and also planned the pre-emptive destruction of potential enemies' less elaborate networks if war should break out. Earlier reliant on cable relay stations in, among other places, Portugal, Spain, Turkey, Iran, Cuba and the United States, the British strove mightily to develop an 'all red' line system which would not rely on basing points in foreign territories, not even in traditionally allied Portugal, nor in the United States.[15] Aside from the fact that Britain deployed far more cable ships than any other power (28 to second-place France's 5) and owned over 60 per cent of the world's cables around 1900, she was able to take great advantage of her global island possessions—Mauritius, the Seychelles, the Maldives, Cocos, Ascension, Malta, Turks, Caicos and others—which were, of course, also very useful for well-spaced coaling operations.[16] The British cable line running from Land's End towards the Far East, for instance, was anchored at the Gambia, Sierra Leone, the Gold Coast, Nigeria, South Africa, Mauritius, the Seychelles and Ceylon; that from Vancouver to Australia across the Pacific Ocean ran through Fanning Island, Fiji and Norfolk Islands.[17]

Britain was not, of course, alone in constructing an elaborate underseas cable network, nor in its efforts at securing the required access points. According to one source, the United States in 1898 annexed Guam and Midway for the specific purpose of providing cable stations *en route* to the Philippines, decades before those islands would become important US air bases.[18] France and Germany also made efforts towards building global systems, but before World War I the latter came to rely more on wireless systems, despite the vulnerability of their communications to interception if decoded. By 1914 the Germans had wireless stations in Togoland, South-West Africa, Tanganyika, Kiung-chow, Yap, Rabaul, Nauru and Samoa, to abet what they knew would be a very vulnerable cable network should war break out.[19]

At the outset of World War I, Britain was able rapidly to sever all of the German underseas cables, while losing only a couple of its own cable stations temporarily, at Cocos and Fanning islands.[20] The redundancy built into Britain's global system, abetted in 1914 by that of France, provided a strong strategic advantage throughout World War I, still one more result of 'indivisible' global naval superiority. Later, in 1919, the German cables were divided as war spoils among the allies as part of the Versailles settlement.

The analogy of these cables to some modern technical facilities; specifically, SOSUS, ground C³I facilities and, of course, satellites, is rather remarkable. As often noted, they are widely perceived as potential objects of 'vertical escalation' in a crisis, hence as contributing to pre-emptive instability, all the more so if striking first may be perceived as an advantage.[21] In particular, the analogy with contemporary scenarios involving space-based wars as a step on the ladder of escalation, that is, ASATs or the use of space mines to 'clear the skies', is particularly striking.

Beyond World War I and up to World War II, increased importance was attached to technical facilities. Long-range radio communications developed apace and with them came the development by major powers of networks of transmitters, receivers, relay stations, and so on. With that came the early development of radio interception facilities—before World War II, the USA worried about German acquisition of interception facilities in the politically unstable Caribbean area, for instance, in Haiti or Colombia.[22] The US breaking of the Japanese code before World War II (which provided what should have been decisive, timely early warning about Pearl Harbor) serves as an additional precursor of subsequent intelligence activities, now far more institutionalized in organizations such as the US National Security Agency (NSA). Japan, meanwhile, in violation of the Washington Naval Agreement, built covert communications facilities on some of its Central Pacific, League of Nations Mandate islands, providing an early problem of arms control verification.[23] On the eve of World War II the USA was beginning to install early-warning radars in some of the bases acquired from the UK as part of the Lend-Lease Agreement.[24] Gradually, one could see movement towards the central importance of C³I today—towards quick if not real-time communications and early warning, and the supersession of human intelligence (HUMINT) as the core of intelligence collection.

The large asymmetry between the USA and the USSR as concerns use of land bases for various communications and intelligence purposes mirrors but is perhaps even greater than that for traditional naval and air bases. There are several reasons for this, all rather obvious yet worth reiterating in combination. First, and again mirroring the balance of traditional bases, there is the approximate heartland/rimland geography of superpower competition and the Soviet Union's continuing relative dearth of overseas allies and clients willing to provide facilities: relatively speaking, the USSR remains less a global power than the USA. For that reason, but also for others (i.e., security of facilities, less reluctance to have military personnel endure lengthy stays at sea) the USSR has long relied on shipborne communications and intelligence facilities. That has involved not only 'regular' units of the Soviet Navy, but also elements of its vast (relative to the USA) fishing fleets, oceanographic research vessels and merchant marine, all under central direction from Moscow.[25] Finally, as regards intelligence facilities, it is obvious that the more open nature of US society reduces the need for technical means of gathering information, relative to what is required by the USA *vis-à-vis* the USSR.

There is another geographical aspect to these questions, and that has to do with the large size of the Soviet land mass, supplemented by that of contiguous allies. That automatically reduces some requirements for communications relays and for satellite tracking and control—again, relative to the USA, and keeping in mind the lesser global nature of its force structure.

In some instances, too, the USSR may simply have been able to concentrate some of its technical functions in a small number of client states, retaining some access to an almost irreducible number in virtually every area of the globe. Cuba, for instance, performs a large C^3I role for Moscow, perhaps to be viewed as combining the importance of several US client states around the near periphery of the USSR—its loss would presumably involve severe reductions in some Soviet capabilities, in the absence of suitable replacements equivalent to those the USA was able to find after the loss of Iran.

Regarding these asymmetries, however, there is now perhaps beginning to emerge a new set of changes, the impact of which may be felt only gradually and over a long period. US defence planners, in looking at the possibilities for protracted conventional and/or nuclear conflicts of various durations and levels of horizontal and vertical escalation have, as noted, become very aware of the political, as well as military, vulnerability in crises or wars caused by moving some functions from the ground to space, that is, missile early-warning, communications relay, and so on. The vulnerability of these space assets to destruction by ASATs and/or jamming is also recognized. That in turn has produced a new emphasis on proliferation, redundancy, mobility, dispersion and concealment of C^3I systems—as exemplified by the US effort embodied in the Ground Wave Emergency Network (GWEN) communications system, and the capability for replacement or 'healing' of systems destroyed in battle.[26] For the USA, that may militate towards greater use of ships (almost in ironic imitation of the USSR) or of larger numbers of mobile ground facilities. Just what the political ramifications of the latter might be with respect to alliance relations is hard to judge.

III. Technical facilities: a breakdown

Most technical facilities can be subsumed under the headings of communications and intelligence/surveillance. Those categories in turn subsume an elaborate variety of activities and functions which require foreign military presence. Under communications, for instance, along the frequency band that runs from ultra-high frequency (UHF) to ELF there are various networks for military and diplomatic communications, some of which involve satellite relays, some of

which are conducted within the atmosphere but require ground-based transmitters, relays and receivers; and some of which are specialized for underseas
communications.[27] Some systems are specialized in connection with strategic
nuclear systems; others are designed in connection with the command and
control of conventional warfare. Generally, satellites, which themselves utilize
ground-links, have been taking over functions previously served by ground-links
alone.

Regarding the broad category of technical intelligence—which, relative to the
once central HUMINT function, now accounts for some 90 per cent of intelligence intake, granted the subjectivity of such numerical comparisons—there
are a number of major functions which are served by foreign facilities.[28] There
is satellite tracking (involving both the tracking of other nations' but also one's
own satellites) by optical devices, lasers, radars, and so on; command and
control of satellites (they can be queried for information or re-positioned); and
data links which relay the data collected by satellites to overseas regional military headquarters or to central headquarters and commands in the homeland.
The data in the latter category can involve imagery from surveillance satellites,
SIGINT interception information, missile telemetry, information on weather,
geodesy, and so on. Additionally, numerous ground-based SIGINT stations
overseas perform similar, related or complementary functions, even if they have
gradually, but by no means completely, been superseded by satellites.

Another broad category of facility requiring overseas access—still another
gradually being superseded by satellites but often requiring ground-based data
links and command and control centres—is that of nuclear detection.[29] This too
subsumes several functions. One has to do with monitoring rivals' (and allies')
nuclear tests, including verification of existing test-ban agreements which limit
tests to the underground and by maximum kilotonnage levels. Second, there is
the current monitoring of the nuclear proliferation activities of hitherto non-
nuclear weapon states, whether or not signatories of the 1968 Treaty on the
Non-Proliferation of Nuclear Weapons (NPT). Third, in the case of actual
nuclear war, limited or otherwise, there would be the requirement for monitoring
the existence, patterns, effectiveness, and so on, of nuclear explosions, that is,
damage assessment, so as to assist planning for additional targeting.

Underwater SOSUS systems constitute still another major category of intelligence activity requiring overseas access for major powers. These are crucial
for tracking the movements of other nations' submarines as they exit from
homeports (often through chokepoints) *en route* to firing stations or patrol areas
in deep ocean areas—not only chokepoints, but also the coastal littorals of
important regions are so covered.[30] Such facilities would be particularly crucial
but also vulnerable during wars or serious crises; for instance, during a protracted conventional phase holding the danger of escalation to the nuclear level.
The systems basically involve large arrays of underseas hydrophones (sonar
listening devices) linked by cable to land-based data processing and analysis
centres, in turn linked to intelligence centres and headquarters in the homeland.

There are still other types of technical facility requiring overseas access.

Radars for strategic or tactical warning are particularly important, and are deployed in large numbers by the rival superpowers within their respective NATO and WTO alliances, and elsewhere in other regions.[31]

For the most part, an analysis of technical C³I facilities as an aspect of FMP is relegated almost entirely to the two superpowers, with the further asymmetry of the much greater reliance by the USA relative to the USSR on foreign facilities for such purposes. Only they deploy global capabilities across the board, involving satellite tracking, ASW, SIGINT, and so on. Among the remaining nations, France and Britain almost alone make some use of overseas facilities, primarily for communications, though Britain has a number of external intelligence facilities (France can use ships for the same purpose). Hence, in this area, relative even to traditional overseas air and naval bases, there is a really pyramidal global division of power, responsibility, presence and perceived requirements. It is for the most part a two-nation game, denoting the fundamental retention of bipolarity in this crucial area of international competition.

IV. US technical facilities abroad

US communications

The USA uses a variety of communications systems and modes, stretching across the frequency spectrum from ELF to super-high frequency (SHF); these variously utilize satellites, ground terminals, shipboard and submarine terminals, and so on.[32] These various frequencies involve trade-offs among a number of variables related to rate of data transmission, vulnerability to jamming, size of transmitter, distance capability, and so on, and tend to be broadly specific for certain functions, that is, land-based tactical communications, those with submerged submarines, and so on. The utilization of various communications modes changes constantly in response to new technological developments; correspondingly, the requirements for FMP access also change.

As ably outlined by Arkin and Fieldhouse, 'In the field of electronic communications, each medium and frequency has advantages and disadvantages.' Varying by wavelength and hence frequency, a number of different paths for communications are provided. According to the same source, 'Radio waves in the four lowest frequency bands travel what are called "groundwaves" and follow the curvature of the earth for long distances beyond the horizon. Thus they are useful for communications with ships far from land. Extremely-low-frequency (ELF) waves (below 300 hertz) can penetrate water to hundreds of feet (perfect for submarine communications), while extremely-high-frequencies (EHF) (above 30 gigahertz) have difficulty penetrating even a heavy rainstorm.[33]

Other than the medium (i.e., water or air) still other conditions determine the most suitable frequency to use. Size of transmitter is important—'for frequencies below the HF band, antennas are too large for ships or aircraft'—the ELF antennas or transmitters considered for emplacement in the northern USA were many miles long.[34] Then, the higher the frequency the higher the data rate. The amount of power required also varies with frequency. For these reasons ELF is not suitable for large-volume commercial communications. There is another variable—reliability—in connection with possible interference, jamming or fading.[35]

HF is widely used by the military—it is long-range, cheap, low-power, small and portable, but requires constant adjustments in specific frequencies to deal with atmospheric conditions,[36] that is, shifting in the ionospheric layers and natural events such as solar flares. This can vary by day, season, location, and so on, so that frequencies must be chosen to best suit the prevailing conditions. For these reasons and others—reliability, 'crowding' of the frequency spectrum, and the advent of computers and satellites (which operate at higher frequencies and data rates)—recent decades have seen a shift away from HF for military purposes. But, the vulnerability of satellites has led to renewed interest, particularly in connection with new technology, that is, 'sounders', solid-state transmitters and microprocessors which can allow for shifting frequencies in response to environmental changes. That interest is underscored by the fact that HF uses the ionosphere for transmission, a medium difficult permanently to interrupt. Finally, in the context of military anxieties about nuclear 'black-out' caused by nuclear blasts during war, mobile or proliferated HF systems are considered one of the more survivable types of communication.[37] Among the HF systems currently used are SAC's Giant Talk/Scope Signal III for strategic bombers, the air/ground/air Global Command and Control System network, the Mystic Star Presidential/VIP network and the Defense Communications System (DCS) 'entry sites'.

Very-low frequency (VLF) and low frequency (LF) are also considered relatively reliable in a nuclear environment and can penetrate sea water as well.[38] Hence, for the USA, a key 'enduring system now envisaged is GWEN (Ground Wave Emergency System), a grid of unmanned relay stations with LF transmitters and receivers hardened to withstand electro-magnetic pulse (EMP)'.[39] When fully proliferated, it will use a system of 'automatic diverse routing' so as to maximize imperviousness to interference even by a full-scale nuclear attack. Still another survivable system envisaged for the USA is 'meteor burst communications', using billions of ionized meteor trails to reflect very-high frequency (VHF) signals.[40] This system would, apparently, even benefit from the increased ionization caused by nuclear war.

Moving up and down the frequency/wavelength band is one way of classifying military communications systems; another is by looking at the corresponding military functions themselves. These range from the very general to the very specific. For instance, the bulk of day-to-day communications within the Defence Communications System are handled by the AUTOVON system (the military's telephone hook-up) and by high-frequency (HF) and VHF-microwave systems. This entails the large volume of overseas traffic from the USA, and traffic within the overseas commands, including that to and from aircraft and surface ships, which tend to use frequencies in the HF/VHF range.[41]

The VHF-microwave system is specifically intended for tactical communications. In all areas where the USA has a large military presence, there are numerous microwave transmitters and relays, the latter required in great density because of the short 'legs' of the microwave transmissions which are bounced off the ionosphere.[42]

There are other more specific, mission-oriented systems. The Strategic Air Command (SAC) has its network of Scope Signal (formerly 'Giant Talk') HF communications facilities, designed to ensure adequate communications with B-52s during a crisis or war (they are 'recallable' systems as distinct from the 'fire and forget' nature of ICBMs and SLBMs).[43] The communications associated with the Defense Satellite Communications System (DSCS) Program, while varied by frequency, involve some very important specific functions, that is, early-warning relay from Defence Support Program (DSP) satellites, communication of SIGINT, telemetry and nuclear detection (NUDET) information, and so on.[44]

There are a number of communications systems used in connection with submarines (SSBNs) on or in transit to or from firing stations, and nuclear attack submarines (SSNs) roaming the various seas. Because of the critical nature of these communications, that is, the perception of SSBNs as the least vulnerable leg of the strategic triad and the one to be used as a strategic reserve ('revenge force') in case of protracted conflict (either for counter-city or counter-value targeting, perhaps also for use in the Central European theatre), considerable layered redundancy has been built into its communications, made all the more important by its one-way nature, that is, SSBNs do not 'talk back' (at least as regards US practice). The latter are all in the VLF to ELF frequency range. Earlier that involved the Omega system superimposed on the LORAN-C navigation positioning system.[45] Omega has now been phased out—as the Navy's new Fleet Satellite Communications (FLTSATCOM) system is phasing in.[46] LORAN-C is still widely in use, its navigation beams superimposed on a communications band which, as used in the Pacific region, goes under the code name of Clarinet Pilgrim.[47] Added to that is the new ELF system, utilizing two transmitters in northern Michigan—that system, once under the code-name Seafarer, was once envisaged as a much larger and more far-reaching one.[48]

US communications with submerged submarines

As noted above, assured communications with submerged submarines is a critical aspect of the US nuclear deterrence posture. This involves the necessity for such communications not only before but also during a nuclear conflict, perhaps one where an adversary's initial strike will have eliminated not only the bulk of ICBM and long-range bomber assets, but much of the nation's command structure as well. This requirement has heretofore normally been perceived in the context of the role of SSBNs as a second-strike, strategic-reserve or 'revenge' force, a situation now being altered as the Trident D-5 missiles provide the USA with some hard-target, that is, first-strike, capability, from under the sea, eventually to involve some 6000 warheads when the Trident fleet is completed.[49] Then, too, some current scenarios of protracted wars envisage the use by SSBNs of reloads stored—perhaps covertly—in globally dispersed locales; also, the possible use of SLBMs for 'tactical' purposes at the Central European forward line of troops (FLOT), sometimes discussed as 'barraging the FLOT'. These functions too would require maintenance of communications contact with command headquarters amid the 'fog of war'. Ensuring the major SSN role in the US ASW effort would also involve a considerable need for adequate communications—in connection with location and targeting of enemy submarines—during an actual war. All of these aspects of submarine warfare communications, of course, ramify back into deterrence, and mutual perceptions thereof.

Throughout most of the 1970s, the USA had eight Omega VLF facilities located overseas. Some of these were phased out beginning in the late 1970s and some have been retained, despite their obsolescence, as backup systems.[50] They were located at: Réunion (Mafate)—operated by the French Navy; Trinidad and Tobago; Liberia (Paynesword); Australia (Woodside); Argentina (Golfo Nuevo, Trelew); Japan (Tsushima Island); and Norway (Bratland).[51] The first three named have been phased out. There was another one at Haiku on Oahu, Hawaii.

Table 15. Location of known Loran C/D transmitters and monitoring stations overseas

Country	Location
Bermuda	Witney's Bay
Canada	Cape Race (Newfoundland), Fox Harbor (Labrador), Montagu (Prince Edward Island), Port Hardy (British Columbia), St. Anthony (New Brunswick), Sandspit (British Columbia), Williams Lake (British Columbia)
Denmark	Ejde (Faeroe Islands)
Greenland	Angissoq
Iceland	Keflavik, Sandur
Italy	Crotone, Lampedusa, Sellia Marina
Japan	Gesaski (Okinawa), Iwo Jima, Marcus Island, Tokachibuto (Hokkaido), Yokota AFB
Johnson Atoll (US owned)	
Norway	Jan Mayen Island
South Korea	Changsan
Spain	Estartit
Turkey	Kargabarun
UK	Sullum Voe (Shetland Islands)
FR Germany	Sylt
Micronesia	Yap Island
Guam (US owned)	Anderson AFB

Source: SIPRI data

There was and remains a far larger global network of LORAN-C/D radio-navigation systems, which are also utilized in connection with aircraft navigation. And as a sub-set, this further involves the Clarinet Pilgrim system in the

Pacific, a shore-to-submarine network (four sites in Japan and one on Yap Island) that works by superimposing data on the waves transmitted by LORAN-C.[52] Some of these are operated by the US Coast Guard, to a degree reflective of the mixed civilian and military navigational aid functions of the LORAN network (still earlier there were some systems designated as LORAN-A).[53] And, as in the case of Omega, some are jointly operated with host-nation personnel. Among the numerous LORAN-C/D transmitters and monitoring stations overseas (there are many others in the USA, including Alaska and Hawaii) are those shown in table 15.

The USA has also utilized some important long-range VLF transmitter sites for communicating with submerged submarines. An important one, in relation particularly to the Indian Ocean, is in Australia—the Harold Holt Naval Communications Station at Exmouth, North West Cape. There are others at Tavolaru, Sardinia; Yosami, Japan; and Helgeland, Norway; and in the USA at Jim Creek, Washington; Cutler, Maine; Annapolis, Maryland; and Wahiawa, Hawaii. There are also some LF transmitters used in connection with submarines at St. George, Bermuda; Kato Souli and Nea Makri, Greece; Grindavik, Iceland; Kamiseya, Yosami and Totsuka, Japan; Kwajalein; Capas Tarlac and San Miguel, Philippines; Isabella and Aguada, Puerto Rico; Guardamar del Segura, Spain; and Thurso, UK.[54]

As a supplement to the VLF and LF transmitters based on land, the US Navy also deploys some 18 TACAMO radio-relay aircraft. These aircraft, retrofitted C-130 transports filled with communications equipment, are meant to provide 'post-attack' communications, particularly as the land-based VLF antennas are vulnerable, soft targets.[55] Usually, one such aircraft is aloft at all times over the Atlantic and Pacific oceans respectively.[56] Outside the USA there are forward-operating bases for the TACAMO aircraft at St. George, Bermuda; Yokota, Japan; and Mildenhall, UK.[57] Guam was earlier similarly used, prior to the deactivation of the Polaris submarine base there. By 1992, the TACAMO aircraft will be replaced by E-6As, which are much faster and have longer range, but there is no indication of a change in basing requirements.[58] The longer ranges and greater power are said to be required by the expanded operating areas of the new Trident submarines.

In the current period, as a replacement for Omega and LORAN-C, the USA is installing its new satellite-based NAVSTAR global positioning system for submarines which, among other things, apparently involves the capability to provide SLBMs with corrective guidance after they surface. The emerging NAVSTAR system has been described as follows:

Essentially, the Navstar GPS is a satellite and ground-based system designed to provide the armed forces with an order of magnitude increase in accuracy over current navigational and position identification capabilities. Now being developed for all US and allied military forces by the Air Force Systems Command's Space Division, GPS will eventually employ at least eighteen satellites in subsynchronous earth orbits of 10, 900 nautical miles to provide global coverage. The satellites will orbit in several distinct planes, be three-axis stabilized, and will circle the globe every twelve hours.

The GPS will provide tactical and strategic forces with accurate position fixes to within fifty-two feet in three dimensions (longitude, latitude, and altitude). In addition, GPS will provide users with velocity data to within 0.3 feet per second, also in three dimensions, and with accurate time to within one millionth of a second.[59]

NAVSTAR's control segment consists of five monitor stations to 'track passively all satellites in view and accumulate ranging data from the navigation signals'.[60] That information is transmitted to the NAVSTAR Master Control Station at Vandenberg Air Force Base, California.[61] The other stations used for tracking, telemetry, control and passive monitoring are at Ascension, Diego Garcia, Kwajalein and Guam, notably all islands controlled by the USA or the UK.[62]

US surface naval communications

Whereas most communications with submarines are conducted along the LF/VLF/ELF end of the spectrum, sea-to-land communications involving surface combatants will usually use high frequency (the corresponding intelligence interception facilities are HF direction finders, that is, HF/DF). The USA has a considerable number of naval HF transmitters and receivers scattered about the globe, most of them near major naval facilities or near bodies of water heavily traversed by US fleet units. They include those shown in table 16.

Table 16. US overseas HF receivers and transmitters

Country	Location
Bermuda	South Hampton
Diego Garcia	
Greece	Nea Makri and Kato Souli
Guam	Barrigada and Finnegayan
Iceland	Grindavik and Sandgerdhi
Italy	Naples (a master station) and Licola
Japan	Iruma, Kamiseya, and Totsuka
Panama	Summit
Philippines	Capas Tarlac and St. Miguel
Portugal (Azores)	Cinco Pincos (Terceira) and Vila Nova
Puerto Rico	Sebana Seca, Isabella, and Aguada
Spain	Guardemar del Segura and Rota
UK	Edzell and Thurso

Source: SIPRI data.

US strategic aircraft—fail-safe communications

SAC controls the strategic bomber force which constitutes the third leg of the familiar 'triad' of nuclear forces—along with SSBNs and ICBMs. Some 264 B-52 and 61 FB-111 bombers are involved, plus some 615 KC-135 tankers, which utilize 19 main air bases in the USA and on Guam, plus numerous 'dispersal' and 'recovery' bases overseas.[63] The bombers are the one 'recoverable' element of the triad, which provides considerable flexibility, as well as an element of coercive diplomacy during crises, when the alert status of the bombers (for instance, the number kept or dispersed aloft) can be raised. The bombers may also increasingly be useful, after the onset of wars, for blasting corridors in foes' defensive shields, and for more flexible and selective targeting. Hence, according to Arkin and Fieldhouse: 'While missiles cannot be recalled or redirected once launched (and thus are "inflexible"), bombers can attack hardened, mobile, or previously unlocated targets and can be called back before reaching them. If they overcome air defences and complete their mission, bombers can return to a "recovery" base and reload for more bombing missions.'[64]

The system used by SAC to implement the concept of 'fail-safe' is otherwise described by the term 'positive control', meaning that bombers go ahead with attack missions only if given 'execution instructions' once aloft and nearing the Soviet Union.[65] As they enter the Arctic region, they are supposed to get orders on the SAC 'Green Pine' network, some of the main bases of which have been identified at Argentia and Melville, Newfoundland; Cambridge Bay, Cape Dyer, Cape Perry and Hall Beach (all in Canada's Northwest Territories); and Grindavik, Iceland.[66] According to Ford, this consists of 'radio beacons set out in a chain extending from Adak in the Aleutians to Keflavik, Iceland'.[67] These have only short-range transmission capability. Otherwise, airborne command posts may be utilized as part of a 'hand-off' procedure, as may also the attacking bombers themselves, which can pass instructions along in a line, from bombers at the end of a line of attack to lead bombers.[68]

In addition SAC bombers and tankers utilize a global system of HF communications called 'Giant Talk'/Scope Signal III, a system of some 14 stations with coverage in all areas of the world other than the Arctic.[69] The stations are listed in table 17. This globally dispersed network clearly corresponds to flexible approach routes towards the USSR by B-52s and/or their successors armed with stand-off ALCMs.

Table 17. Giant Talk/Scope Signal III stations

Country	Location
Ascension	
Azores	Lajes, Cinco Pincos
Greenland	Thule
Guam	Andersen AFB, Barrigada, Nimitz Hill
Japan	Owada, Tokorozawa, Yokota
Okinawa	Kadena
Panama	Howard and Albrook AFBs
Philippines	Clark AFB, Cubi Point, Camp O'Donnell
Spain	Torrejon
Turkey	Incirlik
UK	RAF Croughton, Mildenhall, Barford St John

Source: SIPRI data.

FLTSATCOM and AFSATCOM

These two communications networks are primary systems utilized by the US Air Force and Navy, respectively.

The Air Force Satellite Communications System (AFSATCOM), which operates at UHF, is a network devoted particularly to strategic nuclear-related purposes. Put into operation in 1979, it does not have its own dedicated satellites; rather, there are AFSATCOM repeaters on military and commercial 'host' satellites, with, according to one source, some 900 terminals located in nuclear command centres, storage sites, and so on.[70] More specifically, this involves terminals at major Air Force Command headquarters, on E-4 and EC-135 Command aircraft, on EC-130 TACAMO aircraft, on most B-52 bombers, and at Minuteman launch control centres. The AFSATCOM transponder packages are said to be hosted by DSCS III, the Satellite Data System (SDS), the Fleet Satellite Communications System (FLTSATCOM), and still other satellites.[71] The transponders are used to repeat or relay messages, and are designed to overwhelm jamming through a system known as a regenerative repeater. Generally, AFSATCOM has been criticized, however, not only in relation to vulnerability to jamming, but also to upcoming Soviet ASAT capabilities.[72]

The above-named satellites used as hosts for AFSATCOM direct attention to its dependence on a number of overseas facilities, that is, Landstuhl (FR Germany) and Clark Air Base (Philippines) in connection with DSCS and Finnegayan (Guam), Bagnoli (Italy) and Diego Garcia with FLTSATCOM.[73] There may be others if AFSATCOM transponders have been put on still other satellites, that is, GPS. And, Ford points to four control stations that manage the operation of AFSATCOM—at Offut, Barksdale, March, and Anderson (Guam) Air Force Bases, none of which involves foreign facilities.[74]

FLTSATCOM consists of four satellites parked in geosynchronous orbit all around the equator and provides world-wide coverage except in the polar regions—three more are planned to be put into orbit.[75] These provide, mostly for the US Navy, communications by digitalized voice, teleprinter and other techniques, and operate at UHF. These satellites are also important hosts for AFSATCOM transponders. Indeed, according to one report, each FLTSATCOM satellite has 23 channels, 10 of which are allotted to the Navy for command of its air, ground and sea force; 12 to AFSATCOM for nuclear-related communications; and one reserved for the National Command Authorities.[76]

One particularly important function for FLTSATCOM—along with the DSCS satellites—is the relaying of data from SOSUS and SURTASS (surveillance towed array) hydrophone systems to the Central Shore Station or Acoustic Research Center at Moffett Field, California, 'where it is integrated with data from other sources and processed by the ILLIAC 4 computer complex to provide a real-time submarine monitoring capability'.[77] There is also real-time transmission of data and displays from ocean-surveillance satellites provided to US surface and submarine fleets.

FLTSATCOM utilizes several control or receiver sites. There are several in the USA at Norfolk, Wahiawa (Hawaii), Stockton, California and another at Finnegayan in Guam. Under the heading of FMP, there are additional stations at Bagnoli, Italy and at Diego Garcia, and an AN/MSC-61 system located at Exmouth, Northwest Cape, Australia.[78]

Tactical and intra-theatre communications

Collocated with the main concentrations of US overseas land and air forces—in NATO Europe and along the Pacific rim running from Japan to Korea to Okinawa to the Philippines—are a bewildering number of (often interconnected) communications systems and their associated facilities. These are in many cases specialized or demarcated along several dividing lines: nuclear-strategic and tactical; national and multinational (as with NATO); basically on the ground, underwater or overhead; radio, telephone and cable; army, navy and air force; secure and not-so-secure; and so on. In an area in which the open-source literature is rather sparse and lacking in detail, there is also the problem, for purposes of description and analysis, that some of these systems are by design overlapping or redundant—also, there are constant changes as newer systems are phased in to replace old ones. Particularly difficult to analyse are the interfaces between systems and the degree of interoperability with other nations' systems.

A full description of the myriad US communications nodes overseas—transmitters, receivers, relay stations, switching points, and so on—would be a monumental task and would overwhelm the space limitations of this chapter.[79] Further, it is no simple matter to separate some communications systems—elsewhere discussed—devoted primarily to nuclear forces from those within-theatre facilities devoted mostly to conventional or 'tactical' purposes.[80] Hence, we can here merely attempt to illustrate or outline what is involved, particularly as pertains to key systems and key nodal points which might, among other things, be perceived as critical targets for early interdiction in a major war; by nuclear, chemical or conventional weapons, or even by previously infiltrated *Spetsznaz* forces.

To illustrate the complexity of what is involved, first for NATO Europe, table 18 lists the communications systems and sub-systems documented in one recent US government report, alphabetically by acronym—and the list is not necessarily fully current or exhaustive. (Still another such list would be required to deal with US Pacific forces.) The parentheses indicate to which country or alliance the system belongs.

AUTOVON, AUTODIN, AUTOSEVOCOM

A large part of the day-to-day volume of US military communications is transmitted over the Automatic Voice Switching Network (AUTOVON). According to Jane's, 'during peacetime the network is the primary means of satisfying operations and other types of official calling requirements . . . Excluding the switch at Hawaii, the part of the network outside the USA consists of government-owned switching centres and transmission facilities supplemented by leased transmission facilities.'[81] Further, there are the related Automatic Digital Network (AUTODIN), used for transmission of data, and for more sensitive communications, the Automatic Secure Voice Communications (AUTOSEVOCOM) system. The AUTOSEVOCOM system, an integral part

Table 18. Some major communications systems and sub-systems

Acronym	System name
ACE HIGH	Allied Command Europe Communications Network (NATO)
AOTN	ACE Operational Telegraph Network (NATO)
AMPE	Automatic Message Processing Equipment (USA)
ASCON	Automatic Switched Communication Network (Netherlands)
ATACS	Army Tactical Communication System (USA)
AUTODIN	Automatic Digital Network (USA)
AUTOSEVOCOM	Automatic Secure Voice Communications (USA)
AUTOVON	Automatic Voice Network (USA)
BOXER	A planned microwave system in the UK (See MUKRCS) (UK)
CIP-67	Analog radio system in European Central Region (NATO)
CRITICOM	Critical Intelligence Communications Network (USA)
DCN	Defence Communications Network (UK)
DRAMA	Digital Radio and Multiplex Acquisition (USA)
DSCS	Defense Satellite Communications System (USA)
DSN	Defense Switched Network (USA)
DSSCS	Defense Special Security Communication System (USA)
ETS	European Telephone System (FRG/USA)
FIKS	Defence Integrated Communications System (Denmark)
FKV	Frankfurt, Koenigstuhl, Vaihingen Digital Transmission Link (USA)
FSTS	Federal Secure Telephone System (USA)
FGAFDIN	German Air Force Digital Network (FRG)
IAS	Integrated AUTODIN System (USA)
IDHS	Data Handling System (USA)
I-S/A AMPE	Inter-Service/Agency Automated Message Processing Exchange (USA)
IVSN	Initial Voice Switched Network (NATO)
JINTACCS	Joint Interoperability of Tactical Command and Control Systems (USA)
JCCSA	Joint Communications Contingency Station Assets (USA)
JMTSS	Joint Multichannel Trunking and Switching System (USA)
JTIDS	Joint Tactical Information Distribution System (USA)
MUKRCS	Military United Kingdom Radio Communications System (UK)
NEACP	National Emergency Airborne Command Post (USA)
NCCIS	NATO Command, Control, and Information System (NATO)
NCS	National Communications System (NATO)
NICS	NATO Integrated Communications System (NATO)
NMCS	National Military Command System (the priority component of WWMCCS) (USA)
NODCN	Norwegian Defence Communications Network (Norway)
NTS	Naval Telecommunications System (USA)
RBAFRR	Royal Belgian Air Force Radio Relay Network (Belgium)
SCARS	Status, Control, Alerting and Reporting System (NATO)
SAMHS	Standard Automatic Message Handling System (USA)
SAMSON	Message Switching Network (Canada)
SATCOM	Satellite Communications (NATO)
SPINTCOM	Special Intelligence Telecommunications Network (USA)
STARRNET	UK Radio Relay Network—Germany (UK)
TARE	Telegraph Automatic Relay Equipment (NATO)
Tri-Service	Italian Tri-Service Radio Relay System (Italy)
TRI-TAC	Joint Tactical Communications Program (USA)
WWMCCS	Worldwide Military Command and Control System (USA)

Source: Defense Communications Agency, 'Defense Communications System/European Communication Systems: Interoperability Baseline', Washington, DC, 1 Feb. 1981.

of the Defence Communications System, consists of switching centres, transmission facilities and subscriber terminals. According to Jane's:

. . . the network consists of 11 automatic government-owned switches, one leased automatic switch in the Pentagon, and 101 manual government-owned switches. There are 1460 authorised wide-band subscribers, of which 1347 are operational and served by the AUTOSEVOCOM switches; 276 authorised narrow-band subscribers, of which 239 are operational and served by the AUTOVON switches; and 236 authorised access lines with 224 operational from the AUTOVON switches to the AUTOSEVOCOM switches . . . Long-distance narrow-band AUTOSEVOCOM calls are placed through the AUTOVON system. Long-distance wide-band AUTOSEVOCOM calls are placed through the wide-band 50 kilobit-per-second circuits between the AUTOSEVOCOM switches.[82]

According to the US Defense Communications Agency, the European AUTOSEVOCOM system consists of about 225 wideband subscriber terminals 'homed on four AN/FTC-31 switches and sixteen SECORDS providing secure voice service . . . another 85 subscribers . . . are provided worldwide secure voice access through 10 AUTOVON switches'.[83] Locations of the main switching centres for the AUTOVON network are listed in table 19.

Table 19. Location of the main switching centres for the AUTOVON network

Country	Location
Japan	Fuchu AS, Camp Drake (moving to Yokota)
Okinawa	Grass Mountain or Ft Buckner
Philippines	Clark AFB
Panama	Corozal
Spain	Humosa
UK	Martlesham Heath, Hillingdon, RAF Croughton
FR Germany	Schoenfeld, Feldberg, Donnersberg, Pirmasens, Langerkopf
Italy	Coltano, Mt. Vergine
Greece	Mt. Pateras
Guam	Finnegayan

Source: Defense Communications Agency, 'Defense Communications System/European Communication Systems: Interoperability Baseline', Washington, DC, 1 Feb. 1981; and *Jane's Military Communications, 1981* (Macdonald: London, 1981).

Croughton, Pirmasens, and Coltano are listed by the Defense Communications Agency as the primary routing centres for the AUTODIN system. At the next level, Northwood (UK), Kolsaas (Norway) and Maastricht (Netherlands) are linked under Croughton; Kindsbach (FRG) under Pirmasens; and Naples, Verona and Izmir under Coltano.[84] Figure 6 outlines the related AUTOSEVOCOM Europe network.

Another major system is TARE (Telegraph Automatic Relay Equipment), also listed in the aforementioned report as using a number of overseas facilities as major: Verona (Italy), Kolsaas (Norway), Ankara (Turkey), Lisbon (Portugal), Maastricht (Netherlands), Athens (Greece), Naples (Italy), Izmir (Turkey), Edinburgh (UK), Baumholder (FRG), Latrina (Italy), NATO HQ (Belgium), Viborg (Denmark), Brussels (Evere, Belgium), Senden (FRG),

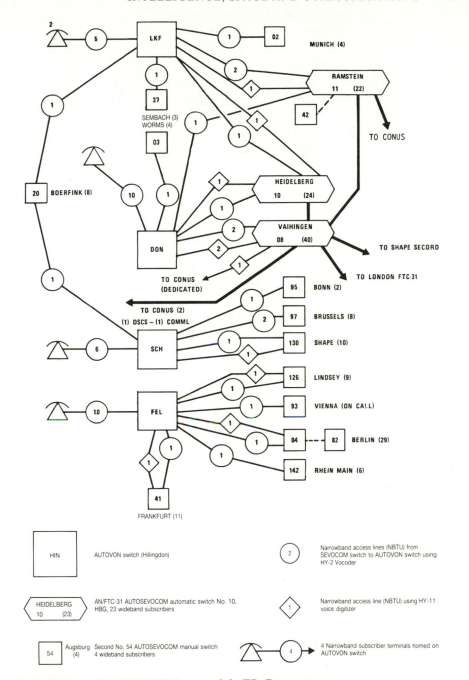

Figure 6. The AUTOSEVOCOM network in FR Germany

Source: Defense Communications Agency, *Defense Communications System/European Communications Systems: Interoperability Baseline* (Defense Communications Agency: Washington, DC, 1 Feb. 1981).

Reitan (Norway), Northwood (UK), and the Supreme HQ Allied Powers in Europe—SHAPE (Belgium).

One of the major US uses of overseas theatre communications is that involved in the highly proliferated microwave/troposcatter systems used to link US and other allied forces within the European and Pacific theatres. This in turn involves a number of sub-systems, perhaps the best known of which is the NATO ACE HIGH system within Europe. According to Jane's,

ACE HIGH is a 60-voice-channel tropospheric scatter/microwave link system which dates back to 1956 when SHAPE developed a plan for an exclusive communication system which would comprise the minimum essential circuits of early warning and alert and implementation of the tripwire retaliation strike plan. The network extends from northern Norway and through Central Europe to Eastern Turkey.[85]

All of the US NATO allies host numerous troposcatter relay links—there are some 40 in FR Germany, 6 in Belgium, 8 in Greece, 16 in Italy, 15 in Turkey, and so on. (Earlier there were some 30 such links in France.[86]) These types of link also run from the continental USA via Greenland, Iceland, the Faeroes and the UK to Europe; indeed, they were originally designed as one link in the Ballistic Missile Early Warning System (BMEWs). In Iceland, it is reported that each such North Atlantic Relay System (NARS) installation consists of four large 'billboard' troposcatter antennas.[87] Parts of the troposcatter network are now being modernized as the Digital European Backbone System (DEBS).

Table 20. Interconnections between ACE HIGH and DCS

DCS	ACE HIGH
Mormond Hill (UK)	Mormond Hill (UK)
Cold Blow Lane (UK)	Maidstone (UK)
SHAPE (Belgium)	Costeau (Belgium)
Bonn (FRG)	Kindsbach (FRG)
Aviano (Italy)	Aviano (Italy)
Naples (Bagnoli, Italy)	Bagnoli (Italy)
Izmir (Turkey)	Izmir (Turkey)
Incirlik (Turkey)	Adana (Turkey)

Sources: Defense Communications Agency, 'Defense Communications System/European Communication Systems: Interoperability Baseline', Washington, DC, 1 Feb. 1981; and *Jane's Military Communications, 1981* (Macdonald: London, 1981).

The NATO ACE HIGH ground-based system is reported interconnected with the US Defense Communications System (DCS) at eight locations; the interconnections are said to be mostly effected by cable, a few by microwave link. Interconnections between ACE HIGH and DCS are listed in table 20, and the coverage of the ACE HIGH and Tare systems are further illustrated in figure 7.

There are additional microwave/troposcatter links spanning the main areas of US force concentrations in the Pacific Ocean; in Japan, South Korea, Okinawa, the Philippines and (earlier) Taiwan, in turn linked to the DCS network. Some of this network is reported to have been superseded by broad-band cables,

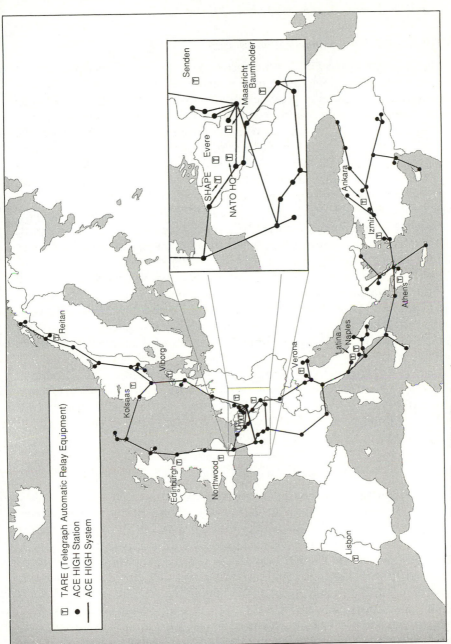

Figure 7. The NATO ACE HIGH and TARE networks

Source: NATO

but Japan and Korea retain some 10–15 troposcatter relay stations apiece.[88] In Alaska, meanwhile, the US Air Force maintains its 'White Alice' troposcatter/ microwave relay system, comprising over 50 relay facilities.[89]

US Defence Satellite Communications System

One key element of the US satellite-based communications system is that of the Defence Satellite Communications System.[90] This involves the placing of communications satellites in geosynchronous orbits 'that would allow a single satellite to relay messages continuously over a wide area of the globe; four such satellites could provide worldwide communications capability'.[91] Earlier, the DSCS II programme initiated in 1969 had resulted in two satellites being placed in such orbits, one over the Western Pacific and another over the Atlantic Ocean. The more recently deployed DSCS III system—considered more effectively hardened and survivable—involves a constellation of four satellites placed in synchronous orbits over the Atlantic, East and West Pacific and Indian oceans.[92] This satellite system operates in the SHF range. According to one press report, DSCS has a 'single channel transponder to send emergency action messages from the President to the nation's nuclear forces'.

The USA utilizes a number of ground nodes in connection with the DSCS satellites. Among them are facilities at Exmouth, North West Cape (Australia), Kester (Belgium), Diego Garcia, Clark AFB (Philippines), Diyarbakir (Turkey), Thurso and Oakhanger in the UK, Keflavik (Iceland), Kwajalein, Howard AFB (Panama), Song So and Yongsan (South Korea), Camp Zama (Japan), Episcopi (Cyprus), Antigua, Cinco Pincos and Vila Nova (Azores), and Landstuhl and Stuttgart (FR Germany). The terminal at Diyarbakir is linked to Lakehurst, New Jersey. That at Kester is the central master station for NATO communications satellites and the NATO control terminal for DSCS. Like the DSP satellite down-links and SOSUS processing stations, some of these might be priority targets at the outset of a major war.[93]

The future—US communications facilities

In a period seeing rapid changes in communications technology, the USA is preparing to deploy still newer satellite-based communications systems, driven by the fear of vulnerability to disruption at the outset of or during a nuclear war. The FMP implications of these changes are not yet apparent.

One new system, the GWEN network, is reported to consist of 'numerous unmanned LF radio sites hardened against electromagnetic pulse, which will ultimately connect warning sensors such as PAVE PAWS radars with NORAD [North American Air Defense Command], national command centres, SAC headquarters, and bomber and ICBM bases'.[94] Its LF ground radio wave will permit secure low-data-rate communications in a nuclear environment, and its main utility is that of resistance to indirect nuclear effects, that is, EMP, during the short period that precedes weapon impact. So far, it appears that this system may be built largely if not entirely within the USA. But, according to Arkin and Fieldhouse, 'GWEN is planned to extend into Canada to connect with Canadian Air Defense Forces'.[95]

Clearly with more important if not yet distinct FMP implications is the emerging MILSTAR communications satellite system, for which the Reagan Administration is reported to have spent $1.5 billion on satellites and communications equipment, and whose ultimate cost is pegged at $15-20 billion. It is described by one source as follows:

Imagine two networks, one in space, one on Earth. The first is a constellation of eight satellites, strategically placed in orbits around the Earth, 70,000 miles or more in space. The satellites connect with the second network, thousands of radios and computer terminals in underground bunkers, missile silos, submarines, tractor-trailers and airborne command posts.

Milstar would be the global nuclear-communications switch-board, connecting all the command stations during and after World War III, receiving and relaying the launch orders for nuclear weapons.[96]

Another source reports that MILSTAR 'will operate three times farther out in space than present defense satellites, at much higher than geosynchronous orbit, and at much higher frequencies' . . .'the present DSCS satellites work at super high frequency (SHF), but MILSTAR will use extremely high frequency (ELF), although it will also have some capability to use lower frequencies to be compatible with existing UHF satellite transmitters and receivers.'[97] It is said to feature favourable jam resistance and survivability. Presumably it would require some overseas control facilities as well as its numerous down-links to military units abroad.[98] But MILSTAR will not need to be constantly linked to major ground tracking stations since it is being designed to operate for weeks without ground involvement and to accept telemetry, tracking and mission data from multiple portable terminals.[99]

Presumably, some of the 'multiple, portable terminals' would be outside the USA, but that is not clear.

VOA facilities

The transmission, relay and reception of *strictly military* and diplomatic messages does not exhaust the uses to which overseas facilities are put within the broad domain of communications. Basing diplomacy has also entered the news in connection with broadcast communications. This can take any of several forms, for instance, the major powers' use of foreign territories for clandestine radio transmitters, particularly adjacent to rivals' territories or those where civil wars are in progress. (In the 1987 US Congressional Iran/'Contragate' hearings, information emerged about the CIA-run clandestine transmitters in Central America and in the Caribbean directed against Nicaragua and Cuba.) On a more overt basis, this has involved, at least as pertains to the US side, the global transmission network of the government's Voice of America (VOA). There are Soviet, French and British counterparts.

Access for VOA transmitters, even despite the absence of obvious military implications, is not always a simple matter. Soviet and other nations' sensitivities to radio-broadcast intrusion are such that a nation hosting a VOA facility will risk a degree of displeasure.[100]

For its short-wave broadcasts, the VOA has six main 500-kilowatt transmitters; additionally a variety of some 100 antennas and relay stations in Asia, Africa and Central America.[101] As indicated in figure 8, the VOA has overseas radio stations in Antigua, Thailand, Botswana, Greece (2), FR Germany, the Philippines (2), Costa Rica, Sri Lanka, Morocco, Belize and the UK (and now also Israel). In 1984–85 as the Central America crisis intensified, it was reported that Costa Rica and Belize had agreed to host VOA broadcast relay stations—in addition, VOA had obtained agreements to construct relay stations in Sri Lanka, Israel, Morocco and Thailand. That in Liberia has been described as the largest US transmitter in the world.[102] That in Israel came to figure in arguments on behalf of Jerusalem's strategic value to the USA, but the project seemed fated to abortion by 1987 amid the seeming thaw in US–Soviet relations wrought by Gorbachev's peace offensive.[103] Those in Greece (located in Thrace and on Rhodes) figured in the Papandreou government's threats to close down all US facilities.

The VOA was reported in 1985 to broadcast 989 hours a week in 42 languages (Radio Moscow broadcasts 2175 hours a week in 81 languages).[104] Another report citing VOA's six 500-kilowatt transmitters said the USSR has 37 for similar short-wave broadcasting, France 11 and Britain 8.[105]

US intelligence

The USA relies on a variety of technical methods for intelligence collection (i.e., other than HUMINT) which involve the use of overseas facilities. These involve the domains of imaging or photographic reconnaissance, signals intelligence, ocean surveillance, space surveillance, nuclear detonation and monitoring.[106] Variously, cutting across these categories and intersecting those analysed in previous chapters, this involves fixed land-based facilities, air bases and naval facilities. In some cases, the utilization of foreign facilities for specific purposes is well-known, as for instance in the cases of large strategic radars or air bases used to stage photo-reconnaissance flights. In others, however, data are more limited—this is particularly true regarding the relay of data from satellites to major headquarters in the US homeland. And, it must be stressed, this is a subject which is in fairly constant flux, and where the redundancy built into some systems renders difficult a judgement on the importance or irreplaceability of specific facilities. Figure 9 maps the main US global facilities for C³I.

Imaging/photographic reconnaissance

As noted in one recent article, 'in theory, imaging satellites can be employed to obtain visible light, infra-red, or radar imagery of a variety of military related activities'.[107] And, for the USA, reconnaissance satellites are of three types: area surveillance, close-look and real-time.

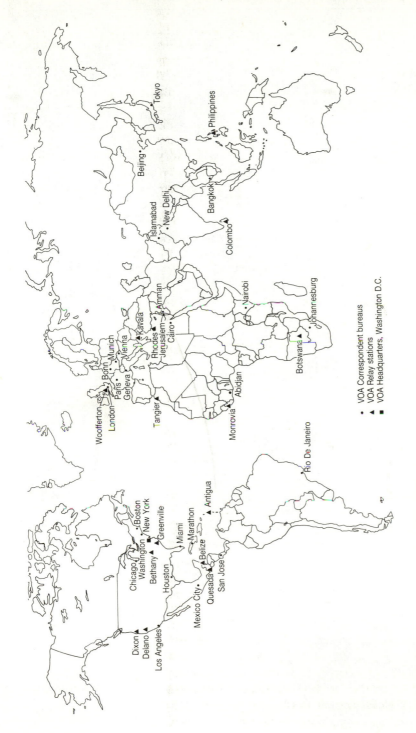

Figure 8. Voice of America facilities throughout the world

Source: Voice of America

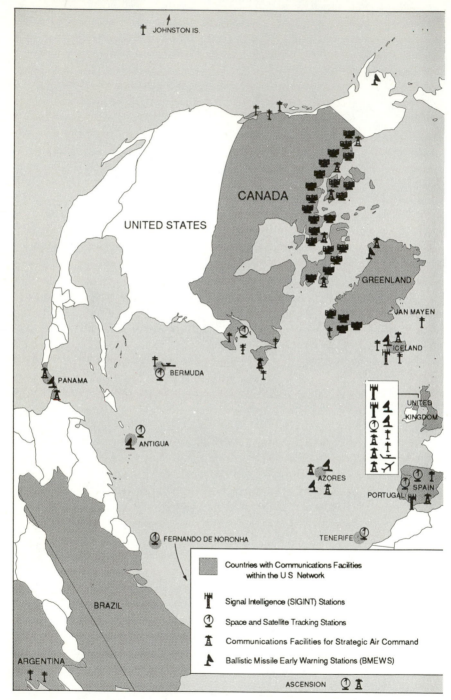

Figure 9. US global facilities for C³I

Source: SIPRI data

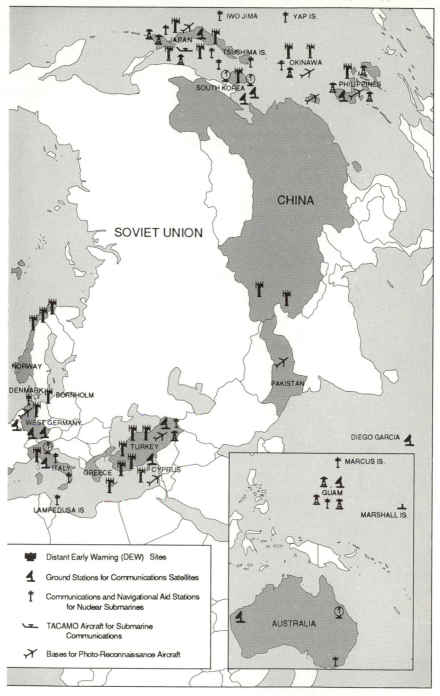

There have been several generations of the first two types, most recently the Keyhole-9 (KH-9) and KH-8 systems devoted to area-surveillance and close-look functions, respectively. These apparently both utilized returnable film capsules, recovered either in mid-air (by Lockheed C-130s stationed in Hawaii) or by frogmen.[108]

The KH-9 (Big Bird) and KH-8 (Close Look) systems are now being superseded by KH-11 spacecraft first introduced in 1976, which fly in 160–400-mile polar orbits. Normally there are two in orbit but, recently, the USA has had to make do with only one.[109] KH-11 pictures are transmitted in real time to facilities in the USA, involving digital radio pulses rather than films. These are, however, relayed via Satellite Data System (SDS) spacecraft and thus appear not to require use of foreign facilities.[110] The same appears true for new imaging systems now coming on stream: the KH-12 (Ikon) close-look satellite to be placed in orbit by a space-shuttle flight, and a new imaging radar satellite. (The high resolution KH-12 will be able to swoop into lower orbits on command, and 'the planned fleet of four satellites will be able to cover any designated area within 20 minutes of receiving an order'.)[111]

While the Keyhole-series satellites are the most productive photo-reconnaissance/imaging systems, can overfly targets without hindrance, and can now provide real-time intelligence, they do have some limitations. To supplement them, aircraft are used to cover critical events at short notice (the onset of crises or wars in the Third World, and key battles in such wars), that is, to provide a focused, quick-reaction capability.

The USA has utilized two aircraft for strategic photo-reconnaissance: the U-2 and the SR-71 Blackbird. The former became operational in 1956 and began to overfly the USSR that year, observing airfields, submarine production facilities, missile silos, and so on, before the advent of reconnaissance satellites. It can fly at more than 70 000 feet, can provide slant or side-angle photography, and has a range of 3000 miles.[112] The newer SR-71s, meanwhile, first made operational in 1966, can fly at a speed of Mach 4 (about 4160 km per hour), at a height of over 25 000 m.[113] In other words, they can survey 256 000 km^2 from an altitude of 24 km in only one hour, and can track SAM missiles at a distance of up to 160 km.[114] They reportedly also have radar detectors, a variety of ECMs and a synthetic-aperture radar for high-altitude night imaging. None have ever been shot down.

The U-2s have now been flying for over 30 years. Some 55 are reported to have been built, though only 7–8 are now operational. Earlier, in 1960, the U-2 gained fame when Gary Powers' plane was shot down *en route* from Peshawar, Pakistan to Bodø, Norway. Since then, U-2s have been flown from bases in Cyprus (Akrotiri), Turkey (Incirlik), Pakistan (Peshawar), Japan (Atsugi), Taiwan, Okinawa, the Philippines (Clark AFB), FR Germany (Wiesbaden), the UK (Mildenhall), and Alaska.[115] At various times, they have flown missions in relation to wars or crises in the Caribbean and Central America, the Middle East, Korea, and so on, as well as the earlier overflights over the USSR, and over the PRC prior to the Sino–American rapprochement. Fifteen to nineteen

SR-71s are now operational. They use many of the same facilities as the U-2s; for instance, those at Mildenhall in the UK, Kadena on Okinawa and Akrotiri on Cyprus. So too do the still newer TR-1A reconnaissance aircraft, of which some 14 are now deployed.[116]

More recently, it has been reported that the roles of the U-2s and SR-71s have been enhanced because of the fact that the USA was down to one KH-11 (its intended companion was destroyed in the failure of a Titan 34 D rocket), itself nearing the end of its life span. The use of the one remaining KH-11 was being restricted so as to extend its life, and the decrease in its coverage was being compensated for by increased use of spy planes, particularly with regard to Cuba and Central America.

Otherwise, the USA has also compensated for loss of KH-11 capabilities by increased purchase of space photographs from civilian remote-sensing satellites, such as the US Landsat and the French SPOT satellite.[117] In the latter case there may also be some new dependence for overseas facilities. Similarly, there has been increased reliance on civilian satellite-communications systems, which the US military is said to have leased in increasing numbers even before the rocket and shuttle failures.

Signals intelligence

The term SIGINT subsumes a number of technical activities, with a commonly utilized breakdown between communications intelligence (COMINT) and electronic intelligence (ELINT). COMINT typically involves interception of various types of communications (encrypted or not)—diplomatic, commercial, and so on, and by radio, telephone, underseas cable, and so on. ELINT involves primarily radar intelligence (RADINT), but also telemetry intelligence (TELINT) and foreign instrumentation signals intelligence (FISINT).[118]

As summarized by one source, RADINT involves 'the mapping of locations and hence targeting of early-warning stations, air-defense systems, ABM systems, airfields, air bases, satellite tracking and control stations, and ships at sea . . . Recording their frequencies, signal strengths, pulse lengths, pulse rates and other specifications allows for the ability to jam the transmitters in the event of war.'[119]

According to the same source, TELINT involves interception of the set of signals by which a missile, a stage of a missile, or a missile warhead sends data back to earth about its performance during a test flight.[120] The data relate to such features as structural stress, rocket motor thrust, fuel consumption, guidance system performance and the physical conditions of the ambient environment. Intercepted telemetry can provide intelligence on such questions as the number of warheads carried by a given missile, the range of the missile, its payload and throw-weight, and hence the probable size of its warheads and the accuracy with which the warheads are guided at the point of release from the missile's post-boost vehicles.

FISINT involves 'electromagnetic emissions associated with the testing and operational deployment of aerospace, surface, and subsurface systems that may have military or civilian application. FISINT includes, but is not limited to, telemetry, beaconing, electronic interrogators, tracking-fusing-aiming-command systems, and video data links.'[121]

SIGINT is performed by a number of systems—satellites, aircraft, ships and land facilities—some of each type involving some use of foreign bases, in the US case at least.

Satellites used for SIGINT fall into two basic types: high-orbiting systems with apogees of 20 000 miles and low-orbiting systems with apogees under 1000 miles.[122] In the former category are the Rhyolite satellites made famous when their capabilities were revealed to the Soviet Union in the espionage operation involving Christopher Boyce and Andrew Lee of 'the falcon and the snowman' fame.[123] Rhyolite is reported capable of being targeted against telemetry, radars and communications; its interception capability in the latter category is said to extend across the VHF, UHF and microwave frequency range, among other things allowing for interception of telephone traffic throughout most of the Soviet realm.[124]

Rhyolite is reported to be controlled from ground stations at Pine Gap, Australia and at Buckley Air National Guard Base in Colorado.[125]

Other identified high-orbiting US SIGINT systems are the Chalet satellite series initiated in 1979; the Satellite Data System programme which performs communications links for SAC aircraft as well as transmission of KH-11 photography; a revised version of the Argus system; and still others called Ferret and Magnum/Aquacade.[126] There are also low-orbiting ferret satellites used to map Soviet, Chinese and other radars, in orbits of only 300–400 miles, some of which have been launched on-board KH-9 photo-reconnaissance satellites. These are higher orbits than for the KH series, but lower than most other satellites, far lower than Rhyolite.

The USA has also long used aircraft for SIGINT missions; indeed, these obviously preceded the ferret satellites which came into operation only in the 1960s and 1970s. Indeed, McGarvey, Bamford and others who have written about early post-war US intelligence operations have detailed the grim and tense history of these operations along the periphery of the USSR and China, where the shooting down of aircraft led to serious diplomatic incidents.[127]

Nowadays, a number of US aircraft types are still used for SIGINT operations, supplementing the task of satellites. The previously discussed U-2s and SR-71s have SIGINT as well as PHOTINT capabilities; the latter are reported to fly along the Soviet periphery to pinpoint potentially hostile signal emitters. Richelson reports that the U-2s based at Mildenhall and Akrotiri have been upgraded by the SENIOR RUBY ELINT system; perhaps too with telemetry interception capability as was reported in 1979 when alternatives to lost Iranian bases were being proposed.[128] The latter illustrated the interchangeability of ground and air-based SIGINT systems, perhaps prior to the development of adequate satellite capability.

Other US aircraft used for SIGINT collection are the EC-135, the RC-135 and the EC-121—the latter has recently been retired.[129] The RC-135, a modified

Boeing 707 with COMINT and ELINT capability, is now the most important. The 18 such aircraft now in use utilize bases at Mildenhall (UK), Hellenikon (Greece) and Kadena (Okinawa) in addition to others in the continental USA and in Alaska.[130] One flying a TELINT mission in August 1983 in connection with an anticipated Soviet ICBM test, flew a parallel course to the doomed Korean Airlines flight 007.[131] Seven operational EC-135Ns, modified KC-135 tankers, have also been used to monitor US as well as Soviet missile tests and space activities.[132]

Table 21. Land-based SIGINT facilities

Country	Location/comments
Australia	North West Cape
The Azores	Villa Nova
Canada	Massett, Argentia, Whitehorse, Leitrim
China	Korla, Qitai
Cuba	Guantanamo
Cyprus	Five stations
Denmark	Bornholm
Diego Garcia	
Honduras	Palmerola
Kwajalein	
Midway	
FR Germany	Augsburg, Hof, a network called La Faire Vite to monitor WTO communications, and others
UK	Cheltenham, Wincombe, Morwenstow, Kirknewton
Greece	Iraklion and Nea Makri
Iceland	Keflavik, Stokknes
Italy	San Vito, Vicenza, Treviso
Japan	Misawa, Camp Zama, Hakata, Sakata, Wakkanei, Kamiseya
South Korea	Yonchon, Camp Humphreys, Pyongtaek, Sinsan-ni, Kangwha
Morocco	Kenitra
Norway	Vardø, Vadsø, Viksjøfjellet
Oman	Al Khasab, Umm Al-Ranam Island
Panama	Corozol, Fort Clayton, Galeta Island
Pakistan	Bada Biea
Philippines	San Miguel, Clark AB, John May Camp
Okinawa	Torii, Hanza, Sobe, Onna Point
Spain	Rota, El Casar del Talamanca
Taiwan	Shou Lin Kou, Taipeh, Nan Szu Pu
Turkey	Sinop, Dyarbakir, Samsun, Karamursel, Antalya, Agri, Kars, Edirne, Ankara

Source: SIPRI data and Richelson, J. T. and Ball, D., *The Ties That Bind* (Allen and Unwin: Boston, Mass., 1985), appendix 1.

Ground-based SIGINT collectors are also important, involving radars and antennas all over the world. Most notable are the Cobra Dane and Cobra Judy phased-array systems located at Shemya Island in the Aleutians and in Hawaii; hence, not involving FMP.[133] But there are a number of other SIGINT radars which do utilize foreign access, mostly around the Eurasian rimland.

These facilities are operated under the National Security Agency, by the service Commands, that is, the Air Force's Electronic Security Command (ESC), the Navy's Naval Security Group (NSG) and the Army's Intelligence and Security Command (INSCOM). Some are multi-purpose, others more specialized at various points along the frequency spectrum or with regard to one or another politico–military function, that is, troop communications, political intelligence, commercial communications, and so on.[134]

Although there are diverse types and mixes of these facilities, a few widely deployed types are notable. One involves a combination of AN/FLR-9 HF and VHF interception and direction-finding system (DF) with the CDAA (Circularly Disposed Antenna Array) known as an 'elephant cage'. Another involves telemetry interception capability with combined VHF–UHF–SHF receivers, used to monitor missile launches.[135] Then there are FPS-17 detection radars and FPS-79 tracking radars also used in connection with missile launches. There are also a considerable number of AN/FLR-15 antennas.[136]

The identifiable land-based SIGINT facilities include those shown in table 21. In some of these cases—Canada, the UK, Turkey, perhaps Japan—SIGINT stations are jointly operated with host personnel, and the data intake shared to one degree or another, no doubt negotiated on a case-by-case basis and subject to periodic renewal; hence, a function of the state of political relationships and associated reciprocal leverage.

Some of these SIGINT stations are thought to be particularly important. Karamursel is used to cover the vital Turkish Straits through which Soviet fleet units move.[137] Iraklion in Greece is used to monitor HF, UHF and SHF (for intercepting telemetry from Soviet missile launches at Kapustin Yar and Tyuratam) and as a receiving station for data gathered by EC-130 ELINT aircraft.[138] Those at Keflavik in Iceland and Rota in Spain are used for ocean surveillance;[139] that on Denmark's Bornholm Island to monitor missile launches from Plesetsk.[140] That at Kamiseya in Japan monitors HF traffic, but also is involved in analysing data gathered by P-3Cs, SOSUS terminals and other SIGINT stations.[141] Generally, the existence of critical SIGINT operations both in Greece and Turkey spotlights the US political dilemma of having to steer a course between two mutually hostile NATO allies. Other political problems are obvious—Panama, Morocco, Taiwan (where a continued US presence is apparently kept quiet),[142] the Philippines, Oman, and so on.

Turkey hosts a number of important SIGINT facilities. Hence, according to one recent source:

Intelligence collection sites in Turkey are those at Sinop and Samsun on the Black Sea Coast in north central Turkey, Belbasi in central Turkey, Diyarbakir in south-eastern Turkey and Karamursel in north-western Turkey. The Sinop facility is operated by INSCOM and collects data on Soviet air and naval activities in the Black Sea area. It also has HF receivers to record the telemetry of missiles launched from Kapustin Yar and Tyuratam.

Associated with Sinop is Samsun—a communications site manned by the Air Force ECS. The Diyarbakir site is operated by INSCOM and consists of an FPS-17 detection radar and FPS-79 tracking radar both of which are targeted against missiles launched from Kapustin Yar and Tyuratam. Telemetry from missiles launched from those sites are intercepted by VHF–UHF–SHF receivers at the Karamursel facilities, which has both NSG and ESC contingents.[143]

There have been additional COMINT sites at Antalya, Agoi, Kars and Edirna.[144]

There are also important SIGINT facilities in China and Norway. Agreement was reached with the People's Republic of China in 1979 (after the Iranian revolution) for the erection of two SIGINT stations at Korla and Qitai in the Sinkiang Province of western China near the Soviet border, directed at Soviet missiles tested at Leninsk and Sary Shagan as well as at military communications. The data from these operations are shared by the USA and the PRC.[145]

There are a number of important US SIGINT installations in Norway. These variously involve HF listening equipment and VHF/UHF antennas (the former can monitor long-distance radio communications, and ship-to-ship, ship-to-shore, and air-to-ground communications). These are pointed towards the Kola Peninsula and the Barents Sea, in connection with the huge concentration of Soviet military activity there and with missile tests. Thus, according to Richelson and Ball:

The NSA network in Norway apparently consists of eight stations, including three in the northern corner of Norway—Vardø, Vadsø and Viksjøfjellet. These facilities are operated for the USA by Norwegian technicians. VHF–UHF–SHF receivers at Viksjøfjellet and Vardø intercept the telemetry of missile launches from the Barents Sea, White Sea, and Plesetsk. HF receivers at Vadsø record count-down communications from these same locations.[146]

Japan on the Asian rim is also a particularly important hub of US SIGINT activity. Citing the same source as above:

Japan is host to numerous sites, the most important being the INSCOM facility at Torii Station, Okinawa. This facility has an AN/FLR-9 HF and VHF intercept and DF system, codenamed 'Kinsfolk'. Other Japanese facilities include NSG facilities at Sobe, Okinawa (with HF-DF and COMSEC functions) and Kamiseya as well as an INSCOM facility at Atsugi and ESC sites at Misawa Air Base, and Kadena AFB, Okinawa. From these facilities the US is able to monitor radar signals from both Soviet ground installations and aircraft. In addition, some antennas at these facilities are tuned to intercept the generally uncoded radio transmissions between Soviet air defence installations and interceptor aircraft.[147]

There are other CDAAs in the Philippines (Clark AFB), the UK (Menwith Hill and Chicksands), Japan, South Korea, FR Germany (Augsburg) and Italy (San Vito).[148] Over the years, the USA has lost access to important SIGINT stations in a number of places, casualties to wars, coups and other political problems. The Kagnew Station in Ethiopia was once a key post, with a large aperture CDAA, as was a facility at Ramasun in Thailand which involved a phased-array radar, Cobra Talon.[149] The same was true of another at Peshawar, Pakistan used to monitor Soviet and Chinese missile tests, though it may now have been restored.[150] The Silvermine base in South Africa was earlier used for NATO monitoring of ship communications traffic in the South Atlantic. The USA had numerous SIGINT facilities in Viet Nam and, of course, in Iran up to 1979. There, the USA had access to the Tacksman I and II telemetry interception facilities; others at Kharabad, Mochan, Shahrabad, Astara, Tumb Islands and Fassabad; and the widespread IBEX system which utilized both specially configured C-130s and ground stations.[151] There were other earlier SIGINT stations in Japan (Tokorozawa), Thailand (Nakhon Phonon, Khon Khaen), on Grand Bahama and Easter Islands, in Honduras (Swan Island), in Morocco (Sidi Yahya), and in Spain (San Pablo)—which also hosted an over-the-horizon (OTH) radar installation used to monitor Soviet missile launches.[152] Increasing US reliance on satellite-based SIGINT has presumably compensated for loss of access to ground-based facilities; at any rate, that trend has been determined by changing technology, which has resulted in greater reliance on satellites, political conditions notwithstanding.

Some US ships are also used for SIGINT purposes as well as for providing tracking data on US missile and space launches. The NSA spy ships *Liberty* and *Pueblo* earlier achieved notoriety in connection with crises and incidents in the Mediterranean and off North Korea, respectively.[153] Some US submarines, code-named under the Holystone, Pinnacle and Bollard programmes, have also been used for SIGINT operations, to plug into Soviet cables on the ocean bottom in the Kola area and in the Sea of Okhotsk.[154] To the extent these surface ships and submarines rely on overseas port calls for maintenance, repair and provisioning (or rely on tenders which in turn utilize foreign ports), then they too, if only indirectly, may rely on FMP.

Ocean-surface surveillance

The USA has a number of systems—satellites, aircraft, ground stations and ships—for observing the world's ocean surfaces, that is, for tracking Soviet warships, auxiliary intelligence ships, merchant and fishing vessels, and so on. Operationally, the goal is to know the location of all Soviet ships at any time. In normal conditions, one major purpose is to track the itineraries of Soviet ships carrying arms to clients—this is a key item of intelligence. In crises or, hypothetically, at the outset of a major war, the hair-trigger, pre-emptive nature of modern naval warfare—nuclear or non-nuclear—would put a premium on real-time location and targeting of rival fleets, in all weathers. Contrariwise, both sides would work hard to devise methods for eluding detection, again, particularly during wartime conditions.

Overseas facilities play a major role here. The USA utilizes its White Cloud satellite system, part of its larger Classic Wizard system, for ocean surveillance, involving a variety of ELINT functions as well as use of interferometry techniques to locate Soviet or other vessels.[155] This system comprises four satellites. The US Naval Security Group operates ground stations which are part of this system at Diego Garcia and Edzell, Scotland, as well as at Guam, Adak and Winter Harbor, Maine.[156]

Various aircraft—some used for other purposes as well—are utilized for ocean surveillance: EP-3Es, EA-3Bs, P-3Cs and U-2s. The EP-3E and EA-3Bs operate out of Rota (Spain), Guam and Atsugi (Japan); the latter also operate from fleet aircraft carriers.[157]

The P-3C Orion, known mostly for its ASW role, is also utilized for ocean surveillance. It has access to bases throughout the world: Clark AFB (the Philippines), Misawa (Japan), Kadena (Okinawa), Keflavik (Iceland), Rota (Spain), Sigonella (Italy), Ascension and Diego Garcia Islands, Cocos Islands (Australia), Masirah (Oman), Mogadiscu (Somalia) and several others.[158] U-2s are flown from their usual facilities, such as Akrotiri (Cyprus) and Mildenhall (UK).

For land-based ocean surveillance considerable use is made of HF/DF systems, which are also mounted on ships which, again, utilize various overseas port-facilities. Among the land-based HF/DF locales are those at Diego Garcia, Rota (Spain), Edzell (Scotland), Keflavik (Iceland), Brawdy (Wales), Japan and Guam.[159] Those in Scotland, Wales and Iceland can, notably, be seen located near the crucial GIUK-gap chokepoint, which would presumably be a major point of contention at the outset of a major war in relation to North Atlantic sea lines of communication and the Soviet submarine bastions near the Kola Peninsula. Richelson and Ball actually report on some 40–50 HF/DF sites for ocean surveillance said to be operated by the combined assets of the USA, UK, Canada, Australia and New Zealand.[160]

Space surveillance

In recent years the proliferation of satellites and other man-made 'space objects' has made their tracking and identification more vital. The USA has an extensive programme intended to detect and track its own satellites, but also Soviet and other nations' space vehicles.

In the security realm this has a number of dimensions. Of course, both sides wish to mask some of their ground activities from surveillance and therefore seek the capability to operate during gaps in surveillance. By detecting and tracking Soviet satellites the US Satellite Reconnaissance Advance Notice (SATRAN) System allows the USA to avoid Soviet coverage of US military activities.[161] As expectations mount about a future which may see large-scale militarization of space, both sides increasingly perceive an interest in real-time surveillance of each others' satellites, in the context of possible later hair-trigger pre-emptive situations as applied to mutual interdiction of satellites. Of course, both sides desire maximally effective intelligence on the others' various military activities conducted from space: communications, ocean surveillance, SIGINT, nuclear detection, and so on.

In summary, as stated by Richelson:

. . . space surveillance helps provide the United States with intelligence on the characteristics and capabilities of Soviet space systems and their contribution to overall Soviet military capabilities . . . Such data aid the United States in developing countermeasures to Soviet systems, provide a database for U.S. ASAT targeting, and allow the United States to assess the threat represented by Soviet ASAT systems.[162]

For the time being, the US mechanisms for tracking and detecting Soviet satellites are almost entirely ground-based, though some space-based capability has already been demonstrated by the KH-11 reconnaissance satellite. For the future, the US Air Force is planning a space-based satellite surveillance system, in the form of its Space Infra-red Surveillance Program, to involve, initially, four satellites in low-altitude equatorial orbits with long-wave infra-red sensors.[163]

At present, the varied ground-based system falls under the overall rubric of SPADATS—the Space Detection and Tracking System. According to the typology utilized by Richelson, that involves three types of sensor—dedicated, collateral and contributing—respectively involving sensors whose primary mission is space surveillance, SAC sensors with a secondary space-surveillance role, and non-SAC sensors with a secondary space-surveillance role.[164]

For many years the heart of the dedicated sensor system was a group of Baker-Nunn optical cameras, huge cameras which, according to one source, could 'photograph, at night, a lighted object the size of a basketball over 20,000 miles in space'.[165] In addition to the two in California and New Mexico, these cameras were located outside the USA in New Zealand (Mt. John), South Korea (Pulmosan), Canada (St. Margarets, New Brunswick) and Italy (San Vito).[166] The latter two are still utilized, along with another at Choejong-San, South Korea. Earlier there were others on Johnston Island, in Alaska, and in Argentina, Brazil, Chile, Ethiopia, Greece, Iran, South Africa, Upper Volta and Curaçao in the Lesser Antilles, among others.[167] Because of its limitations—slowness in data acquisition, processing and response time; absence of all-weather capability and inflexible tracking capability—this system is now being replaced by the Ground-based Electro-Optical Deep Space Surveillance (GEODSS) system.[168]

GEODSS, also to have five locations, will overcome several of the Baker-Nunn system's shortcomings by allowing real-time data, better search capability and more rapid coverage of larger areas of space—but it will still be limited by adverse atmospheric conditions. It is actually a system of three linked telescopes at each site, providing variable coverage by altitude. The five locations will be in Hawaii (Maui) and New Mexico (White Sands), within the USA, and externally in South Korea (Taegu), Diego Garcia and Portugal.[169]

Richelson mentions three other sets of dedicated sensors. There are the Naval Space Surveillance (NAVSPASUR) and some 'optical radars' located in New Mexico and Hawaii (the former is characterized as an electronic fence, which consists of an unsteerable fan-shaped radar beam with a 6000-mile range that extends in an east–west direction from California to Georgia). These systems do not, apparently, involve access to foreign facilities.[170]

A more recently installed system of dedicated sensors is the Pacific Radar Barrier (PACBAR), which involves radars on Guam, in the Philippines (San Miguel) and on Kwajalein. These will enable determination of the orbit of a satellite within its first revolution, according to Richelson.[171] Earlier, up to 1976, such a function was performed by the 'Cobra Talon' facility at Ko Kha in Thailand, which tracked Soviet satellites being launched into orbit from Tyuratam.[172]

Systems used primarily for early warning—BMEWS, FSS-7, PAVE PAWS, Enhanced Perimeter Acquisition Radar Attack Characterization System (EPARCS) and FPS-85 radars—are all usable as collateral space-tracking sensors. Of these, BMEWS—based at Thule (Greenland), Fylingdales (UK) and Clear (Alaska)—involves extensive use of foreign access.[173] Additionally, COBRA DANE (Shemya Island, Aleutians—120° arc, 46 000-km range against space targets) and also the AN/FPS-79 (Pincirlik/Diyarbakir, Turkey) radar are usable in a space-surveillance role, as supplementary to the primary missions of monitoring missile-test re-entry trajectories.[174] The contributing sensors from the Richelson typology, meanwhile, all appear to be located within the USA.

In addition to the above SPADATS installations directed at surveillance of foreign, that is, Soviet, space activities, numerous other foreign facilities are used—or have been used—as part of the US Satellite Tracking and Data Acquisition Network (STADAN) network of installations used to track and monitor US space activities, including the down-range course of launches. Among these are facilities in: Australia (Orooral Valley, Toowoomba), the UK (Winkfield), Ascension, Bermuda, the Canaries (Tenerife), Spain (Madrid), Brazil (Fernando de Noronha) and Antigua.[175] In connection with space surveillance and under the heading of 'miscellaneous radars', a recent IISS publication mentions radars in Kwajalein, Ascension and Antigua, in addition to those at Kaena Point in Hawaii and at MIT's Lincoln Laboratory.[176] Earlier, STADAN tracking facilities were operated, among other places, in Chile, Ecuador, the Malagasy Republic, Grand Turk Island, South Africa and Zaïre.[177] The (quantitative) requirements for these facilities have been lessened by the advent of the Tracking Data and Relay Satellite System.[178] Additionally, these activities have been supplemented by the Cobra Ball airborne system utilizing RC-135 aircraft.[179]

Satellite control stations

One of the more secret or classified areas of FMP is that of satellite control stations. Ford, in his work on command and control, in analysing the vulnerable and non-redundant nature of the US early-warning system involving the DSP East satellite, its down-link facility in Australia and the communications link from there to the satellite control facility in Sunnyvale, California, provides some indication of what is involved. Thus, according to him,

There are several dozen U.S. defense satellites now in orbit—providing communications, photoreconnaissance, electronic intelligence, navigational, meteorological, and other data—and they require contact with the Sunnyvale ground control station and its seven substations around the globe in order to remain functional. A great deal of fine-tuning, for example, is needed to steer the satellites in precise orbits and to keep their sensors and antennas aimed properly. . . . A catastrophic loss of this control center would result in a major disruption of communications, tracking, and control of its space systems . . .[180]

And further:

Other officials are less optimistic. 'We lose the SCF and the satellites basically go haywire', a Pentagon expert who has studied this subject told me. 'The communications satellites drift off to Pluto.' Certain intelligence-gathering satellites in low-earth orbit would be in especially bad shape, he said, since the Sunnyvale facility has to 'feed them' with instructions every time they complete an orbit. 'You should see them scrambling when one of these satellites comes within range.' Desmond Ball estimated that the typical US defense satellite might be able to remain in operation for three to four days without the Sunnyvale SCF; the most critical satellites, such as DSP East, which require a great deal of caretaking attention from the ground, could go out of service within hours.[181]

The seven sub-stations linked to Sunnyvale comprise three within the USA— at Manchester AF Station in New Hampshire, Kaena Point in Hawaii, and Vandenberg Air Force Base (AFB) in California. Others outside the USA are at Thule, Greenland—collocated with various other technical facilities as well as a bomber and tanker base—at Guam at Andersen AFB, at Oakhanger in the UK and at Mahe in the Seychelles.[182] Mahe has long hosted a US satellite control facility (SCF) collocated with a DSCS ground terminal. This facility was apparently important in relation to reconnaissance satellites and for monitoring injection into orbit of satellites launched from Cape Canaveral.[183] The US lease for this site had been extended to 1990, but in the interim, political changes have moved the Seychelles out of the Western orbit and towards close links with the USSR and Tanzania.[184] Earlier, up to 1975, the USA also had what apparently was an SCF at Majunga in the Malagasy Republic, one also used to monitor satellites launched from Cape Canaveral.[185] US access to this facility was then lost at a time when Tananarive shifted towards an arms-supply relationship with the USSR. Still earlier, the USA apparently had a similar SCF on Zanzibar Island, within Tanzania.[186] Access there was lost for similar reasons.

Also, earlier on, it is possible that the major US SIGINT base at Ramasun in Thailand also served as a satellite control facility, as well as housing receivers for data collected by U-2 and SR-71 spy planes.[187] It was shut down in 1976 along with other US bases in the wake of the Viet Nam débâcle, perhaps thereafter used for some purposes by Thai personnel.

It is clear that most satellite control functions (repositioning, switching functions on and off, querying for data, and so on) are performed from the aforementioned network. But, Stares lists a range of additional facilities used as 'control or receiver sites' with reference to all of the main US satellite programmes—photo-reconnaissance (Keyhole), SIGINT (Chalet, Magnum, Jumpseat), ocean-reconnaissance (Whitecloud), early-warning (DSP), communications (DSCS, FLTSATCOM, Leased Satellite System), navigation (Transit-Nova and NAVSTAR GPS) and meteorology (Defense Meteorological Satellite Program—DMSP). Their overseas facilities are noted elsewhere in this chapter. Some or most no doubt have control functions to supplement those provided by the SCF network.[188]

Strategic early warning

One of the most obviously critical areas of intelligence involving foreign bases is that of strategic early warning, that is, warning of impending or unfolding nuclear attack. Both superpowers have had to construct elaborate systems of surveillance so as to detect such attacks, systems directed against all three legs of the triad, that is, ICBMs, SLBMs and long-range bombers. Such intelligence is, clearly, not merely important to damage-limitation, but also to deterrence, as maximum warning time can translate into capability for launch-on-warning and launch-under-attack, which is itself, to the extent credible, a powerful deterrent. It is also important for planning a retaliatory attack, that is, for effective targeting of the opponents' strategic reserve.

Here, as in so many areas of military endeavour, the USA is asymmetrically dependent on foreign access, and crucially so. Indeed, this has long been the case—even before the advent of intercontinental missilry, the USA relied on radars in Canada and Greenland for warning of approaching bombers at a time when such warning could provide several hours of response time.[189] The asymmetries are partly because of the larger relative size of the USSR and partly because of the location of critical foreign terrain—Canada, Greenland, Iceland—between the USA and the trans-Arctic routes that would be traversed by missiles and bombers across the Arctic regions between the superpowers.

Several key US early-warning systems utilize foreign access: ground stations used to relay data from early-warning satellites; the BMEWS radar system directed against Soviet ICBMs; the several layers of radar pickets used to detect bombers *en route* to the USA from the Arctic region; and a variety of other sensors, which might be used in collateral or supplementary roles. More recently, of course, much attention has been devoted to new, emerging US defensive requirements in relation to cruise missiles, SLBM launches and Soviet bombers (probably armed with ACLMs) which might approach the USA on more southerly routes. The first two named have impelled development of the PAVE PAWS (Phased Array Warning System) and OTH-B systems, respectively based, or planned to be based, within the USA. PAVE PAWS, located at Beale AFB in California and at Otis AFB on Cape Cod, utilize AN/FPS-115 radars similar to Cobra Dane.[190] The latter is used mostly to monitor Soviet ICBM tests, but all three are also part of the strategic early-warning system, with PAVE PAWS acting as a back-up to BMEWS for detecting ICBM warheads.[191] OTH-B, if deployed, will be utilized for detection of bombers and air-breathing weapon systems, that is, cruise missiles.[192]

Regarding early-warning satellites, the USA relies primarily on what have become known as DSP East and DSP West (earlier these were called MIDAS satellites). The former has the primary task of watching for ICBM launches; the latter for SLBM launches in the Atlantic.[193]

The Code 647 Defence Support Program satellite—DSP East—sits some 23 000 miles above the Indian Ocean in geosynchronous orbit, monitoring the eastern hemisphere. It contains an infra-red telescope equipped with thousands

of tiny lead-sulphide detectors designed to pick up the hot exhaust flame produced by large rocket engines, during the boost phase of their flights. It has full
coverage of Soviet missile fields from an orbit more or less above the equator
and, in the case of mass launchings, can tell what kinds of missile have been
launched and from where.[194] Hence, DSP East could also provide valuable
information about what kind of attack had been launched, that is, the likely
targeting mix. That would in turn guide the targeting of a US counterforce
response.

Although there is only one DSP East functioning at any given time, older
ones have been left in orbit. They might, in an emergency, be turned back on
by ground controllers and returned to service, that is, could act as back-ups in
case the extant DSP satellite was rendered inoperative.[195] DSP East is dependent
on a single satellite control facility (SCF) located at Sunnyvale, California. That
SCF is critical to repositioning DSP satellites, that is, fine-tuning to keep them
in precise orbits and to keep their sensors and antennas aimed properly.[196] And
in turn, the data from DSP East's sensors must be transmitted to NORAD
headquarters at Cheyenne Mountain, Wyoming, but first via Buckley AFB,
Colorado.[197]

The principal and necessary link between DSP East and NORAD is the
down-link facility at Nurrungar, Australia (there are also control and tracking
functions at Pine Gap and on Guam) described as a highly vulnerable set of
antennas, transmitters and computational facilities.[198] This 'readout station' in
turn must relay data to NORAD, variously by underseas cable, by HF radio
links or via the Defense Satellite Communications System and in turn via a
switching station in Hawaii.[199] These various alternative communications links
between Nurrungar and Buckley AFB in Colorado involve foreign access to
New Zealand, Fiji, Norfolk Island and Canada's British Columbia at Port
Alberni.[200] In recent years, however, another down-link for DSP East (called
the Simplified Processing Station) has been made operational at Kapaun, FR
Germany.[201] The DSP West satellites, which watch for SLBM launches, do not
require foreign access for data down-links.

Recently, the US system of three DSP satellites has—as in the case of other
satellite systems—been jeopardized by ageing and by the restrictions on replacement caused by the shuttle and launcher rocket failures. But, according to
one report, 'the military does have "spares", however, which are basically old
models that have some chance of being revived in space'.[202] Further, there are
plans for six mobile ground terminals to back up the down-link at Nurrungar.[203]

A second major US strategic warning system used to monitor ICBM launches
is BMEWS which comprises three major radars (located at Clear, Alaska; Thule,
Greenland; and Fylingdales Moor, UK).[204] These radars became operational in
1960 and have 4800-km ranges. The USA is in the process of upgrading them,
which has sparked some controversy in the context of remaining within the
limits of the ABM Treaty (the upgrading of Fylingdales would double the scope
of coverage to 360 degrees and increase the radar's range by one-third to over
10 000 km).[205] A current BMEWS facility includes four AN FPS-50 detec-

tion radars and an AN/FPS-49 tracking radar—these also act as contributing sensors for the SPADATS system.[206] Altogether, there are now 12 radars with ranges of 4800 km.

Finally, the USA has long relied—primarily for warning of the approach of bombers—on the series of radar picket lines across the Arctic known as the Distant Early Warning (DEW) and Continental Air Defense Integration North (CADIN) Pinetree lines. These have been located across Alaska, Canada and Greenland; with a few additional outposts in Iceland and the Faeroe Islands (the locations of the sites in Canada, Greenland and Iceland are listed in table 22). The DEW Line has 31 radars, some 21 of which are in Canada and four in Greenland (several also are used as relays for troposcatter communications relays); in the 1950s submarines on the surface filled gaps in the DEW Line—they could submerge after reporting incoming aircraft.[207] As they are somewhat outdated and, in particular, limited in ability to detect low-flying aircraft, some of these facilities are being upgraded with newer radars. Now the system is to be supplemented by 39 auxiliary short-range radars with 110-150 km ranges.[208]

Table 22. Locations of DEW Line and CADIN Pinetree Line radar sites in Canada and Greenland, 1985

DEW Line	Pinetree Line
Canada	
Broughton Island	Alsask
Byron Bay	Armstrong
Cambridge Bay	Baldy Hughes
Cape Dyer	Barrington
Cape Hooper	Beausejour
Cape Perry	Beaver Lodge
Cape Young	Chibougamau
Clinton Point	Dana
Dewar Lakes	Falconbridge
Gladman Point	Gander Air Base
Hall Beach	Goose Bay AB
Jenny Lind Island	Gypsumville
Komakuk Beach	Holberg
Lady Franklin Point	Kamloops
Longstaff Bluff	Lac St Denis
Mackar Inlet	Moisie
Nicholson Peninsula	Montapica
Pelly Bay	Moosonee
Shepherd Bay	Ramore
Shingle Point	Senneterre
Tuktoyaktuk	Sioux Lookout
	Yorkton
Greenland	
Easterly	
Kulusuk Island (Dye-4)	
Qiquatoqoq (Holsteinsberg-Dye-1)	
Westerly	

Source: Arkin, W. M. and Fieldhouse, R. W., *Nuclear Battlefields: Global Links in the Arms Race* (Ballinger: Cambridge, Mass., 1985), appendix A.

The CADIN Pinetree Line of air surveillance radars in Canada, has constituted a second line of warning behind the DEW Line and comprises some 22 stations operated by Canadian personnel for NORAD.[209]

The upgrading of the almost 30-year old DEW Line is being impelled by cruise-missile developments and by new Soviet Backfire bombers capable of penetrating the old barrier, and it preceded the advent of the Strategic Defense Initiative (SDI). A new system, projected to cost $1.8 billion would involve a network of 52 new long- and short-range radar stations overlapping Alaska, Canada and Greenland, and is called the North Warning System.[210] It utilizes many of the hub facilities of the DEW Line, but with upgraded modern radars and independent power systems.

The North Warning System will consist of 13 Seek Igloo AN/FPS-117 automated (minimally attended radar-MAR) systems in Alaska, 13 more in Canada (to be supplemented by 39 auxiliary unmanned short-range radars (110 to 150 km), 4 in Greenland, 1 in Scotland and 2 in Iceland, roughly along the 70°N parallel from Point Lay, Alaska to Greenland, then on to Iceland and Scotland.[211]

Tactical radars

In close association with the locations of major overseas US ground force deployments and tactical aircraft bases, the USA also requires access for numerous tactical early-warning radars. Actually, many of these are enmeshed within the NATO Air Defence Ground Environment (NADGE) system (the British component is called UKADGE), which involves a complex interrelated system of radars in Turkey (with some 14 NADGE radar sites), Greece (now all operated by Greek personnel), Italy, FR Germany, the Netherlands, Denmark and the Faeroe Islands, Belgium, and so on. According to one source this involves, totally, a network of 42 radars extending from Norway to Turkey, with France's radar system additionally tied into it.[212]

There are other scattered US-operated tactical radars in the Azores (Portallo Nova), the Philippines (Wallace Air Station and others), the Ryukyus, South Korea, Iceland, and so on.[213] In Japan, there is the BADGE radar network, and in Spain, there is the Combat Grande network of seven air-surveillance radar stations located around its periphery, connected by 63 microwave relay sites to a combat communications centre located at Torrejon Air Base, but now operated by Spanish forces.[214] This is tied into the NATO system. Eastern radars are similarly linked to the Soviet defence radar system.

Anti-submarine warfare

The United States has perhaps the world's most extensive and effective global ASW capability, which requires access to land facilities around the world: staging bases for aircraft, and processing stations for acoustic and electronic data. Regarding acoustic data, it relies heavily on its SOSUS networks, often alternatively referred to as Caesar. These, going way back to 1954, involve networks of hydrophonic arrays which feed back oceanographic and acoustic data to shore processing facilities, that is, large computer analysis centres. These data and others are correlated at regional processing centres (including those in Hawaii, Wales, Newfoundland and Iceland) and then forwarded to a main processing centre at Moffett Field, California via FLTSATCOM and DSCS satellites.[215]

SOSUS, though augmented by other systems noted below, is the backbone of the US ASW detection capability. It has been described by SIPRI as follows:

Each SOSUS installation consists of an array of hundreds of hydrophones laid out on the sea floor, or moored at depths most conducive to sound propagation, and connected by submarine cables for transmission of telemetry. In such an array a sound wave arriving from a distant submarine will be successively detected by different hydrophones according to their geometric relationship to the direction from which the wave arrives. This direction can be determined by noting the order in which the wave is detected at the different hydrophones. In practice the sensitivity of the array is enhanced many times by adding the signals from several individual hydrophones after introducing appropriate time delays between them. The result is a listening 'beam' that can be 'steered' in various directions towards various sectors of the ocean by varying the pattern of time delays. The distance from the array to the sound source can be calculated by measuring the divergence of the sound rays within the array or by triangulating from adjacent arrays.[216]

The first SOSUS systems were completed on the continental shelf off the east coast of the USA in 1954.[217] Others were later installed off both US shores and at Brawdy, Wales—the Pacific Coast system came to be known by the code-name of Colossus.[218] A jointly-operated US–Canadian array came to be centred at Argentia, Newfoundland; others at Hawaii, the Bahamas and the Azores.[219]

By 1974, it was stated that there were 22 SOSUS installations located along the east and west coasts of the USA and near various chokepoints around the world—another 14 are identified by Richelson and others.[220] Foreign-based SOSUS installations are located at Ascension, in the Azores (Santa Maria), the Bahamas (Andros Island), Barbados, Bermuda, Canada (Argentia), Denmark, Diego Garcia, Gibraltar, Guam (Ratidian Point), Iceland (Keflavik), Italy, Japan (sonar chains across the Tsugaru and Tsushima Straits), Norway, Panama (Galeta), the Philippines, the Ryukyus, Turkey, the UK (Scatsa, Shetland) and Brawdy, Wales). In addition to this list, a facility has been operated in the 'northeastern part of the Indian Ocean', and perhaps another astride Indonesia's critical straits or at Australia's Christmas Island. Others have at times been operated on Grand Turk Island, Antigua, Bahamas (Eleuthera) and Barbados; and maybe on the Canary Islands at Punta de Tero. And the USA may possibly be quietly operating still other barrier sonars, for instance, in the central Mediterranean from Lampedusa and/or Pantelleria Islands, and on Midway Island in the central Pacific Ocean.

Burrows describes as follows the basic geometry of the US SOSUS network which monitors Soviet egress from the Eurasian bastion:

There are actually two SOSUS arrays moored across the approaches to Polyarnyy: one between Norway and Bear Island, and the other linking northern Scotland, Iceland, and Greenland. Submarines whose home port is Petropavlovsk are monitored by hydrophones strung from the southeastern tip of Hokkaido, along a line parallel to the Kuriles, and then up toward the northeast, off the Aleutian coast. Still others stretch from southern Japan to the Philippines, covering the approaches to China and Indochina. And there are also SOSUS installations on the Atlantic side of Gibraltar, others about halfway between Italy and Corsica, and still others at the mouth of the Bosporus, off Diego Garcia in the Indian Ocean, and not so far from Hawaii. The Navy keeps the precise locations of its SOSUS equipment a closely guarded secret, since interfering with it would be a logical Soviet subject.[221]

According to Richelson, 'data from these shore facilities are transmitted via FLTSATCOM and DSCS satellites to a "central shore station" at the Acoustic Research Center (ARC) at Moffett Field, California, where they are integrated with data from other sources and processed by the Iliac 4 computer complex to provide a real-time submarine monitoring capability.'[222] These facilities are said to be able to detect submarines out to 3000 miles or more (meaning close to full coverage of most of the world's seas from the above points), and to be able to localize detection down to 10 miles.[223] Figure 10, not entirely complete, presents a simple graphic picture of US coverage, obviously centred on choke-points and on the known patrol areas of Soviet SSBNs and SSNs.

There are some other complementary or supplementary US ASW systems which involve FMP requirements. This is important as the locations of the main SOSUS centres are known and would be vulnerable to interdiction during a war or crisis; indeed, might be prominent targets for tit-for-tat exchanges during protracted 'conventional phases' in which each side tries to degrade the strategic nuclear capabilities of the other. (This in turn, in those countries hosting major SOSUS terminals, might raise the questions of threats and of possible intra-war 'decoupling'.) Those systems are the Rapidly Deployable Surveillance System (RDSS) and the Surface Towed Array Sensor System (SURTASS)—together with SOSUS they form the Integrated Underseas Surveillance System whose data are sent by FLTSATCOM and DSCS satellites to the Central Shore Station at Moffett Field, California.[224]

RDSS, designed to operate in areas where fixed or manned systems cannot operate reliably, consists of large sonabuoys remotely deployed by aircraft or ships, or even launched through submarine torpedo tubes. Regarding FMP, this would in particular direct attention to P-3C air facilities, which in a crisis, would also be used for forward deployment of nuclear ASW weapons. Indeed, in case of war, acoustical coverage of the oceans could be rapidly expanded by air-dropping moored sonabuoys over strategic areas. SURTASS, designed to be used where SOSUS is unavailable or inoperative, involves the eventual acquisition of 18 ships, or tugs, designated T-AGOS (geodetic oceanographic ships) designed to tow large hydrophone arrays by lengthy cables.[225] As these are designed to operate for 90 days on station, moving slowly, they would presumably have only minimal shore-based support requirements—FMP in connection with ASW involves, most importantly, SOSUS and aircraft-based RDSS systems, that is, sonabuoys.

If it is the case that the now longer ranges of the missiles of Soviet SSBNs such as the Typhoon have reduced Soviet reliance on use of patrol stations far from the main SSBN bastions (and reduced Soviet use of some external facilities

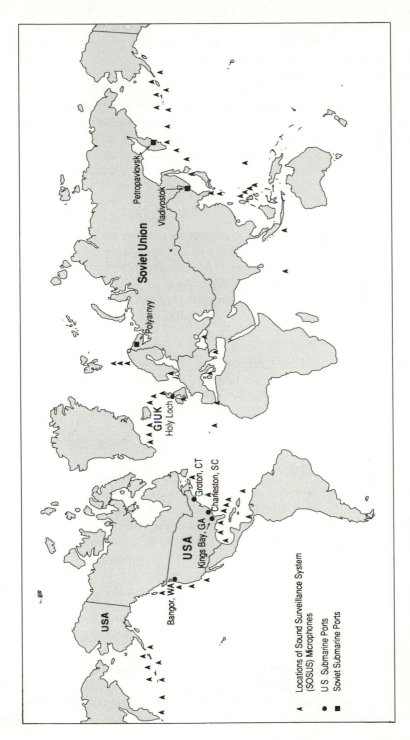

Figure 10. The US Sound Surveillance System

Source: SIPRI data

for SSNs used to guard SSBNs) it may then be the case that the importance of US SOSUS facilities in some areas, that is, the western Atlantic, may have declined a bit. But even in the latter case, the potential role of Soviet SSNs for interdicting SLOCs *en route* to Europe would presumably serve to sustain the importance of such facilities.

Generally speaking, recent reports on US ASW capabilities, and new Soviet developments meant to overcome them, are somewhat pessimistic from the US perspective. Soviet submarine engines are becoming quieter (perhaps abetted by the intelligence coup related to the Toshiba affair), and like the USA they are working on radical new approaches to reduce submarine skin friction so as to increase both quietness and speed.[226] Although new Soviet submarines are increasingly fast and quiet, none can dive deeper than or withstand a hit from modern US torpedoes. But the acoustic systems, both active and passive, are also being improved; and there is increasing attention to 'broad-band' signal processors that would apparently allow sensors to hear a wide spectrum of enemy submarine noises, instead of trying to focus narrowly on particular noises, such as the whine of an engine.[227] Perhaps most important in connection with FMP, a recent report alludes to 'Navy plans to build a network of sensors that will be placed on the ocean floor and connected by miles of fiber optic cables.'[228] The ultimate implications of that for basing access are not clear.

Nuclear detection

One important, but seldom commented upon aspect of the overall US intelligence effort, is that connected with the detection of nuclear explosions. This involves several separate lines of activity.

First, there is the matter of verification of existing arms control treaties, that is, the Limited Test Ban Treaty of 1963 which bans atmospheric testing, and the Threshold Test Ban Treaty of 1974, never ratified by the US Senate (but tacitly adhered to in the manner of SALT II), which bars underground testing of nuclear devices of over 150 kilotons. Second, there is the monitoring of horizontal nuclear proliferation activities of hitherto non-nuclear states, as well as of the non-signatory but nuclear states, China and France. Third—and this has received greater attention of late—there is the contingency of protracted nuclear war during which the USA would want to determine the locations and frequencies of nuclear detonations on both sides and to assess resultant damage, among other reasons, to aid subsequent targeting decisions.

Several interrelated systems are used to pursue the above ends, involving satellites, aircraft and ground stations; the use of ships is also not ruled out. Use of satellites, in connection with FMP, raises the question of external facilities for data down-links and command and control; that of aircraft involves, obviously, bases as well.

According to Richelson, the US space-based nuclear-detection system involves, variously, the various components of the VELA satellite programme begun in the early 1960s; the previously mentioned DSP satellites primarily intended for early warning of missile launches, and the now emerging

NAVSTAR global positioning system.[229] Only two Velas, launched in 1970, remain operational, armed with detectors sensitive to x-rays, gamma rays, neutrons and EMP, and Bhangmeters sensitive to intense bursts of light.[230] As the Vela systems have been in orbit for many years, well preceding the era of inter-satellite communications relay, and are in deep orbit, they presumably require data down-links with some ground stations, details of which are not available.

Later, it is expected that the USA will heavily utilize the GPS satellites (NAVSTAR) for nuclear detection—these will, presumably, be less dependent on ground stations and able to relay communications via DSCS or other satellites. That segment of GPS involved in nuclear detection is called the Integrated Operational NUDETS Detection System (IONDS).[231] The GPS system will consist of 18 satellites (8 are now operational) in 17 610-mile orbits, deployed in three planes, to be used for navigation, targeting, nuclear explosion location (potential damage assessment) and communications.[232] According to Richelson, 'the arrangement will guarantee that at least four to six satellites are in view at all times from any point on or near the earth'.[233] Further, in stating that this 'will allow the detection of nuclear weapons detonations anywhere in the world at any time', it was further stated that the data 'will be reported on a real-time basis, either directly to ground stations or first to airborne terminals or other GPS satellites for subsequent downlink transmissions'.[234] Regarding the DSP, use of DSP East, on geosynchronous station over the Indian Ocean, presumably means use of down-link relays via Nurrungar in Australia and/or Kapaun in FR Germany or, alternatively, via DSCS satellites. The FMP implications of emerging NAVSTAR facilities in this context are not clear, but are probably negligible because of the availability of numerous satellite data links (but there are NAVSTAR command and control or receiver facilities on Ascension, Diego Garcia and Kwajalein as well as in Hawaii (Kaena Point), Guam (Andersen AFB) and Alaska (Adak).[235]

Numerous aircraft types can be used to detect airborne atomic debris left in the wake of explosions (if only the venting of imperfectly conducted underground blasts). One source says that these include the U-2, P-3C, C-135, B-52 and also an HC-130 configured as a sea-water sampler to monitor underwater nuclear tests (monitoring of plutonium-239 separation via krypton-85 analysis is presumably also similarly conducted).[236] For instance, SAC U-2s apparently have operated out of Australian facilities at Sale and Laverton, gathering radio-nuclides as part of a High Altitude Sampling Program.[237] These aircraft are operated by the Air Force Technical Applications Center (AFTAC) and can presumably avail themselves of virtually all the airfields normally open to US use throughout the world. Some of these operations no doubt involve *ad hoc* staging through facilities after an 'event', and the diplomacy of access involved is obscure. But, as there is general convergence of overall interest by most nations with regard to monitoring others' nuclear tests, access in these cases is likely to be permissive.

More germane to FMP are the various US seismic arrays and seismometers located around the world, as well as within the USA.[238] This involves such sub-systems as the Large Aperture Seismic Array in Monterey, the Alaska Long Period Array, and the Norwegian Seismic Array (NORSAR) consisting of seven sub-arrays, centred on Hamar and Karasjok.[239] Additionally, AFTAC operates numerous foreign-based seismometers and seismic arrays, the main locations of which are shown in table 23. Apparently there are also some unmanned detection sites and numerous microbarographs. And, one might assume an impending emphasis on more mobile, covert sites, as one additional aspect of preparation for protracted conflict requiring dispersion, mobility and redundancy.

Table 23. Foreign-based AFTAC seismometers and seismic arrays

Country	Location/details
Australia	Alice Springs, Narrogin, Charters Towers, Amberly and Pearce
Canada	The US Department of Energy operates a station for its Regional Seismic Test Network at Yellowknife Northwest Territories
FR Germany	Wiesbaden (European HQ for nuclear test detection)
Greece	Iraklion
Japan	Misawa and Yokota
Nepal	Earlier microbarograph site for monitoring Chinese atmospheric nuclear tests
Okinawa	Kadena
Panama	Fort Randolph, Howard AFB
Philippines	Clark AFB, Del Monte, and Bukidnon
South Korea	Wongju
Spain	Torrejon AB
Turkey	Belbasi
UK	Lakenheath

Source: SIPRI data and Arkin, W. M. and Fieldhouse, R. W., *Nuclear Battlefields: Global Links in the Arms Race* (Ballinger: Cambridge, Mass., 1985), appendix A.

Geographically and politically speaking, one new focus of US efforts to acquire new access for seismic devices has been China. Thus according to one press report,

The United States is conducting sensitive negotiations to install new seismic devices in China to monitor Soviet underground nuclear tests, according to Reagan Administration and Congressional sources . . . The seismic center, which would be similar to one that went into operation last year in Norway, could help verify Soviet compliance with treaties that currently limit and could eventually ban underground nuclear tests . . . A China-based seismic center would strengthen the U.S. ability to detect and measure Soviet tests at the Semipalatinsk test site in East Kazahkstan . . . The closest seismic base to the main Soviet test site now is in Norway.[240]

This report was verified in 1987 by another stating that seismic devices manned by Chinese workers had been deployed in China's Xingjian Uygur Autonomous Region. This source claimed that the USA actually had nine monitoring sites in China, some for peaceful purposes such as studying earthquakes.[241] It further referred to other seismic research installations in Norway, Pakistan, Turkey, South Korea, India and Japan, among other countries, and said in addition that 'the Air Force operates secret installations around the world to monitor Soviet tests'.[242]

The same article further referred to US efforts at acquiring access to Finland some 1500 miles from another Soviet test site at Novaya Zemlya.[243] It also claimed that AFTAC has 'older, less sophisticated seismic detectors in about 35 countries', a number substantially higher than the countries cited above from open sources.[244] One possible additional site might be at Chiang Mai in Thailand, used to monitor Soviet and Chinese underground nuclear tests, US access to which was apparently retained after the USA lost access to most Thai facilities in 1976.[245] This, the Finnish example cited above and the well-known earlier US use of nuclear monitoring facilities in India (at Nanda Devi and Nanda Kot) illustrate an important point.[246] Nations will often grant access for this purpose even where political ties are weak and other types of access non-existent, because their own interests dictate attention to nuclear activities in surrounding countries and because non-proliferation is one issue where there is little conflict between US and Soviet interests and policies. One such site lost to the USA, that point notwithstanding, was the former Iranian Long-Period Array operated at the University of Tehran to monitor Soviet nuclear tests.

In addition to seismic arrays, the USA also has access overseas to other ground facilities which abet aircraft in monitoring above-ground nuclear explosions. There is one at Mildura in Australia and another at Cagayan de Oro in the Philippines involving radio, atmospheric fluorescense and microbarometric procedures.[247] A facility at Woodbourne in New Zealand has been used to monitor French atmospheric nuclear tests, as was earlier another on Chile's Easter Island.[248]

It is reported that the US Government has established a Regional Seismic Test Network (RSTN) for 'learning how an "in-country" system might be used for monitoring compliance with a comprehensive nuclear test ban treaty', or presumably, something short of that along the lines of the Threshold Test Ban Treaty (TTBT).[249] This, of course, raises the prospect of a wholly new genre of FMP, one that would be located within a rival nation's territory as part of an arms control regime.[250]

V. Soviet technical facilities abroad

As noted, the USSR makes much less use of foreign facilities for technical functions—communications, space, anti-submarine warfare, nuclear detection, and so on—than does the USA. The various reasons, to a degree paralleling those pertaining to air and naval bases, are: much greater utilization of shipboard facilities; the larger (relative to the USA) Soviet land mass in relation to the major focus of the superpower competition along the Eurasian rim, which allows many functions to be performed within the USSR; the still lesser number of aligned client states available to the Soviet Union in the Third World; the practice of utilizing larger numbers of satellites with shorter lives; and the more open nature of Western societies which reduces the (relative) Soviet requirements for proliferated intelligence facilities. Additionally, however, it must be stressed that open-source knowledge of Soviet technical facilities is somewhat limited, so that it is quite possible that scholars tend to underestimate the extent of such Soviet access, particularly where small, mobile and concealable facilities are involved. Ironically, whereas the USSR has striven in recent years to achieve greater land-based access for C³I facilities, the USA—deemed conscious of the political vulnerability of some of its points of access—may now be considering enhanced use of ships for some of these purposes.

Soviet anti-submarine warfare

There is little public information available on a Soviet equivalent to the US SOSUS system, particularly as pertains to land-based systems outside the USSR. Thus, Daniel Ford concludes that: 'the Soviets have no comparable means for the open-ocean tracking of U.S. submarines.'[251] There was, however, a 1978 press report of a Soviet hydrophone apparatus washed ashore in Iceland; whether it was derived from a land- or ship-based array was not clear.[252] It would seem likely that the USSR would desire such systems in or near areas known to be prowling grounds for US submarines, perhaps particularly areas where SSNs patrol in or around the Soviet SSBN bastions in the Norwegian and Barents Seas, and the Sea of Okhotsk. One might similarly assume such installations in Cuba and Viet Nam to be deemed useful, if technically feasible. Again, the information is sparse, and it is likely that the Soviet Union relies on surface ships and perhaps also submarines and aircraft-sown sonabuoys for detection of US submarines, in an area of technical expertise in which the USSR is long thought to have lagged behind the USA. One report states that the Soviet Union uses about 50 auxiliary intelligence ships for ASW work, which maintain a constant presence near important continental US bases such as Charleston, South Carolina; Kings Bay, Georgia; Norfolk, Virginia; Mayport, Florida; and Bangor, Washington; as well as at Holy Loch, Scotland.[253]

Soviet communications with submarines

Unlike the USA, the USSR apparently makes no use of external communications and/or navigation facilities in connection with submarines on patrol. Several sources report that communications with submarines stationed at great distances from the USSR are handled by a network of some 26 VLF and LF transmitters within the USSR itself, apparently sufficient to cover the patrol areas of Soviet SSBNs and SSNs; in the former case, most are kept close to home in the 'bastions', or on stations in the Atlantic or Pacific oceans within range of the home communications stations.[254] Ford refers to six long-range radio transmitters (at Petropavlovsk, Vladivostok, Dikson Ostrov, Kaliningrad, Matochin Shar, and Arkhangelsk) that give orders to Soviet submarines.[255] In addition, Arkin and Fieldhouse report a three-station network of 'Omega-type'

VLF transmitters at Krasnodar, Komsomolsk and Rostov.[256] They also detail a considerable number of LORAN-C type 'Pulsed Phase Radio Navigation System' stations, organized by chains along the western and eastern littorals of the USSR, used to position submarines.[257]

Soviet submarines apparently also receive communications from satellites during brief surfacings. And, one source has indicated the possibility of Soviet use of command and control submarines for relaying communications to other underseas craft within communications distance.[258]

It is hard to say what the contrast between US and Soviet practice in these areas means in relation to targeting. Presumably, much of the Soviet SSBN force, in parallel to its US counterpart, is conceived as a strategic reserve or 'revenge force', that is, one geared to counter-city missions in the absence of hard-target capability. But, Soviet SSBNs located in the Western Atlantic have long been considered as close-in threats to US B-52 bomber bases, critical C³I nodes, and to Washington itself. Those missions would, presumably, require accurate targeting and, hence, the accurate positioning presumably provided by the Loran-C-like networks noted above.

Soviet nuclear detection

As in so many related areas of technical facilities, the USSR appears to deploy far fewer assets on foreign soil for nuclear detection than does the USA, a circumstance only partly explicable by its relatively smaller needs to verify its rival's tests. Hence, according to Richelson:

There are large gaps in Western knowledge concerning the specifics of the Soviet nuclear detonation detection monitoring program. It is not known, at least on an unclassified basis, whether any Soviet satellites (including early warning satellites) are equipped with nuclear detection packages, as are U.S. Defense Support Program, Global Positioning System, Vela, and other satellites. Also, the extent to which reconnaissance aircraft are outfitted with filters and other sensors for detection of nuclear particles in the atmosphere is not known.[259]

Not precluded, however, is Soviet use of other COSMOS satellites for this purpose.

Here too, the USSR makes extensive use of shipborne systems, which according to one US governmental source preceded the 1963 signing of the Partial Test Ban Treaty. Hence, it was earlier reported that: 'Three Soviet ships have appeared within a few miles of the area set aside in the Pacific for U.S. nuclear testing. They reportedly are heavily equipped to monitor U.S. activities in progress and have been actively engaged in obtaining what information is possible on our tests.'[260]

This report noted the capabilities of the 3600-ton hydrometeorological ship *Shokal'skiy*, which was claimed to perform radio-chemical analysis of the debris from explosions so as to provide information on bomb design, yield and similar data and which could also locate the time and approximate locale of explosions from electro-magnetic pulses.[261] It could also launch meteorological rockets to study nuclear effects in the upper atmosphere.

Of course, these ships might, indirectly, be dependent on overseas bases for fuel, water, occasional maintenance, and so on—or, at one level removed, their support ships could also be so dependent, though these operations could, presumably, be independently sustained for reasonable periods of time. But mostly, the Soviet nuclear-detection system depends on its home-based seismographic station network known as the Unified Seismic Observation System—according to Richelson, there are some '168 such stations, 114 of which are regional, which are managed by institutes within each zone'.[262]

There is no clear picture of the emerging Soviet capability for monitoring the progress of a nuclear war via nuclear detection analysis, equivalent to that now being mounted on US satellites. Presumably, ships mounting such capabilities would be highly vulnerable targets, more so than satellites, but the latter are probably the preferred system so as to provide real-time analysis.

Soviet space tracking and other communications

The Soviet global ground network of space-tracking and satellite control facilities is, of course, far less extensive than that of the USA.[263] Again, this is a function of the far more extensive use of shipborne facilities as well as of the lesser external needs dictated by the larger land mass of the USSR, particularly in relation to many satellite orbits which allow direct transmission to the USSR.

At the core of the Soviet space-surveillance system is a network of at least 12 sites within the USSR claimed to be 'equipped with receivers to measure Doppler shifts in radio signals, tracking radars, and photo theodolites and which transmit data to a central computation center'.[264] Additionally, radars associated with anti-ballistic missiles (ABM)—Pushkino, Hen House, Try Add and Dog House—are said to have space-tracking capabilities, along with the controversial (in the context of ABM treaty verification) radar at Abalakova.[265]

Outside the USSR, there are or have been a number of tracking stations in foreign countries. These have been reported in Egypt (Helwan and Aswan) before the Egypto-Soviet break, Mali, Guinea, Cuba and Chad, as well as in Czechoslovakia and Poland.[266] At Santiago de Cuba, for instance, there is an Interkosmos laser radar and also a KIM-3 tracking camera, presumably functionally equivalent to the US Baker-Nunn or GEODSS systems.[267] Perhaps overlapping this grouping, there have been reports of an Interkosmos laser tracking programme (using a laser rangefinder) involving facilities in Egypt, Bolivia, India and Cuba (Santiago de Cuba).[268] And, according to a US government report, 'there have been rumors and reports that the Russians put out feelers that they might like to establish tracking stations in such countries as Indonesia, Australia and Chile'.[269] It is believed that tracking is, or has been, carried out at Khartoum in the Sudan, Afgoi in Somalia, Kerguelen (South Indian Ocean) and Mirnyy (Antarctica).[270] The latter is reported to be an optical tracking facility, probably used in connection with geodetic research.

Noteworthy here is the either existing or aspired-to access for space tracking in countries only weakly aligned with the USSR, or in some cases, aligned with the West. To a degree this may reflect the lesser (relative to naval and air bases) political visibility of such facilities. Or, the Soviet Union may have acquired access in some places by stressing the commercial and/or co-operative multi-national aspects of these activities. Or, such access may have reflected an only temporary phase of alignment with the USSR. Bolivia, during the 1970s, during a somewhat radical political phase, provided the USSR with access for an Interkosmos laser satellite-tracking radar.[271] Chile, from 1970 to 1973, during its more leftist phase, was reported by one source as having provided the USSR with a facility for a transit circle, sited for very precise determination of star positions, to provide accurate data on stars for stellar inertial guidance for some Soviet submarine-launched missiles.[272] The tracking station in Chad during the 1960s and 1970s may have had non-military purposes.[273] India earlier provided a facility at Kavalur for a laser radar, probably for geodetic observation of potential use in calculating strategic missile trajectories.[274] Soviet use of a tracking station in Mali appears to have ceased in 1977.[275] Most baffling was the satellite-tracking station run jointly by France and the USSR on Kerguelen Island in the 1960s, which in studying VLF signals, may have had some relevance for strategic submarine communications systems.[276]

But just because the Soviet Union is reluctant to become too dependent on foreign land-based stations, it has placed considerable emphasis upon ship-borne space-tracking (and also missile-tracking) systems. This involves more than 10 ships—a Soviet source notes that even despite the nation's large land mass, space vehicles are within direct visibility from Soviet territory only for about 9 hours out of 24.[277]

According to one report, one of the major Soviet tracking ships, the *Kosmonaut Vladimir Komarov*, mounted with massive radomes, often frequents Havana harbour, indicating that these operations require some FMP even if, as the same report notes, such ships have ranges of 22 500 nautical miles and 'are capable of 120 days of independent navigation without replacement'.[278]

Concerning Soviet satellite-control functions (that is, reprogramming, repositioning, etc.) there is little publicly available information—the Soviet practice of utilizing numerous satellites for shorter periods probably translates into a lesser requirement for this function, relative to the USA. But it is possible that major satellite ground stations identified in Cuba and Viet Nam may serve that purpose. Ships are apparently also used for this purpose. One report on the *Kosmonaut Pavel Belayev* says one prime function was to 'receive signals from Soyuz spacecraft, while they are out of range of tracking stations on Soviet territory, and to transmit commands to them, acting as a relay between the crew in space and flight controllers on the ground'.[279] Ford, however, pinpoints the principal ground control stations for Soviet satellites—presumably functionally equivalent to the US operation at Sunnyvale, California—at Kalinin north-west of Moscow and at Yevpatoriya in the Crimea.[280]

In the field of communications too, the Soviet Union is far less dependent on foreign land bases than is the USA; correspondingly, far more reliant on ship-borne systems (an exception, of course, are the VLF facilities used to communicate with submarines, perhaps too large to be placed aboard ships). As it is, however, relative to what is known about the USA, there is scant information on how the USSR utilizes the whole of the frequency spectrum for various purposes, how it tries to circumvent countermeasures by redundancy, and so forth.

For the most part, Soviet use of overseas communications facilities focuses on the down-links for the Molniya communications satellites, of which there have been some 50 aloft at a given time in recent years. As it happens, there appears some uncertainty about the respective division of military and civilian usage of the Molniya systems, which is in turn reflected in the difficulties of interpreting the politics of the use of ground stations in other countries. According to Jane's, 'because of their increasing numbers it is certain that the military use them, particularly since there appears to have been no increase in Molniya satellite use for civil communications and broadcasting'.[281] There are some 33 Molniya I satellites, 15 Molniya IIs, and four Molniya IIIs, each with very large payloads. These make two orbits daily, one over the USSR and the other over North America, even as the USSR now moves towards deployment of synchronous satellites for the first time. The new Volna satellites are being positioned respectively over the Atlantic, Pacific and Indian oceans.

Arkin and Fieldhouse identify several satellite ground stations for the Molniya II system located outside the USSR. These are in the German Democratic Republic (Furstenwald), Poland (Kielce), Czechoslovakia (Prague) and perhaps also in Cuba and/or Angola.[282] There are reported satellite communications centres in Ethiopia and Viet Nam as well, perhaps also Mongolia in the form of an 'Orbita' ground station used to relay TV programmes.[283]

Of course, like the USA, the USSR utilizes extensive FMP for communications facilities associated with its large-scale troop and aircraft deployments throughout Eastern Europe, and also in Mongolia and Afghanistan, all areas directly contiguous to the USSR proper. Though there is very little publicly available information on these systems and the location of their facilities, it may be assumed they are similar to the US and NATO infrastructure in Western Europe featuring HF, VLF/microwave and AUTOVON (telephone) systems. Overseas, the facility at Lourdes, Cuba, has been identified as involved in relaying microwave communications to Soviet diplomatic missions elsewhere in Latin America.[284] In South Yemen, the Soviet Navy has an HF radio transmitting and receiving station in the Bir Fuqum area.[285]

But again, ships play an important role. According to one source, regarding the *Kosmonaut Vladimir Komarov*:

The Russians have also said that communications between some spacecraft and Moscow can be maintained on a realtime basis even when not in direct view of the Soviet Union by having the *Kosmonaut Vladimir Komarov* serve as a relay point on Earth, with a further relay from the ship via one of the Molniya I satellites which shares mutual visibility between the ship and the Soviet Union. This type of relay was first mentioned in connection with the Soyuz 6-7-8 flights of October 1969.[286]

And, more recently, with reference to the *Kosmonaut Yuriy Gagarin*:

The ship was described as having over 100 antennas, and via Molniya satellites could reach almost any telephone in the Soviet Union around the clock. It was capable of receiving high data rates from satellites and amplifying weak signals at planetary distances . . . Its automatic systems are said to make it possible to pick up signals from space with high precision even during Force 7 storms and communications are possible simultaneously with two or more satellites. With all four dish antennae facing forward the speed is reduced by two knots.[287]

In discussing four more Soviet ships, all named after cosmonauts who had died, the same report shows that the Soviet ships have very diverse communications capabilities. Thus, for example, there is a reference to a four-dish antenna with 'feeds for the dishes', involving log-periodic antennas providing wide-band coverage from the VHF to UHF ranges up to microwave frequencies.[288] These presumably are closely interconnected with the Molniya satellite network.

The US government report cited above provides some information (and a map) on the general locations of Soviet tracking ships and, hence, of the locales where they might seek port access or at least mooring buoys. Among them: off Sable Island, Nova Scotia; in the western Mediterranean near Gibraltar; the Gulf of Guinea; off Mozambique and Madagascar; off Honduras; east of the Philippines; and north of New Zealand.[289] Large tracking ships apparently moor at Havana and/or Santiago while tracking some flights; Trinidad is also mentioned in this context.[290] Some of the other locations would provide rationales for periodic access to Conakry or Maputo, maybe also to Nicaragua, as well as providing further indications of the Soviet need for access somewhere in the South Pacific. (The US government report states that three large Soviet ships take turns serving in the Caribbean area to extend Soviet deep-space coverage.[291])

Soviet early-warning and space military support systems

Regarding early-warning satellites' down-links, the USSR does not have an equivalent to the US instantaneous photo-reconnaissance capability nor early-warning or electronic-intelligence satellites in geosynchronous orbit.[292] Instead, film packets are 'dropped back to earth, retrieved, and then processed'. Most likely this does not ever require foreign access, though it is to be noted that in some instances, Soviet space-tracking ships have been used to retrieve space capsules, which have then been airlifted home to the USSR from other nations such as India.[293] Whether this could be done with sensitive information, that is, photo-reconnaissance or ELINT data, outside normal peacetime conditions is not easily ascertained.

In recent years, the USSR has moved to deploy some newer space-based military support systems. The most recent Pentagon *Soviet Military Power* refers to a radar ocean-reconnaissance satellite (RORSAT) and an electronic-intelligence ocean-reconnaissance satellite (EORSAT), 'used to locate naval forces that could be targeted for destruction by anti-ship weapons launched from Soviet platforms'.[294] The USA is said not to have comparable capability. But, there is no evidence of Soviet use of external facilities in this connection, neither is there any open-source information regarding satellite imagery, reconnaissance and space-based electronic-intelligence assets.

The same source reports on ongoing Soviet deployment of the global navigation satellite system known as GLONASS, the Soviet equivalent of the US NAVSTAR global positioning system.[295] This may eventually involve more than 20 satellites, but so far there is no evidence of requirements for external ground stations.

Soviet Military Power also reports Soviet plans for a space-based geosynchronous launch-detection satellite system by the end of the 1980s, presumably one similar to the US DSP satellites.[296] It may not yet be clear whether like DSP (which utilizes ground relay stations in Australia and FR Germany), the Soviet equivalent will require ground access, say, in Cuba. The same publication reports impending Soviet expansion of the number of communications satellites to involve some 100 new payloads 'in more than 25 positions in the geostationary orbit belt'.[297] Some of these will be used, similar to US practice, as relays between ground and ship stations, presumably lessening the long-term need for the latter.

Soviet SIGINT

The USSR depends considerably less on land-based SIGINT collection stations than the USA, though, like the latter, it utilizes a variety of means: satellites, surface ships and submarines, aircraft, equipment based in embassies, and so on. And again, similar to the situation with respect to space tracking and early warning, one must be aware of the sometimes only indirect importance of external access; for instance, for fuelling ships used in lieu of land facilities.

At any given time, the USSR operates six SIGINT satellites—roughly equivalent in purpose to the US Rhyolite systems—and one of which passes over the USA daily to monitor the emissions of important US radars such as Cobra Dane and the PAVE PAWS SLBM warning radars.[298] As mentioned above, considerable ELINT collection is performed by aircraft—Tu-95Ds which also perform photo-reconnaissance, and the IL-18 Coot A, which has a primary ELINT mission.[299] Aeroflot planes may also be involved in monitoring VHF and UHF bands in Europe. At sea, the Soviet Union maintains some 61 auxiliary intelligence ships (AGIs) plus other vessels presumed to have SIGINT capabilities, that is, naval survey, naval research, even covert tramp steamers and depot ships—the AGIs in turn perform ocean-surveillance functions as well.[300] The latter have also been used to monitor submarine missile launches and emissions during wars in the Third World, such as those in the Middle East.

Even submarines can be used for these purposes, that is, telemetry collection, monitoring of port and base areas, tapping into cable lines, and underwater positioning of sensors.

The USSR has been reported to have major SIGINT facilities at Lourdes, Cuba; Cam Ranh Bay, Viet Nam; Ethiopia (2); South Yemen; Syria; and Afghanistan.[301] That at Lourdes is reported to be devoted to interpretation of satellite communications.[302] There may be additional ground stations in Libya and Iraq, though the fate of the latter might be questioned since Moscow has given only modest support to Iraq in its war with Iran, particularly in the early stages, in part because of the cross-pressures from its relationships with Libya and Syria.

The Lourdes facility is a large one, operated by some 2000 Soviet personnel— it became a prominent issue in 1979 at the time of the imbroglio in the USA over the Soviet 'Cuban brigade' amid the SALT II confirmation hearings. The facility of 50 buildings houses an antenna field, satellite receiver, and so on and targets US civilian and military communications, that is, B-52 communications, Fort Benning and Cape Canaveral, the naval headquarters at Norfolk, and so on.[303] According to Richelson, the Lourdes facility, complemented by a similar one in the USSR, 'gives complete coverage of the global beams of all US geosynchronous communications satellites'.[304]

At Cam Ranh Bay, the Soviet Union has an important facility from which to monitor both land and ocean-based emissions—there are two HF/DF sites used to gain locational data on US fleet units in the Pacific.[305] The US bases in the Philippines are obvious targets.

The four sites in Afghanistan aid collection, variously, vis-à-vis China, Pakistan, Iran and the Persian Gulf area.[306] And, of course, these sites merely add to the capabilities of hundreds of SIGINT sites located within the USSR.

Finally, though not really qualifying as FMP as such, it is to be noted that the Soviet Union has long made extensive use of embassies for intelligence collection—for that reason Moscow tries to get its embassies located on high ground. The embassy in Washington, in particular, is considered highly capable of intercepting all manner of communications, including considerable government traffic in Washington. There is a massive capability for intercepting and recording microwave telephone conversations, among other things obviously very useful for industrial espionage.

Aside from those mentioned above, the Soviet Union has some other land-based intelligence-interception facilities located outside the USSR. In Laos, there is an air-surveillance radar, obviously directed against the PRC.[307] According to the IISS, there is a Soviet monitoring station (elsewhere identified as a radar site) in São Tomé and Príncipe, even despite the latter's recent political shift away from Soviet tutelage.[308] In Cuba, along with the Lourdes facility, there are also air-defence surveillance radars, the Tall King system, apparently operated by Soviet personnel.[309] In the GDR, there are HF-finding antennas used in connection with jamming operations; in Poland, a SIGINT station and HF direction-finder at Sinajscie, and at Bierdzany a receiver site for a Soviet

OTH radar transmitter located at Kiev.[310] Throughout Eastern Europe, there are large numbers of air-surveillance radars equivalent to the NATO NADGE system—in Hungary, for instance, some 130 sites manned by Soviet personnel are reported.[311]

The Soviet fishing fleet and communications/intelligence: general

The preceding discussions have indicated that the Soviet Union uses fishing fleets—also merchant vessels and oceanographic research ships—for a variety of functions related to communications and intelligence; including space tracking, nuclear detection, perhaps satellite control, telemetry interception in connection with missile tests, and so on. As noted, these narrowly or specifically technical functions must be juxtaposed to an identifiably broader purpose for fishing fleets, that of serving as an initial wedge for access in new places *en route* to larger-scale access involving more explicitly military purposes. And, of course, access for fishing fleets and utilization of foreign facilities for crew rotation and R&R will presumably enhance the possibilities for HUMINT operations as well.

Because of the chronic shortcomings of Soviet agriculture—reflected, until recently at least, in nearly annual efforts to import grains—Soviet people have long depended on the protein derived from fish—to a much greater extent than that common to US and European dietary norms. A vast Soviet fishing fleet has been developed (abetted by Cuban and other East Bloc vessels) which roams the world's fishing grounds and provides huge annual catches. That fleet grew from some 358 units in 1950 to some 4500 by the late 1970s, and now accounts for more than half the world's tonnage, albeit still a lesser annual fishing catch than that of rival Japan.[312]

The large Soviet fishing trawlers have, as noted, long been assumed to carry sophisticated SIGINT gear, radars, ASW equipment (hydrophones, and so on). But because of their ostensible peaceful purpose, they have been able to gain access where overt military access would presumably be denied, for instance, in Spain's Canary Islands and nowadays (see below) in the south-west Pacific.[313]

The Soviet fishing fleet, believed to be co-ordinated by a centralized command and control system, conducts virtually global operations. East of the Atlantic Ocean, it has concentrated in the North Sea, the English Channel, in the Great Sole Bank and off the Shetland Islands; off the United States and Canada, in the Grand, Sable Island and Georges Banks. Other more recent favourite fishing grounds have been off the west coast of Africa, near Walvis Bay, the Gulf of Guinea, the Cape Verde area, and the Canary Islands; in the South Atlantic,[314] Soviet fishing boats prowl near the Falkland Islands and South Georgia. Soviet whaling fleets operate off Antarctica. In the Indian Ocean, the Soviet Union exploits fisheries near Farquhar Island, near the Seychelles and Mauritius, near Kerguelen Island on the Madagascar plateau, in the Mozambique Channel, and off the Australian North West Cape. In the Pacific Ocean, fishing operations used to be concentrated in the Bering Sea and off the US West Coast, but have now declined.[315]

The new 200-mile exclusive economic zones (EEZs), introduced by the UN Convention on the Law of the Sea and enforced by many nations (including the USA and Canada), have forced the Soviet Union (and others) out of some formerly used fishing grounds and prompted a search for new ones, in some cases at great distances from Soviet home ports. And, the size of the Soviet fishing fleet, its far-flung operations, and the demands for its efficient utilization, have dictated requirements for replenishment, repairs, and rotation of crews, so as not to have to bring the fishing ships all the way home.

Partly to offset the impact of EEZs (but in many cases preceding their introduction), the USSR has offered fishing aid to—or entered joint fishing ventures with—a large number of nations. Some of these are allies or states closely aligned with the USSR: Algeria, Angola, Guinea, Guinea-Bissau, India, Iraq, Mozambique, Peru, South Yemen, Syria, Tanzania, Viet Nam, and so on.[316] The list also includes numerous pro-Western and neutralist states: Argentina, Benin, Chile, the Gambia, Ghana, Greece, Kenya, Mauritania, Mauritius, Morocco, North Yemen, Pakistan, the Philippines, Portugal, Senegal, Sierra Leone, Singapore, Somalia, Sri Lanka, Sudan, Tunisia, and so on.[317] In many cases, from the host's perspective (or the partner in a joint venture), economic rationales presumably outweigh or at least overshadow, political ones.

In 1987, what is involved—particularly as it is perceived by Western security analysts—was made prominent by Soviet efforts at acquiring a toehold for fishing access in the newly independent (since 1980) nation of Vanuatu, formerly known as the New Hebrides.[318] The latter signed an agreement to give Soviet fishing vessels access for buying bait and making repairs. (There had been a previous similar arrangement with nearby Kiribati.[319]) The commander of the US Pacific fleet was quoted as ridiculing the description of the accord as commercial, saying 'they are certainly after more than fish'.[320]

The agreement, involving a $1.5 million deal, gave Soviet fishing boats rights to fish inside Vanuatu's 200-mile EEZ, and to use its ports for provisioning and repairs.[321] Beyond that there were disagreements over what level of intelligence work might be involved (on land or at sea); or rather, whether the 'opening wedge' argument regarding enlarged naval access was the main point. A geopolitical analysis of the military implications involved, at least hypothetically, might cover satellite positions, ASW possibilities, the proximity to Kwajalein, Australia, New Zealand, and so on.

By 1988, however, because of a new trend running counter to the above discussion, the USSR appeared to be meeting increasing problems regarding access for its fishing fleets; specifically in Africa. One article details the cancellation of, or limitations on, Soviet fishing access to waters offshore of Equatorial Guinea, Guinea-Bissau, Liberia, Morocco, Senegal and Sierra Leone.[322] The first two of these countries were believed to have provided the USSR with naval access in addition to the possible intelligence access associated with fishing fleets.

Intelligence-collection ships

Compared with the USA, with its heavy reliance on satellites and land-based facilities, the USSR relies considerably on intelligence-collection ships—'spy ships'—normally designated 'AGIs', for signals intelligence. These ships regularly patrol off US submarine bases such as Holy Loch, Guam and Charleston, and monitor aircraft carriers operating near Virginia and Florida, and missile activity at Cape Canaveral.

The importance of this AGI fleet has been stated as follows in one authoritative recent publication,

A significant element of the unparalleled growth of Soviet sea power since 1956 has been the emphasis placed on expanding the country's intelligence-collection fleet. Although Moscow has often used submarines, surface ships, and aircraft for intelligence gathering, this fleet, under the centralized control of the Soviet Navy, remains the principal 'eyes and ears of Soviet naval intelligence'. The core of this fleet is a rapidly growing number of passive intelligence collection ships, which are dedicated to the collection of signal intelligence (SIGINT), electronic intelligence (ELINT), and communications intelligence (COMINT). The Soviet Union currently have more than fifty of these ships.[323]

As shown in table 24, there are 10 classes of Soviet AGIs, most of which are converted trawlers, whalers, tugs and oceanographic survey ships. Only recently, however, has the Soviet Union begun building intelligence collectors from the keel up, such as with the Primorye and Balzam classes.[324] These classes are also far larger than their predecessors, and 'these tremendous increases in size mean that the newer ships have much greater collection and processing capabilities and are able not only to collect but also to process and analyze information'.[325] They are also now armed, with short-range SAMs and Gatling guns, another change from past practice.[326]

The Soviet AGIs have near global patrolling areas. There is a concentrated

Table 24. Soviet intelligence-collection ships

Class	Ship's name
Alpinist	GS 7, GS 39
Balzam	*Balzam* SSV 516
Dnepr	*Izmeritel, Protraktor*
Mayak	*Aneroid, Khersones, Kurs, Kursograf, Ladoga*, GS 239, GS 242, GS 439 (ex *Girorulevoy*)
Mirnyy	*Bakan, Lotsman, Val, Vertikal*
Modified Pamir	SSV 480 (ex-*Gidrograf*), *Peleng*
Moma	SSV 512 (ex-*Arkhipelag*), *Ekvator, Ilmen, Kildin, Nakhodka, Pelorus, Seliger* SSV 504, *Vega, Yupiter*
Nikolai Zubov	SSV . . . *Gavril Sarychev* (mod), SSV 503 *Khariton Laptev*, SSV 469 *Semen Chelyushkin*
Primorye	*Primorye* SSV 501, *Kavkaz* SSV 591, *Krim, Zabaikalye* SSV 464, *Zakarpatye, Zaporozhiye*
Okean	*Alidada, Ampermetr, Barograf, Barometr, Deflektor, Ekholot, Gidrofon, Krenometr, Linza, Lotlin, Reduktor, Repiter, Teodolit, Traverz, Zond*

Source: Watson, B. and Watson, S., *The Soviet Navy* (Westview Press: Boulder, Colo., 1986), p. 110.

effort to monitor off the south-eastern coast of the USA (where US surface and submarine units are concentrated); in the English Channel, the Norwegian Sea and off Holy Loch. In the Indian Ocean and Mediterranean Sea, Western naval movements are monitored particularly near the straits of Gibraltar, Hormuz and Bab El Mandeb, and the Suez Canal. In the Pacific Ocean, there is corresponding emphasis off the coasts of China, Japan, Guam and in the waters around Viet Nam.[327]

The dependence of these 'spy ships' on provisioning from foreign ports is difficult to gauge, but must certainly be considerable. As noted by one source, the Soviet Union has chosen 'not to build an auxiliary fleet of the size necessary to reduce out-of-area base support to a manageable minimum . . .Ship designs, both for ease of maintenance and for reasons of habitability, still are notoriously poor . . . Unlike U.S. ships, most Soviet ships cannot distill enough fresh water and are dependent upon water tankers.'[328]

This situation has necessitated frequent operational port visits by auxiliaries to take on food and fresh water, which are then transferred to combatants, presumably also AGIs, at roadsteads or at sea.[329] This presumably further directs attention to the main Soviet basing hosts and clients—Cuba, Angola, Syria, Viet Nam, South Yemen, and so on—as critical to fuelling and otherwise provisioning the Soviet Union's global AGI effort.

Soviet broadcasting facilities

Although the Soviet Union is engaged in a much more ambitious effort at foreign broadcasting—as measured by programme hours, transmitters, numbers of languages covered, and so on—than is the USA with its Voice of America, there appears somewhat less dependence on access to overseas facilities.[330] In part this has to do with the power and modernity of home-based Soviet transmitters, which can bounce short-wave transmissions off the ionosphere at 2000-km hops.[331] Because the Soviet Union encounters few problems with jamming (China may be an exception), there is a lesser need for relay stations to amplify broadcasts and, hence, to overcome the jamming.

Recently, however, the USSR has begun to use transmitters in Cuba for broadcasts to the USA (these will not be jammed in exchange for a Soviet promise not to jam VOA broadcasts to the USSR).[332] And it is believed that the Soviet Union used Cuban relay transmitters for earlier broadcasts elsewhere to Latin America.

These relay stations, while not directly constituting FMP, have important implications in connection with basing access. The broadcasts are one important vehicle for denying such bases to rival powers. Soviet broadcasts to the Third World harp constantly on the theme of the alleged menace of various US overseas facilities in an effort to create internal political opposition to them and, hence, to alter government policies.[333]

VI. British, French and other nations' technical facilities abroad

For the most part, the global competition for access for C^3I and space-related facilities is a two-nation game. But there are some instances of British and French facilities in these categories, even if not intended to support a truly global military presence either at the conventional or nuclear level.

The UK

The UK, for instance, which deploys SSBNs and SSNs in the eastern Atlantic, has LF transmitters at Bermuda and Gibraltar; the latter are capable of reaching across the Mediterranean to the Indian Ocean (until 1976 the UK had naval communications facilities at Mauritius and Singapore, when it also still maintained a naval presence east of Suez).[334] It has another at Port Stanley in the Falklands, which would obviously be of value in case of resumption of hostilities in that area.[335] It also deploys an RAF/UKADGE early-warning radar at Sornfelli in the Danish-controlled Faeroe Islands.[336]

Britain also fields some additional, scattered C^3I assets overseas. It has a major SIGINT site on Cyprus at Pergamos/Dhekelia.[337] Elsewhere on Cyprus, the UK has a troposcatter communications relay, a Skynet satellite-communications terminal and an OTH radar in the Troodos Mountains capable of monitoring missile tests within the USSR.[338] There are reported Government Communications Headquarters (GCHQ) SIGINT stations on Ascension (Two Boats) and St. Helena Islands; also at Darwin, Australia (earlier, there were others in Botswana, Aden, Bahrain, Malta, Mauritius, Singapore and on Oman's Masirah Island).[339] There is a COMINT and HF/DF facility at Gibraltar.[340] Two other SIGINT stations are located at Hong Kong (at Little Sai Wan and Tai Mo Shan) for interception of radio traffic within China, and there is a major one at Diepholz in FR Germany, along with other signals units at Teufelsberg, Jever, Celle, Darnenberg and Gorleben.[341] A former US-run nuclear-detection site at Pearce, Australia is now operated by the British Atomic Energy Authority.[342] Earlier, there was a communications relay facility on Mauritius.

Britain also contributes to the overall Western intelligence effort via some jointly operated facilities. In conjunction with Australia, it operates an ocean-surveillance radar at Hong Kong, once directed against the People's Republic of China, now used to monitor Soviet fleet movements in the SLOCs between Siberia and Viet Nam.[343] (Australia and New Zealand jointly operate a similar facility at Singapore.) The USA and UK jointly operate such a facility at Diego Garcia. These and other such facilities—an Australian installation at Darwin, US-operated bases at Edzell, Scotland and Brawdy, Wales, constitute a global system code-named Bullseye for direction-finding interception of ships at sea.[344] These and related activities are discussed by Richelson and Ball in the context of the multilateral UKUSA arrangement entered into by the USA, UK, Canada, .

Australia and New Zealand in 1947 in the aftermath of World War II.[345]

In common with the USA, the USSR and perhaps other powers, the UK operates SIGINT facilities in numerous embassies throughout the world. Among those singled out by Richelson and Ball are those in Czechoslovakia, Egypt, Ghana, Hungary, Kenya, Malawi, Poland, Saudi Arabia, Sierra Leone, South Africa and the USSR.[346]

The UK does use some overseas communications facilities in connection with its Skynet satellites. These transportable stations have operated at Cyprus, Singapore and Hong Kong; earlier at Bahrain and Gan in the Maldives Islands.[347] These stations, perhaps somewhat in imitation of Soviet practice, have been supplemented by the SCOT shipborne satellite communications system designed for installation on ships down to frigate size. The Royal Navy is reported planning procurement of some 40 of these units.[348]

The Skynet system was conceived in the 1960s, and it was only in 1974 that the British-built Skynet 2B was successfully launched into orbit.[349] It was stationed over the Seychelles, and has two channels in the HF frequency range. It is controlled from the Oakhanger control station in the UK, that is, London has had no need for external access to a satellite control facility.[350]

Britain apparently plans on moving ahead with a Skynet 3 system as Skynet 2 approaches the end of its useful life, and as it appears that NATO and the DSCS satellites will not be able to provide the UK, particularly the Royal Navy, with the additional capacity it will need.[351]

In 1987, reports emerged—on the basis of leaked information—about plans to launch the first British spy satellite, a SIGINT satellite with the code name Zircon, claimed to be for the interception of radio signals and other communications from the USSR, Eastern Europe and the Middle East.[352] It was not immediately clear whether that would require utilization of related external ground relay or control stations, given the proximity of the targeted areas to the UK itself.

Otherwise, Britain has long operated at least two other technical facilities within closely allied Canada. There is an LF transmitter used for North Atlantic Fleet broadcasts at Halifax, and a seismic array at Yellowknife used to collect data on Soviet underground nuclear tests.[353]

France

France, once the possessor of a colonial empire and corresponding basing network second only to Britain's, now has a quasi-global military presence perhaps equal to that of the latter, if only a far smaller presence than that of the two superpowers. France's naval presence in the Indian Ocean and its deployments of aircraft in Africa are described above. Additionally, France has some overseas facilities associated with communications, intelligence and satellite tracking, control, and launching, and so on. This tends, furthermore, to be a somewhat independent presence, in contrast to the UK, some of whose technical facilities are linked to those of the USA, Canada and Australia through the UKUSA and other co-operative arrangements, and whose missile and nuclear weapons testing have also been conducted in or from allies' territories (often Commonwealth).

To support the deployment of its SSBNs and SSNs operative in the eastern Atlantic, along with its surface fleets, France has a number of VLF and LF communications transmitters within France itself. Some of these can presumably be used to contact submarines far from France. There are LF transmitters at Brest (Finistère), Cherbourg and La Regine (Aude), and Toulon, the latter two for the Mediterranean.[354] There are VLF transmitters at S'Assise, Rosnay, and Kerlouan (Finistère); and VLF/LF at Croix d'Hins (Gironde).[355] Paris is also apparently moving towards ELF capability at Rosnay for submarine communications; the latter is further abetted by four Transall C-160s modified for VLF airborne relay similar to the US TACAMO system for emergency communications with submarines.[356]

There are also a couple of Loran-C facilities within France to assist positioning of submarines, at Lessay (Manche) and Soustons (Landes).[357]

The overseas structure for such activities is not large. There are LF transmitters at Papeete, Tahiti; New Caledonia, Senegal and Martinique, corresponding to fairly major French naval deployments.[358] France also operates the Omega station at Mafate, Réunion, once part of the now somewhat obsolete US global Omega network.[359] It is to be noted, of course, that most of these facilities—Senegal excluded—are within French overseas *départements* or remnant colonial possessions; hence, excluded from the quid pro quo diplomacy of FMP.

France does have a number of overseas fleet broadcast system facilities associated with its global OMAR (Organization Mondiale Inter-Armee de Transmissions) and OMIT (Organization Maritime de Transmissions) HF communications system for its surface fleets, some of these collocated with the above VLF/LF systems directed mostly to submarines. The OMAR links are at Djibouti, Guadeloupe, Martinique (apparently used as a relay to French possessions in the Pacific), New Caledonia, Papeete, Réunion, Dakar (Senegal) and Kerguelen Island in the southern Indian Ocean.[360] There are a number of ground links to the Symphonie-2 satellite communications system, for instance, at Guadeloupe and Réunion (on Réunion at Saint Denis there is also a French Air Force communications relay station for communications between French bases throughout Africa and the Indian Ocean area); there is an apparent optical satellite-tracking station at Padefontin, South Africa; additionally, there are several other space-tracking and satellite telemetry stations in relation to the Symphonie satellite programme: Las Palmas (Canary Islands), Brazzaville (Congo); Kourou (French Guyana) and at Ouagadougou (Upper Volta).[361] These latter are part of the 'Iris' network of satellite telemetry receiving stations.[362] The facility at Ouagadougou had long co-existed with a US Baker-Nunn satellite-tracking camera located there.[363]

Command and control of French satellites is apparently handled entirely from a number of stations within France, under the *Centre de Détection et de Control* (CDC), some of these collocated with early-warning radars. Arkin and Fieldhouse cite primary control centres at Brest, Cinq-Mars-La-Pile, Contrexeville, Doullens, Drachenbronn and Mt. Angel (Nice); secondary centres at Narbonne and Prunay.[364] Some of the radars are linked to the NATO NADGE system for early warning.[365]

The degree of dependence by France on foreign facilities for SIGINT is not clear—there is little information available in the public domain. Similarly unclear are French capabilities for satellite reconnaissance—important, for instance, for nuclear targeting in the USSR. There are no reported existing ground stations for such purposes, though it is possible that such activities might be collocated with other technical facilities, for instance, the VLF stations in French outposts such as Martinique. It is also possible that SIGINT interception capability could have been 'hung' on to the Symphonie satellites. Otherwise, France probably bases some SIGINT capability on ships operating out of ports such as Djibouti, Réunion, Dakar, and so on. Though it is shrouded in secrecy, it is probable that France is availed of NATO or US-based data for SIGINT, targeting and so on, despite France's withdrawal from military cooperation with NATO.

Regarding satellites, it is important to note that the French-controlled facility at Kourou, French Guyana, is the rocket-launching pad for the European Space Agency (ESA), especially for its Ariane rockets carrying satellites into orbit.[366] It is now being considered for launching some US satellites. As is discussed in chapter 7, this type of facility, of which globally there are a limited number, may now increasingly be discussed in the context of protracted war scenarios, conventional or nuclear, wherein major powers may perceive the requirement for launching replacement satellites so as to 'heal' or replenish destroyed reconnaissance and SIGINT assets.

VII. Other nations' C³I and space facilities

While the bulk of any discussion about C³I and satellite-related external facilities pertains to the USA and the USSR, much less so to the UK and France, it is worth noting that the ongoing pace of military technological development, and the diffusion of military capabilities to second-tier powers, raise the issue of whether other nations will seek facilities of these sorts.

Of course, there are some jointly fielded and used NATO facilities juxtaposed to those of the UK and the USA—these constitute a form of FMP for the remaining NATO nations. In the 1960s, there was the Initial Defense Communication Satellite Program (IDCSP), which used two transportable earth stations known as MASCOT. In a phase II for NATO, two medium-capacity satellites similar to Skynet II were launched, with 12 earth terminals, and a more elaborate phase III is imminent.[367]

The PRC has some 10 satellite-tracking stations within its borders; also some five VLF transmitters for communications with naval forces.[368] Presumably there are also land-based SIGINT stations within the PRC itself. But again, there are no such facilities on foreign soil, which would at any rate not be expected given the PRC's lack of colonial possessions, and its paucity of arms transfer clients and/or formal alliances. Recently, however, the PRC has become a dominant supplier of arms to Iran and, to a lesser degree, Iraq. It had long been a key arms supplier to Pakistan. Whether in the former cases facilities near the USSR are involved or aspired to, is not here known. One recent report merely cited commercial rationales, and that of putting additional pressure on the USSR in connection with the latter's involvement in Afghanistan. (China hosts US facilities on a joint basis and presumably shares some intelligence on the USSR.)

Japan may some day become a far more important military power—obviously, it has the technical wherewithal to compete in areas such as space, submarines, surface navies, and so on. Though it too will no doubt initially have a regionally based military force, it is at least possible it will require an external presence in some areas, particularly given the small size of its homeland, which makes effective space-tracking and other functions difficult. If so, that could eventually drive a much larger arms selling effort by Japan which, obviously, has enormous latent potential in that area.

The British Commonwealth states—which, as noted, are partners to the UKUSA arrangements—make some use of foreign access. There have been Australian SIGINT facilities in Malaysia and Singapore (collocated with an air force presence but closed in 1975),[369] Papua (Port Moresby) and Hong Kong (operated with British GCHQ), and Canada operates a similar facility at Bermuda.[370]

Otherwise, there are as yet few if any examples of smaller or Third World countries utilizing external access for C³I facilities. Earlier, for instance, there were some vague reports of Israeli use of access to some Ethiopian-owned islands in the Red Sea, during the reign of Haile Selassie, possibly in connection with intelligence or communications functions.[371]

VIII. Conclusions

Amid the blizzard of detail describing the communications, intelligence and space facilities used 'out of area' or 'out of country' by the major powers, several main points or trends appear to stand out. These points for the most part merely parallel or follow upon conclusions emerging from the analysis of 'non-technical', that is, 'traditional' naval and air bases in chapters 2 and 3.

First, it is clear that the whole subject of foreign-based C³I and related facilities for the most part involves a two-nation global contest—in a way, the rival networks so very well reflect the bipolar and global nature of the struggle for influence and access between the superpowers. France and the UK each have far fewer such assets, they are less global in scope and purpose, and they reflect very specific regional and or functional purposes, that is, the maintenance of a modicum of deterrence *vis-à-vis* the USSR by SSBNs in the eastern Atlantic, France's nuclear testing apparatus in the south-west Pacific, and so on. The bulk of French and British facilities are domiciled in the remnants of former empires: Ascension, Bermuda, Diego Garcia, Gibraltar, Hong Kong and others in the one case; French Guyana, Guadeloupe, New Caledonia, Réunion and Tahiti in the other. There are very few exceptions, for example, France's access to Senegal and Djibouti, both former Francophone colonies which are now independent. Generally speaking, it is only the superpowers who, on a large scale, have competed on the basis of alignments with ideologically like-minded clients, usually cemented by arms transfer relations, but with access a constantly contingent and bargained-over matter.

Because only the superpowers are engaged in a fully global contest, not only for political influence but also for the contingency of actual conflict anywhere along the escalation ladder from localized conventional war to all-out nuclear war, it is they alone who deploy a significant number of global technical systems. Only they have elaborate early-warning systems—in space and on the ground—in connection with initiation of a nuclear war. Only they have global SIGINT capabilities conducted from a variety of platforms against a variety of signals for various reasons. Only they have global nuclear-detection capabilities and elaborate capabilities for ASW *vis-à-vis* rivals' SSBNs and SSNs. Only they have the capability for RORSAT and EORSAT necessary to conduct a serious global naval engagement, whether at the conventional or nuclear level. And, of course, only they are beginning to move ahead with ASATs, the inevitable contingency planning for space war, and the corresponding variety of requirements for external land access. The medium powers, by comparison, have facilities concentrated for the purposes of communications with surface fleets and small SSBN forces; they can at any rate rely upon and tie in with superpower capabilities. Some medium powers, such as the PRC, FR Germany and Japan, have essentially nothing in the way of access to technical facilities, their military requirements being correspondingly narrow.

There has appeared an ineluctable trend in recent years towards the attachment of more and more importance to satellites, including supersession by the latter of some functions—in whole or part—previously served by land-based facilities. Indeed, the political problems and economic costs of the latter—including the contingent nature of access during crisis or war—have been instrumental in driving the increased reliance on satellites: communication of early warning of missile launches, SIGINT and nuclear detection. But, both superpowers have stressed overlapping and redundant systems, wherein both rely somewhat equally on satellites, but with the USA reliance on overseas land facilities matched by the relatively much greater use of ships by the Soviet Union.

For all the obvious reasons—geography; power-over-distance factors in relation to Europe and the Persian Gulf; the smaller size of the US homeland relative to the USSR; the closed nature of the Soviet political system, placing relatively greater demands on the USA for technical means of surveillance; the US role as a maritime power and the Soviet role as a continental land power; the greater US reliance on technology and qualitative military factors—the USA still fields a much larger network of overseas technical facilities than does the USSR. This parallels the much larger external presence of the United States as measured by air and naval bases, and by the various measures of naval 'presence', that is, ship-days at sea and port calls. The greater Soviet reliance on surface naval ships, fishing vessels, AGIs, and so on, magnifies the impact of these factors.

In the late 1980s a new trend towards dispersion, concealment and proliferation of technical facilities, that is, C^3I, is apparent. This reflects the heightened interest in protracted war, conventional or nuclear; the increasingly contingent nature of access, particularly in crisis conditions, that is, the 'decoupling' phenomenon; and growing concerns about the vulnerability of satellites to pre-emptive attack and also significant intra-war attrition in conditions not easily lending themselves to reconstitution of such assets. Whether this will in the future lead to a resurgence of efforts at acquiring land-based C^3I assets, or, rather, to moving them out to sea—or both—is not yet clear. Such trends will be driven by still newer technological developments as well as by those pertaining to the politics of access. Most likely, full or partial withdrawal of US forces from Western Europe—whether at US or European initiative—would result in some increased US reliance on shipborne systems in the numerous technical areas discussed here.

It is important to note, of course, that this trend towards mobility is by no means restricted to C^3I systems; rather, is also reflected in newer ICBM models (deployed on the Soviet side, talked about on the US side), in the deployment of SLCMs at sea (on submarines and also such as the US TLAMs based on surface ships) in lieu of land-based intermediate nuclear forces, and so on. These trends promise to be continued.

Notes and references

[1] This recognition has been reflected in the publication of a number of prominent works to be cited extensively throughout this chapter: Arkin, W. M. and Fieldhouse, R. W., *Nuclear Battlefields: Global Links in the Arms Race* (Ballinger: Cambridge, Mass., 1985); Ford, D., *The Button* (Simon and Schuster: New York, 1985); Stares, P. B., *Space and National Security* (Brookings Institution: Washington, DC, 1987); Richelson, J. T., *The U.S. Intelligence Community* (Ballinger: Cambridge, Mass., 1985); Richelson, J. T., *Sword and Shield: The Soviet Intelligence and Security Apparatus* (Ballinger: Cambridge, Mass., 1986); Richelson, J. T. and Ball, D., *The Ties That Bind* (Allen and Unwin: Boston, Mass., 1985); Bracken, P., *The Command and Control of Nuclear Forces* (Yale University Press: New Haven, Conn., 1983); and Blair, B., *Strategic Command and Control* (Brookings Institution: Washington, DC, 1985).

[2] EMP is discussed in Blair (note 1), at various points in relation to aircraft vulnerability, AUTOVON, hardened aircraft, Minuteman vulnerability, submarine vulnerability, etc. Regarding the possible use of meteorites for monitoring radio communications during a nuclear war in which EMP blanked out ordinary signals, see 'Radio signal transmitted by meteor', *International Herald Tribune*, 21 Aug. 1986, p. 7.

[3] Blair (note 1), especially chapters 8 and 9.

[4] Blair (note 1), pp. 234–38; and Ford (note 1), pp. 36–39, 44.

5 Frei, D., *Risks of Unintentional Nuclear War* (Croom Helm: London, 1983), especially chapter 6 under 'Nuclear accidents and incidents'.

6 See the works of Blair and Ford (note 1) in particular.

7 Steinbruner, J., 'Nuclear decapitation', *Foreign Policy*, winter 1981/82, pp. 16–28; and Ball, D. and Richelson, J. (eds), *Strategic Nuclear Targeting* (Cornell University Press: Ithaca, N.Y., 1986), especially the chapters by Richelson, J. T., 'The dilemmas of counter power targeting', pp. 159–70, and Gray, C., 'Targeting problems for central war', pp. 171–93.

8 Shukman, D., 'Nuclear strategy and the problem of command and control', *Survival*, vol. 29, no. 4 (July/Aug. 1987), pp. 336–59.

9 Epstein, J. M., 'Horizontal escalation', eds S. E. Miller and S. Van Evera, *Naval Strategy and National Security* (Princeton University Press: Princeton, N.J., 1988), pp. 102–14.

10 Among numerous sources, see Bellamy, C., *The Future of Land Warfare* (St. Martin's: New York, 1987), chapter 7; and Gabriel, R., *Operation Peace for Galilee* (Hill and Wang: New York, 1984).

11 See the map in Arkin and Fieldhouse (note 1), pp. 4–5.

12 This issue has arisen particularly in US negotiations with Greece and Turkey in recent years.

13 Wilkes, O., 'A checklist of U.S. military activities', unpublished manuscript, SIPRI, 1974; and Richelson and Ball (note 1).

14 See 'U.S. prepares for protracted nuclear war', *International Herald Tribune*, 29 July 1986, p. 1, which discusses the Ground Wave Emergency Network (GWEN), Milstar satellites, a satellite-based nuclear detection system and various other measures.

15 Kennedy, P. M., 'Imperial cable communications and strategy, 1870–1914', *The English Historical Review*, vol. 86, no. 141 (1971), pp. 728–52; Kemp, G. and Maurer, J., 'The logistics of Pax Brittanica: lessons for America', paper presented at Fletcher School Annual Conference, 23–25 Apr. 1980, Boston, Mass.; and Cole, D. H., *Imperial Military Geography*, 12th edn (Sifton Praed: London, 1956), chapter 12, under 'Cables and wireless'.

16 Kennedy (note 15), p. 731.

17 Kennedy (note 15), p. 740.

18 Kennedy (note 15), p. 748.

19 Kennedy (note 15), p. 749. See also Carroll, J. M., *Secrets of Electronic Espionage* (E. P. Dutton: New York, 1966), pp. 19–21, who cites the West German chain of global radio stations keyed on a transmitter near Berlin and involving overseas stations at Kamina, Togo, and Windhoek, S.W. Africa.

20 Kennedy (note 15), p. 751.

21 This is implied in the discussion in Ford (note 1), pp. 133–34.

22 This is discussed in Harkavy, R. E., *Great Power Competition for Overseas Bases: The Geopolitics of Access Diplomacy* (Pergamon: New York, 1982), pp. 68–69.

23 Harkavy (note 22), p. 77.

24 Harkavy (note 22), p. 27. Bamford, J., *The Puzzle Palace* (Houghton-Mifflin: Boston, Mass., 1982), pp. 32–33, discusses some pre-World War II SIGINT activities, involving facilities in Panama and the Philippines as well as along both US coasts.

25 See *Soviet Space Programs: 1976–1980*, US Senate, Committee on Commerce, Science and Transportation, 97th Congress, 2nd Session (US Government Printing Office: Washington, DC, Dec. 1982); and Davidchik, M. and Mahoney, R., 'Soviet civil fleets and the Third World', eds B. Dismukes and J. McConnell, *Soviet Naval Diplomacy* (Pergamon: New York, 1979).

26 Arkin and Fieldhouse (note 1), pp. 31–32.

27 See Arkin and Fieldhouse (note 1), pp. 28–33.

28 Perhaps the best brief review is in Richelson, J., 'Technical collection and arms control', ed. W. Potter, *Verification and Arms Control* (D. C. Heath: Lexington, Mass., 1985), pp. 169–216. See also Richelson and Ball (note 1); and Burrows, W., *Deep Black* (Random House: New York, 1985), especially pp. 174–98.

29 Richelson in Potter (note 28), pp. 194–98.

30 Richelson in Potter (note 28), pp. 186–90.

31 Arkin and Fieldhouse (note 1), pp. 77, note NATO's NADGE network and other systems tied into US networks such as Combat Grande in Spain, BADGE in Japan and another in the Philippines.

32 See also, for the pluses and minuses of various frequency ranges, Ford (note 1), especially pp. 152–57.

33 Arkin and Fieldhouse (note 1), p. 28.

34 Arkin and Fieldhouse (note 1), p. 28.

[35] Arkin and Fieldhouse (note 1), p. 29.

[36] Arkin and Fieldhouse (note 1), p. 29.

[37] Blair (note 1), pp. 103–104, 265 and 278.

[38] See Ford (note 1), p. 155; and Blair (note 1), pp. 198–99.

[39] Ford (note 1), pp. 225–27; Arkin and Fieldhouse (note 1), pp. 31–32; Blair (note 1), especially pp. 254–55; and Ulsamer, E., 'C³I survivability in the budget wars', *Air Force Magazine*, June 1983, pp. 39–40.

[40] Arkin and Fieldhouse (note 1), p. 33; and Blair (note 1), p. 279.

[41] For a full description, see the recent editions of *Jane's Military Communications* (Macdonald: London).

[42] Ford (note 1), p. 153; Blair (note 1), p. 279.

[43] Arkin and Fieldhouse (note 1), pp. 80, 128.

[44] DSCS is discussed in 'Satellite delays may erode U.S. warning system', *Washington Post*, 12 May 1986, p. A16. During wartime it provides secure voice and data communications for DOD; in peacetime it carries embassy and intelligence messages. By 1986, there were seven DSCS II satellites, four operational and three spares. See also Ford (note 1), pp. 68, 152 and 187–88; and Blair (note 1), pp. 253–66.

[45] One description of Omega is in 'Coast Guard worried over Hawaii project near transmitter', *New York Times*, 24 Oct. 1986, p. A18.

[46] Blair (note 1), pp. 187, 203 and 266.

[47] Arkin and Fieldhouse (note 1), pp. 80, 128.

[48] Arkin and Fieldhouse (note 1), pp. 28–29, 80; and Velocci, T., 'The state of the nation's C³I', *National Defense*, Oct. 1982, p. 22.

[49] Arkin and Fieldhouse (note 1), p. 45, use the figure of 5500 nuclear warheads based on 36 submarines total and 640 launch tubes as of 1985. A figure of 5632 warheads is used in 'Submarines now dominate U.S. nuclear forces', *New York Times*, 27 Nov. 1987, p. A32.

[50] SIPRI data; Arkin and Fieldhouse (note 1), appendix A; and Langer, A., Wilkes, O. and Gleditsch, N. P., *The Military Functions of Omega and Loran-C* (Peace Research Institute: Oslo, 1976).

[51] That in Liberia is noted in 'U.S. ties with Liberia put under new strain', *New York Times*, 16 May 1987, p. 2.

[52] Arkin and Fieldhouse (note 1), pp. 128, 148; SIPRI data; and Blair (note 1), p. 170.

[53] LORAN is discussed by Hersh, S., *The Target is Destroyed* (Random House: New York, 1986), pp. 7–8, who notes that, as pertains to aircraft navigation, it has been superseded by the Inertial Navigation System (INS) by 1978.

[54] SIPRI data; and Arkin and Fieldhouse (note 1), p. 127. The role of Nea Makri is noted in 'U.S. gets ready to lose its bases in Greece', *Daily Telegraph*, 16 Feb. 1985, p. 6; and 'Dispute may close U.S. base', *Centre Daily Times*, 28 Mar. 1987, p. 1, which discusses Greece's threat to close the facility down amid the Greece–Turkey crisis over the Aegean.

[55] SIPRI data; Arkin and Fieldhouse (note 1), p. 80 and appendix A; Blair (note 1), pp. 156–57, 169–75 and 198–201.

[56] Ford (note 1), p. 96.

[57] Arkin and Fieldhouse (note 1), p. 127 and appendix A.

[58] Blair (note 1), p. 295, discusses long-term plans for a newer TACAMO ECX craft, 15 of which are to be purchased. See also Ford (note 1), p. 196.

[59] 'The Air Force satellite systems', *Air Force Magazine*, June 1982, p. 52. See also Stares (note 1), p. 29, who says that Navstar's sensors will be able to provide, in real time, information on the yield, height and location of nuclear bursts to within 100 metres anywhere in the world.

[60] 'The Air Force satellite systems' (note 59), p. 54.

[61] 'The Air Force satellite systems' (note 59), p. 54.

[62] Stares (note 1), p. 188.

[63] International Institute for Strategic Studies, *The Military Balance: 1986–1987* (IISS: London, 1986), p. 20.

[64] Arkin and Fieldhouse (note 1), p. 51.

[65] Ford (note 1), p. 150.

[66] SIPRI data; and *Jane's Military Communications, 1981* (Macdonald: London, 1981), p. 589.

[67] Ford (note 1), p. 150.

[68] Ford (note 1), pp. 150–51.

[69] Arkin and Fieldhouse (note 1), p. 80 and appendix A; and *Jane's Military Communications, 1981* (note 66), p. 589.

[70] Arkin and Fieldhouse (note 1), pp. 77–78.
[71] Stares (note 1), pp. 30, 193; Ford (note 1), p. 224; and Blair (note 1), p. 203.
[72] Ford (note 1), p. 224; Stares (note 1), pp. 193–94; and Blair (note 1), pp. 204–205.
[73] 'Satellite delays may erode U.S. warning system' (note 44), p. A1.
[74] Ford (note 1), p. 224.
[75] Blair (note 1), p. 203.
[76] *Jane's Military Communications, 1981* (note 66), p. 589.
[77] Richelson and Ball (note 1), p. 201.
[78] Stares (note 1), p. 188.
[79] One point of departure is an unclassified paper by the Defense Communications Agency, 'Defense Communications System/European Communication Systems: Interoperability Baseline', Washington, DC, 1 Feb. 1981, hereinafter referred to as 'DCA Paper'; another is *Jane's Military Communications, 1981* (note 66).
[80] Regarding complexity and overlap, see 'Military's message system is overloaded, officers say', *New York Times*, 25 Nov. 1985, p. A17.
[81] *Jane's Military Communications, 1981* (note 66), p. 591.
[82] *Jane's Military Communications, 1981* (note 66), p. 593.
[83] DCA paper (note 79), p. S-1.
[84] DCA paper (note 79), p. S-1; and *Jane's Military Communications, 1981* (note 66), pp. 594–95.
[85] *Jane's Military Communications, 1981* (note 66), p. 579.
[86] SIPRI data.
[87] SIPRI data on Iceland.
[88] SIPRI data.
[89] SIPRI data on Alaska.
[90] *Jane's Military Communications, 1981* (note 66), pp. 274–75.
[91] See 'Satellite delays may erode U.S. warning system' (note 44), p. A1.
[92] See 'Military role widened by an aggressive G.E.', *New York Times*, 27 Mar. 1985, p. D9; and '4th space shuttle starts secret mission', *New York Times*, 4 Oct. 1985, p. B5, which reports on the space shuttle *Atlantis* carrying two DSCS III satellites.
[93] 'U.S. prepares for protracted nuclear war' (note 14), p. 1. See also Carnes Lord's review of Blair, *Strategic Command and Control* (note 1) in *Strategic Review*, fall 1985, pp. 79–84, who argues that the vulnerabilities of the US C³I network provide one argument in favour of strategic defence.
[94] Blair (note 1), p. 254.
[95] Arkin and Fieldhouse (note 1), p. 79. Further regarding GWEN, see Ford (note 1), pp. 225–26.
[96] 'Pentagon plans for WW IV', *Centre Daily Times*, 22 Feb. 1987, p. B7. See also Arkin and Fieldhouse (note 1), p. 80; and 'U.S. prepares for protracted nuclear war' (note 14), in which Milstar is described as 'the first communications satellite able to support a "multiple-exchange campaign", in which adversaries would fire nuclear weapons in salvos'.
[97] Ford (note 1), p. 215.
[98] See also Blair (note 1), pp. 264, 267; and Stares (note 1), p. 194, which states that 'the ground segment will be dispersed, hardened and proliferated'. Similarly, on p. 196, 'The Navstar GPS spacecraft will use many of the standard measures to reduce dependence on ground stations'.
[99] Blair (note 1), pp. 276–77.
[100] See, for instance, regarding negotiations over a VOA station in Greece, 'Greek leader asserts the U.S. shows favoritism to Turkey', *New York Times*, 9 Mar. 1987, p. A11. Such broadcasts are also often jammed—see 'Soviet "Voice" jammers shift to "Liberty"', *New York Times*, 2 June 1987, p. A12. Some are run on a more or less clandestine basis—see 'The trail so far', *New York Times*, 8 May 1987, p. A14, which discusses the plan for a broadcasting station in an unnamed Caribbean station intended to beam programmes into Cuba.
[101] See Reston, J., 'The other Star War', *New York Times*, 20 Mar. 1985, p. A27, which says that the VOA has a total of 108 transmitters. See also 'VOA to expand radio relay stations', *Daily Collegian*, 17 Sep. 1984, p. 7.
[102] A VOA transmitter in Liberia is mentioned in 'U.S. ties with Liberia put under new strain', *New York Times*, 16 May 1987, p. 2.
[103] See Safire, W., 'Detente's first victim', *New York Times*, 30 Sep. 1987, p. A31, which also notes new VOA construction in Morocco, Botswana, Thailand and Sri Lanka.
[104] Reston (note 101).
[105] 'New tenor, new tone at the Voice of America', *New York Times*, 31 Aug. 1984, p. A14.

[106] This typology is drawn from Richelson, *The U.S. Intelligence Community* (note 1), chapters 7 and 8; and Richelson in Potter (note 28), pp. 169–216.

[107] Richelson in Potter (note 28), p. 173.

[108] Richelson in Potter (note 28), p. 173; Richelson, *The U.S. Intelligence Community* (note 1), pp. 114–15; and in particular, Burrows (note 28), pp. 199–224.

[109] See 'U.S. satellite photographed details of Soviet disaster', *Centre Daily Times*, 1 May 1986, p. A11, wherein Richelson is cited as claiming that electronic signals from KH-11 are relayed to the Satellite Data System (SDS), and then to Ft Belvoir, Virginia, where the television images can be made into photographs. See also Richelson in Potter (note 28), p. 176; 'U.S. says intelligence units did not detect the accident', *New York Times*, 2 May 1986, p. A9; and '2 years of failure end as U.S. lofts big Titan rocket', *New York Times*, 27 Oct. 1987, p. A1, which reports the probable insertion in space of a badly needed second KH-11. See also 'U.S. designs spy satellites to be more secret than ever', *New York Times*, 3 Nov. 1987, p. C1, which discusses KH-11 and the newer KH-12; and 'Pentagon nursing an aging network of key satellites', *New York Times*, 20 July 1987, p. A1. Regarding the latter, see also Richelson in Potter (note 28), pp. 176–77, who also discusses US plans for an imaging radar satellite.

[110] *Centre Daily Times* (note 109); Richelson in Potter (note 28); see also Burrows (note 28), pp. 225–51, especially p. 227.

[111] 'Pentagon fears delays on future spy satellites', *New York Times*, 24 Feb. 1986, p. B6.

[112] Richelson in Potter (note 28), p. 178.

[113] 'Our spy on high', *New York Times Magazine*, 10 May 1987, pp. 30–34.

[114] 'Our spy on high' (note 113), p. 32. See also Richelson in Potter (note 28), p. 177.

[115] The issue of US U-2 flights over Turkey to monitor the SALT II Treaty after the loss of access to Iran is discussed in 'U.S. reported to drop U-2 plan', *International Herald Tribune*, 13 Sep. 1979; 'U.S. panel says Turkey to allow flights by U-2s', *International Herald Tribune*, 5–6 July 1980; and 'Turkey refuses to consult Russians about spy flights', *The Times*, 5 July 1980. Use of U-2s based in Cyprus for monitoring the Sinai is noted in 'U.S. Air Force U-2 crashes on Cyprus; 5 killed 7 injured', *International Herald Tribune*, 8 Dec. 1977; and 'U.S. plans to use new U-2s to monitor Soviet missiles', *International Herald Tribune*, 6 Apr. 1979.

[116] Burrows (note 28), pp. 153–69. See also 'Second SR-71 deployed to England', *Aviation Week & Space Technology*, 31 Jan. 1983, p. 59; and 'Spy planes sent to Britain', *Daily Telegraph*, 13 Mar. 1979.

[117] 'Civilians use satellite photos for spying on Soviet military', *New York Times*, 7 Apr. 1986, p. A1; Burrows (note 28), pp. 324–27. US provision of data to China from the Landsat D satellite is mentioned in 'U.S. looks to China for aid to Pakistan', *New York Times*, 3 Jan. 1980, p. 9. See also 'U.S. designs spy satellites to be more secret than ever' (note 109).

[118] Richelson in Potter (note 28), pp. 178–79.

[119] Richelson in Potter (note 28), p. 179.

[120] Richelson in Potter (note 28), p. 179.

[121] Richelson in Potter (note 28), p. 179.

[122] Richelson in Potter (note 28), p. 180.

[123] Richelson in Potter (note 28), p. 180.

[124] Richelson in Potter (note 28), p. 180.

[125] Richelson in Potter (note 28), p. 180. See also Stares (note 1), p. 188, who identifies control or receiver cites at Pine Gap, Australia, and Menwith Hill, UK, as well as at Ft Meade, Md.

[126] IISS (note 63), p. 21; Richelson in Potter (note 28), p. 181; and Burrows (note 28), pp. 192, 198.

[127] McGarvey, P., *CIA: The Myth and The Madness* (Penguin: Baltimore, Md., 1972), pp. 49–52; and regarding the famous RB-47 incident, in which one US aircraft was shot down near the Kola Peninsula, see Hersh (note 53), p. 11. See also Bamford (note 24), pp. 178–86, for a brief history of several of the more celebrated incidents involving ELINT craft.

[128] Richelson in Potter (note 28), pp. 182–83. An impending follow-on to the SR-71, with stealth capabilities, is discussed in 'New uncertainty on Lockheed', *New York Times*, 20 Jan. 1988, p. D8.

[129] Richelson in Potter (note 28), p. 183; and Burrows (note 28), p. 176, who discusses the past roles of the EC-47, EC-121, EC-130, RB-57 and RB-66. Burrows counts the bases used by these aircraft by the end of the 1960s as including Alconbury and Mildenhall in the UK, Rota (Spain), Hellenikon (Greece), Akrotiri (Cyprus), Incirlik (Turkey), Kadena (Okinawa), Atsugi (Japan), Osan (South Korea), and others in Iceland, FR Germany, Norway, Iran and Pakistan.

[130] According to Burrows (note 28), p. 171, 14 of the RC-135s are 'U' models, operating in a programme called Rivet, also extensively discussed by Hersh (note 53), pp. 8–11. These operate

out of Mildenhall, Kadena, Hellenikon and Alaska—those in Greece, for instance, are targeted against the south-western USSR, the Near East and the Mahgreb; those from Okinawa monitor Sakhalin. Hersh (note 53), p. 9, also claims that the USA was by mid-1984 flying 12 RC-135 'Rivet Joint' flights a month out of Howard AFB in Panama in support of government troops in El Salvador and the rebel contras in Nicaragua.

[131] Richelson in Potter (note 28), p. 183; and Hersh (note 53), chapter 1.

[132] Richelson in Potter (note 28), p. 183.

[133] Richelson in Potter (note 28), pp. 183–84. See also IISS (note 63), pp. 20–21.

[134] Richelson and Ball (note 1), p. 106. Their appendix also identifies service intelligence units associated with specific facilities. See also Bamford (note 24), chapter 5.

[135] Richelson in Potter (note 28), p. 185; Richelson and Ball (note 1), pp. 184–85.

[136] Richelson in Potter (note 28), p. 185; Richelson in Ball (note 1), pp. 184–85; and Richelson, *The U.S. Intelligence Community* (note 1), pp. 126–27.

[137] Richelson in Potter (note 28), p. 185; SIPRI data; and Richelson, *The U.S. Intelligence Community* (note 1), p. 127.

[138] Richelson in Potter (note 28), p. 185; SIPRI data; and Richelson, *The U.S. Intelligence Community* (note 1), p. 127. Iraklion's role of monitoring Soviet fleet movements in the Mediterranean is also noted in 'Anti-Americanism menaces Crete bases', *International Herald Tribune*, 26 Aug. 1975; and 'U.S. forces keep low profile in Greek areas', *International Herald Tribune*, 20 Feb. 1976.

[139] SIPRI data; Richelson in Potter (note 28), p. 188.

[140] SIPRI data.

[141] SIPRI data.

[142] Regarding continued use of the listening post at Shu Lin Kou in Taiwan, see 'U.S. base maintained on Taiwan', *International Herald Tribune*, 21 Feb. 1979; and 'Listening post in Taiwan helps offset loss of Iran sites', *Washington Star*, 18 Apr. 1979.

[143] Richelson and Ball (note 1), p. 188.

[144] SIPRI data. See also, 'Morale hit by loss of bases', *Washington Post*, 5 Feb. 1976, p. 17; 'Defence pact with Turkey brings U.S. bases', *London Daily Telegraph*, 31 Mar. 1980; 'How important are those U.S. bases in Turkey?', *Christian Science Monitor*, 11 Aug. 1975; and Bamford (note 24), pp. 159–60.

[145] SIPRI data; and Richelson and Ball (note 1), p. 323. See also Bamford (note 24), p. 201.

[146] Richelson and Ball (note 1), p. 188. The Vadsø facility is also discussed in Hersh (note 53), p. 4, wherein: 'Vadso, for example, is close enough to the Soviet Union to intercept the ultra-high-frequency (UHF) communications from Soviet aircraft to ground stations'. He cites another station at Barhauge, which monitors 'an advanced Soviet data-link communications system that enables ground controllers to exercise enormous control over the fighters above'.

[147] Richelson and Ball (note 1), p. 188. The US use of the Japanese facility at Wakkanai, Hokkaido, during the KAL 007 incident is also noted in 'How the U.S. listened in', *Newsweek*, 12 Sep. 1983, p. 25; and Hersh (note 53), especially pp. 60–61. See also Hersh (note 53), p. 47, for a detailed description of AN/FLR sites and their global network as it operated during the KAL 007 crisis.

[148] Richelson and Ball (note 1), appendix; Richelson in Potter (note 28), p. 185. For a more graphic description, see Bamford (note 24), pp. 161–67, particularly regarding the facility at Menwith Hill, UK.

[149] Richelson in Potter (note 28), p. 193, which reports that the COBRA Talon radar was moved from Thailand to San Miguel in the Philippines after the Viet Nam War. The seeming loss of US access to Ramasun after the close of the Viet Nam War is discussed in 'Thailand rejects bid by U.S. to keep using radar station', *International Herald Tribune*, 2 June 1976. See also 'GIs at secret base—plenty of time to worry', *Washington Post*, 14 Sep. 1972, p. E1; and 'U.S. shuts Thailand bases', *Baltimore Sun*, 21 June 1976, p. 4.

[150] The US loss of the Peshawar listening post called Bada Beir in 1968 is discussed in 'U.S. to hand over "Site 23" to Turk', *New York Times*, 10 June 1968; and 'U.S. base in Pakistan phasing out after 10 years', *Christian Science Monitor*, 27 June 1969. Regarding the reported restoration of US access to Peshawar, see Harrison, S., 'Needless offense to India', *New York Times*, 25 Nov. 1986, p. A27.

[151] Richelson and Ball (note 1), pp. 324–25; and Bamford (note 24), pp. 199–200. See also 'Iranian listening posts aren't needed to verify SALT', *Los Angeles Times*, 11 Mar. 1979, Part VI, p. 2. Hersh (note 53), p. 41, also discusses the past role of Tacksman I which had monitored the Soviet

space centre and ICBM launch facilities at Tyuratam, providing 'first burn data' on launches of liquid-fuelled missiles.

[152] SIPRI data. Regarding the earlier (up to 1965) listening post at Morocco's Kenitra, see 'U.S. to quit military base in Morocco', *Atlanta Journal*, 23 Apr. 1978, p. 25. According to Richelson and Ball (note 1), p. 327, the US SIGINT facilities in Morocco, closed in 1978, may have been reopened in 1982.

[153] Regarding the *Pueblo* and *Liberty* incidents, see Bamford (note 24), pp. 212-35. He describes the global patterns of the several sea-based SIGINT platforms used earlier by the NSA. On pages 216-17 are noted port calls by SIGINT ships at Capetown, Dakar, Aden (pre-independence) and Abidjan.

[154] The Holystone project is discussed by Richelson in Potter (note 28), p. 186. See also 'Pelton admits telling Soviets of one project of data interception', *Washington Post*, 3 June 1986, p. A1.

[155] Classic Wizard is discussed in Karas, T. H., 'Implications of Space Technology for Strategic Nuclear Competition', the Stanley Foundation, Occasional Paper No. 25, Muscatine, Iowa, July 1981. He says 'the program uses satellites to help fuse acoustic data from navy sensors around the world . . . Computers attempt to sort the data patterns which help locate and track the submarines. Indirect assistance in this task is provided by oceanographic satellites which have improved understanding of the ocean characteristics which affect how sound travels through the water.' See also Richelson and Ball (note 1), pp. 214-16.

[156] Richelson in Potter (note 28), p. 188; SIPRI data; and Burrows (note 28), p. 269, who characterizes Classic Wizard as the US equivalent to the Soviet EORSAT and RORSAT programmes. See also Richelson and Ball (note 1), pp. 206-207. The latter claims that additional facilities in Japan—Hanza, Misawa, Kamiseya—are also part of the Classic Wizard system.

[157] Richelson in Potter (note 28), p. 188; and Richelson and Ball (note 1), appendix.

[158] Richelson in Potter (note 28), p. 188; Richelson and Ball (note 1), appendix; and Burrows (note 28), p. 176. 'U.S. stepping up Indian Ocean activity', *Los Angeles Times*, 25 June 1978, discusses US P-3 ocean reconnaissance planes' use of Singapore.

[159] Richelson in Potter (note 28), p. 188; and Richelson and Ball (note 1), appendix. The latter discusses the Bullseye HF/DF system and identifies in that regard facilities in Japan at Hanza, Futenma and Sobe. It also cites San Miguel in the Philippines, Pearce in Australia and Tangimoana in New Zealand as additional HF/DF sites.

[160] Richelson and Ball (note 1), pp. 202-10.

[161] Richelson in Potter (note 28), pp. 190-91.

[162] Richelson in Potter (note 28), p. 190.

[163] Richelson in Potter (note 28), p. 191; and Burrows (note 28), especially pp. 245-46.

[164] Richelson in Potter (note 28), pp. 191-92.

[165] Richelson in Potter (note 28), p. 192.

[166] Richelson in Potter (note 28), p. 192; and SIPRI data.

[167] SIPRI data.

[168] Richelson in Potter (note 28), p. 192; and Burrows (note 28), pp. 275-76. The latter also discusses two highly classified telescopic cameras code-named Teal Amber and Teal Blue in Florida and Hawaii, respectively, hence not involving FMP. The future of technology in this area is previewed in 'Radically new telescope heralds great sharpness', *New York Times*, 23 Sep. 1986, p. C1, which discusses the technique called optical interferometry; and 'New space challenge: monitoring weapons', *New York Times*, 8 Dec. 1987, p. C1.

[169] Richelson in Potter (note 28), p. 192; and IISS (note 63), p. 21.

[170] Richelson in Potter (note 28), p. 193.

[171] Richelson in Potter (note 28), p. 193; and IISS (note 63), p. 20.

[172] Richelson in Potter (note 28), p. 193; and Richelson and Ball (note 1), p. 189.

[173] Richelson in Potter (note 28), p. 193; and IISS (note 63), pp. 20-21.

[174] Richelson in Potter (note 28), p. 194.

[175] SIPRI data.

[176] IISS (note 63), p. 21; and Richelson in Potter (note 28), p. 194. Regarding the tracking station in Antigua, see 'New nation gets $19 million gift', *Miami Herald*, 2 Nov. 1981.

[177] SIPRI data. The earlier use of a station on Grand Turk Island is noted in 'In old pirate haunt, daunting news of drug trade', *New York Times*, 13 Mar. 1985, p. A2.

[178] Richelson in Potter (note 28), p. 177; and Burrows (note 28), p. 273.

[179] Cobra Ball is discussed in Burrows (note 28), pp. 172-73; and Hersh (note 53), especially pp. 37-42.

[180] Ford (note 1), pp. 64-65.

[181] Ford (note 1), p. 65.

[182] Ford (note 1); Stares (note 1), pp. 187–89; and Richelson, *The U.S. Intelligence Community* (note 1), p. 203. The latter, discussing the Oakhanger SCF, says it has five functions: tracking, telemetry, command, recovery and radiometric testing. He also says it comprises 'eleven remote tracking stations, including four double stations'.

[183] SIPRI data on the Seychelles.

[184] See 'Lease for U.S. tracking station in Seychelles extended to 1990', *New York Times*, 20 June 1981, p. 2; and 'Seychelles: new outpost for Russians?', *U.S. News and World Report*, 24 Mar. 1980, p. 36.

[185] 'Space base "destroyed"', *The Times*, 26 July 1975, describes the destruction of the facility on Madagascar by US technicians fearing it might fall into communist hands.

[186] SIPRI data.

[187] 'U.S. shuts Thailand bases', *Baltimore Sun*, 21 June 1976, p. 4; and SIPRI data. Stares (note 1), p. 188. Regarding the orbital heights of different satellites (and thus their relative vulnerability to anti-satellite activities), see 'The satellite sky', *Centre Daily Times*, 5 July 1987, p. D1.

[188] Stares (note 1), p. 188. Regarding the orbital heights of different satellites (and thus their relative vulnerability to anti-satellite activities), see 'The satellite sky', *Centre Daily Times*, 5 July 1987, p. D1.

[189] Ford (note 1), p. 208; Arkin and Fieldhouse (note 1), pp. 74–76.

[190] Arkin and Fieldhouse (note 1), pp. 74–76; Ford (note 1), pp. 76–78.

[191] Arkin and Fieldhouse (note 1), pp. 74–76; Ford (note 1), pp. 76–78.

[192] Ford (note 1), pp. 212–13; IISS (note 63), p. 21; Arkin and Fieldhouse (note 1), p. 31.

[193] Full details on the DSP programme (now apparently alternatively known as SEWS—Satellite Early Warning System) can be gleaned from Ball, D., *A Base for Debate: The U.S. Satellite Station at Nurrungar* (Allen and Unwin: Sydney, 1987). See also Ford (note 1), pp. 61–64, 70–72 and 201–204.

[194] Ball (note 193), pp. 70–72, under 'DSP and nuclear war-fighting'.

[195] Ford (note 1), p. 64.

[196] Ford (note 1), p. 64.

[197] Ford (note 1), p. 71.

[198] Ford (note 1), p. 66.

[199] Ford (note 1), p. 48.

[200] See the relevant map in Ball (note 193), p. 48. But he also notes, pp. 36–37, the newer development of satellite-to-satellite crosslinks, hence mitigating US dependence on foreign access for DSP communications.

[201] Ball (note 193), pp. 4, 59–62. See also 'U.S. bases in Australia "potential priority targets"', *Financial Times*, 7 June 1984.

[202] See 'Satellite delays may erode U.S. warning system' (note 44), p. A1, which notes that 'having an "ideal" system means having three operating DSP satellites and one reserve in orbit'.

[203] Ball (note 193), pp. 62–63.

[204] The BMEWS site in Greenland is discussed in 'Owned by Denmark: greatest empire left', *International Herald Tribune*, 16–17 Aug. 1975.

[205] 'Moscow offers to end a dispute on Siberia radar', *New York Times*, 29 Oct. 1985, p. A1.

[206] Richelson in Potter (note 28), pp. 192–93. For the early post-war period, see Engelbardt, S., *Strategic Defenses* (Thos. Crowell: New York, 1966), chapter 10.

[207] SIPRI data; Arkin and Fieldhouse (note 1), p. 76.

[208] SIPRI data; Arkin and Fieldhouse (note 1), p. 79.

[209] Arkin and Fieldhouse (note 1), p. 79.

[210] See also 'In remote outposts, U.S. is upgrading vigil', *New York Times*, 12 Feb. 1986, p. A27; 'Update defenses, Canada is urged', *New York Times*, 28 Jan. 1985, p. A5; and 'Echo in Arctic tundra of new military goals', *New York Times*, 6 July 1987, p. 2.

[211] IISS (note 63), p. 21.

[212] Arkin and Fieldhouse (note 1), p. 77.

[213] SIPRI data.

[214] SIPRI data; and Arkin and Fieldhouse (note 1), p. 77. in 'U.S. sets up new facilities', *International Herald Tribune*, 3 Feb. 1984, p. 1, it is reported that the USA operated a radar at Tiger Island on the Honduran Pacific coast near Nicaragua. An air defence radar at Hofn, Iceland, is noted in 'Iceland: close Nato ally', *USA Today*, 1 Oct. 1986, p. 2A.

[215] Richelson and Ball (note 1), pp. 200–202.

[216] SIPRI, *World Armaments and Disarmament: SIPRI Yearbook 1979* (Taylor & Francis: London, 1979), p. 430.

[217] Richelson and Ball (note 1), p. 200.

[218] Richelson and Ball (note 1), p. 200. See also Burrows (note 28), p. 178, who notes that the first SOSUS hydrophones laid on the continental shelf along the Atlantic and Gulf coasts of the USA in the 1950s and 1960s were code-named 'Caesar'.

[219] Richelson in Potter (note 28), p. 189. See also Arkin and Fieldhouse (note 1), pp. 72–73.

[220] Richelson in Potter (note 28), p. 189. The sonar listening post on Santa Maria island in the Azores is noted in 'Portugal bargains for U.S. military aid with strategic mid-Atlantic base', *Christian Science Monitor*, 24 Mar. 1981, p. 9. That near Keflavik in Iceland is noted in Gunnarsson, G., 'Icelandic security and the Arctic', ed. K. Motolla, *The Arctic Challenge: Nordic and Canadian Approaches to Security and Cooperation* (Westview: Boulder, Colo., 1988). The facilities on Italy's Lampedusa Island, which figured in the US–Libyan crisis in 1986, may include a sonar barrier—see 'Libya's raid did not escape Crete's notice', *New York Times*, 21 Apr. 1986, p. A7. See also Lukacs, J., 'The Lampedusa mystery', *New York Times*, 7 May 1986, p. A31, which merely hints at an intelligence station of some sort, not necessarily involving ASW.

[221] Burrows (note 28), p. 179.

[222] Richelson in Potter (note 28), pp. 189–90.

[223] Richelson and Ball (note 1), p. 201; and Richelson in Potter (note 28), p. 190.

[224] 'Deadly game of hide-and-seek', *U.S. News and World Report*, 15 June 1987, pp. 36–41; Richelson and Ball (note 1), p. 201; and Burrows (note 28), p. 181.

[225] 'In battle of wits, submarines evade advanced efforts at detection', *New York Times*, 1 Apr. 1986, p. C1. See also 'Sonar sales to Chinese concern U.S. Allies', *Defense Week*, vol. 6, no. 3 (21 Jan. 1985), p. 1; and 'Defense Department says Soviet sub may have hit a U.S. sonar device', *New York Times*, 5 Nov. 1983, p. 10. RDSS—an ASW system that uses a sonabuoy tossed from an aircraft and moored to the sea bottom, is discussed in 'Sonabuoy bobs back up again', *Defense Week*, vol. 6, no. 3 (21 Jan. 1985), p. 16.

[226] 'In battle of wits, submarines evade advanced efforts at detection' (note 225).

[227] 'Navy warns of crisis in anti-submarine warfare', *New York Times*, 19 Mar. 1987, p. A19.

[228] 'Navy warns of crisis in anti-submarine warfare' (note 227); and 'Can submarines stay hidden?', *New York Times*, 11 Dec. 1984, p. C1.

[229] Richelson in Potter (note 28), pp. 195–96; and Burrows (note 28), pp. 183–84. The latter notes three components of the programme: (*a*) Vela Uniform's seismic detectors for underground and underwater explosions; (*b*) Vela Sierra's riometers and other equipment to detect atmospheric and space-related detonations; and (*c*) Vela Hotel's pairs of satellites to detect nuclear explosions in space or on the earth's surface.

[230] Richelson in Potter (note 28), p. 195.

[231] Burrows (note 28), p. 185; and Arkin and Fieldhouse (note 1), p. 20.

[232] Richelson, *The U.S. Intelligence Community* (note 1), p. 158.

[233] Richelson, *The U.S. Intelligence Community* (note 1), p. 158.

[234] Richelson, *The U.S. Intelligence Community* (note 1), p. 159.

[235] Stares (note 1), p. 188.

[236] Richelson in Potter (note 28), p. 197.

[237] SIPRI data.

[238] According to one source, 'the backbone of the U.S. detection system consists of seismic facilities in 35 countries, manned by the air force's Technical Applications Center at Patrick Air Force Base in Florida'. See *International Herald Tribune*, 13 Aug. 1985, p. 6.

[239] See *International Herald Tribune* (note 238), regarding the Norwegian arrays, said to measure high-frequency signals and to be able to detect extremely low-yield explosions at long distances.

[240] 'U.S., China discuss tracking Soviet tests', *International Herald Tribune*, 20 Mar. 1986, p. 1.

[241] 'U.S. uses seismic devices in China to estimate size of Soviet A-tests', *New York Times*, 4 Apr. 1987, p. 1, which sites the facility at Urumqi. It also refers to another device, in Manchuria, which would allow the USA to 'learn more about the geology of the Soviet Union'.

[242] 'U.S. uses seismic devices in China to estimate size of Soviet A-tests' (note 241).

[243] 'U.S., China discuss tracking Soviet tests' (note 240), p. 1.

[244] 'U.S., China discuss tracking Soviet tests' (note 240), p. 1.

[245] U.S. retention of Chiang Mai is discussed in 'U.S. presence in Thailand cut to bone', *Washington Star*, 17 July 1976, p. 3.

[246] SIPRI data.

[247] SIPRI data.

[248] SIPRI data.

[249] See Arkin and Fieldhouse (note 1), p. 79, regarding RSTN facilities at Yellowknife and Red Lake (Ontario), Canada.

[250] Similarly, regarding the prospective START treaty under negotiation, see 'U.S. verification proposal calls for joint access to bases', *International Herald Tribune*, 22 Mar. 1988, p. 1.

[251] Ford (note 1), p. 133.

[252] Burns, T. S., *The Secret War for the Ocean Depths* (Rawson: New York, 1978), p. 311, which reported on a string of 32 hydrophones, 11 feet long, weighing more than a ton. See also 'A Soviet sub-detection system?', *Newsweek*, 8 Sep. 1980, p. 15, which at that point said that US officials thought that 'the Soviets still lack the land-based technology necessary to make a detection system work properly'.

[253] Stuart, G. and Taylor, L., 'The Soviet naval auxiliary force', eds B. Watson and S. Watson, *The Soviet Navy: Strengths and Liabilities* (Westview Press: Boulder, Colo., 1986), pp. 109–12; and Arkin and Fieldhouse (note 1), p. 73.

[254] Arkin and Fieldhouse (note 1), appendix B.

[255] Ford (note 1), p. 139.

[256] Arkin and Fieldhouse (note 1), appendix B.

[257] Arkin and Fieldhouse (note 1), appendix B.

[258] Meyer, S. M., 'Soviet nuclear operations', ed. S. Cimbala, *Soviet C³* (AFCEA International Press: Washington, DC, 1987), p. 148; and Friedman, N., 'Soviet naval command and control', in Cimbala, p. 289, which says that the Soviets have 'converted two Golf class diesel power ballistic missile submarines into survivable command ships or communications relays'.

[259] Richelson, *Sword and Shield* (note 1), p. 110.

[260] Richelson, *Sword and Shield* (note 1), p. 110.

[261] Richelson, *Sword and Shield* (note 1), p. 110.

[262] Richelson, *Sword and Shield* (note 1), p. 110.

[263] But overall, the Soviet military space effort is very impressive and growing as note, for instance, 'Soviets' space program forging ahead of U.S.', *Centre Daily Times*, 27 Apr. 1986, p. B-7. An opposite view is provided by Stares, P., 'A Soviet lead in space? The facts belie it', *International Herald Tribune*, 21 Aug. 1986, p. 4. See also Stares (note 1), p. 199, wherein: 'Because of the paucity of information on Soviet satellite survivability powers, one can only infer their general approach to this problem. Some insurance against the loss of satellites is provided by the size of most Soviet constellations.'

[264] Richelson, *Sword and Shield* (note 1), p. 108.

[265] Richelson, *Sword and Shield* (note 1), p. 108.

[266] *Soviet Space Programs: 1976–1980* (note 25), p. 124; and Jasani, B., SIPRI, *Outer Space— Battlefield of the Future?* (Taylor & Francis: London, 1978), p. 179. The former discusses the Czech role in this 'Great Arc' programme. See also, Richelson, *Sword and Shield* (note 1), p. 124.

[267] *Soviet Space Programs: 1976–1980* (note 25), p. 124.

[268] *Soviet Space Programs: 1976–1980* (note 25), p. 124; and Richelson, *Sword and Shield* (note 1), p. 109.

[269] *Soviet Space Programs: 1976–1980* (note 25), p. 124.

[270] *Soviet Space Programs: 1976–1980* (note 25), p. 124.

[271] SIPRI data; and Richelson, *Sword and Shield* (note 1), p. 109.

[272] SIPRI data on Chile.

[273] SIPRI data on Chad. Richelson, *Sword and Shield* (note 1), p. 109, sites the facility at Fort Lamy in Chad.

[274] SIPRI data on India.

[275] SIPRI data on Mali; and *Soviet Space Programs: 1976–1980* (note 25), p. 124.

[276] SIPRI data on Kerguelen; and *Soviet Space Programs: 1976–1980* (note 25), p. 124.

[277] *Soviet Space Programs: 1976–1980* (note 25), p. 126.

[278] *Soviet Space Programs: 1976–1980* (note 25), p. 128.

[279] *Soviet Space Programs: 1976–1980* (note 25), p. 130.

[280] Ford (note 1), p. 139.

[281] *Jane's Military Communications, 1981* (note 66), p. 269. See also Johnson, N. L., 'C³ in space: the Soviet approach', in Cimbala (note 258), p. 344.

[282] Arkin and Fieldhouse (note 1), appendix B.

[283] Arkin and Fieldhouse (note 1), appendix B, regarding a satellite ground station in Hanoi; and SIPRI data on Mongolia and Ethiopia.

[284] US Department of Defense, *Soviet Military Power 1985*, 4th edn (US Government Printing

Office, Washington, DC, 1985), p. 120; SIPRI data; and 'Senate panel calls hearings on Soviet troops in Cuba', *New York Times*, 7 Sep. 1979.

[285] *Soviet Military Power 1985* (note 284), p. 128.

[286] *Soviet Space Programs: 1976–1980* (note 25), p. 127.

[287] *Soviet Space Programs: 1976–1980* (note 25), p. 129.

[288] *Soviet Space Programs: 1976–1980* (note 25), p. 130.

[289] *Soviet Space Programs: 1976–1980* (note 25), p. 136.

[290] *Soviet Space Programs: 1976–1980* (note 25), p. 136.

[291] *Soviet Space Programs: 1976–1980* (note 25), p. 138.

[292] Richelson, *Sword and Shield* (note 1), pp. 91–92. Johnson, N. L., 'C³ in space: the Soviet approach', in Cimbala (note 258), p. 348, says the Soviet Union has had a 'semi-operational' early-warning system using the nine Molniya launch detection satellites, but that only at the end of the 1980s would it have a geostationary warning system. Jasani (note 266), p. 47, discusses the possible role of Molniya satellites for missile detection and says that the Cosmos 775 satellite was probably the first Soviet early-warning satellite in synchronous orbit.

[293] *Soviet Space Programs: 1976–1980* (note 25), p. 136, wherein: 'it was the Borovichi that made the pickup, but the capsule was transferred to a Soviet meteorological service ship, the Vasiliy Golovnin for carriage to Bombay, from where it was air-lifted home.'

[294] US Department of Defense, *Soviet Military Power 1987*, 6th edn (US Government Printing Office, Washington, DC, 1987), p. 53; and see also Richelson, *Sword and Shield* (note 1), pp. 103–105.

[295] US Department of Defense, *Soviet Military Power 1988*, 7th edn (US Government Printing Office, Washington, DC, 1988), p. 63, anticipates initial deployment of 9–12 satellites to provide two-dimensional navigational capacity, and says that for three-dimensional approaches it would require 18–24 satellites.

[296] *Soviet Military Power 1987* (note 294), p. 54.

[297] *Soviet Military Power 1987* (note 294).

[298] Richelson, *Sword and Shield* (note 1), p. 97; and Jasani (note 266), pp. 41–43.

[299] See also, 'Spy planes a threat to U.S.', *Washington Post*, 14 Sep. 1979, p. D15. Specifically, regarding Tu-95 Bear D and Tu-95 Bear F flights out of Cam Ranh Bay, see 'Soviet air spies over S.E. Asia', *Daily Telegraph*, 4 Nov. 1983. See also Richelson, *Sword and Shield* (note 1), p. 89.

[300] Richelson, *Sword and Shield* (note 1), p. 98.

[301] Richelson, *Sword and Shield* (note 1), p. 100.

[302] Richelson, *Sword and Shield* (note 1), p. 100. The facility at Lourdes, said to include 'large dish-shaped radar receiver terminals at a site called Torrens for intercepting communications from American missile tests and from satellites', is discussed in 'Soviet brigade: how the U.S. traced it', *New York Times*, 13 Sep. 1979, p. 16; and 'Russians in Cuba', *Asahi*, 17 Sep. 1979. Arkin and Fieldhouse (note 1), p. 264, note the role of Lourdes in monitoring US missile tests from Cape Canaveral.

[303] Richelson, *Sword and Shield* (note 1), p. 100.

[304] Richelson, *Sword and Shield* (note 1), p. 100.

[305] Richelson, *Sword and Shield* (note 1), p. 101, and p. 107 notes the probable ocean-surveillance roles of facilities at Cam Ranh Bay, Lourdes (Cuba) and another in S. Yemen.

[306] Richelson, *Sword and Shield* (note 1), p. 101; and 'Tuning in: Soviets set up spy station', *Time*, 8 Mar. 1982, p. 32.

[307] Haselkorn, A., *The Evolution of Soviet Security Strategy, 1965–1975* (Crane, Russak: New York, 1978), p. 132.

[308] IISS (note 63), p. 113.

[309] SIPRI data on Cuba.

[310] SIPRI data on Poland.

[311] SIPRI data on Hungary.

[312] Davidchik, M. D. and Mahoney, R. B., 'Soviet civil fleets and the Third World', in Dismukes and McConnell (note 25), p. 324.

[313] Haselkorn (note 307), p. 106; 'Spain charges Soviets monitoring hot spots', *Washington Post*, 31 Jan. 1976, p. A5; and 'Spanish leader hoping for entry to NATO in '81', *New York Times*, 14 Apr. 1981, p. A8. See also Carnes, C. F., 'Soviet naval intelligence', in Watson and Watson (note 253), p. 172; and 'Canaries counting on Soviet shipping', *The Times*, 14 June 1983.

[314] Davidchik and Mahoney (note 25), p. 325.

[315] Davidchik and Mahoney (note 25), p. 325.

[316] Davidchik and Mahoney (note 25), p. 329.

[317] Davidchik and Mahoney (note 25), p. 329.

[318] 'Vanuatu may open port to Soviet Pacific trawlers', *International Herald Tribune*, 31 July 1986, p. 6; 'South Pacific: America may have missed the boat', *International Herald Tribune*, 1 Aug. 1986, p. 4; 'Pacific isle anti-communists chase off Soviet cruise ship', *New York Times*, 3 Feb. 1987, p. A3; 'Fishing yields Soviet a South Pacific toehold', *New York Times*, 17 May 1987, p. 22.

[319] 'Soviet seeks a larger role in Southeast Asia', *New York Times*, 8 Apr. 1986, p. A17.

[320] 'Fishing yields Soviet a South Pacific toehold' (note 318).

[321] 'Fishing yields Soviet a South Pacific toehold' (note 318).

[322] 'Soviet is losing rights to fish off West Africa', *New York Times*, 13 Jan. 1988.

[323] Stuart and Taylor (note 253), p. 109.

[324] The Balzan's shadowing of US ships off the US eastern coast is discussed in 'NATO war games begin off Boston', *New Orleans Times Picayune*, 30 Aug. 1985, p. A8. See also 'Disabled Soviet sub surfaces off South Carolina', *New York Times*, 4 Nov. 1983, p. A1.

[325] Stuart and Taylor (note 253), p. 111.

[326] Stuart and Taylor (note 253), p. 111.

[327] Stuart and Taylor (note 253), p. 112.

[328] Petersen, C. C., 'Trends in Soviet naval operations', in Dismukes and McConnell (note 313), p. 64.

[329] Petersen, C. C., 'Trends in Soviet naval operations', in Dismukes and McConnell (note 312), p. 64; and Stuart and Taylor (note 253), pp. 106–108.

[330] See 'New tenor, new tone at the Voice of America' (note 105), which reports that the USSR has 37 transmitters for short-wave broadcasts, vs. 6 for VOA, 11 for France and 8 for Britain.

[331] Private communication, VOA official.

[332] VOA (note 331); and 'Soviet starts radio broadcasts to U.S. from Cuba', *New York Times*, 27 May 1987, p. A15.

[333] See subsequent discussion in chapter 10, based on analysis of the US Governments' FBIS (Foreign Broadcast Information System).

[334] SIPRI data.

[335] Arkin and Fieldhouse (note 1), p. 278, identified as an LF transmitter.

[336] SIPRI data on the Faeroe Islands; and Arkin and Fieldhouse (note 1), p. 278.

[337] Richelson and Ball (note 1), p. 335.

[338] Richelson and Ball (note 1), p. 335; and 'What was all the fuss about', *Daily Telegraph*, 19 Nov. 1978, centred on the GCHQ operation at Ayios Nikolaos on eastern Cyprus but noting a network of intercept bases around the world in Hong Kong, Australia, Ascension, South Africa, Iran, FR Germany, Malta and Cyprus. See also 'Bitter lemons', *Guardian*, 29 May 1976.

[339] Richelson and Ball (note 1), p. 535. The Mauritius facility is sited by the SIPRI data at Plaissance.

[340] The communications facilities on Gibraltar are noted in 'The cloudy outlook for Gibraltar's commanding view', *New York Times*, 10 Feb. 1985, p. E5.

[341] Richelson and Ball (note 1), pp. 194, 336, and which also reports on joint NSA–GCHQ operations at Diego Garcia and Ascension, and a GCHQ unit at Sinop, Turkey.

[342] SIPRI data on Australia.

[343] Richelson and Ball (note 1), p. 194.

[344] Richelson and Ball (note 1), p. 206.

[345] Richelson and Ball (note 1), p. 206.

[346] Richelson and Ball (note 1), pp. 335–36. The additional intelligence facility at Silvermine, South Africa, said built with aid from NATO countries in 1973, is noted in 'Not singling out Israel', *Near East Report*, 6 Apr. 1987, p. 55.

[347] *Jane's Military Communications, 1981* (note 66), p. 271.

[348] *Jane's Military Communications, 1981* (note 66), pp. 40–41.

[349] Jasani (note 266), p. 111.

[350] The role of Oakhanger as a control facility for Skynet is discussed in 'RAF Oakhanger', *Spaceflight*, vol. 12, no. 2 (Feb. 1970), pp. 72–73. See also, 'Skynet: the U.K. defense satellite communications system', *Spaceflight*, vol. 11, no. 8 (Aug. 1969), pp. 291–93, which also discusses the use of shipboard and mobile, transportable ground stations linked to Oakhanger.

[351] 'British to supply NATO satellites', *New York Times*, 20 Jan. 1987, p. D4, discusses the still newer Skynet 4 satellite and a planned NATO-4 version.

[352] 'British spy agency's leak sought', *Harrisburg Patriot-News*, 25 Jan. 1987, p. D6.

[353] SIPRI data on Canada.

[354] Arkin and Fieldhouse (note 1), appendix D.

[355] Arkin and Fieldhouse (note 1), appendix D.

[356] Arkin and Fieldhouse (note 1), p. 283, based at Evreux Air Base.

[357] Arkin and Fieldhouse (note 1), appendix D.

[358] Arkin and Fieldhouse (note 1), p. 288.

[359] Arkin and Fieldhouse (note 1), p. 288.

[360] SIPRI data; and Arkin and Fieldhouse (note 1), p. 288.

[361] SIPRI data.

[362] SIPRI data.

[363] SIPRI data on Upper Volta.

[364] Arkin and Fieldhouse (note 1), appendix D.

[365] Arkin and Fieldhouse (note 1), p. 287, in relation to the National Military Command Center at Taverny.

[366] SIPRI data; 'Misguided rocket destroyed', *Centre Daily Times*, 13 Sep. 1985, p. A2; 'From jungle outpost, Europe readies a space age challenge', *New York Times*, 16 June 1981, p. C1; 'Competitor in the Cosmos: Europe's Arianespace is giving NASA a run for the money', *Time*, 26 Nov. 1984, p. 33; and 'Europeans weighing an expanded role in space', *New York Times*, 21 Sep. 1987, p. A6.

[367] *Jane's Military Communications, 1981* (note 66), p. 268, under 'NATO satellites'.

[368] Arkin and Fieldhouse (note 1), appendix E.

[369] Richelson and Ball (note 1), p. 337, who also refer to additional facilities at the Australian embassies in Thailand and Indonesia.

[370] Richelson and Ball (note 1), p. 337.

[371] 'Ethiopia: Israeli bases in operation?', *Defense and Foreign Affairs' Weekly Report on Strategic Middle Eastern Affairs*, vol. 2, no. 3 (19 Jan. 1977).

7. Research and environmental facilities

I. Introduction

Largely obscured from public view and rarely catalogued, much less discussed, in the national security literature are the overlapping but still essentially distinct categories of overseas research and environmental facilities. Involved here are a plethora of functions and purposes, many both esoteric and vital: missile ranges for ICBMs and SLBMs; underground and above-ground nuclear test facilities; weather stations; facilities related to geodesy, terrestrial mapping and the monitoring of solar flares; those involved in measuring the atmospheric effects of nuclear explosions; facilities utilized for medical and biological warfare research; those for researching combat conditions in the Arctic, the desert and the tropics; and facilities related to anti-submarine warfare in the oceanic depths. There are also many, many others; indeed, many perhaps not easily found in open source materials.

As noted, there is a distinction between facilities primarily devoted to research and those devoted to the environment. The former—really referring more broadly to research *and* development (R&D)—is presumably more or less self-explanatory; indeed, it will subsume some research on environmental matters, for instance, that on new meteorological techniques. It pertains centrally to R&D of new weapons, tactics, C^3I; indeed, the various categories for which the use of foreign facilities is analysed in this book. Environmental facilities, on the other hand, can involve 'finished' and deployed technologies which make an ongoing, current contribution to a nation's readiness or defence posture; for instance, the roles weather stations, seismic sensors and solar flare sensors might play amid a nuclear crisis or war, or for deterrence of same. In short, environmental facilities will usually involve the continuous monitoring of the environment in connection with ongoing military activities; otherwise, various calibrations in connection with readiness.

Many research and environmental activities can, of course, be conducted within the superpowers' homelands. The USSR has a large land mass incorporating diverse climates and topographies. So does the USA, albeit with less space and a greater population density. France, Britain and other second-tier powers, on the other hand, have limited space and far less diverse climates and terrain, and require external facilities for those purposes. However, as they are not global powers and do not field the full range of military capabilities available to the superpowers, they may have reduced needs for research and environmental monitoring.

Generally, the need for external facilities in these areas results from one or more of several general factors: (*a*) weather or climate, (*b*) topography or terrain,

(c) physical space—land, sea or air, and (d) location or position—as with polar opposite requirements and in relation to foes' military deployments.

All but the last of these criteria is self-evident in nature. Regarding location, for example, if one major power deploys submarines in the Indian Ocean, it may then require research on the propagation of VLF communications specific to that ocean. If SSBNs must be located in Arctic waters for geographic reasons related to targeting, then that may impel research on underwater Arctic conditions. The expected routes of ICBMs during war will dictate specific geodetic research in line with those trajectories.

II. Research

Testing and evaluation of weapons

One of the major categories of research facilities is that having to do with testing and evaluation of weapons, again, for whatever reason, where external access is required. In the US case, this importantly involves tracking and impact facilities connected to testing of long-range missiles—ICBMs and SLBMs—with ranges of over 4800 km, clearly requiring some external access. Earlier, before atmospheric testing of nuclear weapons was proscribed by the Partial Test Ban Treaty, the USA required testing facilities outside the continental USA where populations would not be threatened by down-wind radiation. Various weapons and tactics associated with ASW or, generally, the combat operations of submarines, have required external access where ocean spaces were available in proximity to land facilities. Finally, some facilities have been utilized for testing a variety of weapons—down to the level of small arms—where specific climatic conditions not readily available in the USA can be found elsewhere, that is, tropical jungles, vast deserts, the Arctic, and so on. The main US research and environmental facilities around the world are located in figure 11.

Generally, the USSR has made much less use of external facilities of these sorts than has the USA. Its ICBMs, fired from launcher pads in the western part of the USSR at Plesetsk and Tyuratam, have overflown Soviet territory and impacted in the northern Pacific without needing external tracking bases.[1] Its nuclear tests have all been conducted within the USSR, for instance, at Novaya Zemlya in the far north, and at Semipalatinsk in Siberia's Yakut Autonomous Region.[2] There has also been considerable testing of weapons such as ship-to-ship missiles in the Black Sea, among other locales. There is little evidence of Soviet requirements for testing weapons in climates not found in the USSR being fulfilled elsewhere, for instance, tropical jungles (which are found within some Soviet client states and basing hosts, i.e., Cuba, Guinea, Viet Nam). However, there have been some earlier reports of Soviet utilization of South Yemen's Socotra Island for amphibious training under conditions not replicable within the USSR.[3]

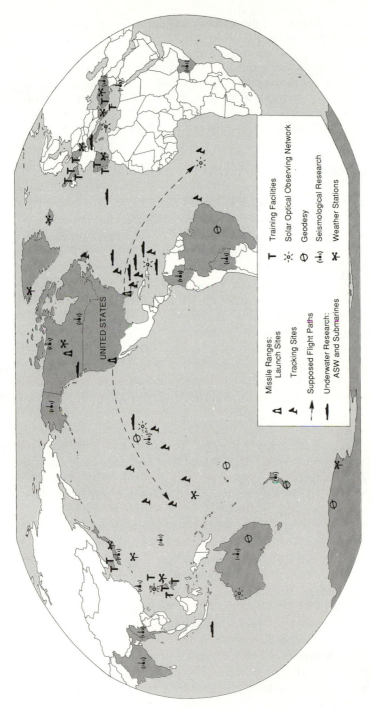

Figure 11. US research and environmental facilities

Source: SIPRI data

Missile ranges

As indicated by Arkin and Fieldhouse, nuclear delivery vehicles have a testing infrastructure which spans the globe. Thus:

The test ranges contain instruments to record every possible facet of a weapon's operation: They photograph the launch, track the missile by radar, and measure its range and accuracy . . . During test flights a missile sends diagnostic data on its internal workings (called telemetry) to observers on land, on tracking ships, and on special aircraft. After collecting and analyzing the test data the military adjusts the weapon to refine accuracy and reliability.[4]

Generally speaking, the USA operates two major long-range missile ranges: the Eastern and Western Test Ranges. These involve down-range tracking facilities and impact points for missiles launched from Cape Canaveral, Florida, and Vandenberg Air Force Base in southern California, respectively. Missiles launched from Cape Canaveral are generally fired in a south-easterly direction towards the South Atlantic; those from Vandenberg in a south-westerly direction towards Kwajalein Island.[5]

Numerous facilities are utilized in connection with tracking and telemetry of missiles tested from Cape Canaveral (from where SLBMs and Pershing IIs have been tested), among them, at Ascension, Grand Turk Island, Bermuda, Newfoundland (Argentia), Fernando de Noronha (belonging to Brazil), Antigua (a Missile Impact Location System—MILS—facility), the Grand Bahamas, and elsewhere in the Bahamas at San Salvador, Great Abaco, Eleuthera, Mayaguana, Great Stirrup Cay and Freeport, where timing transponders are sited.[6] Earlier, there were additional such facilities in South Africa and Puerto Rico.[7]

At Ascension, for instance, there are tracking radars, optical equipment, MILS arrays and telemetry antennas.[8] Bermuda has a tracking station and range safety station.[9] Grand Turk Island had an underwater cable serving the Eastern Test Range and a command station for ordering destruction of off-course test missiles as well as associated communications and an auxiliary airfield, apparently closed in 1983.[10]

Concerning the Western Test Range, Kwajalein Island in the Carolines is a critical basing point. It is a target point for ICBMs launched from Vandenberg and SLBMs launched from submarines off the coast of California which ascend to 7000 km before their re-entry vehicles (RVs) plunge into Kwajalein Lagoon. Several large radars, airborne equipment and optical sensors monitor the re-entries.[11] Much of the development of the Polaris, Poseidon, Trident, Minuteman and MX missiles has been carried out here, where tracking systems are said to be more sensitive than those on the eastern range.[12] Further, Kwajalein is also a major testing facility for defensive strategic missile systems, that is, for ABMs—the Sprint/Spartan/Safeguard systems were tested here, as well as more recently developed ABM technologies.[13] The Memorandum of Understanding regarding the establishment of the data base for the 1987 INF Treaty listed Roi

Namur on Kwajalein and Wake Island as missile research and development sites.[14]

There are other facilities associated with the Western Test Range in the former Gilbert Islands at Birnie, Hull and Enderbury; Wake, Midway and Johnston Islands; and on Hawaii.[15] At Midway and Wake, for instance, there are sensors for the MILS system of the Western Test Range, involving underwater hydrophone target arrays.[16] And at Johnston Island facilities include launch pads for Athena rockets launched towards Kwajalein, to serve as targets for ABM detection systems and to test ABM missiles.[17]

The USA does require some external access for testing missiles other than long-range ballistic missiles. In recent years, it has used overhead access and aiming points for the testing of cruise missiles. That has involved use of the Primrose Lake (Alberta) Weapons Evaluation Range in Canada, which is the target point for ALCM test flights launched from the Canadian Arctic—its 10 000 km^2 is also used for aircraft and artillery testing. The Primrose range allows for simulation of Soviet Arctic terrain.[18]

In the area of missile testing, as in so many others, the USA has experienced some pressures on its once taken-for-granted access. For instance, in 1983, the USA sought and obtained some limited use of Australian facilities in connection with tests of the then new MX missile. It involved support for mobile telemetry ships operating in international waters and operation of surveillance aircraft out of a Sydney base to monitor the last stages of the test flights. Access was quietly granted on condition that the test was kept out of Australia's 200-mile zone, but it led to a subsequent political crisis.[19]

British-owned Christmas Island has been used to host equipment for down-range tracking of missiles launched from the opposite direction—Woomera in Australia, including ELDO space launches.[20] The nearby island of Maribu has been used for meteorological work in relation to these tests.[21]

The foregoing illustrates the critical strategic importance of numerous oceanic islands for still another purpose—additionally, many of the same islands have derived importance in connection with aerial staging and refuelling, SIGINT, communications and ASW. It also provides an obvious basis for the emergent Soviet interest in acquiring access to Pacific islands, particularly in proximity to the critical US facility at Kwajalein now extensively used for ABM/SDI research.

France has also made use of external research facilities for missile tracking and telemetry monitoring. From 1959 to 1967, it utilized a tracking and tele-metry station at Hammaguir in Algeria.[22] Afterwards, the telemetry equipment was shifted to Las Palmas in the Canaries, and the tracking equipment to French Guyana.[23] Facilities in Portugal's Azores have also been used by France for such purposes, involving SLBM and IRBM tests in the Atlantic launched from France's Atlantic coast.[24]

Nuclear testing

Whereas both the USSR and China (the latter in its western desert province of Sinkiang) have been availed of domestic space for nuclear testing (first in the atmosphere, later underground), all three of the Western nuclear powers have made extensive use of external access for such purposes. For the USA, this was limited to the earlier period of above-ground testing; since that time it has conducted its underground nuclear tests at sites in Nevada and in Alaska at Amchitka Island.

In the early part of the nuclear era, the USA conducted tests at several Pacific islands acquired at the end of World War II, that is, Eniwetok, Bikini and Johnston. Eniwetok was used for 34 tests, including the first thermonuclear explosion; Bikini for 23, above and below water, including those involving large numbers of ships; and Johnston for 12, including some at high altitudes which produced the first data on the electromagnetic pulse.[25] After the PTBT came into being, Johnston Island was kept as a National Nuclear Test Readiness Center in case such testing was later resumed.[26]

France and Britain, for obvious reasons having to do with land size and the absence of unpopulated space, have both required overseas access for nuclear testing. Earlier on, France tested its first five nuclear bombs at Reggane in Algeria around 1960-61, then 13 more at Ahaggar in Algeria, some underground.[27] Afterwards the nuclear testing was shifted to the French Polynesian islands in the south-west Pacific, particularly at Muroroa Atoll, but also earlier at Fangataufa Island.[28] Several other islands—Papeete, Hao and Mangareva—have hosted facilities associated with the programme, which has involved more than 40 tests since 1966, but which, since 1974, have all been underground.[29] These tests have created considerable political ferment in the south-west Pacific and Oceania, and in 1987 reports surfaced alleging a US offer to allow France to test in Nevada, so as to obviate its political problems in the Pacific.[30]

Britain, meanwhile, has made extensive use of access to Australia for its nuclear testing, at Maralinga, Monte Bello Island and Emu Field.[31] Monte Bello was the site for the very first British test in 1952.[32] In recent years, Britain's nuclear testing has been conducted in the USA at the Nevada Test Site (and its strategic missiles tested from Cape Canaveral).[33]

Generally speaking, all of the extant nuclear powers have come under increasing pressures—on environmental as well as arms control grounds—with regard to nuclear testing. This is the case even though atmospheric testing has been more or less completely eliminated and the occasional problem of 'venting' of underground tests has caused no major fall-out problems. Britain was earlier subjected to pressures about testing in Australia; France has had political problems in New Zealand and in South-East Asia because of its testing at Muroroa. Perhaps ironically, domestic pressures on US testing in Nevada have been less severe, though not non-existent, leaving one to wonder whether the USA will henceforth take on the role as test-ground for all its NATO Allies. Meanwhile, progress towards a comprehensive test ban treaty has been slow—the military on both sides is reluctant to abandon weapon evaluation and calibration, both for new and for long-stockpiled weapons. It remains to be seen whether the seemingly improved overall climate for arms control in the late 1980s will have an impact here or whether there will be further multilateral pressures on external testing (particularly that by the UK and France).

There has been some speculation about additional (FMP) access provided for nuclear testing. In 1979, there was the *cause célèbre* of the flash over the ocean in waters adjacent to South Africa, commonly ascribed to an Israeli or joint Israeli–South African nuclear test. There have been no definitive answers. If the 'flash' did involve Israeli nuclear testing, it may have involved access to South African facilities, if only for associated logistics.[34] Reports of 'private' missile testing by a German firm—OTRAG—in Zaïre fall into a similar category.[35] One way or another, the problems of space for smaller powers' missile or weapon testing and the related diplomatic requirements—are highlighted.

Underwater research: ASW and submarines

The USA has utilized a varied network of test facilities in connection with underwater research which subsumes ASW (acoustics, that is, sonars, hydrophones, sonabuoys, etc.) and also various weapons utilized by or against submarines, that is, torpedoes, Harpoon missiles, the anti-submarine rocket (ASROC), the Navy's UUM-44A underwater-to-air-underwater missile (SUBROC), and so on. Those facilities have been concentrated in the Caribbean, the Pacific, and the Canadian north-west, but have also involved the Azores as well as (not involving FMP) Alaska and Hawaii.

Most notable in this regard is the Atlantic Underseas Test and Evaluation Center (AUTEC) centred on various sites in the Bahamas, which plays a central role in submarine training, testing and certification, and in SOSUS research. According to one source AUTEC, on Andros Island, involves a:

... deep water range for submarine systems undersea R&D, only permanent underwater noise measuring facility on the east coast of the U.S., used for Trident submarine certification trials, also key station in the missile submarine security and silencing programs and sonar testing, ASROC and SUBROC testing, instrumentation includes a hydrophone acoustic array fixed to a single cable which is buoyed 50 feet below the surface and anchored to the ocean floor. Weapons Range is a 5 by 15 mile tracking range used for ASW training and certification against mobile targets.[36]

US underseas research is also conducted in a number of other locales. US Navy submarine torpedoes are tested in US-owned Saint Croix.[37] In the Azores, in connection with the Azores Fixed Acoustic Range, research is carried out on LF sonar.[38] Similar research is underway in Hawaii, which also hosts the Barking Sands facility devoted to work on torpedoes, ASROC, SUBROC and Harpoon missiles.[39] Underwater acoustics research is conducted in the Virgin Islands, at Eleuthera in the Bahamas and on Christmas Island—where a hydrophone array is used to calibrate a sonar array at Diego Garcia.[40] A station at Tudor Hill, Bermuda is said to be used to monitor long-range sonar propagation by recording signals from a sonar transmitter in Eleuthera.[41] According to Arkin and Fieldhouse, at a complex involving Nanoose Bay, Jervis Inlet and Winchelsea Island in British Columbia, there is a joint US–Canadian testing centre which: '. . . includes a 15-mile range in the Strait of Georgia which varies from 2–5 miles wide and about 1,400 feet deep used for testing underwater detection systems and ASW weapons including air-dropped sonabuoys, NUWES Keyport, WA uses Nanoose for RDT & E of ASW weapons including ASROC and SUBROC missiles.'[42]

Finally, under NATO auspices but presumably dominated by the USA, there is at La Spezia, Italy, a SACLANT (Supreme Allied Command Atlantic) Anti-Submarine Warfare Research Centre, involving nine NATO governments: the USA, Canada, Denmark, France, FR Germany, Italy, Netherlands, Norway, and the UK.[43]

Training facilities

While some overseas facilities are required for research and testing of weapons because of location, climate, and so on, there is also the need for continual weapons training in proximity to existing overseas air, land and sea military deployments. Mostly this involves bombing practice and tactical missile ranges in proximity to major air and missile deployments.

The USA holds nuclear bombing or air-to-surface missile firing exercises in a number of overseas locales: South Korea (Koon-ni and Osan), Spain (Bardenas Reales), the UK (Holbeach, Jurby, Wainfleet), Netherlands (Vlieland), Philippines (Crow Valley, Las Fraites, Tarbones, Nazosa Bay), Japan (Ie Shima), Guam (Anderson) and Italy (Decimannu, Maniago).[44] At Konya, Turkey the USA has an air-to-ground bombing and strafing range acquired to replace facilities lost at Wheelus AFB in Libya, now used mainly for F-111 low-level operation exercises.[45] According to Arkin and Fieldhouse, 'at a major nuclear bombing range at Crow Valley in the Philippines, targets include mock railyards and military bases'.[46] Lance and Honest John missiles have been test-fired at NATO's NAMFI facility on Crete; there is a NATO missile test facility in Portugal.[47] The USSR also uses external facilities for simulated nuclear weapon training. According to the same report, ' . . . in East Germany, for instance, Soviet aircraft and missiles are known to conduct simulated nuclear missions at ranges in Belgern, Retzow, Rossow, Sperenberg, and Letzlinger Heide'.[48]

VLF communications research

Use of VLF communications is crucial to communications with submerged submarines during crises, and the survivability of C^3I after a first strike is a major area of concern. (This remains the case for the USA despite a move towards alternative reliance on ELF based in Michigan and Wisconsin.) In this connection, knowledge of the specific conditions or configurations of various oceanic or sea bodies of water is important—this may also apply to the ability to intercept the communications of rivals.

Hence, the US Naval Research Laboratory has operated VLF research facilities in connection with various bodies of water where its submarines prowl.

One at Bahrain, for instance, earlier (up to 1963) monitored VLF radio propagation to determine its adequacy for communications with Polaris submarines in the Arabian Sea.[49] During the same period of time, long-distance VLF propagation from Jim Creek, Washington, and from Panama was monitored at a facility in Santiago, Chile.[50] Other facilities in Israel and Italy served the same purpose for submarine communications in the Mediterranean; one in Japan served for the Pacific Ocean; another at Tananarive, Madagascar for the Indian Ocean.[51] These have apparently now been phased out.

Earlier on, there was additional, related research on VLF (also ELF) transmissions over longer distances, which utilized geomagnetically conjugate facilities in the far north of the globe and the far south. At Longwire in Antarctica, there was a 35-km long VLF radio antenna, fed by a VLF transmitter, used for research in magnetosphere propagation of VLF and ELF wavelengths, which was located geomagnetically conjugate to the Great Whale Station in Canada.[52] Another at Siple Station in Antarctica was geomagnetically conjugate to one at Robeval in Canada; another at Eights Station in Antarctica conjugate to one at Luther, Maine.[53] There was a similar relationship between a station at Naseby in New Zealand and one at Cold Bay in Alaska.[54] Still another VLF-related station at Santiago, Chile monitored long-distance signals from Jim Creek, Maine, to test the adequacy of communications to Polaris submarines.[55] Earlier, there was a VLF-related facility in Botswana, antipodal to one in Hawaii.[56]

Climate-related research

The USA operates or participates in research at a number of facilities clearly involving broad military implications and applications emerging from various climatic conditions. Mostly, this has involved the extremes of climate and terrain, that is, the Arctic and tropical jungles.

In Alaska within the USA, there is the US Arctic Test Center and Permafrost Research Station.[57] In Canada, the USA has facilities at Fort Churchill for research on 'polar cap absorptions', which simulate the effects of nuclear explosions on the ionosphere.[58] In Canada and Greenland there are ground stations for the high-altitude research satellite (HILAT), which investigates the aurora borealis.[59] In Greenland there is an experimental army camp constructed in tunnels excavated within the ice cap, and a seismic research site to determine the suitability of an ice cap location for underground nuclear test detection seismic arrays.[60] At the other extreme are a tropical exposure station in Panama and, in Australia, a Joint Tropical Research Unit.[61] Arkin and Fieldhouse report that climatic testing of aircraft, missiles and nuclear artillery takes place in Canada, Panama and the Philippines.[62] In a related vein, US forces have long utilized areas in Panama, Palau, Okinawa and elsewhere for jungle combat training and related amphibious landings; and areas in Norway for similar training under Arctic conditions.

Beyond the obvious, there are other research facilities devoted to the esoteric characteristics of areas deemed possible future locales of conflict. In Egypt, for instance, at Hurghada, the US Naval Marine Laboratory carries out research on Red Sea marine biology, including venomous animals, shark behaviour, and boring and fouling organisms.[63]

Medical research

Various US medical research units have conducted research around the globe, usually with reference to conditions and diseases found in specific places. This is a sensitive and contentious subject, given the thin line between medical and biological warfare (BW) research (the one is inherently the obverse of the other) and the fact that preventative or defensive research is allowed under the BW Convention.

Over the years the USA has had medical research facilities in, among other places, Bangladesh, Ethiopia, Indonesia, Japan, Malaysia, Panama and Egypt. That in Bangladesh, up to the latter's acquiring of independence in 1971, was a SEATO Cholera Research Laboratory.[64] That in Ethiopia up to its revolution in 1977 conducted research on local infectious diseases, perhaps including Rift Valley fever.[65] Those in Panama, Indonesia and Malaysia dealt with tropical diseases; that in Egypt with the indigenous bilharzia; that in Japan apparently dealt with beta encephalitis, perhaps with BW-related implications.[66]

Whether the USSR conducts similar medical research around the world is not here known, particularly as it concerns the BW connection. There have been allegations of such 'research' in Afghanistan and Laos, that is, the controversies over 'yellow rain'.[67]

Geodesy

One of the least publicized functions of satellites has to do with the science of geodesy, defined by Jasani as 'the branch of applied mathematics that deals with the shape of the earth, its gravitational field, and the exact positions of various points on the Earth's surface'.[68] Critically involved is the fact that the earth's rotation has distorted it from a sphere to a slightly flattened ellipsoid, and the fact that the earth's uneven surface, uneven climate, and so on, make for complexities in gauging gravitational pulls at various points along the earth's surface and in the atmosphere. According to Jasani:

Geodetic satellites . . . are able to provide greater accuracy over a much wider area. By using maps with grids accurately to locate specific places, and by obtaining knowledge of the Earth's gravitational field through satellites, the military are able to gain a more accurate cartographical picture, an essential requirement, for example, in the development of long-range ballistic missiles.[69]

Both the USA and the USSR use satellites to acquire such extremely precise data on the size and shape of the earth's surface and its gravitational fields. The USA earlier relied on GEOS and Pageos satellites; more recently on Geosat spacecraft to supply new geodetic data for its Trident II programme, which will operate from large, unsurveyed areas of the ocean.[70] The USSR launches one or two geodetic satellites a year; France has also launched a number of them.[71]

A number of ground research facilities have been associated with the satellite-based US geodetic programme, and have involved access to foreign facilities. This pertains to so-called tracking network (TRANET) geodetic facilities, using Doppler tracking methods in relation to Transit satellites; and others related to the Pageos satellites. These have been identified in Antarctica, Australia, Hawaii (Wahiawa), American Samoa (Pago Pago) and perhaps in Brazil, involving obvious concentration in the southern hemisphere.[72] In the past, several TRANET stations were operated in Australia at Smithfield, Perth, Darwin, Rockhampton, Canberra, Adelaide and Woomera. These apparently operated only up to 1971.[73]

The USA also formerly operated a number of BC-4 ballistic cameras for observation of the Pageos geodetic satellites. These were at Vanuatu, Macquarie Island and Pitcairn Island.[74] Earlier, at Perth in Australia, there was a telemetry station for observations of the Indian Ocean with the GEOS-3 satellite.[75]

Still another related type of research facility are those described as transit circle and astrograph sites, for making accurate measurements of southern hemisphere star locations, hence providing data for improved accuracy of new strategic systems, specifically, the stellar inertial guidance system of the Trident SLBM. There is one at Black Birch Mountain in New Zealand.[76]

A similar facility was apparently utilized by the USSR in Chile during the Allende period, 1970–73, to provide accurate data on stars for the Soviet SS-N-8 and other ballistic missiles.[77]

While most of the geodetic information is now obtained by satellite, the USA had earlier carried out land survey in some areas, to provide more accurate maps particularly of remote regions. The USAF Aerospace Cartographic and Geodetic Service has, for such purposes, had access to Bolivia, Chile, Colombia, Ecuador, Ethiopia, Paraguay and other countries.[78] Australia has enjoyed access to East Irian for similar purposes.[79]

The Soviet Union also does extensive work in geodesy and mapping, reportedly utilizing Cosmos and perhaps also navigation satellites. This is important for ICBM targeting in connection with gravitational fields around launch and target areas, and 'since the missile fields in the Soviet Union are spread over a wide geographical area, the use of geodetic satellites becomes almost essential'.[80]

The Soviet Union also apparently makes some use of external access for work in geodesy. Hence, according to one source,

The Polish contribution to geodesy under the aegis of the Interkosmos program was described in an article by Dr. Olgierd Wolczek. Observations of the orbits of artificial satellites made by the Agricultural Academy in Olsztyn, the Adam Mickiewicz Astronomical Observatory in Poznan, and the Institute of Geophysics in Borowicz were used to study the effect upon the orbits of the Earth's gravitational field, luni-solar gravitational fields, solar radiation pressure and drag in the upper layers of the atmosphere. To this end, a laser-measuring apparatus was installed at Borowicz in 1975 giving an accuracy of 1.2 meters.[81]

III. Environmental facilities

Seismological

Chapter 6 details the various systems and assorted access related to detection of nuclear explosions, involving seismological facilities for underground blasts, satellites which can detect detonations above ground, aircraft for gathering down-wind air samples, and so on. That, in turn, is related to the purposes of non-proliferation monitoring, verification of test bans and intra-war targeting requirements.

In addition, a number of other, related facilities associated with the DARPA/ Vela-Uniform program for seismological research have been identified. The extent to which some of these facilities may have quasi-military implications, beyond research in connection with earthquakes, may not be entirely clear. But at any rate, such facilities have been hosted in Australia and Colombia (seismic-research observatories), Bolivia, Canada (Yellowknife and Red Lake), India, Iran (earlier), Israel, Japan, Kenya, New Zealand, Taiwan, Thailand and Turkey, as well as in Alaska, Hawaii and Guam.[82] Most of these involve high-gain, long-period seismometers utilizable for monitoring underground nuclear tests or for developing technologies therefor. Some have apparently been operated primarily by host-country personnel.

In a somewhat related vein, some US facilities were earlier devoted to gauging the impact of atmospheric nuclear tests on the ionosphere—among other things, this involved research on the post-event implications for communications utilizing the ionosphere. In this regard the USA operated a system of some 19 foreign facilities within the Pacific Riometer Network (collocated were related facilities to monitor geomagnetic micropulsations). Among them were those located, up to about 1972, in Canada (Resolute), Raratonga, Tonga (Tongatapu and Acaria), Peru (several stations up to 1967) and Canton Island (Kiribati).[83] The last of these facilities were phased out in about 1979.

The USA has also operated additional facilities for monitoring fall-out from nuclear tests. A chain of stations monitoring radio-nuclides comprised stations in Bolivia, Peru, Chile, Ecuador and Panama until about 1963, when US atmospheric nuclear tests in the Pacific Ocean were discontinued. It was designated the '80th meridian airborne radionucleide sampling program'.[84]

Weather stations

The various US services continue to operate a number of weather stations around the world, even as meteorological work has increasingly been assumed by satellites which themselves utilize overseas down-links. Indeed, the military's infrastructure for weather forecasting involves ground observations and radar, upper-air sensors (aircraft, balloons and rockets), specialized weather-reconnaissance aircraft and satellites. All of these are dependent on FMP. According to Arkin and Fieldhouse, this is particularly important to strategic nuclear activities, in that forecasting of cloud cover is crucial to aiming of reconnaissance satellites, while prediction of low-altitude weather systems is important to aid low-level bomber and cruise-missile penetrations.[85]

Over the years the USA has used weather stations in Antarctica, Canada (six stations earlier in connection with B-52 operations), FR Germany (several stations), Iceland, Spain (a fleet weather station and another for the USAF), Iwo Jima and Nauru (in connection with the Western Test Range).[86] But the DMSP satellite programme—which relies on some overseas facilities—is the Pentagon's most important source of weather data for tactical and strategic forces:[87]

Its two operational satellites, which fly a near-polar orbit about 450 miles above Earth, cover the globe 14 times a day and send current meteorological, space, environmental, and oceanographic data to Air Force and Navy forecasting centers. Additional capability is being added to allow transmissions to local Air Force, Navy, and Marine Corps operating units equipped with special receiving units.[88]

In connection with the DMSP satellites, there is a major weather satellite tracking and receiving facility at Bann in FR Germany, and a satellite control or receiver site at Thule, Greenland.[89] (There are others in Hawaii, Wisconsin, California, Maine and Nebraska, with the latter one, at Omaha, designated as the Air Force Global Weather Control.) Stares reports on plans to harden a new weather command, control and data processing facility at Fairchild AFB, Washington State.[90]

The USA also operates a number of overseas facilities designated as 'weather intercept stations'. These bases, actually involving a form of (overt and un-threatening) intelligence activity, are devoted to monitoring weather broadcasts by other nations, so as to reduce the US need for more comprehensive, global meteorological coverage. Such facilities have been operated in Greece (Nea Makri), Japan (Owada, Honshu), Philippines (Dau, San Miguel in Luzon), Spain (Torrejon) and Turkey (Incirclik). Most of these are collocated with other facilities, such as major air bases.[91]

In a related, more specialized vein, the USA operates Arctic Ice Patrol aircraft from a facility in Iceland, presumably related both to surface and sub-surface naval operations.[92]

Other nations also operate overseas weather stations. France has such stations on Amsterdam, Kerguelen and Crozet islands.[93]

Regarding Soviet weather-related foreign facilities, information is sparse. Jasani has outlined the Soviet meteorological satellite programme, begun in 1966 with the Cosmos programme and involving Molniya and Meteor satellites. Regarding the more recent Meteor 2 satellite programme, he reports that 'the image resolution from these satellites will be comparable to that obtained by

U.S. weather satellites', and that 'the new system will also be able to transmit automatically photographs of weather conditions on Earth so that weather imagery will be received by Soviet ground- or ship-based stations around the world'.[94] There are reportedly three Meteor ground receiving stations within the USSR, at Novosibirsk, Moscow and Khavarovsk. Additionally, according to one US government report, 'a Polish report in 1978 instanced plans to construct a satellite data reception center in Cracow designed to collect information from meteorological satellites'.[95] There may be others outside the USSR in addition to those aboard ships.

SOFNET and SOON—solar flares and interruptions of communications

Since the early 1970s, the USA has operated a global system of facilities to monitor solar emissions or 'flares' which can cause magnetic storms and, in some circumstances, could interfere with critical communications by causing temporary black-outs. This is specifically critical in connection with HF communications, for which frequencies need to be changed continuously so as to maximize reliable and clear transmissions. Earlier, up to around 1977, this involved the Solar Flare Network (SOFNET); subsequently this function has been performed by solar observations within the Solar Optical Observing Network (SOON). A typical facility might be equipped with a solar telescope and some antennas for monitoring emissions. Thus, according to Arkin and Fieldhouse:

The U.S. military operates its own solar observation network: the Space Environmental Support System, for observing solar flares and activity, and for detection and forecasting of auroral activity. Outbursts of solar energy, equivalent to billions of nuclear explosions, constantly strike the earth's upper atmosphere and affect a variety of military systems. When these energy particles become trapped in the ionosphere, they can result in a visible Aurora Borealis ('northern lights'), which affects high-frequency (HF) and short-wave communications, satellite orbits, and radar operations. Solar flare activity occurs in eleven-year cycles, and the early 1980s is a high point of activity. From six locations around the world, Air Force solar telescopes observe the sun around-the-clock. By measuring light intensity and wavelength (to one-ten-billionth of one meter), these sites can alert the military to adverse conditions.[96]

The earlier SOFNET system incorporated facilities in Australia, Greece and Puerto Rico.[97] The SOON network comprises facilities with solar telescopes in Australia (Learmouth), Hawaii, Ascension Island, Italy (San Vito), Philippines (Manila) and Puerto Rico (Point Borinquen).[98] That at San Vito was relocated from Iran after the 1979 revolution.[99]

IV. Miscellany

The aforementioned research and environmental activities and associated utilization of external facilities is not comprehensive. There are others. And, though the discussion of such facilities here has emphasized US activities because of the greater availability of information, it may be assumed that other major powers, including the USSR, conduct numerous such activities outside their borders. For instance, there is evidence that the USSR has conducted oceanographic research from Guinea in connection with fisheries activities.[100]

One US government source, for instance, reported on a Soviet facility in Czechoslovakia utilized for ionospheric research, as follows:

The Czechoslovakian station is located at Panska Ves in Northern Bohemia and is described as the ionospheric observatory of the Geophysical Institute of the Czechoslovak Academy of Sciences. This station was responsible for controlling the Magion satellite with which it made contact four times daily. The station had its last contact with Magion on September 10, 1981, just before it decayed after nearly 3 years in orbit and making more than 16,000 orbits.[101]

Various miscellaneous research and environmental activities can be identified which are not easily categorized, nor do they fit into easily recognizable global systems. Argentina and Chile have some scientific stations—perhaps in part to underscore a presence—in Antarctica.[102] The USA has operated ionospheric laboratories in Labrador and Greenland which, among other things, involves testing of backscatter radars as part of the 'Polar Fox' programme.[103] There was earlier another facility related to OTH propagation located on Australia's Norfolk Island.[104] It has also apparently tested chemical and BW weapons in Canada, also on Baker Island in the Pacific.[105] NATO's SHAPE Technical Center in the Netherlands conducts research for NATO communications.[106] Chemical warfare (CW) research has been carried out in Panama.[107] France once had a research rocket range in Argentina, and during the Viet Nam period the USA had facilities in Thailand to test defoliation techniques, and a tribal research centre in connection with counter-insurgency.[108] There have also been reports of a jointly operated Franco–Soviet VLF research facility on Kerguelen Island in the southern Indian Ocean and similar Soviet activity on Australia's Macquarie Island, both in the guise of non-military research.[109]

Looking to the future, one interesting question may be the extent to which the major powers will require access for research and environmental facilities related to emerging space-based missile defence systems. Little concrete information has yet emerged, but one might speculate on near-global requirements for testing land-based lasers and related geodetic requirements.[110]

Notes and references

[1] Arkin, W. M. and Fieldhouse, R. W., *Nuclear Battlefields: Global Links in the Arms Race* (Ballinger: Cambridge, Mass., 1985), appendix B, and see also the map on pp. 70–71.

[2] Arkin and Fieldhouse (note 1), p. 68, noting that 'The Soviets have tested nuclear warheads at twenty sites, including East and West Kazakh, five sites in Siberia, Semipalatinsk, and two on the island of Novaya Zemlya.' See also, 'Soviets conduct nuclear test blast', *Centre Daily Times*, 8 July 1987, p. A9, regarding a test in the Yakut Autonomous region.

[3] Harkavy, R. E., *Great Power Competition for Overseas Bases: The Geopolitics of Access Diplomacy* (Pergamon: New York, 1982), p. 190.

[4] Arkin and Fieldhouse (note 1), pp. 68–69.

[5] Arkin and Fieldhouse (note 1), p. 69 and appendix A. Herein, Canaveral is said to have

supported tests of Pershing I and II, Trident I and II, Poseidon, British Polaris and Chevaline, SRAMs and small ICBMs; and Vandenberg of MX, Titan II, Minuteman and cruise missiles. See also, 'U.S. protests Soviet missile tests near Hawaii', *New York Times*, 2 Oct. 1987, p. A6.

[6] SIPRI data; and Arkin and Fieldhouse (note 1), appendix A.

[7] SIPRI data.

[8] SIPRI data; and Arkin and Fieldhouse (note 1), appendix A.

[9] SIPRI data; and Arkin and Fieldhouse (note 1), appendix A.

[10] SIPRI data; and Arkin and Fieldhouse (note 1), appendix A.

[11] SIPRI data; and Arkin and Fieldhouse (note 1), appendix A. See also, 'U.S. to open Kwajalein range parley', *Aviation Week & Space Technology*, 12 July 1982, p. 61.

[12] SIPRI data; and Arkin and Fieldhouse (note 1), appendix A.

[13] SIPRI data; and Arkin and Fieldhouse (note 1), appendix A. See also, 'U.S. intercepts warhead in test attack', *International Herald Tribune*, 12 June 1984, p. 1.

[14] See 'Locations of sites named in arms agreement', *New York Times*, 11 Dec. 1987, p. A25.

[15] SIPRI data.

[16] SIPRI data; and Arkin and Fieldhouse (note 1), appendix A.

[17] SIPRI data; and Arkin and Fieldhouse (note 1), appendix A.

[18] SIPRI data; and Arkin and Fieldhouse (note 1), appendix A. See also, 'Cruise missile lands in Canada', *Centre Daily Times*, 23 Jan. 1986, p. A2.

[19] Alves, D., *Anti-Nuclear Attitudes in New Zealand and Australia* (National Defense University Press: Washington, DC, 1985), pp. 45–48. See also, 'Australia backs down on offer to support MX', *Centre Daily Times*, 6 Feb. 1985, p. A2.

[20] SIPRI data.

[21] SIPRI data.

[22] SIPRI data.

[23] SIPRI data.

[24] Arkin and Fieldhouse (note 1), p. 288, siting a missile-tracking station at Flores, and an airfield at Santa Maria for aircraft used in tracking and telemetry collection in connection with missile testing.

[25] SIPRI data.

[26] SIPRI data.

[27] SIPRI data.

[28] SIPRI data. See also, 'French nuclear tests wearing out atoll', *International Herald Tribune*, 14 May 1980.

[29] SIPRI data; and 'Paris to continue Pacific N-Tests', *International Herald Tribune*, 11 Apr. 1979. See also, 'New Pacific N-test site?' *Christchurch Press*, 15 Dec. 1978, which discusses the alternative French plans for testing in the Marquesas island group. 'France may shift bomb test site', *Philadelphia Inquirer*, 21 Dec. 1981, p. 10, discusses Kerguelen Island as another possibility.

[30] 'U.S. offered Nevada site for French nuclear tests', *International Herald Tribune*, 22 June 1987, p. 1; and 'Test site report denied by France', *International Herald Tribune*, 23 June 1987, p. 2.

[31] SIPRI data.

[32] SIPRI data.

[33] SIPRI data; and Arkin and Fieldhouse (note 1), p. 278 and p. 68, wherein: 'All U.S. and British warheads are detonated at the Nevada Test Site.'

[34] This subject is summarized in, among others, Joseph, B. M., *Besieged Bedfellows: Israel and the Land of Apartheid* (Greenwood Press: New York, 1988), especially chapter 7 under 'The ultimate weapon: Don't push us too far'. Later, there were reports of joint Israeli–South African activities on remote Marion Island near Antarctica, perhaps involving missiles to be armed with nuclear warheads, see, 'S. Africa/nuclear weapons', in Department of Defense, *Wire News Highlights*, 29 Dec. 1986.

[35] SIPRI data on Zaïre indicate that these activities were halted in 1979. But, according to Karp, A., 'Ballistic missile development', *Journal of Defense and Diplomacy*, vol. 5, no. 12 (1987), p. 17, OTRAG had set up a new operation in Libya beginning in 1979.

[36] Arkin and Fieldhouse (note 1), p. 215. See also, 'Bahamas still seeks more for U.S. bases', *Chicago Tribune*, 16 Sep. 1977, p. 8; and 'U.S. and Bahamas in accord', *New York Times*, 21 July 1981, p. 8.

[37] SIPRI data.

[38] SIPRI data; and Arkin and Fieldhouse (note 1), p. 229.

[39] SIPRI data; and Arkin and Fieldhouse (note 1), p. 186.

[40] SIPRI data.

[41] SIPRI data; and Arkin and Fieldhouse (note 1), p. 216.
[42] Arkin and Fieldhouse (note 1), p. 218.
[43] SIPRI data on Italy.
[44] SIPRI data; and Arkin and Fieldhouse (note 1), appendix A.
[45] SIPRI data; and Arkin and Fieldhouse (note 1), appendix A.
[46] Arkin and Fieldhouse (note 1), p. 69.
[47] SIPRI data; and Arkin and Fieldhouse (note 1), appendix A.
[48] Arkin and Fieldhouse (note 1), p. 69.
[49] SIPRI data.
[50] SIPRI data.
[51] SIPRI data.
[52] SIPRI data.
[53] SIPRI data.
[54] SIPRI data.
[55] SIPRI data.
[56] SIPRI data.
[57] SIPRI data.
[58] SIPRI data.
[59] Arkin and Fieldhouse (note 1), p. 31.
[60] SIPRI data.
[61] SIPRI data.
[62] Arkin and Fieldhouse (note 1), p. 69.
[63] SIPRI data.
[64] SIPRI data.
[65] SIPRI data.
[66] SIPRI data.
[67] The yellow rain allegations are covered in, among other sources, Seagrave, S., *Yellow Rain* (M. Evans: New York, 1981). See also, 'Bee feces theory of yellow rain is reasserted', *International Herald Tribune*, 13 Aug. 1985, p. 6.
[68] Jasani, B., SIPRI, *Outer Space—Battlefield of the Future?* (Taylor and Francis: London, 1978), p. 158.
[69] Jasani (note 68).
[70] Jasani (note 68), pp. 160–62; and Stares, P., *Space and National Security*, pp. 37–39.
[71] Jasani (note 68), p. 162; and Stares (note 70), p. 39, who states that 'other spacecraft, such as the Salyut space station, may also provide geodetic data'.
[72] SIPRI data. See also Hendrickson, W., 'Satellites and the sea', *National Defense*, Oct. 1982, pp. 27–28.
[73] SIPRI data.
[74] SIPRI data.
[75] SIPRI data.
[76] SIPRI data.
[77] Sited at Santiago (SIPRI data).
[78] SIPRI data.
[79] SIPRI data.
[80] Jasani (note 68), p. 162.
[81] *Soviet Space Programs: 1976–1980*, US Senate, Committee on Commerce, Science and Transportation, 97th Congress, 2nd Session (US Government Printing Office: Washington, DC, Dec. 1982), p. 124.
[82] SIPRI data.
[83] SIPRI data.
[84] SIPRI data.
[85] Arkin and Fieldhouse (note 1), p. 18.
[86] SIPRI data.
[87] See Stares (note 70), pp. 35–36. See also, Jasani (note 68), pp. 144–46.
[88] 'Weather Service to drop NASA for satellites', *New York Times*, 27 Mar. 1987, p. A15.
[89] Stares (note 70), p. 188; Arkin and Fieldhouse (note 1), p. 237.
[90] Stares (note 70), p. 199.
[91] Arkin and Fieldhouse (note 1), appendix A.
[92] SIPRI data.
[93] SIPRI data.

[94] Jasani (note 68), pp. 148–49. See also Stares (note 70), pp. 36–37.

[95] *Soviet Space Programs: 1976–1980* (note 81), p. 125.

[96] Arkin and Fieldhouse (note 1), p. 28. See also, 'Solar flare expected to disrupt systems of communication', *New York Times*, 27 June 1988, p. A10; and 'Solar discharge sends storm over Earth', *New York Times*, 7 May 1988, p. 36.

[97] SIPRI data.

[98] Arkin and Fieldhouse (note 1), appendix A.

[99] Arkin and Fieldhouse (note 1), p. 224.

[100] SIPRI data on Guinea report that this activity ended in 1981 and was of ambiguous military relevance.

[101] *Soviet Space Programs: 1976–1980* (note 81), p. 125.

[102] SIPRI data.

[103] SIPRI data.

[104] SIPRI data.

[105] SIPRI data.

[106] SIPRI data.

[107] SIPRI data.

[108] SIPRI data.

[109] SIPRI data.

[110] For a preview of some possibilities, see 'New clues on a Soviet laser complex', *New York Times*, 23 Oct. 1987, p. A14.

8. Nuclear-related FMP: deterrence and defence

I. Introduction

In this and the next chapter, we move towards a more broadly 'functional' description and analysis of the major powers' basing systems. Whereas chapters 2–7 describe such systems according to a traditional service breakdown (army, navy, air force); or one centred on types of weapon or technology (missiles, communications, intelligence, research, etc.); chapters 8 and 9 move to integrate those data according to the two broad 'functional' areas of military endeavour: the strategic nuclear balance and conventional power projection. While many issues—and many external facilities—fall into a grey area between, or span both, these categories (some intelligence and communications installations, for instance, are used for both), there appear few if any facilities whose purpose does not apply to either. Indeed, the dualism appears more or less all-inclusive. We begin on the nuclear side of the equation.

There are a number of ways in which nuclear-related facilities can be classified. There is, of course, the by now familiar division between strategic, theatre and tactical nuclear forces (and the C^3I and other activities associated with them); granted the potential use of some weapons and related facilities in more than one of these categories. To a degree, some division between first- and second-strike-related forces may be assayed; similarly, a distinction can be made between forces devoted to deterrence and defence or war-fighting, respectively. The latter distinction is by no means abstract or theoretical—many facilities useful and usable for deterrence purposes during normal peacetime conditions might not be available to the nuclear superpowers either at the outset of or during a nuclear war, as presumably frightened and intimidated client states 'decoupled' in the face of threats and the terror of atomic holocaust.

Also worth looking at here is a gradient of necessity as applied to nuclear-related threats. Some facilities are more or less expendable than others, either in conditions of peace (deterrence) or war. The new interest in a possible 'Europe without America' now also directs attention to the question of which facilities—on either side—are vitally necessary and irreplaceable—and which can be replaced and at what cost, either via new technology or political developments.[1]

Since the data are organized on a system-by-system basis (pertaining either to weapon or support systems) in other chapters, here more attention is devoted to the roles—in the nuclear context—of individual nations and also regions which host nuclear-related facilities for either the USA or the USSR. Together with the traditional definition of geopolitics as having to do with 'the world that matters'[2]—this allows for a focus on those nations that, for either side, are most crucial to the superpowers' nuclear postures. In other words, emphasis here is on the strategic value of various locales in the nuclear–strategic context.

One final point about organization of the data bears mention. The chapters on naval, air and ground-force presence, including nuclear facilities, do not provide details on storage of nuclear weapons, that is, warheads. To the extent possible, and relying on some excellent recent research which has surfaced in the open literature, that is done here.

The fuzziness of the dividing line between nuclear-related facilities and those ostensibly devoted to conventional power projection must be stressed. That can easily be illustrated merely by reviewing the by now almost 'standard' scenario for the beginning of a 'central' war between the superpowers which might escalate up the ladder from conventional to tactical, to theatre and then to strategic nuclear weapons. Such scenarios often focus on the need for the USA to reinforce NATO by sea; hence, on protection of the Atlantic SLOCs. They also often focus on US offensive naval operations in the Norwegian and Barents seas, involving the combined use of airpower (land- and sea-based), surface fleets (carrier battle groups) and attack submarines to 'roll back' Soviet naval forces and to whittle down the Soviet SSBN force in the 'bastions'. The Soviet Union, on the other hand, is commonly portrayed as going all out to seize forward positions in Norway and perhaps Iceland, so as to extend defences forward and better to conduct operations against the Atlantic SLOCs by breaching the NATO barriers across the GIUK–Norway 'gaps'. It is also portrayed as utilizing *Spetsnaz* forces to destroy NATO nuclear facilities in Europe. So far these are conventional operations, but they involve numerous nuclear-related facilities, that is, SOSUS networks usable both against SSBNs and SSNs (and against surface ships with or without nuclear weapons); bases for dual-purpose aircraft such as P-3C Orion ASW craft and Soviet equivalents; air tanker facilities usable either in connection with conventional or nuclear strikes; and so on.

For these reasons, the division between nuclear–strategic and conventional-power projection related facilities can—to a partial degree—be correlated, respectively, with major power activities in Europe and/or related to the prospect of an all-out war in Europe; and activities related to the major powers' force projection in the Third World.

II. Historical background

The utilization of overseas facilities in connection with the superpowers' nuclear competition began immediately after the close of World War II. During the late 1940s, prior to the Soviet Union's development of a deployed nuclear military capability, the US forward-based some nuclear-armed B-29 aircraft in the UK in an effort to deter feared Soviet advances in Europe. By 1950, B-29s were based at Brize Norton, Upper Heyford, Mildenhall, Lakenheath, Fairford, Chelveston and Sculthorpe.[3] There were also reserve B-29 bases at other British bases. There were related depots at Burtonwood and Alconbury, and also related LORAN navigational facilities at Angle, Pembrokeshire and in the Hebrides.[4] That provided a clear first-strike deterrent capability for the USA well into the 1950s.

During the 1950s, the B-47 bombers became the backbone of SAC, and while their effective ranges were greatly extended by the aerial refuelling techniques then emerging, the USA then determined on forward deployment to enhance its chances for penetration and to lessen its vulnerability to a Soviet first strike. This so-called 'reflex force' rotated between US home bases and those in the UK (Fairford, Upper Heyford), Morocco (Sidi Slimane, Benguerir, Ben Slimane, Nouasseur), Spain (Torrejon, Zaragoza, Moron de la Frontera), Greenland (Thule) and Goose Bay, Labrador.[5] (F-84 fighters used as bomber escorts were also based at Nouasseur until US access to Morocco was lost in 1963.[6]) Related US tankers (then mostly KC-97s) were based primarily at Thule, Greenland and Goose Bay, Labrador; and also at several other Canadian bases: Namao, Churchill, Harmon, Cold Lake and Frobischer.[7] Though the subsequently deployed B-52s which began entering inventories in 1955 did not require forward main basing, they too utilized trans-Arctic tanker facilities (including one at Sondrestrom in Greenland) as well as contingency recovery bases in Spain and elsewhere.[8]

It is obvious that in the earlier part of the post-war period the USA greatly depended on foreign bases for its nuclear deterrence—because of the then shorter ranges of bombers and (from the 1960s) the shorter ranges of submarine-launched missiles. These rationales no longer apply. Since the USA and its NATO Allies still have a strong desire to use US nuclear forces to deter the Soviet (conventional or nuclear) threat to Western Europe, this has involved maintenance of some US forward-based systems in Europe with the capability to project nuclear force into the USSR: GLCMs and Pershing IIs, F-111 bombers, attack aircraft on land and aboard carriers.

The Soviet Union did not utilize forward strategic-bomber facilities during this period. Indeed, early Soviet bombers, such as the 4500-km range Tu-4, could only reach the US Pacific north-west from Siberia and, even then, by conceding several hours' warning time because of US radar coverage in Alaska.[9]

During this period and for a long time thereafter, the USA also relied on foreign access for strategic defence, primarily in Canada, Greenland and Iceland—that involved the DEW Line, Mid-Canada, and Pinetree Line strings of electronic listening posts, all under the US Air Defence Command, which worked closely with SAC.[10] In addition, some US interceptor aircraft were deployed at Canadian bases such as Goose Bay, and at bases in Greenland and Iceland, for perimeter early defence, well forward of the large-scale interceptor deployments around major US urban areas.[11] The location of DEW Line and Pinetree Line sites in Canada and Greenland, put into operation in 1956 and 1960, respectively, are listed above in table 22.

By the late-1950s, Soviet missile developments had rendered somewhat obsolete the three-layered radar early-warning system across the Canadian Arctic, which had been constructed to provide several hours' warning of bomber attacks. To cope with the missile threat, the USA built, beginning around 1958, the Ballistic Missile Early Warning System (BMEWS), the three hinges of which were in Fairbanks (Alaska), Thule (Greenland) and Fylingdales Moor (Yorkshire, UK).[12]

In the mid- to late-1950s, the USA underwent its famed 'missile-gap scare', following the Soviet Union's initial testing of IRBMs and ICBMs, and the launching of the first 'Sputnik' satellite. Coming before the deployments of Atlas, Titan and Minuteman ICBMs and Polaris SLBMs, this created a perceived 'window of vulnerability' which, in turn, impelled the short-term solution of US installation of IRBMs in Europe adjacent to the Soviet Union. Specifically, this involved emplacement in 1958 of sixty 2400-km range Thor missiles in the UK at 20 bases, with headquarters at Great Driffield, North Luffenham, Hemswell and Feltwell; 30 Jupiter missiles in Italy (at Gioia del Colle); and 15 Jupiters in Turkey, installed in 1961 at Cigli Air Base (these were removed as part of the deal in which the USSR removed IRBMs and also IL-28 aircraft from Cuba, after the Cuban missile crisis of October 1962—though the orders for their removal had apparently been given earlier).[13]

Late in 1960 the USA deployed its first Polaris submarines and then its long-range, counter-value Atlas and Titan ICBMs, thus quickly defusing the 'missile-gap scare'—though the forward-based IRBMs were to remain in place for an additional two to three years.[14]

As noted in chapter 6, US overseas facilities also played a crucial role during this period in the surveillance of the Soviet buildup of strategic bombers and missiles, prior to the utilization of the first spy satellites which began in the early 1960s. Specifically, this involved U-2 surveillance flights and those of 'ferret', that is, ELINT aircraft. Subsequently, early ground activities related to satellite reconnaissance were established.

The U-2, which began its career in 1956, served to compensate for the US disadvantage vis-à-vis the USSR with respect to strategic intelligence, resulting from the 'closed' nature of Soviet frontiers and society, which could only in part be made up for by intelligence from human sources. In 1957, U-2 flights operating out of Peshawar in Pakistan overflew the then new Soviet missile test site at Tyuratam near the Aral Sea and revealed the progress of the Soviet ICBM programme which hitherto had been monitored by a giant radar at Diyarbakir on the Turkish Black Sea coast.[15] These flights continued until 1960, ending with the fateful mission in which Gary Powers was shot down by missiles over Sverdlovsk while en route from Peshawar to Bodø, Norway.[16]

During this period—and well after—U-2 missions were flown from bases in Pakistan (Peshawar), Turkey (Adana), Norway (Bodø), FR Germany (Wiesbaden), Cyprus (Akrotiri), the UK (Alconbury) and Japan (Atsugi), among other places. Even without overflights of Soviet territory, these aircraft could take pictures of targets as far as 100 miles away by means of oblique-angle photography from high altitudes.[17]

In connection with emerging satellite developments, the USA made early use of external facilities for radio transmissions and for mid-air physical recovery procedures. In connection with the former, ground stations were deployed (supplementing those in New Hampshire, California, Alaska, Hawaii and Guam) in the British-held Seychelles Islands, and in at least one African country.[18] From 1964 several shipboard stations with 30-foot antennas were also used, and these too presumably relied—either directly or indirectly—on foreign ports for refuelling, food and water supplies.[19]

Complementary to BMEWS, the USA developed early-warning satellites under the MIDAS satellite programme. This involved combined use of infra-red sensors and telephoto lenses for immediate detection of missile-launching tracks and transmission of this information to US decision-makers. Launched by Atlas/Agena D missiles, advanced MIDAS satellites deployed in 1969 could be 'parked' in synchronous orbits, allowing for continuous coverage of the western USSR and the China–Siberia region as well as areas where Soviet submarines lurked in firing positions.[20] As noted in chapter 6, this involved the critical data down-link in Australia at Nurrungar, a related control facility in Guam and an underwater cable terminal near Vancouver in Canada.

One other key element of the strategic deterrence system came to depend upon overseas access: long-distance and protracted deployment of the Polaris nuclear-submarine force. The Polaris submarines were initially deployed early in the Kennedy Administration. The proportion of that fleet which the USA was able to deploy at any given time was enhanced by replenishment and repair facilities at Holy Loch, Scotland; Rota, Spain; and at Guam. Indeed, the asymmetries which these facilities created *vis-à-vis* subsequent Soviet SSBN deployment allowed the USA to negotiate that part of the SALT I Treaty which gave the USSR a 62 to 44 advantage in strategic submarines, but which was claimed to be counterbalanced by the efficiencies accruing to the USA from its overseas replenishment facilities.[21]

Throughout the early post-war period, the USSR lacked overseas facilities which might have served to moderate the unfavourable strategic balance it confronted. Indeed, throughout much of the 1950s its deterrent capability was based on bombers which could fly only one-way missions against the USA. The Soviet Union also lagged behind the USA in tanker-refuelling capability.

In the early 1960s, after the brief US missile-gap scare, the Soviet Union underwent a scare period of its own, as several US strategic programmes were phased in. To compensate, Moscow gambled with the introduction in 1962 of some 40 MRBMs into Cuba at several installations, precipitating the Cuban missile crisis.[22] (One recent report claims that these missiles were not accompanied by nuclear warheads.[23]) The history of that crisis bears no repeating here, but it is worth noting that only by the early 1960s did the Cuban revolution avail the USSR of its first valuable overseas assets applicable to the strategic nuclear equation. Henceforth, Cuba would become a very valuable Soviet base, its proximity to the USA providing irreplaceable assets related to intelligence, communications, naval replenishment, and so on, along with contingent bomber recovery bases in the event of a major war.

During the early post-war period, the USA made use of numerous nuclear-related intelligence and communications facilities around the Eurasian periphery—directed against the USSR, China and North Korea—mostly in the SIGINT (ELINT and COMINT) categories. These are discussed in detail for the more recent period in chapter 6. Earlier, both U-2 and other aircraft such as the RB-47 were flown from bases in Europe and Asia to 'tickle' Soviet early-warning radars and, in the case of the U-2s, to test radars well inside the USSR which might be of different types than the Soviet Union's peripheral early-warning systems.[24] By so doing, US planners might ascertain weaknesses and ranges, and scan patterns in the Soviet radar network which could be valuable for planning the penetration routes for a nuclear-bomber attack.

These exercises in low-level brinkmanship—apparently involving some mock 'raids' mounted by US units in Turkey and elsewhere—resulted in some serious incidents in which US ferret aircraft were shot down and their crews killed or captured. Some flights originating at Brize Norton in the UK apparently traversed the entire Soviet Arctic coastline, emerging at the Barents Sea.[25] The area between the Caspian Sea and the Sea of Azov was also apparently a focal point of US surveillance missions utilizing Turkish and Iranian airspace, some staged originally from FR Germany and Cyprus.[26]

Soviet ferret missions, on the other hand, operating out of Siberia towards Alaska, are believed rarely to have penetrated US airspace. At any rate, Moscow had no bases from which to fly missions intended to test US radars in such places as Canada and Greenland.

Satellites have by now largely but by no means entirely replaced the missions of ELINT aircraft. The same holds true for communications interception—chapter 6 notes the numerous existing US land-based SIGINT facilities.

US use of ground-based SIGINT stations, obviously crucial to various aspects of nuclear deterrence, dates well back into the post-war period. One source reported that this had earlier involved some 40 stations in at least 14 countries, ranging from small, mobile field units to sprawling complexes such as the Air Force Security Headquarters in FR Germany.[27] These were said to have involved some 30 000 personnel, with a minimum of 4000 radio-interception consoles operated in such varied locales as northern Japan, the Khyber Pass in Pakistan, and an island in the Yellow Sea off the coast of Korea.[28]

Further, these COMINT land stations had to be supplemented by numerous airborne and seaborne radio-interception facilities, particularly after Soviet and aligned nations' military forces switched to VHF radios during the 1950s, after which adequate coverage demanded getting closer to transmitters and overcoming terrain features such as mountains.[29] At any time, several dozen airborne listening posts were said to have been in intermittent operation, flying out of such bases as Kimpo Airfield in Korea, Clark AFB in the Philippines, and many others.[30] Added to these were some 12 to 15 spy ships such as the ill-fated *Pueblo* and *Liberty*, which also presumably required access to foreign ports for replenishment.[31]

It is obvious that the USA long enjoyed a large advantage over the USSR in the strategic equation by the asymmetric facts of basing access. Not surprisingly, in 1958 when President Eisenhower first proposed a ban on the use of outer space for military purposes, the Soviet Union insisted that such a measure be accompanied by 'liquidation' of foreign military bases in Europe, the Middle East and North Africa.[32] At that time, such a measure would have been very disadvantageous to the USA, given its noted reliance on B-47 and related tanker bases, and the whole vast network of C³I and other technical facilities around the Eurasian rim. Once the Soviet Union became more competitive in acquiring a rival basing access network, albeit on a smaller scale, it became more reserved about proposing formal arrangements which might mutually cancel out the superpowers' overseas nuclear-related facilities.

III. Extant nuclear forces

Both the USA and the USSR rely on numerous foreign facilities in connection with their nuclear deterrence and/or defence postures, along the spectrum from strategic, theatre and battlefield designated forces. The facilities also span the various functions or categories discussed in other chapters: aircraft bases, surface and submarine naval facilities, missile bases, and a variety of installations involving communications, intelligence, space-tracking, research and environmental facilities, and so on. As noted above, many of these facilities serve both nuclear and non-nuclear forces, so that it is not easy to ascertain discrete boundaries for the former.

Strategic nuclear forces: launchers and platforms

Generally speaking, the present period sees both the USA and the USSR left with only minimal dependence on foreign facilities—Soviet dependence is relatively less—for their strategic nuclear launchers, involving the familiar triad of ICBMs, SLBMs and long-range bombers. Of course, this is not to ignore the fact, particularly as it pertains to US forces, that some launchers designated as 'theatre' weapons can serve 'strategic' purposes in that their warheads can be delivered into the Soviet Union.

All of the US ICBMs (450 Minuteman IIs, 550 Minuteman IIIs and a few remnant Titan IIs now being phased out as the new MX-Peacekeeper is phased in) are housed in silos within the continental USA—they represent over 2100 accurate warheads. Similarly, the Soviet ICBM force (448 SS-11s, 60 SS-13s, 150 SS-17s, 308 SS-18s, 360 SS-19s, 72 SS-25s with more to come) of some 1398 ICBMs with some 6354 warheads, is sited entirely within the USSR.[33]

The Soviet SSBN force (983 SLBMs in 77 submarines, of which 944 SLBMs and 62 submarines are under the SALT Treaty; and 39 SLBMs on 15 submarines are outside it) is based entirely at Soviet homeland bases, in the Kola Peninsula area at Polyarny and Severomorsk, and at Petropavlovsk and Vladivostok in the Far East.[34] No foreign bases are used for refuelling, maintenance or crew changes. By contrast to the USA, only some 15–20 Soviet submarines are normally away from their bases; perhaps 10–12 on station at any given time.[35]

The US SSBN force, which earlier made extensive use of facilities at Holy Loch (Scotland), Rota (Spain) and at US-owned Guam, now utilizes only the first-named of these with its other three main bases in the continental USA at Kings Bay (Georgia), Bangor (Washington) and Charleston (South Carolina).[36] The development of the longer-range Poseidon and Trident missiles (with ranges of 4000 miles) has allowed for utilization of firing stations nearer US bases and further from the USSR, hence reducing requirements for firing stations in the Western Pacific (Guam) and in the Mediterranean (Rota). That force, which earlier deployed 41 Polaris submarines, now fields 640 SLBMs in 36 SSBNs, comprising 8 Ohio class submarines with Trident missiles; and 28 Franklin, Madison and Lafayette class submarines with a mix of Trident I and Poseidon C-3 missiles, amounting to some 6300 warheads.[37]

According to Arkin and Fieldhouse, little is publicly known about where these submarines patrol, but they are thought to transit to firing stations in the Arctic, North Atlantic and North Pacific oceans and in the Mediterranean Sea with about 30 per cent of the force 'on station' on day-to-day alert, and a roughly equal proportion in transit or on training missions.[38] The use of Holy Loch as a forward base (for submarines homeported at Groton, Connecticut) allows more to be on station than otherwise would be feasible, and it is also to be noted that 400 Poseidon warheads deployed on submarines operating out of Holy Loch are designated for NATO targeting, presumably either for 'theatre' targeting or for battlefield use along the Forward Line of Troops (FLOT) in central Germany.[39]

The second-tier nuclear powers—Britain, France and China—base all of their smaller SSBN forces at home bases. Britain has four SSBNs, which operate out of Faslane in Scotland near Holy Loch; France's five Redoubtable SSBNs operate out of Ile Longue in Brest (Brittany); China's two SSBNs are also based at home.[40] In all three cases, firing stations are easily accessible from home bases.

The long-range bomber forces of the USA and the USSR are based primarily within their respective homelands though in both cases, in the event of war, use of external dispersal or recovery bases may be envisaged.

At the strategic level, the USA now deploys some 260 long-range bombers (some 20 B-1Bs and some 240 B-52G/Hs), and some 55 medium-range FB-111A bombers.[41] Most of the B-52s carry up to 20 ALCMs; others carry a similar number of short-range attack missiles (SRAMs); and some, armed with Harpoon missiles, are operational in a conventional mode. This bomber force is supported by some 663 tankers (centrally comprising some 487 KC-135s and 48 KC-10s) of which some 125 are operated by the Air National Guard or Air Force Reserve, the primary role of which is to support the US nuclear-deterrence posture.[42]

This bomber force, which carries over 5000 nuclear warheads, is main-based at 19 air bases in 13 states and at Andersen AFB in Guam; but numerous 'dispersal' (pre-attack or crisis) and 'recovery' (post-attack) bases, or 'forward operating bases', are involved.[43] Some of these are outside the USA, for instance in Canada at Cold Lake (Alberta), Goose Bay (Labrador), Namao (Alberta) and Whitehorse (Yukon); in Greenland at Sondrestrom; in the UK at Brize Norton, Marham and Fairford; in Spain at Moron and Zaragoza.[44] But numerous others could, on the basis of *ad hoc* contingency planning, be made available, the politics of the moment so availing. Similarly, the USA is availed of numerous tanker bases—or their dispersal bases—in connection with the SAC bomber force; at some of the above-mentioned Canadian bases at Namao and Goose Bay; at Mildenhall and Fairford in the UK; Zaragoza in Spain; Clark AFB in the Philippines; Kadena in Okinawa; Diego Garcia; Keflavik (Iceland), Guam, Thule (Greenland), and so on.[45] Clearly, whereas in earlier years the bulk of tanker operations were in connection with Trans-Arctic routes, the development of more omnidirectional approaches to the USSR allowed for by longer-range stand-off weapons has impelled increased use of a more globally dispersed tanker force in connection with SAC bombers.

The USA forward-bases some 156 of the nuclear-armed F-111E/Fs in the UK, which are actually tactical fighter bombers designated for missions in Central Europe. These are stationed at Upper Heyford and Lakenheath in the UK, which host some 72 and 84 aircraft, respectively, involving in each case the storage of some 300 nuclear bombs.[46] Additionally, there are contingency plans for rotation forward in a crisis of some 60 FB-111s, the strategic version of the F-111E. These carry four SRAMs and two bombs, and would be moved forward from bases in Plattsburgh, N.Y. and Pease AFB, New Hampshire.[47]

By comparison, the Soviet Union makes little use of external facilities for its long-range strategic bomber force, which consists of some 160 aircraft: 140 Tu-95 Bear A/B/C/G/Hs armed either with ALCMs or air-to-surface missiles; and 20 Mya-4 Bisons (these will later be superseded by the Blackjack strategic bomber now being developed).[48] The same is true of the some 230 Backfire, Badger and Blinder bombers—some of the former are assigned to Soviet long-range aviation. These strategic bombers utilize five northern staging and dispersal bases within the USSR from which attacks could be mounted on the USA.[49]

The Soviet Union now has some 50 tankers (30 Mya-4s, 20 Tu-16s) with which to extend the range of the bombers. None of these now utilize external dispersal bases. Cuban airfields could, at least hypothetically, be used as recovery or forward dispersal bases for Soviet bombers (including Backfires) and tankers in the case of actual conflict, though the near-proximity to US air power might render such activities highly vulnerable. Soviet acquisition of additional air bases in, for instance, Central America or the Western Pacific, could, at least hypothetically, open up additional possibilities.

Britain earlier deployed long-range strategic bombers in the form of its 'V-bomber' force. That now defunct force utilized bases only in the UK.

Theatre and tactical or battlefield nuclear forces—platforms and launchers

Numerous standard analyses and associated game-based scenarios utilize the somewhat arbitrary and also fuzzy distinction between theatre and tactical (or battlefield) nuclear weapons. That distinction is to some degree based on sheer range considerations, at least as pertains to missiles (battlefield weapons are in the range of, say, 50-150 miles). Otherwise, by now standard usage defines NATO's (or the West's) theatre weapons as those which, based in Europe or in the Far East, can deliver nuclear warheads into the USSR proper as well as deep behind the lines in Eastern Europe; and, similarly, can do so from forward US bases in the Far East, for example, Korea or Okinawa. Soviet theatre nuclear weapons, on the other hand, are those that can deliver warheads well beyond the (hypothetical) Central European battlefield throughout Western Europe, from bases either within the USSR or 'forward' within Eastern Europe, or perhaps Mongolia in relation to China. No theatre weapons are based in the USA, nor are any now deployed which can reach the USA. Hence, further, the West's theatre weapons are effectively, or at least in a supplementary sense, 'strategic' in that they can reach targets within the USSR. Soviet theatre weapons are, however, 'strategic' as pertains to Western Europe or the Far East, as they can be targeted on rivals' cities, military command centres or nuclear forces themselves. Amid all of this definitional confusion, Europe plays a key role, while Asia plays a secondary but increasingly important role.

On a broader basis, involving the spectrum of weapon platforms running from 'strategic' to 'battlefield', several classes of weapon are involved: (a) surface-to-surface missiles—both ballistic and air-breathers/cruise missiles—of various ranges, some of them MIRVed; (b) aircraft—medium bombers, attack fighters/interceptors—configured with nuclear weapons, either based on land or at sea on aircraft carriers, and which can be used on the battlefield, or for long-range interdiction missions; (c) various forms of nuclear artillery involving howitzers or guns of various calibres, some towed by truck and some self-propelled and hence more mobile; and (d) nuclear mines, dubbed ADMs, i.e., atomic demolition munitions, in fixed emplacements along expected routes of invasion.

There are still other types of nuclear weapon which are located 'in-theatre': (a) nuclear-armed SAMs for interdiction of opponents' nuclear-armed aircraft, usually based in proximity to important bases or command centres; (b) land-based naval aircraft which can carry nuclear depth charges over adjacent waters to interdict opponents' submarines; and (c) attack submarines which carry nuclear-armed missiles or torpedoes usable both against enemy submarines and surface fleets.

Regarding forward emplacement of US nuclear weapons, primarily in Europe, there are several distinct types of circumstance in which they may be based, involving the issues of dual control or the 'two-key' system, and the politics of nuclear basing on other nations' soil. First, there is the actual forward basing of US aircraft, missiles or artillery—fully manned by US personnel, involving organic US military units but based on foreign soil and in circumstances in which *ad hoc* permission for actual combat must be assumed. Next, there are the numerous circumstances in which other nations—FR Germany, Belgium, the Netherlands, Italy, Turkey, Greece, etc.—deploy nuclear weapons on aircraft, missiles, howitzers, and so on, but where the strictures of the nuclear non-proliferation regime dictate a US custodial presence and the use of a two-key system, further implying a veto on actual use by either the USA or its nuclear partner. Some of these situations involve Allied nuclear systems based within the host nations' borders as, for example, in Turkey or Greece; others involve Allied forward basing of nuclear systems within FR Germany, as with Belgian or Dutch nuclear-armed artillery. Some nations, such as Norway and Denmark, do not allow nuclear weapons or foreign military bases on their soil during peacetime. Others, such as Iceland, do not allow nuclear weapons on their soil but have contingency provisions for forward-basing of nuclear weapons for 'wartime ASW operations'.[50] Portugal is an anomaly in not allowing nuclear weapons to be based on its (continental) home soil, but in allowing such basing in the Azores.[51] In short, the politics of the basing of nuclear weapons, juxtaposed to the various types of such weapon and their missions, is seen to be rather complex.

Table 25. US Pershing II and West German Pershing 1a facilities in FR Germany, 1985

Site	Facilities
Arsbeck, NW	West German Pershing 1a support site for Tevren
Bodeslberg, Bay	West German Pershing 1a support site for Landsberg
Frankfurt-Hausen, Hess	Pershing modification and exchange facility
Heilbronn, BaWü	18 US Pershing II launchers, weapon storage
Kleingartach, BaWü	Pershing 1a Combat Alert Status site
Landsberg/Lech, Bay	US custodian, West German Pershing 1a unit, 36 launchers
Lehmgrube, BaWü	US Pershing II Combat Alert Status site
Mutlangen, BaWü	US Pershing deployment and training site
Neckarsulm, BaWü	18 Pershing II launchers and warhead storage
Oberoth/Kettershausen, Bay	US Pershing II Combat Alert Status site
Schwäbisch-Gmünd, BaWü	36 US Pershing II launchers
Schweinsburg, BaWü	Pershing missile training area
Teveren, NW	US custodian, West German Pershing 1a unit
Waldheide/Heilbronn, BaWü	Pershing missile training area
Weilerbach, RhPf	Pershing storage; missile and warhead support

Source: Arkin, W. M. and Fieldhouse, R. W., *Nuclear Battlefields: Global Links in the Arms Race* (Ballinger: Cambridge, Mass., 1985), appendix A.

As identified in chapter 5, the primary land-based US theatre weapons were, until recently, the Pershing II and ground-launched cruise missiles now to be eliminated in connection with the INF Treaty. These were, of course, all foreign-based, involving the 108 Pershings (plus 12 spares) at several sites in FR Germany (Heilbronn, Waldheide, Neckars-Ulm, Schwäbisch-Gmünd), and the already deployed and planned GLCMs there (at Woescheim), and in the UK (Greenham Common, Molesworth), Belgium (Florennes), the Netherlands (Woendsrecht) and Sicily (Comiso). Additionally, launcher repair facilities had been identified at EMC Hansen, Frankfurt (FRG) and at SABCA, Gossens, Belgium, and a missile storage site at Weilerbach in FR Germany.[52] Originally this called for 464 GLCMs overall, based on 116 launchers, with perhaps nearly double that number of warheads, though by the time of the 1987 INF Treaty only some 309 missiles and 109 launchers had been deployed. The Pershing missiles with ranges capable of reaching well into the USSR, indeed, as far as Moscow, may have been perceived as having 'strategic' implications, albeit based outside the USA. Additionally, there were the remnant German Pershing 1as, under US custodian control (with about two warheads per launcher), with shorter reaches well short of being able to target the USSR proper (these too will be eliminated under the new INF accord). Table 25 describes the various facilities involved in the Pershing 1a and II programmes. It should also be noted that Arkin and Fieldhouse reported on 36 wartime dispersal sites, the precise locations of which were not cited.[53]

Otherwise, the USA bases a considerable number of nuclear-capable aircraft forward in Western Europe, that is, those manned directly by USAF personnel, which involves the forward deployment of some 1700 nuclear bombs.[54] These are, obviously, usable for tactical purposes along or directly behind the FLOT, but—particularly with the aid of aerial refuelling—also capable of deep interdiction missions throughout Eastern Europe and well into the Soviet Union proper. Some 72 F-16 fighter-attack aircraft and some 150 nuclear bombs are stored at both Hahn and Ramstein air bases; at Spangdahlem, a similar number of F-4Es (to be replaced with F-16s) with some 150 weapons are stored.[55] At Aviano in Italy, some 200 weapons are said to be stored in connection with nuclear-capable F-16s, previously rotated forward from Spain but now to be based in Italy.[56] In Turkey, the base at Incirlik supports some 36 nuclear-capable F-4s or F-16s which can be loaded with the weapons on quick-reaction alert after being rotated forward, while another base at Cigli, Izmir acts as a dispersal base for nuclear-capable aircraft.[57] Some 200 nuclear bombs are stored at Incirlik.[58]

Of course, land-based aircraft are not the only forward-based US nuclear-armed aircraft. There are also US aircraft carriers in the Mediterranean Sea and the Atlantic Ocean. Typically, there are two carriers on station in the Mediterranean—utilizing ports such as Naples, Souda Bay, Rota—which can launch A-6E, A-7 and F/A-18 aircraft carrying nuclear weapons, with respective ranges of 3200, 2800, and 1000 km.[59] With the capability to strike the Soviet homeland if within range, each carrier deploys over 100 nuclear bombs.[60]

A number of the NATO allies deploy nuclear-capable aircraft and store nuclear weapons for the USA, under the two-key system involving US custodial control. According to the IISS, this involves the older F-104G/Ss, F-4E/Fs and F-16s. FR Germany (90), Greece (66), Italy (18) and Turkey (97) have nuclear-capable F-104s; FR Germany (60), Greece (47) and Turkey (60) have F-4E/Fs; and Belgium (36), Denmark (64), the Netherlands (75) and Norway (65) have F-16s.[61] Additionally, Britain, the FRG and Italy deploy nuclear-capable (and jointly developed) Tornado aircraft, with some of the RAF planes forward-based in FR Germany, in this case not requiring US 'two-key' custodial control.

In Turkey, F-104G/Ss are based and 25 nuclear bombs are stored at Balikesir and Murted.[62] Similar numbers of such bombs are stored at other bases at Erhac/Malatya and Eskisehir, where F-4Es are based.[63] In Greece, there is also a wing of F-104Gs at Araxos AB, where 25 nuclear bombs are also deployed in a custodial relationship with the USA.[64] Similarly, there is an equivalent wing of F-104G/Ss in Italy, at Rimini, also with 25 nuclear bombs.[65] FR Germany deploys nuclear-capable F-104s at Bueckel AB and Memmingen, and nuclear-certified Tornados (converted from F-104Gs) at Lechfeld AB and Norvenich AB, each in connection with 25 stored nuclear bombs.[66] Belgium's F-16s (and 25 nuclear bombs) are at Kleine Brogel AB; the Netherlands' F-16s (and 25 nuclear bombs), are based at Volkel.[67] Norway and Denmark, while deploying nuclear-capable F-16s, do not apparently store designated nuclear weapons on their territories. Britain, meanwhile, deploys several squadrons of Tornado strike aircraft, along with nuclear weapons, at bases in FR Germany—at RAF Brueggen and RAF Laarbruch.[68] Nuclear-capable Harrier GR.5 jump-jets are also now being deployed at RAF Gutersloh.[69] Italy, also a co-producer of Tornados, deploys some at a base at Ghedi-Torre, backed up by 25 US nuclear bombs.[70] All in all, it can be seen that NATO forces in Europe, albeit mostly in line with US custodianship, field a formidable force of nuclear-armed strike aircraft, many of which—for instance, those in Turkey—are capable of penetration deep into the Soviet homeland, if only in the face of formidable Soviet air defences. Combined, the US Air Force and its allies maintain nuclear-armed aircraft on alert at all times at some 17 bases in Europe.[71]

As well as nuclear-armed aircraft, there are the numerous US and other NATO nations' ASW aircraft, involving the US P-3C Orions and the British Nimrods. In a conflict, these would be vital to NATO efforts at securing North Atlantic SLOCs against interdiction by Soviet attack submarines. US and Dutch P-3Cs and British Nimrods are based at or staged through British bases at St. Mawgan and Machrihanish (the latter in the Strathclyde area of Scotland)—some 63 US nuclear depth bombs are stored at each base.[72] Additional US-manned and -operated P-3Cs with forward-stored nuclear depth charges are based at Keflavik, Iceland (48 bombs), Sigonella on Sicily (63 bombs) and Rota, Spain (32 bombs).[73] Other US P-3Cs are rotated through Andøya and Bodø in Norway, Souda Bay on Crete, and Montigo, Portugal, while some 32 nuclear depth bombs are stored at Lajes in the Azores for wartime operations.[74]

Other NATO nations also deploy ASW aircraft with such nuclear weapons, mostly with US custodianship. Dutch P-3Cs operate out of a home base at Valkenburg, but their bombs are stored in the UK.[75] Italy flies nuclear-armed Breguet Atlantique aircraft out of Sigonella and Catania, from which British Nimrods also operate.[76] Canada operates nuclear-capable ASW aircraft, again with US custodianship, out of bases at Greenwood, Nova Scotia, and Comox in British Columbia (hence, covering both ocean areas)—these bases are also thought to be contingency bases for nuclear weapons supporting US P-3Cs during wartime.[77] And, of course, US P-3Cs with nuclear weapons operate out of numerous bases outside CONUS and the immediate NATO area: Diego Garcia (with 'wartime deployment' allowed as in Lajes), Ascension, Guam, Midway and Masirah Island (Oman), among others.[78] Guam is apparently used for storage of numerous nuclear depth charges.[79] According to Arkin and Fieldhouse, despite Japan's strict non-nuclear policies 'the facility at Misawa also appears to be prepared to receive nuclear depth bombs in wartime'.[80] Earlier, in the 1960s, US nuclear weapons were reported stored at Iwakuni Marine Air Station.[81]

Otherwise, South Korea also hosts some forward-based nuclear-capable US aircraft, themselves capable of strike missions within the Soviet homeland. Indeed, the Republic of Korea is now the only US forward (of Guam) base in Asia. Nuclear-capable F-16s are based at Kunsan, and F-4Es at Taegu AB, with some 60 bombs stored at the former.[82] That alone provides a formidable deterrent to conventional attack across the FLOT in the narrow Korean peninsula.

Soviet forward-based nuclear-capable aircraft

According to the IISS, the USSR has several types of land-based strike aircraft capable of being configured with nuclear weapons, each of which can carry two nuclear bombs. These are the Su-7 Fitter A (80), the MiG-21 Fishbed L (135), the MiG-27 Flogger D/J (810), the Su-17 Fitter D/H (900) and the Su-24 Fencer (700)—a total of 2625 such aircraft.[83] Of the 700 Fencers, 450 fall under the control of Strategic Aviation. Over 1000 Soviet tactical fighter aircraft are forward-based at a large number of facilities in the GDR, Czechoslovakia, Poland and Hungary, as listed in chapter 3.

According to Arkin and Fieldhouse, nuclear-capable Su-24 Fencers are stationed at Szprotawa AB and Zagan AB in Poland, at Debrecen in Hungary and at Brand-Briesen AB in the GDR, in each case involving associated nuclear storage sites (the latter base was said to have been converted from Su-7s in 1982).[84] In the GDR, nuclear-capable MiG-27 Flogger D/J regiments and nuclear-bomb storage sites are at Finsterwalde AB and Mirow-Rechlin Larz AB; Su-17 Fitter D regiments are located at Grossenhain AB, Neuruppin AB and Templin-Gross Dolln AB.[85] An additional possible nuclear-bomb storage site is identified at Parchim AB.[86] The number of stored nuclear bombs at these sites does not seem to be publicly available by contrast with available information for comparable NATO deployments.

The IISS also notes that several of the non-Soviet WTO nations deploy nuclear-capable aircraft, perhaps involving something like a two-key system, under Soviet custodianship. Czechoslovakia (50) and Poland (40) have Su-7 Fitters; Poland (40) Su-20 Fitter Cs; and Bulgaria (45), Czechoslovakia (40) and the GDR (24) MiG-23 Flogger F/As.[87] The IISS also notes that 'the total actually available as nuclear-strike aircraft may be lower than the figure shown'.[88] It is possible that the Soviet air force could itself use these aircraft in a nuclear mode if war erupted.

Outside the WTO area, the USSR also deploys some 16 Tu-16 Badger bombers in Viet Nam, which are capable of nuclear missions, perhaps against China or the US basing structure in the Philippines.[89]

The USSR also utilizes several external bases for nuclear-capable ASW aircraft. Bear-F aircraft, for instance, utilize Cuban bases at San Antonio de los Banos and Havana's Jose Marti airport.[90] Nuclear-capable IL-38 May ASW aircraft regularly operate out of Aden and Al Anad in South Yemen, Asmara in Ethiopia, Okba ben Nafi in Libya and Tiyas in Syria.[91] There is no publicly available information about whether nuclear depth charges are permanently stored at any of these facilities.

Battlefield artillery

As noted in chapter 4, the USA and its allies deploy a formidable arsenal of battlefield nuclear-capable artillery in Western Europe (for the USA, also in South Korea). This has involved several types of howitzer—the 155-mm and the larger 8-inch (or 203-mm) types. These involve warheads with explosive capabilities in a range between 0.1 kt and 10 kt, that is, from weapons only marginally more destructive than large conventional explosives to others of the order of magnitude of a Hiroshima-sized weapon. In various versions, these howitzers have ranges up to about 30 km, and CEPs (circular error probable) as small as 170 m.[92]

According to recent IISS data, the USA has over 4000 such dual-capable howitzers, and its NATO allies about another 2000.[93] As can be seen in table 26 the bulk of these weapons are deployed in FR Germany; others are based in Greece, Italy, the Netherlands, Turkey and South Korea. They are widely deployed in infantry, armoured and mechanized divisions. Arkin and Fieldhouse report that there are some 1500 nuclear-certified guns in FR Germany and about 1200 155-mm and 8-inch nuclear artillery projectiles.[94] There are also about 43 such projectiles in Greece, around 80 in Italy, 14 in the Netherlands, 57 in Turkey and some 70 in South Korea. This involves several types of facility, mostly in FR Germany: US nuclear artillery units and their maintenance and storage sites; other nations' (FR Germany, Britain, the Netherlands) artillery units and support facilities; and US custodian units assigned—in connection with the two-key system—to the artillery units of its NATO allies, involving Greece, Turkey, the Netherlands and Italy. Altogether, outside of US artillery units, some 570 warheads are designated for NATO in the forces of Belgium, Britain, Greece, Italy, the Netherlands, Turkey and FR Germany.[95] And, according to Collins, with reference to the mobility of these systems, there are some 600 aiming points where they are 'registered in'.[96]

The status of Soviet and allied WTO nuclear artillery is less clear, though it is assumed that the Eastern bloc has developed major capabilities in this area. According to the IISS, the USSR has several types of nuclear-capable artillery

Table 26. US foreign-based nuclear field artillery (155-mm and 8-in./203-mm), 1985

Country/site	Facilities
FR Germany	
Albersdorf, SchH	W German 8-in. artillery unit
Amberg, Bay	US 155-mm artillery unit
Ansbach, Bay	US 155-mm artillery unit
Arolsen, Hess	W German 155-mm artillery unit
Augsburg, Bay	US 155-mm and 8-in. artillery units
Augustdorf, NW	W German 155-mm artillery unit
Babenhausen, Hess	US 8-in. artillery unit
Bad Hersfeld, Hess	US 155-mm artillery unit
Bad Kissingen, Bay	US 155-mm artillery unit
Bad Kreuznach, RhPf	US nuclear artillery units
Bad Reichenhall, Bay	W German 155-mm artillery unit
Bamberg, Bay	US 155-mm and 8-in. artillery units
Baumholder, RhPf	US 155-mm and 8-in. artillery units
Bayreuth, Bay	US 155-mm artillery unit
Bergen, Ndsa	US custodian for British artillery units
Bindlach, Bay	US 155-mm artillery unit
Boostedt, SchH	W German 155-mm artillery unit
Braunschweig, Ndsa	W German 155-mm artillery unit
Butzbach, Hess	US 155-mm artillery unit
Dahn/Pirmasens, RhPf	US nuclear storage, support
Dedelstorf, Ndsa	W German 155-mm artillery unit
Deilinghofen-Menden, NW	US custodian for British artillery units
Dellbrück-Küln, NW	US custodian for Belgian artillery units
Donauworth, Bay	W German 155-mm artillery unit
Doerverden, Ndsa	US custodian for W German artillery units
Dülmen, NW	US custodian for W German artillery units
Dünsen Bassum, Ndsa	US custodian for W German artillery units
Flensburg-Meyn, SchH	US nuclear weapons storage for W German artillery
Flensburg-Weiche, SchH	US custodian for W German 8-in. artillery units
Frankfurt, Hess	US HQ, nuclear artillery support
Friedberg, Hess	US 155-mm artillery unit
Fulda, Hess	US 155-mm artillery unit
Füssen, Bay	W German 155-mm artillery unit
Garlstedt, Ndsa	US 155-mm artillery unit
Gelnhausen, Hess	US 155-mm artillery unit
Giessen, Hess	US 155-mm and 8-in. artillery unit
Güppingen, BaWü	US nuclear artillery units
Güttingen, Ndsa	W German 155-mm artillery unit
Grossauheim, Hess	US nuclear storage
Günzburg, Bay	US nuclear artillery support for W German artillery
Hamburg-Fischbek	W German 155-mm artillery unit
Hamburg-Rahlstedt	W German 155-mm artillery unit
Hanau, Hess	US 155-mm and 8-in. artillery units
Hemau, Bay	US custodian unit for W German nuclear artillery
Hemer Menden, NW	US nuclear storage for British Army
Herzogenaurach, Bay	US 8-in. artillery unit
Homberg, Hess	W German 155-mm artillery unit
Idar Obserstein, RhPf	US 155-mm artillery unit
Immendingen, Bay	W German 155-mm artillery unit
Kellinghusen, SchH	US custodian unit for W German nuclear artillery
Kempten, Bay	W German 155-mm artillery unit
Kirsch-Göns, Hess	US 155-mm artillery unit
Kitzingen, Bay	US 8-in. artillery unit
Kriegsfeld-Gerbach, RhPf	US nuclear weapons storage
Lahn Ems/Soegel, Ndsa	US custodian for W German nuclear artillery

Country/site	Facilities
Landshut, Bay	W German 155-mm artillery unit
Lippstadt, NW	British 155-mm and 8-in. artillery units
Luttmersen, Ndsa	W German 155-mm artillery unit
Münchweiler, RhPf	US nuclear warhead support
Münster-Dieberg, Hess	US nuclear warhead support
Münster-Handorf, NW	US custodian for British, Belgian, W German nuclear units
Münsingen, BaWü	W German 155-mm artillery unit
Naumburg, Hess	W German 155-mm artillery unit
Neu-Ulm, BaWü	US 155-mm artillery unit
Neunburg-vorm-Wald, Bay	W German 155-mm artillery unit
Nürnberg-Fürth, Bay	US 8-in. artillery unit
Oldenburg, Ndsa	W German 8-in. artillery unit
Paderborn, NW	US custodian, British army units
Pfullendorf, Bay	US custodian, W German artillery units
Phillipsburg, BaWü	US custodian, W German artillery units
Regensburg, Bay	US 8-in. artillery unit
Schwabach, BaWü	US 155-mm artillery unit
Schwabstadl, Bay	US custodian, W German nuclear artillery units
Schweinfurt, Bay	US 155-mm artillery units
Siegelsbach/Heilbronn, BaWü	US nuclear weapons support site
Stadtallendorf, Hess	W German 8-in. artillery unit
Tauberbischofsheim, BaWü	W German 8-in. artillery unit
Treysa/Schwalmstadt, Hess	US custodian, W German nuclear artillery units
Walldürn, BaWü	W German 155-mm artillery unit
Weiden, Bay	W German 155-mm artillery unit
Wentorf, SchH	W German 155-mm artillery unit
Werl, NW	US custodian, Belgian 155-mm and 8-in. artillery units
Wertheim	US 8-in. artillery units
Wetzlar, Hess	W German 155-mm artillery unit
Wildeshausen, Ndsa	W German 155-mm artillery unit
Würzburg, Bay	US nuclear artillery unit
Zirndorf/Nürnburg, Bay	US 155-mm artillery unit
Greece	
Elefsis	Storage, maintenance, (43) 8-in. projectiles
Yiannitsa	Nuclear warhead custodian unit—8-in.
Italy	
Longare	Fifty 155-mm projectiles for US forces, support for 29 Italian 8-in. projectiles
Sciaves	Nuclear warhead custodian unit—8-in.
Vicenza	HQ—control of Italian nuclear weapons
Netherlands	
t'Harde	Nuclear warhead custodian unit—8-in., support for 14 Netherlands 8-in. projectiles
South Korea	
Camp Ames, Taejon	Nuclear weapons support unit
Camp Casey, Tongduchon	Nuclear artillery units
Camp Essayons, Uijongbu	8-in. artillery unit
Camp Stanley, Uijongbu	Nuclear artillery units
Kunsan AB	Storage of 155-mm nuclear projectiles
Tobongsan	Standby forward nuclear storage site
Turkey	
Cakmakli	Storage, maintenance, 57 8-in. projectiles

Source: Arkin, W. M. and Fieldhouse, R. F., *Nuclear Battlefields: Global Links in the Arms Race* (Ballinger: Cambridge, Mass., 1985), appendix A.

(some of which can also utilize chemical shells)—several towed and self-propelled types of 152-mm gun; and a 203-mm self-propelled howitzer and a 240-mm self-propelled mortar.[97] These can be fitted with nuclear projectiles in the 2–5 kt range, with ranges up to 27 km. The Soviet Union has some 10 000 such nuclear-capable weapons, and their WTO allies (Bulgaria, the GDR, Hungary and Romania) several hundred more.[98] These guns and their nuclear ammunition are assumed assigned to Front and Army units throughout the GDR, Czechoslovakia and Hungary. According to Arkin and Fieldhouse, 'each motorized rifle and tank division in the GDR has also received a battalion of 152-mm nuclear-capable artillery in its artillery regiment'.[99] (There are some 20 such divisions in the GDR.) Otherwise, the some 400 203-mm systems are also considered crucial nuclear-capable battlefield systems.

The IISS also notes that the Soviet Union's WTO allies deploy a number of M-1955 (D-20) 152-mm towed guns and howitzers, with the capability for launching 2-kt projectiles. There are some 220 all told; around 20 with Bulgarian forces, 50 each in Romania and the GDR and 100 in Hungary.[100] The IISS refers to nuclear warheads held in Soviet custody, but with no numbers on warheads provided.[101] Altogether, the IISS reports that the USSR has over 3700 nuclear-capable artillery pieces facing NATO, and its allies an additional 164.[102]

Atomic demolition munitions

In recent years US forces have been armed with atomic demolition munitions (ADMs), basically tantamount to nuclear land mines. The tripwire nature of these weapons was assumed to have a strong deterrent effect. These munitions were deployed in FR Germany, Italy and South Korea, and came in two versions, called the Medium and Special Atomic Demolition Munitions (MADMs and SADMs), the latter man-portable.[103] They were assigned, variously, to corps, division, armoured cavalry regiment and special forces group headquarters. At the peak of deployment in the early 1980s, NATO had some 350 ADMs deployed in FR Germany and 24 more in Italy.[104] Another 21 were in South Korea. Table 27 indicates the sites at which these mines were stored in the early to mid-1980s.

All of these ADMs are now apparently in the process of being withdrawn from US and also from West German forces (among US allies only the latter deployed ADMs). Some critics, in viewing the negotiations over arms control draw-downs of short-range ballistic missiles were to regret this decision—claimed, at least in the case of ADM deployments, to have been made on the basis that ADMs, by their very nature, seemed to reinforce or to institutionalize the idea of a permanently divided Germany.[105] Others have seen a declining utility for battlefield nuclear weapons; variously because of the preferable alternatives provided by enhanced radiation weapons, the associated vulnerability of troops carrying such weapons near the line of battle; and generally, a lack of acceptable political and military doctrine for their use.

Table 27. US foreign-based atomic demolition mines, 1985

Country/site	Facilities
FR Germany	
Bad Kreuznach, RhPf	US ADM unit
Bad Tölz, Bay	US ADM unit
Frankfurt, Hess	US ADM unit
Göppingen, BaWü	US ADM unit
Hanau, Hess	US ADM unit
Herbornseelbach, Hess	US support, W German ADM units
Kornwestheim, BaWü	US ADM unit
Minden, NW	W German ADM unit
Nürnberg, Bay	US ADM unit
Wildflecken, Bay	US ADM unit
Würzburg, Bay	Nuclear units include ADMs
Italy	
Longare	Storage, 24 ADMs
Vicenza	ADM engineering unit
South Korea	
Camp Casey	ADM engineering unit
Kunsan AB	Storage, 21 ADMs

Source: Arkin, W. M. and Fieldhouse, R. F., *Nuclear Battlefields: Global Links in the Arms Race* (Ballinger: Cambridge, Mass., 1985), appendix A.

The USSR has apparently not deployed ADMs with its forces in the GDR, which may or may not reflect the commonly assumed less defensive character of those deployments (but there have been some reports of such deployments). That also apparently applies to North Korea. Neither France nor China appear to utilize such munitions, though the US Government has hinted at such deployments in the case of the latter.[106]

Nuclear air defence

Preceding the current era of controversy over ballistic-missile defence, the USA and its allies have long deployed nuclear-armed systems for defence against incoming nuclear-armed aircraft. Earlier, Nike missile batteries ringed many US cities, before the acceptance of MAD (mutual assured destruction) led to their abandonment in the face of the corollary futility of defence of cities against long-range missiles. The Nike missiles originally were intended for interdiction of relatively high-flying formations of incoming aircraft; hence, they have been rendered obsolete by low-level penetration aircraft. Earlier, they were positioned well behind the FLOT, behind a picket fence of tactical radars and an I-HAWK SAM belt.[107]

In recent years, however, the USA and its NATO allies had continued to deploy nuclear-armed Nike-Hercules air defence missiles, with slant ranges of up to 140 km.[108] These had first been deployed in 1962, and in the early 1980s there were some 320 Nike-Hercules missiles in FR Germany alone.[109] As of 1988, they appeared to be in the process gradually of being phased out, to be replaced by conventional 'improved HAWK' and Patriot missiles. According to the IISS, however, as of 1987, some 443 Nike-Hercules launchers were still deployed with NATO forces: Belgium (36), the FRG (216), Italy (96), the Netherlands (23) and Turkey (72)—the Belgian and Dutch missiles were then *en route* to being phased out.[110] Greece earlier also hosted such missiles, while South Korea has 100 of them, with no nuclear weapons held for them despite their still having a theoretical nuclear capability.[111]

The various and numerous facilities connected to Nike-Hercules missiles are listed in table 28, including some only recently phased out. As is indicated, all of the Belgian and Dutch missiles of this type had been forward deployed in FR Germany. And, of course, US custodian units were located in proximity to all of the Allied units equipped with Nike-Hercules missiles.

Table 28. US foreign-based Nike-Hercules missiles, 1985

Country/site	Facilities
FR Germany	
Adelheide/Delmenhorst, SchH	Former US custodian, W German unit
Barnstorf/Diepholz, Ndsa	US custodian, W German unit
Baumholder, RhPf	Former Nike Hercules tactical firing site
Borgholzhausen, NW	Former custodian for Dutch Nike-Hercules unit
Bramsche, NW	HQ, Dutch Nike-Hercules unit
Büren, NW	US storage and warhead custodial site
Burbach/Lipper Hohe, NW	US custodian, W German unit
Dallau Eltzal, BaWü	US former Nike-Hercules unit
Darmstadt, Hess	US Nike-Hercules, HQ
Datteln-Ahsen, NW	W German Nike-Hercules unit
Dexheim, RhPf	Former US Nike-Hercules unit
Dichtelbach, RhPf	Former US Nike-Hercules unit
Dornum, Ndsa	US custodian, W German unit
Düren Drove, NW	US custodian, Belgian Nike-Hercules unit
Erle-Schermbeck, NW	Belgian Nike-Hercules unit
Euskirchen-Billig, NW	US custodian, Belgian Nike-Hercules unit
Geinsheim/Hassloch, RhPf	Former US Nike-Hercules unit
Grefrath/Hinsbeck, NW	Former US custodian, Belgian Nike-Hercules unit
Gross Sachsenheim, BaWü	Former US Nike-Hercules unit
Hardheim, BaWü	Former US Nike-Hercules unit
Hohenkirchen, Ndsa	US custodian, W German Nike-Hercules unit
Hontheim, RhPf	Former US Nike-Hercules unit
Kapellen-Erft, NW	Former Belgian Nike-Hercules unit
Kaster, NW	Former US custodian, Belgian Nike-Hercules unit
Kemel, Hess	W German Nike-Hercules unit
Kilianstädten, Hess	US custodian, W German Nike-Hercules unit
Körbecke, NW	US custodian, W German Nike-Hercules unit
Landau, RhPf	Former US Nike-Hercules unit
Lich, Hess	W German Nike-Hercules unit
Liebenau, Ndsa	W German Nike-Hercules unit
Lohne-Vechta, Ndsa	W German Nike-Hercules unit
Marienheide, NW	W German Nike-Hercules unit
Miesau, RhPf	US Nike Hercules support unit
Mulheim/Blankenheim, NW	Former US custodian, Belgian Nike-Hercules unit
Oberauerbach, RhPf	Former US Nike-Hercules unit
Obersayn, RhPf	W German Nike-Hercules unit
Oedingen-Elspe, NW	W German Nike-Hercules unit
Pforzheim, BaWü	Former US Nike-Hercules unit
Putz/Bedburg, NW	Belgian Nike-Hercules unit

Country/site	Facilities
Quirnheim/Grünstadt, RhPf	Former US Nike-Hercules unit
Rheine-Elte, NW	Former Dutch Nike-Hercules unit
Salzwoog-Lembürg, RhPf	Former US Nike-Hercules unit
Schönborn, RhPf	Former US Nike-Hercules unit
Greece	
Elefsis	Storage, 30 Nike-Hercules warheads
Erithea	US custodian unit, Greek Nike Hercules
Karatea	US custodian unit, Greek Nike Hercules
Katsimidhi	US custodian unit, Greek Nike Hercules
Koropi	US custodian unit, Greek Nike Hercules
Italy	
Bovolone	US custodian unit for Italian Nike Hercules
Catron (Montichiari)	US custodian unit for Italian Nike Hercules
Ceggia	US custodian unit for Italian Nike Hercules
Chioggia	US custodian unit for Italian Nike Hercules
Conselve	US custodian unit for Italian Nike Hercules
Cordovado	US custodian unit for Italian Nike Hercules
Longare	Storage and support, 60 Nike Hercules
Monte Calvarina	US custodian unit, Nike Hercules

Source: Arkin, W. M. and Fieldhouse, R. F., *Nuclear Battlefields: Global Links in the Arms Race* (Ballinger: Cambridge, Mass., 1985), appendix A.

Until recently, the Genie short-range, unguided, air-to-air rockets designed for strategic interception of bombers were deployed by the US and Canadian air forces in NORAD. These had earlier been deployed aboard US F-106A, F-4 and F-15 fighters, and also Canada's CF-101s.[112] As late as 1983, some 200 Genie nuclear warheads were still operational, though their production had ended in 1962.[113] Only in 1984 were the weapons withdrawn as the Canadian Air Force converted from CF-101s to CF-18s. Until then, Genies had been stored at Canadian bases at Bagotville, Quebec; Comox, Lazo, British Columbia, and Chatham, New Brunswick; other bases at Gander and Harmony, Newfoundland and Goose Bay, Labrador were utilized as strategic interceptor dispersal bases.[114]

The USSR has also developed several models of nuclear-armed SAMs: the ABM-1B Galosh (Moscow only), the SH-04/08, SA-10, and the SA-5 Gammon, the latter two of which may alternatively be deployed with conventional warheads. (Arkin and Fieldhouse note 'numerous reports of the existence of nuclear warheads for Soviet SAMs, particularly the SA-2 Mod-4 and SA-5 systems.[115]) There is no publicly available information indicating that any nuclear-armed SAMs are forward-based in Eastern Europe or in Mongolia—in the Western theatre of military operations (TVD) alone, which incorporates the GDR, Poland and Czechoslovakia, the Soviet Union deploys a total of 2500 SAMs, many of which are nuclear-capable.[116] Altogether, the USSR has 735 and 2050, respectively, of the newer SA-10 and older SA-5 systems.[117] Generally speaking, nuclear warheads mounted on these systems would not appear usable against low-flying attack aircraft in the Central European arena.

Tactical nuclear-armed missiles

In the mid-1970s, the USA and its allies began to replace the long-deployed Honest John battlefield weapons with the short-range Lance missile. Even in the early 1980s, some Honest Johns, with 40-m ranges, were still deployed by the allied forces of Greece and Turkey, in connection with US custodianship. By 1987, these had been withdrawn, and only in South Korea were there a small number (12) of these missiles, for which no nuclear weapons were held.[118]

Table 29. US foreign-based tactical or battlefield missiles, 1985

Country/site	Facilities
FR Germany	
Aachen, NW	W German Lance missile ground support, equipment training
Aschaffenburg, Bay	6 US Lance launchers
Crailsheim, BaWü	6 US Lance launchers
Eschweiler, NW	W German Lance electronic components maintenance training
Flensburg-Meyn, SchH	W German Lance missile storage
Flensburg-Weiche, SchH	US custodian, W German Lance missile unit
Frankfurt, Hess	US Lance missile units
Giessen, Hess	6 US Lance launchers; US custodian, W German Lance missile unit
Grossengstingen, BaWü	US custodian, W German Lance missile unit
Hanau, Hess	US (6) Lance launchers
Herzogenaurach, Bay	US (6) Lance launchers
Montabaur, RhPf	US custodian, W German Lance missile unit
Sennelager, NW	US custodian, British Lance missile unit
Werl, NW	US custodian, Belgian Lance missile unit
Wesel, NW	US custodian, W German Lance missile unit
Wiesbaden, Hess	US (6) Lance launchers
Greece	
Agyroupolis	US custodian, Greek Honest John unit
Canea, Souda Bay, Crete	Training range, Honest John and Lance missiles
Drama	US custodian, Greek Honest John unit
Elefsis	Storage, maintenance, 66 Honest John warheads
Perivolaki	US custodian, Greek Honest John unit
Italy	
Codogne	US custodian, Italian Lance missile unit
Longare	Storage, maintenance support 42 Lance missiles
Oderzo	US custodian, Italian Lance missile unit
Portogruaro	HQ, Italian Lance missile brigade
Netherlands	
Havelteberg	US custodian, Dutch Lance missile unit, 42 warheads
South Korea	
Camp Page, Chunchon	Former HQ, controlled Honest John missiles
Turkey	
Cakmakli	Storage, assembly, maintenance, 132 Honest John warheads
Corlu	US custodian, Turkish Honest John unit
Erzurum	US custodian, Turkish Honest John unit
Izmit	US custodian, Turkish Honest John unit
Ortakoy	US custodian, Turkish Honest John unit

Source: Arkin, W. M. and Fieldhouse, R. F., *Nuclear Battlefields: Global Links in the Arms Race* (Ballinger: Cambridge, Mass., 1985), appendix A.

The newer Lance missiles, first deployed in 1972, have a range of 110 km and CEPs in the range of 150–400 m.[119] The USA has some 144 of these launchers for its own forces world-wide, of which 36 are in FR Germany; US allies deploy another 55 in Europe as a whole: Belgium (5), Britain (12), FR Germany (26), Italy (6) and the Netherlands (6).[120] Britain and Belgium base Lances in FR Germany, while the Dutch Lances are based within the Netherlands.[121] Each launcher appears to have some seven warheads, allowing for significant reload capability. Altogether, NATO has some 692 Lance warheads, 608 of which are in FR Germany deployed with the forces of Belgium, Britain, Italy, the Netherlands, FR Germany and the USA.[122]

The present Lance and recent Honest John missile sites are listed in table 29.

As outlined in chapter 5, the Soviet Union forward bases, within Eastern Europe, several types of battlefield (up to 100-km range) and medium-range (100–1000 km) missile. In the former category are the Frog-3/7 battlefield missiles now being superseded by the SS-21. In the latter category are the Scud A/B/C and Scaleboard missiles, which were in the process of being replaced by the SS-22 and SS-23, but which will be eliminated by the INF Treaty. The Soviet Union has also developed GLCMs, specifically, the SS-C-1b Sepal. According to the Memorandum of Understanding Regarding the Establishment of the Data Base for the Treaty, that involved 84 missiles which had been tested but not deployed.[123]

The 70-km range Soviet Frog missiles, as noted in chapter 5, are deployed in large numbers in the GDR, Poland, Hungary, Czechoslovakia, Bulgaria and Mongolia—in the first-named alone there are some 90 launchers at over 20 sites.[124] These carry 200-kt warheads, with CEPs of around 400 m; the successor SS-21s with 120-km ranges carry 100-kt warheads, with 300-m CEPs.[125] No precise information is available on the total number of warheads involved for these two systems, but it clearly is in the range of several hundred, based on a total of 350 launchers.[126] Additionally, the non-Soviet WTO countries have another 214 Frog 3/5/7 launchers of their own.[127]

The longer-range Scud-B (300-km range, 900-m CEP), which was being replaced by the SS-23 (500-km range, 350-m CEP), was widely based, as noted above, in the GDR, Poland and Czechoslovakia. There were two brigades (nine missiles apiece) in the GDR, a similar number in Czechoslovakia and a smaller number in Poland. Altogether, there were, prior to the INF Treaty, some 375 Soviet SS-23/Scud A/Bs within the WTO facing NATO; plus another 143 Scud B/Cs in the hands of the other WTO forces.[128]

The larger SS-12 mod Scaleboard has a range of 900 km, and a CEP of 300 m. The USSR has 130 of these, with 1-Mt warheads, some of which were forward-based in Eastern Europe facing NATO, mainly involving one brigade each in the GDR and Czechoslovakia.[129]

According to the Memorandum of Understanding attached to the INF Treaty, Soviet missile bases subject to inspection were at Hranice in Czechoslovakia and at Bischofswerde, Jena Forst, Königsbrück, Waren, Weissenfels and Wokuhl in the GDR.[130]

Additional foreign-based naval nuclear forces

The foreign basing implications of some naval nuclear forces are discussed in chapters 2 and 3: the US SSBN bases; bases for aircraft carriers deploying nuclear-armed aircraft; and those for land-based ASW aircraft which can deliver nuclear depth charges, in the latter case involving facilities used by both superpowers.

In addition there is some forward deployment of nuclear weapons carried aboard attack submarines for use against rival submarines. US attack submarines carry SUBROC (underwater–air–underwater) rockets and, according to one source, the base at La Maddalena on Sardinia involves storage of some 15 out of a global total of some 285 such weapons.[131] Others may be stored on Guam and perhaps at Subic Bay.[132] The Soviet Union has an equivalent ASW rocket (the SS-N-15) carried aboard some 65 attack submarines. There is no information as to whether reloads for such weapons are stored at ports regularly used by Soviet attack submarines such as Cienfuegos, Cuba; Cam Ranh Bay, Viet Nam; Aden, and so on.

Numerous US surface ships also carry ASROC (the surface ASW version of SUBROC missiles)—Arkin and Fieldhouse claim that some 150 US ships carry these weapons, involving a total of some 575 warheads.[133] These ships will, of course, make regular port calls wherever nuclear-armed ship visits are normally allowed. The same is true for nuclear depth charges. For both types of these weapon, for instance, Cubi Point in the Philippines is said to serve as a stand-by storage site.[134] In addition the USA has deployed ship-based nuclear-armed SAMs such as the now obsolete Terrier missile.[135] Generally speaking, the Soviet Navy has not been subjected to public criticism in its allied nations over use of facilities by nuclear-armed ships.

Recent years have seen increased attention given to the prospect of possibly protracted nuclear war; in turn presupposing an increased emphasis on mobility and dispersion. On both sides of the nuclear divide this points to increasing emphasis on the use of reloads both for aircraft and ships, and hence, to storage of weapons at dispersed external bases, the politics of access so allowing.

Nuclear-related technical facilities: intelligence, communications, space

Chapters 6 and 7 outline the major powers' global networks of a variety of facilities falling, variously, under the headings of intelligence, space, communications, and research and the environment. Many of these facilities, of course, perform functions in relation to the powers' nuclear forces—strategic, theatre, tactical—either during normal peacetime conditions or, provisionally or hypothetically, during a general war either before or amid resort to nuclear weapons. But many are also dual-purpose in relation to nuclear and non-nuclear roles. Space and land-based SIGINT systems, for instance, can collect information valuable for planning in relation to nuclear deterrence or war-fighting, but also useful for conventional purposes or for those more aptly described as 'political' or even economic or commercial. Photo-reconnaissance aircraft can be detailed, specifically, to photograph nuclear facilities, but they can acquire information for many other purposes. SOSUS networks can monitor the movements of submarines (nuclear-powered or not, nuclear-armed or not) during 'conventional phases' of a general conflict or amid a nuclear exchange. Nuclear weapon test facilities, on the other hand, are just that.

The outline of technical and research/environmental facilities given in other chapters is reviewed and supplemented here, with specific reference to the existing nuclear balance. It is emphasized that while the USA relies on a vast and proliferated global network of nuclear-related technical facilities, the USSR— in connection with an at least equally massive nuclear arsenal as measured by launcher platforms, warheads, aggregate megatonnage, etc.—manages with a far smaller external presence, counterbalanced by reliance on its larger homeland area and, more importantly, by more extensive use of shipboard facilities.

For early warning of nuclear attack and assessment of such attacks, for instance, the USA relies on foreign facilities for several functions: ground downlinks for early-warning satellites (in Australia and FR Germany); the ballistic missile early-warning system—BMEWS—in Greenland and the UK; and several strings of radars stretching across Canada, Greenland and Iceland from Alaska—to detect *en route* bombers. The Soviet Union fields a similar capability, but with no discernible dependence on overseas access; indeed, at home, it has some 7000 radars for early warning.[136]

At the theatre level within Europe, and in relation to the contingency of war between the NATO and WTO alliances, both sides utilize external facilities for early warning. The NATO NADGE network is balanced by the WTO air defence radars in Eastern Europe.[137] Depending upon the scenario, these rival networks could be construed either as nuclear-related or not—most standard scenarios for European conflict assume sequential escalation from conventional to nuclear conflict (or, alternatively, a conflict kept below the nuclear threshold); much rarer, a nuclear assault to initiate a war within Europe.

Intelligence facilities are crucial to nuclear postures on both sides, but the USA has a much greater dependence on external facilities. As noted, it has an elaborate network of SOSUS installations, most in proximity to chokepoints or SLOCs in such disparate places as the Bahamas, the UK, Turkey, Japan, Bermuda, Norway, Iceland, Italy, Panama and so on, all of which relay data on the movements of Soviet submarines back to central processing and analysis centres in the USA.[138] The USSR has, apparently, nothing equivalent to SOSUS—perhaps more a function of access and the facts of geography than of technical capability or cost—and relies instead on a large fleet of intelligence ships, that is, AGIs, which prowl in proximity to US submarine bases.[139]

The same asymmetry obtains with regard to monitoring of strategic missile tests. In this area, US use of major radar installations in Turkey, Norway, China and the Marshall Islands is balanced by the Soviet Union's far more extensive use of shipboard systems. China too, entirely bereft of foreign facilities, makes extensive use of telemetry and missile-tracking ships, both for monitoring its own and rivals' activities.[140]

The same asymmetries hold true for nuclear explosion detection capabilities, which could pertain both to weapon testing and to targeting intelligence during a war. As noted, the USA fields a truly massive global network of seismic arrays in, among other places, Spain, the UK, Norway, Turkey, Australia, Japan, South Korea, the Philippines, China, Panama and so on.[141] Again, the USSR relies primarily, if not entirely, on its large fleet of intelligence vessels to supplement home-based seismic systems.[142]

In the field of space-tracking, however (potentially important in nuclear war scenarios, for instance, in relation to interdiction of ocean-reconnaissance or other satellites), both the USA and the USSR utilize foreign facilities. The USA has numerous (dedicated, collateral or contributing) radars for this purpose, for instance, the BMEWS radars and the large AN/FPS-79 in Turkey, as well as the global optical systems represented first by the Baker-Nunn cameras and now by GEODSS cameras emplaced in South Korea, Portugal and Diego Garcia.[143] By contrast, whereas the USSR makes extensive use of its ships for space-tracking, it has also utilized land-based facilities in Cuba, Mali, Guinea, Chad, Poland and Czechoslovakia for laser radars and tracking cameras.[144]

The USSR also has a number of land-based SIGINT stations, for instance, in Cuba, Viet Nam, South Yemen, Syria and Afghanistan, but a smaller number than the more proliferated US network.[145] Some of these are HF/DF sites usable for location of fleet units (supplementing data provided by ocean-surveillance satellites which could be knocked out in a war); in turn, these could be crucial to nuclear attacks on fleet concentrations if a central war should escalate at sea to the nuclear level.

As earlier noted, the major powers utilize complex, proliferated and often redundant communications systems across the entirety of the frequency spectrum. As ably portrayed by Arkin and Fieldhouse, in emphasizing the complexity of what is involved:

Tying all the weapons, test ranges, surveillance, and early warning systems together is a vast communications network of wires, submarine cables, radio stations, and satellites. Satellites, now only two decades old, link the entire globe with instantaneous communication. According to Admiral Gordon Nagler, chief of Naval communications, 'we can talk to any ship any place on the surface of the Earth, 365 days a year, 24 hours a day'.

The largest communications system in the world is that of the United States. The Defense Communications System, a peacetime and crisis operations network, serves 3,161 locations in seventy-five countries and islands. Nearly two-thirds of it is overseas. It combines many lesser networks comprising 35 million miles of circuits, operated by 15,000 people. Every command center, headquarters, submarine, missile silo, or bomber constantly receives messages over it.[146]

Some of the frequency ranges—and their associated transmitters, relays and receivers—are utilized for a variety of generalized purposes. This is true for the HF and VHF/microwave systems, not to mention the telephone and data links embodied in the US AUTOVON/AUTOSEVOCOM systems and their counterparts. Numerous uses may be envisaged for these systems in relation to nuclear forces, either during peace or war.

Otherwise, however, there are some communications systems, some space-based and others not, which may be identified in relation to specific components of the US nuclear posture and for which Soviet counterparts may be assumed, even if they are not easily identified from now public sources. As stated by Arkin and Fieldhouse, 'the day-to-day networks are supplemented by a bewildering array of special networks that support nuclear weapons'.[147] Chapter 6 outlines the US SAC force's Green Pine and Giant Talk/Scope Signal 'fail safe' communications networks, the former with locations in Canada and Iceland along expected and long-maintained trans-Arctic routes; the latter in various nations—Spain, Turkey, Japan, the Philippines, etc.—allowing for more omnidirectional approaches to the USSR.[148] AFSATCOM (Air Force Communications System) is also noted, a network devoted *primarily* to nuclear forces, with satellite linkages to some 900 terminals in nuclear storage sites, command centres, and so on.[149] Some of the control and receiver sites related to FLTSATCOM satellites (which have AFSATCOM transponders plus functions in relation to National Command Authorities, ocean reconnaissance, relay of SOSUS data, etc.), are located in foreign facilities in Italy and Diego Garcia.[150] (AFSATCOM is about to be superseded by the MILSTAR system deemed better for managing a nuclear war. The implications of this system for FMP are unclear but it will probably involve external control facilities.)

Several communications systems are used in connection with control of underwater submarines on patrol, at or *en route* from firing stations, some requiring associated foreign access. Newer ELF transmitters are located in Michigan and Wisconsin, but there are important VLF facilities in Australia, Sardinia, Japan and Norway; and several LF facilities in Bermuda, Greece, Iceland, Japan, the Philippines, Spain and the UK.[151] As noted, the US TACAMO aircraft utilize forward operating bases in Bermuda, Japan and the UK; the now somewhat obsolete Omega and Loran-C systems used for accurate positioning of submarines utilized numerous foreign facilities, as does the Clarinet Pilgrim system in the Pacific, involving facilities in several places such as Japan.[152] The important NAVSTAR Global Positioning System involves satellite monitoring stations overseas at Ascension and Diego Garcia as well as at Kwajalein and Guam.[153] Meanwhile, US surface naval forces—some armed, obviously, with nuclear weapons—utilize important HF receivers and transmitters in various foreign locales: Bermuda, Diego Garcia, Greece, Guam, Iceland, Italy, Japan, Panama, the Philippines, the Azores, Spain and the UK.[154]

The Soviet Union is also heavily dependent on communications in relation to its nuclear posture, and is reported to make extensive use of buried cables, 'special networks', airborne command posts, and radio relays. It is reported that the USSR is moving much of its communications infrastructure into space, in parallel with US practice. Soviet communications with submarines are apparently conducted entirely by home-based transmitters.[155] Molniya satellites have some down-links in countries such as the GDR, Poland, Czechoslovakia and Cuba, but the linkages to Soviet nuclear forces are not clear.[156] Neither is it apparent from the open literature whether or not the Soviet Union has some sort of 'fail-safe' communications with heavy bombers requiring external access, say in Cuba.

Noteworthy on the US side are the external satellite control facilities linked to the master station at Sunnyvale, California: in Greenland, the UK and the Seychelles.[157] The USSR does not appear to have equivalents outside the USSR, again, mostly a function of its favourably large land mass.

In the nuclear-related areas of research and environmental activities requiring extensive networks of facilities, the USA also makes greater use of external access. As noted, though it now conducts nuclear tests at home, its eastern and western missile ranges utilize access to facilities in a number of places: several Caribbean nations, Bermuda, Brazil and Ascension in the east; Kwajalein and other islands in the west.[158] Testing of cruise missiles has required access to the Canadian north; that of a variety of submarine and ASW functions has needed access to several Caribbean nations, including the Bahamas.[159] The USSR tests its nuclear weapons at home. Its large and (in Siberia) relatively sparsely populated territory allows overhead missile flights which terminate in the Pacific, without involvement of foreign facilities for range instrumentation or impact location analysis. France, on the other hand, constrained by its geography, conducts nuclear tests overseas at Muroroa, while its strategic missile testing utilizes access to the Azores.[160]

In chapter 7, various other nuclear-related research and environmental activities are indicated which, mostly in the US case, involve external access. They include: weather stations; the SOON and SOFNET networks for detecting solar flares which might interrupt critical communications; facilities for geodetic research in connection with the accuracy of long-range missiles; ASW, including long-range underwater communications; and so on.[161] The locations of these activities, almost ironically, tend to be more global than some others which fit the pattern of heartland and rimland, i.e., as with SIGINT and fail-safe communications. The USSR, meanwhile, does have geodesy-related facilities in several other countries, perhaps just because of specific locational requirements for that science. There is no open-source evidence for its use of facilities equivalent to the US SOON/SOFNET system for detecting solar flares; neither for weather stations. In the latter area, the USSR apparently makes heavy use of shipboard facilities for transmitting weather data collected by satellites.

IV. Necessity, redundancy and decoupling: the geopolitics of nuclear basing

The brief review of nuclear-related facilities above is, for the most part, organized according to clusters of facilities associated with types of weapon (strategic bombers, tactical missiles, etc.) or associated support facilities (SIGINT, submarine communications, etc.). This provides a picture of the extent to which the superpowers depend on external access for the conduct of one or another such activity, and of the number of other nations required for fully effective and adequate use of particular weapons or systems.

One could equally examine the reliance of either superpower on particular allies or client states, the most important of which host numerous and diverse nuclear-related facilities on behalf of a nuclear superpower. Of course, in many cases, both superpowers have redundant points of access (or alternative uses of land-based, shipboard and space-based systems in some cases) or have some flexibility in substituting for various weapon or support systems. For example, the USA, having lost access for theatre missile emplacements in Europe, might compensate by deploying additional cruise missiles on ships, or nuclear-armed aircraft aboard carriers, but these too may now become subjects of arms control negotiations.

These caveats notwithstanding, it is still possible to survey the whole range of external nuclear-related facilities, and make some rough judgements on the particular overall importance of some basing host states. Or, stated another way, one can assess the vulnerability of either superpower to the loss (total or partial) of access in some places, a timely matter, particularly on the US side, amid a seemingly escalating trend towards decoupling.

US nuclear access

On the US side, not surprisingly, the geopolitics of nuclear access point to the particular importance of a number of countries located around the Eurasian rimlands in proximity to the USSR and (somewhat overlapping the previous point) of several nations located astride the trans-arctic sea and air routes between the Soviet and US heartlands. In the former category are Norway, the UK, FR Germany, Italy, Spain, Portugal, Greece, Turkey, the Philippines, Japan, South Korea, Australia, and also Belgium and the Netherlands; in the latter, additionally, Iceland, Greenland and Canada. Otherwise noteworthy are the key roles played in certain respects by a number of oceanic islands, some but not all under British control: Ascension, the Azores, Bermuda, Diego Garcia, Kwajalein, the Seychelles and some in the Caribbean.

Norway, with its critical location on NATO's northern flank and in near proximity to the Soviet cluster of naval and air bases in the Kola Peninsula area, hosts a variety of important nuclear-related facilities: bases for P-3C ASW aircraft, SIGINT and nuclear-detection facilities, VLF communications and a forward base for AWACS. In a major crisis it would have a crucial Northern Flank reinforcement role, emphasizing a designated Marine Amphibious Brigade and collocated operating bases for aircraft to be rotated forward from the USA.[162] Ironically, this nation, though generally speaking politically receptive to the US presence, does not allow nuclear weapons on its soil, nor for that matter, foreign bases identified with one nation—it provides access for NATO use.[163]

The UK hosts a profuse variety of nuclear-related facilities, with a not unexpected close integration of US and British forces and bases. There are F-111E bomber bases, SAC standby bases, that is, collocated operating bases, and bases for ground-launched cruise missiles, and the important Poseidon SSBN base at Holy Loch. There are air bases and nuclear storage sites for P-3C ASW craft, other bases for EF-111 'Raven' electronic warfare and command and control aircraft, and for tankers and TACAMO aircraft. In addition, there is a profusion of C³I and space-related facilities: SOSUS, Giant Talk/Scope Signal transmitters for SAC, nuclear test detection stations, LORAN-C, BMEWS, AUTODIN, a satellite control facility and weather interception control units. There are also a number of important headquarters, for instance, that for US Naval Forces Europe/US Commander Eastern Atlantic. For the US nuclear posture, access to the UK is crucial and perhaps in some ways irreplaceable.[164]

FR Germany, of course, while hosting the large US Seventh Army and its associated facilities, is also vital to the US nuclear posture. It hosts numerous nuclear-armed strike aircraft (Pershing missiles and GLCMs are now being removed), as well as numerous tactical and battlefield nuclear systems, that is, Lance missiles, nuclear-capable howitzers, atomic demolition missiles, and so on. Otherwise, there are also vital SIGINT and communications facilities, the early-warning satellite down-link at Kapaun, bases for AWACS and U-2s, LORAN-C and a host of important headquarters and command centres. Generally speaking, however, FR Germany's importance to the USA in this respect has been concentrated in the areas of theatre and tactical nuclear capability, that is, with regard to the defence of FR Germany and Europe itself.[165]

The several US NATO allies in the southern flank/Mediterranean area (Spain, Portugal, Italy, Greece and Turkey) all host crucial US facilities, albeit perhaps with a degree of (actual or potential) redundancy now threatened by political problems militating towards decoupling, particularly in the cases of Spain and Greece, but still potentially with Portugal and perhaps Italy. Further, these problems may now acquire added importance just because of the new arms control arrangements for Central Europe—the USA may be ill able to afford, simultaneously, a reduction of its nuclear forces in FR Germany and the decoupling of its Mediterranean alliances and loss of part of the attendant base structure.

Spain has provided important air bases; until recently for F-16s rotated forward to Italy and Turkey, for KC-135 tankers and for SAC bomber recovery, and for P-3C ASW operations. It also provides facilities for naval HF and for SAC's fail-safe communications, interception of weather broadcasts, nuclear bombing practice, nuclear detection and satellite-communications control centres. The F-16s will now be removed—it remains to be seen whether there will be further pressures on the US basing presence.

Portugal provides only a part-time P-3C rotational base on its mainland, but the Azores host a number of crucial nuclear facilities: SOSUS, missile tracking, satellite control, P-3Cs and HF transmitters. The functions related to ASW and ocean surveillance are crucial for obvious geographical reasons, and paralleled by other islands such as Diego Garcia, Ascension and Bermuda. Lisbon also allows the US Navy visiting rights.

Italy is a crucial hub of US/NATO nuclear activities: there are Lance missiles, nuclear artillery, F-16 rotational bases and nuclear storage, a vital attack submarine base on Sardinia, another for P-3C and other ASW aircraft, ground-launched cruise missiles, a variety of communications and surveillance functions, LORAN-C, a SOON observatory, and a homeport for the US Sixth Fleet's carrier battle group along with that fleet's headquarters. It is the hub of NATO's operations in southern Europe and the Mediterranean and ranks third in nuclear warheads deployed in overseas countries, behind FR Germany and the UK.

Greece, somewhat politically estranged from the USA under its present regime, still provides NATO and the USA access to vital nuclear facilities. There are tactical fighters armed with two-key nuclear weapons, though the Nike Hercules and Honest John missiles have been phased out. There is a vital base for rotation of P-3 aircraft, a NATO missile training range, HF and LF naval transmitters (some used for submarines), facilities for KC-135 tankers and strategic reconnaissance aircraft, weather intercepts, an AWACS forward base and some headquarters functions. Rival Turkey is equally if not more important, with five bases for nuclear-armed strike aircraft, a DSCS satellite communications down-link, Giant Talk/Scope Signal III, an AWACS forward base, critical SIGINT stations and radars vital for missile telemetry and satellite tracking, early-warning radars and NADGE tactical radars, nuclear detection and LORAN-C. Incirlik is a crucial air-staging base for US Middle Eastern operations, as well as a communications hub, and Pirinclik is critical for monitoring Soviet missile tests. It would be difficult to overestimate Turkey's role in supporting NATO's nuclear posture.

In the Asia–Pacific area, Australia, the Philippines and Japan—to a lesser degree South Korea—are crucial to various aspects of the US nuclear posture. Australia hosts the critical satellite-related facilities at Nurrungar (DSP early warning) and Pine Gap (SIGINT and reconnaissance satellite down-links); allows B-52 transits through Darwin; and also provides access for an important VLF transmitter, Omega, seismic detectors, a SOON laboratory, P-3C flights, and FLTSATCOM and DSCS facilities. Japan provides major naval and tactical fighter air bases, important communications and satellite-related facilities (including B-52 fail-safe communications, VLF/HF transmitters, AFSATCOM ground terminals), nuclear detection, LORAN-C/D, Omega, Clarinet Pilgrim, P-3C and TACAMO bases, SOSUS terminals, and an air base on Okinawa where tankers, SR-71s, RC-135s and P-3Cs are deployed. The Philippines hosts the major naval base at Subic Bay and Clark AFB, plus the whole gamut of technical facilities: fail-safe communications, SIGINT, nuclear detection, strategic-related radars, HF and LF facilities, a SOON facility, weather interception control, a DSCS satellite operation, and so on. In South Korea, there are bases for nuclear-armed strike aircraft which can reach the USSR, plus LORAN C/D, a GEODSS facility, nuclear-test detection, storage sites for army-related nuclear weapons and a variety of nuclear-related communications facilities.

Otherwise—and in line with the obvious facts of geography which render those areas astride the great circle routes between the US and Soviet core areas important—Canada, Greenland and Iceland are all vital to the US nuclear posture. Canada, which provides a massive land barrier to the north of the

USA, but also a jumping-off point *en route* to the USSR over the Arctic, hosts a perhaps surprising number of vital US nuclear facilities. Among them are the DEW Line and CADIN Pinetree Line radars (now to become the North Warning System), the Green Pine fail-safe communications network, dispersal bases for B-52s and KC-135s, fighter-interceptor bases, SOSUS and valuable research and environmental facilities used to test, among other things, ALCMs and ASW technologies.[166] Greenland hosts DEW radars, BMEWS, LORAN-C, an Air Force Satellite Control facility, SAC fail-safe communications, and a bomber and tanker dispersal base, even though actual nuclear weapon deployments are restricted. Iceland provides the USA access for HF and LF communications, Green Pine, LORAN-C, early-warning radars, a SOSUS processing facility, basing for tactical fighters, P-3Cs and AWACS. Altogether, Keflavik itself is one of the several most important US basing hubs in the world. Iceland and Greenland, along with the UK and Norway, of course, derive immense importance from their locations adjacent to the crucial North Atlantic SLOCs and the chokepoints associated with the GIUK–Norway gaps.

Otherwise, and as bruited in some of the explicitly geopolitical writings of Geoffrey Kemp and others, a number of well-located islands in the various oceans have assumed great importance for the US nuclear posture.[167] In particular, and aside from the US territory of Guam, these are Ascension, the Azores, Bermuda, Diego Garcia and Kwajalein; and perhaps to a lesser extent Barbados, Oman's Masirah, the Seychelles, and others. It is to be noted that three of the five most important islands involve US access to British territory. Ascension provides access for P-3Cs and tankers, satellite control, NAVSTAR, tracking radars in relation to missile tests, MILS, a SOON observatory, and a weather interception facility. Bermuda hosts air bases for P-3Cs and TACAMO, SOSUS, HF and LF radio, ASW research and tracking radars for the Eastern Space and Missile Center (ESMC). Diego Garcia provides access for nuclear depth bomb storage, P-3Cs, KC-135s, Maritime Prepositioning Ships, a carrier battle group, GEODSS, a DSCS station, an HF transmitter and receiver, and a NAVSTAR facility. Kwajalein, with a narrower range of activities, hosts an LF transmitter, a NAVSTAR facility, a missile-range terminus and satellite-tracking facilities. The dispersal of these facilities throughout all the major oceans is worth noting, as is their virtually irreplaceable nature.

Soviet nuclear access

By contrast to the dominant geographical patterns of US nuclear-related facilities (the rimlands, trans-Arctic territories and mid-ocean islands), the USSR relies first on contiguous allies in Eastern Europe and Mongolia, and then on a handful of states defined more randomly (and without a discernible geographical pattern) by ideological affinity. In the former category, particularly the GDR, Czechoslovakia, Hungary and Poland provide the USSR with a wide variety of nuclear-related facilities. There are bases for theatre and tactical missiles, for nuclear-armed strike aircraft and nuclear artillery, bombing ranges, and so on. In addition, these nations host numerous tactical radars and communications hubs, nuclear storage sites, SIGINT stations, and so on. The GDR and Poland also host Molniya satellite down-links. Generally speaking, publicly available information on such technical facilities is sparser than is the case for NATO facilities in Western Europe.

Cuba, of course, particularly as it alone provides access in close proximity to the USA, is a vital hub of Soviet FMP.[168] It provides air bases for ocean-surveillance and nuclear-armed ASW aircraft, SIGINT, satellite ground stations, missile tracking near Cape Canaveral and naval access both for submarines and surface ships. Otherwise, Viet Nam, South Yemen, Ethiopia and Angola are, in particular, valuable for Soviet air and naval access, and for some C³I functions. One notes the almost fortuitous global dispersion of these external Soviet positions, providing access to several major ocean littorals. All in all, Cuba and Viet Nam appear the most important of the Soviet overseas basing hosts; the one near the USA, the other astride the important East Asian SLOCs and near to the major US bases in the Philippines and Guam.

V. Port visits: on-board nuclear weapons and nuclear propulsion systems

The USA faces some serious problems regarding other nations' restrictions on access to their territories for nuclear weapons. This problem is noted with regard to Norway, Denmark, Iceland, Spain, Portugal (mainland only) and Japan, all of which restrict storage or regular deployment of US warheads for nuclear depth charges, bombs for tactical aircraft, and so on, albeit in some cases with provisional exceptions for emergency or high-alert circumstances.

There is a further, perhaps only emerging, problem regarding visits by warships (surface ships and submarines) which carry nuclear weapons and in some cases with regard to ships with nuclear propulsion systems. Restrictions in the latter case are more likely to be based on environmental grounds, if not on purist aspirations for 'nuclear-free zones', even if not within an agreed-upon (i.e., a treaty) regional arrangement.

The recent legislation in New Zealand barring nuclear-capable ships (or aircraft carrying nuclear weapons) is one example, in a situation which created a serious political rift with an old US ally.[169] The issue has also arisen elsewhere, in Denmark, with respect to current negotiations over the future of newly independent Belau and, earlier, in connection with interpretations of the Tlatelolco Treaty establishing a nuclear-free zone in Latin America.[170] It also arose recently in connection with the initiation of US naval unit visits to Chinese ports.[171]

Further complications are presented by a US Navy policy of neither confirming nor denying the presence or absence of nuclear weapons aboard ships (the presence of nuclear-propulsion systems is always obvious). Even aside from the classified nature of the subject, the author has learned by inquiring within the US Government which nations do or do not allow nuclear-armed or

-propelled ships to visit, that the answers are not always easily ascertainable. In some cases, apparently, requests for visits are turned down with vague explanations which leave unclear the role played by the nuclear issue.[172] In other cases US nuclear-propelled ships do not visit certain ports for unspecified technical reasons, perhaps because of the density of populations in close proximity to those places where a nuclear-propelled ship could be berthed. That is, restrictions on US nuclear-propelled ships tend, more often than not, to be self-imposed. Otherwise, with regard to nuclear weapons, it remains to be seen whether the New Zealand case is an anomaly, or a harbinger of things to come.

The list in table 30 was provided by the US Navy from an open briefing, detailing those places the US Atlantic submarine force has been able to visit in the recent past to provide liberty to sailors. There are few surprises, save perhaps the level of access to Latin America.[173]

Table 30. Foreign liberty ports used by the US submarine force in 1986

26 countries in which 54 ports were visited			
Canada	France	Curacao	Venezuela
Norway	Bahamas	Belgium	Brazil
Scotland	Gibraltar	Chile	Ecuador
Bermuda	Portugal	Jamaica	Peru
England	Italy	Panama	Colombia
Netherlands	Turkey	Cuba (Guantanamo)	
FR Germany	Barbados	NL Antilles	

Source: US Navy.

Some similar issues have arisen with regard to transit of nuclear-armed aircraft; New Zealand denies that too. All in all, there appears some trend towards greater restraints in this area, howsoever to be interpreted on political or more narrowly environmental grounds.

There is no evidence that the USSR labours under any restrictions regarding nuclear weapons or propulsion systems in connection with ship port visits or aircraft transit. The governments of the nations to which it has access tend to be mute—and certainly unaffected by public opinion—on these issues.

VI. Other weapons of mass destruction: foreign-based chemical weapons

By 1988 the subject of chemical weapons and warfare (CW) had seemed to acquire a more prominent place in the news and scholarly journals than had long been the case. This resulted from the conjunction of several trends and events.

The Iraq-Iran War had, by 1988, seen the open use of chemical weapons to produce mass casualties, primarily involving Iraqi use of air-delivered poison gas.[174] Following upon the previous allegations of Soviet use of 'yellow rain' toxins in Afghanistan and (with Viet Nam) perhaps also Laos, this appeared to represent a crucial loosening of the international norms which had prevailed since World War I, the reported exceptions in Ethiopia (by Italy), Manchuria (by Japan) and Yemen (by Egypt) notwithstanding. By 1988 there were also other signs of movement towards acquisition of possible CW delivery vehicles by other nations deemed anxious to acquire a 'poor man's A-bomb': Syria had acquired Soviet SS-21 missiles assumed intended to carry CW warheads for use against Israel; and Saudi Arabia had acquired long-range Chinese missiles, apparently for similar purposes as well as for deterrence against Iran.[175]

The flurry of arms control activity centred on Central Europe—the signing of the INF Treaty, and talk or negotiations about a follow-on 'triple-zero' option to eliminate battlefield weapons—also had ramifications for CW deployment and possible control. Critics of the INF Treaty pointed to the huge asymmetries in the NATO/WTO chemical-warfare balance, claiming that the partial or full denuclearization of Central Europe might serve to enhance the significance of those asymmetries along with those in conventional forces (there were conflicting views on the value of chemical warfare for offensive operations at the FLOT, as some claimed their main provisional value was at the theatre level for interdiction of logistics and embarkation points or for interdiction of rivals' air bases). Hence, there was also increased discussion of the need for CW arms control agreements to supplement INF (and perhaps possible conventional force agreements) even as some sceptics denied the viability of any verification regime in this area, as applied to NATO and the WTO, or to a more global chemical warfare control arrangement.

Table 31. US CW facilities abroad, 1988

Location	Unit/activity
Dahn, FRG	Storage?
Fischbach, FRG	64th Ordnance Company munitions depot
Hanau, FRG	Storage
RAF Lakenheath, UK	Storage
RAF Molesworth, UK	C-warfare central security control facility
	C-warfare wing command post facility
Mannheim, FRG	Storage
Okinawa, Japan	Bulk storage of VX
Pirmasens, FRG	Storage
Spangdahlem AB, FRG	C-warfare squadron operations facility
	F-4 with VX spray tanks
Torrejon AFB, Spain	Biological warfare squadron
Viernheim, FRG	191 Ordnance Battalion chemical depot
RAF Welford, UK	7551st Ammo Supply Squadron
	BLU/80-B Bigeye VX aviation bomb
Zweibrücken AFB, FRG	C-warfare air-photo interpretation facility
	C-warfare squadron operations facility

Source: Mallory, C. K., 'CBW study: interim report', SIPRI internal working paper, 1988, p. 43.

Though largely ignored in the literature, CW deployment patterns by both the USA and the USSR have implications for FMP; indeed, on the Western side at least, such deployment has led to some thorny political problems parallel to those involving nuclear weapons. According to one source, the USA has an estimated 28 000 to 42 000 agent-ton stockpile of chemical weapons (down from an earlier unofficial estimate of 80 000 tons), 'the useful portions of which are roughly 2000 agent-tons of nerve-agent-filled artillery projectiles and about 1500 agent-tons of nonpersistent nerve-agent bombs.[176] For practical purposes, this is said to translate into about 600 000 rounds of 155-mm GB howitzer ammunition and 900 or so modern Weteye 500-pound GB bombs (all missile systems have been destroyed and there is no serviceable multiple rocket launcher capability).[177]

Mallory, in his research for SIPRI, has pointed to an overseas US chemical weapon supply structure which, actually, has its origins in the storing of such weapons in the UK during World War II.[178] He claims that in time of war US chemical weapons could presumably pass through the UK, or be transported directly to FR Germany for combat purposes.[179] He cites a number of locations outside the USA alleged to have a connection to chemical warfare or to be 'agent storage depots'—these are listed in table 31.

The USSR has a relatively far larger chemical warfare structure, involving some 85 000 dedicated CW personnel (the comparable US figure is around 2000)[180] and a chemical weapon stockpile which has been variously estimated from as low as '20 000 tons of chemical nerve agents to 350 000 tons of all types of agents, to over 700 000 tons', in turn based on 14 chemical-agent production facilities.[181] These agents can be delivered by mortars, howitzers, guns, multiple rocket launchers, and surface-to-surface missiles, as well as by aircraft. Mallory cites, in particular, the roles of 122-mm and 152-mm artillery pieces, the BM-21 Grad multiple rocket launcher, the SS-21 missile, and Mi-24 Hind helicopter as preferred delivery systems.[182] He also cites the US Defense Intelligence Agency's allegation of some 39 Soviet-controlled chemical warfare or biological warfare weapons' dumps, 30 of which are alleged to be in Eastern Europe. Some of these depots are listed in table 32.[183]

Table 32. Soviet-controlled CW and BW weapon depots in Eastern Europe, 1988

Location	Country	Location	Country
Presov	Czechoslovakia	Kosice	Czechoslovakia
Sliac	Czechoslovakia	Zvolen	Czechoslovakia
Mlada-Boleslav	Czechoslovakia	Milovice	Czechoslovakia
Pilzen-Dobrany	Czechoslovakia	Neubrandenburg	GDR
Rechlin-Larz	GDR	Dessau-Zerbst	GDR
Sondershausen	GDR	Brand-Briesen	GDR
Mockrehna-Brandis	GDR	Riesa-Grossenhain	GDR
Dresden-Hermsdorf	GDR		

Source: Mallory, C. K., 'CBW study: interim report', SIPRI internal working paper, 1988.

In recent years the USA in particular has moved towards modernization of its chemical weapon stockpile: these plans have centred on binary 155-mm howitzer ammunition and the Bigeye binary VX bomb (binaries are composed of two chemicals which are much less toxic than nerve gas and produce the latter only when combined).[184] This greatly reduces the hazards of storage and transportation. There are also plans for delivering binary weapons by multiple rocket launchers or by missiles. Forward deployment of binaries in NATO has encountered political opposition, however. In Europe, only France deploys sizeable numbers of CW weapons (none outside France); Belgium reportedly has some small stocks.[185] The FRG, where US stocks are deployed, has formally renounced them, even while supporting in principle US modernization efforts so as to balance off the huge Soviet chemical weapon arsenal.

VII. Summary: advantage and vulnerability in peacetime and wartime

The USA enjoys a fully global network of nuclear-related facilities, many favourably located around the long arc of the Soviet Eurasian borders. That network remains substantially intact despite some long-term erosion caused by political defections from the Western bloc (such as Iran, Pakistan, Viet Nam), but it is under some pressure because of various political problems, such as at present in Spain and Greece. As is elaborated upon in chapter 10, the USA has been forced to bargain harder and to offer larger amounts of economic and security aid, just to retain the current peacetime status of many of its overseas nuclear facilities. There is a trend towards decoupling; this is based variously on a perceived decline in cold war tensions, strivings for sovereignty underpinned by nationalism, environmental concerns, and perhaps the evident decline in US prestige and authority in the post-Viet Nam period. But, as noted, many of the most vital US facilities are hosted by long-term close allies such as the UK, FR Germany and Canada, though even in these countries there have been demands for the reduction of the US presence.

Generally speaking, the main threats to the continuing US presence now appear to be on NATO's Southern Flank where the USA faces complex negotiations with Spain, Greece, Portugal (re the Azores) and Turkey. This could involve more restrictive agreements (regarding out-of-area operations) but perhaps also the dismissal of some installations; for instance, nuclear-related facilities in Greece.

The USSR is far less reliant on overseas access; as noted, it relies instead on its huge land mass and a massive array of ships for various C^3I and space-related functions. Otherwise, the political nature of its key allies—Cuba, Viet Nam, Ethiopia, etc.—perhaps renders it less vulnerable to the kinds of public political pressures the USA has faced in Spain and Greece; not only as pertains to withdrawal, but also in connection with the narrower questions of nuclear weapon storage and transit. But it too must bargain with the governments of its base host states, and as exemplified by the histories of Egypt and Somalia, it too can face the loss of access.

Those are peacetime conditions in relation to deterrence. If war should erupt, particularly one involving a protracted conventional phase or one only slowly escalating to the nuclear level at the lower rungs of the ladder, it is now standard fare to assume US vulnerability to decoupling under Soviet threats—just where and to what extent is argued. But there may be other conditions less often discussed in open-source journals. If a contest of tit-for-tat destruction of overseas facilities should erupt as both sides strive to improve their end of the intra-war nuclear balance, the paucity of Soviet external facilities might create instability in that it might tempt NATO to initiate interdiction of Soviet homeland facilities, perhaps in the Far East or in the Kola area. In addition, the extent to which the USSR relies heavily on its AGI fleet and other support vessels, raises the question of *their* vulnerability at the outset of a conflict, particularly as many habitually steam in waters close to the USA and to some of its allies. That question, rarely addressed, appears to focus attention particularly on ocean-surveillance capabilities and, hence, anti-satellite operations. But it also illustrates what might be the sharp distinction between the peacetime (deterrence) and wartime (war-fighting) functions of nuclear-related FMP. The hypothetical politics of the latter are vague indeed and difficult to anticipate. It is perhaps only in recent years that the withering of long-existent alliances has begun to feed those questions back into the deterrence equation.

Notes and references

[1] This by now increasingly common term/question was broached in John Palmer, 'Europe without America?' (Oxford University Press: New York, 1987).

[2] This definition comes from Cohen, S., *Geography and Politics in a World Divided* (Random House: New York, 1963), p. 26.

[3] SIPRI data, and Campbell, D., *The Unsinkable Aircraft Carrier: American Military Power in Britain* (Paladin: London, 1986), pp. 31, 39 and map, pp. 36–37. Also cited in the latter are fighter bases at Woodbridge, Carnaby and Manston, and transport bases at Stornaway, Heathrow, Prestwick Valley and Nutts Corner (Northern Ireland).

[4] Campbell (note 3).

[5] SIPRI data and Goodie, C. B., *Strategic Air Command* (Simon and Schuster: New York, 1965), pp. 12, 14, 24, 42 and 52.

[6] SIPRI data.

[7] SIPRI data.

[8] SIPRI data.

[9] See Holst, J. J., *Comparative U.S. and Soviet Deployments, Doctrines, and Arms Limitation* (University of Chicago: Chicago, Ill, 1971), Occasional Paper of the Center for Policy Study, and Klass, P., *Secret Sentries in Space* (Random House: New York, 1971), pp. 5–8.

[10] SIPRI data and Arkin, W. M. and Fieldhouse, R. F., *Nuclear Battlefields: Global Links in the Arms Race* (Ballinger: Cambridge, Mass., 1985), pp. 76–79.

[11] Arkin and Fieldhouse (note 10); and Cochran, T. B., Arkin, W. M. and Hoenig, M. M., *Nuclear Weapons Databook, vol. 1: U.S. Nuclear Forces and Capabilities* (Ballinger: Cambridge, Mass., 1984), p. 41.

[12] Among others, see Richelson, J., 'Technical collection and arms control', ed. W. Potter, *Verification and Arms Control* (D. C. Heath: Lexington, Mass., 1985), p. 193; and Ford, D., *The Button* (Simon and Schuster: New York, 1985), pp. 74–75.

[13] Campbell (note 3), pp. 70–75; and SIPRI data.

[14] This history is reviewed in, among others, Klass (note 9); and Holst (note 9).

[15] Klass (note 9), pp. 50–51.

[16] Klass (note 9), pp. 50–51. See also Infield, G. B., *Unarmed and Unafraid* (Macmillan: New York, 1970), especially chapter 10.

[17] Klass (note 9), p. 84; SIPRI data; and Richelson (note 12), pp. 177–78.

[18] Klass (note 9), p. 136.

[19] Klass (note 14), p. 136.

[20] Klass (note 14), pp. 91, 104–105 and 124.

[21] See Newhouse, J., *Cold Dawn: The Story of SALT* (Holt, Rinehart and Winston: New York, 1973), pp. 22, 245; and Rhinelander, J. B., 'The SALT I Agreements', eds M. Willrich and J. B. Rhinelander, *SALT: The Moscow Agreements and Beyond* (The Free Press: New York, 1974), pp. 125–59, especially p. 149, which discusses the 'on-station' advantages the USA enjoyed as a result of bases in Holy Loch, Rota and Guam.

[22] Klass (note 9), chapter 12, and Allison, G. T., 'Conceptual models and the Cuban missile crisis', *American Political Science Review*, vol. 63, no. 3 (Sep. 1969), pp. 689–718.

[23] See Lukas, J. H., 'Class reunion: Kennedy's men relive the Cuban missile crisis', *The New York Times Magazine*, 30 Aug. 1987, pp. 22ff. For an opposite view, that the USSR *did* have nuclear weapons in Cuba, see ''62 missile crisis yields new puzzle', *New York Times*, 30 Jan. 1989, p. A2.

[24] McGarvey, P., *CIA: The Myth and the Madness* (Penguin: Baltimore, Md., 1972), pp. 49–50; and Hersh, S., *The Target is Destroyed* (Random House: New York, 1986), p. 11.

[25] See Carroll, J., *Secrets of Electronic Espionage* (Dutton: New York, 1966), p. 175.

[26] Carroll (note 25), p. 167; and Klass (note 9), pp. 51–52.

[27] McGarvey (note 24).

[28] McGarvey (note 24), chapters 2 and 5.

[29] McGarvey (note 24), p. 47.

[30] McGarvey (note 24), p. 47.

[31] McGarvey (note 24), p. 49; and Bamford, J., *The Puzzle Palace* (Houghton-Mifflin: Boston, Mass., 1982), pp. 212–35.

[32] Klass (note 9), p. 34.

[33] International Institute for Strategic Studies, *The Military Balance: 1986–1987* (IISS: London, 1986), pp. 200, 204.

[34] IISS (note 33), p. 36; and Arkin and Fieldhouse (note 10), pp. 46–47.

[35] Arkin and Fieldhouse (note 10), p. 46.

[36] Arkin and Fieldhouse (note 10), p. 45.

[37] Arkin and Fieldhouse (note 10), p. 45, and IISS (note 33), pp. 19–20.

[38] Arkin and Fieldhouse (note 10), p. 45.

[39] Arkin and Fieldhouse (note 10), p. 47. See also Collins, J. M., *U.S.–Soviet Military Balance: 1980–1985* (Pergamon-Brassey's: Washington, DC, 1985), p. 69.

[40] Arkin and Fieldhouse (note 10), p. 47.

[41] IISS (note 33), p. 20.

[42] IISS (note 33), p. 20.

[43] Arkin and Fieldhouse (note 10), p. 51.

[44] SIPRI data, and Arkin and Fieldhouse (note 10), appendix A.

[45] SIPRI data, and Arkin and Fieldhouse (note 10), appendix A.

[46] Arkin and Fieldhouse (note 10), p. 234; Cochran, Arkin and Hoenig (note 11), pp. 232–33; and Campbell (note 3), pp. 230–40.

[47] See Campbell (note 3), p. 268.

[48] IISS (note 33), p. 37.

[49] Arkin and Fieldhouse (note 10), p. 52.

[50] Arkin and Fieldhouse (note 10), p. 222.

[51] Arkin and Fieldhouse (note 10), p. 229.

[52] For accurate details, see 'Treaty Between the United States of America and the Union of Soviet Socialist Republics on the Elimination of Their Intermediate-Range and Shorter-Range Missiles', Department of State Publication 9555, Bureau of Public Affairs, Washington, DC, Dec. 1987.

[53] Arkin and Fieldhouse (note 10), p. 54.

[54] Arkin and Fieldhouse (note 10), p. 56.

[55] Arkin and Fieldhouse (note 10), appendix A.

[56] Arkin and Fieldhouse (note 10), p. 222.

[57] Arkin and Fieldhouse (note 10), p. 233.

[58] Arkin and Fieldhouse (note 10), p. 233.

[59] IISS (note 33), p. 201.

[60] Arkin and Fieldhouse (note 10), p. 57; and Cochran, Arkin and Hoenig (note 11), pp. 251–54.

[61] IISS (note 33), p. 202.

[62] Arkin and Fieldhouse (note 10), pp. 232–33.

[63] Arkin and Fieldhouse (note 10), pp. 232–33.
[64] Arkin and Fieldhouse (note 10), pp. 219–20.
[65] Arkin and Fieldhouse (note 10), p. 224.
[66] Arkin and Fieldhouse (note 10), pp. 236–45.
[67] Arkin and Fieldhouse (note 10), pp. 216, 227.
[68] Arkin and Fieldhouse (note 10), p. 279.
[69] Arkin and Fieldhouse (note 10), p. 279.
[70] Arkin and Fieldhouse (note 10), p. 223.
[71] Arkin and Fieldhouse (note 10), p. 57, and appendix A.
[72] Arkin and Fieldhouse (note 10), p. 235.
[73] Arkin and Fieldhouse (note 10), p. 222.
[74] Arkin and Fieldhouse (note 10), appendix A.
[75] Arkin and Fieldhouse (note 10), p. 227.
[76] Arkin and Fieldhouse (note 10), p. 223.
[77] Arkin and Fieldhouse (note 10), p. 217.
[78] Arkin and Fieldhouse (note 10), appendix A.
[79] Arkin and Fieldhouse (note 10), p. 221, sited at NAS Agana/Brewer Field/Guam IAP.
[80] Arkin and Fieldhouse (note 10), pp. 224–25.
[81] Arkin and Fieldhouse (note 10), p. 225.
[82] Arkin and Fieldhouse (note 10), p. 231.
[83] IISS (note 33), p. 206.
[84] Arkin and Fieldhouse (note 10), appendix B.
[85] Arkin and Fieldhouse (note 10), pp. 265–66.
[86] Arkin and Fieldhouse (note 10), p. 266.
[87] IISS (note 33), p. 207.
[88] IISS (note 33), p. 207, note f.
[89] Arkin and Fieldhouse (note 10), p. 267.
[90] Arkin and Fieldhouse (note 10), p. 264.
[91] Arkin and Fieldhouse (note 10), appendix B, and US Department of Defense, *Soviet Military Power 1985*, 4th edn (US Government Printing Office, Washington, DC, 1985), chapter VII.
[92] IISS (note 33), p. 200, and Cochran, Arkin and Hoenig (note 11), pp. 300–308.
[93] IISS (note 33), pp. 200, 202.
[94] Arkin and Fieldhouse (note 10), p. 236.
[95] Arkin and Fieldhouse (note 10), p. 61.
[96] Collins (note 39), p. 70.
[97] IISS (note 33), p. 205.
[98] IISS (note 33), p. 206.
[99] Arkin and Fieldhouse (note 10), p. 265.
[100] IISS (note 33), p. 206.
[101] IISS (note 33), p. 207, note k.
[102] IISS (note 33), pp. 205–207.
[103] Cochran, Arkin and Hoenig (note 11), especially p. 281.
[104] Arkin and Fieldhouse (note 10), p. 61.
[105] This point was made to the author by several Pentagon officials in private conversations.
[106] Arkin and Fieldhouse (note 10), pp. 61–62.
[107] The Improved Hawk SAM belt is illustrated by a map showing the increasing vulnerability of NATO air in Karber, P. A. and Whitley, A. G., 'Operational continuity and change within the Central European conventional arms control competition', notes prepared for the West Point Conference on 'NATO at Forty', New York, 4–7 June 1987.
[108] IISS (note 33), p. 202.
[109] Arkin and Fieldhouse (note 10), p. 236. By 1987, according to IISS (note 33), p. 202, this number had been reduced to 216.
[110] IISS (note 33), p. 202.
[111] IISS (note 33), p. 202.
[112] Cochran, Arkin and Hoenig (note 11), pp. 88, 213, 214, 218, 230 and 231.
[113] Cochran, Arkin and Hoenig (note 11), p. 168.
[114] Arkin and Fieldhouse (note 10), pp. 216–19.
[115] Arkin and Fieldhouse (note 10), p. 61.
[116] IISS (note 33), p. 205.
[117] IISS (note 33), p. 205.

[118] IISS (note 33), p. 204.

[119] IISS (note 33), p. 202.

[120] IISS (note 33), p. 202.

[121] Arkin and Fieldhouse (note 10), appendices A and C.

[122] Arkin and Fieldhouse (note 10), p. 60.

[123] INF Treaty (note 52), p. 37.

[124] IISS (note 33), pp. 42, 205.

[125] IISS (note 33), p. 205.

[126] IISS (note 33), p. 42, and Arkin and Fieldhouse (note 10), appendix B and p. 60.

[127] IISS (note 33), p. 42, and Arkin and Fieldhouse (note 10), appendix B and p. 60.

[128] IISS (note 33), p. 206.

[129] IISS (note 33), p. 205, and INF Treaty (note 52), p. 37, which notes 93 missiles and 58 launchers forward-based in the GDR and Czechoslovakia.

[130] INF Treaty (note 52).

[131] Arkin and Fieldhouse (note 10), p. 223. Cochran, Arkin and Hoenig (note 11), p. 269, estimate a global total of 400.

[132] Cochran, Arkin and Hoenig (note 11), p. 94; Arkin and Fieldhouse (note 10), p. 221.

[133] Arkin and Fieldhouse (note 10), p. 62.

[134] Arkin and Fieldhouse (note 10), p. 228.

[135] Arkin and Fieldhouse (note 10), p. 63.

[136] IISS (note 33), p. 38. See also, Arkin and Fieldhouse (note 10), pp. 74–75; Richelson, J. T., *Sword and Shield: The Soviet Intelligence and Security Apparatus* (Ballinger: Cambridge, Mass., 1986), p. 108.

[137] Noted in SIPRI data and Arkin and Fieldhouse (note 10), p. 77.

[138] Richelson, J. T. and Ball, D., *The Ties That Bind* (Allen and Unwin: Boston, 1985), pp. 199–201.

[139] Some evidence for an incipient Soviet SOSUS is provided in Burns, T. S., *The Secret War For The Ocean Depths* (Rawson: New York, 1978), p. 311; and 'A Soviet sub-detection system?' *Newsweek*, 8 Sep. 1980, p. 15.

[140] Muller, D., *China as a Maritime Power* (Westview: Boulder, Colo., 1983), p. 109, which notes that by 1971 the Chinese had converted a merchant cargo ship into a down-range missile instrumentation ship for testing ICBMs.

[141] Richelson (note 12), pp. 194–98.

[142] Richelson (note 136), pp. 106–107.

[143] Richelson (note 12), pp. 192–93.

[144] *Soviet Space Programs: 1976–1980*, US Senate, Committee on Commerce, Science and Transportation, 97th Congress, 2nd Session (US Government Printing Office: Washington, DC, Dec. 1982), p. 124.

[145] Richelson (note 136), p. 100.

[146] Arkin and Fieldhouse (note 10), p. 77.

[147] Arkin and Fieldhouse (note 10), p. 77.

[148] Arkin and Fieldhouse (note 10), p. 80, and appendix A; and SIPRI data.

[149] Arkin and Fieldhouse (note 10), pp. 77–78; and Ford (note 12), pp. 223–24.

[150] Stares, P. B., *Space and National Security* (Brookings Institution: Washington, DC, 1987), p. 188.

[151] Arkin and Fieldhouse (note 10), appendix A and SIPRI data.

[152] Arkin and Fieldhouse (note 10), pp. 80, 128, and SIPRI data.

[153] Stares (note 150), p. 188.

[154] SIPRI data; Arkin and Fieldhouse (note 10), appendix A.

[155] Arkin and Fieldhouse (note 10), appendix B; and Friedman, N., 'Soviet naval command and control', ed. S. Cimbala, *Soviet C^3I* (AFCEA International Press: Washington, DC, 1987), p. 285, and Meyer, S. M., 'Soviet nuclear operations', in Cimbala, p. 148.

[156] SIPRI data; Arkin and Fieldhouse (note 10), appendix B.

[157] Stares (note 150), p. 188; and Ford (note 12), pp. 64–71.

[158] SIPRI data; Arkin and Fieldhouse (note 10), appendix A.

[159] Arkin and Fieldhouse (note 10), pp. 79, 215.

[160] SIPRI data; Arkin and Fieldhouse (note 10), p. 288.

[161] SIPRI data; Arkin and Fieldhouse (note 10), p. 78; and various sources otherwise cited in chapter 7.

[162] See 'Danish Defense', special issue of *Defense Today*, Aug. 1986, p. 27, which refers to a US 'Marine Amphibious Force' of 40 000 men, and planes to match, one-third of which is said permanently to have been allocated to Norway, while 'the other two-thirds can be deployed in various places in the Northern Region, including Denmark'.

[163] Arkin and Fieldhouse (note 10), p. 227.

[164] Campbell (note 3), p. 286, provides a list of US headquarters, administration, and command and control centres in the UK.

[165] The data for this section are extensively referenced in other chapters; SIPRI data and Arkin and Fieldhouse (note 10), appendix A are particularly used.

[166] Regarding the various US nuclear-related facilities in Canada, see Arkin and Fieldhouse (note 10), pp. 78–79; and SIPRI data.

[167] Kemp, G., 'The new strategic map', *Survival*, vol. 19, no. 2 (Mar./Apr., 1977), pp. 50–59.

[168] Arkin and Fieldhouse (note 10), appendix B; and *Soviet Military Power 1985* (note 91), pp. 115, 119–20.

[169] Among other sources, see Alves, D., *Anti-Nuclear Attitudes in New Zealand and Australia*, A National Security Affairs Monograph (National Defense University Press: Washington, DC, 1985); and 'New Zealand rebuff: A baffling furor', *New York Times*, 7 Feb. 1985, p. A10.

[170] See, regarding Denmark, 'Danish voting Tuesday centers on military issues', *New York Times*, 9 May 1988, p. A9; 'Slicing NATO too thin in Denmark', *New York Times*, 9 May 1988, p. A18; and 'NATO: Alliance a la carte?' *Newsweek*, 23 May 1988, p. 27. Regarding Belau, see 'Vote to end Pacific islands' atom-arms ban is challenged', *New York Times*, 13 Oct. 1987, p. A19; and 'Pacific isle blocks nuclear accord with U.S.', *New York Times*, 18 Sep. 1986, p. A21.

[171] 'China said to bar visits by a-weapon ships', *Washington Post*, 29 Mar. 1986; and 'Vessey starts talks', *New York Times*, 13 Jan. 1985, p. 12.

[172] This point emerged from a conversation with Captain Harry Bergbauer, USN, retired, State College, Pa.

[173] These data were provided by memorandum from Commander, Submarine Force, Atlantic Fleet, Norfolk, Va.

[174] Among numerous recent sources, see 'Chemical warfare: The specter looms', *New York Times*, 5 Aug. 1988, p. A8, which discusses the widespread fear of a precedent having been set in the Iraq–Iran conflict.

[175] 'Countering a missile threat', *Near East Report*, vol. 31, no. 19 (11 May 1987), p. 75; 'Bio-chemical warfare must be examined, controlled', *Journal of Defense and Diplomacy*, vol. 6, no. 1 (1988), pp. 56–57; and 'The danger grows', *Near East Report*, vol. 32, no. 26 (27 June 1988), p. 107. See also Mallory, C. K., *CBW Study: Interim Report*, unpublished manuscript, SIPRI, 1988, introduction.

[176] Stringer, H., *Deterring Chemical Warfare: US Policy Options for the 1990s* (Pergamon-Brassey's: Washington, DC, 1986), for the Institute for Foreign Policy Analysis.

[177] Stringer (note 176).

[178] Mallory (note 175).

[179] Mallory (note 175), p. 41.

[180] Stringer (note 176), p. 34. See also Department of Defense, *Soviet Military Power 1987*, 6th edn (US Government Printing Office, Washington, DC), p. 89.

[181] Stringer (note 176), p. 36. According to 'Chemical arms: To have fewer, first have more?', *International Herald Tribune*, 15 Mar. 1988, p. 4; 'Western intelligence services estimate that the Soviet Union has about 300,000 tons of nerve agents', while the USA is said to have 30 500 tons, 6 500 tons of which are in FR Germany. See also, Collins, J. M., *U.S.–Soviet Military Balance: 1980–1985* (Pergamon-Brassey's: Washington, DC, 1985), pp. 86–95. See also, *Soviet Military Power 1987* (note 178), pp. 89–90.

[182] Mallory (note 175), pp. 20–24.

[183] Mallory (note 174), p. 29.

[184] Mallory (note 174), pp. 33–34, and 'Chemical arms: To have fewer, first have more?', *International Herald Tribune*, 15 Mar. 1988, p. 4.

[185] *International Herald Tribune* (note 181), reports on a French chemical rearmament programme announced by Prime Minister Jacques Chirac in November 1986.

9. Conventional FMP: power projection

I. Introduction

As a counterpart to the function of nuclear deterrence, that of conventional power projection constitutes the other major, general purpose served by integrated FMP, spanning the realms of ground, naval and air forces, and those of the various 'technical' activities mostly subsumed under the heading of C³I. As noted, many overseas facilities and the forces and systems associated with them, serve dually in relation to nuclear and conventional missions.

Generally speaking, several categories of FMP are involved:

1. The large, stationary 'forward' conventional forces in Western and Eastern Europe, Korea, Mongolia, and so on—and their associated tactical air power—deployed for the eventuality of major conventional warfare;

2. Foreign deployments of the US and Soviet navies in connection with possible large-scale conventional naval conflict or assistance in the deterrence of general war;

3. The logistics of pre-positioned *matériel* (weapons, ammunition, POL—petroleum, oil and lubricants—etc.), usable for general war between the superpowers or for more limited 'regional' contingencies;

4. Air and naval staging bases in connection with the logistics for possible superpower interventions in Third World areas, i.e., direct interventions;

5. Air staging and overflight rights in relation to major powers' arms resupply of friends and clients in conflict; also used for normal peacetime arms transfers;

6. The stationing and provisioning of 'surrogate' or 'proxy' forces in the Third World, i.e., indirect interventions;

7. Coercive diplomacy—the use of external bases for various manifestations of gunboat diplomacy, or for subtler but similar forms of deterrence;

8. 'Presence'—naval and other visits.

As the chapters on land, naval and air forces separately describe the FMP in those individual categories, this chapter serves to integrate those data along the lines of the above categories of conventional power projection, some of which involve 'combined arms' operations spanning the functions of the traditional services. It also focuses on foreign logistics facilities, particularly those related to pre-positioning of ordnance and other *matériel* by the respective powers.

Curiously, the terminology of 'power projection' has acquired common usage only in the past decade or so. It was seemingly inspired by the enormous attention in the USA and elsewhere in the West given to the problem of defending the Persian Gulf against possible Soviet invasion from the north. That in turn appeared to revive scholarly interest in the traditional corpus of writings on geopolitical theory, and in turn in the measuring of costs, time constraints, and so on, involved in 'projecting' power over great distances. The difficulties in overcoming the 'power over distance gradient' or 'loss of strength gradient' has, in turn, produced a large and growing interest in the forward pre-positioning of *matériel* by all the major powers.

The Pentagon's somewhat formal definition of conventional power projection is somewhat different from that used here. Here, no clear distinction is made between Europe and the Third World in this regard, or between those places where the major powers have regularly deployed forces and long-held per-manent facilities, and others. The Pentagon, by contrast, tends to define the 'projection' of force as applicable where 'the U.S. has little or no nearby military infrastructure or, in some cases, maintains no presence at all'.[1] Hence, 'there are many locations where we might need to project force, not only in SWA (Southwest Asia) and the Middle East, but also in Africa, Central America, South America, the Caribbean and elsewhere'.[2]

Otherwise stated, in line with common current usage, conventional power projection has to do with 'mobility forces' or 'inter-theatre mobility', that is, situations where forces are moved to combat theatres rather than positioned along or behind a stationary border or long-entrenched Forward Line of Troops (FLOT).[3] A broader view is taken here, however.

II. Forward-based army, navy and air force combat units: permanent deployments under stable alliances

In other chapters, the external deployments of the land, naval, air and missile forces of the major powers are separately reviewed. Taken together, some of these forces would, of course, be vital to the conduct of a nuclear war, at levels ranging from battlefield to theatre or strategic use. Many of the same forces, or elements of them, can also be seen as providing the wherewithal for fighting or deterring various levels of conventional warfare, from low-intensity to high-intensity combat. Some of these forces, as with the US armies in Europe, are in place to defend specific territories. But, under certain circumstances, elements of these forces can be seen as providing the potential—along with others based at home—for projecting power elsewhere, that is, in NATO terminology, 'out of area', or 'inter-theater'.[4] In short, the power of some of these forces may be viewed as already having been projected, as being in place for a possible war, if only as a 'tripwire' to convey seriousness of intent or to fight a holding action until larger reserves may be sent. Otherwise, the power of elements of these forces, already deployed overseas, may be seen as capable of projecting power elsewhere, entailing a less onerous 'loss of strength gradient' than would be the case if the power had to be projected all the way from home.[5]

It is important to note, however, that the by now long-term (over 40-year) stationing of large-scale forces in Central-Europe—and in Korea—is historically unique, at least for the recent period. The Romans, of course, may be said to have enjoyed foreign military presence in Europe for more than a millennium, but that did not involve alliances between sovereign political entities. But there has been no precedent in recent centuries; certainly not in the inter-war period, nor in the nineteenth century, nor in the period preceding the Napoleonic wars, nor at any time since the beginnings of the global system which has evolved since the Age of Exploration in the sixteenth century. Even the bipolarization of the European system preceding World War I, and the correspondingly tight alliances, were not accompanied by forward stationing of forces within allied borders. Usually, the explanation provided therefor by international relations theorists centres on the facts of a relatively rigid bipolar system which has existed since 1945, featuring two dominant superpowers, an ideological basis for big power rivalry, the rigidity of alliances, the stability provided by mutual nuclear deterrence and the lingering effective roles of some forces as occupying forces.[6] The nature of the anomaly is worth keeping in mind at a point in history which sees considerable speculation about the break-up of long-standing alliances, ideological convergence, and a possible trend towards neutralization of Central Europe.

Chapter 4 on ground forces outlines the deployments of the large-scale land-force deployments of the rival NATO and WTO alliances, centrally involving US, Canadian, Dutch, Belgian, French and British forces in FR Germany (also US forces in Italy); their Soviet counterparts in the GDR, Poland, Czechoslovakia, and Hungary; and also the large-scale US deployments in South Korea and the Soviet presence in Mongolia. Partially by way of review, but also to present more graphically the FMP implications, figure 12 displays the recent disposition of these forces, according to the various unit-type designations shown in the legend, that is, tank/armoured, mechanized, artillery divisions, and so on. In NATO's case, one sees the interspersion of US, Canadian, British, French, Belgian and Dutch forces with those of West German units; with US, Canadian and French forces concentrated in the south; British, Dutch and Belgian forces in the north. Only recently have some large-scale US forces come to be stationed further north, in the NORTHAG sector.

In the East, one sees a somewhat similar dispersion of Soviet with allied East German and Czechoslovak forces. But, Soviet forces make up a far higher proportion of the WTO deployments than do the US units in the West. Interestingly, whereas Soviet forces dominate near the FLOT along the East German border with FR Germany; they are located further back in Czechoslovakia, allowing Czechoslovak forces to dominate the forward border areas.

Chapter 8, on nuclear-related FMP, notes the concerns of some that the mutual reduction in theatre and short-range nuclear missiles represented by the 1987 INF Treaty might serve to enhance the importance of the WTO's conventional force preponderance in Central Europe. Indeed, that fear along with those related to verification and the possible enhancing of neutralist sentiment in Western Europe, seemed the primary argument of the treaty opponents.[7] Table 33, on conventional forces in Europe, includes the ratios for all of the various subcategories under manpower and ground-force equipment.

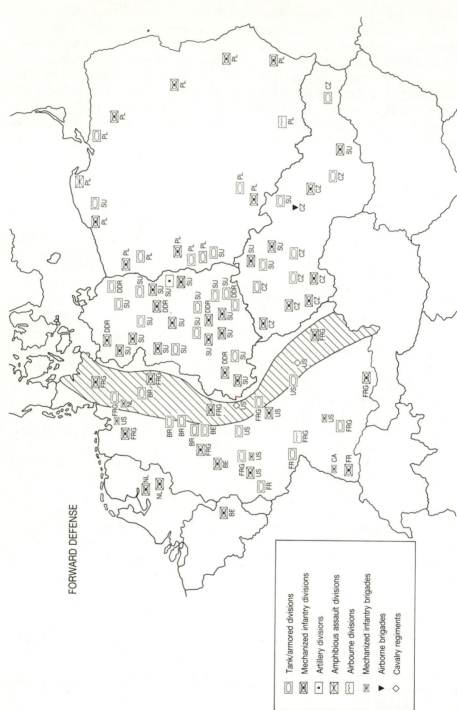

FORWARD DEFENSE

▯	Tank/armored divisions
▨	Mechanized infantry divisions
·	Artillery divisions
⊠	Amphibious assault divisions
{	Airbourne divisions
▨	Mechanized infantry brigades
►	Airborne brigades
◇	Cavalry regiments

Figure 12. Central European military balance, 1980

Source: Karber, P. A. and Whitley, A. G., 'Operational continuity and change within the Central European conventional arms control competition', notes prepared for the West Point Conf.

Table 33. Conventional force data: NATO and the WTO, 1987

	NATO Guidelines Area (NGA)		Atlantic to Urals		Global	
	NATO[a]	WTO	NATO[a]	WTO	NATO[a]	WTO
Manpower (000s)						
Total active ground forces[b]	796	995	2 385	2 292	2 992	2 829
Total ground-force reserves[c]	992	1 030	4 371	4 276	5 502	5 348
Divisions[d]						
Manned in peacetime[e]	32$1/3$	48$2/3$	107$2/3$	101$1/3$	127$1/3$	131
Manned on mobilization of reserves[f]	12	8	41?	100	72	137
Total, war mobilized[f]	44$1/3$	56$2/3$	149	201$1/3$	199$1/3$	268
Ground force equipment[g]						
Main battle tanks	12 700	18 000	22 200	52 200	30 500	68 300
MICV	3 400	8 000	4 200	25 800	8 000	34 400
Artillery, MRL, ATK guns	3 600	9 500	11 100	37 000	21 500	50 400
Mor (120-mm and over)	1 200	2 200	2 600	9 500	2 600	13 600
ATGW: ground-based[h]	6 500	4 500	10 100	16 600	18 500	23 600
ATGW: hel-borne	300	270	470	1 050	1 620	1 370
AA guns	3 100	3 400	7 400	12 000	8 400	15 100
SAM[i]	1 350	2 200	2 250	12 850	3 000	16 150
Armed helicopters[j]	550	430	780	1 630	2 020	2 130
Land combat aircraft[k]						
Bombers[k]	72	225	285	450	518	1 182
Attack[k]	901	799	2 108	2 144	5 157	3 119
Interceptors/fighters[k]	304	1 020	899	4 930	1 763	5 265

Note: This table presents aggregated data for a large number of national forces, divided on the basis of their geographical deployment. The level of confidence as to the many components varies: the aggregated figures therefore embody a measure of estimation.

[a] French and Spanish forces are not part of NATO's integrated military command, but are included insofar as they are deployed in the relevant geographical area. French forces in FR Germany are included in the NGA column by virtue of their deployment but are not subject to the MBFR negotiations.

[b] Ground forces exclude paramilitary forces, border guards and security forces. WTO figures would be increased by some 500 000–700 000 (Atlantic to Urals) and some 800 000 to 1.5 million (global) by the inclusion of an assumed ground force 'slice' of Soviet railroad, construction, labour, command and general support troops—all of which are uniformed, armed and have undergone at least basic military training. Reserves could arguably be increased in proportion.

[c] Reserves do not generally include personnel beyond a five-year post-service period, whether or not they are assigned to units.

[d] Divisions are not a standard formation between armies, nor do divisions contain comparable numbers or types of equipment or personnel. For the purposes of this table, three brigades or regiments are considered to be a divisional equivalent.

[e] 'Manned in peacetime' includes all Soviet and WTO Category 2 divisions in the relevant geographical area.

[f] Comprises only forces mobilized *within* relevant geographical areas. North American-based US and Canadian formations earmarked for reinforcement of Europe on or after mobilization are therefore shown under 'global' rather than in the 'NGA' or 'Atlantic to Urals' columns.

[g] Figures include equipment in storage or reserve where known.

[h] ATGW proliferation presents particular difficulties for realistic counting rules. The figures shown are estimated aggregates of all dismounted ATGW and those vehicle-mounted weapons with a primary ATK role. Soviet Category 3 divisions are assumed to hold a reduced (50%) scale of dismounted weapons. Totals exclude ATGW on MICV (e.g. M-2/-3 *Bradley*, BMP, BMD) or fired by main battle tank main armament (e.g. T-80) and do not, therefore, represent total available ATGW for either side.

i SAM launchers exclude shoulder-launched weapons. They include Air Force and Air Defence Force weapons.

j Comprises all helicopters whose primary function is close air support or anti-tank (i.e. *includes* hel-borne ATGW shown in earlier line).

k The categorization of aircraft between roles reflects that shown in the country entries, but the figures should be used with care. Many of the aircraft are multi-role: primary roles for similar aircraft vary between countries, and distinctions between attack and bomber and between fighter and fighter ground attack (FGA = attack) cannot be drawn with certainty. Moreover, training aircraft have been excluded, although they could provide some reinforcement or replacements in operations.

Source: International Institute for Strategic Studies, *The Military Balance 1987–1988* (IISS: London, 1987), p. 231. These data are published annually by the IISS, the most recent being set out in *The Military Balance 1988–89*, pp. 236–37.

Most salient are the ratios for the critical categories of main battle tanks (52 200 to 22 200) and artillery (37 000 to 11 100) in the area from the Atlantic to the Urals; the former are usually deemed the most crucial component of modern land warfare. From another angle, figure 13 provides a picture of the tank imbalance in Central Europe, as depicted according to battalion-size tank units. The overwhelming concentration of Soviet forward-based armoured units in the GDR and Czechoslovakia stands out.

In the wake of the INF Treaty, there has been some talk of a matching conventional arms limitation agreement, now to be negotiated in a new forum to supersede MBFR. If that were to occur, it would need to address centrally the possibilities for mutual withdrawals of Soviet and US (perhaps also other Western nations') forces from Central Europe, amounting to a reduction of the long-stable FMP in this region.[8]

Both the superpowers, as noted, make extensive use of forward air bases in Europe, deploying aircraft which, for the most part, can be configured either for conventional or nuclear use. For the USA, this involves the stationing of 324 combat aircraft in FR Germany (F-16A/Bs, F-4Gs, F-15C/Ds, RF-4Cs, etc.), 292 in the UK (F-111E/Fs, EF-111s, A-10s, F-5Es, etc.), 24 in the Netherlands (F-15C/Ds), 72 in Spain (F-16A/Bs), 18 in Iceland (F-15s) and a scattering elsewhere—a total of about 735 combat aircraft.[9] Those in Spain will be moved to Italy. Additionally, the UK forward deploys its Tornados, Phantoms, Jaguars and Harriers in FR Germany, most of which are dual-configured for nuclear or conventional use.[10]

Some of these aircraft deployments—in addition to constituting a crucial part of the NATO deterrence/defence scheme *vis-à-vis* the USSR in Central Europe—may be envisioned for purposes of conventional-force projection else-where. For instance, US aircraft which may be rotated from Italy or Spain or elsewhere to bases in Eastern Turkey, would be crucial to interdiction of a Soviet advance through Iran to the Persian Gulf (if Turkish use for this purpose was granted), perhaps in the absence of fighting between NATO and the WTO in Central Europe, though further horizontal escalation to that level would be a serious concern.[11] The US use of British-based F-111s for its raid on Libya is a further example.

The USSR, as noted, deploys massive numbers of fighter aircraft in Eastern

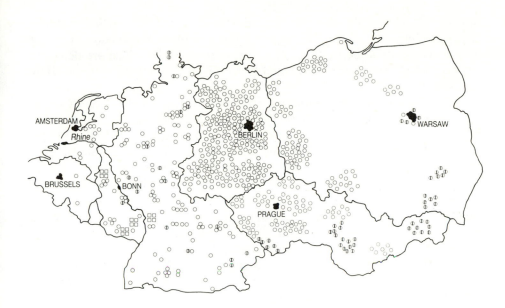

●   Active units

⊕   Units manned at around 50 per cent in peacetime (NATO-committed HSB in the FRG, Polish and Czech cadre divisions)

○   Units virtually unmanned in peacetime (Belgian mobilization units;
     Dutch RIM and mobilization units; most·HSB in the FRG)

□   US POMCUS tank battalions

Figure 13. Tank imbalance in Central Europe

Source: Karber, P. A. and Whitley, A. G., 'Operational continuity and change within the Central European conventional arms control competition', notes prepared for the West Point Conference on 'NATO at Forty', New York, 4–7 June 1987.

Note: Approximate numbers of tanks per NATO unit: Belgian armoured battalions—40; Canadian battalions—57; Dutch armoured battalions—53–56; French armoured regiments—54; FRG armoured battalions—54; FRG armoured reconnaissance squadrons—31; British armoured regiments—57; British armoured battalions—54–58; British armoured cavalry squadrons—43; US POMCUS tank battalions—54.

Approximate numbers of tanks per WTO unit: Soviet tank regiments—31; Soviet motorized rifle regiments—40; Soviet independent tank battalions—51; GDR, Poland and Czechoslovakia—31 in tank regiments, 40 in motorized rifle regiments.

HSB = Heimat Schützen Brigaden; RIM = Rechstreeks Instromend Mobilisabel.

Europe, most of which could be used for purely conventional purposes against NATO. This involves some 685 combat aircraft in the GDR (Su-17s, Su-24s, Su-25s, Mig-27s, MiG-21s, MiG-25s, MiG-23s, MiG-29s), 105 in Czechoslovakia (MiG-27s, MiG-23s, Su-17s) and 90 in Hungary (Su-17s, Su-24s, MiG-21/23/29s, etc.), in addition to large numbers of other Soviet aircraft in the USSR itself within the western and south-western TVDs which are deployed against NATO and which easily could be rotated forward to bases in the GDR and Czechoslovakia.[12]

In the Far East also, both superpowers forward deploy combat aircraft usable for conventional purposes. As previously noted, this involves Soviet basing of aircraft in Mongolia, Viet Nam (which hosts one squadron of MiG-23 Floggers) and in the disputed Kurile Islands.[13] On the US side there are forward deployments in Japan (72 F-15C/Ds, 2 F-16s, 18 RF-4Cs), South Korea (36 F-4E/RF-4Es, 48 F-16s, 24 A-10s, 24 OA-37s); the Philippines (2 squadrons of F-4E/Gs, and a training group including 15 F-5Es).[14] Also usable for conventional operations, the USAF deploys tactical airlift units with C-130s in the Philippines (16), Japan (16), the UK (16) and FR Germany (16 plus 18 C-23A Sherpas).[15] Units of KC-135 tankers usable for conventional operations are based in the UK (29), Japan and Guam;[16] AWACS in Iceland and Japan; F-111E/Fs in the UK; additionally, units of search and rescue helicopters (HC-13s, HH-53s) are deployed in Japan, the UK, Spain, Iceland and South Korea.[17]

All of the forward surface naval deployments noted for the USA and the USSR in chapter 2 are, of course, available for conventional power projection purposes, either for general war between the superpowers, or for operations, interventions or coercive diplomacy in the Third World. That involves, most crucially, the major US naval bases at such locales as Yokosuka (Japan), Subic Bay (the Philippines), Diego Garcia, Souda Bay (Greece), Naples (Italy), and so on, and their Soviet counterparts in Viet Nam, South Yemen (Aden), Ethiopia (Dahlak Archipelago), Angola (Luanda), and so on, and whatever refuelling and maintenance facilities might be provided elsewhere under a variety of circumstances ranging from all-out war to limited shows of force. Both superpowers have, for instance, utilized fleet movements in the Mediterranean for coercive or signalling purposes during various past Middle Eastern crises.

But, as is further discussed in chapter 10, the USA is finding it increasingly difficult to maintain fleet access in numerous places long considered secure, including Spain, Greece, Turkey and the Philippines.[18] Such access has, even where nominally retained, become more restricted, contingent and expensive. At a time when Pentagon budgets are being cut, and the hoped-for 600-ship navy (and 15 carrier battle-group navy) are in jeopardy, these increasing restraints on access are perceived by the US Navy as all the more serious, particularly where forward conventional power projection is concerned. Hence, according to former Assistant Secretary Richard Perle, in noting that losing bases would weaken Washington's ability to protect its interests around the world, 'It may mean that there are parts of the world we simply can't get to as rapidly with significant firepower.'[19] Added US Rear Admiral Edward Baker, 'The distances are the thing that kill you. If ships have to commute from farther away, you need more ships and more aircraft.'[20]

Hence, in the same vein according to one source:

Navy officials argue that the trend of declining basing privileges logically translates into a greater reliance on the fleet, with more auxiliary ships to carry ammunition, supplies and fuel, as well as more aircraft carriers to project power. 'When the welcome mats roll up, the carrier admirals see the cash registers ringing,' says Mr. Perle.

But the continuing budget crunch rules out any expansion of the fleet for the next decade. Last month a Senate financing committee actually shrank the fleet when it voted to mothball a World War II-era carrier ahead of schedule.[21]

On the reverse side, as noted below, the USSR's conventional power projection capability, as embodied in its growing fleets, would appear more jeopardized by domestic economic constraints than by a trend towards decoupling on the part of its friends and allies.

Of course, the forward-based conventional forces in Europe can be used to project conventional power into other areas. Specifically, and practically speaking, this has pertained to the use of US military power in the Middle East. For example, in 1958, some US forces used for an intervention in Lebanon, which also heralded the advent of the 'Eisenhower Doctrine', were flown there from FR Germany, staged via Turkey.[22] Indeed, airborne units located near the main air bases at Frankfurt and Wiesbaden were long designated as potential quick reaction forces for contingencies in the Middle East, in a period preceding the development of now far better long-range logistics from the USA itself. More recently, in 1973, massive amounts of ordnance were moved from US stocks in FR Germany to resupply Israel in its war with Egypt and Syria; indeed, that was done in the face of resistance by most US European allies.[23] Still more recently, the US raid on Libya which utilized F-111 attack bombers flown from the UK further illustrated Washington's use of its standard NATO deployments for conventional power projection in adjacent regions. However, the illustrative value of the Libya raid as an 'out-of-area' operation may be limited. It may have been a one-off event, one that could only have been mounted from Britain, given the special historical and diplomatic ties involved and perhaps too the debt owed the USA for its aid to the Falklands campaign. Arguably, the raid on Libya may have made the European powers more restrictive in their attitude towards out-of-area operations. The record of European co-operation on such ventures is not good, and some countries are now insisting on 'no out-of-area' clauses in their base agreements with the USA.[24] The geography of Moscow's East European allies allows for no such comparable activity, though the Soviet use of Yugoslav airspace and, perhaps too, staging bases (also obviously involving WTO airspace and perhaps other facilities) in the 1973 war is worth noting.

Needless to say, a number of the C³I and space-related facilities discussed in chapters 6 and 8 would be vital to the conduct of conventional war in the

European and/or Korean theatres; many, indeed, have alternative conventional and nuclear roles. These include the vast HF and VHF/microwave, and AUTODIN/AUTOVON communications systems (and their Soviet counterparts); land-based SIGINT stations, SOSUS, facilities related to ocean-reconnaissance and photo-reconnaissance satellites, tactical radars, and so on. One interesting question is thereby posed in relation to the fire-break between conventional and nuclear war, and to escalation ladder paths. Both sides might have a great interest in knocking down surveillance satellites used to observe conventional force deployments, and/or their down-links. But in doing so, there might be some loss to rivals' nuclear early warning, perhaps in turn providing some impetus to nuclear pre-emption. Generally, the possible place of anti-satellite activities along the (hypothetical) ladder of escalation is rather unclear or unformulated.

Mobility forces and inter-theatre mobility

On the US side, however, most of the attention paid in recent years to the basing aspects of conventional power projection has been to the evolvement of Rapid Deployment Force (now under the US Central Command) capabilities for projecting power to the oil-rich South-West Asia/Persian Gulf region or otherwise for alternative conflict scenarios in the Middle East involving Egypt, Lebanon, Israel, Jordan, and so on.[25]

In recent annual Pentagon documents, the role of mobility forces has been discussed, as noted, in the context of 'intertheater mobility', referring 'to the movement of forces between major geographic regions or theaters of conflict'. Further according to the Pentagon, 'the scenario we consider most important in our mobility planning and programming is a U.S. reinforcement of NATO Europe to counter a Warsaw Pact buildup or attack, preceded by a deployment of U.S. forces to Southwest Asia (SWA) to counter Soviet aggression in that region.'[26]

The Pentagon, recognizing the critical nature of access problems in relation to projection of forces to South-West Asia, states that

Although SWA is the focus of our rapid deployment planning, we presently have no agreements to station our combat forces ashore in the area and, therefore, maintain only a limited sea-based presence there. Furthermore, political conditions and agreements with our friends and allies near the region, in Europe, and elsewhere along vital lines of communication (LOCs) influence the availability of important resources and transit facilities necessary to support our rapid deployment strategy. As a result, many of our programs emphasize mobility and achieving access to countries en route to and near that distant region.[27]

It then proceeds to outline its objectives in the South-West Asian theatre, recognizing the limitations imposed by the fact that the US presence in that area is mostly limited to seaborne forces:

— Developing mobility capabilities to deploy forces rapidly to and within SWA over extended air and sea lines of communication (ALOCs/SLOCs) and to sustain them in combat;

— Locating, obtaining approval for, and developing land-based prepositioning sites;

— Obtaining both overflight rights and *en route* access from several additional countries;

— Securing lengthy ALOCs/SLOCs during the conflict to sustain combat operations;

— Obtaining access to and improving in-theatre airfields and seaports;

— Obtaining host nation support agreements with countries en route to and in SWA; and

— Improving our cargo loading and unloading capabilities to compensate for the lack of local infrastructure and trained personnel.[28]

In recent years, of course, beginning with the latter years of the Carter Administration, the USA has moved ambitiously to enhance its power projection forces, again, with South-West Asian scenarios primarily in mind. By 1987 that involved having met 60 per cent of a stated goal of 66 million-ton-miles-per-day of airlift based on a strategic airlift force of 234 C-141 Star-lifters, 80 C-5 Galaxies (66 C-5As and 14 C-5Bs), and 57 KC-10 aircraft capable of serving either as cargo lifters, tankers, or both.[29] Additionally, in an emergency, the USA could utilize its civilian reserve air force (CRAF) fleet of 227 passenger and 78 cargo aircraft.[30] For moving troops and supplies within theatres, and for use with shorter runways, there are 520 shorter-range C-130s and some 700 helicopters (CH-46s, CH-47s, CH-53s, CH-54s).[31] The USA has also moved to enhance its sea-lift capacity. By 1988 its Military Sealift Command and Maritime Administration maintained some 108 dry cargo ships and 33 tankers, with 116 cargo ships available in the National Defence Reserve Fleet that could be augmented in an emergency by a civil fleet of about 200 dry cargo ships and 120 tankers, mostly by charter or under government contract under the Sealift Readiness Program.[32]

In the early 1980s, as the USA moved to beef up its air and sea-lift capabilities for projecting forces in South-West Asia, it also had to seek additional facilities along the ALOCs and SLOCs to and within South-West Asia, from which to support deployment of its forces. This involved aircraft and ship staging facilities, overflight rights, and also locations for conducting air-based ASW and maritime patrol aircraft operations. It also involved in-theatre facilities, such as airfields and debarkation points, for reception of incoming units, stockpiling of combat supplies, and provision of sites from which to launch combat operations.[33]

This involved negotiations about facilities—variously for prepositioning of *matériel*, use of facilities during crises, or use for training exercises—with several nations in the South-West Asian area, though no new US bases *per se* were created. The earlier focus of those efforts was mostly on Egypt (Ras Banas), Oman, Kenya, Somalia, Diego Garcia, the Azores (Lajes) and several other locations such as that involving contingent *en route* access to airfields in Morocco, with which the USA has an 'access and transit agreement' which allows the USA staging access with *ad hoc* permission.[34] And, indeed, as is further pursued in chapter 10, this involved in each of these cases offers of (and demands for) increased security assistance. Access to Ras Banas did not pan out, but other Egyptian air bases were vital for mounting the abortive Iran hostage raid in 1980.[35] In the other cases, important air and naval access was acquired, though use in specific circumstances might still require host nations' permission and in some cases might involve sticky diplomatic issues, for instance, US use of Lajes or Diego Garcia in connection with assistance to Israel, or very visible use of Omani facilities in connection with some scenarios involving other Arab countries.

There are, of course, other regions to which the USA requires access for conventional power projection purposes not immediately related to the possibility of large-scale war with the USSR, and where in all cases, *ad hoc* permission for that access would presumably be required. Japan remains a vital forward staging area for any possible re-involvement of US combat forces in Korea. The facilities in the Philippines would be vital for any further US involvement in South-East Asia and for numerous scenarios around the Indian Ocean and in South-West Asia. Those in Kenya and Somalia might be usable for conflicts in the Red Sea area or along Africa's eastern coast; Ascension and perhaps Roberts Field, Liberia and also Dakar, Senegal might later be involved in US conventional operations further south along Africa's west coast. Facilities in Honduras and Panama would, of course, be vital to any possible US combat operations in Central America; again, requiring accommodating policies by the host nations at the relevant time.

The Soviet Union has not, of course, perceived a requirement for near-global conventional power projection on a level equal to the USA, not least because of its heartland geographical position and its long tradition as a land power. But, since the 1960s, it has greatly enhanced its airlift and sea-lift capabilities; and, hence, its long-range power projection potential. More recently, though its capabilities in these areas have continued to grow, at least some writers—not necessarily a majority—have, paradoxically, perceived a waning of the Soviet thrust towards overseas power projection capability, whether a function of Moscow's domestic politics or of a changed overall global security strategy may be debatable.

But, as noted, the assets are now in place and are growing, as is annually detailed by the IISS and by the Pentagon's now annual *Soviet Military Power*. The Soviet VTA long-range transport aircraft force now consists of some 610 medium- and long-range cargo transports: 210 AN-12 medium-range turboprops; 340 IL-76 Candid long-range jets which are replacing the AN-12s; 55 AN-22 Cock long-range turboprops; and about 5 AN-24 Condors which entered production only in 1987.[36] The latter are comparable to the US C-5A Galaxies, and will significantly upgrade VTA's heavy-lift capabilities, as has the AN-22, which is 'the only Soviet transport able to carry out-sized cargo such as tanks or large missiles'.[37] This VTA fleet is supplemented by Aeroflot's civilian fleet of some 1600 medium- and long-range passenger aircraft, which includes some

Soviet military transport aircraft

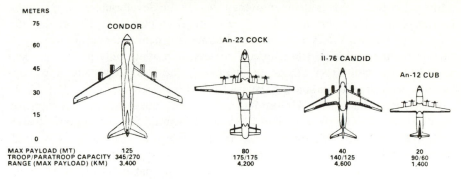

MAX PAYLOAD (MT)	125	80	40	20
TROOP/PARATROOP CAPACITY	345/270	175/175	140/125	90/60
RANGE (MAX PAYLOAD) (KM)	3,400	4,200	4,600	1,400

US military transport aircraft

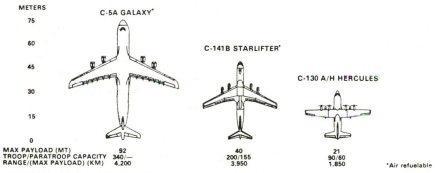

MAX PAYLOAD (MT)	92	40	21
TROOP/PARATROOP CAPACITY	340/—	200/155	90/60
RANGE/(MAX PAYLOAD) (KM)	4,200	3,950	1,850

*Air refuelable

Figure 14. Soviet and US military transport aircraft

Source: US Department of Defense: *Soviet Military Power 1985*, 4th edn (US Government Printing Office: Washington DC, 1985), p. 83.

200 Cubs and Candids.[38] Figure 14 graphically compares US and Soviet long-range air transport assets.

Until recently, Soviet maritime power projection capabilities had been rather meagre, relative to those of the USA and, hence, basing requirements had been less demanding. As stated by John Collins,

Soviet forces rely very little on sea lanes and a lot on land transportation. Relatively short lines lead to NATO Europe through Warsaw Pact partners, to outposts along the frontier they share with China, and almost every other locale where Soviet forces presently are deployed or could become militarily involved on a large scale in the foreseeable future. Even the 1000-mile link between the Transcaucasus and Kuwait is much shorter than the most direct routes from our east coast (6,700 NM by air, 8,580 NM by sea). Logistic support for distant Third World supplicants is politically important, but not militarily imperative. Only the Soviet Far East demands long-haul transportation.[39]

None-the-less, Soviet maritime projection capabilities are growing, as some pundits see political and economic considerations dictating a levelling off of this now lengthy trend development. The growth of the Soviet surface combat navy and its associated basing structure are detailed in chapter 2, but it is worth adding that the USSR is slowly moving towards the development of significant carrier forces. There are now four 37 000-ton Kiev-class aircraft carriers, deploying 13 Yak-38 V/STOL fighters and numerous helicopters and a variety of missiles; and two 17 000-ton Moskva carriers, deploying only helicopters and missiles.[40] But still larger carriers are expected, and their implications for continuous deployments and basing remain to be seen.

Otherwise, the Soviet Union has developed immense sea-lift capacity. MORFLOT, the Soviet Merchant Marine, has some 2500 ocean-going vessels with larger ones replacing smaller ones on a relatively one-for-one basis. According to the IISS, this includes 81 ramp-fitted and roll-on/roll-off (RO-RO) ships, some with rails for railroad cars; and seven float-on/float-off (FLO-FLO) barge carriers.[41] Nine more RO-RO and nine more ramp-fitted support merchant ships are on order.[42] And, the once nugatory Soviet amphibious force capability is also growing. There are now some 77 amphibious ships, including a couple of the large Ivan Rogov LPDs (amphibious transport docks), 33 Alligator and Repucha LSTs (landing ship tanks) and 42 Polnocny LSMs (landing ship medium).[43] An Ivan Rogov can carry 2–3 KA-27 Helix helicopters and can accommodate two air cushion vehicles as well as being able to transport over 500 troops and their equipment.[44] Indeed, the Soviet Navy is now the world's largest operator of military air cushion vehicles.

These are now backed up by some 18 000 naval infantry, including armoured and *Spetsnaz* units.[45] One naval infantry detachment is forward-based in Ethiopia, but there are large such units attached to each of the Soviet fleets (the Pacific Ocean Fleet contains a 7000-man division).[46]

As noted, the Soviet Navy has important forward bases in Cuba, Ethiopia, Angola, South Yemen, Syria and Viet Nam, all of which can be used to project power into neighbouring areas. While it is true that, heretofore, the USSR has acted cautiously and sparingly in this area, the newer capabilities may provide for greater freedom of action. For example, when the Rene government in the Seychelles (long host to an important US satellite control facility) has been threatened by insurrections, the USSR has sent amphibious ships and naval infantry (based in Ethiopia and South Yemen) to offer support.[47] Naval infantry based continuously on ships have conducted amphibious exercises in Viet Nam and on South Yemen's Socotra Island and have maintained a presence in the Mediterranean and off the West African Coast. But so far, there are few indications of Soviet ambitions or capabilities to conduct large-scale, long-distance power projection operations.

As noted, the USSR has been cautious so far about long-range, out-of-area or inter-theatre power projection operations and one sees little in the way of a focused effort to prepare for *one* particular contingency equivalent to the US concentration upon scenarios for South-West Asia. Regarding airlifts involving Soviet forces, one could, however, point to the logistics operation used to support Soviet forces in Afghanistan; also, the airlift of Soviet forces into Prague at the outset of the operation used to squelch the liberalization movement in Czechoslovakia in 1968.

Mostly, however—and with particular and specific reference to basing assets—Soviet long-range airlift in connection with power projection has come prominently into play with the several large-scale arms resupply operations on behalf of Third World clients in combat. Several of these operations were 'time-urgent', and involved not only the use of air-staging bases for refuelling, maintenance, and so on, but also *en route* overflights.

In 1973, the USSR—then much weaker as concerns air transport capability but able to rely heavily on the huge, lumbering AN-22s—mounted a massive arms resupply operation to Egypt and Syria, ultimately simultaneous with and competitive with the US airlift on behalf of Israel. According to various reports, this involved crucial use of Turkish and Yugoslav airspaces as well as those of East European allies and combatant Arab nations such as Iraq.[48] The relatively short distances involved precluded the need for staging points with the possible exception of Yugoslavia.

In 1975-76, the Soviet Union (and Cuba) mounted a massive arms airlift on behalf of the Marxist Neto forces fighting a multifront civil war in Angola. That involved staging points in, and overflights of, a number of *en route* African nations. Among those publicly mentioned in various reports were Algeria, Mali, Benin, Equatorial Guinea, Guinea, Sierra Leone, Guinea-Bissau and the Congo—there may have been others.[49] Another such air resupply on behalf of Ethiopia in 1977-78 during its war with Somalia apparently involved crucial access, on land and above, provided by Iraq and South Yemen, and perhaps unauthorized flights over some among Iran, Pakistan, Egypt and Sudan.[50] In 1979, still another airlift to Viet Nam during its brief war with China apparently involved overflights and perhaps staging points provided by India; and perhaps unauthorized or forced use of the airspace of some other *en route* nations.[51]

Until now, the most important component of Soviet overseas maritime power projection has been that of arms resupply by sea. Whereas massive airlifts have been critical in some urgent situations (1973 to Egypt and Syria, Ethiopia in 1977, etc.), sea-lift has provided the main basis for arming Soviet clients during normal conditions, and for less urgent resupply operations in connection with sustained combat. The Pentagon's annual *Soviet Military Power* has, for instance, detailed the growing military tonnages delivered by Soviet ships to Nicaragua in recent years, said to have reached 33 000 tonnes by 1984.[52] Arms-carrying ships have, similarly, been vital to supplying weapons to a variety of Soviet clients—including Angola, Ethiopia and Mozambique. Often, as noted before, these ships will visit several client states during one journey, with fuel and provisioning taken on at each stop. As noted, the Soviet Union now has a truly global network of facilities for these purposes.

The USA has also utilized critical access to staging points and overhead airspace in connection with some support operations on behalf of its allies, in some cases involving difficult political problems with nervous and cross-pressured client states. The use of Lajes in the Azores for the resupply of Israel in 1973 has often been commented upon;[53] additionally, there were conflicting reports about US tankers' use of Spanish bases at that time.[54] During the Carter Administration, the USA and France made crucial use of Dakar in moving forces and *matériel* to beleaguered allies in Zaïre's Shaba province.[55] There have been other such cases.

Sometimes, both long-time US and Soviet client states have refused access to their mentors during crises or in connection with resupply operations. Guinea and Senegal are reported to have refused refuelling access to Soviet aircraft during the Cuban missile crisis.[56] As noted, some of the USA's West European NATO allies refused Washington access both in 1973 and then in 1986 for its bombing raid against Libya. In other cases, access has been granted, but only quietly and reluctantly; nervousness was evident in Egypt, Saudi Arabia and Oman when reports surfaced of their granting the US staging and overflight access for the ill-fated Iran hostage raid.

As indicated in figure 14, the two largest US transport aircraft, the C-5A and C-141, have a refuelling capability not matched by any of the Soviet transport aircraft. This further corresponds with the much larger US tanker fleet (KC-10s and KC-135s) relative to the USSR, some of which are forward-based in Iceland, Spain, the UK, Japan, and so on, and are a key element in the US capability for global power projection. The USSR uses tankers primarily for its strategic bomber force, not for long-range logistics. But, as its requirements for the latter relate mostly to the periphery of the Soviet heartland, this is not much of a disadvantage, particularly as the larger Soviet transport aircraft—Condors, Candids, An-22s—have ranges, carrying maximum payload, of between 3400 and 4600 km (comparable US aircraft have similar ranges but with trans-oceanic refuelling requirements). In the one region where it might be required, for logistical operations to southern Africa, the USSR is availed of numerous staging points provided by ideological allies and arms client states (including Libya, Algeria, Ethiopia, Guinea, Tanzania and Angola), but could have some conceivable problems with overflight rights.

Generally speaking, numerous C^3I and space-related facilities are vital to these types of conventional power projection, that is, direct intervention and arms resupply to client states. Photo-reconnaissance is vital for intelligence in both cases; hence too, the importance of their satellite down-links. Communications involving such systems as NAVSTAR are similarly vital. And, where wars between Third World states are involved, the superpowers are increasingly utilizing the leverage that goes with provision of battlefield satellite or aircraft reconnaissance—Israel and Iraq have benefited from such US assistance, and Argentina perhaps received such help from the USSR during the 1982 Falklands War, as did the UK from the USA.[57]

Both Britain and France, as second-tier powers, have made some use of external facilities for conventional power projection purposes in recent years, though neither aspires to global capabilities of this sort. Britain's use of Ascension for staging air and naval operations to the Falklands (including its use for V-bomber operations) is well documented.[58] And the British naval contribution to the Western Persian Gulf escort operations has, it would appear, involved some access to Oman and Bahrain.

France, meanwhile, has utilized air bases in West Africa (notably, Dakar) for moving *matériel* and Moroccan forces to trouble spots in Zaïre's Katanga Province.[59] It has also apparently utilized such access in support of Chadian forces fighting Libya; for instance, for transit of *matériel* through the Cameroons.[60] Though nothing has been made public, it is also obvious that overflight rights have been granted to France for several of its operations in support of Zaïre and Chad. France's naval force in Djibouti, meanwhile—and its marine infantry units in Djibouti, Gabon, the Ivory Coast and Senegal—are clearly positioned for nearby combat operations as well as for support of friendly, incumbent political regimes. They are, as noted, supported by Jaguar attack aircraft and provided mobility by C-160 transport aircraft and helicopters. Indeed, France has been involved in some minor combat operations in recent years, in Chad and in Mauritania, as well as in Katanga.

Generally speaking, British and French utilization of external access for power projection has involved either remnant control of 'colonial' holdings (Ascension, Belize) or spheres of influence involving such former holdings, as with France's activities in Francophone Africa.

There have been a few scattered instances of smaller powers' use of external facilities for power projection. Israel clearly utilized access to Kenyan airspace and staging points to assist its Entebbe hostage raid.[61] Cuba, howsoever acting as a Soviet surrogate, utilized numerous staging points in mounting an airlift to Angola in the mid-1970s: Barbados, Guyana, Cape Verde, Sierra Leone and the Congo were mentioned in press reports.[62] As several recent Third World wars have seemed to demonstrate, however, most smaller nations have great difficulty projecting power even small distances beyond their own borders, even into contiguous states, and little capability for combined arms operations. Where basing access for such purposes is concerned, it remains largely a big-power game.

Forward logistics and prepositioning of matériel and fuel

In recent years, the major US efforts at prepositioning war stocks—variously, for use in Western Europe, the Middle East and Europe's northern flank—have received extensive attention, much of it in connection with the Rapid Deployment Joint Task Force (RDJTF) and with the build-up of *matériel* in FR Germany which could be 'married', in a crisis, to troop units flown from the USA. Such arrangements are designed to provide for effective power projection without the permanent large-scale stationing of full combat units in proximity to possible battle areas, or at least a lessening of those requirements.

The prepositioning of fuel and munitions is not necessarily a uniquely contemporary phenomenon. Indeed, before World War II, US intelligence reports devoted considerable attention to rumoured German and Japanese 'secret' storage of fuel for submarines in areas close to the Panama Canal; in Colombia,

Panama, and some of the other Central American nations; and in Brazil.[63] Some of these activities were thought conducted with the use of 'private' ranches and other such land-holdings along strategic stretches of ocean frontage. Still earlier, the imperial British Navy, in the heyday of its maritime dominance, had coal bunkering storage sites throughout the globe—a predecessor to today's fuel storage sites.

In the present period, prepositioning of *matériel* has tended to take any of several forms along a spectrum. In Europe and Korea (and on the Soviet side in Eastern Europe), there is stockpiling of reserve stocks of equipment and munitions amid the massive force deployments on either side. These stocks are intended to sustain deployed units for lengthy periods of combat, during which attrition of ammunition, spare parts, and so on, as well as of trucks, artillery pieces, tanks, and so on, would presumably be heavy. Second, however, the USA also extensively stores munitions and fuel all along the logistics routes between the continental USA and its main force deployments in Europe and Korea—much of it on oceanic islands or in coastal areas—so as to make much easier and less costly and time-consuming the resupply of embattled forces should a war erupt. (Contrariwise, this provides stocks of munitions and fuel well away from battle areas where they cannot easily be overrun.) Third, the USA also forward positions equipment for entire units—division size combat units—so that troops can be flown to and married to that equipment, hence avoiding the burden of having to conduct a massive movement of *matériel* at the outset of a conflict. The type of prepositioning represented by this third category, in contrast to the first two, is a relatively recent phenomenon, one undertaken only in the past two decades, beginning in the 1960s. There is also a fourth category, that of (effectively) prepositioned *matériel* in the guise of excessive arms transfers to client states located favourably in relation to potential combat zones.

Regarding the first category, that of (traditional) war reserve stocks, the main components of 'sustainment' are ammunition, POL, and major items and repair parts. Hence, according to one recent US Army publication: 'War reserve stocks are established in strategic locations worldwide to provide an immediate supply of ammunition, weapons, fuel and secondary items during the initial days of combat for wartime consumption until the supply pipeline can be filled from CONUS depots and manufacturers.'[64]

Not surprisingly, most of the war reserve stocks in these categories are collocated with major US force deployments: in FR Germany, Italy, the UK, South Korea, Japan, the Philippines and other allied countries.

In FR Germany, the USA has an elaborate infrastructure of munitions storage sites and POL depots. Air force munitions for the bases at Sembach, Hahn and Bitburg, respectively, are stored nearby at Hochspeyer, Wuscheim and Motsch.[65] There are various other munitions depots, most of them army-related, at: Werigerath, Aschaffenberg, Bamberg, Baumholder, Münster, Olfen, Siegelsbach, Miesau, Lubberstedt, Walsrode, Dahn, Bad Kissingen, Kirschheimbolln, Ingolstadt and Wahrendal.[66] Some of these, as noted, are nuclear as well as conventional weapon storage sites. Aircraft fuel is stored at, among other places, Philipsheim and Neuhemsbach, near the air bases at Spangdahlem and Sembach respectively.[67] In the north at Bremerhaven, the port of entry for most supplies to US bases in central and southern FR Germany, there are large-scale docks, warehouses and troop staging areas.[68]

In the UK, there is a munitions storage depot at Welford, and naval armaments depots at Broughton Moor and Glen Douglas, along with various other storage sites, some located near the main air bases.[69] In Italy, there is a USAF storage site at Avellino, a naval depot on Caprera Island near La Maddalena, and a major US Army depot at Leghorn, part of the 8th Logistics Command; also a large NATO munitions and fuel storage depot at Augusta Bay.[70] In Greece, US forces have large fuel storage depots; similarly, NATO has a fuel storage depot in Vandel in Denmark.[71]

In the Far East, the USA has a similar infrastructure for its war reserve stocks. In South Korea, there are fuel storage depots, terminals and pump stations at Pohang, Waegwan, Taegon, Seoul and Kusan; munitions and ordnance depots at Sacheon (near Kunsan AB), Osan-ni (near Osan AB), Inchon, Pusan, Taegu, Taejon, Uijong-ni, Waegwan, Amyong-up, Mason, Chonwon and Kumchon-ni.[72] In Japan, there are naval fuel depots at Tsurumi and Koshiba; army munitions sites at Akizuki, Kawakami, Kure and Hiro.[73] (Up to the early 1970s, there were numerous other naval munitions, mine storage and fuel storage sites, but these are now operated by the Japanese Defence Facilities Administration Agency on behalf of the USA.) In the Philippines the USA has a major fuel storage site at Subic Bay, and a munitions storage site at Camayan Point.[74]

Otherwise, as noted, the USA maintains very important war-reserve storage sites along the main lines of logistics both in the Atlantic and Pacific oceans, in many cases involving islands (or island nations) or littoral states well removed from expected initial theatres of combat. In the Atlantic area, for example, there are munitions storage sites at Portugal's Madeira Island and in the Azores (Aguava and Caldera in proximity to Lajes AB), in Northern Ireland at Ben Bradagh (an underground tunnel), along Portugal's Tagus River (naval munitions), at Iceland's Patterson Airfield and at Erzurum in Turkey.[75] There are fuel storage sites at Bermuda, Madeira (Porto Santo), Faial in the Azores, in Iceland at Hvalfjordur and Stakksfjordur, and in Turkey at Iskenderun, where 20 per cent of the 6th Fleet's fuel is stored.[76] At Stakksfjordur the USA is said to have constructed an off-shore fuel terminal and fuel storage site with 200 000-ton capacity, the bulk of it for aviation fuel, financed under the NATO infrastructure programme[77] (still another underground fuel depot is now being built in Hofn). In the Pacific, there are munitions depots on Okinawa and Taiwan, supplementing those on US territory at Guam and Hawaii.[78] On Guam, the USA has major weapon storage depots, involving naval ammunition, bombs for B-52s, mines, and so on; there are similar sites in Hawaii at West Loch and Lualualei.[79] Hawaii's Red Hill site is the largest fuel storage depot in the world.[80] Air and naval fuel for the region are stored at Wake Island and Okinawa, as well as in Japan, South Korea and the Philippines.[81] Diego Garcia, meanwhile, has become a major site for munitions and fuel storage in relation to contingencies in South-West Asia. The USA also has an additional fuel depot in this region at Berbera in Somalia; perhaps also at Kuwait.[82]

Two general comments may be made in relation to the FMP implications of siting war reserve stocks along logistics routes leading to major force deployments and areas of potential conflict. First—and perhaps particularly in the cases of islands such as Madeira, Wake, Diego Garcia, Bermuda, and so on—these may be highly vulnerable to interdiction in wartime. Tunnelling and revetment in addition to location may render this a manageable problem if only conventional weapons are involved. In a nuclear environment, these facilities would presumably be priority, vulnerable targets—but so would many other facilities. Second, it is possible that the aforementioned munitions and fuel storage points are only a sample of a much larger number of such sites— there is obviously a current thrust towards mobility and dispersion, albeit the countering trend towards political counter-pressures.

Some of the overseas fuel storage sites are on a large scale. That in Hawaii holds over 900 000 tons of petrol; that near Subic Bay in the Philippines over 400 000 tons; and that in Ireland around 200 000 tons.[83]

The fuel storage sites are, in some areas, abetted by another important feature of the infrastructure of the Western alliances, that of fuel pipelines. In France, even after the latter's partial withdrawal from NATO, a French corporation under contract operates for NATO the Donges–Metz pipeline which runs on into FR Germany and connects with NATO pipelines. Along its length there are major fuel storage sites at Donges, Melun and Chalons.[84] In FR Germany is the Zweibrücken–Huttenheim pipeline for supply of aviation fuels to US air bases and NATO forces.[85] In Turkey there is a fuel pipeline system, running from the southern coast to military bases in the interior, consisting of a north–south line in the west and a 'Y'-shaped line in the east—2300 km total with 29 storage locations and 34 pumping stations.[86] There is also a POL line in Spain running from Rota to the major air bases at Zaragoza and Torrejon and to La Muela.[87] The USA maintains some 400 km of fuel pipelines in South Korea, and in the Philippines there is a 70-km fuel pipeline linking the main bases at Subic Bay and Clark AFB.[88] This kind of infrastructure clearly is reflective of the expectation if not the fact of durable long-term alliances and foreign military presences.

In recent years, the USA has, as noted, in several areas, moved towards prepositioning of extensive caches of *matériel* to be married during crises to large combat units moved from the USA. This involves, most saliently, POMCUS stocks, described or defined by one US government publication as follows:

POMCUS is organizational equipment stored in company and battalion size packages, in a ready-for-use condition. The purpose of POMCUS is to position the majority of a unit's organizational equipment forward, so that in time of crisis only unit personnel, with minimum equipment, will require airlift to meet the requirements of a NATO contingency.[89]

Aside from the economics of it, this kind of prepositioning can sharply reduce response times in the initial stages of an overseas deployment. Hence, as noted by the Pentagon, the storing of the heavy equipment of mechanized divisions in Europe can cut each division's transit time from several weeks to two or three days.

The USA actually began to preposition equipment in Europe in the 1960s, in response to the realization that theatre forces were inadequate to match those of the WTO. Hence, as explained in the most recent annual report to Congress by the Secretary of Defense:

Under the POMCUS (Prepositioning of Materiel Configured to Unit Sets) program, the Army stores heavy items of equipment—such as tanks, personnel carriers, and trucks—in dehumidified warehouses in Europe. The equipment is arranged in unit sets, ready to be moved rapidly out of storage to marshalling areas. This means that only the troops themselves, their personal equipment, and any remaining materiel not suitable for prepositioning—such as helicopters and electronic gear—would have to be airlifted to the theater at the outbreak of a crisis. On arriving in Europe, the forces would be trucked to the marshalling areas, where they would pick up their prepositioned equipment, assemble into units, and move forward.[90]

By 1988, the USA was nearing completion of its plan to provide POMCUS equipment for six US-based Army divisions and supporting units. Four of these sets are in FR Germany; as shown above on the map in figure 13 these are concentrated in Pfalz, Hesse (near Frankfurt) and in Nord-Rhein/Westphalia west of the Rhine River. The last two of the six division sets are being located in Belgium and the Netherlands.[91] There is an additional large POMCUS depot in Luxembourg,[92] and at Burtonwood in the UK, according to Campbell, there is a vast POMCUS equipment depot which has '2 million square feet for equipment storage and covers 5 square miles'.[93] Additionally, the US Air Force is prepositioning equipment and consumables in Europe: engineering, ground support, medical equipment, munitions, and so on. In the event of a war, the USA plans not only an initial reinforcement of the six Army divisions, but also of 60 tactical fighter squadrons and a Marine Amphibious Brigade (MAB).[94] After that, follow-on reinforcements would rely largely on movement by sea.

There is some apparent disagreement among analysts over the completeness and also the vulnerability of the US POMCUS stocks.[95] Apparently they do lack some of their army aviation components, for instance, helicopter gunships.

POMCUS has now entered the realm of conventional arms control proposals. Some have suggested that it and its Soviet counterparts be made part of any mutual conventional force limitations in Central Europe.

Matériel for the MAB mentioned above is prepositioned in Norway. This reflects the huge importance now attached by both the USA and the USSR to control over the northern Norwegian coast during the initial phases of a war, in relation to the North Atlantic SLOCs (i.e., reinforcement of NATO) and to naval warfare in the Norwegian and Barents Seas near to the Soviet submarine bastions and Kola Peninsula basing complex.

The third major locale of extensive US prepositioning is that of the so-called 'Near-Term Prepositioning Force' (NTPF) at Diego Garcia. Initially, in 1980, this involved seven charter ships in support of what was then called the Rapid Deployment Joint Task Force. Later there were 18 ships loaded with rations, fuel and water for the Army and Air Force elements of the Central Command (11 ships) as well as the supplies for a MAB. Six of these ships carry unit equipment, medical facilities and supplies for a heavily mechanized MAB. The eighteenth NTPF ship has been stationed in the Mediterranean.[96] Now, 13 larger Maritime Prepositioning Ships (MPS) are being deployed to enable outfitting of two more MABs of 16 000 men each.[97] These would be capable of allowing for unopposed landings ashore or for off-loading in primitive ports or over-the-shore via causeways and lighters. When the force is expanded to provide for three MABs, some of the equipment will be stationed at locations other than Diego Garcia, but where they would still be available for contingencies in South-West Asia. At present, just two smaller Marine Amphibious Units (MAUs)—one in the Pacific and one in the Mediterranean—are regularly constituted, with about 2000 personnel apiece.[98]

Still another locale for large-scale prepositioning of US *matériel* appears in the making in Thailand. According to one report, this could include a large munition and weapon stockpile to cost $100 million over five years, presumably to be made available for contingencies throughout South-East and South Asia. Further, it is said that 'it will be the first in a country where foreign forces are not based', referring to the closing of US bases in Thailand in 1976 after the communist takeover in Viet Nam.[99]

Less easily measured, there is one other (real or hypothetical) form of prepositioning which has been used, or at least considered, by the major powers. That has to do with the practice, in some cases, of providing what would appear excessive or even superfluous levels of arms to well-placed client states, with the (spoken or unspoken) understanding that they provide a forward-based cache for movement elsewhere. It is difficult to prove that such arrangements exist, as they are not publicly enunciated. Yet, for instance, in recent years, huge Soviet-origin arms inventories piled up in Libya have been viewed by some as constituting a prepositioned arms stockpile, elements of which could be moved further south in Africa, or elsewhere in the Middle East. South Yemen and Syria have been discussed along similar lines.[100]

Libya, for instance, has some 2200 T-54/55/62 tanks plus 160 newer T-72s, some 1500 Soviet armoured personnel carriers, and a huge arsenal of self-propelled artillery, for an army of only 55 000 men.[101] South Yemen's still smaller army has 470 Soviet tanks and 400 APCs.[102] Syria has an incredible 4200 Soviet tanks, 3800 artillery pieces and about 3500 armoured personnel carriers, mechanized infantry combat vehicles and reconnaissance vehicles.[103] Fractions of these arsenals could be decisive in some potential Third World conflicts, say in Africa.

Earlier, Israeli scholar Avigdor Haselkorn analysed what he perceived as an elaborate Soviet strategy along these lines, involving an interlocking network of arms client states. For example, he detailed the movement of Soviet arms from Egypt to India during the latter's 1971 war with Pakistan; others later noted the movement of Soviet arms from South Yemen to Ethiopia in 1977 during the so-called 'Horn War', at a time when there was extensive involvement of Cuban troops and Soviet advisors.[104]

There have also been allegations that the USA has also utilized arms transfers as a cover for forward prepositioning of *matériel*. There has been some discussion about Israel in this context in relation to the Persian Gulf, which discussions have commonly revolved about allegedly stockpiled *matériel* at Israel's Hatserim air base in the Negev.[105] Massive Saudi arms inventories have inspired similar, more tentative discussions.[106] Also, the USA apparently once envisioned the buildup of a large facility at Ras Banas, Egypt, on the Red Sea Coast as not only a forward transit or jumping-off base but perhaps also as a forward (in relation to the Persian Gulf or Saudi Arabia) depot for stockpiled *matériel*.[107] Indeed, Britain had used its massive Suez Canal base (particularly the huge ordnance depot at Tel El Kebir) up to the early 1950s for precisely such purposes, that is, as a central weapon supply depot for its forces throughout the Middle East.[108] In none of these cases is there the equivalent to the explicit marrying of troop units to designated weapons as is the case for POMCUS or for the MAB stockpiles on Diego Garcia or in Norway.

The USA is not entirely alone in its use of external facilities for storing munitions and fuel in Western Europe, nor is FR Germany only a host for such activities. The West German *Bundeswehr*, which deploys major combat units in Schleswig-Holstein near the Danish border, utilizes several large depots in Denmark as fall-back positions for storage of munitions, fuel and medical equipment, in an area where there is little geographic depth to NATO's forward positions.[109] FR Germany similarly has weapon depots in Belgium and the Netherlands—the latter is also involved in West German naval logistics.[110]

Miscellaneous logistics facilities

In addition to war reserve stocks, prepositioned *matériel*, and fuel depots and pipelines, there are some other scattered categories of logistics facilities which involve foreign presences. The most important of these are military hospitals and a variety of foreign-based headquarters or administrative centres, ranging from the major to the minor. Otherwise, there are such disparate cases as a milk reconstitution plant in South Korea, and a depot for the USAF Postal and Courier Service at Sydney, Australia.[111]

Several of the main US allies host major US military hospitals, obviously usable during peacetime as well as war and, in some cases, providing a regional medical capability which may obviate the need for transporting wounded military personnel all the way back to the USA say, from the Middle East. In FR Germany, the US Army has some 10 hospitals: Bad Kreuznach, Baumholder,

Hoppstadten, Frankfurt, Heidelberg, Landstuhl, Bremerhaven, Münchweiler, Nürnberg and Bad Cannstadt; the USAF has another at Wiesbaden.[112] In the UK, aside from major US military hospitals at Lakenheath and Wethersfield, Campbell notes a 500-bed contingency hospital (an additional 500-bed aeromedical evacuation unit is also planned) at Little Rissington, and several other 500-bed wartime contingency hospitals at Bicester, Borden, Feltwell, Kemble, Newton, Nocton Hall, Upwood, Waterbeach, Bulford, Colerne, Cosford, Tidworth and (a navy hospital) at Locking.[113] There are others in the Far East.

Israel has offered the USA the use of its medical facilities for crises in the Middle East, and this may now involve some prepositioned medical *matériel*. On the other hand, at the time of the bombing of the US Marine barracks in Beirut, political exigencies dictated the Pentagon's moving of wounded personnel to US hospitals in FR Germany, the added time and distance notwithstanding.[114]

Otherwise, all of the nations where the USA has a major military presence host the gamut of administrative and support facilities, including major headquarters for the various services. For example, in Turkey, the USAF has administrative offices in Izmir and Salipazari (Istanbul), and in Ankara, a major support facility which houses the Turkish–US Logistics Group (TUSLOG), the central logistics and support hub for all US activities in that country including hospital, family housing, maintenance, recreation and flight support annexes.[115] In the category of larger headquarters, there are the 6th and 7th Fleet Headquarters in Gaeta, Italy and Yokosuka, Japan, respectively.[116]

Campbell's detailed study of the US basing structure in the UK notes the large infrastructure of US headquarters, and administration and command and control centres. They include a USAF Third Air Force Headquarters and operations centre at Mildenhall; another at Ruislip; a US European Command war headquarters under construction underground at High Wycombe; the US Naval Headquarters Europe and US Eastern Atlantic naval commander at Grosvenor Square, London; various naval administrative and intelligence-related offices at Northwood, and so on.[117] (There are, additionally, some 30 family housing annexes.) There are equivalently large headquarters and administrative centres in FR Germany and Japan, and on an important scale in Belgium, Italy, Japan, South Korea, and so on.

The USSR, of course, also forward positions war-reserve stocks in Eastern Europe (and also in Mongolia and Afghanistan), though the locations for munitions and fuel depots are not easily discernible from public documents. There are, however, no indications of a Soviet equivalent to the US POMCUS stocks—Soviet proximity to the central military arena in Europe appears to preclude that need.

As it happens, there appears considerable disagreement among Western analysts as to the size and location of Soviet war reserve stocks in Eastern Europe. It is widely assumed that such stocks are kept in underground tunnels, hence, impervious to satellite reconnaissance, if not to HUMINT.[118] This uncertainty has acquired additional importance of late because of the growing debate over

Soviet capability to launch a sudden, massive attack against NATO without providing the warning which, almost certainly, would result from mobilization and forward movement of troops and *matériel*.

The Soviet Union also has some specialized logistics facilities in Eastern Europe worth noting. For instance, they have rebuilt several East-West railway lines and converted from standard Polish gauge to the wider Soviet gauge, so as to facilitate the westward movement of Soviet troops and supplies in time of war. There is one such line between Kaliningrad and Berlin passing through northern Poland; another between Terespol and Berlin passing through northern Poland (the main line Moscow-Warsaw-Berlin); and another between Hrubieszow and Katowice, passing through south-east Poland.[119]

III. Conclusion

In the current global context, conventional power projection requirements exist on two separate, connected levels which provide different problems for the major powers just as they relate to very different geographical situations and to different mixes of military capability.

On one level—as noted, this appears historically unique—the two superpowers maintain and dominate long-held alliances in Central Europe (and to a lesser degree in the Far East), in the context of a bipolar global structure. Based on ideological affinity, these alliances have provided the superpowers with an elaborate infrastructure of competing forward bases, across the spectrum of land, air, naval and 'technical' facilities. At present, the USA appears to be having relatively more trouble maintaining its side of the forward presence because of trends towards neutralization and decoupling and because the longevity of these relationships may have taken its toll in bruised national sensitivities and weariness with a foreign presence. There is increased and seemingly more serious talk about significant reduction of the US presence in Europe; less about a reduction of the Soviet presence in Eastern Europe, at least outside a formal conventional arms reduction pact.[120] There, more than mere geographical propinquity appears at stake, that is, the whole question of continuing Soviet control of Eastern Europe along the lines of the Brezhnev doctrine.

At the other level is the competition between the powers for global maritime and aircraft access, all revolving about the traditional themes of classical geopolitics: heartland and rimland, land versus maritime power, horizontal escalation in the case of general war, 'showing the flag', a struggle over resources, and the claimed indivisibility of global sea control. In this realm, the USA has long held some advantages: its more advanced and more numerous navy and long-range air transport corresponding to historical geopolitical realities and traditions; its initially more numerous footholds in the Third World based on the legacy of Western colonialism and traditional lines of clientship. Even today, one notes its large advantage as measured by carrier battle groups, amphibious forces, and aerial tankers, all mainstays of power projection.

But Moscow has been catching up in all these areas; indeed, has taken advantage of anti-Western sentiment in post-colonial areas to establish *points d'appui* in all areas of the globe, just as *its* capabilities in surface naval forces, long-range transportation, and so on, have begun to climb towards parity with the USA. But more recently, Soviet attempts to maintain the Brezhnev Doctrine (that once a country has become socialist it must remain so forever, as a historical 'law' and as a Soviet security imperative) have run up against the countervailing Reagan Doctrine (Angola, Nicaragua, Afghanistan, Cambodia) just as economic pressures in connection with the Soviet domestic economy could no longer be ignored. What this will mean for the future power projection competition around the rimlands remains to be seen. The USA too, however, has increasingly found it difficult to maintain (economically reasonable) access in the Third World, leading to some speculation that *both* superpowers may face declining access in a more decoupled but also familiar (traditional) global international structure.

Notes and references

[1] Weinberger, C. W., Secretary of Defense, *Annual Report to the Congress—Fiscal Year 1984* (US Government Printing Office: Washington, DC, 1983), p. 191.

[2] Weinberger (note 1).

[3] Weinberger (note 1), pp. 207–208. Herein, mobility forces are those that 'allow us to project power worldwide—even to austere regions—and sustain that power over long periods'. And, 'the term "intertheater mobility" refers to the movement of forces and materiel between major geographic regions or theaters of conflict'.

[4] See Kupchan, C., *The Persian Gulf and the West* (Allen and Unwin: Boston, Mass., 1987), chapter 8, under 'The out-of-area problem for NATO'.

[5] One early discussion of this concept, alternatively called 'power-over-distance gradient', is Wohlstetter, A., 'Illusions of distance', *Foreign Affairs*, vol. 46, no. 2 (Jan. 1968), pp. 242–55. See also Gray, C. S., *Maritime Strategy, Geopolitics and the Defense of the West* (National Strategy Information Center: New York, 1986), pp. 14–16.

[6] This is discussed at greater length in Harkavy, R. E., *Great Power Competition for Overseas Bases: The Geopolitics of Access Diplomacy* (Pergamon: New York, 1982), chapters 1 and 3.

[7] But, by mid-1988, there was considerable talk about a fundamental shift by the Soviet Union from an offensive to a defensive conventional posture in Europe. See, for instance, 'The big shake-up', *Time*, 8 Aug. 1988, pp. 20–22; and 'A strategic shift observed in Moscow', *International Herald Tribune*, 8 Mar. 1988, p. 1.

[8] 'Issue of conventional forces is a priority at NATO Summit', *International Herald Tribune*, 1 Mar. 1988, p. 2; and 'Gorbachev seeks Europe arms talks', *New York Times*, 12 July 1988, p. A3.

[9] International Institute for Strategic Studies, *The Military Balance: 1986-1987* (IISS: London, 1986), p. 79.

[10] IISS (note 9), p. 60.

[11] See the map in Arkin, W. M. and Fieldhouse, R. W., *Nuclear Battlefields: Global Links in the Arms Race* (Ballinger: Cambridge, Mass., 1985), p. 141.

[12] IISS (note 9), pp. 41–45.

[13] IISS (note 9), pp. 45–46.

[14] IISS (note 9), pp. 29–30.

[15] IISS (note 9), pp. 29–30.

[16] IISS (note 9), pp. 29–30.

[17] IISS (note 9), pp. 29–30.

[18] One good summary is 'Shrinking power: network of U.S. bases overseas is unraveling as need for it grows', *Wall Street Journal*, 29 Dec. 1987, p. 1.

[19] Note 18.

[20] Note 18.

[21] Note 18, p. 5.

[22] The role of the Adana base in this operation is discussed in 'Atomic unit in Germany among forces dispatched', *New York Times*, 17 July 1958, p. A1.

[23] Laqueur, W., *Confrontation: The Middle East and World Politics* (Quadrangle/The New York Times Book Co: New York, 1974), pp. 178 and 207, which states that US war *matériel* was shipped by way of Bremerhaven, and that FR Germany protested.

[24] Discussions with Simon Duke, SIPRI.

[25] Among others, see McNaugher, T., *Arms and Oil: U.S. Military Strategy and the Persian Gulf* (Brookings Institution: Washington, DC, 1985).

[26] Weinberger (note 1), p. 207.

[27] Weinberger (note 1), p. 192.

[28] Weinberger (note 1), p. 196.

[29] Weinberger, C. W., *Annual Report to the Congress: Fiscal Year 1988* (US Government Printing Office: Washington, DC, 1987), p. 229.

[30] Weinberger (note 29).

[31] Weinberger (note 29).

[32] Weinberger (note 29), pp. 229–30.

[33] Weinberger, C. W., *Annual Report to the Congress: Fiscal Year 1985* (US Government Printing Office: Washington, DC, 1984), pp. 210–216; and McNaugher (note 25).

[34] Weinberger (note 33), pp. 213–14.

[35] 'U.S. military is no secret in Egypt', *Washington Post*, 20 June 1980, p. 1.

[36] US Department of Defense, *Soviet Military Power 1987*, 6th edn (US Government Printing Office, Washington, DC), pp. 98–100.

[37] US Department of Defense, *Soviet Military Power 1985*, 4th edn (US Government Printing Office, Washington, DC, 1985), p. 83.

[38] *Soviet Military Power 1987* (note 36), pp. 99–100.

[39] Collins, J., *U.S.–Soviet Military Balance: 1980–1985* (Pergamon-Brassey's: Washington, DC, 1985), p. 115.

[40] *Soviet Military Power 1987* (note 36), pp. 85–86; and IISS (note 9), pp. 39–40.

[41] IISS (note 9), p. 40.

[42] IISS (note 9), p. 40.

[43] IISS (note 9), p. 40.

[44] IISS (note 9), p. 40.

[45] IISS (note 9), p. 39.

[46] IISS (note 9), p. 46.

[47] *Soviet Military Power 1985* (note 37), pp. 123–24.

[48] Silberman, L., 'Yugoslavia's "old" communism', *Foreign Policy*, no. 26 (spring 1977), pp. 3–27.

[49] 'Soviet tightens grasp in Africa', *New York Times* , 14 Dec. 1975; and Shulsky, A., 'Coercive diplomacy', eds B. Dismukes and J. McConnell, *Soviet Naval Diplomacy* (Pergamon: New York, 1979), pp. 144–51; 'Guyana denies aid by Cubans', *International Herald Tribune*, 8 Mar. 1976.

[50] 'U.S. charges Soviet mounts big airlift to Ethiopian army', *New York Times*, 14 Dec. 1977, p. A1.

[51] 'Soviet arms airlift to Vietnam hinted as combat goes on', *New York Times*, 23 Feb. 1979, p. A1; and 'Soviets pouring aid into Viet', *Pittsburgh Press*, 3 Sep. 1978, p. B4.

[52] *Soviet Military Power 1985* (note 37), p. 121.

[53] Among numerous sources, see Luttwak, E. and Laqueur, W., 'Kissinger and the Yom Kippur War', *Commentary*, vol. 58, no. 3 (Sep. 1974), pp. 33–40; 'Portugal bargains for U.S. military aid with strategic mid-Atlantic base', *Christian Science Monitor*, 24 Mar. 1981; 'NATO looks to Azores as fortress', *Philadelphia Inquirer*, 8 Sep. 1980; 'U.S. seeks access to bases in Azores, Indian Ocean', *International Herald Tribune*, 26–27 Jan. 1980; 'Accord reached on Portugal's Azores Air Base', *Financial Times*, 14 Dec. 1983.

[54] 'Spain reportedly urges U.S. to quit air base near Madrid', *International Herald Tribune*, 25 Feb. 1975; 'Secret U.S.–Spain airlift accord told', *Washington Post*, 11 Oct. 1976, p. A24; and 'No secret pact on bases, Spain says', *Washington Post*, 14 Oct. 1976, p. A25.

[55] Mangold, P., 'Shaba I and Shaba II', *Survival*, vol. 21, no. 3 (May/June 1979), pp. 107–115. According to SIPRI data, based on US congressional documents, the African airfields used for the Zaïre operation were at Dakar, Roberts IAP (Liberia) and Kinshasa.

[56] Dinerstein, H., *The Making of a Missile Crisis: October 1962* (Johns Hopkins University Press: Baltimore, Md., 1976), p. 223.

[57] US provision of information about the positions of Egyptian armoured divisions prior to the 1973 crossing of the Suez Canal, obtained by SR-71 reconnaissance flights, is alleged in El Shazly, Lt. Gen. S., *The Crossing of the Suez* (American Mideast Research: San Francisco, Calif., 1980), p. 252; and Heikal M., *The Road to Ramadan* (Collins: London, 1975), pp. 229, 251, respectively regarding satellites and reconnaissance aircraft. Regarding US aid to Britain during the Falklands War, see 'U.S. providing British a wide range of intelligence', *New York Times*, 15 Apr. 1982, p. A11; and 'Argentina holding U.S. responsible for upsets', *New York Times*, 30 May 1982, p. 16. Regarding alleged Soviet satellite assistance to Argentina, see Jack Anderson's column, *Centre Daily Times*, 16 Jan. 1984, p. A4.

[58] Among numerous sources, see Vaux, N., *Take That Hill: Royal Marines in the Falklands War* (Pergamon-Brassey's: Washington, DC, 1986), especially chapter 4.

[59] 'U.S. role in Zaire grows with Gabon, Senegal airlift', *Washington Post*, 7 June 1978, p. A21.

[60] Information provided by Prof. Anthony Williams, Dept. of Geography, Pennsylvania State University, recently resident in Cameroons. See also, 'Heavy fighting rocks town in Northern Chad', *International Herald Tribune*, 11 Aug. 1983.

[61] 'The rescue: "We do the impossible"', *Time Magazine*, 12 July 1976, pp. 21–22.

[62] 'Cuban flights to Angola said to refuel in Guyana', *Washington Post*, 24 Dec. 1975, p. A8; 'Guyana stop', *Washington Post*, 31 Dec. 1975; and 'Cubans face test in Angola', *Washington Post*, 21 Dec. 1975, p. F5. Further Cuban use of a Canadian staging point in Newfoundland is noted in 'Canada bars Cuban flights to Angola', *Washington Post*, 31 Jan. 1976, p. A5.

[63] This can be seen throughout the pre-World War II intelligence files—see the US National Archives, Navy and Old Army Branch, Record Group 165 (Records of the War Department, General and Special Staffs), Military Intelligence Division (MID) (Washington, DC, 1920–40).

[64] *The United States Army Posture Statement: Fiscal Year 1988*, Joint Statement by the Chief of Staff, US Army, and Secretary of the Army (US Government Printing Office: Washington, DC, 1987), p. 39, under 'War reserve stocks'.

[65] SIPRI data on FR Germany.

[66] SIPRI data on FR Germany.

[67] SIPRI data on FR Germany.

[68] SIPRI data on FR Germany.

[69] SIPRI data on the UK.

[70] SIPRI data on Italy.

[71] SIPRI data on Denmark.

[72] SIPRI data on South Korea.

[73] SIPRI data on Japan.

[74] SIPRI data on the Philippines.

[75] SIPRI data.

[76] SIPRI data.

[77] SIPRI data on Iceland.

[78] SIPRI data.

[79] SIPRI data.

[80] SIPRI data.

[81] SIPRI data.

[82] SIPRI data on bunkering facilities.

[83] SIPRI data.

[84] SIPRI data.

[85] SIPRI data.

[86] SIPRI data on Turkey.

[87] SIPRI data on Spain and additional data provided by Simon Duke.

[88] SIPRI data on the Philippines.

[89] *The United States Army Posture Statement: Fiscal Year 1988* (note 64), p. 37.

[90] Weinberger, C. W., *Annual Report to the Congress: Fiscal Year 1987* (US Government Printing Office: Washington, DC, 1986), p. 239.

[91] Weinberger (note 90), p. 239.

[92] SIPRI data.

[93] Campbell, D., *The Unsinkable Aircraft Carrier: American Military Power in Britain* (Paladin: London, 1986), p. 290.

[94] The Organization of the Joint Chiefs of Staff, *United States Military Posture Fiscal Year 1985* (US Government Printing Office: Washington, DC, 1984), p. 71.

[95] Regarding vulnerability, see US Senate Committee on Armed Services, *Department of Defense*

Authorization For Appropriations For Fiscal Year 1986, 99th Congress, 1st Session (US Government Printing Office: Washington, DC, 27, 28 Feb.; 1 Mar. 1985), pp. 1435, 1447.

[96] By 1988, the Pentagon reported it had prepositioned equipment for three Marine brigades afloat, in three squadrons of maritime prepositioning ships. One brigade set was prepositioned at Diego Garcia for use in South West Asia; the other two sets are maintained in the Atlantic and Pacific. In addition it was further reported that the USA also has prepositioned afloat 7000 tons of Army equipment for port-opening and clearance units. See also, 'Marines prepare for duty in Asia', *New York Times*, 10 Apr. 1985, p. A17. See Weinberger (note 29), p. 230.

[97] The Organization of the Joint Chiefs of Staff, *United States Military Posture: FY 1987* (US Government Printing Office: Washington, DC, 1986), p. 69.

[98] 'Marines train for swift raids and hostage rescues', *New York Times*, 6 Aug. 1987, p. 6.

[99] 'The U.S. steps up its power projection capability', *Pacific Defence Reporter*, vol. 13, no. 8 (Feb. 1987), p. 7; and 'Weinberger assures Thais on arms stockpile', *Far Eastern Economic Review*, 9 July 1987, p. 6.

[100] This is explicitly discussed in 'Soviet said to build arms caches in Libya, Syria, Persian Gulf Area', *New York Times*, 14 Mar. 1980, in which it is reported that 'Col. Muammar al-Qaddafi, the Libyan leader, has said that the arms have been assembled so that his country can serve as "the arsenal of Islam" in a new war with Israel'. The huge Libyan air force was said to rely on Soviet, North Korean, Palestinian and Pakistani airmen. See also, 'Syria continues military expansion', *Near East Report*, vol. 29, no. 4 (28 Jan. 1985), p. 14.

[101] IISS (note 9), p. 103.

[102] IISS (note 9), p. 112.

[103] IISS (note 9), p. 109.

[104] Haselkorn, A., 'The Soviet collective security system', *Orbis*, vol. 19, no. 1 (spring 1975), pp. 231–54.

[105] 'Israel's desire for a strategic relationship with U.S. is taken more seriously than ever', *International Herald Tribune*, 2 Oct. 1981. 'Israelis put strategic arms cooperation terms to U.S.', *The Times*, 19 Nov. 1981; 'Administration drops plan for bases in Egypt, Israel', *Washington Star*, 10 Jan. 1980, p. 1; 'Begin offers air cover, arms storage to U.S.', *International Herald Tribune*, 13 Sep. 1981. This issue arose again during the 1988 election campaign, during which the Bush campaign endorsed prepositioning of US *matériel* in Israel; see 'Bush issues pro-Israel paper', *Near East Report*, vol. 32, no. 31 (1 Aug. 1988). See also, 'Build-up of arms urged by Sharon', *Daily Telegraph*, 1 Dec. 1981.

[106] See 'Saudis to let U.S. use bases in crisis', *New York Times*, 5 Sep. 1985, p. 1; and 'U.S. Saudi bases?" *Near East Report*, vol. 29, no. 36 (9 Sep. 1985).

[107] 'Secret U.S. air base is revealed in Egypt amid broader buildup', *International Herald Tribune*, 24 June 1983; 'U.S. suspends talks on use of Egypt base', *International Herald Tribune*, 22 May 1983, p. 21; and 'House panel cuts money for bases', *New York Times*, 17 May 1984, p. A7.

[108] Blaxland, G., *The Regiments Depart* (William Kimber: London, 1971), pp. 215–36.

[109] SIPRI data.

[110] SIPRI data.

[111] SIPRI data.

[112] SIPRI data on FR Germany.

[113] Campbell (note 93), pp. 291–92.

[114] 'Israelis on sidelines' and '36 wounded airlifted to West Germany', *New York Times*, 25 Oct. 1983, p. A14.

[115] SIPRI data on Turkey.

[116] SIPRI data.

[117] Campbell (note 93), p. 286.

[118] This was conveyed to the author in a conversation with Mr. Stephen Bowman, Congressional Research Service, Library of Congress.

[119] SIPRI data.

[120] But, note, by way of mitigation, 'U.S. says Soviets may pull troops out of Hungary', *New York Times*, 9 July 1988, p. A1.

10. The politics and economics of foreign military presence

I. Introduction

This book concentrates on description and enumeration of the thousands of facilities, bases and other forms of FMP provided, for the most part, to the two superpowers and the other major powers whose security requirements involve a reach and presence beyond their own borders. These presences are shown to involve a complex concatenation of functions: naval, air, ground-force, missile, C³I, environmental, research, logistical, and so on, cutting across the broader functions of nuclear deterrence and warfighting and of conventional power projection.

Juxtaposed upon this blizzard of detail, however, are some additional important questions: centrally and specifically, what is the basis for access in these varied situations? What, indeed, can one say about the politics and economics of foreign military presence; that is, who provides access (and what degree of access) to whom, and at what cost or under what terms? What is the relationship of FMP to formal alliances and/or defence agreements, to other indicators of the strength of relationships between nations, such as overall trade, investment, or memberships in international or non-governmental organizations? What is the relationship to arms transfer patterns or, more broadly, to security assistance including training missions, economic aid, and so on? And, at still another level, what can one say about the historical development of some of these questions? What is similar to or different from the patterns of 1970, or 1945? How can one relate some of these changes to the emerging macro-political trends discussed in chapter 1? These are complex matters. This chapter both raises questions and provides some of the answers.

Historical development: recapitulation

In chapter 1, a somewhat simplified outline of the progression of basing diplomacy in this century is advanced. It focuses on the question of what has been central or vital to an explanation of the patterns of who provides access to whom, or of the main underpinnings of the relationships between user and host nations. A progression is outlined from (a) a pre-World War II phase, when most FMP was determined by colonial relationships and little by bargained arrangements between sovereign states; (b) a second phase, covering the first two decades or so of the post-war period, when FMP was determined by convergent security interests within hierarchical alliances as well as by the dwindling remnants of colonialism;[1] (c) a third phase in which a more symmetrical bargaining relationship emerged between host and user nations, and arms transfers became closely linked to basing access; to (d) a perhaps emerging fourth phase, telescoped to the third, in which many former access relationships seem to be decoupling and others seem to be moving towards a more commercial basis and away from a basis of mutual security interests.[2] Needless to say, the complexities of FMP access at any point do not easily lend themselves to such simple classification—we are dealing here with relative but noticeable tendencies, cautiously advanced. Temporal dividing lines between these phases are fuzzy and telescoped—in fact they gradually merge into one another.

Formal alliances

Not surprisingly, there is a close relationship between formal alliances and patterns of access. A formal alliance strongly implies a close security relationship as well as the likelihood of an arms transfer tie, particularly where there are asymmetries of power within the alliance translating into hierarchical and dependent relationships.

One historical point, a somewhat esoteric one, intervenes here. The present diplomatic epoch is characterized by a lessened overall propensity by most nations to engage in formal security pacts.[3] The reasons for this are obscure (and beyond the scope of this chapter) and paralleled by a lesser frequency of declarations of war, or of formal peace treaties to end them. These questions relate to subjective tendencies involving practices of international law, the 'norms' of international behaviour, and so on; that is, 'the way the game is played'.

Although there may have been a lessened frequency of alliance formation in the post-war period, those alliances which have been entered into have tended to be long-term and stable, corresponding to the nature of the post-war global system, characterized as it has been by bipolarity and stable ideological rigidity.

In some cases, of course, the linkage of basing access to formal alliances is altogether obvious; indeed, NATO and WTO countries, respectively, account for a significant proportion of US and Soviet external facilities.[4] Almost all of Washington's NATO Allies in Europe provide vital facilities, though some (Denmark, Iceland, Norway, Portugal and Spain) maintain restrictions on the deployment of nuclear weapons, or have recently either curtailed US access or raised the costs (Greece, Portugal and Spain). NATO Allies other than the USA are also provided access by their Alliance partners: Belgium, Canada, France, the Netherlands and the UK have access to FR Germany; the UK also has access to Italy and Iceland; and there are a number of other examples. The USSR has extensive, counterpart access within the WTO—Romania, however, is an exception with only a small, remnant Soviet military presence.

Of the remaining nations of Europe—Albania, Austria, Cyprus, Finland, Ireland, Malta, Sweden, Switzerland and Yugoslavia—only Cyprus hosts a foreign military presence, that is, the two British bases also utilized by the USA.

These emerged from the Treaty of Guarantee signed by Britain, Greece and Turkey in 1959 assuring the independence, territorial integrity and security of Cyprus, which agreement specifically provides for a British presence.[5] It is not an alliance. Albania once hosted Soviet bases while it was a WTO member, but it dropped out in 1968, moving into a close relationship with China.[6] Malta hosted British bases up to 1979, but in 1984 it signed a Treaty of Co-operation and Friendship with Libya, under which it agreed to *exclude* foreign bases.[7] This is an example of base denial activity, a subject returned to below.

In the Middle East, the USSR has signed Treaties of Friendship and Co-operation with Syria, South Yemen, Iraq and North Yemen.[8] The first two named have been associated with major access, the last-named with only limited access, that is, port visits. Iraq earlier provided fairly extensive access for the Soviet Navy at Umm Quasr, but this has declined apparently in part because of periodically strained relations, but also because Iraq's ports in the Persian Gulf have been blocked by the war with Iran since 1980.[9]

The USA has defence agreements of various sorts with Israel, Egypt, Morocco, Oman and Bahrain.[10] All have provided Washington some access, but only under strict conditions in the cases of Egypt and Morocco, and only for some purposes in those of Oman and Bahrain. No major permanent facilities are involved in these cases, nor in the case of Tunisia, with which the USA has a strategic co-operation agreement.[11]

Britain has treaties of friendship with Bahrain, Quatar and the United Arab Emirates—only the first involves some limited access, as does a defence co-operation agreement with Oman.[12] China has treaties of friendship or defence co-operation agreements with North Yemen, Egypt and Sudan, in no case involving military access which would anyway be largely irrelevant because of Peking's lack of long-range power-projection capability.[13]

In Africa, where there are a number of multilateral regional agreements, some of which have security as well as economic provisions (at least on paper), there are a number of bilateral external agreements. The USA has mutual defence and assistance agreements with Kenya (1980) and Somalia (1980), both of which provide Washington with limited access to naval and air facilities[14] (Djibouti, Liberia, Somalia and Senegal, among others, have also provided some access in the absence of such formal ties).

The Soviet Union has Treaties of Friendship and Co-operation with Angola (1976), Ethiopia (1978) and Mozambique (1977), all of which, particularly the two first-named, have provided Moscow with extensive basing access.[15] But the USSR has also had limited access in a number of other places—including the Congo, Guinea, Guinea-Bissau, Mali, Somalia (up to 1977) and São Tomé and Príncipe—without an associated security treaty. France, meanwhile, has signed defence agreements with Cameroon (1974), the Central African Republic (1960), Chad (1960), the Comoro Islands (1978), Djibouti (1977), Gabon (1974), the Ivory Coast (1961), Senegal (1974) and Togo (1963), most of which (excepting perhaps Togo and the Comoro Islands) have provided varying levels of access.[16]

In Asia, the USA has mutual security and co-operation treaties with Japan (1951), South Korea (1954), the Philippines (1951), Australia (1952) and (until 1987) New Zealand (1952), all of which have provided basing access.[17] So too has Thailand (now at a lower level), in connection with the now lapsed SEATO Pact (earlier, Pakistan, as a member both of SEATO and CENTO, provided some bases to Washington). Meanwhile, the Five Power Defence Arrangement (between Australia, New Zealand, Malaysia, Singapore and Britain) begun in 1971 has provided an umbrella for access to the South-East Asian nations by Australia and New Zealand.[18]

The USSR has Treaties of Friendship and Co-operation with Afghanistan (1978), Mongolia (1966), North Korea (1961), Viet Nam (1978) and India (1971), and has had extensive access to all but India, where its presence has been limited to naval port visits and aircraft overflights.[19] But China has had similar agreements with Afghanistan (1960), Burma (1960), North Korea (1961), Nepal (1960) and Kampuchea (Khmer Rouge—1961), but with no military presence.[20]

In Latin America, the USA is connected to most of the region's nations by the 1947 Inter-American Treaty of Reciprocal Assistance (Treaty of Rio) and the 1945 Act of Chapultepec, which are interlocking mutual security pacts.[21] But in some contrast to patterns elsewhere, these arrangements have not resulted in extensive granting of basing access, perhaps in part because the more benign security environment, that is, the absence of a significant Soviet presence outside of Cuba and Nicaragua, does not require it. But the USA does have some military access in Panama, Honduras, several states where there are minor technical facilities and in several of the Caribbean nations, several of which are now themselves bound together in the 1982 Regional Security System (RSS).[22] In addition, the USA has recently concluded a status-of-forces agreement with Antigua (1978), and a defence treaty with Honduras (1985), both of which arrangements are tied to US military access.[23] The USSR has no formal defence agreements with any of the states in the area. Britain has an arrangement called the 'Commonwealth Pact' (also involving Barbados, Bahamas, Canada, Guyana, Jamaica and Trinidad and Tobago), which allows it continued FMP in Belize under a multilateral consultative arrangement.[24]

A few generalizations can be made involving the relationship between FMP and formal alliances/defence pacts/treaties of 'friendship and co-op-eration', and so on. First, most states which provide major basing access to the USA and the USSR are tied to the respective superpower by some type of formal security treaty. There are some exceptions on both sides, that is, alliances without bases and bases without alliances, but not many. However, both superpowers are availed of more minor forms of access (small 'technical' or research facilities, port visits, routine overflights, etc.) in numerous places without the tie of security pacts.

Otherwise, there are numerous (too numerous to enumerate here) security arrangements or non-aggression pacts *among* Third World states, in most cases not involving military access, partly because most such states are not capable of, or do not want, an extended military reach. For example, Cuba and Viet Nam have a Treaty of Friendship and Co-operation (1987); as does North Korea with Libya, Tanzania and Cuba respectively.[25] The above-mentioned RSS in the Caribbean involves Antigua-Barbuda, Barbados, Dominica, Grenada,[26] St Lucia, St Vincent and St Kitts-Nevis—with little or no mutual access (there are similar arrangements among some groups of African states). As stressed, most FMP involves the USSR, the USA, France and Britain as user states, with only a few other states having such access. Where the big powers are involved there is usually a formal security pact as part of the arrangement which, of course, normally provides a defence commitment for the host, linked to the larger power through a web of arms transfer and other security assistance arrangements.

II. Arms transfers and FMP

Cause versus correlation

In recent years, there has been considerable discussion about the relationship between arms sales, or more broadly, security assistance including economic aid, and the acquisition and retention of basing access. The literature and the author's discussions with US government officials in the course of researching this book reveal a certain amount of disagreement about the general strength of this relationship.

To some degree, the disagreements appear to result from the typical confusion of the empirical and normative aspects of analytical questions of this sort. Some policy makers and academic analysts with a policy preference for controlling conventional arms sales are resistant to the utilization of such sales for acquiring bases and tend to downgrade the very efficacy of such use of weapon transfers. Those concerned about the loss of access—or the necessity for more of it—on the other hand, are inclined to see arms transfers as a near-panacea for access problems in an era witnessing increased pressures for decoupling throughout the world.[27]

Other analysts, while acknowledging the obviously significant correlation between arms transfer and access patterns, tend to play down a causal link, preferring to see the diplomacy of these two domains as running on separate tracks. This perspective tends to emphasize the economic rationales for arms transfers—more geopolitically inspired explanations tend to attribute greater importance to the causal nexus between the two domains.

What this all adds up to, of course, is the necessity for examining many situations on a case-by-case basis, to determine the extent to which basing access is causally connected to weapon sales or, again, more broadly to security and economic assistance (themselves not easily separated in practice). Space does not permit such case studies here and in many cases, particularly involving Soviet access in the Third World but in some cases also involving US access, the full picture is not clear. Data and records are scarce and hard to come by, and one enters, in many instances, the realm of classified data and secret diplomacy. This is, of course, particularly the case where sensitive intelligence, research and space-related facilities are involved, but also for aircraft overflights and staging of war *matériel* to Third World combatants. Almost unavoidably, we are forced back to an analysis of correlations, in an only roughly empirical sense, without sophisticated statistical techniques.

Several related and important questions arise, however. One has to do with what, in various circumstances, has led or driven what when it comes to the relationship between the two security domains. Have a priori arms transfer relations tended eventually to lead to FMP? Or, in other cases, has FMP come first, followed thereafter by arms sales? Or, have they tended to be initiated simultaneously? Again, a full analysis is beyond the scope of this work.

There are also qualitative as well as quantitative aspects to this relationship. Some host nations, in many cases already or long since an arms client of the base user state, may utilize the bait of continued or upgraded access in an effort to get more sophisticated types of weapon, wholly aside from the matter of cost. Or, the bargaining may be over the user providing the host with technology transfer which may enable the latter to embark upon indigenous production of weaponry.[28] These important and subtle aspects of FMP diplomacy will not be picked up in an aggregate data analysis of the nexus in question; they would rather have to be dealt with case-by-case.

Arms transfer and FMP patterns: a cross-cutting typology and matrix

It may be useful, juxtaposing global FMP patterns with those of arms transfers, to utilize a typology developed in the early 1970s by the present author to describe various patterns of arms-supply relationships. From the perspective of the arms recipients (mostly those states which also host FMP), this involves basic questions of how many suppliers a given recipient relies upon, and in what proportions, and how these patterns vary over time.[29] There are also, as is explained below, some important political ramifications associated with various arms-supply patterns, and they in turn are closely related to questions of granting access to major powers. As an initial caveat, however, it is also very much the case that classifying arms-trade patterns is a difficult and daunting problem, wherein even the most complex matrices may not capture all that is important.

At one end of the spectrum, there are sole-source relationships, that is, where *all* of a recipient's arms are acquired from one supplier. Of course, there are some situations in which almost all of the arms come from one source; and perhaps just a minor item or two from another. Here, the political implications may be the same as for the sole source.[30] Further along the spectrum, there are predominant source patterns in which, say, 60 per cent or more of a nation's weapons come from one source, but a significant amount comes from one or more other sources.

In terms of the political meaning of such a predominant pattern, there is one major point of possible variation. If there are, let us say, two or three suppliers of which one is predominant, they may all come from within the US/NATO bloc, from within the Soviet/WTO bloc, from both blocs or (assuming that China and the USSR are no longer *en bloc*) from a West–China or Sino–Soviet combination. There are, of course, other possible patterns, that is, a predominant US or Soviet supplier role with a secondary role by a Third World power such as Brazil, Israel, Egypt, and so on. There are many possibilities.

Moving still further along the spectrum, one can speak of multiple source acquisitions, where no one supplier accounts for as much as 60 per cent of the market and where a nation's supplies are often drawn from many sources. Here too, the multiple arms sources may all be from within NATO or the WTO, from both blocs, or in one or another of the above combinations. The difference here lies in the absence of a single predominant supplier.

Such a typology involves almost endless complications, some not so trivial for analytical purposes. Some nations, for instance, tend to acquire weapons for one service (army, navy, air force) from one supplier and those for another service from another supplier.[31] There is also the time element—transfers from different sources may be simultaneous or they may be conducted in sequential periods. If one examines a nation's current inventories, presumably comprising weapons acquired over many years, a decade or more, one may be looking at what appears to be a multiple-source style of acquisition. A closer look may divulge segmented periods, where one supplier or bloc may have been dominant for a while, and where there was then a dramatic shift, perhaps as a result of a revolution, coup or other upheaval. Iran, Egypt, Morocco, Pakistan and many other nations have displayed such segmented acquisition patterns at times.

As if these problems were not sufficiently daunting, there are also others involving the various sources for arms trade data and the varying criteria of measurement. Since these methodological issues have been discussed at length in a recent SIPRI book, it will suffice here briefly to summarize those arguments. They centre around the differences between the two most widely used data bases, produced by SIPRI and by the US Arms Control and Disarmament Agency (ACDA), respectively. These differences involve sources, valuation methods, country samples (Third World only versus global), coverage (major weapons only versus all weapons and ammunition), and so on. As both ACDA and SIPRI data are used here, a brief summary of the distinctions follows:

There are large differences between SIPRI-figures and those published by governments. This should be no surprise, given the differences in coverage. There is a pattern of divergence ranging from countries which mostly export major weapons (such as France and the USA) to those which mainly export ammunition, small arms and parts for weapon systems (such as Belgium, Czechoslovakia, Canada, Sweden or Switzerland). In the latter cases, this means that SIPRI figures systematically underrepresent total arms exports from these countries.

ACDA figures should be closer to national data since the definition used by ACDA is wider. While this holds in some cases, in other cases there are large discrepancies between ACDA data and national data resulting from differences in definition, unreliable national data or unreliable ACDA data. In general, ACDA data seem to underestimate the arms exports of some countries, which export mainly weapon components, production technology, small arms and ammunition.[32]

Arms acquisition patterns as illustrated by SIPRI and ACDA data are shown in tables 34 and 35, respectively.

The political ramifications of the various patterns of FMP can be important. A sole-source relationship (or a strongly predominant source and a within-bloc relationship) usually denotes close political ties, more often than not involving a formal alliance/defence treaty/treaty of friendship and co-operation, or other arrangement. Hence, there is usually a security commitment provided by the major-power arms supplier, and where the security *interests* of supplier and recipient are more or less convergent, FMP is very often involved. The big power is welcome, or at least accepted, and its protection desired; hence, the strength of *its* overall power is deemed to be in the interest of the smaller, dependent power. The latter grants its patron access because it is in its *own* interest, at least on balance.

There are, of course, some disadvantages for the recipient (and often base host) in this kind of relationship.[33] A sole or predominant arms supplier has leverage when it comes to arms resupply during crises or wars—it cannot easily or quickly be replaced as, for instance, Israel learned in 1967 when embargoed by France, or as Pakistan learned in 1965 when similarly embargoed by the USA. An army cannot be retrained on a whole new set of weapons overnight, as Iran has learned since 1979 when its US source was largely cut off.[34] In addition, acquiescing to too close an embrace by a major power can often have unsettling domestic political implications—bases are visible and emotion-laden targets of frustration.

Multiple-source acquisition, on the other hand, provides leverage and flexibility for a recipient. There are also disadvantages, that is, the inefficiencies and logistical nightmares involved in training with and maintaining a large variety of weapons. Language can be a problem where numerous training manuals are involved. Most of all, a multiple-source supplier relationship, particularly where the sources are distributed across the blocs, usually denotes the absence of a strong security relationship with a major power, if not neutralism or a fickle shifting of big-power political ties. Hence, such an acquisition pattern would be expected to exclude major-power basing access, particularly as concerns major and visible naval and air facilities.

By comparison with arms-supplier patterns, an equivalent or comparable typology of FMP patterns would appear, at least in some respects, to be relatively simple. For one thing, with a *very* few exceptions, those countries which host FMP do so for only one user nation (or, over a longer span, one at a time). There are, in other words, few equivalents to a predominant or multiple-source arms acquisition pattern; indeed, most basing access, as shown below, *is associated with* a sole or predominant arms supply pattern. There are a few exceptions: FR Germany hosts the forces of several NATO Allies; Italy has US and British facilities; and Oman and Bahrain allow US and British naval access.

Table 34. Arms acquisition patterns based on SIPRI data, 1976–85

Recipient country	Years	Arms suppliers							
		Solely or mainly US (within bloc)	Mainly US (cross-bloc)	Multiple source (within West)	Multiple source (cross-bloc)	Multiple source (within East)	Mainly Soviet (cross-bloc)	Solely or mainly Soviet (within bloc)	Other
Afghanistan	1976–80							X	
	1981–85							X	
Algeria	1976–80				X				
	1981–85						X		
Angola	1976–80							X	
	1981–85							X	
Argentina	1976–80			X					
	1981–85			X					
Bahamas	1976–80								Solely UK
	1981–85								
Bahrain	1976–80								..
	1981–85								Mainly French
Bangladesh	1976–80								Mainly PRC
	1981–85			X					Mainly PRC
Belize	1976–80								..
	1981–85								Solely UK
Benin	1976–80				X				
	1981–85				X				
Bolivia	1976–80								Mainly Third World
	1981–85								Mainly French
Botswana	1976–80								Solely UK
	1981–85				X				
Brazil	1976–80								
	1981–85			X					Mainly UK
Brunei	1976–80			X					
	1981–85								Mainly Third World
Burkina Faso	1976–80			X					
	1981–85			X					
Burma	1976–80			X					
	1981–85			X					Solely UK

Recipient country	Years	Arms suppliers							
		Solely or mainly US (within bloc)	Mainly US (cross-bloc)	Multiple source (within West)	Multiple source (cross-bloc)	Multiple source (within East)	Mainly Soviet (cross-bloc)	Solely or mainly Soviet (within bloc)	Other
Burundi	1976–80							X	
	1981–85								
Cameroon	1976–80			X					
	1981–85			X					
Cape Verde	1976–80							X	
	1981–85							X	
Central African Rep.	1976–80								Mainly Third World
	1981–85								
Chad	1976–80								Mainly French
	1981–85								Mainly French
Chile	1976–80			X					
	1981–85			X					
Colombia	1976–80	X							
	1981–85			X					
Comoros	1976–80								Mainly Italy
	1981–85								Mainly France
Congo	1976–80				X				
	1981–85				X				
Costa Rica	1976–80	X							
	1981–85	X							
Ivory Coast	1976–80								Mainly France
	1981–85								Mainly France
Cuba	1976–80							X	
	1981–85							X	
Djibouti	1976–80								Mainly Third World
	1981–85								Mainly France
Dominican Republic	1976–80	X							
	1981–85	X							
Ecuador	1976–80			X					
	1981–85			X					
Egypt	1976–80				X				
	1981–85		X						

Recipient country	Years	Arms suppliers							
		Solely or mainly US (within bloc)	Mainly US (cross-bloc)	Multiple source (within West)	Multiple source (cross-bloc)	Multiple source (within East)	Mainly Soviet (cross-bloc)	Solely or mainly Soviet (within bloc)	Other
El Salvador	1976–80	X							
	1981–85	X							
Equatorial Guinea	1976–80							X	'Other'
	1981–85								
Ethiopia	1976–80							X	
	1981–85							X	
Gabon	1976–80			X					
	1981–85			X					
Gambia	1976–80								
	1981–85								Mainly UK
Ghana	1976–80			X					
	1981–85								Mainly Italy
Guatemala	1976–80	X							
	1981–85	X							
Guinea	1976–80							X	
	1981–85							X	
Guinea Bissau	1976–80							X	'Other'
	1981–85								
Guyana	1976–80			X					
	1981–85								Mainly Third World
Haiti	1976–80	X							
	1981–85								Mainly Italy
Honduras	1976–80			X					
	1981–85	X							
India	1976–80						X		
	1981–85						X		
Indonesia	1976–80			X					
	1981–85			X					
Iran	1976–80		X						
	1981–85				X				
Iraq	1976–80						X		Mainly PRC
	1981–85								

Recipient country	Years	Arms suppliers							
		Solely or mainly US (within bloc)	Mainly US (cross-bloc)	Multiple source (within West)	Multiple source (cross-bloc)	Multiple source (within East)	Mainly Soviet (cross-bloc)	Solely or mainly Soviet (within bloc)	Other
Israel	1976–80	X							
	1981–85	X							
Jamaica	1976–80	X							
	1981–85	X							
Jordan	1976–80								
	1981–85		X						
Kampuchea	1976–80								Mainly PRC
	1981–85							X	
Kenya	1976–80			X					
	1981–85			X					
North Korea	1976–80							X	
	1981–85							X	
South Korea	1976–80	X							
	1981–85	X							
Kuwait	1976–80				X				
	1981–85				X				
Laos	1976–80							X	
	1981–85							X	
Lebanon	1976–80			X					
	1981–85	X							
Lesotho	1976–80								Mainly UK
	1981–85								Mainly Italy
Liberia	1976–80	X							
	1981–85								Mainly Third World
Libya	1976–80						X		
	1981–85						X		
Madagascar	1976–80						X		
	1981–85								Mainly Third World
Malawi	1976–80								Mainly France
	1981–85								Mainly UK
Malaysia	1976–80			X					
	1981–85			X					

Arms suppliers

Recipient country	Years	Solely or mainly US (within bloc)	Mainly US (cross-bloc)	Multiple source (within West)	Multiple source (cross-bloc)	Multiple source (within East)	Mainly Soviet (cross-bloc)	Solely or mainly Soviet (within bloc)	Other
Mali	1976–80							X	
	1981–85								
Mauritania	1976–80			X					
	1981–85						X		
Mauritius	1976–80								Mainly France
	1981–85								
Mexico	1976–80			X					
	1981–85			X				X	
Morocco	1976–80			X					
	1981–85			X					
Mozambique	1976–80							X	
	1981–85							X	
Nepal	1976–80			X					
	1981–85								
Nicaragua	1976–80			X					
	1981–85								Mainly UK
Niger	1976–80	X							
	1981–85			X			X		
Nigeria	1976–80				X				
	1981–85				X				
Oman	1976–80								Mainly UK
	1981–85								Mainly UK
Pakistan	1976–80				X				
	1981–85				X				
Panama	1976–80			X					
	1981–85								
Papua New Guinea	1976–80	X							Mainly 'other'
	1981–85								Mainly Third World
Paraguay	1976–80	X							Mainly Third World
	1981–85								
Peru	1976–80				X				Mainly Third World
	1981–85				X				

Recipient country	Years	Arms suppliers							
		Solely or mainly US (within bloc)	Mainly US (cross-bloc)	Multiple source (within West)	Multiple source (cross-bloc)	Multiple source (within East)	Mainly Soviet (cross-bloc)	Solely or mainly Soviet (within bloc)	Other
Philippines	1976-80	X							
	1981-85	X							
Qatar	1976-80								Mainly France
	1981-85								Mainly France
Rwanda	1976-80								Mainly UK
	1981-85								Mainly France
Saudi Arabia	1976-80	X							
	1981-85	X							
Senegal	1976-80								Mainly France
	1981-85								Mainly France
Seychelles	1976-80				X				
	1981-85								Mainly Italy
Sierra Leone	1976-80			X					
	1981-85								Mainly France
Singapore	1976-80	X							
	1981-85	X							
Somalia	1976-80				X				
	1981-85			X					
Sri Lanka	1976-80								Mainly PRC
	1981-85			X					
Sudan	1976-80			X					
	1981-85			X					
Suriname	1976-80								Mainly UK
	1981-85			X					
Swaziland	1976-80								..
	1981-85								..
Syria	1976-80						X		
	1981-85							X	
Taiwan	1976-80	X							
	1981-85	X							
Tanzania	1976-80								Mainly PRC
	1981-85								Mainly PRC

Recipient country	Years	Arms suppliers							
		Solely or mainly US (within bloc)	Mainly US (cross-bloc)	Multiple source (within West)	Multiple source (cross-bloc)	Multiple source (within East)	Mainly Soviet (cross-bloc)	Solely or mainly Soviet (within bloc)	Other
Thailand	1976-80	X							
	1981-85								
Togo	1976-80			X					Mainly France
	1981-85			X					'Other'
Trinidad & Tobago	1976-80	X							
	1981-85								
Tunisia	1976-80			X					
	1981-85			X					
Uganda	1976-80				X				
	1981-85	X							
United Arab Emirates	1976-80								Mainly France
	1981-85								
Uruguay	1976-80			X					
	1981-85			X					
Venezuela	1976-80			X					
	1981-85			X					Mainly Italy
Viet Nam	1976-80							X	
	1981-85							X	
North Yemen	1976-80						X		
	1981-85							X	
South Yemen	1976-80							X	
	1981-85							X	
Zaire	1976-80				X				
	1981-85				X				
Zambia	1976-80				X				
	1981-85						X		
Zimbabwe	1976-80								Mainly Third World
	1981-85								Mainly UK

Source: Brzoska, M. and Ohlson, T., SIPRI, Arms Transfers to the Third World: 1971-85 (Oxford University Press: Oxford, 1987).

Table 35. Arms acquisition patterns based on ACDA data, 1987

Country	Arms suppliers							
	Solely or mainly US (within bloc)	Mainly US (cross-bloc)	Multiple source (within West)	Multiple source (cross-bloc)	Multiple source (within East)	Mainly Soviet (cross-bloc)	Solely or mainly Soviet (within bloc)	Other
Afghanistan						X		..
Albania								
Algeria						X		
Angola						X		
Argentina			X					
Australia	X		X					
Austria			X					
Bahrain								
Bangladesh				X				
Barbados								Mainly UK
Belgium	X							
Benin						X		
Bolivia								Mainly 'others'
Botswana						X		
Brazil			X					
Bulgaria							X	
Burkina Faso								Mainly 'other'
Burma								Mainly 'others'
Burundi								
Cambodia							X	
Cameroon			X					
Canada	X							
Cape Verde							X	
Central African Republic								Mainly France
Chad								Mainly France
Chile			X					
China				X				
Colombia								
Congo							X	Mainly FRG
Costa Rica	X							

Country	Arms suppliers							
	Solely or mainly US (within bloc)	Mainly US (cross-bloc)	Multiple source (within West)	Multiple source (cross-bloc)	Multiple source (within East)	Mainly Soviet (cross-bloc)	Solely or mainly Soviet (within bloc)	Other
Cuba					X			
Cyprus								Mainly 'others'
Czechoslovakia							X	
Denmark	X							
Dominican Republic			X					
Ecuador			X					
Egypt				X				
El Salvador	X							
Equatorial Guinea								Predom. 'others'
Ethiopia						X		
Fiji								..
Finland				X				
FR Germany	X							
France	X							
Gabon								Mainly France
Gambia								..
German DR							X	
Ghana			X					
Greece				X				
Guatemala				X				
Guinea							X	Mainly 'others'
Guinea-Bissau						X		
Guyana			X					
Haiti			X					
Honduras			X					
Hungary							X	
Iceland								..
India			X	X				
Indonesia				X				
Iran				X				
Iraq				X				
Ireland								Mainly UK

Arms suppliers

Country	Solely or mainly US (within bloc)	Mainly US (cross-bloc)	Multiple source (within West)	Multiple source (cross-bloc)	Multiple source (within East)	Mainly Soviet (cross-bloc)	Solely or mainly Soviet (within bloc)	Other
Israel	X							
Italy	X							
Ivory Coast								Mainly France
Jamaica	X							
Japan	X							
Jordan				X				
Kenya		X						
North Korea					X			
South Korea	X							
Kuwait				X				
Laos							X	
Lebanon			X					Mainly 'others'
Lesotho			X					
Liberia	X		X					
Libya	X							
Luxembourg	X							
Madagascar						X		
Malawi			X					Mainly France
Malaysia			X					
Mali							X	Mainly 'others'
Malta							X	Mainly 'others'
Mauritania								
Mauritius			X					
Mexico			X					
Mongolia							X	
Morocco			X					
Mozambique			X					
Nepal	X							
Netherlands	X							
New Zealand						X		
Nicaragua			X					
Niger								..

Country	Arms suppliers							
	Solely or mainly US (within bloc)	Mainly US (cross-bloc)	Multiple source (within West)	Multiple source (cross-bloc)	Multiple source (within East)	Mainly Soviet (cross-bloc)	Solely or mainly Soviet (within bloc)	Other
Nigeria				X				
Norway								
Oman			X					
Pakistan								Mainly 'others'
Panama								Mainly 'others'
Papua New Guinea								Mainly 'others'
Paraguay				X				
Peru				X				
Philippines	X							
Poland							X	
Portugal								
Qatar		X						Mainly France
Romania								Mainly France
Rwanda						X		
São Tomé & Príncipe								..
Saudi Arabia			X					
Senegal								Mainly France
Sierra Leone								Mainly France
Singapore	X							
Somalia		X						
South Africa								Mainly WTO
Soviet Union								
Spain			X					
Sri Lanka								Mainly 'others'
Sudan				X				
Suriname								Mainly 'others'
Swaziland								..
Sweden	X							
Switzerland	X							
Syria						X		
Taiwan	X							
Tanzania							X	

Arms suppliers

Country	Solely or mainly US (within bloc)	Mainly US (cross-bloc)	Multiple source (within West)	Multiple source (cross-bloc)	Multiple source (within East)	Mainly Soviet (cross-bloc)	Solely or mainly Soviet (within bloc)	Other
Thailand	X							
Togo								Mainly France
Trinidad & Tobago								..
Tunisia			X					
Turkey		X						
Uganda								Mainly 'others'
United Arab Emirates			X					
United Kingdom	X							
United States			X					
Uruguay			X					
Venezuela			X					
Viet Nam							X	
North Yemen				X				
South Yemen							X	
Yugoslavia				X				
Zaire				X				
Zambia				X				Mainly 'others'
Zimbabwe				X				

Source: ACDA, World Military Expenditures and Arms Transfers (US Government Printing Office: Washington, DC, 1987).

In a rare Third World case, the Seychelles apparently allows both Soviet naval visits and continued US use of a vital satellite control facility. These are exceptions to the rule.[35]

Mostly, the devising of a classification for basing access comes down to the question of a typology to describe the importance or magnitude of the FMP. Some nations host a variety of key facilities, for instance, Iceland and Italy provide the USA with access across the board for large and critical naval, air and C³I installations. At the other extreme, some nations may merely host one rather inconspicuous technical facility, perhaps a seismic detector, a space-tracking facility or a medical research laboratory; or they may allow periodic port visits or aircraft overflights on an *ad hoc*, case-by-case basis. There are various combinations in-between.

Of course—and this is reflected in the associated diplomacy—some host nations may be important to a major power just because they host one vital technical facility, particularly if the host's location could not easily be matched or duplicated by access elsewhere, or if a host is the only potential point of access for a major nation in an entire region. Cuba, for instance, provides the Soviet Union with irreplaceable SIGINT facilities; Ascension is a vital tanker base for the USA, and so on. After the fall of Iran, China became vital to the USA in hosting facilities used to monitor the telemetry of Soviet missile tests.

Somewhat arbitrarily, then, we utilize a three-way typology here, whereby basing hosts will be designated as of major, moderate or minor importance to the user nation. In the 'major' category are those countries which host large air and naval bases, or a variety of key facilities as, for example, is the case for Viet Nam (for the USSR) or the Philippines (for the USA). The 'moderate' category will apply to a host with a smaller number of diverse facilities or perhaps just one major one. The 'minor' category is residual for hosts to one or two inconspicuous or not irreplaceable facilities, or the regular provision of port visits and air staging rights, without a permanent military presence. Categorizations here may be somewhat arbitrary and arguable, unavoidably so.

Arms transfer and FMP patterns: congruence?

Cautionary warnings about the inconclusiveness of a causal relationship between arms supplier markets and basing access notwithstanding, the strong correlation between the two patterns is hard to gainsay. This may be slightly more the case on the Soviet side, but it stands out on the US side as well.

As table 36 shows, all of the nations providing major levels of basing access to the USSR are, without exception, in a sole or predominant arms supplier relationship with Moscow: Angola, Cuba, Ethiopia, Syria, Viet Nam, South Yemen and the several East European WTO states. This is also true of all the states which provide moderate levels of access: Afghanistan, Algeria, Cape Verde, Kampuchea, Laos, Libya, Madagascar, Mongolia, Mozambique, Nicaragua and North Korea.[36] Of these nations Algeria and Madagascar have acquired some arms from Western states in recent years (Algeria from the USA,

France and the UK, Madagascar from France), perhaps reflective of broader albeit cautious shifts in alignment. Libya has bought some of its weapons from France and Italy, relying on the leverage of its oil wealth which provides it some room for diplomatic manœuvre. It is also noteworthy that in the cases of Algeria and Libya, cross-bloc arms acquisitions have been associated with a limited and restrained granting of access to the USSR, particularly as concerns major air and naval facilities.

Of those countries which have provided minor levels of access to Moscow, all have acquired Soviet arms, but in many cases those acquisitions have been balanced by purchases from the West. India (port calls, overflights) purchases a lot of Soviet arms, but also deals with France, the UK and others. Peru (minor naval access) purchases some Soviet weapons, but the bulk of its arms come from France, Italy, FR Germany and the USA. Iraq (earlier port access) still acquires most of its weapons from Moscow, but significant amounts from France, Italy, Brazil, China and others. Guinea-Bissau (some naval access) receives some Soviet arms; Equatorial Guinea (former technical facility) has now shifted to other suppliers such as Spain. Tanzania grants Moscow some access, but has since the early 1970s bought the bulk of its arms from China. Benin has apparently provided some access while purchasing more French than Soviet weapons, but Soviet naval access to Mauritius in the 1980s has been associated with a sole-source arms relationship.[37] The same is true of the Congo, which provided airstaging for the USSR, particularly during the Angolan conflict in 1975–77.[38] North Yemen has bought mostly Soviet arms since the late-1970s, but has granted only limited access, perhaps because of countervailing Saudi pressures.[39] The Seychelles (some naval access) also continues to grant space-related access to the USA while purchasing some arms from the USSR, but more from Italy. Somalia, Sudan and Chad—particularly the former—once hosted a Soviet presence, but in these cases that has disappeared along with arms supplies in response to dramatic political reversals.

There are some nations which have acquired significant amounts of Soviet arms—usually in a cross-bloc pattern—but where military access has been very minimal or non-existent. Among those in this category are: Burundi (1970s), Kuwait (since the late 1970s), Iran (earlier under the Shah), Uganda (up to the late 1970s), Zambia (mid-1970s to the present), Nigeria (since the mid-1960s), Jordan (since the early 1980s), Pakistan (since the late 1960s) and Botswana (since the early 1980s). This list appears to incorporate a couple of discernible types of situation. There are oil-rich states (or their own allies and dependents)—Kuwait, Iran, Jordan and Nigeria—which can increase their leverage with the West but without compromising their own independence in the process, and where ideological ties to Moscow are non-existent. Then, there are small, land-locked African states—Zambia, Botswana, Uganda and Burundi—to which the USSR simply may not need or desire access, or where the possible costs in terms of anxieties in surrounding states may outweigh whatever benefit limited access might provide.

All in all, however, the fit between access and arms transfer patterns involving

Soviet client states is obviously fairly tight, perhaps more so than where US arms and access are involved. The ties that bind in the form of ideology and regime structure would appear to be explanatory here by way of cautious inference. Needless to say, this applies *ipso facto* to the facts of the massive Soviet presence in Eastern Europe and Mongolia.

In the US case too, basing access has, far more often than not, been associated with arms transfers. There are both a larger number of arms recipients and a larger number of basing hosts, whereas by contrast, an overall roughly equivalent volume of Soviet arms sales has long been concentrated among a smaller number of buyers.[40]

In Western Europe, of course, two of the major hosts of US facilities—the UK and FR Germany—produce much of their own weaponry, but the USA is the main supplier of the remainder. As table 36 shows, Washington is similarly the most significant purveyor of arms to Belgium, Denmark, Greece, Italy, Luxembourg, Netherlands, Norway, Portugal, Spain and Turkey. But Greece also purchases heavily from FR Germany and Italy (and a little from the USSR), Turkey from FR Germany and the UK, Portugal from FR Germany and France, and Spain from France in particular. One can see the trend towards arms diversification (within NATO) most clearly in those places where the pressures towards decoupling have been most strongly felt. (Iceland purchases no arms, so pressures there have been divorced from the arms markets.) The same pattern has held for Australia and New Zealand, but almost all of Canada's external purchases are from the USA. Outside NATO and ANZUS, the key providers of basing access to the USA—the Philippines, Japan, South Korea—all purchase the bulk of their arms from the USA.

Table 36. Summary of the arms transfer/FMP nexus for the USSR and the USA, 1981–85

Foreign/host nation	Arms suppliers
(a) The USSR	
Major FMP hosts	
Angola	Mainly USSR, some 'other'
Bulgaria	Mainly USSR, some Poland, FRG
Cuba	Mainly USSR, some 'other'
Czechoslovakia	Mainly USSR, some Poland
Ethiopia	Mainly USSR, some 'other'
German DR	Mainly USSR, some Poland, Czechoslovakia
Hungary	Mainly USSR, some Czechoslovakia, Poland, 'other'
Poland	Mainly USSR, some Czechoslovakia
South Yemen	Mainly USSR, some 'other'
Syria	Mainly USSR, some 'other'
Viet Nam	Solely USSR
Moderate FMP hosts	
Afghanistan	Mainly USSR, some 'other'
Algeria	Multiple source: USSR, USA, France, UK
Cape Verde	Solely USSR
Kampuchea	Solely USSR
Laos	Solely USSR

Foreign/host nation	Arms suppliers
Libya	Mainly USSR, some France, Italy
Madagascar	Mainly USSR, some France, 'other'
Mongolia	Solely USSR
Mozambique	Solely USSR
Nicaragua	Mainly USSR, some France, 'other'
North Korea	Mainly USSR, some China, 'other'

Minor FMP hosts

Benin	Multiple source: France, USSR, 'other'
Congo	Solely USSR
Equatorial Guinea	Mainly 'other', some USSR
Greece	Multiple source: USA, FRG, Italy, USSR, France, 'other'
Guinea-Bissau	Mainly 'other', some USSR, China, France
India	Mainly USSR, some UK, France, USA
Iraq	Multiple source: USSR, France, Italy, China, Brazil, 'other'
Mauritius	Solely USSR
North Yemen	Mainly USSR, some USA, 'other'
Peru	Multiple source: France, Italy, USA, USSR, FRG
Romania	Multiple source: USSR, UK, Czechoslovakia, France
São Tomé & Príncipe	..
Seychelles	Mainly Italy, some USSR, 'other'
Tanzania	Mainly China, some Italy, USA, 'other'
Yugoslavia	Multiple source: USSR, USA, France, 'other'

(b) The USA

Major FMP hosts

Australia	Mainly USA, some UK, FRG, France, Italy
Canada	Mainly USA, some UK
Denmark (Greenland)	Mainly USA, some France, UK, Italy
FR Germany	Mainly USA, some UK, France, Italy
Greece	Multiple source: USA, FRG, Italy, USSR, France
Iceland	..
Italy	Mainly USA, some France
Japan	Mainly USA, some FRG
Luxembourg	Mainly USA
Norway	Mainly USA, some UK, FRG, France
Philippines	Mainly USA, some FRG, UK, 'other'
Portugal (Azores)	Multiple source: USA, FRG, France, UK
South Korea	Mainly USA, some France, UK
Spain	Multiple source: USA, France, FRG, Italy, UK
Turkey	Multiple source: USA, FRG, UK, France
United Kingdom	Mainly USA, some France

Moderate FMP hosts

Bahrain	Multiple source: FRG, USA, France, UK
Belgium	Mainly USA, some France, FRG
China	Multiple source: France, USSR, USA, FRG
Cyprus	Mainly France, some 'other'
Djibouti	Solely France
Honduras	Mainly USA, some France, 'other'
Kenya	Multiple source: UK, France, USA, Italy
Morocco	Multiple source: France, USA, Italy, UK, FRG
Netherlands	Mainly USA, some FRG, UK, Italy, France
New Zealand	Mainly USA, some FRG, UK
Oman	Mainly UK, some FRG, France, USA, China, Italy
Panama	Mainly USA, some 'other'
Singapore	Mainly USA, some France, UK, Italy, 'other'
Somalia	Mainly USA, some China, Italy, 'other'

Foreign/host nation	Arms suppliers
Minor FMP hosts	
Antigua	. .
Argentina	Multiple source: FRG, France, UK, USA, Italy, 'other'
Bahamas	Solely UK
Belize	Solely UK
Bolivia	Mainly France, some USA, 'other'
Botswana	Multiple source: USA, USSR, France, UK
Brazil	Multiple source: FRG, France, Italy, USA, 'other'
Chile	Multiple source: UK, FRG, France, USA
Colombia	Mainly FRG, some USA, France, UK, 'other'
Costa Rica	Solely USA
Ecuador	Multiple source: Italy, France, USA, UK, 'other'
Egypt	Mainly USA, some China, France, UK, Italy, 'other'
El Salvador	Mainly USA, some France, 'other'
France (Réunion)	Mainly USA, some UK
Indonesia	Multiple source: USA, FRG, UK, France, 'other'
Israel	Solely USA
Kuwait	Multiple source: France, USA, FRG, UK, USSR
Lebanon	Mainly USA, some France, 'other'
Liberia	Mainly USA
Malaysia	Multiple source: FRG, USA, Italy, UK, France
Pakistan	Mainly USA, some China, France, UK
Paraguay	Mainly 'other', Third World
Peru	Multiple source: France, Italy, USA, FRG, USSR, 'other'
Saudi Arabia	Mainly USA, some France, UK
Senegal	Mainly France, some 'other'
Seychelles	Mainly Italy, some USSR, 'other'
Sri Lanka	Mainly UK, some 'other'
Sudan	Mainly USA, some FRG, UK, Italy, China, 'other'
Taiwan	Mainly USA, some 'other'
Thailand	Mainly USA, some Italy, UK, China, France
Tunisia	Multiple source: USA, France, 'other'

Source: ACDA, *World Military Expenditures and Arms Transfers* (US Government Printing Office: Washington, DC, 1987); and Brzoska, M. and Ohlson, T., SIPRI, *Arms Transfers to the Third World: 1971–85* (Oxford University Press: Oxford, 1987).

Among the providers of moderate but significant levels of access to US forces, the same patterns generally hold, but one can see more diversified patterns of weapon purchases. Bahrain's (naval access) main recent supplier has been FR Germany, and Morocco's (SIGINT, VOA) has been France. Kenya (naval and air access) relies heavily on London, Paris and Rome as well as Washington. Oman (air and naval access) has purchased arms more from the UK and FR Germany than from the USA, while Somalia has relied increasingly on Italy and China. But the USA is Singapore's largest supplier, followed by France, the UK and Italy. Honduras has relied significantly on Israel as well as the USA. China (SIGINT stations) produces most of its own weapons but does import from the USA, France, and others.

Of those nations providing only relatively minor levels of military access to the USA, there is a mixture of both strong and less significant arms sales relationships; it is clear from table 36 that there are also some cases where such purchases are divided between the West and the Soviet bloc and/or China.

Among those in this category which are very heavily reliant on US weapons are: Israel, Egypt, Taiwan, Thailand, Tunisia (split with France), Saudi Arabia (also France and the UK), Costa Rica, El Salvador, Lebanon (also France) and Liberia. Some nations hosting minor US facilities acquire the bulk of their arms elsewhere: Colombia (FR Germany), Chile (France, the UK and FR Germany), Bahamas (UK), Argentina (FR Germany and France), Brazil (FR Germany, France and Italy), Indonesia (France, FR Germany and the UK), Ecuador (from France and Italy), Senegal (from France), Seychelles (from Italy), Sudan (FR Germany and China), Sri Lanka (UK and others), and so on. Kuwait buys some Soviet arms and Pakistan buys a significant volume from China. A number of these situations are in Latin America, where US arms were once dominant, despite a low US military profile, but where the existence of a small number of US research or other technical facilities (Bolivia, Colombia, Ecuador and Paraguay) is now associated with the predominance of West European arms suppliers.[41] Iran under the Shah was the prime example of significant US FMP juxtaposed to a fairly significant flow of Soviet arms—again, oil leverage is explanatory.

There are some cases where a predominant or very significant US role as arms supplier has been associated with very little or no military access: the Dominican Republic, Guatemala, Haiti, Jamaica, Jordan, Niger, Trinidad and Tobago, and Uganda (recently). Obvious political cross-pressures preclude extensive US access in at least one of these cases (Jordan), while either lack of requirements (i.e., alternative access in nearby states) and/or nationalist sensibilities would presumably provide explanations in several other cases.

Regarding the two other major powers which utilize fairly extensive foreign access—France and the UK—there is also somewhat of a correlation with arms sales patterns, more so in the case of the former. France is a major supplier of arms to the several Francophone African states where it maintains a military presence: Cameroon, the Central African Republic, Chad, Djibouti, Gabon, the Ivory Coast and Senegal; also (where its access is limited) in Mauritania, Niger and Togo. But it is important to note that France is a significant arms seller to numerous nations throughout the world where it *does not* have such access: Algeria, Argentina, Bahrain, Bolivia, Brazil, Burundi, Chile, Congo, Ecuador, India, Indonesia, Iraq, Jordan, Kenya, Kuwait, Lebanon, Libya, Morocco, Nigeria, Oman, Peru, Qatar, Rwanda, Saudi Arabia, Sierra Leone, Singapore, Tunisia, United Arab Emirates, Uruguay, Venezuela, and still others. Among the numerous states which acquire British arms, only two— Belize and Oman—provide military access.

West German, Italian and other European arms sales are totally divorced from basing diplomacy. This point and the above discussion of Britain and France merely remind us of the typology provided by a 1972, seminal SIPRI work on arms transfers, wherein the distinction between 'hegemonic' (geo-political) and 'commercial' national styles of arms supply are discussed.[42] For the USA and the USSR, arms transfers are, more often than not, closely tied to basing access or, more broadly, to the diplomacy of global security alignments. By contrast, whereas some French and British arms sales—mostly to former colonial states—are tied to access, the vast bulk of them have primarily commercial underpinnings, and are conducted where FMP (other than training personnel associated with the arms transfers) is neither desired, sought nor welcomed.[43]

One other point bears mention here in connection with the relationship between arms supplies and FMP. The above discussion focuses entirely on the *relative* proportions of a recipient nation's arms acquisitions which are accounted for by various suppliers; hence too, the breakdown into sole, main and multiple-source acquisition styles. *Absolute* volumes of arms transfers may also be important, but large countries acquire more arms and may also be more likely, in many cases, to provide a diverse collection of facilities to one of the major powers. These are (statistically) complicated matters, beyond the scope of this work.

It is worth reiterating that, in some cases, a major power which can attain the position of sole or predominant arms supplier to a small state may thereby gain access for one or a few critical facilities, particularly C^3I or other technical facilities which require neither much space nor a particular type of terrain or topography, that is, a harbour or room for an airstrip. Hence, the arms acquisition patterns of states such as Mauritius, the Seychelles or Cyprus can become rather interesting. The USSR, on the other hand, has established FMP in a relatively small number of states by pouring in massive weapon supplies (in relation to the size of those states) that are in turn underpinned by Moscow's mammoth annual arms production in most categories of weapons such as tanks, artillery pieces, SAMs, and so on. On the US side too, it is noteworthy that relatively modest levels of arms supplies to nations such as Honduras, Kenya, Oman, Singapore, Somalia, Thailand, and so on, have resulted in access to some vital pieces of terrain.

III. Security assistance policies: the trend towards commercialization of FMP

The above analysis of the relationship between FMP and arms sales policy is in accordance with the somewhat esoteric conceptual terminology of contemporary international relations theory, at the 'systems level of analysis'. At that level, we deal for the most part with aggregate data and with 'transactions' between arms suppliers and recipients, and base users and hosts. At another level, one can examine national policies as viewed from the inside. On a much larger scale, this could involve analysis of the bureaucratic and interest group politics of numerous users and providers of basing access, and of decision-making in general. Given the limitations of space, we devote some attention here to the recent FMP policies of the USA and the USSR, both treated for the most part as 'unitary actors', that is, without particular attention to the respective domestic and organizational politics in Washington and Moscow that are involved in this area.

The above analysis also examines arms transfers without reference to the nature of, or basis of, those transfers; specifically, the relative trade and aid components involved. Proceeding to an examination of the aid component—often discussed under the rubric of 'security assistance'—allows us to focus on the extent to which the major powers have utilized such aid as an instrument in acquiring and retaining foreign access at a time, as noted, when such access has often been put on a more commercial basis.

On the US side, the mid-1980s saw increasing attention—reflected in numerous press reports and scholarly writings—being given to the use of security assistance in acquiring or retaining access to foreign facilities.[44] This attention has been focused, as noted, by the increasing restrictions and costs associated with the US overseas basing structure, particularly with regard to several key nations which host US facilities:[45] Portugal, Spain, Greece, Turkey, the Philippines (the issue of 'decoupling' exemplified by the New Zealand case involves separate matters, albeit related in the sense of being one more aspect of an overall trend towards a more restricted climate for basing). Then too, as the Reagan era proceeded towards a climax, Washington's economic problems—the falling dollar, budget deficits, trade deficits, etc.—resulted in massive pressures on the defence budget itself, and also on the always (politically) insecure security assistance budget. As the assistance levels for Egypt and Israel—justified as an underpinning for the Camp David accords—remained sacrosanct and intact, the reductions in security assistance had to come from elsewhere. By 1988, that was placing tremendous pressures on the USA's ability to sustain that part of the security assistance budget intended to support its critical FMP, particularly in the key nations mentioned above, some of which were, for other reasons, becoming more reluctant to provide Washington with continued access at the same levels.

US economic and military assistance for fiscal year 1988

As revealed by the fiscal year (FY) 1988 *Congressional Presentation for Security Assistance Programs*, and as explained in the framework of US global strategy, the US security assistance budget was based on six broad policy goals:

1. To promote peace in the Middle East;
2. To enhance co-operative defence and security;
3. To deter and combat aggression;
4. To promote regional stability;
5. To promote key interests through Foreign Military Sales (FMS), cash sales and commercial military exports; and
6. To promote professional military relationships through grant training.[46]

The FY 1988 security assistance programme budget, as submitted to the US Congress by the Reagan Administration, is given in table 37 and provides the basis for a discussion of its relationship to the USA's current FMP diplomacy.

Although all of these categories impinge in one way or another on access matters, the second-, third- and fourth-named are most crucial in this context, particularly the second.

The promotion of peace in the Middle East

Four countries have been involved in this policy goal—Egypt, Israel, Jordan and Lebanon—none of which has provided the USA with major basing access (Egypt has allowed port visits, large-scale joint manœuvres and air staging access; and Israel has allowed port visits, a VOA transmitter, hospital contingency access, etc.). But the $5.2 billion annual budget in this area now accounts for more than half the US global annual total of some $9.4 billion in economic and military assistance.

Enhancing co-operative defence and security

The second category involves 13 countries, all of them significant hosts of a US military presence which, increasingly, has had to be underpinned by security assistance, whether or not formally defined as 'rent'. As indicated, the total aid figure of some $2.3 billion is less than half that devoted to supporting Middle East peace efforts, and it is here that the US security assistance budget has been put under pressure. The heart of the justification in the congressional presentation reads as follows:

In NATO and elsewhere in the world, countries with whom this country has significant security assistance relationships provide the United States with basing, transit, overflight, port call and exercise facilities—most often near strategic air and sea lines of communications. Some make available sites for invaluable military navigation and communications operations. Without these facilities, the United States could not reach or cover some areas of the globe with our strategic airlift, tactical fighter wings, and seaborne units. In their absence, the United States would have to develop a much larger lift and underway replenishment capacity than it has today.

For example, the bases at Subic Bay in the Philippines and Rota, Spain give the United States the capability to offload aircraft directly from a carrier onto an air station for major repair or training. U.S. ability to project power in defence of the strategic sea and air lines of communication in the Pacific and Indian Oceans directly depends, in fact, on access to the base facilities in the Philippines. Similarly, U.S. cooperation with Oman supports the shared goal of maintaining security, stability and freedom of navigation in the Persian Gulf, especially in the vital Straits of Hormuz. In Panama, our security arrangements are embodied in the Canal treaties and are designed to protect that strategic waterway.

The host countries generally see their cooperation in making such facilities available to U.S. forces and the security assistance provided by the United States as reciprocal manifestations of a security partnership; there is, sometimes, an explicit linkage. Security assistance, therefore, makes a major contribution to U.S. power projection capabilities and forward deployment strategy.[47]

As indicated by table 37, there is virtually a two-tiered breakdown of the countries in this category. Those receiving aid up in the hundreds of millions of

Table 37. US Security Assistance Programs for FY 1988
Figures are in $ thousands.

Security Assistance Program	Economic support	FMS financing		MAP (grants)	IMETP (grants)	PKO	Total
		Treasury	Concessional				
Promote Middle East peace:							
Egypt	815 000	0	1 300 000[a]	0	1 750	0	2 116 750
Israel	1 200 000	0	1 800 000[a]	0	0	0	3 000 000
Jordan	18 000	0	12 000	40 000	1 800	0	71 800
Lebanon	300	0	0	0	475	0	775
Middle East regional	20 000	0	0	0	0	0	20 000
Total	**2 053 300**	**0**	**3 112 000**	**40 000**	**4 025**	**0**	**5 209 325**
Enhance cooperative defense and security:							
Djibouti	3 000	0	0	2 000	135	0	5 135
Greece	0	0	435 000	0	1 250	0	436 250
Kenya	17 000	0	0	19 000	1 600	0	37 600
Liberia	17 000	0	0	3 000	900	0	20 900
Morocco	20 000	0	0	50 000	1 450	0	71 450
Oman	20 000	0	5 150	0	150	0	25 300
Panama	10 000	0	0	3 000	600	0	13 600
Philippines	124 000	0	0	110 000	2 600	0	236 600
Portugal	80 000	0	40 000	85 000	2 550	0	207 550
Somalia	23 000	0	0	22 000	1 250	0	46 250
Spain	12 000	0	265 000	0	3 000	0	280 000
Sudan	18 000	0	0	10 000	1 000	0	29 000
Turkey	125 000	0	235 000	550 000	3 500	0	913 500
Total	**469 000**	**0**	**980 150**	**854 000**	**19 985**	**0**	**2 323 135**
Deter and combat aggression:							
Cambodian Resistance	5 000	0	0	0	0	0	5 000
Chad	5 000	0	0	9 000	200	0	14 200
Costa Rica	90 000	0	0	2 000	450	0	92 450
El Salvador	200 000	0	0	118 000	1 875	0	319 875
Honduras	100 000	0	0	80 000	1 530	0	181 530
Korea	0	0	0	0	2 000	0	2 000

Security Assistance Program	Economic support	FMS financing		MAP (grants)	IMETP (grants)	PKO	Total
		Treasury	Concessional				
Pakistan	250 000	0	290 000	0	915	0	540 915
Thailand	5 000	0	10 000	50 000	2 200	0	67 200
Tunisia	20 000	0	0	40 000	1 450	0	61 450
Yemen	0	0	0	3 000	1 100	0	4 100
Total	**675 000**	**0**	**300 000**	**302 000**	**11 720**	**0**	**1 288 720**
Promote regional stability:							
Afghan Humanitarian	15 000	0	0	0	0	0	15 000
Africa Civic Action/Health	0	0	0	6 000	0	0	6 000
Antigua-Barbuda	0	0	0	1 850	50	0	1 900
Barbados	0	0	0	850	70	0	920
Belize	2 000	0	0	1 000	70	0	3 070
Bolivia	30 000	0	0	8 000	400	0	38 400
Botswana	0	0	0	5 000	335	0	5 335
Burma	0	0	0	0	260	0	260
Cameroon	0	0	2 500	0	250	0	2 750
Central African Republic	0	0	0	1 000	125	0	1 125
Central America Regional	20 000	0	0	0	0	0	20 000
Colombia	0	0	0	7 500	1 400	0	8 900
Cyprus	10 000	0	0	0	0	0	10 000
Dominica	0	0	0	850	50	0	900
Dominican Republic	35 000	0	0	2 000	1 000	0	38 000
Eastern Caribbean	25 000	0	0	0	0	0	25 000
Ecuador	17 000	0	0	7 500	950	0	25 450
Equatorial Guinea	0	0	0	1 000	75	0	1 075
Fiji	1 500	0	0	300	100	0	1 900
Gabon	0	0	2 500	0	150	0	2 650
Grenada	0	0	0	850	80	0	930
Guatemala	80 000	0	0	7 000	600	0	87 600
Guinea	0	0	0	3 000	150	0	3 150
Haiti	30 000	0	0	4 000	550	0	34 550
Indonesia	0	0	20 000	0	2 000	0	22 000
Jamaica	45 000	0	0	6 000	300	0	51 300
Latin America and Caribbean regional	6 000	0	0	0	0	0	6 000
Madagascar	0	0	0	1 000	75	0	1 075

Security Assistance Program	Economic support	FMS financing		MAP (grants)	IMETP (grants)	PKO	Total
		Treasury	Concessional				
Malawi	0	0	0	1 000	200	0	1 200
Malaysia	0	0	4 000	0	1 000	0	5 000
Niger	0	0	0	3 000	250	0	3 250
Peru	10 000	0	0	3 000	700	0	13 700
S. Pacific regional fisheries development	1 500	0	0	0	0	0	1 500
S. Pacific Tuna Treaty	10 000	0	0	0	0	0	10 000
S. Pacific oceanographic research	200	0	0	0	0	0	200
Senegal	14 000	0	0	2 000	475	0	16 475
Seychelles	3 000	0	0	0	35	0	3 035
St Christopher-Nevis	0	0	0	850	50	0	900
St Lucia	0	0	0	850	50	0	900
St Vincent and Grenadines	0	0	0	900	50	0	950
Uruguay	0	0	0	1 500	125	0	1 625
Zaire	0	0	0	10 000	1 300	0	11 300
Zimbabwe	0	0	0	0	175	0	175
Total	**355 200**	**0**	**29 000**	**87 800**	**13 450**	**0**	**485 450**
Promote key interests through foreign military cash sales/commercial exports:							
Algeria	0	0	0	0	100	0	100
Argentina	0	0	0	0	50	0	50
Austria	0	0	0	0	60	0	60
Brazil	0	0	0	0	50	0	50
Finland	0	0	0	0	60	0	60
India	0	0	0	0	500	0	500
Ireland	35 000	0	0	0	30	0	35 030
Luxembourg	0	0	0	0	30	0	30
Mexico	0	0	0	0	275	0	275
Paraguay	0	0	0	0	150	0	150
Singapore	0	0	0	0	50	0	50
Venezuela	0	0	0	0	200	0	200
Yugoslavia	0	0	0	0	100	0	100
Total	**35 000**	**0**	**0**	**0**	**1 655**	**0**	**36 655**
Promote professional military relationships through grant training:							
Bahamas	0	0	0	0	100	0	100

Security Assistance Program	Economic support	FMS financing		MAP (grants)	IMETP (grants)	PKO	Total
		Treasury	Concessional				
Bangladesh	0	0	0	0	300	0	300
Benin	0	0	0	0	75	0	75
Burkina Faso	0	0	0	0	50	0	50
Burundi	0	0	0	0	140	0	140
Cape Verde	0	0	0	0	50	0	50
Chile	0	0	0	0	50	0	50
Comoros	0	0	0	0	40	0	40
Congo	0	0	0	0	40	0	40
Gambia	0	0	0	0	60	0	60
Ghana	0	0	0	0	225	0	225
Guinea-Bissau	0	0	0	0	30	0	30
Guyana	0	0	0	0	50	0	50
Iceland	0	0	0	0	40	0	40
Ivory Coast	0	0	0	0	150	0	150
Lesotho	0	0	0	0	50	0	50
Maldives	0	0	0	0	30	0	30
Mali	0	0	0	0	150	0	150
Mauritania	0	0	0	0	75	0	75
Nepal	0	0	0	0	100	0	100
Nigeria	0	0	0	0	100	0	100
Pacams	0	0	0	0	2 100	0	2 100
Papua New Guinea	0	0	0	0	50	0	50
Rwanda	0	0	0	0	75	0	75
Sao Tome	0	0	0	0	50	0	50
Sierra Leone	0	0	0	0	70	0	70
Solomon Islands	0	0	0	0	30	0	30
Sri Lanka	0	0	0	0	160	0	160
Suriname	0	0	0	0	50	0	50
Swaziland	0	0	0	0	50	0	50
Tanzania	0	0	0	0	35	0	35
Togo	0	0	0	0	60	0	60
Tonga	0	0	0	0	50	0	50

Security Assistance Program	Economic support	FMS financing		MAP (grants)	IMETP (grants)	PKO	Total
		Treasury	Concessional				
Trinidad and Tobago	0	0	0	0	50	0	50
Uganda	0	0	0	0	100	0	100
Total	**0**	**0**	**0**	**0**	**4 835**	**0**	**4 835**
Other:							
Deob/Reob authority	12 500	0	0	0	0	0	12 500
General costs	0	0	0	46 000	330	0	46 330
Multinational force and observers (MFO)	0	0	0	0	0	35 623	35 623
UN forces in Cyprus	0	0	0	0	0	10 688	10 688
Total	**12 500**	**0**	**0**	**46 000**	**330**	**46 311**	**105 141**
Total budget authority	**3 600 000**	**0**	**4 421 150**	**1 329 800**	**56 000**	**46 311**	**9 453 261**

a Repayment forgiven.

FMS: Foreign Military Sales; MAP: Military Assistance Program; IMETP: International Military Education and Training Program; PKO: Peacekeeping Operations.

Source: United States of America, *Congressional Presentation for Security Assistance Programs: Fiscal Year 1988* (US Government Printing Office: Washington, DC, 1987), pp. 4–6.

dollars—Greece, Philippines, Portugal, Spain and Turkey—have come to be thought of as constituting the heart of the US problem, where 'rents' are involved. The others involve smaller sums, and also an identifiable sub-grouping—Djibouti, Kenya, Morocco, Oman and Somalia—related to power projection problems in connection with South-West Asia.

All of the five largest recipients in this category have constituted major political problems for the USA in recent years. Turkey was earlier angry over US aid restrictions after its invasion of Cyprus,[48] while Greece's relations with Washington have soured during the era of Prime Minister Andreas Papandreou, who has periodically threatened to close all US bases.[49] US access to Portugal's Azores was earlier threatened after the overthrow of the Salazar regime and the subsequent political turmoil;[50] similarly, access was threatened in the wake of the overthrow of the Marcos Government in the Philippines.[51] Spain has recently moved to curtail US access; specifically that for the 72 F-16s based at Torrejon, in response to domestic pressures.[52]

Table 38. US aid to countries with US bases, 1980–88
Figures are in US $m.

Country	Fiscal year								
	1980	1981	1982	1983	1984	1985	1986	1987	1988[a]
Turkey	402.3	451.6	708.0	753.0	856.6	878.1	738.0	593.3	569.5
Greece	146.2	177.6	281.2	281.2	501.4	501.4	431.9	344.3	344.3
Spain	129.0	129.5	149.0	414.1	414.4	414.5	396.6	113.0	120.0
Portugal	110.9	88.8	87.4	112.0	147.9	208.0	188.9	147.4	147.4
Philippines	152.6	168.1	206.8	205.8	211.1	268.1	484.7	471.8	289.0[b]

[a] Subcommittee recommendation.
[b] Supplemental funding is expected.

Source: *Wall Street Journal*, 29 Dec. 1987, p. 5.

Amid these continuing political pressures, the security assistance budgets for these countries have not fared well of late because of the domestic economic pressures playing havoc with the Reagan Administration's security policies. The progression of this problem through the Reagan years is shown in table 38. It shows security assistance to these nations as having peaked in 1984–86, then having dropped, dramatically so. Thus, according to the accompanying *Wall Street Journal* article,

. . . foreign assistance has never been popular on Capitol Hill, where legislators have other priorities closer to home. Now, in the face of relentless pressure to cut U.S. spending, legislators resent efforts by foreign governments to raise the price of retaining bases. The administration requested $912 million for Turkey for last year, but Congress approved only $490 million. Overall, the administration requested $2.1 billion for the five basing countries, and Congress approved $1.4 billion.[53]

That is not to say, however, that levels of security assistance are all that is involved in determining the willingness of countries in this category to continue to provide access for US forces. There are also more subtle, psychological and political underpinnings to these relationships, some of them related to unique and idiosyncratic historical circumstances. While discussing these matters with academics and journalists in Spain in 1988, for instance (in the wake of the Spanish Government's withdrawal of access for US F-16s at Torrejon), the author became very much aware of the role played by US support for former President Franco up to 1975 in shaping Spanish sensibilities; similarly the legacy of Spain's defeat by the USA in the war of 1898. Money was rarely mentioned. In Turkey, on the other hand, money seems more important, but here too, other issues are involved: US handling of the Greco-Turkish dispute and of the Kurdish human rights problems, the US role in easing Turkish entry into the EEC, and so on.

Deterring and combatting aggression

Among the countries to which aid is granted to meet this third policy goal— 'deterring and combatting aggression' (i.e., US clients deemed to be immediately threatened by neighbours in regional conflicts)—several nations host important US facilities, particularly South Korea and, to a lesser degree, Thailand, Honduras and perhaps Pakistan. Several other nations in this category—Chad, Costa Rica, Tunisia and Yemen—do not host such a presence.

The promotion of regional stability

In the next category, a vague catch-all advertised as having to do with 'promoting regional stability', there are a number of nations which host minor US facilities or related forms of access: Antigua-Barbuda, Belize, Bolivia, Cyprus, Ecuador, Senegal and the Seychelles. There are also a number of neutral nations which do not host FMP. Curiously, there are also several nations which have provided some access to the USSR: Equatorial Guinea (earlier), Guinea, Madagascar, Peru and the Seychelles.

The promotion of key interests through FMS cash sales and commercial military exports

This category includes only some $36 million of total assistance to 13 countries, comprising a diverse mix of states moderately friendly to the USA (Argentina and Brazil), neutral states (Ireland, Austria, Finland and Yugoslavia) and even states such as India and Algeria which have leaned towards Soviet clientship. Most of the aid goes to Ireland. Of the remaining recipients, only Singapore provides some military access to the USA, that is, staging rights for P-3 ocean-reconnaissance aircraft.

The promotion of professional military relationships through grant training

The list of nations supported to meet this goal includes Benin, Cape Verde, Congo, Guinea-Bissau, Mali, São Tomé and Tanzania, all nations reputed at times to have provided some military access to the USSR, albeit in all cases limited. The security assistance here proferred by Washington, much of it involving token numbers, may perhaps in part be viewed as an effort at 'base denial', that is, at weaning some client states away from Moscow's orbit. This usually involves states which have undergone recent political shifts which might predispose them to change their policies on the granting of external access.

Other factors determining access: varieties of quid pro quo

The above discussions of arms transfers and security assistance do not, however, capture all that may be involved in the quid-pro-quo bargaining over the terms of access. There are many other possibilities: the qualitative aspects of arms transfers; sharing of intelligence information; a variety of possibilities falling under the general heading of economic assistance, including offsets; assistance to indigenous weapon production programmes; diplomatic support; even a reversal of the normal flow of aid from user to host as another type of offset. The possibilities are as numerous and as open-ended as are the ongoing varieties of transactions and bargaining elements between nations, details of which are not always available. And, indeed, the precise nature of what is involved in the granting of access to a facility or of overflights may in many instances never be known. Some arrangements, whether the whole story or not, are made public in formal documents. Others are the results of secret conversations and covenants, which may just possibly one day be made available to historians.

Regarding qualitative levels of arming, it is obvious that in some cases, mere quantification of arms transfers will not tell the whole story. Arms transfer diplomacy, as so often connected to access diplomacy, may also involve the level of sophistication of aircraft or tanks transferred or, for instance, what types of weapon and electronic warfare gear may be put on a platform such as an aircraft or a ship. Such matters have entered into negotiations over US sales of AWACS and F-15s to Saudi Arabia (in the latter case involving conformal fuel tanks, certain kinds of bomb rack, numbers of air-to-surface weapons, etc.), and no doubt figure heavily in associated bargaining over access.[54] The qualitative character of aircraft transfers from the USSR to North Korea has certainly figured in bargaining over enhanced Soviet access.[55] Earlier, the USA had engaged in similar bargaining with the Philippines regarding aircraft, and with Morocco over the nature of counter-insurgency *matériel* for use against the Polisario guerrillas.[56] In recent years, renewed US efforts to re-acquire access for technical facilities in Pakistan have coincided with bargaining over sales of advanced attack aircraft to Islamabad.[57] There may not always be an explicit tie here to access but, unavoidably, the quality of arms transfers is an important part of the context for base negotiations.

The degree of US assistance to burgeoning 'indigenous' weapon production programmes—perhaps involving licensed or assembly production—can also be at issue. An earlier US Defense Cooperation Agreement with Turkey—which provided for renewal of agreements for US access to important communications and intelligence facilities—explicitly committed US assistance to the development of Turkey's arms industries, which has now eventuated in co-production rights for the F-16 fighter. It also involved a commitment by the

US Government to provide, without cost to Turkey, access to the Defense Satellite Communications System.[58]

There have been other 'service-funded' projects used by the USA to facilitate base negotiations. Earlier, the USA agreed to contribute up to $50 million for modernizing an aircraft control and warning network on a matching basis with the Spanish Air Force.[59] In the case of Greece, pre-Papandreou, the US National Aeronautics and Space Administration (NASA) agreed to provide surveillance equipment worth $5.5 million.[60] While such projects may appear minor, they can play an important role in the later stages of negotiations because they are tailored to specific high-priority host country interests.

Some of the recent agreements between the USA and nations such as Turkey and Greece, which host important intelligence facilities, have appeared to offer concessions to the hosts in the form of sharing of the intelligence intake. This too is reported part of the deal between the USA and China as pertains to US use of SIGINT monitoring stations in Sinkiang near the Soviet border.[61]

General diplomatic support is, of course, about the vaguest but also often the most important item of quid pro quo involved in base negotiations. Earlier, at the height of the cold war, it was clear that a common perception of the Soviet threat allowed Washington to maintain facilities in a number of countries without any quid pro quo other than the expectation of mutual security. This was obviously true throughout NATO and with regard to important US Pacific allies such as Australia, New Zealand, Japan, South Korea and Taiwan.

Sometimes, US basing hosts perceive mutual antagonisms to be more important than the threat from Moscow, as for example with the perpetual dispute between Turkey and Greece. Hence, both tend to bargain over access in the context of efforts at achieving support from the USA in its disputes with the other. Earlier, the Philippines, in bargaining over the quid pro quo of military assistance to be given for access to its bases, raised the issues of supporting Filipino claims to various off-shore islands, and of enhanced support for combating the insurgency in Mindanao.[62] These are merely examples of a broader phenomenon, the possibilities for which are nearly endless, albeit often obscured and hidden in the interstices of complex, multifaceted relations between base user and host states.

On another dimension, it can be seen that the US security assistance budget is subdivided into a somewhat complex and confusing set of subcategories. A discussion of the politics and histories of these various programmes—and the rationales for year-to-year distributions of funds through these various budgets—is beyond the scope of this work. But table 37 reveals, even to a cursory review, that a number of somewhat distinct, crucial elements are involved: the old Military Assistance Program (MAP), the concessionary aspects of the Foreign Military Sales (FMS) programme; the Economic Support Fund (ESF) which is centred on Israel and Egypt; and the International Military Education and Training Program (IMET). In a somewhat subsidiary way, there are the varied additional instruments: the PL-480 food assistance programme, the Peace Corps, the programme for international narcotics control, another

for excess defence articles, and so on. Generally speaking, where FMP is concerned (i.e., primarily in the category: 'enhance co-operative defence and security'), there is a channelling of funds through the FMS, MAP, and ESF
programmes, primarily the first two-named. The ESF programme dominates
those assistance programmes to countries listed under 'deter and combat
aggression', which involves a few US basing hosts. The IMET programme, as
can be seen, dominates aid relations to many smaller, non-aligned, and even
Soviet-leaning nations where the USA may be quietly trying to improve
relations.

In some limited cases, there is evidence that trade concessions have been
linked to base negotiations even though this might appear to conflict with the
General Agreement on Tariffs and Trade and other international negotiations,
and might get entangled in the domestic politics of business and labour groups
in the USA. In the late 1950s, for instance, Loftleider, Iceland's North Atlantic
Air Carrier and single greatest foreign currency earning firm, was permitted to
land in the USA without being required to become a member of IATA or to
follow its tariff rates.[63] While this arrangement was not explicitly linked to the
base agreement, it may have had much to do with Iceland's willingness to retain
the US facilities. In another such example, Turkey has attempted to write
a textile quota agreement into the last negotiations over the (still unsigned)
Defense Cooperation Agreement which defines the US basing rights.

Alongside the now habitually prominent issues of security and economic aid
as quid pro quo for basing access, it should not be forgotten that the traditional
'status-of-forces' issues centred on the modalities of extraterritoriality can still
be important. In recent years, the USA has negotiated with the Philippines and
other countries about police and court matters related to bases; indeed about
the territorial sizes of the base complexes themselves.[64] In Greece, the USA has
had severe problems regarding the level of wages for local personnel employed
at US facilities.[65] In Djibouti and perhaps elsewhere, there may be restrictions
on shore leave for sailors while their ships are being refuelled or otherwise
maintained, a matter which ramifies into the sensitivities and pride of peoples
asked to host often rowdy and unruly military personnel.[66] In Iceland, there has
long been a maximum limit on the overall number of US military personnel
and also limitations on their access to the capital city, Reykjavik, reflective of
Icelandic fears that their culture would be overwhelmed by a relatively large
foreign presence.[67] These examples could be multiplied on a global basis, and
not only where US access is involved. The level of Egyptian and Somali access
to Soviet naval and air facilities in their own countries became serious issues
linked in both cases to eventual withdrawal of access rights.

Security assistance in reverse—offsets and FMP

In most cases, the USA (and other major powers) *pays* for its external access,
howsoever measured by 'rent', various forms of security assistance, the quid
pro quo of arms transfers, or the more or less unmeasurable and subjective

aspects of diplomatic support or 'protection'. In a few cases, however, in recent years, the direction of the payments has been in reverse, from base providers to base users. Primarily this has involved Japan and FR Germany, not accidentally those US allies which also have become economic competitors during a period witnessing ballooning US trade and budget deficits and a falling dollar and in both cases where their per capita national incomes now exceed that of the USA. The falling dollar, of course, has rendered US 'rents' for foreign facilities more and more costly just at the point at which domestic political support for financing those 'rents' has been at a low ebb. It was noted, for instance, that US payments to some 21 000 Japanese who work at US bases had in effect doubled as the dollar fell in value in 1986–87.[68]

Aside from their roles as rising economic competitors to the USA, Japan and FR Germany have also represented special cases in a broader, security context. As the defeated powers of World War II, their re-militarization has been restricted, variously, by their own constitutions, their own domestic political pressures, and the fears of even their best friends of the possibly baneful implications of full rearmament. Hence, the USA has assumed the role of protector of Japan, including its vital sea arteries to South-East and South-West Asia. It has also held the role of ultimate defender of FR Germany through its nuclear deterrent, even as Bonn has deployed sizeable conventional forces for its own defence. But as the cost for Washington of maintaining large-scale deployments in Asia and Europe have become ever more burdensome, Japan and FR Germany have come to alleviate the burden through various forms of offsets whereby they finance part of those costs. Recently, indeed, in early 1988, this issue came to the fore amid the tense multifaceted negotiations between Japan and the USA which culminated in the visit to Washington by Japanese Prime Minister Takeshita. He attempted to fend off US congressional pressures regarding trade imbalances and the falling dollar by making further concessions on Japanese offset payments for US forces based in Japan.[69]

By 1988, Tokyo was absorbing some 50 per cent of the personnel fringe-benefit costs, but not salaries, for Japanese workers at US bases, amounting to $165 million in 1987, and expected to rise to $330 million by 1990.[70] Notably, these payment levels are roughly similar to the levels of 'rents' the USA pays to such countries as the Philippines, Portugal, Greece, and so on.

The USA claims these offsets are justified not only by the security provided by Washington to the Japanese homeland, but also because the USA protects Japan's oil lifeline in the Persian Gulf and along the SLOCs leading from there to Japan. Contrariwise, some opponents in Japan prefer to see the US presence there as primarily concerned with US security interests, that is, that Japan's situation is not very distinct from those of numerous countries with which the USA bargains for access related to its nuclear and/or conventional posture *vis-à-vis* the Soviet Union, and where the host nation strives to decouple from the superpower competition.

The USSR, France and Britain, the other major users of basing access, do not receive offsets from host countries in this way. None of the Soviet basing hosts has the combination of security need and economic wherewithal to match the situations of Japan and FR Germany, unless it might be said that a sophisticated analysis of the full range of transfers within the WTO would divulge what, in effect, would be hidden (and also involuntary) subsidies of the Soviet military presence.[71] Generally speaking, though, what it all adds up to is a growing trend towards hard bargaining between hosts and users of bases, involving questions of who needs whom for security (mutual perceptions) and who can shift what burden upon whom (bargaining leverage in a situation of multiple decision formats and types of transaction).

Soviet security assistance

In the absence of an open-source 'congressional presentation', figures for Soviet security assistance to its FMP hosts are hard to come by. Specifically, it is difficult to separate out the aid and trade components of this effort, where there are bewildering complexities of secret agreements regarding barter, trade subsidies, offsets, long-term loans which may or may not be called in, and so on. But on the basis of some available analyses, it is clear that Moscow has a very extensive security assistance effort, one focused on its smaller (relative to the USA) number of important base hosts.

The sheer difficulties involved in estimating Soviet security assistance—as it relates to FMP—are made obvious in a reading of the perhaps most extensive effort made to measure it, that by Charles Wolf, Jr and his RAND Corporation associates in *The Costs and Benefits of the Soviet Empire, 1981-83*.[72] They attempt to guide the reader through the complexities of comparative dollar and rouble valuations of that assistance, and a variety of other methodological and conceptual problems. In this study, the RAND group subdivides the costs of the Soviet empire into several categories:

(1) trade subsidies, calculated as the reduction in prices charged for Soviet fuel exports to Eastern Europe and other parts of the empire, compared with then-prevailing world-market prices, as well as the premium prices paid by the Soviet Union for imports from these countries, compared with prevailing world-market prices for similar products; (2) export credits, construed as the Soviet Union's trade surpluses with communist and Third World countries, where these net surpluses exceeded $10 million in any one year; (3) Soviet economic aid, net of aid repayments; (4) military aid, calculated as total military deliveries minus hard-currency military sales; (5) incremental costs incurred by Soviet military forces in Afghanistan, above what these forces would cost if their normal basing and operational modes were maintained; and finally, (6) a part of total Soviet covert and related activities that, by a series of plausible as well as arguable assumptions, can be assigned to the Soviet imperial enterprise, as distinct from maintenance of the system's control within the Soviet Union itself.[73]

With the exception of the last-named, all of these mechanisms have been used in connection with FMP (the first four generally, the fifth in the case of one country, Afghanistan). These data are then further broken down according to what the RAND group calls the two external Soviet empires, that is, the contiguous one involving Eastern Europe, Mongolia and Afghanistan; and the non-contiguous one involving Soviet client and base-host states such as Viet Nam, Cuba, South Yemen, Ethiopia, Mozambique and Syria.[74]

A number of salient conclusions emerge from this study, the admitted conceptual and measurement problems notwithstanding. First, the cost of this empire for Moscow is seen to be almost staggering, but having peaked in the early 1980s at around $43–44 billion per year it subsequently declined to a level just below $30 billion.[75] The reasons for this decline are seen basically as two: (*a*) a reduction of 40 to 50 per cent in Soviet subsidy of its trade with Eastern Europe resulting from the fall in oil prices; and (*b*) increased resource pressures resulting from growing stringencies in the Soviet economy.[76] Trade credits and subsidies comprise about $20 billion of this aid (over 60 per cent); economic and military aid combined in the neighbourhood of $5 billion (about 18 per cent). Overall, the Soviet (dollar) costs for its empire are seen by the RAND Corporation as having gone slightly over 3 per cent of GNP around 1980, then subsequently to have declined to around 1.85 per cent around 1983 (the rouble costs are more than double these figures). By contrast, the RAND Corporation estimates that the USA spent about 0.3 per cent of GNP on 'its empire' in 1983.[77]

Table 39. Soviet-bloc security assistance to Cuba and Nicaragua, 1982–86
Figures are in US $ thousands.

	1982	1983	1984	1985	1986
Cuba					
Economic assistance	4 665	4 260	4 620	4 545	5 390
Military deliveries	1 650	1 210	1 370	2 100	1 510
(From USSR)	(1 600)	(1 200)	(1 350)	(850)	(1 400)
(From Eastern Europe)	(50)	(10)	(20)	(1 250)	(110)
Total assistance	**6 315**	**5 470**	**5 990**	**6 645**	**6 900**
Nicaragua					
Economic assistance	180	275	325	450	585
Military deliveries	160	260	320	300	590
(From USSR)	(150)	(250)	(300)	(250)	(550)
(From Eastern Europe)	(10)	(10)	(20)	(50)	(40)
Total assistance	**340**	**535**	**645**	**750**	**1 175**

Source: US State Department, *Soviet Bloc Assistance to Cuba and Nicaragua*, Report to US Congress, 12 Aug. 1987.

Overall, the bulk of the trade subsidies have come from the subsidy of oil shipments to, and industrial goods from, Eastern Europe; and the subsidy of oil exports to, and of sugar and nickel imports from, Cuba. Exports of petroleum have also been heavily subsidized in the cases of Viet Nam, Kampuchea, Laos and Mongolia. But whereas subsidies for Eastern Europe and some Third World states appear to have declined in the early- to mid-1980s, they may have risen just in the cases of Cuba and Viet Nam. If that is the case, it appears to underscore the strategic importance these two countries had come to assume for Moscow as vital military basing hubs in the Atlantic and Pacific areas, respectively.

More specifically, and here relying on US Government sources, some figures for Soviet-bloc security and economic assistance to Cuba and Nicaragua are given in table 39. As noted, the numbers appear massive—those for Cuba appear greatly in excess of US aid to any single US ally or client state, and by a wide margin.[78]

Otherwise, the same US Government sources estimate Soviet assistance to Viet Nam at over $1.5 billion a year, including about $1 billion in economic aid.[79] Meanwhile, by 1987–88, Moscow's bill for Afghanistan was reported running at some $4-5 billion per year, whether or not wholly to be construed as a 'cost of empire' or one primarily to be interpreted in the context of FMP and basing.[80]

A few other points bear mention as they emerge from the RAND Corporation study. First, as of around 1983, around 35 per cent of Moscow's military export deliveries were estimated to be in the form of aid, running at over $3 billion per year.[81] Soviet economic aid was estimated to be running at about $1.5 billion per year, some two-thirds to communist countries such as Cuba, Viet Nam and North Korea, and the remainder scattered among a variety of Third World states.[82]

Still another set of data (see table 40), published by the CIA on an open-source basis, provides another angle on Soviet economic aid to less developed countries. By 1986, that aid was seen to be approaching $3 billion a year—by contrast, the same publication gauges Moscow's arms deliveries at around $15 billion per year.[83]

Some interesting points and recent trends are revealed by these data. The amount of Soviet economic aid going to Africa is seen as having dramatically declined, even from 1985 to 1986—this may underscore the now common thesis that the Soviet Union is in retreat there, perhaps less interested in military involvement. The bulk of Soviet aid is shown going to the Middle East and South Asia; the Latin American figures are, however, climbing.[84] Two of the three largest recipients—Brazil and India—provide little or no access to Soviet forces; indeed, Brazil also purchases few if any Soviet weapons. Nicaragua is the third, and even it provides only limited Soviet military access.

All in all, these figures may denote a weakening nexus between Soviet FMP and economic aid, and may reflect a less ideologically oriented and perhaps less security-oriented basis for that aid.

Soviet use of a variety of aid instruments to support allied states is, of course, nothing new. Earlier (and analogous to the Soviet subsidies of Cuban sugar and nickel), much of Egypt's and Sudan's cotton crop was bought up in exchange for access.[85] Viet Nam was earlier apparently provided a market for cheap vodka and light industrial goods, freeing Moscow in the first instance to sell its own (high quality) vodka to acquire hard currency.[86]

Unlike the USA, the USSR has not had to worry as much as has the USA about the balance-of-payments implications of its FMP, at least according to US political economist Robert Gilpin. Hence, according to him,

The Soviet Union, on the other hand, has been generally free of this balance-of-payments problem. The bulk of Soviet military forces have remained within the Soviet Union proper, and foreign aid has been in the form of goods or military equipment. But where the Soviet Union has stationed large military contingents outside the country as in Eastern Europe, it has created a monetary and payments system to support this extension of power. By creating the ruble bloc, manipulating the value of the ruble, and keeping the ruble inconvertible, the Russians have forced the East Europeans to finance their military presence in Eastern Europe. Thus, the extent of Russian influence has been largely determined by the scope of their military rather than their economic power.[87]

The cost of the aid itself has apparently been high, lending credence to current speculation that Moscow is drawing in its horns and modifying its earlier drive to beef up its presence in the Third World. The causal explanation may also be somewhat reversed. As noted, particularly with reference to Africa, numerous erstwhile providers of access to the USSR (including Benin, Congo, Equatorial Guinea, Guinea, Guinea-Bissau, Mozambique, Madagascar and São Tomé and Príncipe) have soured on socialist economics of late and have re-oriented their economies—and politics—towards the West.[88] This has perhaps made Moscow more chary of throwing money at (perhaps fickle) providers of military access, but may also have resulted in redoubled efforts at financing the retention of some key, seemingly stable assets, such as Viet Nam, Ethiopia, South Yemen, and so on. Again, what stands out is the concentrated focus of Soviet aid efforts in connection with a dispersed, taut basing system represented by at least one host in each of the major regions of the Third World.

IV. Base denial activities

Whereas the bulk of this book is devoted to the major powers' acquisition and retention of basing access, it is also the case that they devote considerable efforts to denying or removing rivals' access and presence. Various instruments are used to that end: economic and security inducements, propaganda, threats, encouragement of local protest movements, pre-emptive base acquisitions and pre-emptive arms selling, diplomacy within the UN and other transnational or regional forums and organizations, and so on.[89] There have been successes and failures on both sides. The superpowers are not alone in these endeavours: Third World states have organized themselves to remove big-power presences, as well as to delete or restrict access elsewhere useful to their (regional) rivals' defence efforts.

Generally speaking, recent US efforts at denying or removing Soviet access has centred on economic and security inducements, that is, a broader effort at weaning long-term Soviet basing clients away from socialist economics and ideology; hence, almost automatically, from a Soviet security tie. Soviet denial efforts, on the other hand, have tended to emphasize propaganda and threats, including the threat of internal insurrection or, short of that, protest potentially damaging to an incumbent regime. Of course, the Reagan Doctrine, intended to overturn governments closely tied to Moscow, may also be interpreted largely

Table 40. Soviet economic aid extended to less developed countries, by recipient, 1954–86.
Figures are in US $m.

Recipient	1954–86	1985	1986
Africa	9 548	583	108
Algeria	1 937	340	..
Angola	946	25	7
Burkina Faso	6	—	—
Cameroon	8	..	..
Central African Republic	3	..	..
Congo	74	..	..
Equatorial Guinea	4	—	..
Ethiopia	1 298	—	..
Ghana	110	—	..
Guinea	406	7	..
Madagascar	270	93	69
Mauritania	34	16	..
Morocco	2 098	..	..
Mozambique	337	90	26
Nigeria	1 207	..	..
Senegal	8	..	—
Sierra Leone	35	—	..
Somalia	164	..	..
Sudan	65	..	..
Tanzania	44	..	..
Tunisia	123	..	..
Uganda	35	—	..
Zambia	30	..	..
Other	306	12	6
East Asia	261	..	..
Indonesia	214	..	..
Other	47	..	..
Latin America	3 461	296	613
Argentina	390	..	..
Bolivia	204	—	1
Brazil	708	..	300
Nicaragua	1 268	296	312
Other	891	..	1
Middle East and South Asia	24 412	2 024	2 241
Afghanistan	3 451	325	100
Bangladesh	515	82	..
Egypt	1 439	..	..
India	6 548	1 200	2 126
Iran	1 164	..	..
Iraq	2 726	..	..
North Yemen	197	..	..
Pakistan	1 210	..	..
Sri Lanka	100	..	..
Syria	1 916	..	..
Turkey	3 399	..	..
Other	1 747	418	15
Total	**37 683**	**2 903**	**2 962**

Source: US Central Intelligence Agency, *Handbook of Economic Statistics, 1987* (CIA: Washington, DC, 1987), p. 113.

as a base denial strategy, as might the numerous historical efforts at Moscow-inspired subversion, even as other, related aims have also been involved.

Even a cursory glance at the list of recipients of US security assistance in 1987–88, particularly in the categories to 'promote regional stability', and 'promote professional military relationships through grant training', will reveal a sustained and determined effort at shifting some states out of the Soviet orbit and, hence, denying Moscow access. In the former category are Botswana, Equatorial Guinea, Ethiopia (Public Law-480—PL-480—food aid), Grenada, Guinea, Madagascar, Mauritius, Mozambique, Peru, the Seychelles, Zambia (PL-480) and Zimbabwe (PL-480).[90] Food aid, as noted, is a primary inducement, in an area where the USA obviously has a huge comparative advantage. Recipients of military grant training include such recent and present granters of Soviet access (or recipients of Soviet arms) as Bangladesh, Benin, Burundi, Cape Verde, Congo, Ghana, Guinea-Bissau, Guyana, Mali, Nigeria, São Tomé, Sierra Leone, Tanzania and Uganda.[91]

Indeed, the very language of the budgetary justifications in the congressional presentation is revealingly open on this point. For Guinea-Bissau: 'During the past several years, the Government of Guinea-Bissau has demonstrated a clear desire to move toward genuine nonalignment and broaden its relations with the USA and other Western countries.'[92] Or, for Cape Verde: 'The Government of Cape Verde has been moving steadily away from the Soviet bloc and toward genuine nonalignment.'[93] There are others in the same vein.

The USA has also used threats and overt military action in connection with Soviet access, particularly in places in near proximity to the continental USA: Cuba, Grenada, Guatemala and Nicaragua are obvious examples. It has also used Saudi security assistance and military aid to supplement its own in places such as Egypt, Morocco, Sudan, Somalia, Tunisia, and so on, where Washington and Moscow have competed for access.[94] There are other such examples, for instance, as emerged in the Iran–Contragate hearings, the use of money from Brunei to support efforts at overthrowing Nicaragua's Sandinistas.[95]

In the past, but perhaps less so of late, Moscow has also used aid inducements to loosen Western access. More recently, the focus has been on propaganda, threats and multilateral activities within the UN. On almost any given day, a review of global Soviet media activities—as reviewed in the US Foreign Broadcast Information Service (FBIS)—will reveal a relentless harping on US basing activities. Arab nations are constantly warned that US access in their area will aid Israel. Australia, Norway and others are warned of the dangers of hosting US nuclear facilities lest they become targets in a nuclear war. Italians, Greeks, Turks, Thais, Cypriots and others are cajoled about the threats to their sovereignty and dignity represented by a US presence. In other cases, propaganda harps upon the possible dangers to civilians of US nuclear ships making port calls. In still others, locals are bombarded with data on murders and rapes allegedly committed by US sailors, another kind of appeal to national dignity.

Soviet broadcasts often encourage and reinforce local demonstrations by anti-American domestic forces against US facilities in countries such as Greece,

Italy, Japan, and so on, so as to create a broader base of popular support for eliminating the bases and to tie together elements of political 'popular fronts'. They also amplify statements by prominent Third World leaders demanding withdrawal of the US presence. Earlier, in 1976–77, for instance, a great effort was made to amplify complaints from Madagascar, India, the Seychelles, and Mauritius about the growing US presence in Diego Garcia and the need for 'Indian Ocean demilitarization'.[96]

The tone and thrust of these efforts are aptly conveyed in the following English-language *TASS* report of 19 March 1987 regarding US bases in the Philippines:

The U.S. military presence is a permanent tangible factor in the Philippines. It involves not only permanent military exercises and practice shooting, as a result of which window panes are broken in close-lying houses, and shells fired 'by mistake' sometimes explode in densely populated areas. The U.S. military bases are in addition breeding grounds of banditism, drug addiction and other social scourges. Apart from that the Philippine Health Ministry said, expressing concern over the propagation of AIDS in that country, that the dangerous virus is spread by servicemen from the U.S. bases.

A mass movement led by the coalition against bases incorporating more than 100 organizations and groups, which consistently campaign for the immediate dismantling of the Pentagon nests, is gaining in scope in the Philippines. The groups and organizations call demonstrations and rallies of protest, take an active part in international peace conferences.

Yet there are also forces in the Philippines trying to preserve military presence there. They are chiefly right-wingers who continue whipping up the 'Soviet menace' myth. Some of them were among the special commission, which drafted the Constitution of the Philippines and were trying to have their say in resolving the country's future.[97]

Or, from the 24 March 1987 edition of *Izvestiya*, regarding US access to Diego Garcia:

The Soviet Union's support for Mauritius' rightful demand to have its sovereignty over the Chagos Archipelago, including Diego Garcia Island, restored meets with particular satisfaction among the population of Indian Ocean islands and countries.

The militarization of this region by the Pentagon is dangerously exacerbating the situation in the region. In creating yet another zone for the forward basing of strategic forces, the United States is building up its military presence and sending aircraft carriers, submarines, and shiploads of marines into the area. B-52 strategic bombers fly overhead. Their main stronghold is Diego Garcia—an atoll in the Chagos Archipelago illegally taken from Mauritius by Britain and leased in 1966 to the United States for 50 years. The Americans expelled the indigenous population from the island and set up a major air and naval base there. According to information in the press, nuclear and chemical weapons dumps are maintained on the atoll.[98]

A random perusal (in March 1987) of the Soviet FBIS materials reveals numerous such items, even within the span of a week or so. There are items entitled: 'NATO "cold war" exercises begin in Norway'; 'Weinberger silent on F-16 bombers in Spain'; 'Costa Rica disapproves of U.S. use of territory'; 'Chadian GUNT forces capture US mercenaries', and 'Neutron bomb for

Israel'.[99] The latter, from *TASS*, commenting upon an article which appeared in Egypt's *Al Wafd* on 23 March 1987, claimed that Washington had transferred 1000 neutron bombs to Israel, but had put them at the disposal of the US Rapid Deployment Force, and 'intends to use these weapons itself in the region or to enable Tel Aviv to do so'.[100]

The United Nations has long been a useful forum for Soviet efforts at putting pressure on US and other Western points of access. In particular, various scattered island dependencies and other small enclaves have been targeted as 'remnants of colonialism': Micronesia (i.e., Kwajalein), American Samoa, Puerto Rico, St Helena, Guam, Bermuda, Ascension, Turks and Caicos, Diego Garcia, Gibraltar, and so on. As noted, some of these territories host very important Western facilities and, because of their small size, there has not always been tremendous internal pressure for their independence equivalent to the earlier phases of decolonialization in Africa, the Caribbean and elsewhere.[101]

Other nations too have been involved in the game of base denial, usually where rivals in Third World conflicts exert efforts at denying arms resupply staging points to each other. Arab OPEC nations have been particularly active along these lines in anticipation of future Middle East conflicts which might again see Israel dependent on a US arms airlift. Arab pressures have been directed against US air access in Spain (for tankers) and Portugal (the Azores) while Morocco—in promising staging access to the USA for Persian Gulf contingencies—has made it plain that access would not, of course, be made available on behalf of Israel.[102] Use of British-owned Diego Garcia would, presumably, be subject to similar pressures. Some Arab states have also pressured Egypt and Oman about US access, despite the fact that it is not likely to be relevant to an Arab–Israeli conflict. Libya, as noted above, has given aid to Malta in exchange for a pledge by the latter not to allow Western military access.[103]

In some cases, the pace of Western withdrawals from former basing locales has appeared more affected by the prospect of replacement by Soviet access than by the loss of Western access itself. For that reason Britain only slowly and reluctantly withdrew from Malta, the Maldives, Mauritius, the Seychelles, and so on, with the memory of Aden a salient reminder. France has worried similarly about Djibouti and Comoros, no doubt aware of Soviet inroads in the wake of Portuguese withdrawal from Cape Verde, São Tomé, and so on. Most of all, the USA has only slowly and grudgingly granted various degrees of (existing or promised) independence to the Northern Marianas, Belau and others in the Pacific Ocean, as it warily watches the first signs of a Soviet presence in nearby Vanuatu and Kiribati.

There have also been some examples of regional or multilateral efforts at comprehensive denial of access to *all* of the major powers. Such efforts, of course, may be viewed from a North–South perspective, as some Third World states wish to quarantine their areas from the East–West competition, in a manner perhaps analogous to nuclear weapon-free zones (NWFZs) or to prospective regional arms transfer recipient arrangements such as that broached by Latin Americans at Ayacucho. In 1980, not long after the aborting of US–Soviet talks about Indian Ocean demilitarization, Iraq floated a 'Pan-Arab Charter', the ostensible purpose of which was to keep *all* superpower bases out of the region.[104] The OAU and the Indian Ocean littoral states have made similar declarations and demands; again, this was associated in the late 1970s and early 1980s with the high-water mark of the 'North–South dialogue'. More recently, such efforts appear to have died down even as, on a more practical basis, both the USA and the USSR have had increasing *bilateral* difficulties where it pertains to maintaining access.

V. Summary

One main point stands out from a review of the recent politics and economics of FMP, that is, that *both* superpowers have, lately, appeared to face a gradually more constrained environment for access. In both cases, the pressures for de-coupling have come both from domestic and external forces.

The USSR, with its new drive towards '*perestroika*', clearly has come to perceive the support of a global basing system as increasingly onerous for an already severely strained and burdened economy. These strains have been associated with a widespread perception in the Third World, particularly in Africa, of the inherently flawed nature of Soviet-style socialist economics, which in turn has driven a number of erstwhile providers to Moscow of military access towards reconciliation with the West. The result is a real focus, measured by aid figures and diplomacy, on (expensive) retention of a residual core of key basing hosts in Viet Nam, South Yemen, Syria, Ethiopia, Angola, Cuba and a few others—one notes their global distribution.

The USA, amid mounting payments and budget problems, faces continued trends toward decoupling of basing ties in Portugal, Spain, Turkey, Greece, the Philippines, Panama, New Zealand and elsewhere. Generally, this results from a fading of cold-war ideological ties and of the formerly more strongly shared perception of interests between the USA and many of its long-term allies and clients. Some might characterize this as the result, variously, of declined power, prestige, mystique or cachet, combined with an upsurge of resentful nationalism in many places. But the overall trend is unmistakable.

In a curious way, one might claim that the base denial activities on both sides of the cold-war divide have been (mutually) increasingly successful. From the more theoretical perspective of international systems analysis, that may merely connote a long-term, secular trend towards multipolarity and global diffusion of power. But then, such trends can be extrapolated only with great caution.

Notes and references

[1] Harkavy, R. E., *Great Power Competition for Overseas Bases: The Geopolitics of Access Diplomacy* (Pergamon: New York, 1982), chapter 1, 'Introduction'.

[2] This is stated in a non-theoretical way, in 'Shrinking power: network of U.S. bases overseas is unraveling as need for it grows', *Wall Street Journal*, 29 Dec. 1987, p. 1.

[3] This point is covered, pro and con, in Holsti, O. R., Hoppmann, P. T. and Sullivan, J. D., *Unity and Disintegration in International Alliances: Comparative Studies* (John Wiley: New York, 1973), especially chapters 1 and 2; and Liska, G., *Nations in Alliance* (The Johns Hopkins Press: Baltimore, Md., 1962).

[4] The current state of formal alliances can be read out of the sections entitled, 'Bilateral External Agreements', 'Multilateral Regional Agreements' and 'Bilateral Regional Agreements' at the beginning of each of the region-by-region analyses in International Institute for Strategic Studies, *The Military Balance* (IISS: London, annual).

[5] International Institute for Strategic Studies, *The Military Balance: 1986–1987* (IISS: London, 1986), p. 80.

[6] IISS (note 5). See also, Remnek, R., 'The politics of Soviet access to naval support facilities in the Mediterranean', eds B. Dismukes and J. McConnell, *Soviet Naval Diplomacy* (Pergamon: New York, 1979), pp. 357–403.

[7] IISS (note 5), p. 89.

[8] IISS (note 5), p. 89.

[9] SIPRI data, which also note adjacent Soviet naval access to bases at Al Fao and As Zubayr.

[10] IISS (note 5), p. 89.

[11] IISS (note 5), p. 89.

[12] IISS (note 5), p. 89.

[13] IISS (note 5), p. 89.

[14] IISS (note 5), p. 113.

[15] IISS (note 5), p. 113.

[16] IISS (note 5), p. 113.

[17] IISS (note 5), p. 146.

[18] IISS (note 5), p. 146.

[19] IISS (note 5), p. 146.

[20] IISS (note 5), p. 146.

[21] IISS (note 5), p. 174.

[22] IISS (note 5), p. 175.

[23] IISS (note 5), p. 175.

[24] IISS (note 5), p. 175.

[25] IISS (note 5), p. 175.

[26] IISS (note 5), p. 175.

[27] This emerged from the author's conversations with various government specialists in the Department of Defense and the Department of State, particularly the latter's Office of Politico-Military Affairs (PM), which is at the hub of decision making and diplomacy regarding US overseas bases.

[28] This, for instance, was part of the 1980 Defense and Economic Cooperation Agreement (DECA) signed with Turkey, as outlined in United States of America, *Congressional Presentation for Security Assistance Programs: Fiscal Year 1988* (US Government Printing Office: Washington, DC, 1987), pp. 248–52. See also, 'U.S., Turkey sign accord exchanging bases for aid', *International Herald Tribune*, 31 Mar. 1980.

[29] Harkavy, R. E., *The Arms Trade and International Systems* (Ballinger: Cambridge, Mass., 1975), chapter 4, in turn based upon Leiss, A. C. *et al.*, *Arms Transfers to Less Developed Countries*, C/70-1 (MIT Center for International Studies: Cambridge, Mass., 1970).

[30] Harkavy (note 29).

[31] This appears partly to have been the case for Indonesia during the Sukarno period; and also of late for Saudi Arabia, which has acquired a lot of ground equipment from France, but aircraft first from the USA, more recently from the UK. Such (relative) tendencies elsewhere can be gauged from SIPRI, *Arms Trade Registers: The Arms Trade with the Third World* (The MIT Press: Cambridge, Mass., 1975).

[32] Brzoska, M. and Ohlson, T., SIPRI, *Arms Transfers to the Third World: 1971–85* (Oxford University Press: Oxford, 1987), pp. 367–68.

[33] For a brief discussion, see Kemp, G., 'Arms transfers and the "back-end" problem in developing countries', eds S. Neuman and R. E. Harkavy, *Arms Transfers in the Modern World* (Praeger: New York, 1979), especially pp. 270–73.

[34] Cordesman, A., *The Iran–Iraq War and Western Security* (Jane's: London, 1987); and Staudenmaier, W. O., 'Iran–Iraq', eds R. Harkavy and S. Neuman, *The Lessons of Recent Wars in the Third World: Approaches and Case Studies* (D. C. Heath: Lexington, Mass., 1985), pp. 211–31.

[35] 'Navy docking agreement near in Seychelles', *The Times*, 27 July 1983; 'U.S. renews Seychelles

pact for satellite tracking post', *New York Times*, 24 Nov. 1985, p. I6; 'Russians eye military base in the Seychelles', *Financial Times*, 1 June 1980.

[36] The analysis in this section is based on arms transfer data drawn from Brzoska and Ohlson (note 32), appendix 7; and the recent annual editions of US Arms Control and Disarmament Agency, *World Military Expenditures and Arms Transfers* (US Government Printing Office: Washington, DC, annual).

[37] 'Mauritius set to "regain" Diego Garcia', *Daily Telegraph*, 29 Mar. 1977.

[38] SIPRI data and Brzoska and Ohlson (note 32), appendix 7. The Congo's provision of access to the USSR for arms resupply of Angola is noted in Shulsky, A., 'Coercive diplomacy', in Dismukes and McConnell (note 6), p. 144.

[39] SIPRI data and Brzoska and Ohlson (note 32), appendix 7.

[40] This emerged as a conclusion earlier in Leiss (note 29).

[41] US Department of State, 'Conventional arms transfers in the Third World, 1972–81', Special Report no. 102, Washington, DC, Aug. 1982.

[42] SIPRI, *The Arms Trade with the Third World* (Humanities Press: New York, 1971), pp. 17–41.

[43] For a recent analysis, see Brzoska and Ohlson (note 32), pp. 59–76.

[44] Generally, regarding US security assistance, see Graves E. and Hildreth S. (eds), *U.S. Security Assistance: The Political Process* (D. C. Heath: Lexington, Mass., 1985); and Hammond, P. and Louscher, D., *The Reluctant Supplier: U.S. Decision-Making for Arms Sales* (Oelgeschlager, Gunn and Hain: Cambridge, Mass., 1983), especially chapter 5.

[45] *Wall Street Journal* (note 2), p. 1; '5 allies want U.S. soldiers out', *Centre Daily Times*, 30 Nov. 1987, p. A7; Snyder, J., 'Security slips at NATO's south flank', *Wall Street Journal*, 18 Nov. 1987, p. 33.

[46] *Congressional Presentation 1988* (note 28).

[47] *Congressional Presentation 1988* (note 28), pp. 14–15.

[48] 'U.S. hopes a pledge on military aid will ensure base rights in Turkey', *International Herald Tribune*, 22–23 Mar. 1986, p. 2; 'Turks get briefing from Weinberger', *New York Times*, 19 Mar. 1987, p. A7; 'U.S. reaches agreement on use of Turkish bases', *New York Times*, 17 Dec. 1986, p. A10.

[49] Greece and U.S. delay talks on military bases', *New York Times*, 6 Sep. 1988, p. A17.

[50] 'U.S. renews accord on Azores air base', *New York Times*, 14 Dec. 1983, p. A3; and 'Portuguese Premier talks of annulling U.S. Pact', *New York Times*, 9 Sep. 1987, p. A9.

[51] See 'Manila view: bases go home, slowly', *New York Times*, 6 Aug. 1988, p. 4; 'U.S. offers Philippines aid to retain bases', *Centre Daily Times*, 8 Sep. 1988, p. A9; and 'U.S. eyes pullout over Filipino demands', *Centre Daily Times*, 17 Sep. 1988, p. A10, which says that 'The United States is threatening to abandon its two giant military bases in the Philippines because Philippine officials want at least "1.2 billion a year to keep them open" '. If the bases were closed, according to the article, alternatives might be found in Guam or other Pacific islands. See also, 'Shultz: U.S. won't pay rent for bases', *Centre Daily Times*, 17 June 1988, p. B5; and 'Manila defers talks on U.S. bases until April 5', *International Herald Tribune*, 16 Mar. 1988, p. 2.

[52] 'Spain to press U.S. for a timetable on removal of F-16 Jets near Madrid', *International Herald Tribune*, 26 June 1987, p. 2.

[53] *Wall Street Journal* (note 2), p. 5.

[54] 'Saudis to let U.S. use bases in crisis', *New York Times*, 5 Sep. 1985, p. A1; and 'U.S. expects Saudis to extend protection for AWACs', *International Herald Tribune*, 20–21 June 1987, p. 2.

[55] Jong-Chul Choi, 'United States Security Policy in Asia and the U.S.-Japan-South Korea Collective Security Cooperation System', M.A. thesis, Pennsylvania State University, 1988, p. 29.

[56] Lewis, W. H., 'War in the Western Sahara', in Harkavy and Neuman (note 34), p. 117; and Solarz, S., 'Arms for Morocco?' *Foreign Affairs*, no. 58 (fall 1979–winter 1980), pp. 278–99.

[57] According to Richelson, J. T. and Ball, D., *The Ties That Bind* (Allen and Unwin: Boston, Mass., 1985), p. 327, the NSA presence at Peshawar was removed in 1970, but subsequently re-established. See also, Khalid, Z. A., 'A new round of American installations in Pakistan', *Asian Defence Journal*, May 1982, pp. 29–34.

[58] 'Elements of Quid-Pro-Quo for U.S. Facilities Overseas', unclassified, unpublished State Department paper, 1977, Annex 5, under 'U.S. military assistance included in base agreements', p. 2.

[59] Note 58, p. 1.

[60] Note 58, p. 3.

[61] Richelson and Ball (note 57), p. 172.

[62] This is noted in note 58, p. 2.

[63] This is discussed in note 58, annex 2, p. 3. For a good illustration of the often indirect nexus

of economic issues to those of basing rights, see 'Australia wheat farmers reap bitter feelings', *New York Times*, 2 Feb. 1987, which details the threat to US bases caused by the reaction of Australian farmers to US sales of subsidized wheat to the USSR, Australia's biggest customer. Herein: 'Nobody is seriously talking of closing the United States military bases in Australia. But a growing skepticism is being expressed, especially among younger farmers.' See also, 'Turks link trade to pact on bases, surprising Shultz', *New York Times*, 24 Mar. 1986, p. A1, which discusses Turkish demands for an increase in textile import quotas.

[64] 'Talks on bases spur defiance towards U.S.', *New York Times*, 25 June 1988, p. A1; 'Accord reached in Philippine strike', *New York Times*, 2 Apr. 1986, p. A3; and 'Agreement reached on U.S. use of military bases in Philippines', *International Herald Tribune*, 1 June 1983.

[65] See 'U.S. base in Athens is besieged', *New York Times*, 24 July 1985, p. A5. For a report on similar issues in Panama, see 'Panama canal workers strike as pay is halted', *International Herald Tribune*, 15 Mar. 1988, p. 7.

[66] Among the recent press items detailing US problems with the nationalist sensitivities of various base hosts, see 'Over the screeching jets, Germans cry "enough" ', *New York Times*, 10 Aug. 1988, p. A4; 'Japanese city (roar) wants U.S. jets (roar) to go', *New York Times*, 23 July 1984, p. A2; 'Koreans harbor resentment of the U.S. over their subordinate role in defense', *Wall Street Journal*, 28 July 1987, p. 28; and 'U.S. shifts troops' homes in Panama', *New York Times*, 24 Aug. 1988, p. A3.

[67] Gunnarsson, G., 'Iceland: guarding the gap', eds R. Rudney and L. Reychler, *European Security Beyond the Year 2000* (Praeger: New York, 1988), chapter 11, p. 183.

[68] 'Japan to pay more of U.S. bases' cost', *New York Times*, 9 Jan. 1988, p. 3.

[69] Note 68.

[70] Note 68.

[71] Crane, K., *Military Spending in Eastern Europe*, R-3444/USDP (RAND Corporation: Santa Monica, Calif., May 1987).

[72] Wolf, C., Crane, K., Yeh, K., Anderson, S. and Brunner, E., *The Costs and Benefits of the Soviet Empire, 1981–1983*, R-3419-NA (RAND Corporation: Santa Monica, Calif., Aug. 1986), prepared for the Director of Net Assessment, Office of the Secretary of Defense.

[73] Wolf *et al.* (note 72), p. 3.

[74] This distinction is stated in Wolf *et al.* (note 72), p. 2.

[75] Wolf *et al.* (note 72), 'Summary', p. v.

[76] Wolf *et al.* (note 72), 'Summary', p. v.

[77] Wolf *et al.* (note 72), p. 17.

[78] US State Department, *Soviet Bloc Assistance to Cuba and Nicaragua*, Report to US Congress, 12 Aug. 1987. One other source puts Soviet annual aid to Cuba somewhat lower at $4 billion, and discusses the barter of Cuban sugar for Soviet oil in that context. See 'Global view: Cuba', in *Journal of Defense and Diplomacy*, vol. 5, no. 11 (1987), p. 62. But for a recent and somewhat altered view, see 'Soviets cut economic aid to Cuba, papers show', *International Herald Tribune*, 17 Mar. 1988, p. 3.

[79] *Soviet Bloc Assistance to Cuba and Nicaragua* (note 78).

[80] Wolf *et al.* (note 72), p. 28.

[81] Wolf *et al.* (note 72), p. 29.

[82] Central Intelligence Agency, Directorate of Intelligence, *Handbook of Economic Statistics, 1987* (CIA: Washington, DC, 1987).

[83] CIA (note 82), p. 113.

[84] The growing divorce of Soviet trade and security policies, involving a de-emphasis of ideological considerations, is illustrated in 'Soviet courts South America with an eye for trade', *New York Times*, 4 Oct. 1987, p. E3; and in 'Soviet, in a shift, expands contact with Third World', *New York Times*, 25 May 1987, p. 1.

[85] Joshua, W. and Gibert, S., *Arms for the Third World: Soviet Military Aid Diplomacy* (The Johns Hopkins Press: Baltimore, Md., 1969), pp. 13–14, which reports that Soviet–Egyptian relations were actually strained when Moscow sold Egyptian cotton it had received in exchange for aid, hence, lowering the world cotton price and excluding Egypt from some markets.

[86] 'Soviet imperialism is in the red', *Fortune*, 13 July 1981, pp. 107–108.

[87] Gilpin, R., *U.S. Power and the Multinational Corporation* (Basic Books: New York, 1975), footnote 14, pp. 273–74.

[88] Fukuyama, F., 'Soviet military power in the Middle East; or, Whatever became of power projection?', eds S. Spiegel, M. Heller and J. Goldberg, *The Soviet–American Competition in the Middle East* (D. C. Heath: Lexington, Mass., 1988), pp. 159–82. But for the thesis that there is a

new Soviet Third World policy emphasizing increased trade and influence with influential but non-Marxist states, see 'Soviet courts South America with an eye for trade', *New York Times*, 4 Oct. 1987, p. E3; and 'Soviet in a shift, expands contact with Third World', *New York Times*, 25 May 1987, p. A1.

[89] For an earlier and somewhat more comprehensive discussion, see Harkavy (note 1), pp. 233–37. See also, Cottrell, A., 'Soviet views of U.S. overseas bases', *Orbis*, vol. 7, no. 1 (spring 1963), pp. 77–95.

[90] *Congressional Presentation 1988* (note 28), pp. 375–76.

[91] *Congressional Presentation 1988* (note 28), pp. 376–77.

[92] *Congressional Presentation 1988* (note 28), p. 315.

[93] *Congressional Presentation 1988* (note 28), p. 314.

[94] 'Secret Saudi funding aids U.S. policy goals', *International Herald Tribune*, 22 June 1987, p. 1; and Dawisha, A., 'Saudi Arabia's search for security', Adelphi Paper no. 158 (IISS: London, 1980).

[95] 'Shultz confirms funds from Brunei vanished', *New York Times*, 8 Jan. 1987, p. I10.

[96] Harkavy (note 1), p. 234.

[97] US FBIS, USSR International Affairs: Southeast Asia and Pacific, 19 Mar. 1987, reporting on Moscow TASS in English from 14 Mar. 1987, under 'Anniversary of U.S.-Philippines Agreement noted'.

[98] US FBIS, USSR International Affairs: Sub-Saharan Africa, 26 Mar. 1987, reporting on Moscow *Izvestiya* in Russian from 24 Mar. 1987, under 'Mauritian minister wants Diego Garcia returned'.

[99] FBIS, USSR International Affairs, 18 Mar. and 25 Mar. 1987.

[100] FBIS, USSR International Affairs, 25 Mar. 1987, 'Report on U.S. neutron shells in Israel cited', from Moscow *Sovetskaya Rossiya* in Russian, 24 Mar. 1987, 1st edn, p. 3.

[101] See, for instance, FBIS, USSR International Affairs, 16 Nov. 1976, under 'U.S. attempts to 'annex' Micronesia contradict detente'; or 19 Nov. 1976, under 'Tass reports on U.N. vote on U.S., U.K. possessions', which focuses on the 'right to self-determination of the people of American Samoa;' or 22 Oct. 1976, under 'UNGA condemns French occupation of Mayotte Island'.

[102] 'Lisbon denies Arab offer on U.S. base', *International Herald Tribune*, 24 Aug. 1974; 'Secret U.S.-Spain airlift accord told', *Washington Post*, 11 Oct. 1976, p. A24; and 'No secret pact on bases, Spain says', *Washington Post*, 14 Oct. 1976, p. A25. See also, 'Portugal cool to idea of U.S. sending spare parts to Iran via Azores base', *Christian Science Monitor*, 4 Nov. 1980, p. 11.

[103] 'In Malta, ties to West at issue again', *New York Times*, 11 May 1987, p. A3.

[104] This is discussed in Weinland, R., 'Superpower access to support facilities in the Third World: Effects and their causes', paper delivered at meeting of International Studies Association, Philadelphia, 18–21 Mar. 1981; and in 'Iraq: frustration in the Gulf', *Middle-East Intelligence Survey*, vol. 8, no. 8 (16–31 July 1980), pp. 60–61.

Select Bibliography

Books and reports

Alves, D., *Anti-Nuclear Attitudes in New Zealand and Australia* (National Defense University Press: Washington, DC, 1985).

Arkin, W. M. and Fieldhouse, R. F., *Nuclear Battlefields: Global Links in the Arms Race* (Ballinger: Cambridge, Mass., 1985).

Ball, D., *A Base for Debate: The U.S. Satellite Station at Nurrungar* (Allen and Unwin: Sydney, 1987).

Bamford, J., *The Puzzle Palace* (Houghton-Mifflin: Boston, Mass., 1982).

Barnet, C., *Britain and Her Army: 1509–1970* (William Morrow: New York, 1970).

Blair, B., *Strategic Command and Control* (Brookings Institution: Washington, DC, 1985).

Blaker, J. R., Tsagronis, S. J. and Walter, K. T., *US Global Basing: US Basing Options*, Report for the US Department of Defense, HI-3916-RR, Hudson Institute, Alexandria, Va., Oct. 1987.

Blaxland, G., *The Regiments Depart* (William Kimber: London, 1971).

Blechman, B. M. and Kaplan, S. S., *Force Without War: U.S. Armed Forces as a Political Instrument* (The Brookings Institution: Washington, DC, 1978).

Boxer, C. R., *The Dutch Seaborne Empire: 1600–1800* (Knopf: New York, 1965).

Boxer, C. R., *The Portuguese Seaborne Empire, 1415–1825* (Knopf: New York, 1969).

Bracken, P., *The Command and Control of Nuclear Forces* (Yale University Press: New Haven, Conn., 1983).

Brzoska, M. and Ohlson, T., SIPRI, *Arms Transfers to the Third World: 1971–85* (Oxford University Press: Oxford, 1987).

Burrows, W., *Deep Black* (Random House: New York, 1985).

Campbell, D., *The Unsinkable Aircraft Carrier: American Military Power in Britain* (Paladin: London, 1986).

Carroll, J. M., *Secrets of Electronic Espionage* (Dutton: New York, 1966).

Cimbala, S. (ed.), *Soviet C³* (AFCEA International Press: Washington, DC, 1987).

Clancy, T., *Red Storm Rising* (G. P. Putnam's Sons: New York, 1986).

Cochran, T. B., Arkin, W. M. and Hoenig, M. M., *Nuclear Weapons Databook, Vol. 1: U.S. Nuclear Forces and Capabilities* (Ballinger: Cambridge, Mass., 1984).

Cole, D. H., *Imperial Military Geography*, 12th edn (Sifton Praed: London, 1956).

Collins, J., *U.S.–Soviet Military Balance 1980–1985* (Pergamon-Brassey's: Washington DC, 1985).

Dadant, P. M., *Shrinking International Airspace as a Problem for Future Air Movements– a Briefing*, Report R-2178-AF (RAND Corporation: Santa Monica, Calif., 1978).

Dismukes, B. and McConnell, J. (eds), *Soviet Naval Diplomacy* (Pergamon: New York, 1979).

Ford, D., *The Button* (Simon and Schuster: New York, 1985).

Fukuyama, F., 'Soviet military power in the Middle East; or, Whatever became of power projection?', eds S. Spiegel, M. Heller and J. Goldberg, *The Soviet–American Competition in the Middle East* (D. C. Heath: Lexington, Mass., 1988).

Gilpin, R., *U.S. Power and the Multinational Corporation* (Basic Books: New York, 1975).

Gray, C. S., *Maritime Strategy, Geopolitics and the Defense of the West* (National Strategy Information Center: New York, 1986).

Gray, C., *The Geopolitics of the Nuclear Era* (Crane Russak: New York, 1977).

Gregor, A. J. and Aganon, V., *The Philippines Bases: U.S. Security at Risk* (Ethics and Public Policy Center: Washington, DC, 1987).

Gunnarsson, G., 'Iceland: guarding the gap', eds R. Rudney and L. Reychler, *European Security Beyond the Year 2000* (Praeger: New York, 1988).

Hagerty, H. G., *Forward Deployment in the 1970's and 1980's* (National Defense University: Washington, DC, 1977), National Security Affairs Monograph 77-2.

Harkavy, R. E., *Great Power Competition for Overseas Bases: The Geopolitics of Access Diplomacy* (Pergamon: New York, 1982).

Hersh, S., *The Target is Destroyed* (Random House: New York, 1986).

The International Institute for Strategic Studies, *The Military Balance* (IISS: London, annual).

Jane's Military Communications (Macdonald: London, annual).

Jasani, B., SIPRI, *Outer Space–Battlefield of the Future?* (Taylor and Francis: London, 1978).

Kaplan, S. (ed.), *Diplomacy of Power: Soviet Armed Forces as a Political Instrument* (The Brookings Institution: Washington, DC, 1981).

Karas, T. H., 'Implications of Space Technology for Strategic Nuclear Competition', the Stanley Foundation, Occasional Paper No. 25, Muscatine, Iowa, July 1981.

Kaufmann, W. W., *A Thoroughly Efficient Navy* (The Brookings Institution: Washington, DC, 1987).

Kennedy, P. M., *The Rise and Fall of British Naval Mastery* (Scribner: New York, 1976).

Kidron, M. and Smith, D., *The War Atlas* (Simon and Schuster: New York, 1983).

Klass, P., *Secret Sentries in Space* (Random House: New York, 1971).

Kupchan, C., *The Persian Gulf and the West* (Allen and Unwin: Boston, Mass., 1987).

Langer, A., Wilkes, O. and Gleditsch, N. P., *The Military Functions of Omega and Loran-C* (Peace Research Institute: Oslo, 1976).

MccGuire, M. and McDonnell, J. (eds), *Soviet Naval Influence* (Praeger: New York, 1977).

McNaugher, T. L., *Arms and Oil: U.S. Military Strategy and the Persian Gulf* (Brookings Institution: Washington, DC, 1985).

Miller, S. E. and Van Evera, S. (eds), *Naval Strategy and National Security* (Princeton University Press: Princeton, N.J., 1988).

Neuman, S. and Harkavy, R. (eds), *Arms Transfers in the Modern World* (Praeger: New York, 1979).

Paul, R., *American Military Commitments Abroad* (Rutgers University Press: New Brunswick, N.J., 1973).

Richelson, J. T. and Ball, D., *The Ties that Bind* (Allen and Unwin: Boston, Mass., 1985).

Richelson, J. T., 'Technical collection and arms control', ed. W. Potter, *Verification and Arms Control* (D. C. Heath: Lexington, Mass., 1985).

Richelson, J. T., *Sword and Shield* (Ballinger: Cambridge, Mass., 1986).

Richelson, J. T., *The U.S. Intelligence Community* (Ballinger: Cambridge, Mass., 1985).

Roberts, S. S., 'The decline of the overseas station fleets: the United States Asiatic fleet and the Shanghai crisis, 1932' (Center for Naval Analyses: Arlington, Va., Nov. 1977), Professional Paper No. 208.

Rosinski, H., *The Development of Naval Thought* (Naval War College Press: Newport, R.I., 1977).

Rubinstein, A. Z. and Smith, D. E. (eds), *Anti-Americanism in the Third World* (Praeger: New York, 1986).

Stares, P. B., *Space and National Security* (Brookings Institution: Washington, DC, 1987).

Stettinius, E., *Lend-Lease, Weapons for Victory* (Macmillan: New York, 1944).

Stringer, H., *Deterring Chemical Warfare: US Policy Options for the 1990s* (Pergamon-Brassey's: Washington, DC, 1986).

Tow, W. T. and Feeney, W. R. (eds), *U.S. Foreign Policy and Asian-Pacific Security: A Transregional Approach* (Westview Press: Boulder, Colo., 1982), pp. 163-225.

Watkins, Admiral J. D. (ed.), *The Maritime Strategy* (US Naval Institute: Annapolis, Md., 1986).

Watson, B. W., *Red Navy at Sea: Soviet Naval Operations on the High Seas 1956-80* (Westview Press: Boulder, Colo., 1982).

Watson, B. W. and Watson, S. M. (eds), *The Soviet Navy: Strengths and Liabilities* (Westview Press: Boulder, Colo., 1986).

Weller, G. A., *Bases Overseas: An American Trusteeship in Power* (Harcourt, Brace: New York, 1944).

Wolf, C., Crane, K., Yeh, K., Anderson, S. and Brunner, E., *The Costs and Benefits of the Soviet Empire, 1981-1983*, R-3419-NA (RAND Corporation: Santa Monica, Calif., Aug. 1986).

Articles

'ASW: A deadly underseas game', *US News and World Report*, 15 June 1987, pp. 40-41.

Barnaby, F., 'On target with an Omega station?', *New Scientist*, vol. 109, no. 993 (25 Mar. 1976), pp. 671-72.

Blechman, B. and Weinland, R., 'Why coaling stations are necessary in the nuclear age', *International Security*, no. 2 (1977), pp. 88-99.

Cottrell, A. and Moorer, T. H., 'U.S. overseas bases: problems of projecting American military power abroad', *Washington Papers*, no. 47 (CSIS Georgetown, Washington, DC, 1977).

Cottrell, A., 'Soviet views of U.S. overseas bases', *Orbis*, vol. 7, no. 1 (spring 1963), pp. 77-95.

Friedman, N., 'SOSUS and U.S. ASW tactics', *U.S. Naval Institute Proceedings*, Mar. 1980, pp. 120-22.

Gray, C., 'Maritime strategy', *U.S. Naval Institute Proceedings*, Feb. 1986, pp. 34-42.

Harkavy, R., 'Arms resupply during conflict: A framework for analysis', *The Jerusalem Journal of International Relations*, vol. 7, no. 3 (1985), pp. 5-40.

Haselkorn, A., 'The Soviet collective security system', *Orbis* (spring 1975), p. 240.

'In battle of wits, submarines evade advanced efforts at detection', *New York Times*, 1 Apr. 1986, p. C1.

Kaplan, S., 'The utility of U.S. military bases', *Military Review*, vol. 57, no. 4 (Apr. 1977), pp. 43-57.

Kemp, G., 'The new strategic map', *Survival*, vol. 19, no. 2 (Mar./Apr. 1977), pp. 50–59.

Kennedy, P. M., 'Imperial cable communications and strategy, 1870–1914', *The English Historical Review*, no. 86, vol. 141 (1971), pp. 728–52.

Mearsheimer, J. J., 'A strategic misstep', *International Security*, vol. 2, no. 2 (fall 1986), pp. 3–55.

Moorer, T. and Cottrell, A., 'The search for U.S. bases in the Indian Ocean: a last chance', *Strategic Review*, spring 1980, pp. 36–37.

'Navy warns of crisis in anti-submarine warfare', *New York Times*, 19 Mar. 1987, p. A19.

Patch, B. W., 'American naval and air bases', *Editorial Research Report*, vol. 1, no. 7 (16 Feb. 1939).

Patch, B. W., 'Overseas bases', *Editorial Research Report*, vol. 2, no. 2 (14 July 1951), pp. 441–42.

'Shrinking power: Network of U.S. bases overseas is unraveling as need for it grows', *Wall Street Journal*, 29 Dec. 1987, p. 1.

Siegel, L., 'Diego Garcia', *Pacific Research*, vol. 8, no. 3 (Mar.–Apr. 1977).

Tierney, J., 'The invisible force', *Science 83*, vol. 4, no. 9, pp. 68–78.

Weinland, R. G., 'Land support for naval forces: Egypt and the Soviet Escadra 1962–1976', *Survival*, no. 20 (1978), pp. 73–79.

'When the stepping stones of world power are rocky bases', *US News and World Report*, 23 Nov. 1987, pp. 30–31.

Wohlstetter, A., 'Illusions of distance', *Foreign Affairs*, vol. 46, no. 2 (Jan. 1968), pp. 242–55.

Government reports

Central Intelligence Agency, Directorate of Intelligence, *Handbook of Economic Statistics, 1987* (CIA: Washington, DC, 1987).

Congressional Presentation for Security Assistance Programs: Fiscal Year 1988 (US Government Printing Office: Washington, DC, 1987).

Defense Communications Agency, 'Defense Communications System/European Communication Systems: Interoperability Baseline', Washington, DC, 1 Feb. 1981.

Department of Defense, *Soviet Military Power* (US Government Printing Office: Washington, DC), published annually since September 1981.

Discriminate Deterrence, Report of the Commission on Integrated Long-Term Strategy (Co-Chairmen: Iklé, F. C. and Wohlstetter, A.) (US Government Printing Office: Washington, DC, Jan. 1988).

Soviet Bloc Assistance to Cuba and Nicaragua, US State Department report to US Congress, 12 Aug. 1987.

Soviet Space Programs: 1976–1980, US Senate, Committee on Commerce, Science and Transportation, 97th Congress, 2nd Session (US Government Printing Office: Washington, DC, Dec. 1982).

The Organization of the Joint Chiefs of Staff, *United States Military Posture: FY 1987* (US Government Printing Office: Washington, DC, 1986).

The United States Army Posture Statement: Fiscal Year 1988, Joint Statement by the Chief of Staff, US Army, and Secretary of the Army (US Government Printing Office: Washington, DC, 1987).

Treaty Between the United States of America and the Union of Soviet Socialist Republics on the Elimination of Their Intermediate-Range and Shorter-Range Missiles (the INF Treaty), US Department of State Publication 9555, Bureau of Public Affairs, Washington, DC, Dec. 1987.

United States of America, *Congressional Presentation for Security Assistance Programs: Fiscal Year 1988* (US Government Printing Office: Washington, DC, 1987).

US Department of Defense, *United States Posture, 1988*, prepared by the Joint Staff (US Government Printing Office: Washington, DC, 1987).

US Defense Mapping Agency, *World Port Index*, 10th edn (Defense Mapping Agency: Washington, DC, 1986).

US Department of Defense, Comptroller's Office, *DOD Annual Operating Costs of Maintaining U.S. Military Forces in Foreign Countries and Areas* (US Government Printing Office: Washington, DC, annual.)

US Department of Defense, *Soviet Military Power* (US Government Printing Office: Washington, DC), published annually since September 1981.

US House of Representatives, Committee on Foreign Relations, *Greece and Turkey: Some Military Implications Related to NATO and the Middle East*, report prepared by Congressional Research Service, Library of Congress (US Government Printing Office: Washington, DC, 28 Feb. 1975).

US Senate, Committee on Foreign Relations, *United States Foreign Policy Objectives and Overseas Military Installations*, prepared by the Congressional Research Service, Library of Congress, Washington, DC, 1979.

US Senate, Committee on Foreign Relations, *United States Security Agreements and Commitments Abroad*, Hearings Before the Sub-committee on US Security Agreements and Commitments Abroad, 91st Congress, Volumes I and II (US Government Printing Office: Washington, DC, 1971).

Weinberger, C. W., *Annual Report to the Congress: Fiscal Year 1985* (US Government Printing Office: Washington, DC, 1984).

Weinberger, C. W., *Annual Report to the Congress: Fiscal Year 1988* (US Government Printing Office: Washington, DC, 1987).

Index